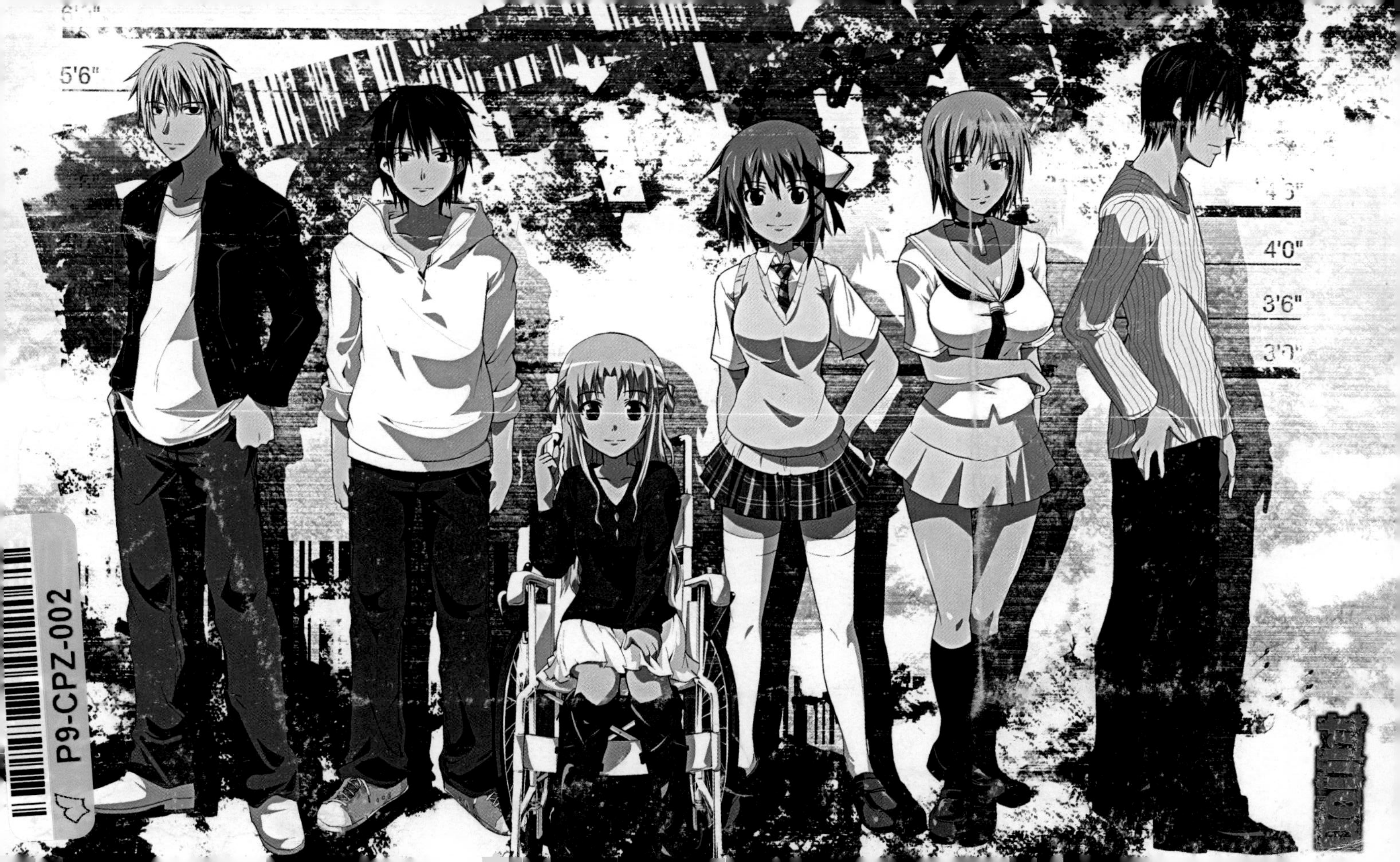
5'6"
4'0"
3'6"

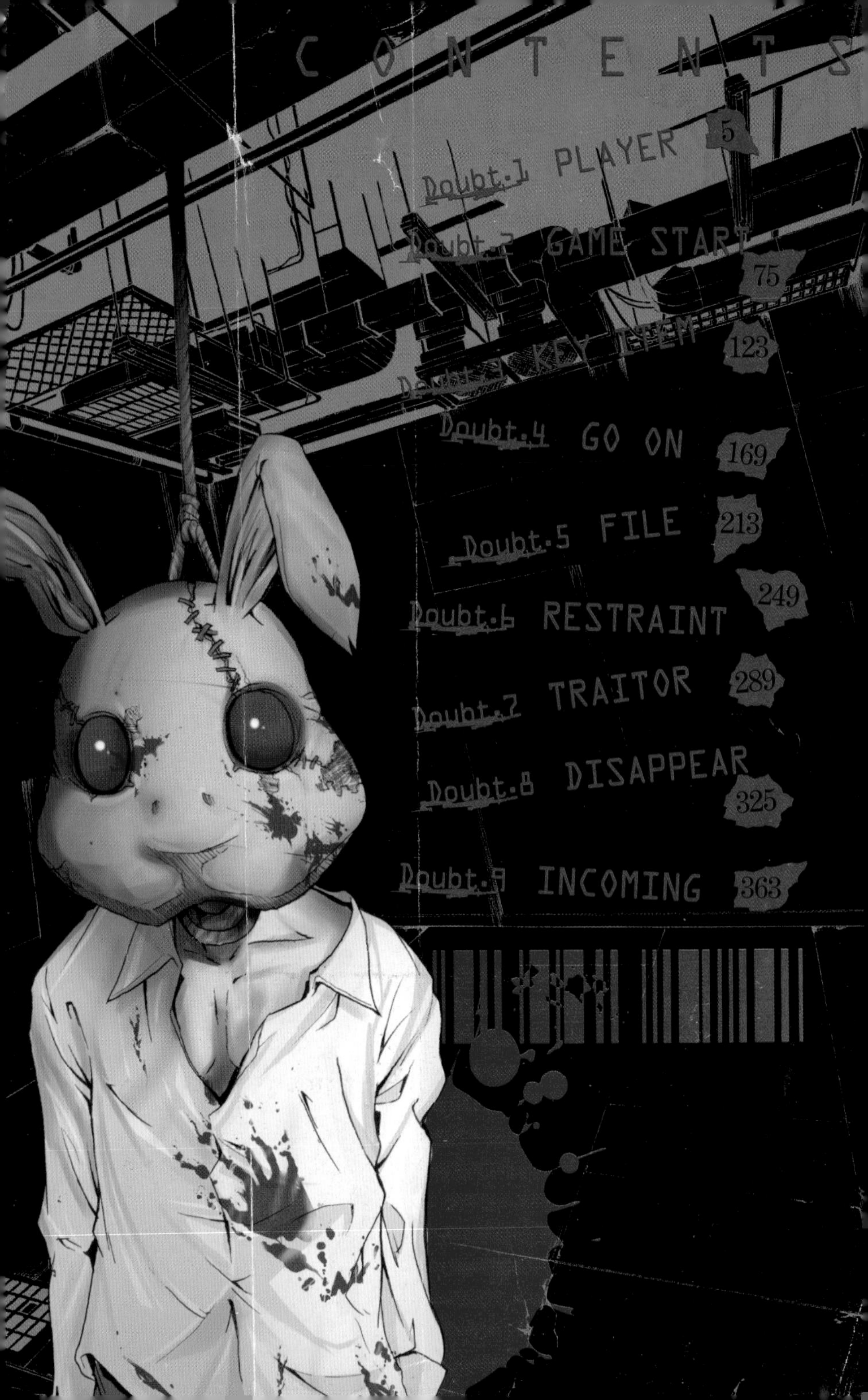

CONTENTS

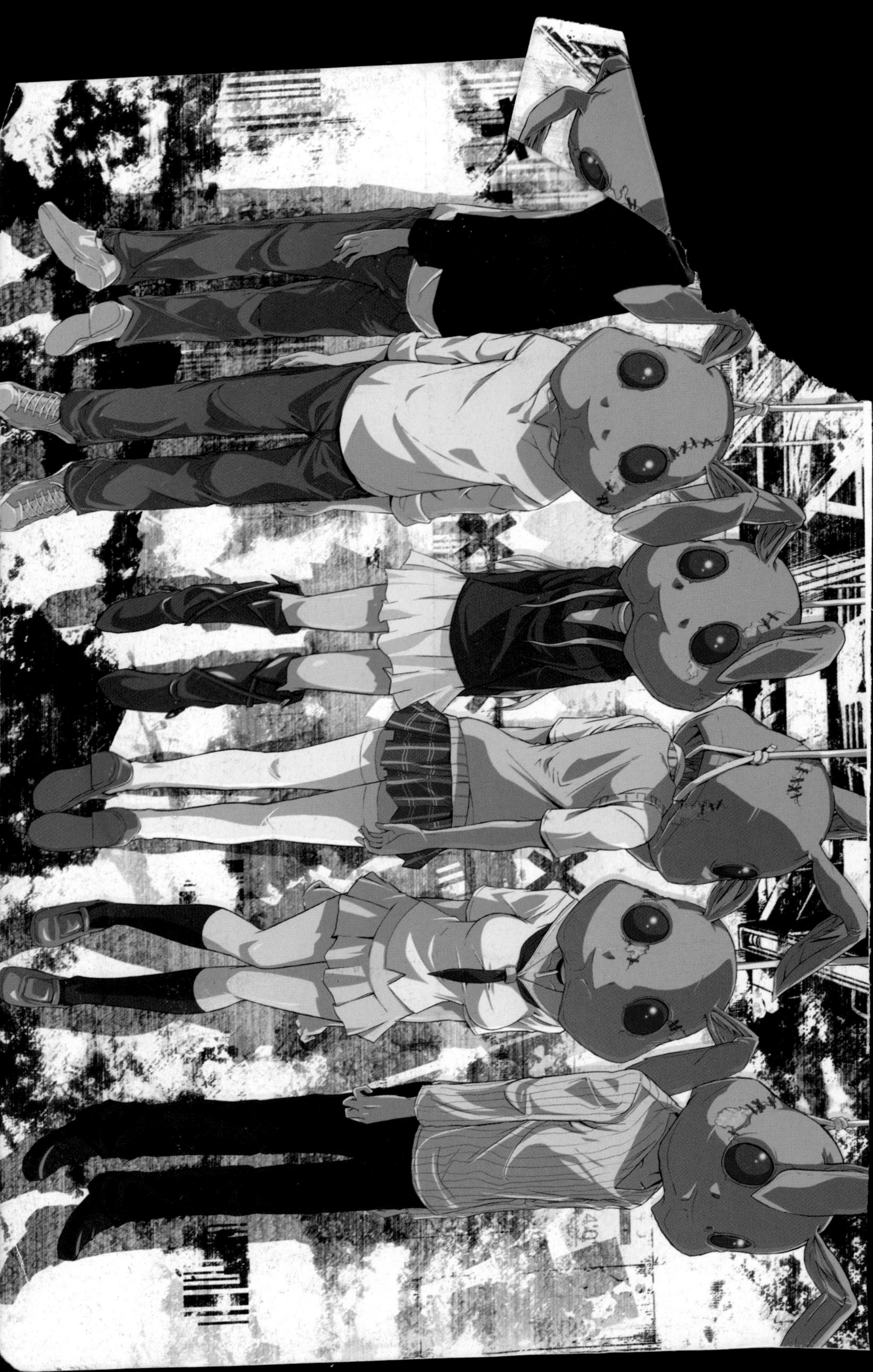

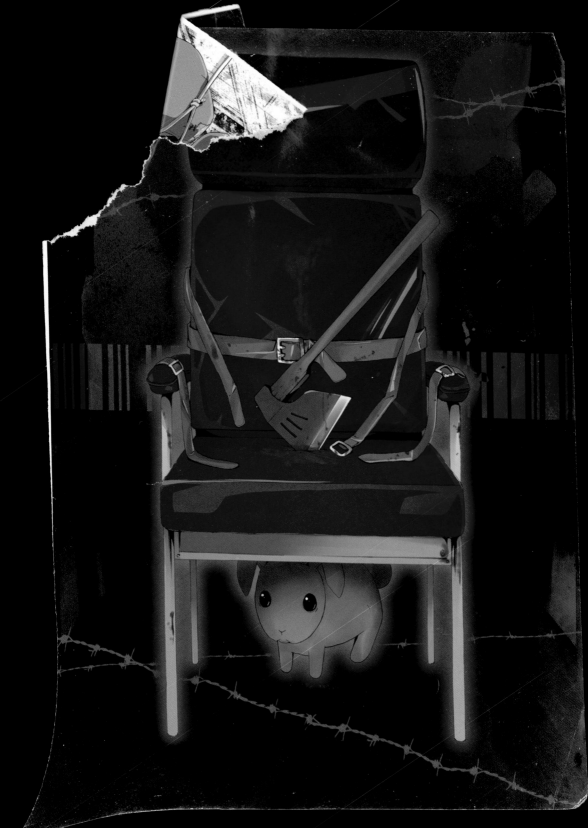

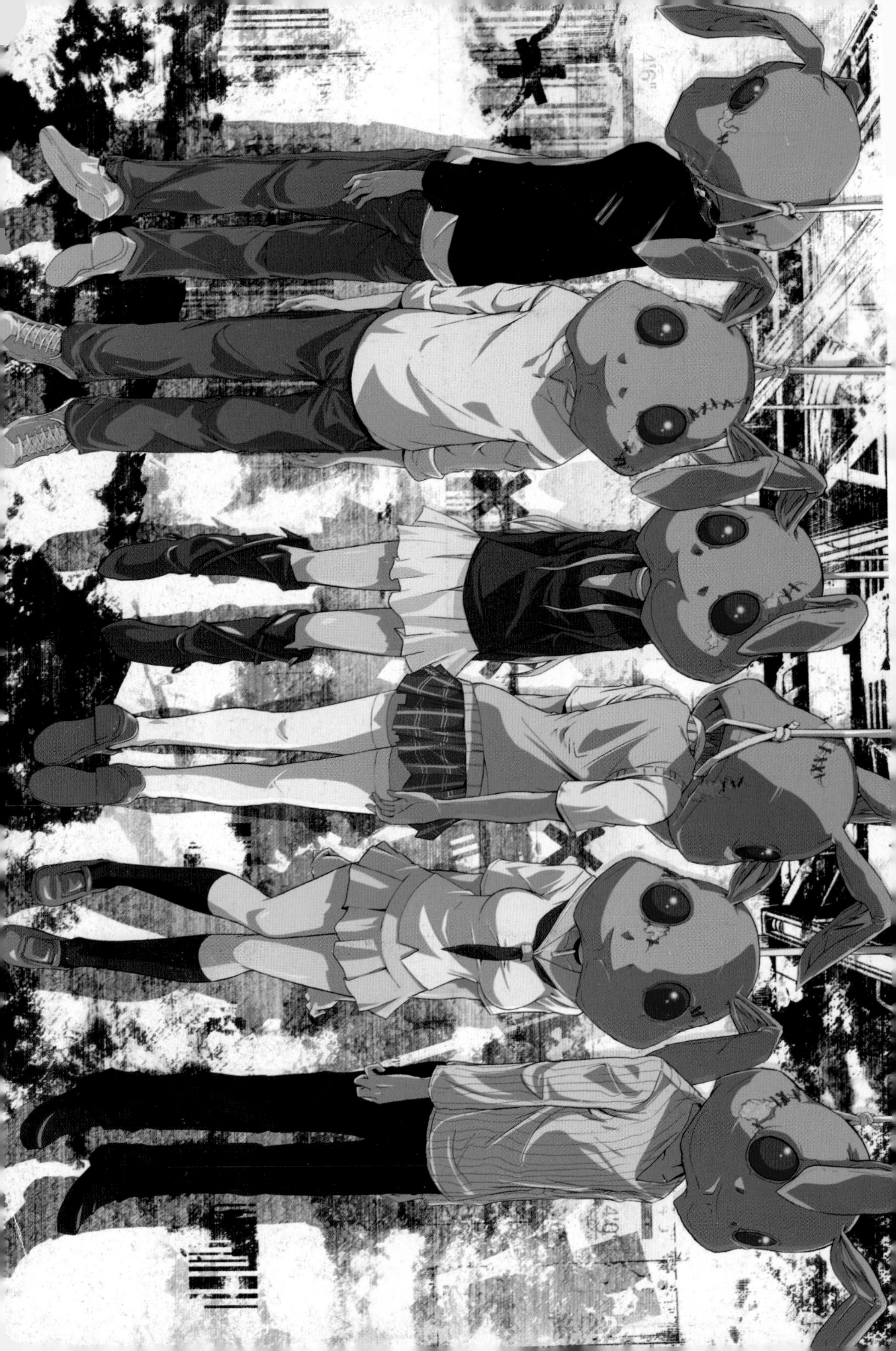

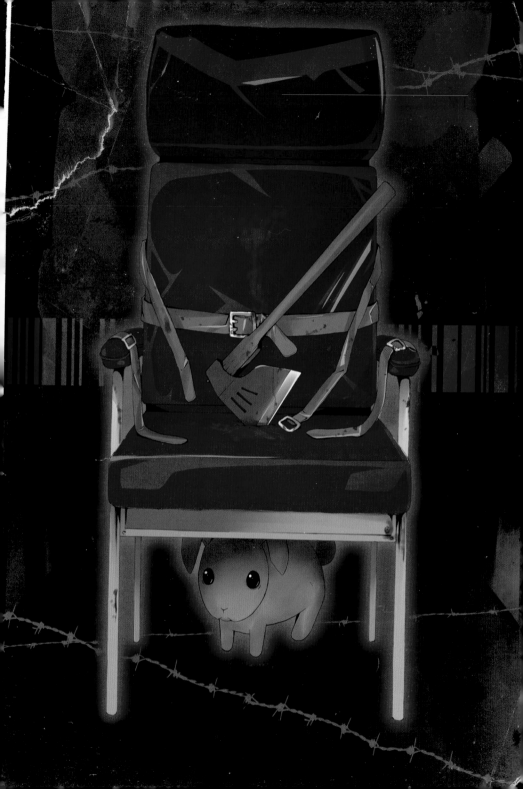

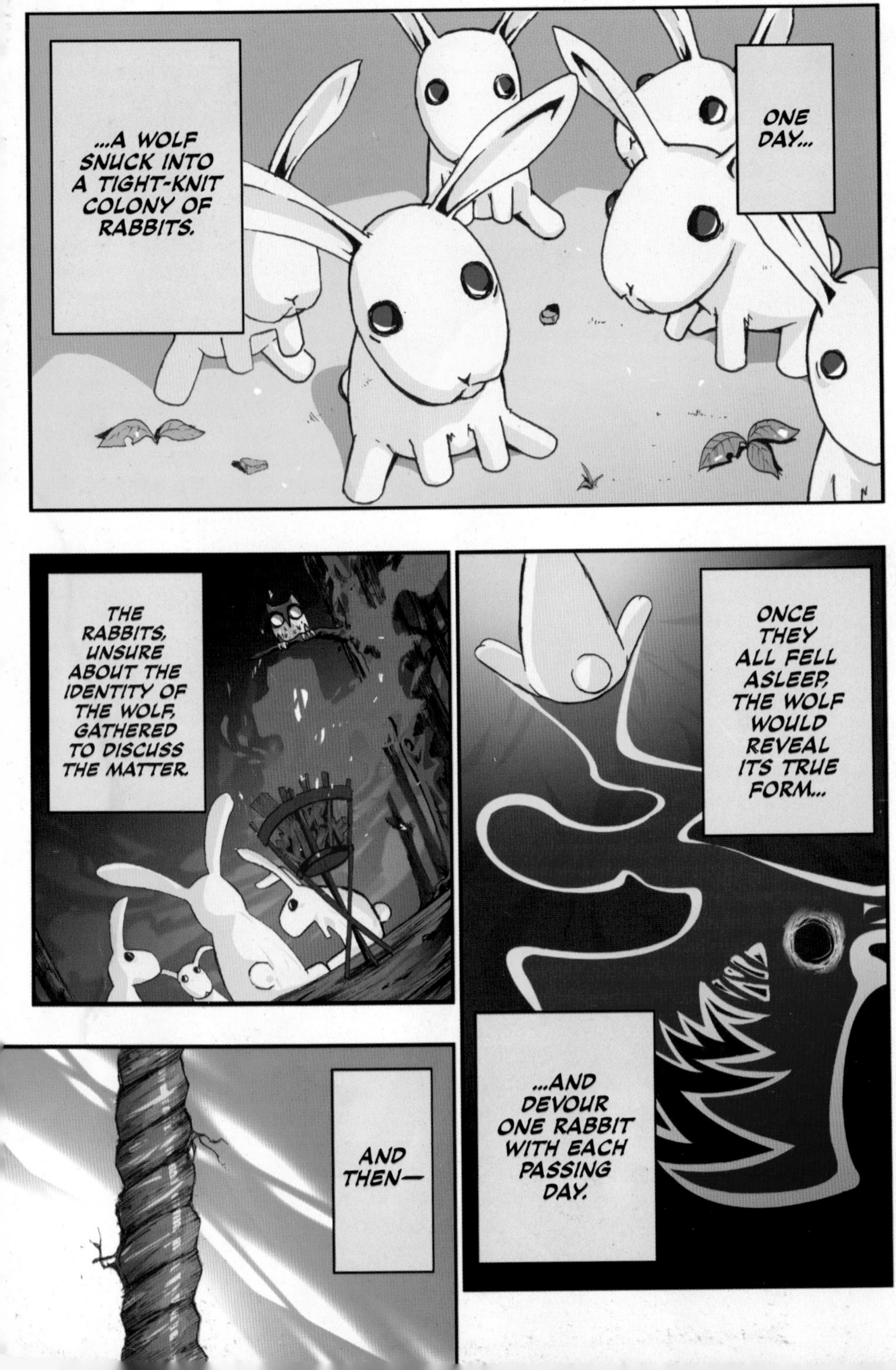
ONE DAY...
...A WOLF SNUCK INTO A TIGHT-KNIT COLONY OF RABBITS.
ONCE THEY ALL FELL ASLEEP, THE WOLF WOULD REVEAL ITS TRUE FORM...
...AND DEVOUR ONE RABBIT WITH EACH PASSING DAY.
THE RABBITS, UNSURE ABOUT THE IDENTITY OF THE WOLF, GATHERED TO DISCUSS THE MATTER.
AND THEN—

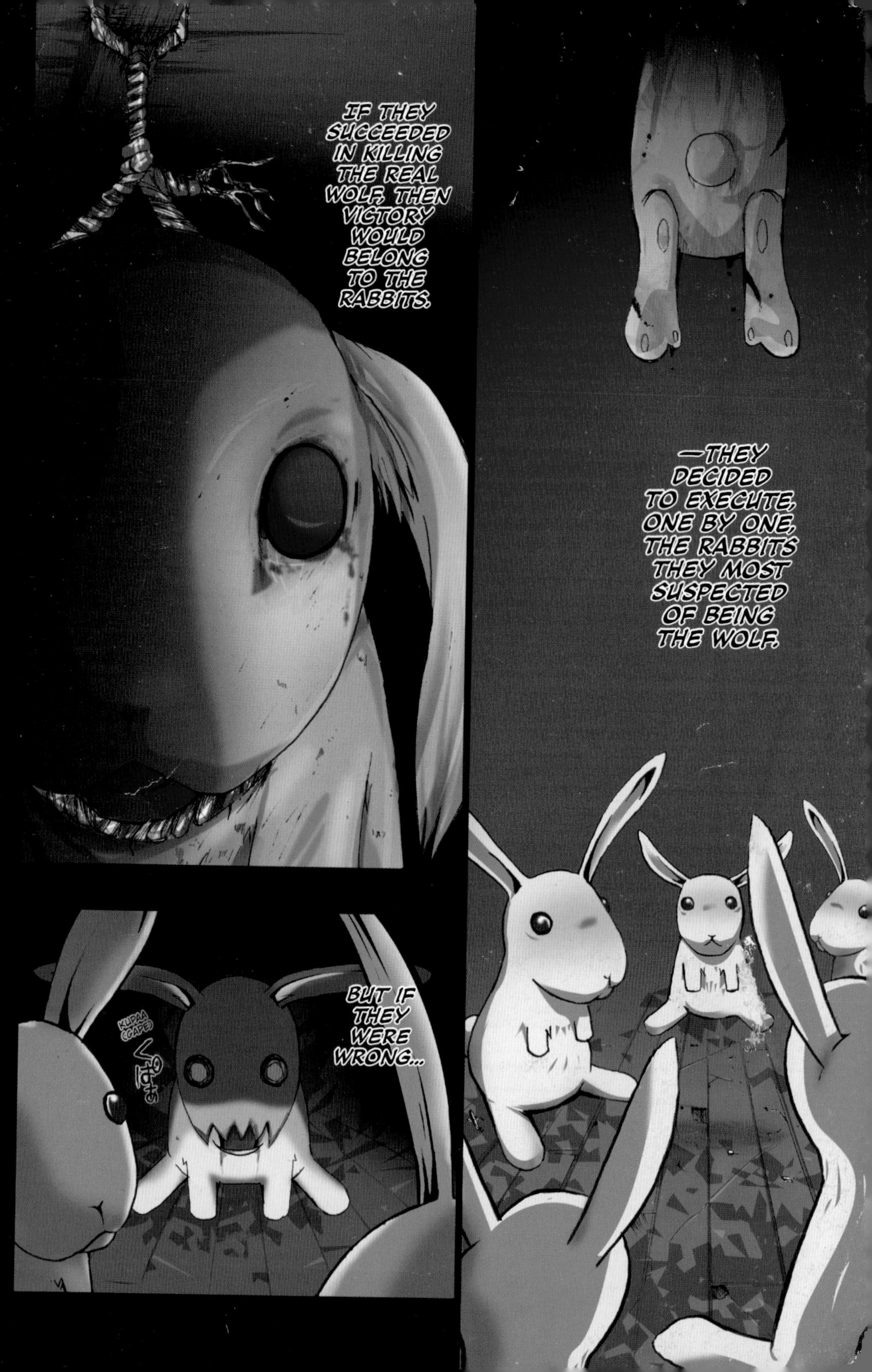
—THEY DECIDED TO EXECUTE, ONE BY ONE, THE RABBITS THEY MOST SUSPECTED OF BEING THE WOLF.
IF THEY SUCCEEDED IN KILLING THE REAL WOLF, THEN VICTORY WOULD BELONG TO THE RABBITS.
BUT IF THEY WERE WRONG...
KUPAA (GAPE)

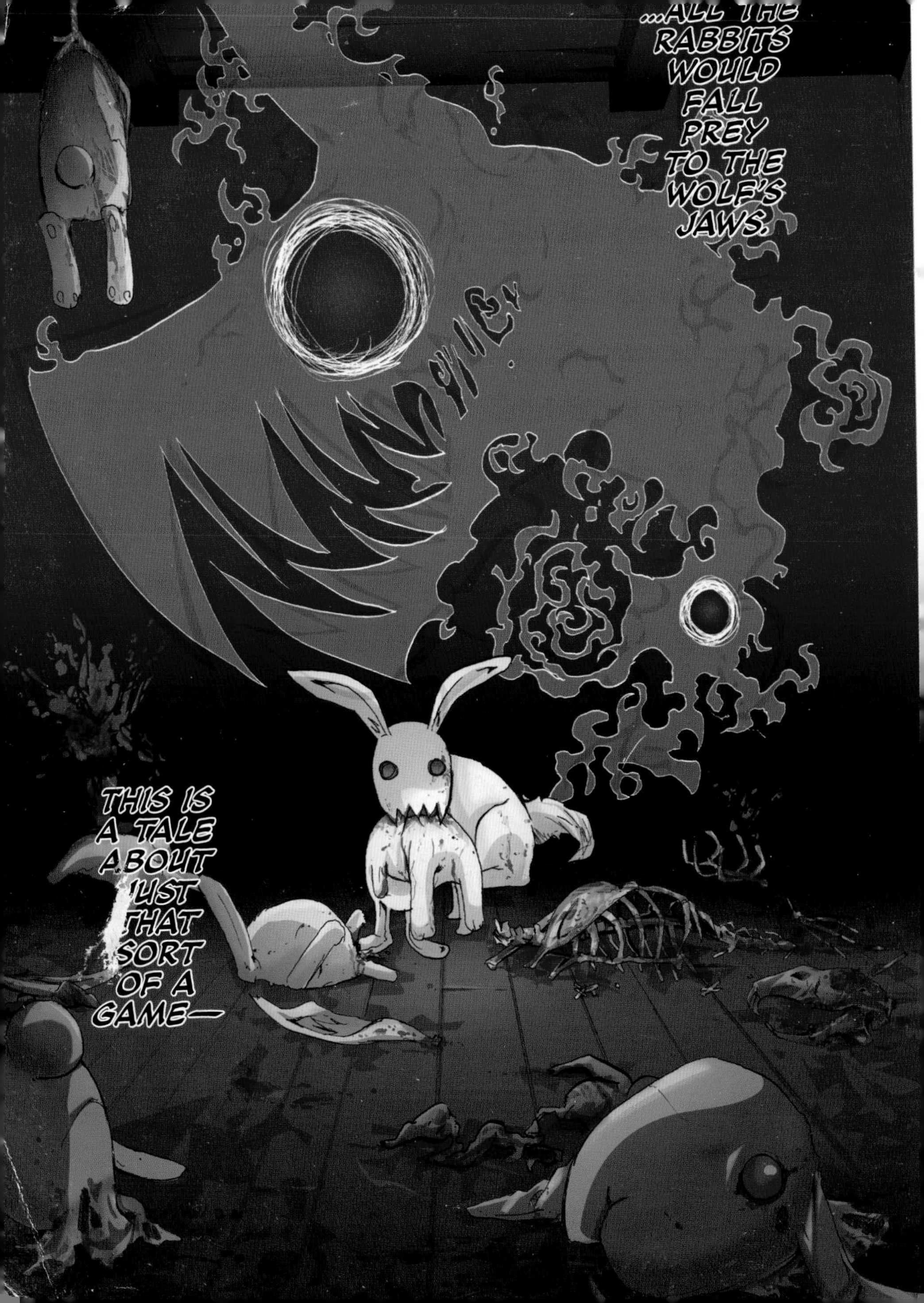
...ALL THE RABBITS WOULD FALL PREY TO THE WOLF'S JAWS.
THIS IS A TALE ABOUT JUST THAT SORT OF A GAME—

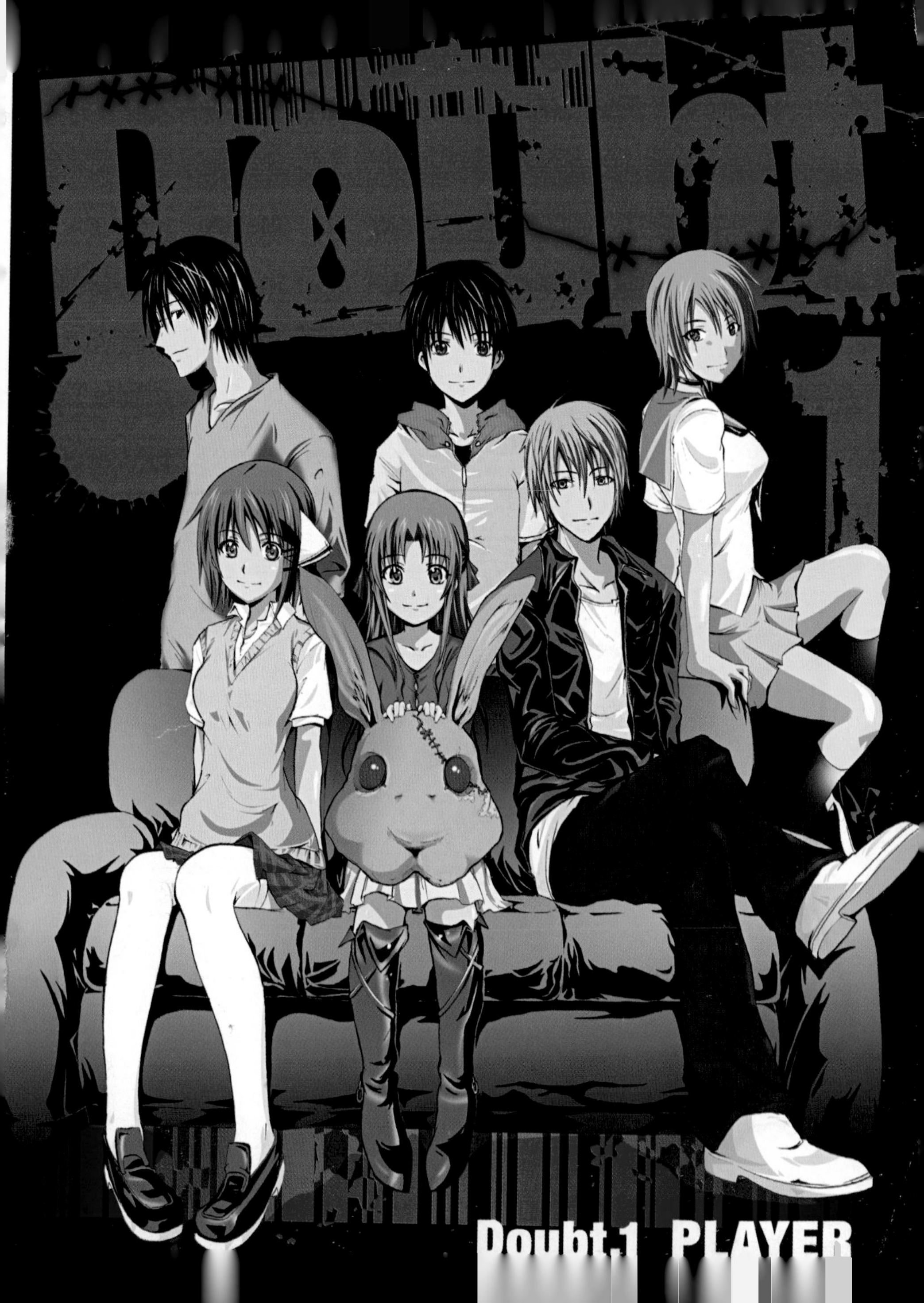
Doubt
Doubt.1 PLAYER

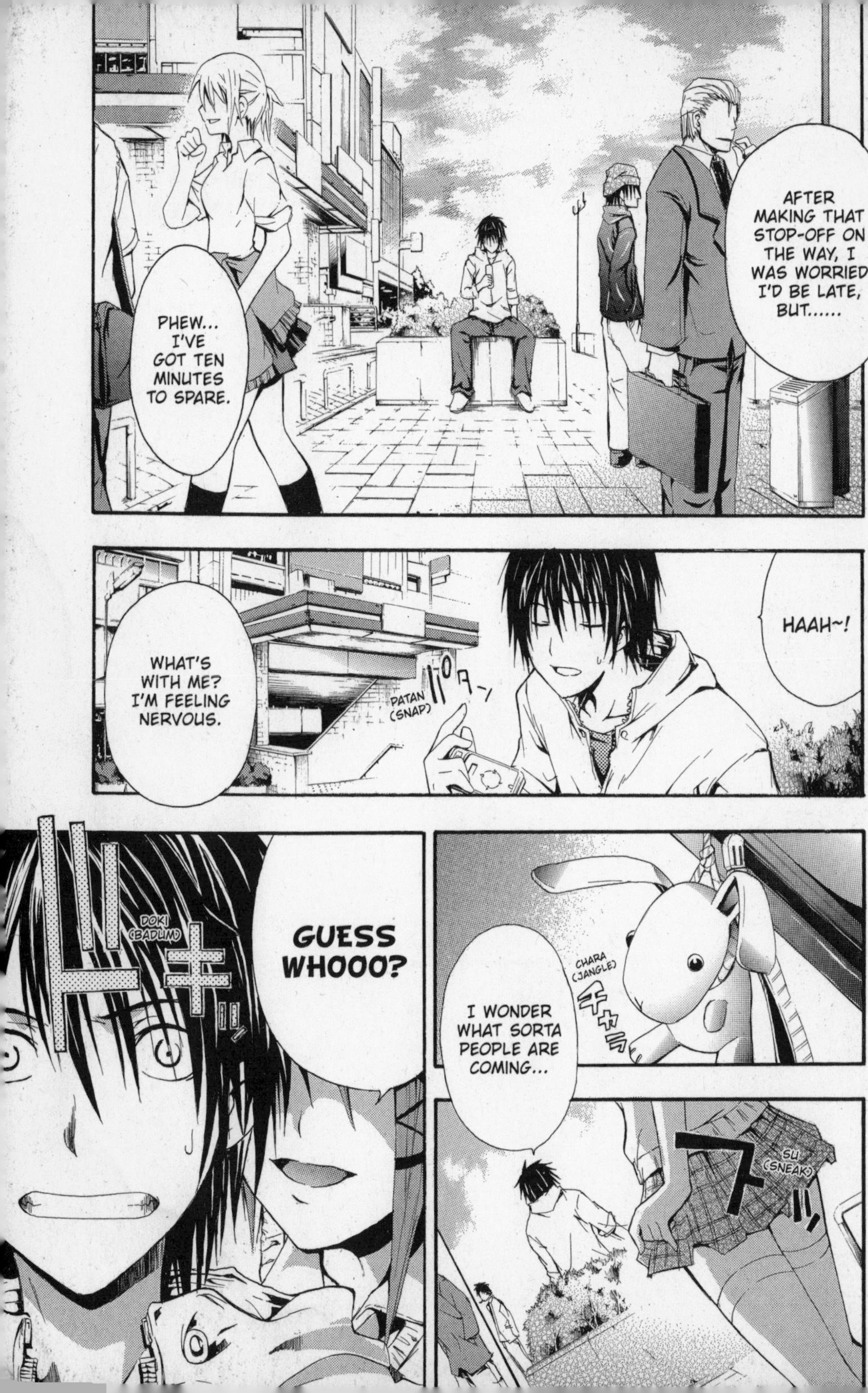
AFTER MAKING THAT STOP-OFF ON THE WAY, I WAS WORRIED I'D BE LATE, BUT......
PHEW... I'VE GOT TEN MINUTES TO SPARE.
HAAH~!
PATAN (SNAP)
WHAT'S WITH ME? I'M FEELING NERVOUS.
CHARA (JANGLE)
I WONDER WHAT SORTA PEOPLE ARE COMING...
SU (SNEAK)
GUESS WHOOO?
DOKI (BADUMP)

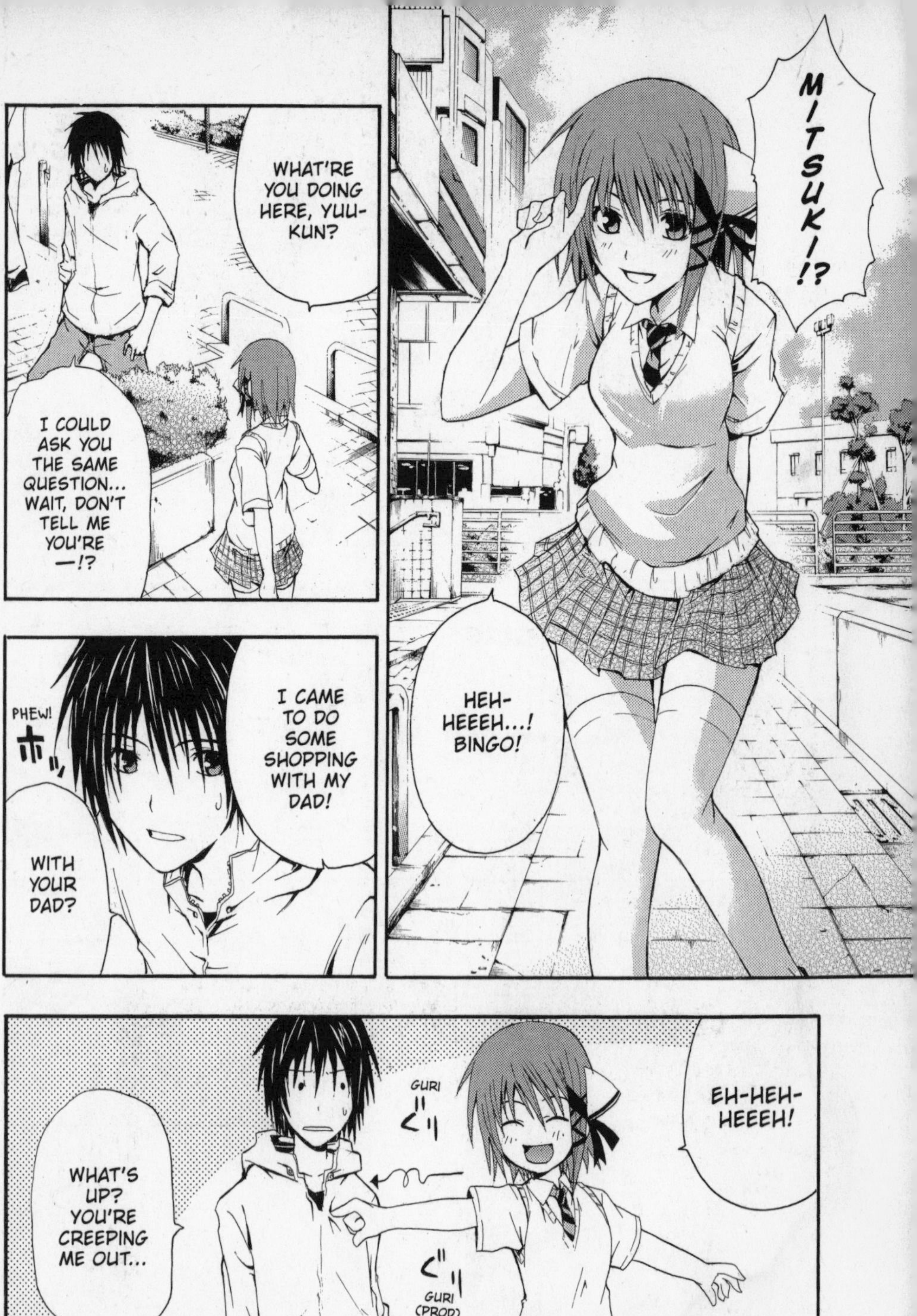
MITSUKI!?
HEH-HEEEH...! BINGO!
WHAT'RE YOU DOING HERE, YUU-KUN?
I COULD ASK YOU THE SAME QUESTION... WAIT, DON'T TELL ME YOU'RE —!?
I CAME TO DO SOME SHOPPING WITH MY DAD!
PHEW!
ホッ
WITH YOUR DAD?
EH-HEH-HEEEH!
GURI
ぐり
WHAT'S UP? YOU'RE CREEPING ME OUT...
ぐり
GURI (PROD)

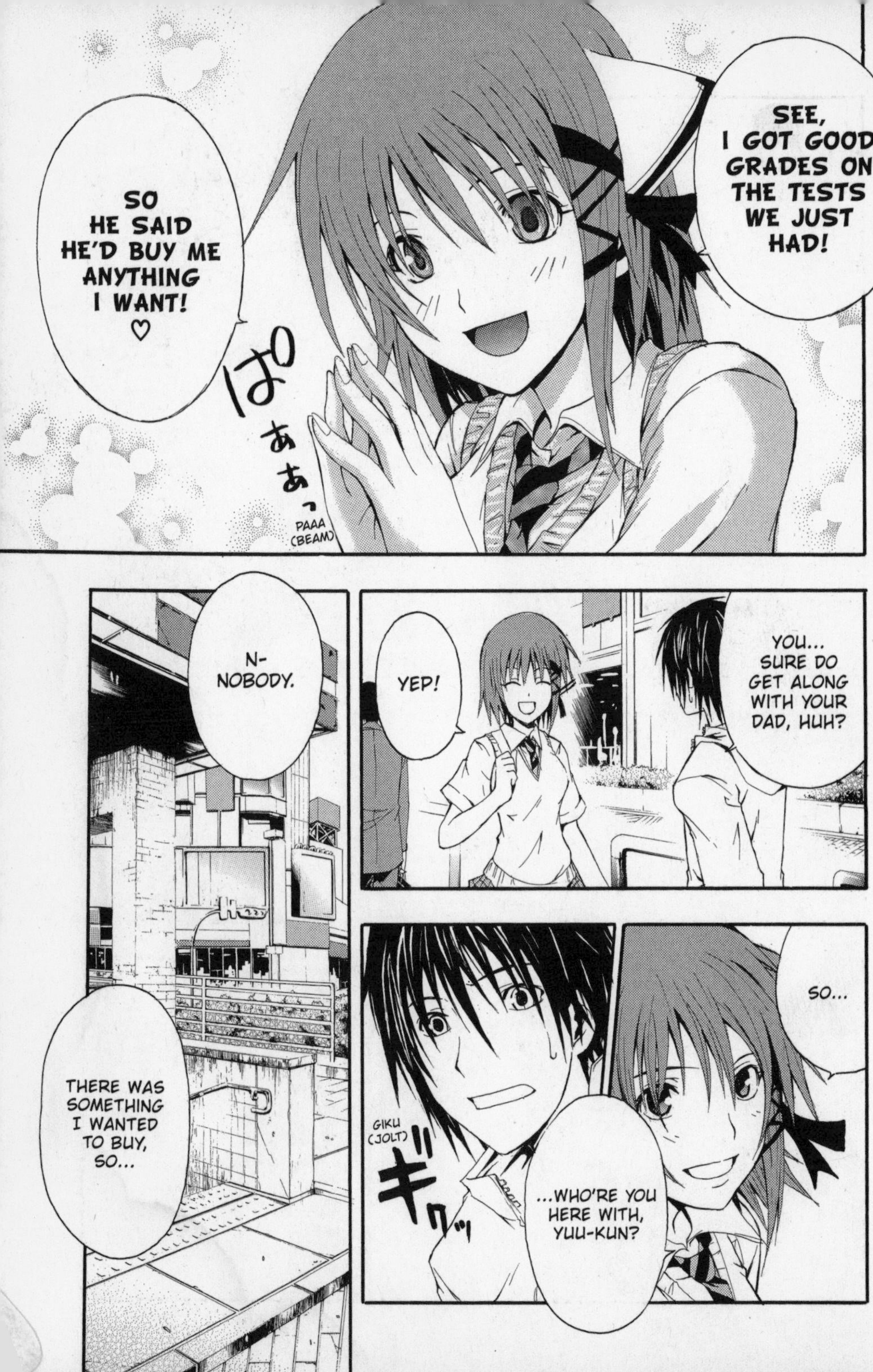
SEE, I GOT GOOD GRADES ON THE TESTS WE JUST HAD!
SO HE SAID HE'D BUY ME ANYTHING I WANT! ♡
ぱあぁっ
PAAA (BEAM)
YOU... SURE DO GET ALONG WITH YOUR DAD, HUH?
YEP!
SO...
...WHO'RE YOU HERE WITH, YUU-KUN?
GIKU (JOLT)
ギクッ
N-NOBODY.
THERE WAS SOMETHING I WANTED TO BUY, SO...

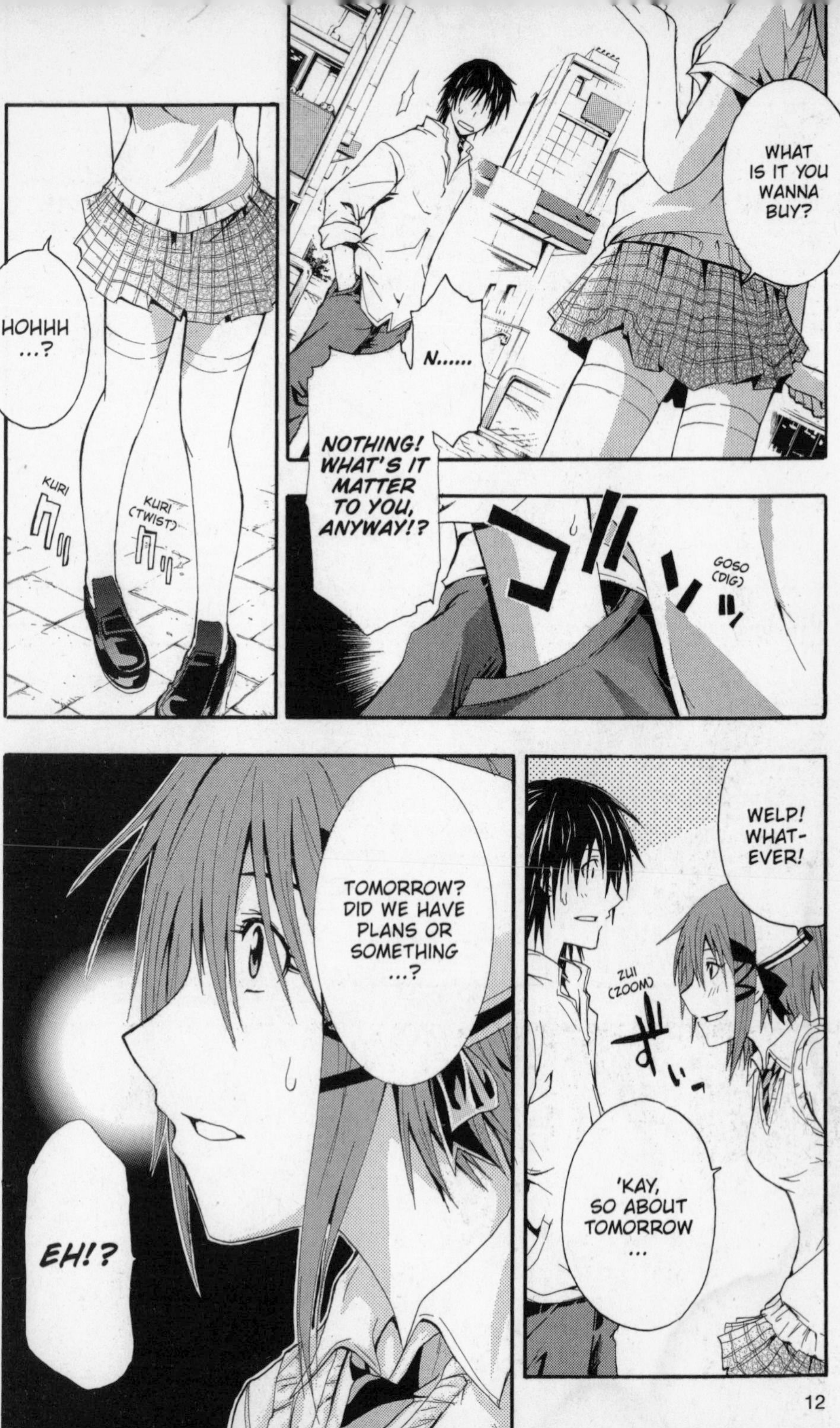
WHAT IS IT YOU WANNA BUY?
N......
NOTHING! WHAT'S IT MATTER TO YOU, ANYWAY!?
GOSO (DIG)
HOHHH ...?
KURI
KURI (TWIST)
WELP! WHAT-EVER!
ZUI (ZOOM)
'KAY, SO ABOUT TOMORROW ...
TOMORROW? DID WE HAVE PLANS OR SOMETHING ...?
EH!?

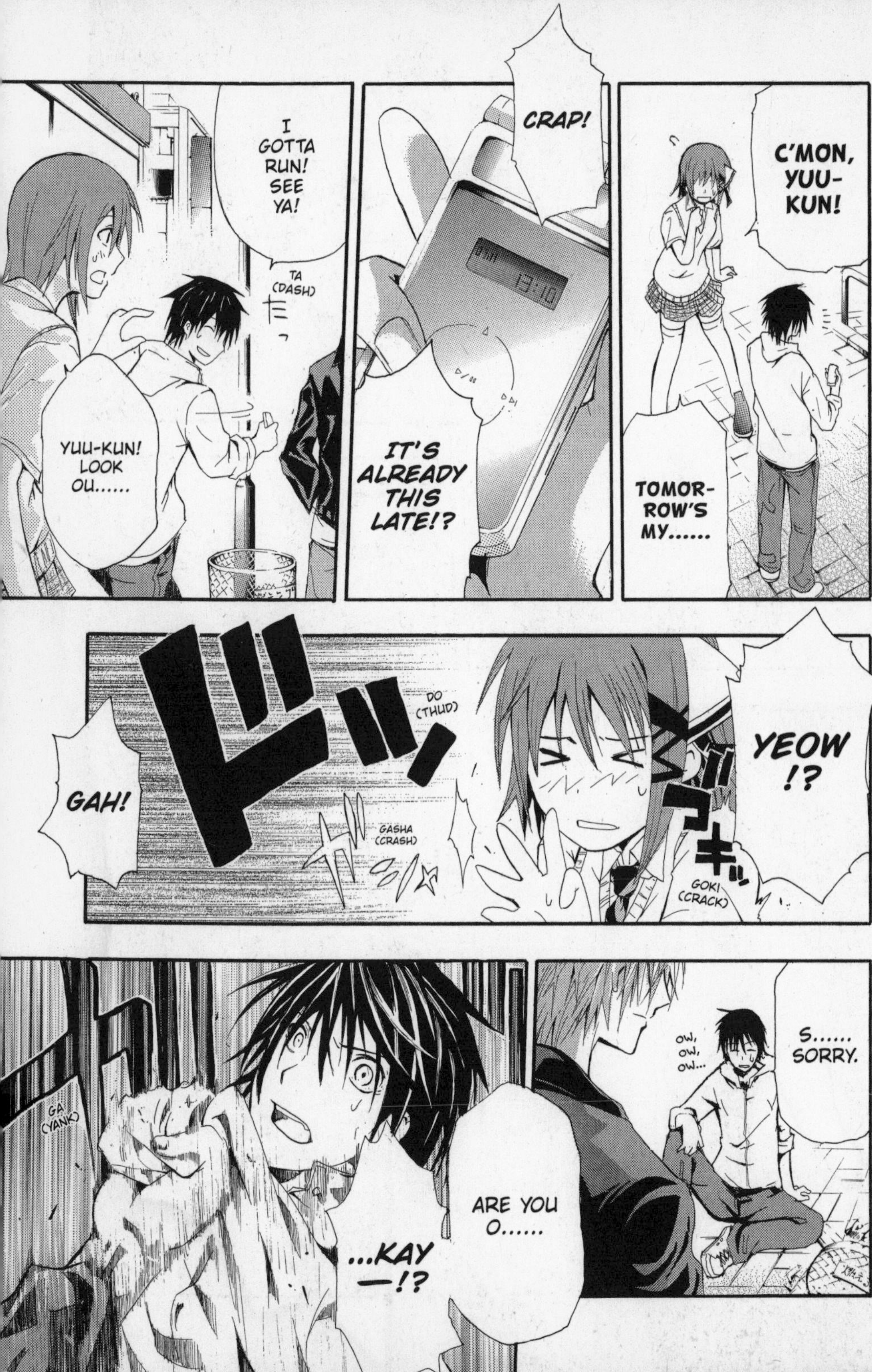
C'MON, YUU-KUN!
TOMOR-ROW'S MY......
CRAP!
IT'S ALREADY THIS LATE!?
I GOTTA RUN! SEE YA!
TA (DASH)
YUU-KUN! LOOK OU......
YEOW !?
GOKI (CRACK)
DO (THUD)
GASHA (CRASH)
GAH!
S...... SORRY.
OW, OW, OW...
ARE YOU O......
...KAY —!?
GA (YANK)

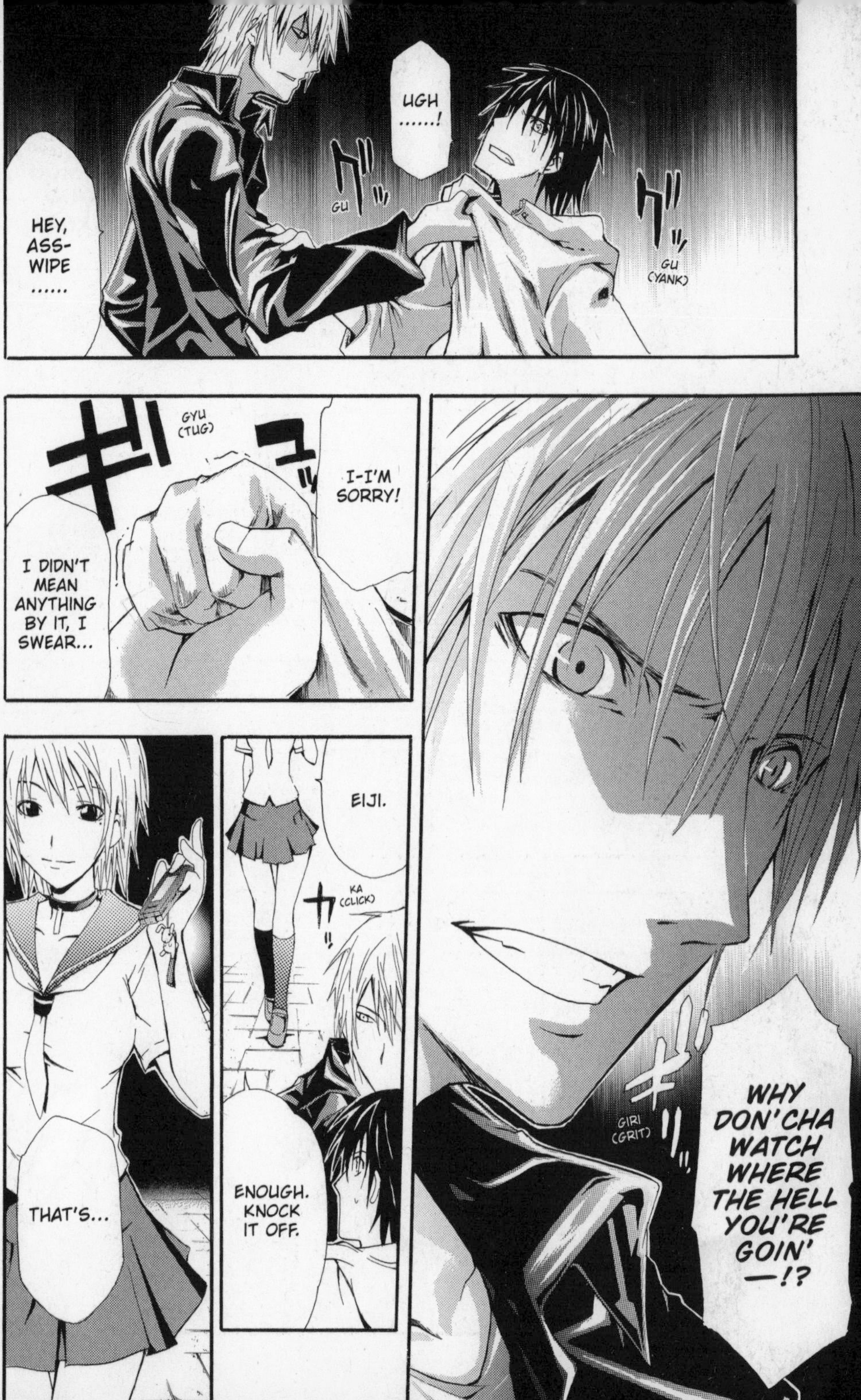

UGH ......!
GU (YANK)
GU
HEY, ASS-WIPE ......
GIRI (GRIT)
WHY DON'CHA WATCH WHERE THE HELL YOU'RE GOIN' —!?
GYU (TUG)
I-I'M SORRY!
I DIDN'T MEAN ANYTHING BY IT, I SWEAR...
EIJI.
KA (CLICK)
ENOUGH. KNOCK IT OFF.
THAT'S...

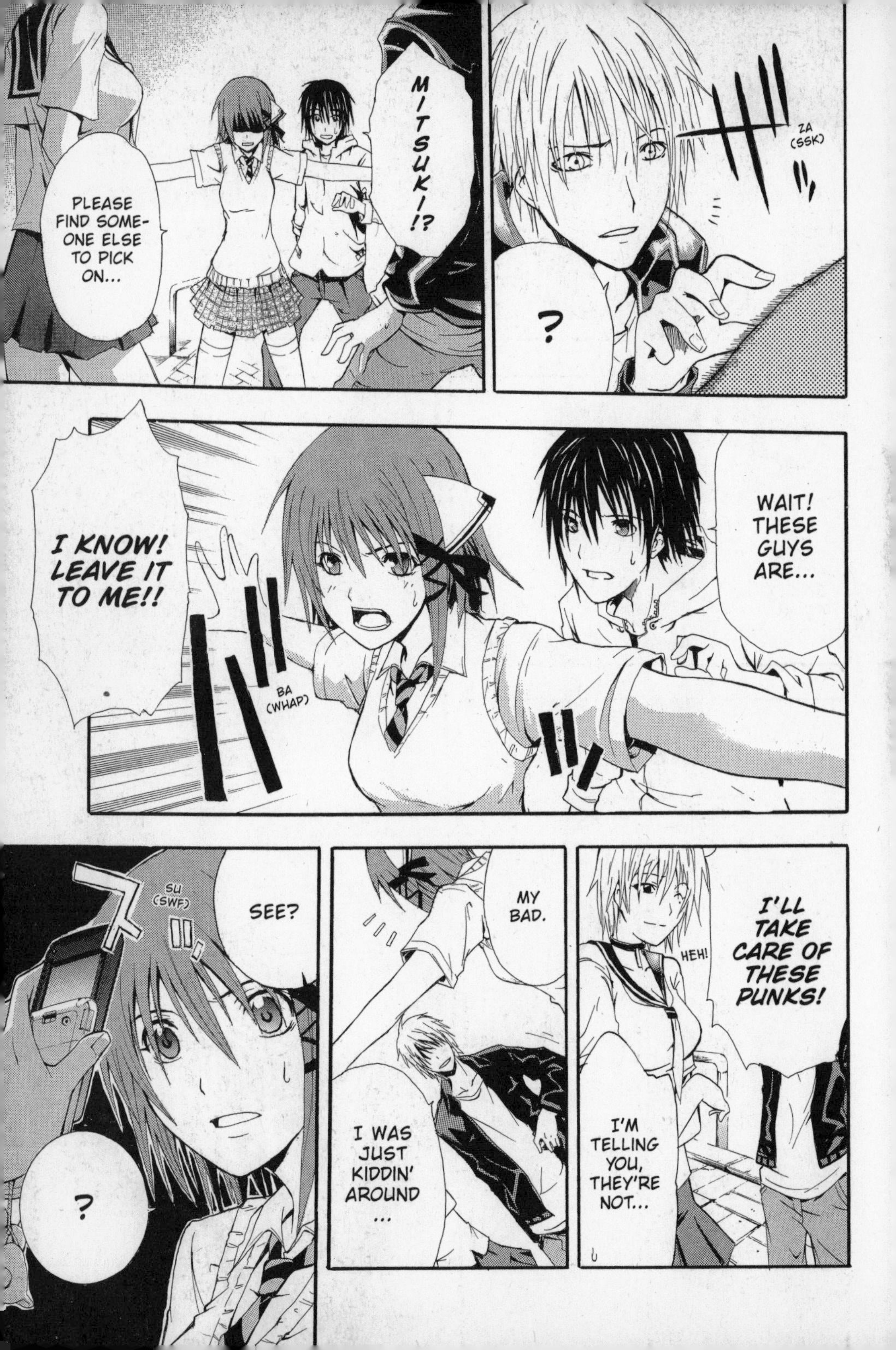
ZA (SSK)
?
MITSUKI!?
PLEASE FIND SOME-ONE ELSE TO PICK ON...
WAIT! THESE GUYS ARE...
BA (WHAP)
I KNOW! LEAVE IT TO ME!!
I'LL TAKE CARE OF THESE PUNKS!
HEH!
I'M TELLING YOU, THEY'RE NOT...
MY BAD.
I WAS JUST KIDDIN' AROUND...
SEE?
SU (SWF)
?

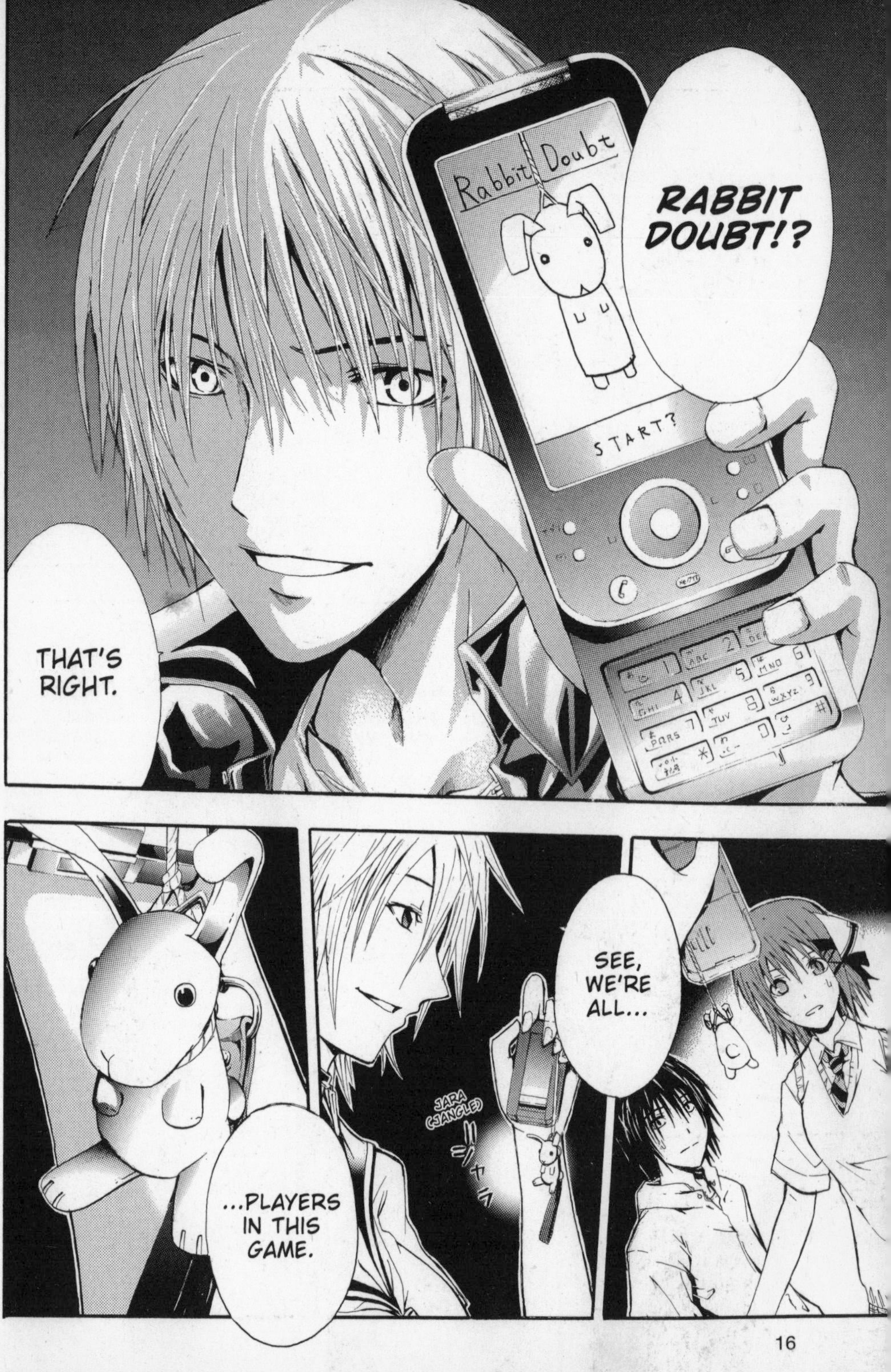
RABBIT DOUBT!?
Rabbit Doubt
START?
THAT'S RIGHT.
SEE, WE'RE ALL...
JARA (JANGLE)
...PLAYERS IN THIS GAME.

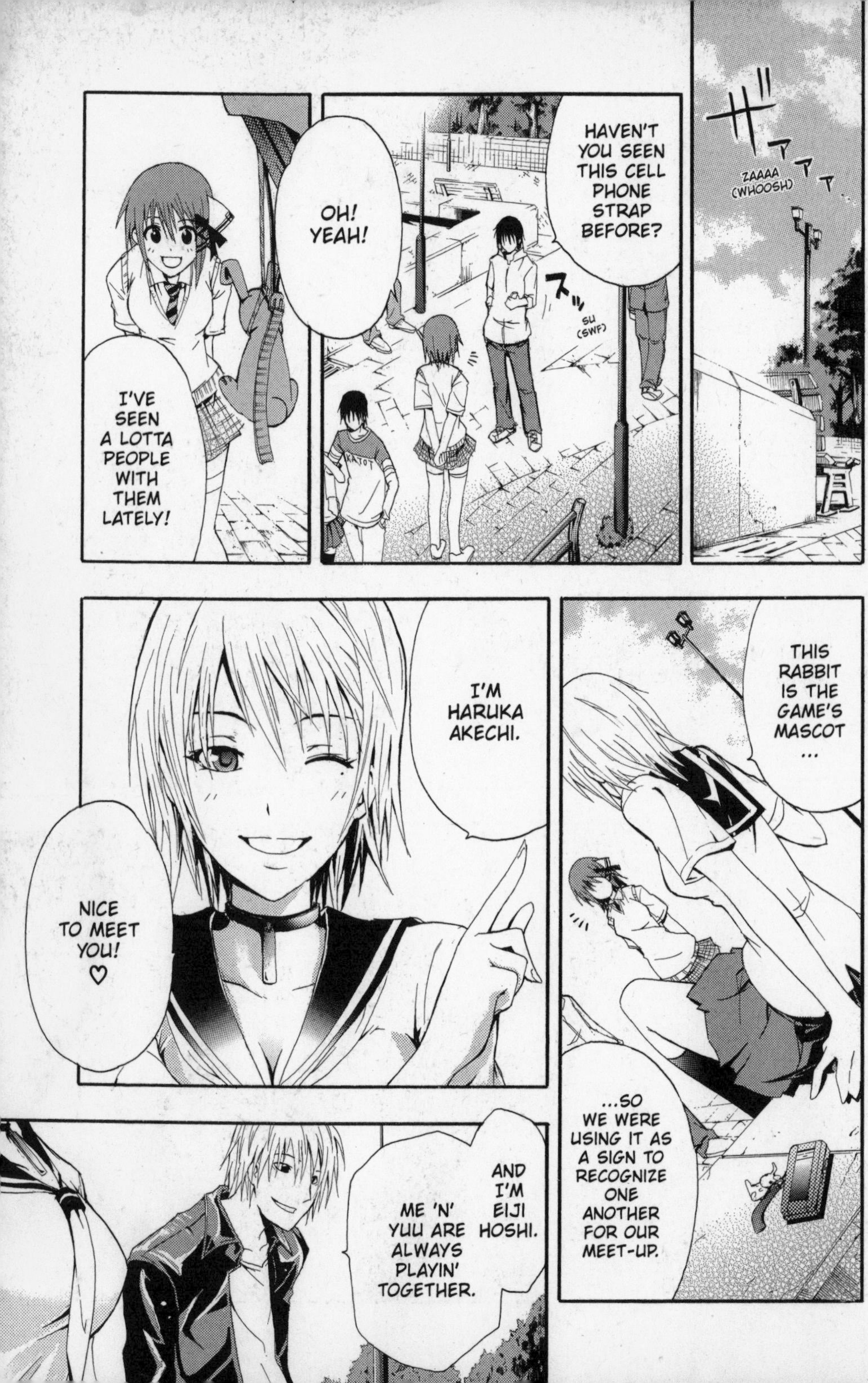
ザァァァ
ZAAAA (WHOOSH)
HAVEN'T YOU SEEN THIS CELL PHONE STRAP BEFORE?
スッ
SU (SWF)
OH! YEAH!
I'VE SEEN A LOTTA PEOPLE WITH THEM LATELY!
THIS RABBIT IS THE GAME'S MASCOT ...
...SO WE WERE USING IT AS A SIGN TO RECOGNIZE ONE ANOTHER FOR OUR MEET-UP.
I'M HARUKA AKECHI.
NICE TO MEET YOU! ♡
AND I'M EIJI HOSHI.
ME 'N' YUU ARE ALWAYS PLAYIN' TOGETHER.

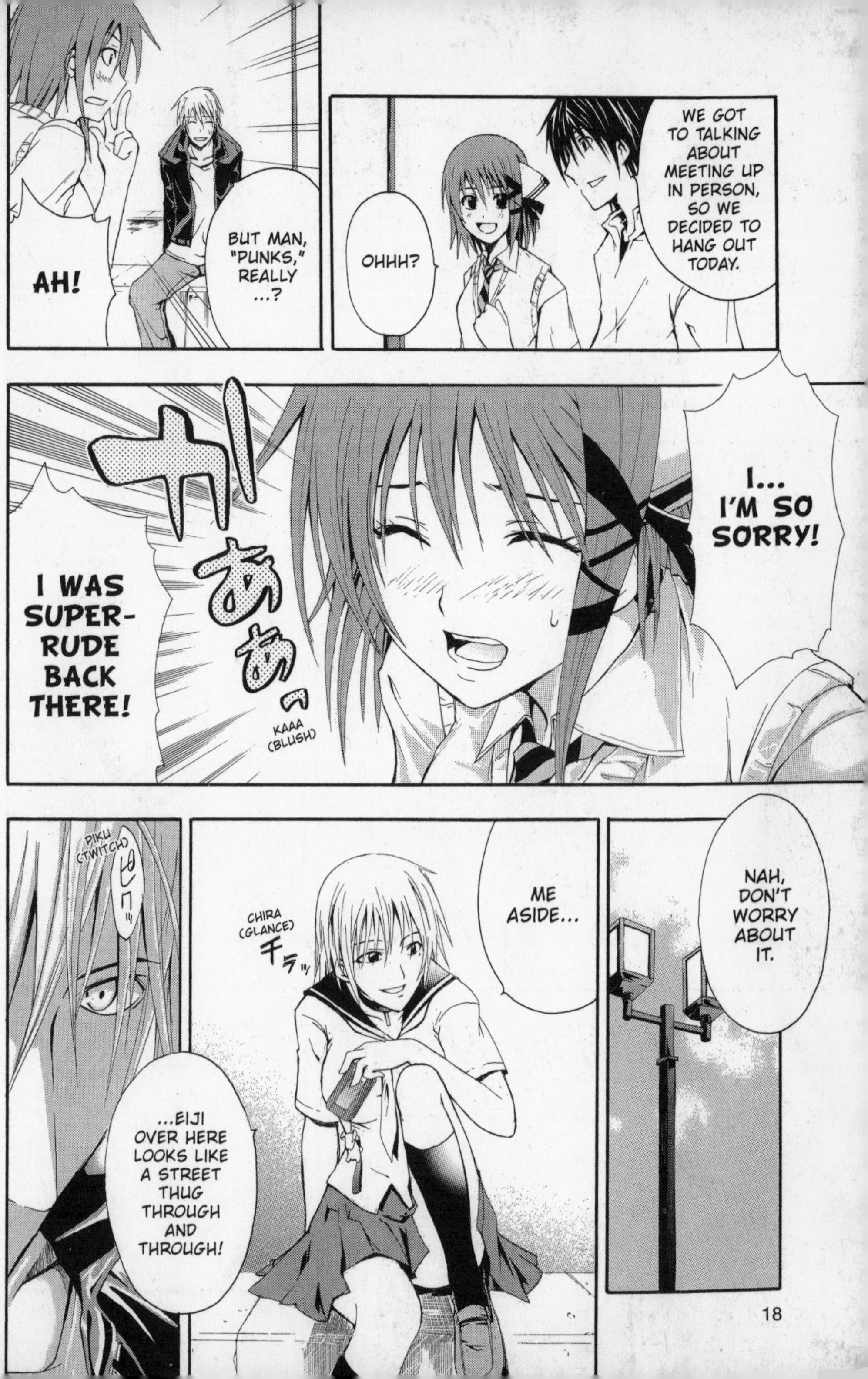
WE GOT TO TALKING ABOUT MEETING UP IN PERSON, SO WE DECIDED TO HANG OUT TODAY.
OHHH?
BUT MAN, "PUNKS," REALLY ...?
AH!
I... I'M SO SORRY!
I WAS SUPER-RUDE BACK THERE!
かあぁ
KAAA (BLUSH)
NAH, DON'T WORRY ABOUT IT.
ME ASIDE...
チラッ
CHIRA (GLANCE)
ピクッ
PIKU (TWITCH)
...EIJI OVER HERE LOOKS LIKE A STREET THUG THROUGH AND THROUGH!

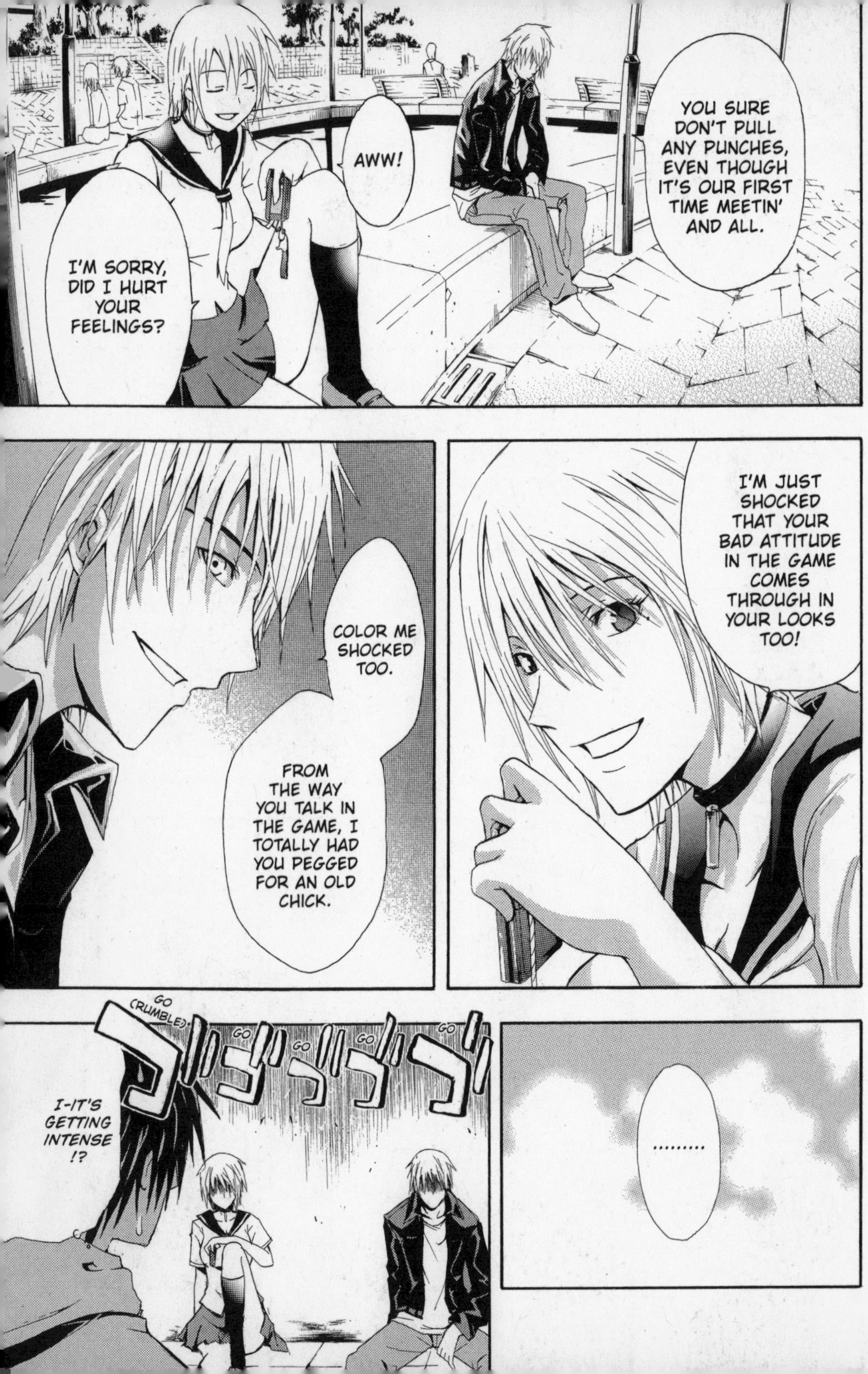
YOU SURE DON'T PULL ANY PUNCHES, EVEN THOUGH IT'S OUR FIRST TIME MEETIN' AND ALL.
AWW!
I'M SORRY, DID I HURT YOUR FEELINGS?
I'M JUST SHOCKED THAT YOUR BAD ATTITUDE IN THE GAME COMES THROUGH IN YOUR LOOKS TOO!
COLOR ME SHOCKED TOO.
FROM THE WAY YOU TALK IN THE GAME, I TOTALLY HAD YOU PEGGED FOR AN OLD CHICK.
....
GO GO GO GO GO (RUMBLE)
I-IT'S GETTING INTENSE !?

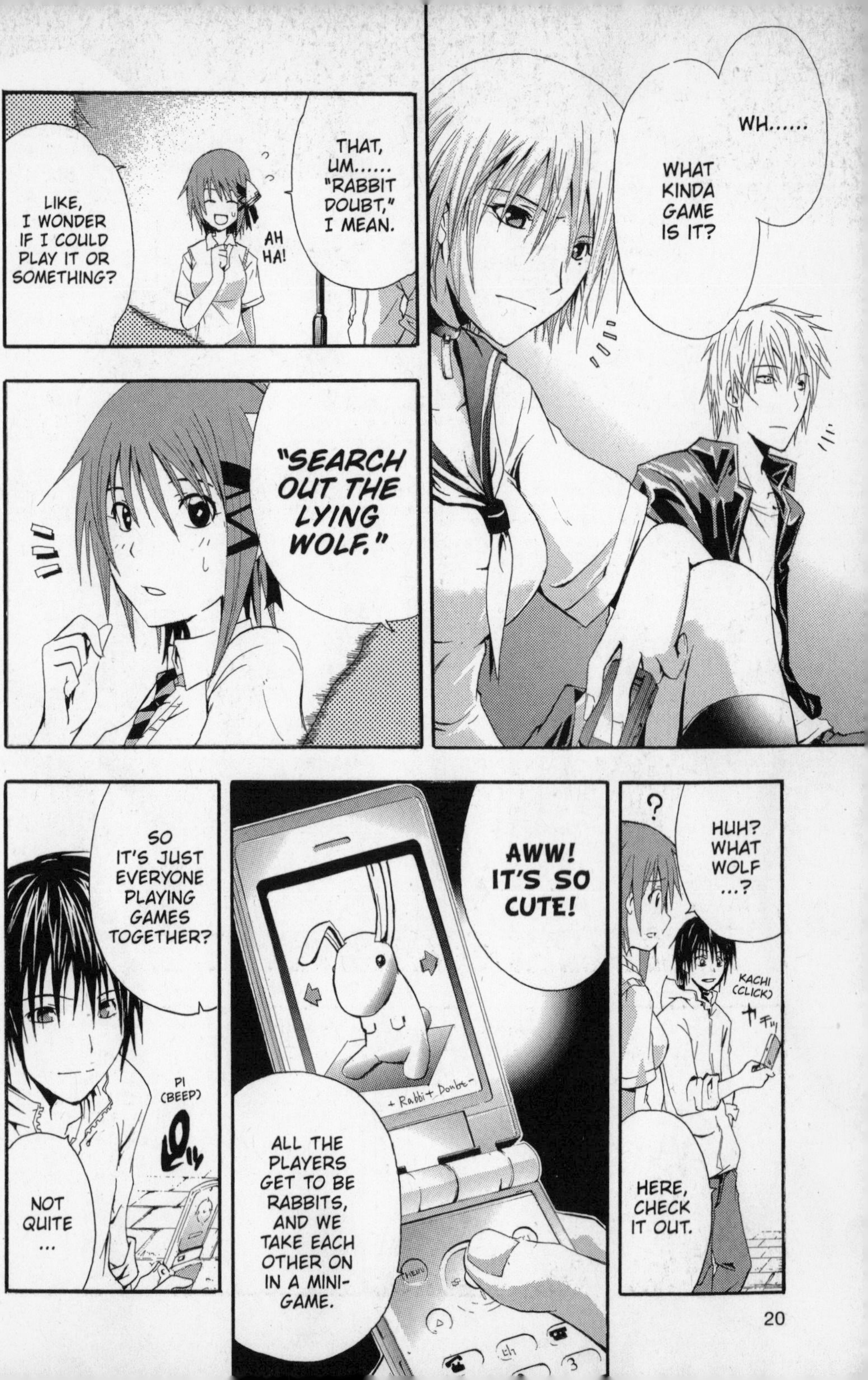

WH......
WHAT KINDA GAME IS IT?
THAT, UM...... "RABBIT DOUBT," I MEAN.
AH HA!
LIKE, I WONDER IF I COULD PLAY IT OR SOMETHING?
"SEARCH OUT THE LYING WOLF."
HUH? WHAT WOLF ...?
KACHI (CLICK)
HERE, CHECK IT OUT.
AWW! IT'S SO CUTE!
+ Rabbit Doubt -
ALL THE PLAYERS GET TO BE RABBITS, AND WE TAKE EACH OTHER ON IN A MINI-GAME.
SO IT'S JUST EVERYONE PLAYING GAMES TOGETHER?
PI (BEEP)
NOT QUITE ...

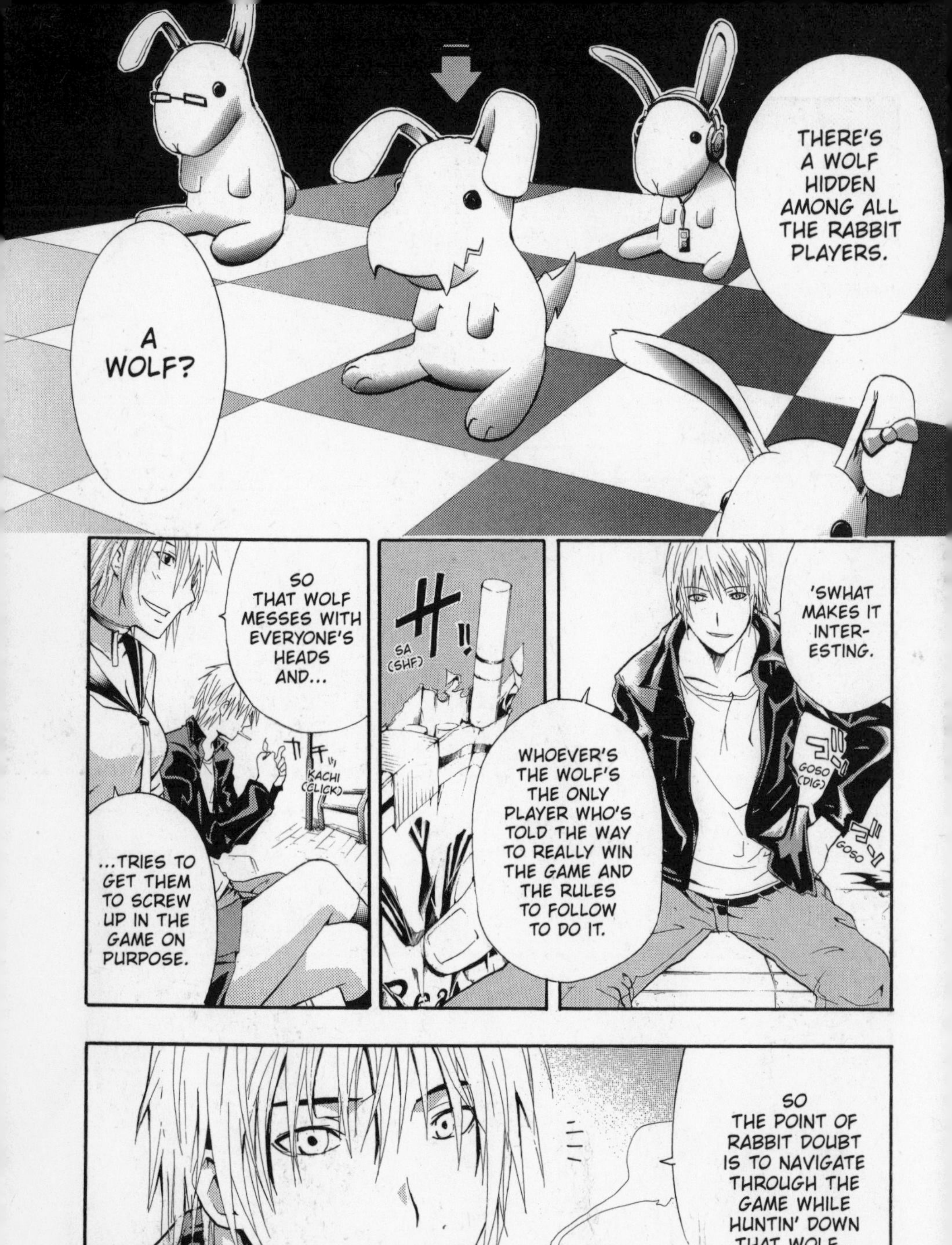
THERE'S A WOLF HIDDEN AMONG ALL THE RABBIT PLAYERS.
A WOLF?
'SWHAT MAKES IT INTER-ESTING.
GOSO (DIG)
GOSO
SA (SHF)
WHOEVER'S THE WOLF'S THE ONLY PLAYER WHO'S TOLD THE WAY TO REALLY WIN THE GAME AND THE RULES TO FOLLOW TO DO IT.
SO THAT WOLF MESSES WITH EVERYONE'S HEADS AND...
KACHI (CLICK)
...TRIES TO GET THEM TO SCREW UP IN THE GAME ON PURPOSE.
SO THE POINT OF RABBIT DOUBT IS TO NAVIGATE THROUGH THE GAME WHILE HUNTIN' DOWN THAT WOLF...

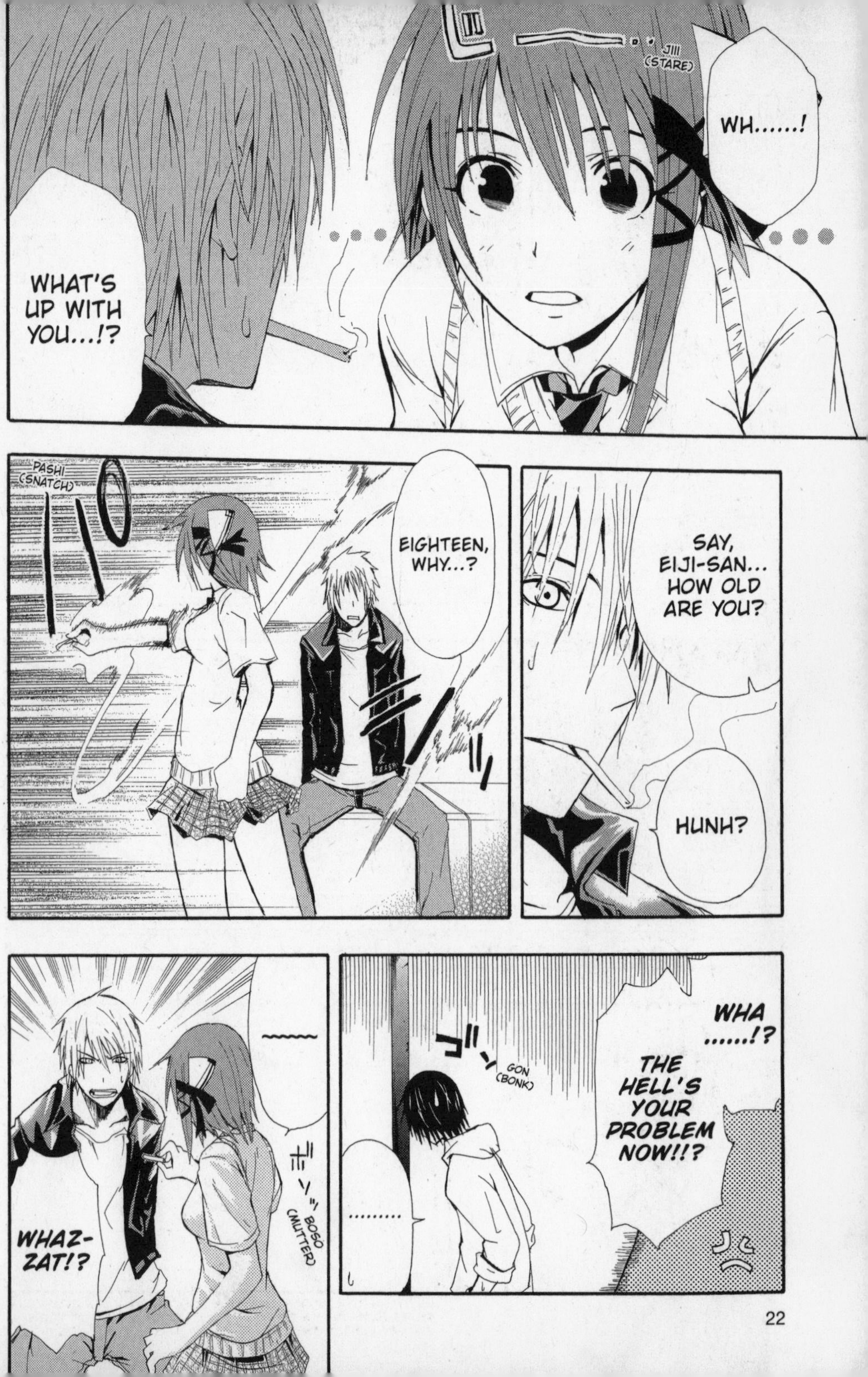
JIII (STARE)
WH......!
• • •
• • •
WHAT'S UP WITH YOU...!?
SAY, EIJI-SAN... HOW OLD ARE YOU?
HUNH?
EIGHTEEN, WHY...?
PASHI (SNATCH)
WHA ......!?
THE HELL'S YOUR PROBLEM NOW!!?
GON (BONK)
....
~~~~~
BOSO (MUTTER)
WHAZ-ZAT!?
~~~~~

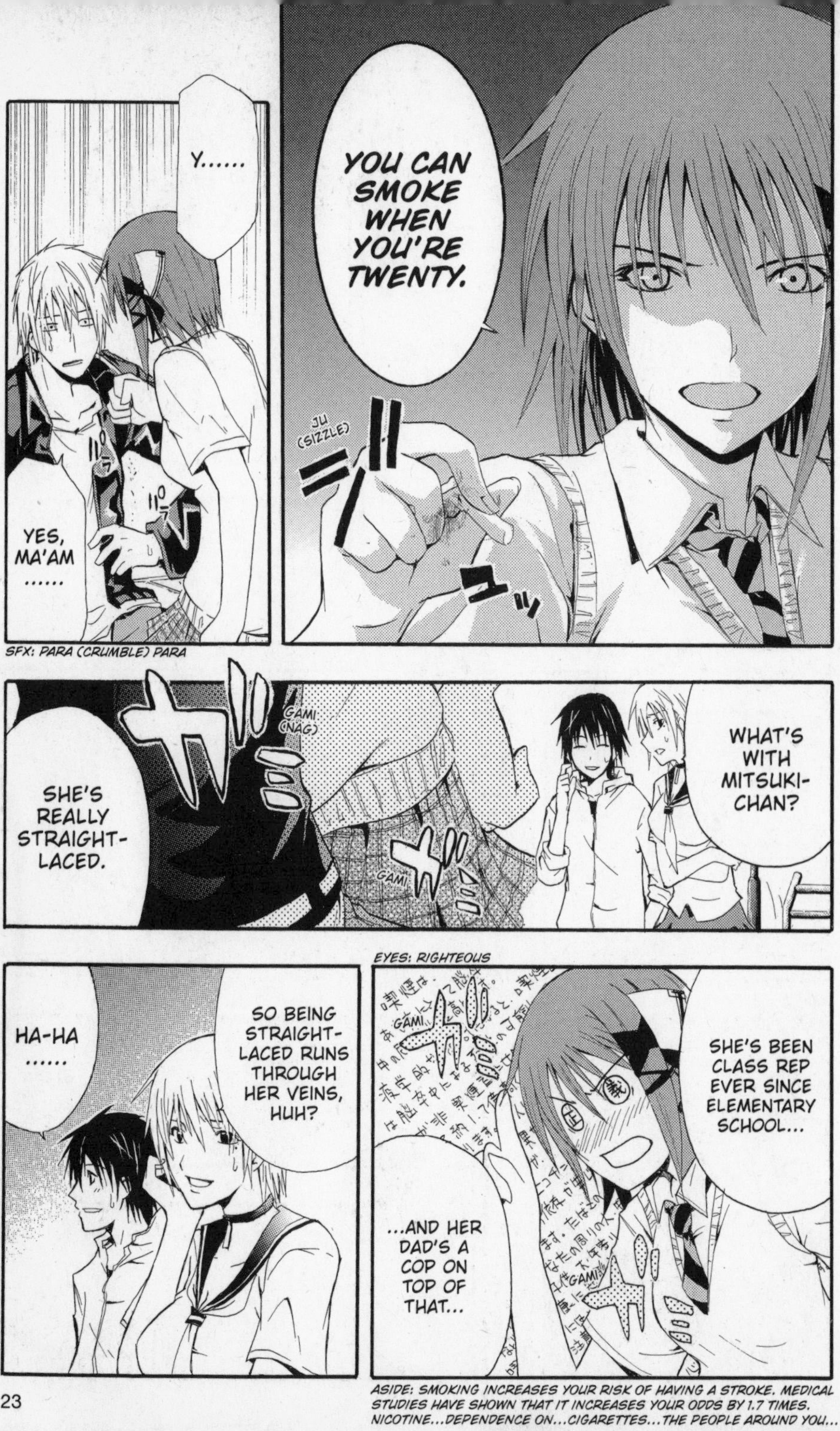
YOU CAN SMOKE WHEN YOU'RE TWENTY.
JU (SIZZLE)
Y......
YES, MA'AM ......
SFX: PARA (CRUMBLE) PARA
WHAT'S WITH MITSUKI-CHAN?
GAMI (NAG)
GAMI
SHE'S REALLY STRAIGHT-LACED.
EYES: RIGHTEOUS
SHE'S BEEN CLASS REP EVER SINCE ELEMENTARY SCHOOL...
GAMI
GAMI
...AND HER DAD'S A COP ON TOP OF THAT...
SO BEING STRAIGHT-LACED RUNS THROUGH HER VEINS, HUH?
HA-HA ......

ASIDE: SMOKING INCREASES YOUR RISK OF HAVING A STROKE. MEDICAL STUDIES HAVE SHOWN THAT IT INCREASES YOUR ODDS BY 1.7 TIMES. NICOTINE...DEPENDENCE ON...CIGARETTES...THE PEOPLE AROUND YOU...

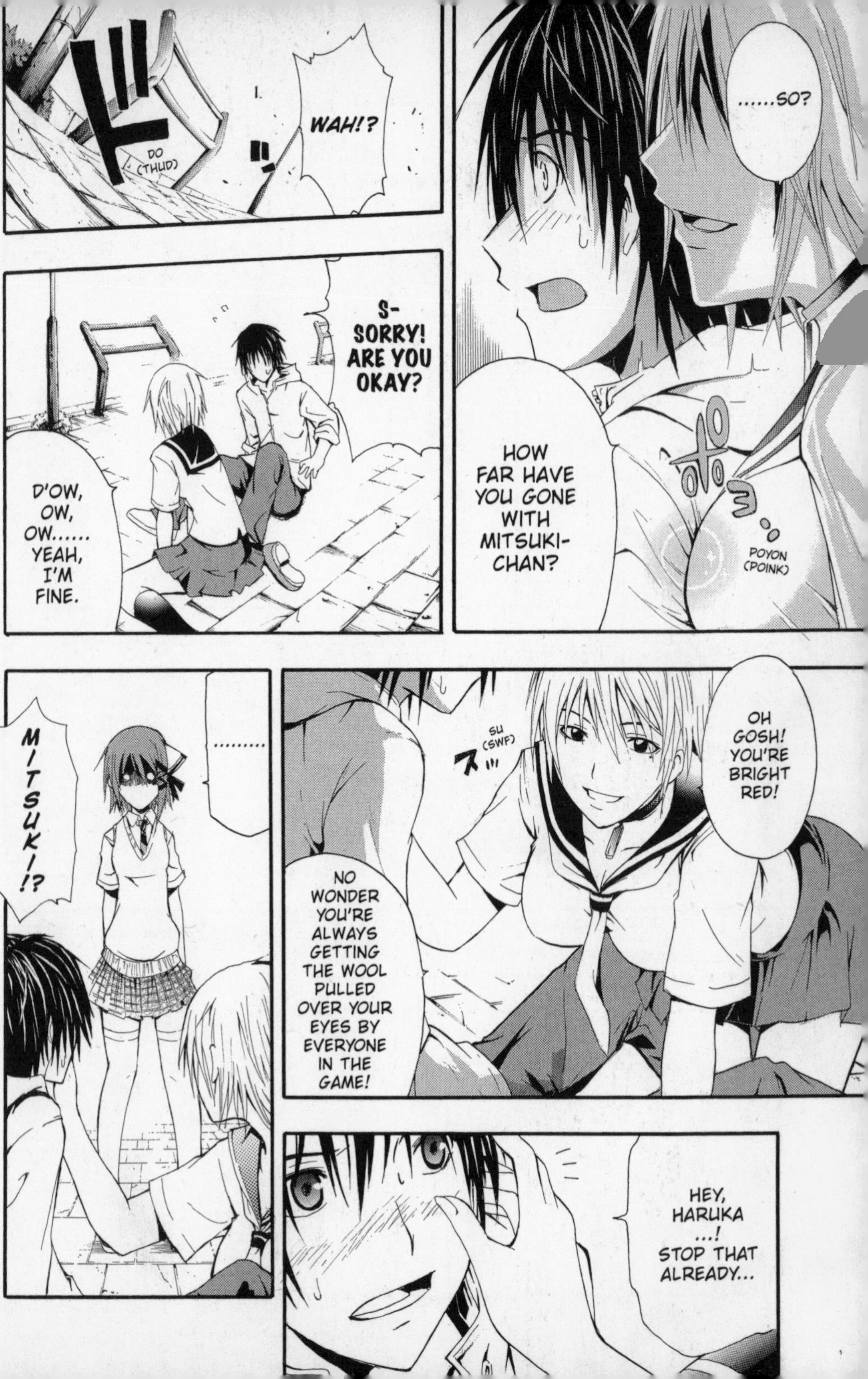
......SO?
HOW FAR HAVE YOU GONE WITH MITSUKI-CHAN?
POYON (POINK)
WAH!?
DO (THUD)
S-SORRY! ARE YOU OKAY?
D'OW, OW, OW...... YEAH, I'M FINE.
OH GOSH! YOU'RE BRIGHT RED!
SU (SWF)
NO WONDER YOU'RE ALWAYS GETTING THE WOOL PULLED OVER YOUR EYES BY EVERYONE IN THE GAME!
HEY, HARUKA ...! STOP THAT ALREADY...
....
MITSUKI!?

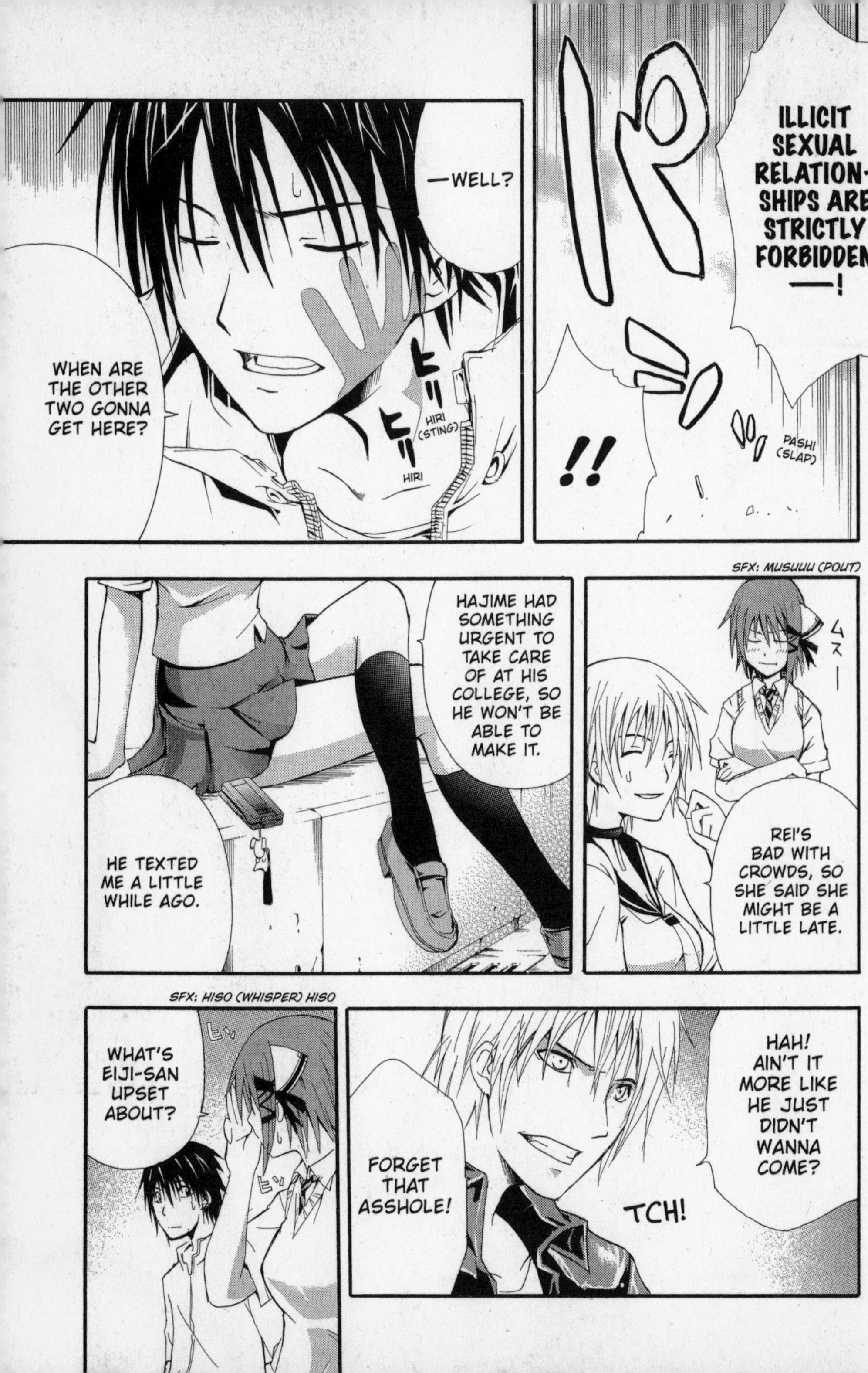

!!
PASHI (SLAP)
ILLICIT SEXUAL RELATION-SHIPS ARE STRICTLY FORBIDDEN—!
—WELL?
HIRI (STING)
HIRI
WHEN ARE THE OTHER TWO GONNA GET HERE?
SFX: MUSUUU (POUT)
REI'S BAD WITH CROWDS, SO SHE SAID SHE MIGHT BE A LITTLE LATE.
HAJIME HAD SOMETHING URGENT TO TAKE CARE OF AT HIS COLLEGE, SO HE WON'T BE ABLE TO MAKE IT.
HE TEXTED ME A LITTLE WHILE AGO.
HAH! AIN'T IT MORE LIKE HE JUST DIDN'T WANNA COME?
TCH!
FORGET THAT ASSHOLE!
SFX: HISO (WHISPER) HISO
WHAT'S EIJI-SAN UPSET ABOUT?

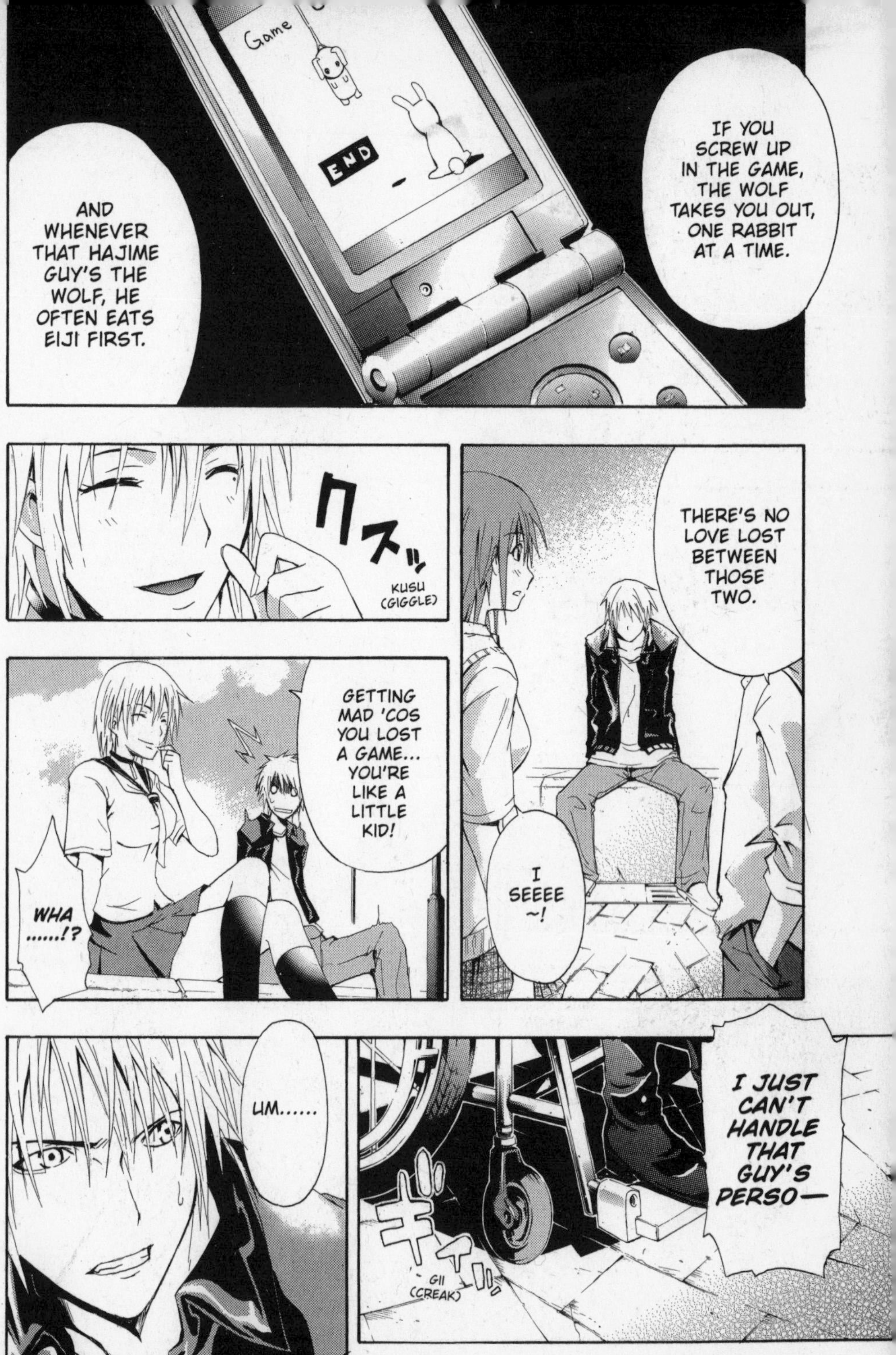

Game
END
IF YOU SCREW UP IN THE GAME, THE WOLF TAKES YOU OUT, ONE RABBIT AT A TIME.
AND WHENEVER THAT HAJIME GUY'S THE WOLF, HE OFTEN EATS EIJI FIRST.
THERE'S NO LOVE LOST BETWEEN THOSE TWO.
I SEEEE ~!
クスッ
KUSU (GIGGLE)
GETTING MAD 'COS YOU LOST A GAME... YOU'RE LIKE A LITTLE KID!
WHA ......!?
I JUST CAN'T HANDLE THAT GUY'S PERSO—
ギィ
GII (CREAK)
UM......

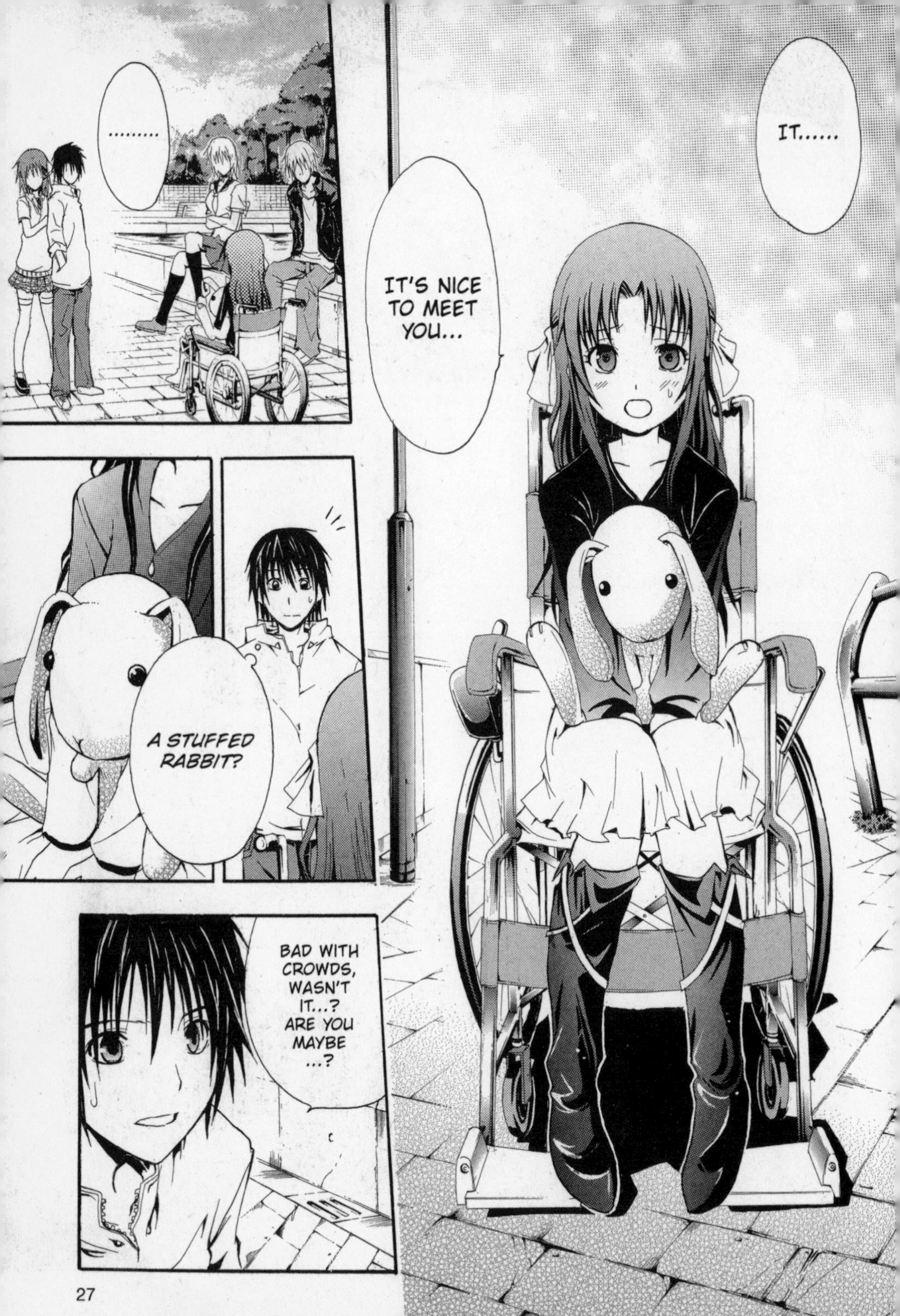
IT......
IT'S NICE TO MEET YOU...
....
A STUFFED RABBIT?
BAD WITH CROWDS, WASN'T IT...? ARE YOU MAYBE ...?

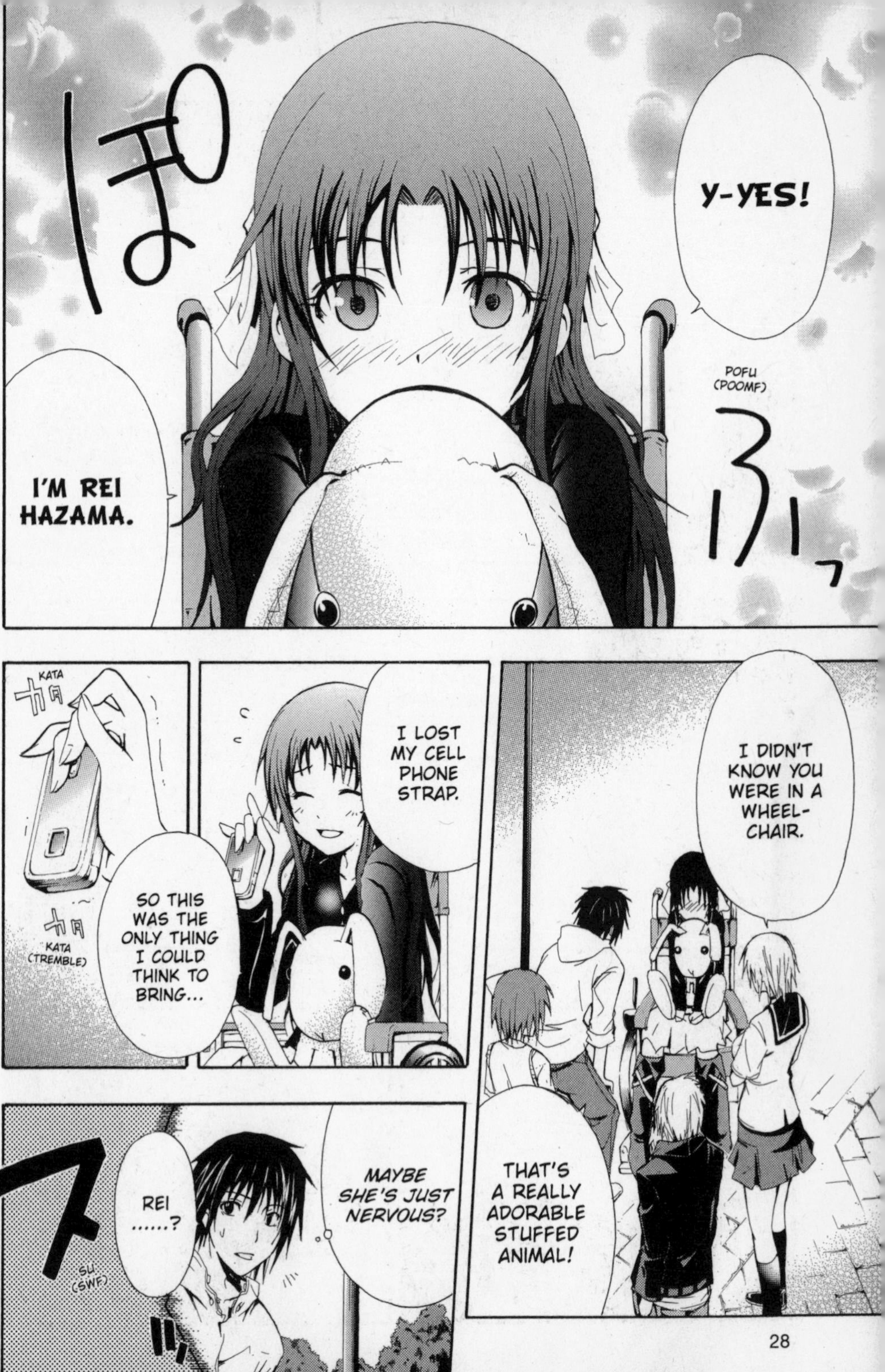
Y-YES!
POFU (POOMF)
I'M REI HAZAMA.
I DIDN'T KNOW YOU WERE IN A WHEEL-CHAIR.
I LOST MY CELL PHONE STRAP.
SO THIS WAS THE ONLY THING I COULD THINK TO BRING...
KATA
KATA (TREMBLE)
THAT'S A REALLY ADORABLE STUFFED ANIMAL!
MAYBE SHE'S JUST NERVOUS?
REI ......?
SU (SWF)

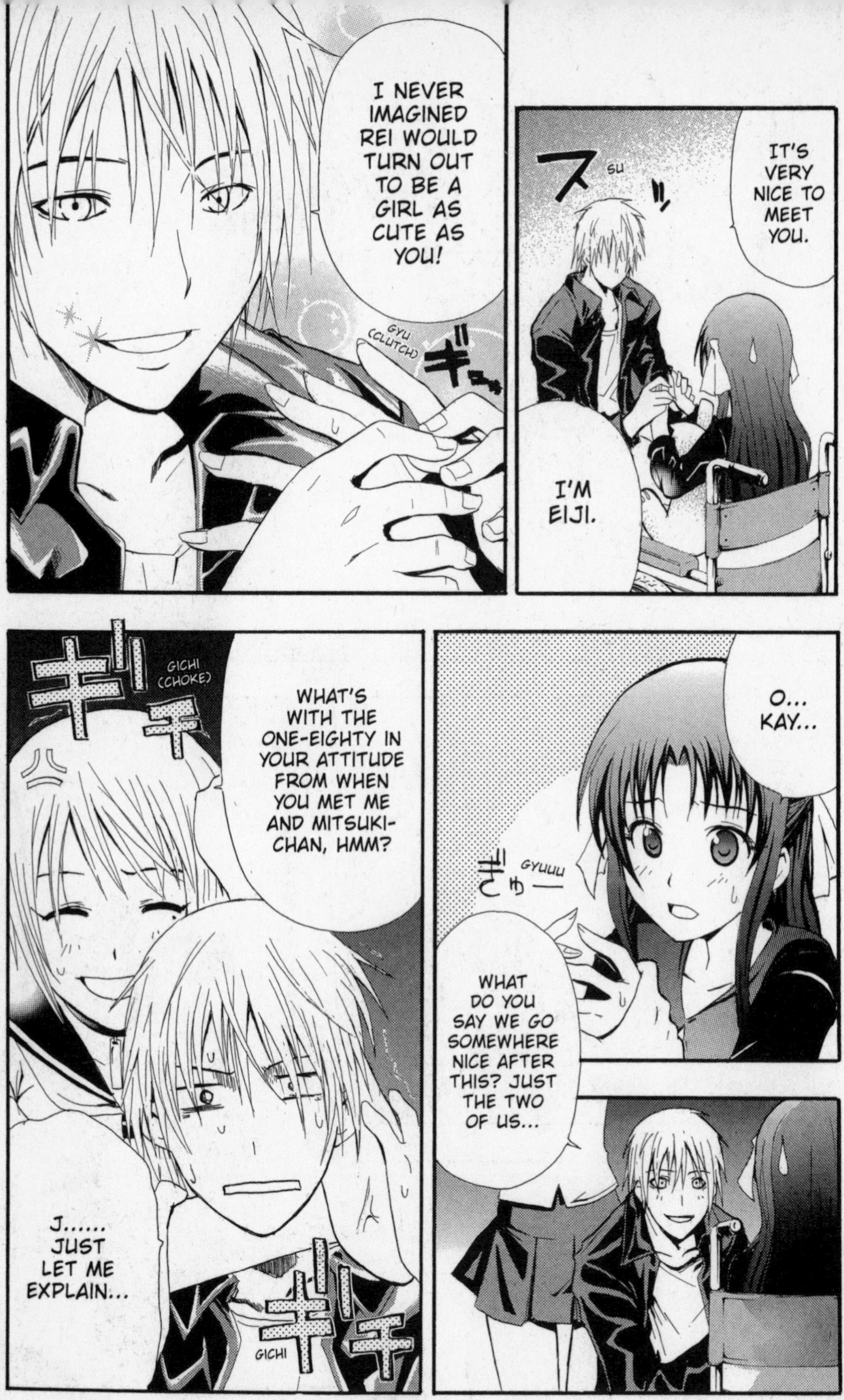
IT'S VERY NICE TO MEET YOU.
ス
SU
I'M EIJI.
I NEVER IMAGINED REI WOULD TURN OUT TO BE A GIRL AS CUTE AS YOU!
ギュ
GYU (CLUTCH)
O... KAY...
ぎゅー
GYUUU
WHAT DO YOU SAY WE GO SOMEWHERE NICE AFTER THIS? JUST THE TWO OF US...
ギチ
GICHI (CHOKE)
WHAT'S WITH THE ONE-EIGHTY IN YOUR ATTITUDE FROM WHEN YOU MET ME AND MITSUKI-CHAN, HMM?
J...... JUST LET ME EXPLAIN...
ギチ
GICHI

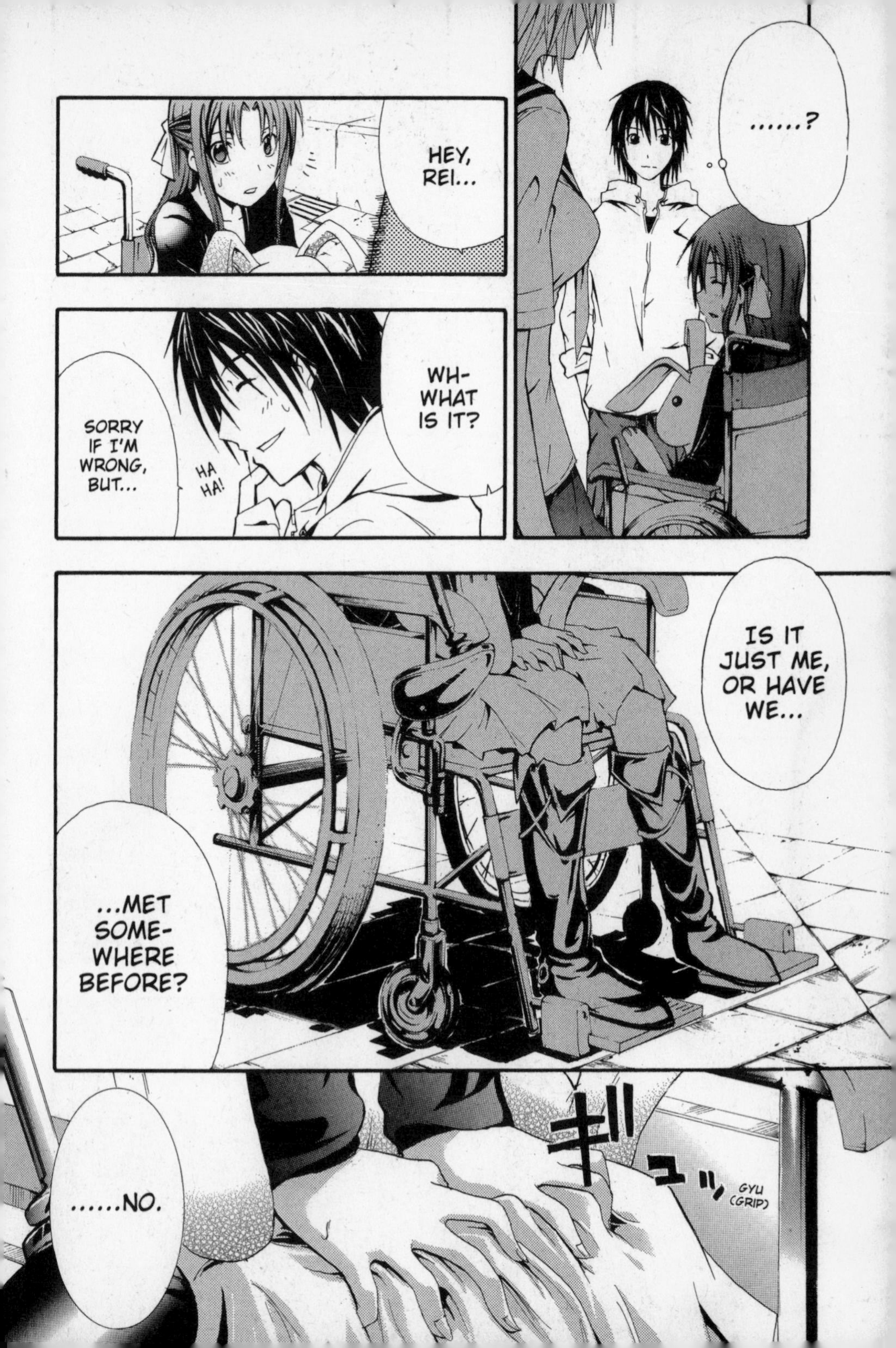
......?
HEY, REI...
WH- WHAT IS IT?
SORRY IF I'M WRONG, BUT...
HA HA!
IS IT JUST ME, OR HAVE WE...
...MET SOME- WHERE BEFORE?
ギュッ
GYU (GRIP)
......NO.

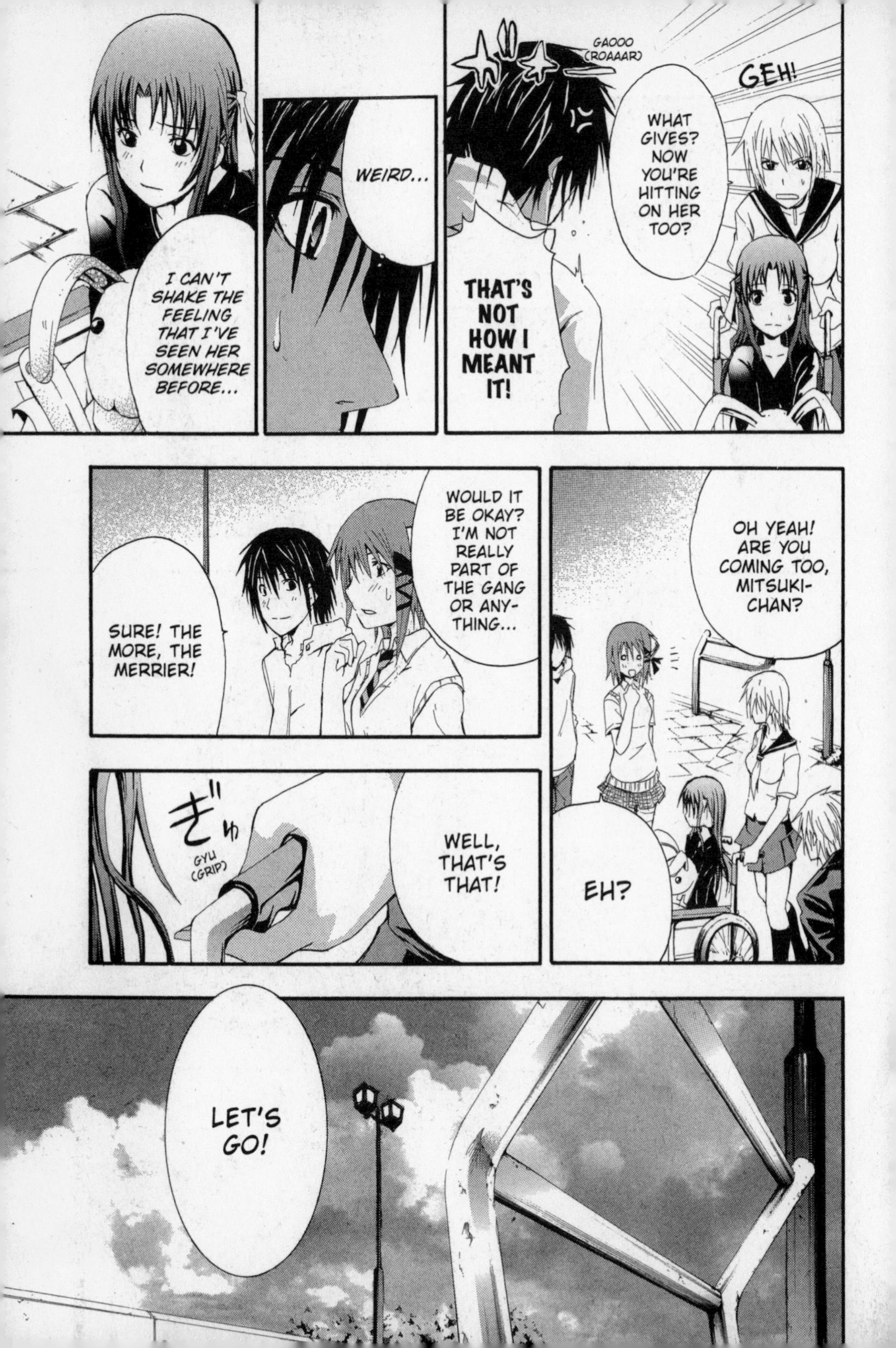
GEH!
WHAT GIVES? NOW YOU'RE HITTING ON HER TOO?
GAOOO (ROAAAR)
THAT'S NOT HOW I MEANT IT!
WEIRD...
I CAN'T SHAKE THE FEELING THAT I'VE SEEN HER SOMEWHERE BEFORE...
OH YEAH! ARE YOU COMING TOO, MITSUKI-CHAN?
EH?
WOULD IT BE OKAY? I'M NOT REALLY PART OF THE GANG OR ANY-THING...
SURE! THE MORE, THE MERRIER!
WELL, THAT'S THAT!
ぎゅ
GYU (GRIP)
LET'S GO!

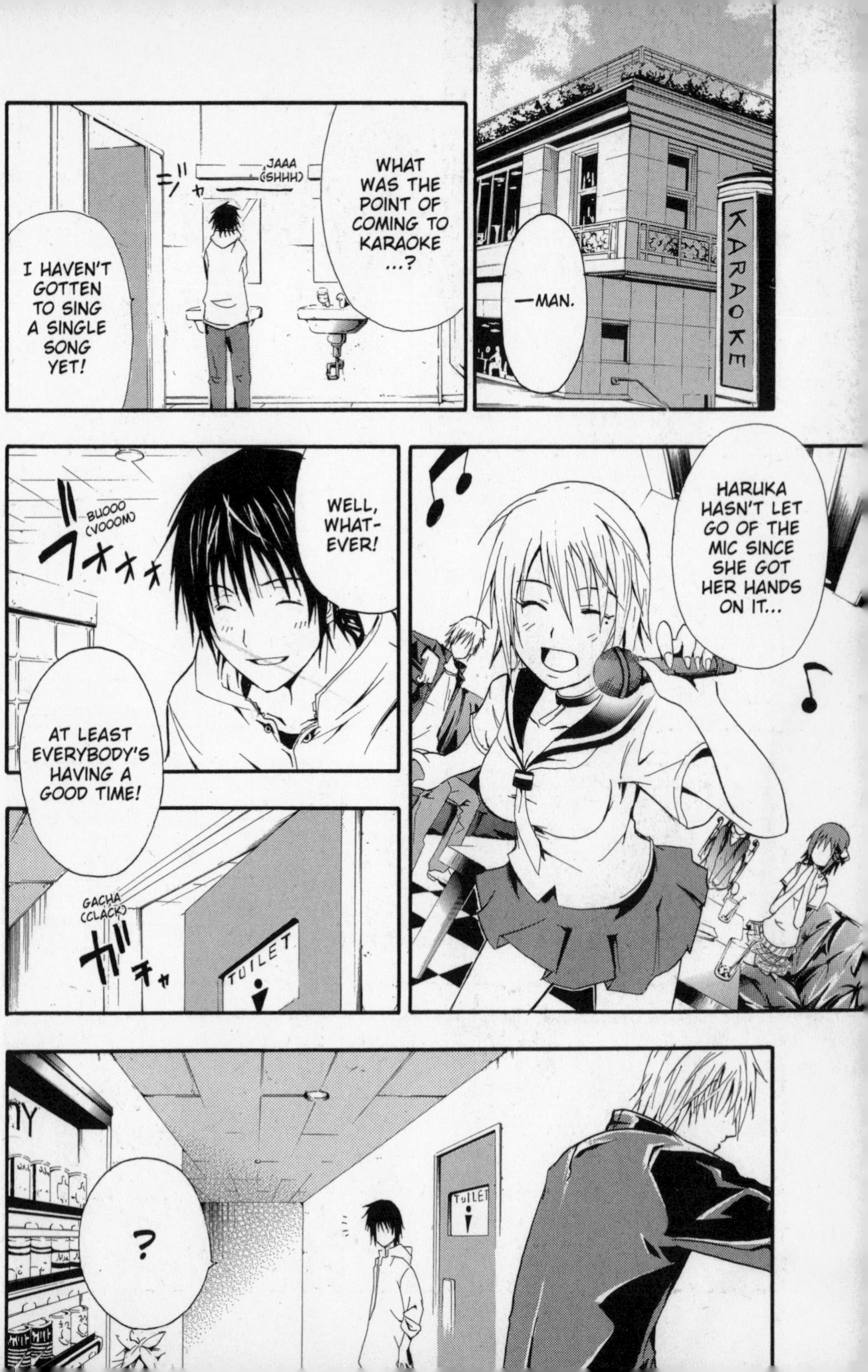

KARAOKE
—MAN.
WHAT WAS THE POINT OF COMING TO KARAOKE ...?
JAAA (SHHH)
I HAVEN'T GOTTEN TO SING A SINGLE SONG YET!
HARUKA HASN'T LET GO OF THE MIC SINCE SHE GOT HER HANDS ON IT...
WELL, WHAT-EVER!
BUOOO (VOOOM)
AT LEAST EVERYBODY'S HAVING A GOOD TIME!
GACHA (CLACK)
TOILET
?
TOILET

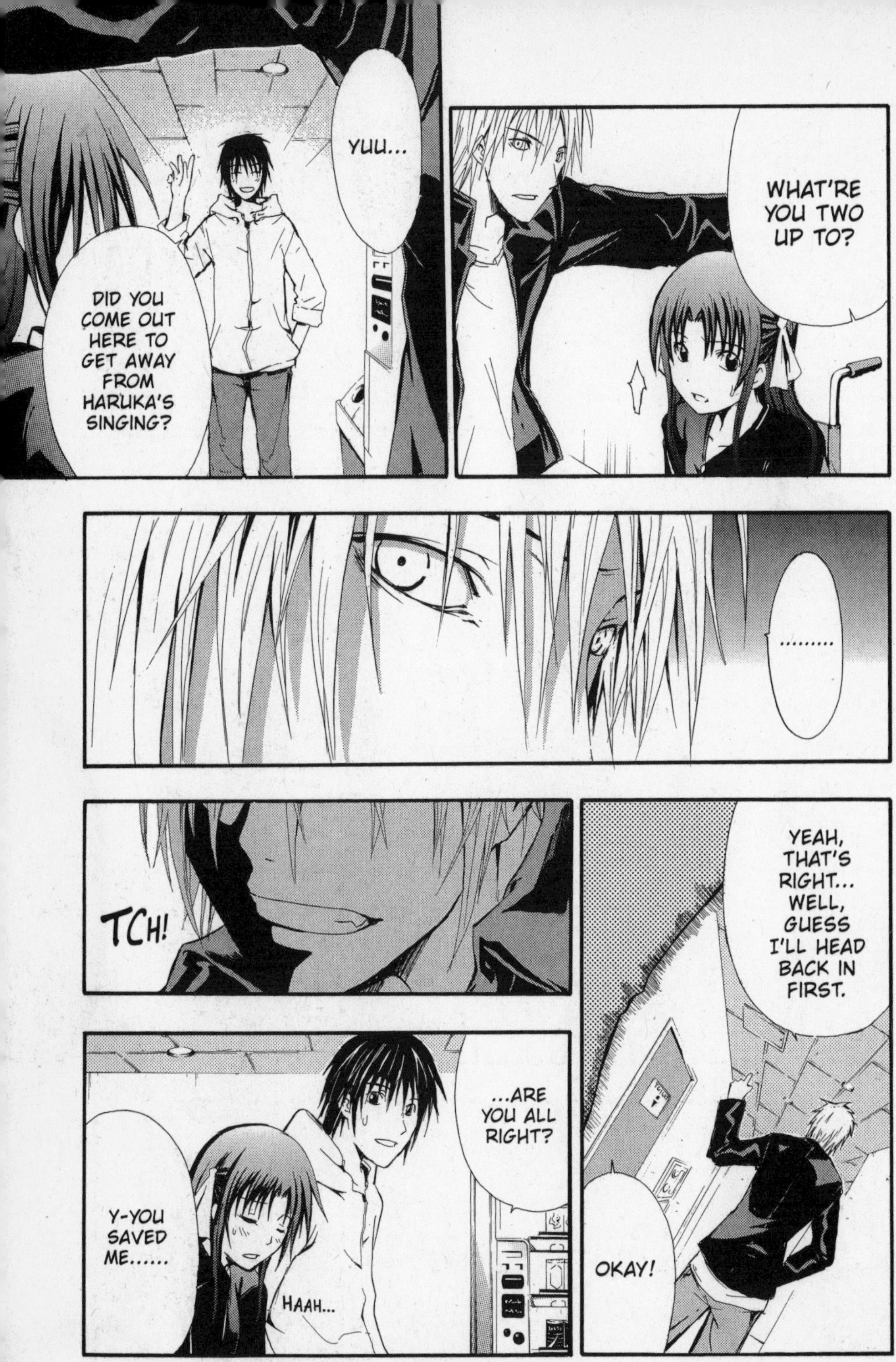
WHAT'RE YOU TWO UP TO?
YUU...
DID YOU COME OUT HERE TO GET AWAY FROM HARUKA'S SINGING?
....
YEAH, THAT'S RIGHT... WELL, GUESS I'LL HEAD BACK IN FIRST.
OKAY!
TCH!
...ARE YOU ALL RIGHT?
Y-YOU SAVED ME......
HAAH...

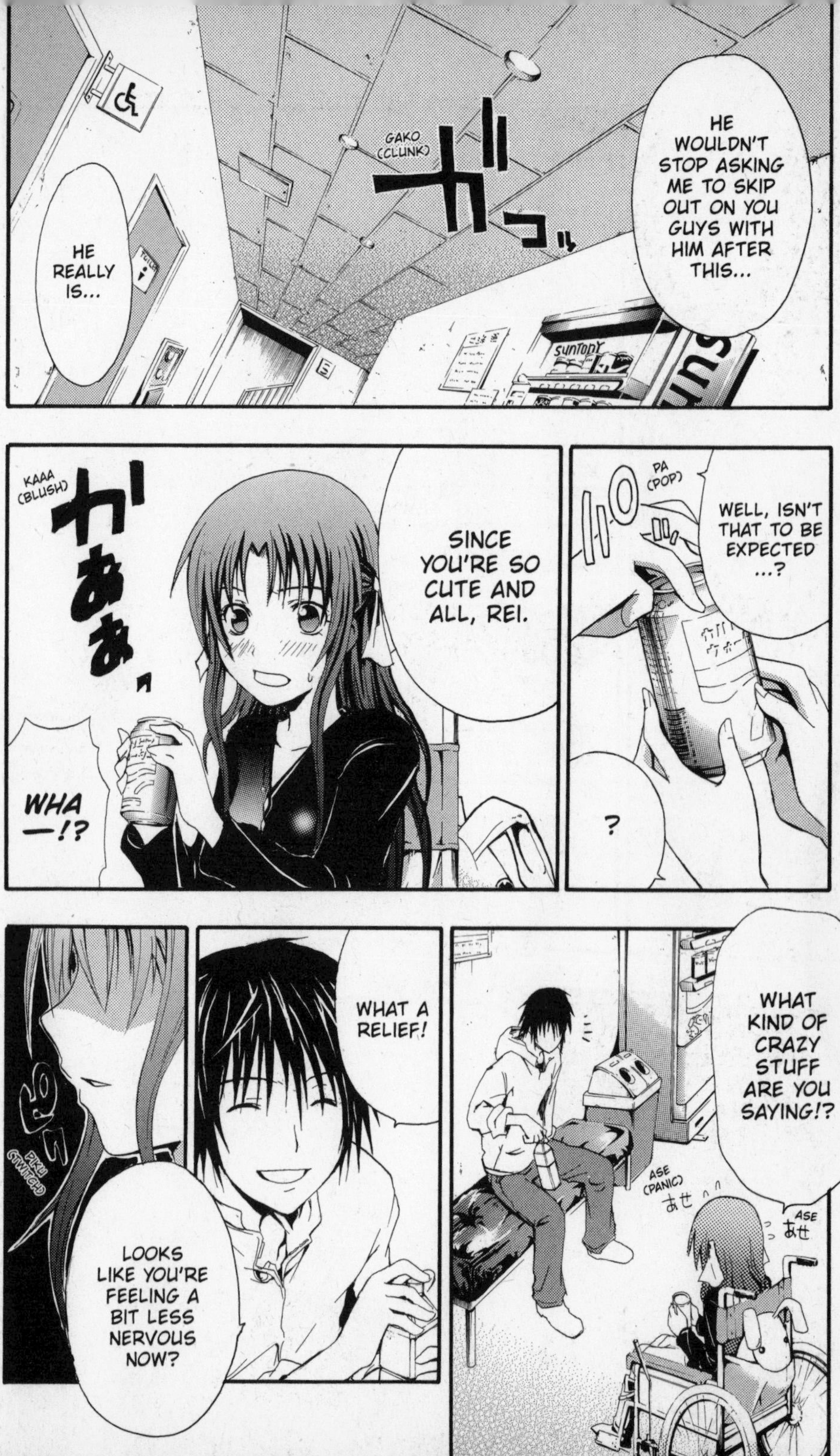
HE WOULDN'T STOP ASKING ME TO SKIP OUT ON YOU GUYS WITH HIM AFTER THIS...
GAKO (CLUNK)
HE REALLY IS...
PA (POP)
WELL, ISN'T THAT TO BE EXPECTED ...?
?
SINCE YOU'RE SO CUTE AND ALL, REI.
KAAA (BLUSH)
WHA—!?
WHAT KIND OF CRAZY STUFF ARE YOU SAYING!?
ASE (PANIC) あせ
ASE あせ
WHAT A RELIEF!
LOOKS LIKE YOU'RE FEELING A BIT LESS NERVOUS NOW?
PIKU (TWITCH)

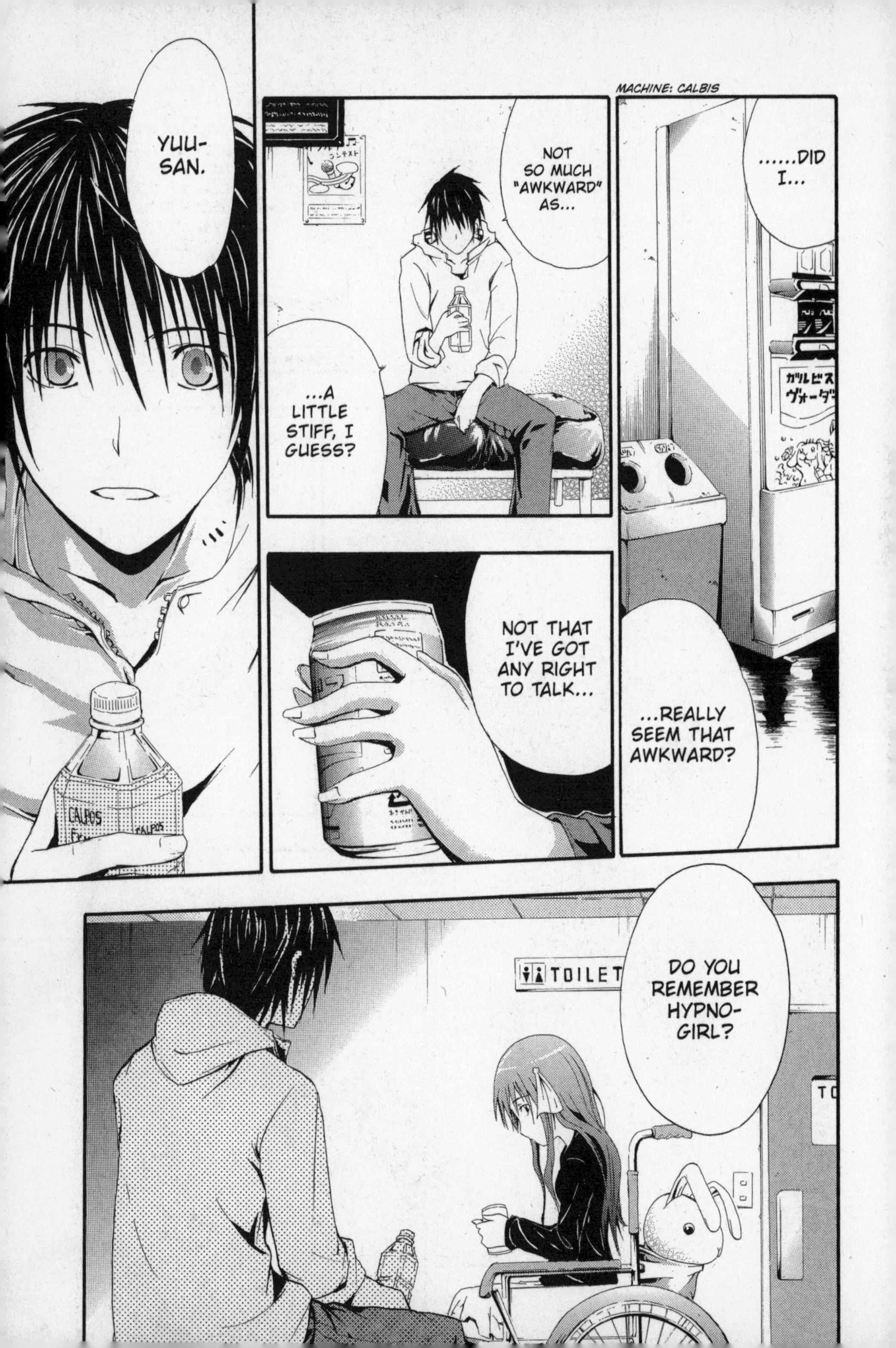
MACHINE: CALBIS
......DID I...
...REALLY SEEM THAT AWKWARD?
NOT SO MUCH "AWKWARD" AS...
...A LITTLE STIFF, I GUESS?
NOT THAT I'VE GOT ANY RIGHT TO TALK...
YUU-SAN.
DO YOU REMEMBER HYPNO-GIRL?
TOILET

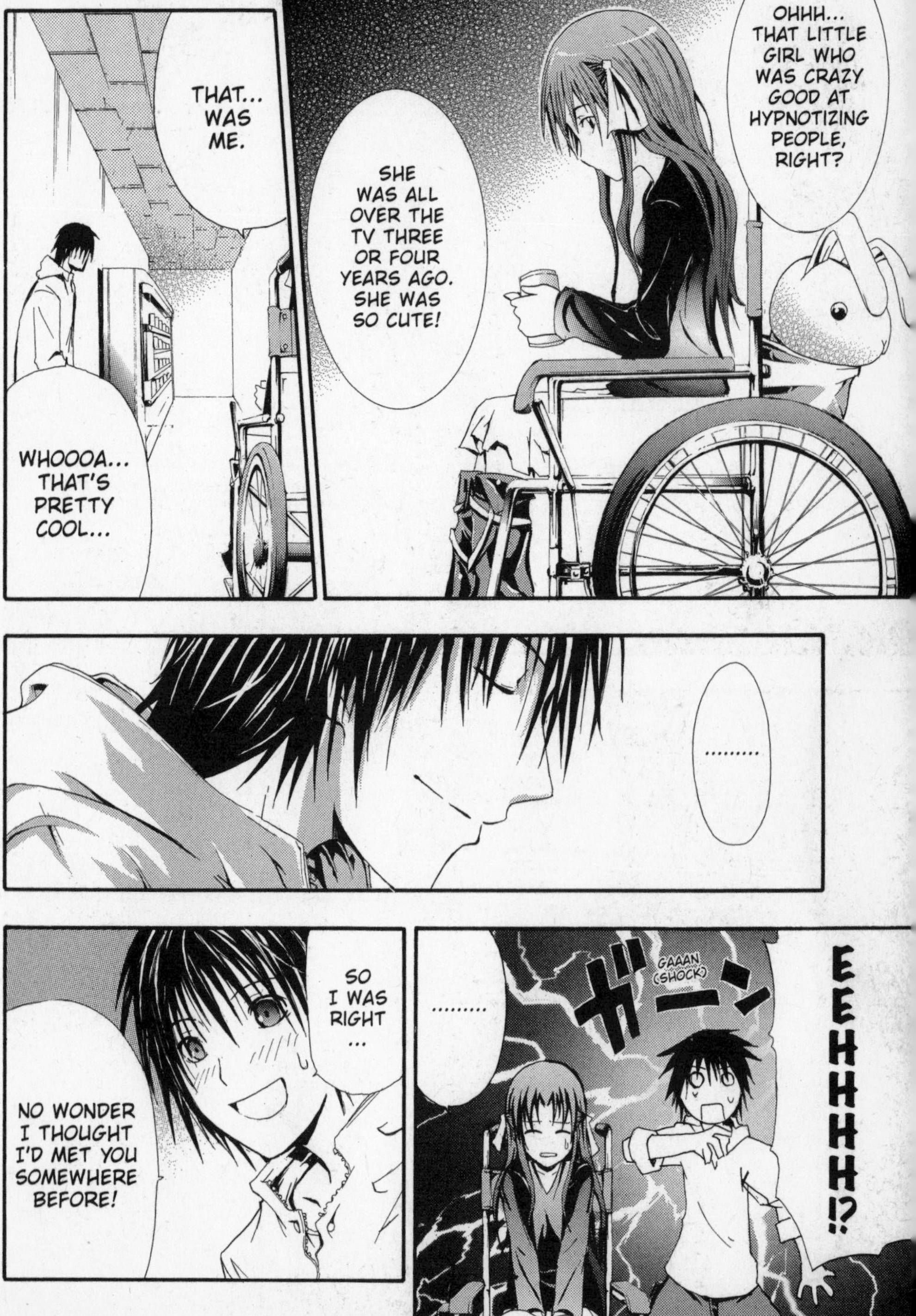
OHHH... THAT LITTLE GIRL WHO WAS CRAZY GOOD AT HYPNOTIZING PEOPLE, RIGHT?
SHE WAS ALL OVER THE TV THREE OR FOUR YEARS AGO. SHE WAS SO CUTE!
THAT... WAS ME.
WHOOOA... THAT'S PRETTY COOL...
....
EEHHHHH!?
ガーン
GAAAN (SHOCK)
....
SO I WAS RIGHT ...
NO WONDER I THOUGHT I'D MET YOU SOMEWHERE BEFORE!

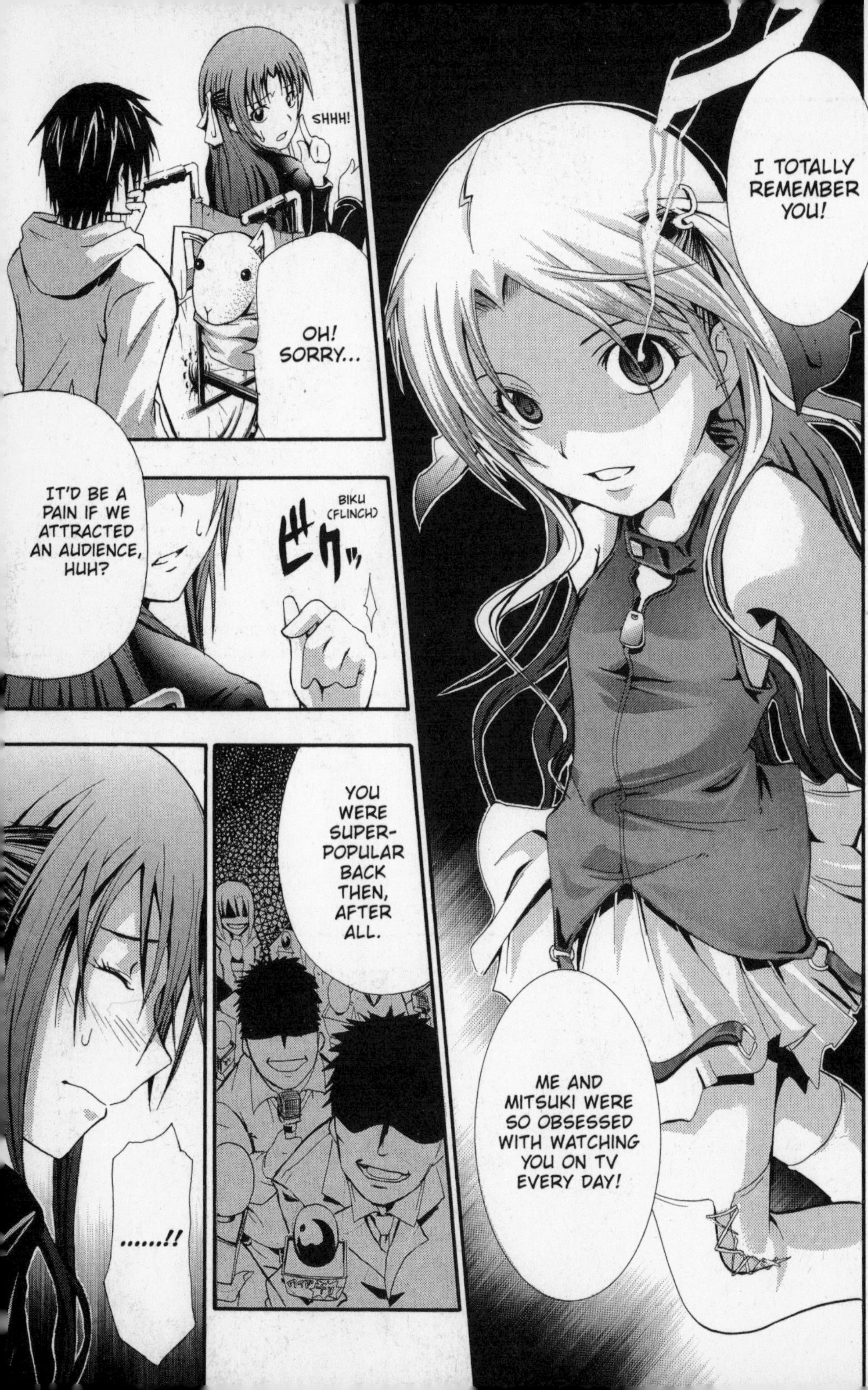
I TOTALLY REMEMBER YOU!
ME AND MITSUKI WERE SO OBSESSED WITH WATCHING YOU ON TV EVERY DAY!
SHHH!
OH! SORRY...
IT'D BE A PAIN IF WE ATTRACTED AN AUDIENCE, HUH?
BIKU (FLINCH)
YOU WERE SUPER-POPULAR BACK THEN, AFTER ALL.
......!!

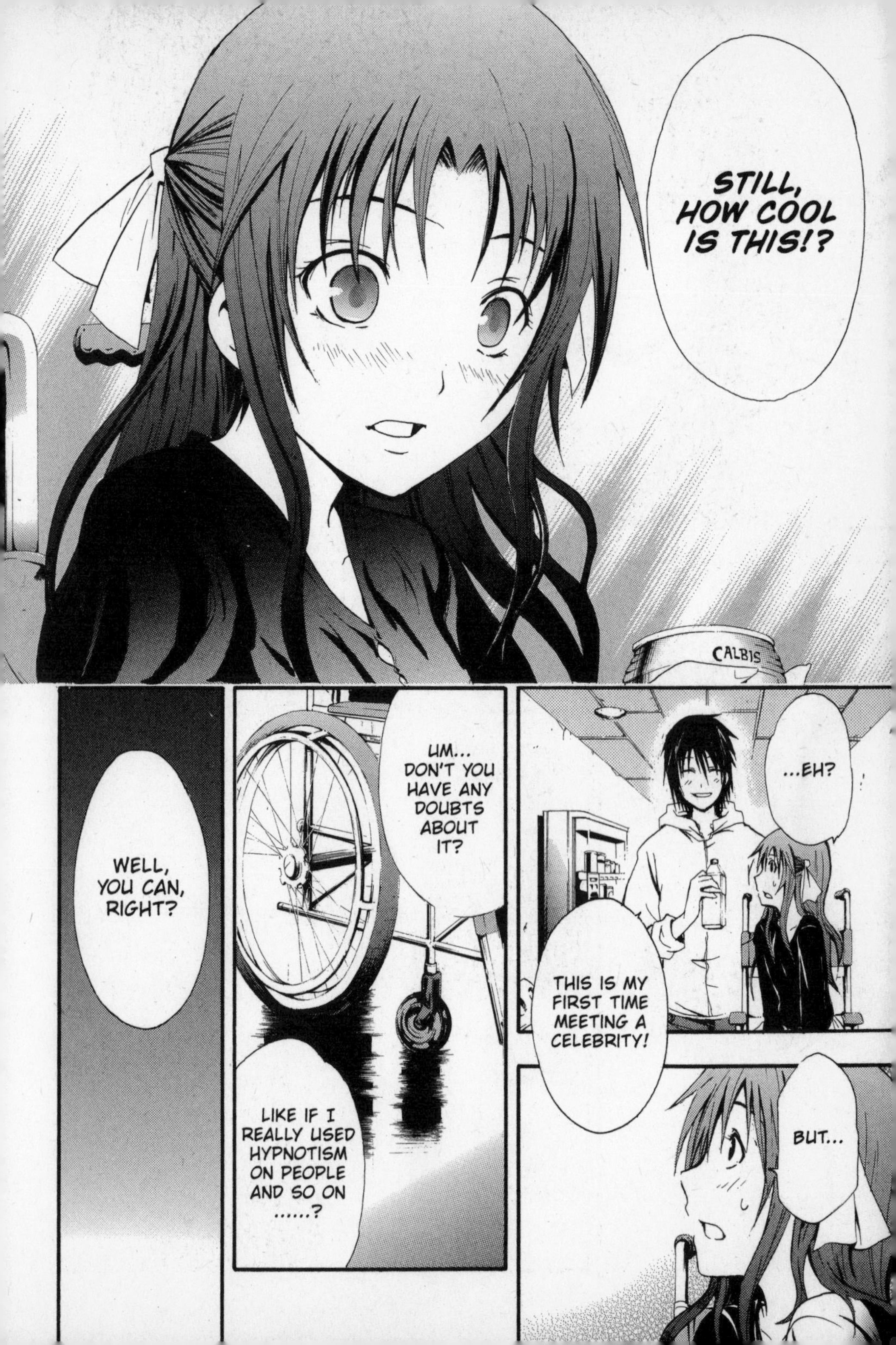
STILL, HOW COOL IS THIS!?
CALBIS
...EH?
THIS IS MY FIRST TIME MEETING A CELEBRITY!
BUT...
UM... DON'T YOU HAVE ANY DOUBTS ABOUT IT?
LIKE IF I REALLY USED HYPNOTISM ON PEOPLE AND SO ON ......?
WELL, YOU CAN, RIGHT?

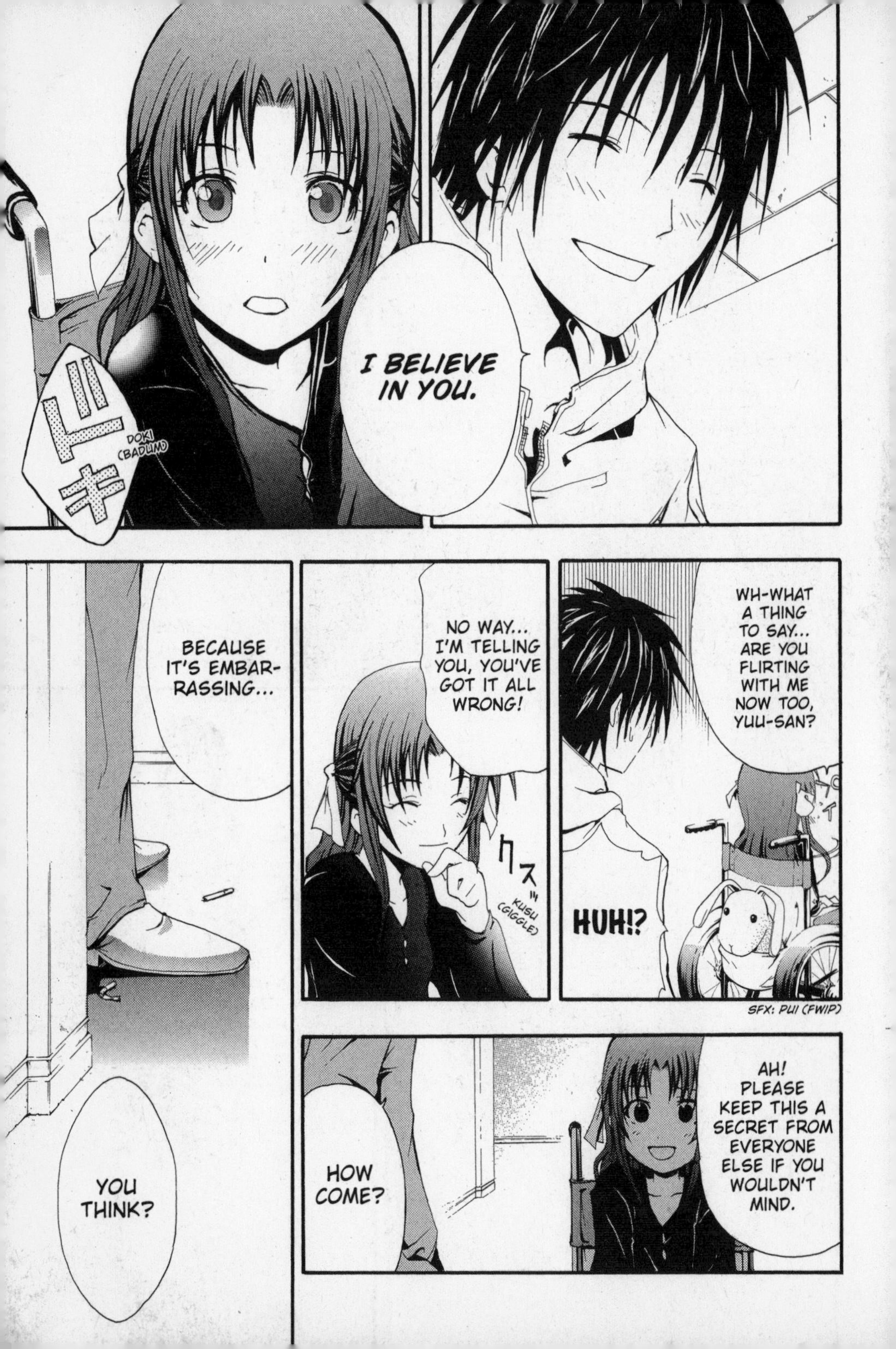
I BELIEVE IN YOU.
ドキ
DOKI (BADUM)
WH-WHAT A THING TO SAY... ARE YOU FLIRTING WITH ME NOW TOO, YUU-SAN?
HUH!?
SFX: PUI (FWIP)
NO WAY... I'M TELLING YOU, YOU'VE GOT IT ALL WRONG!
クスッ
KUSU (GIGGLE)
AH! PLEASE KEEP THIS A SECRET FROM EVERYONE ELSE IF YOU WOULDN'T MIND.
HOW COME?
BECAUSE IT'S EMBARRASSING...
YOU THINK?

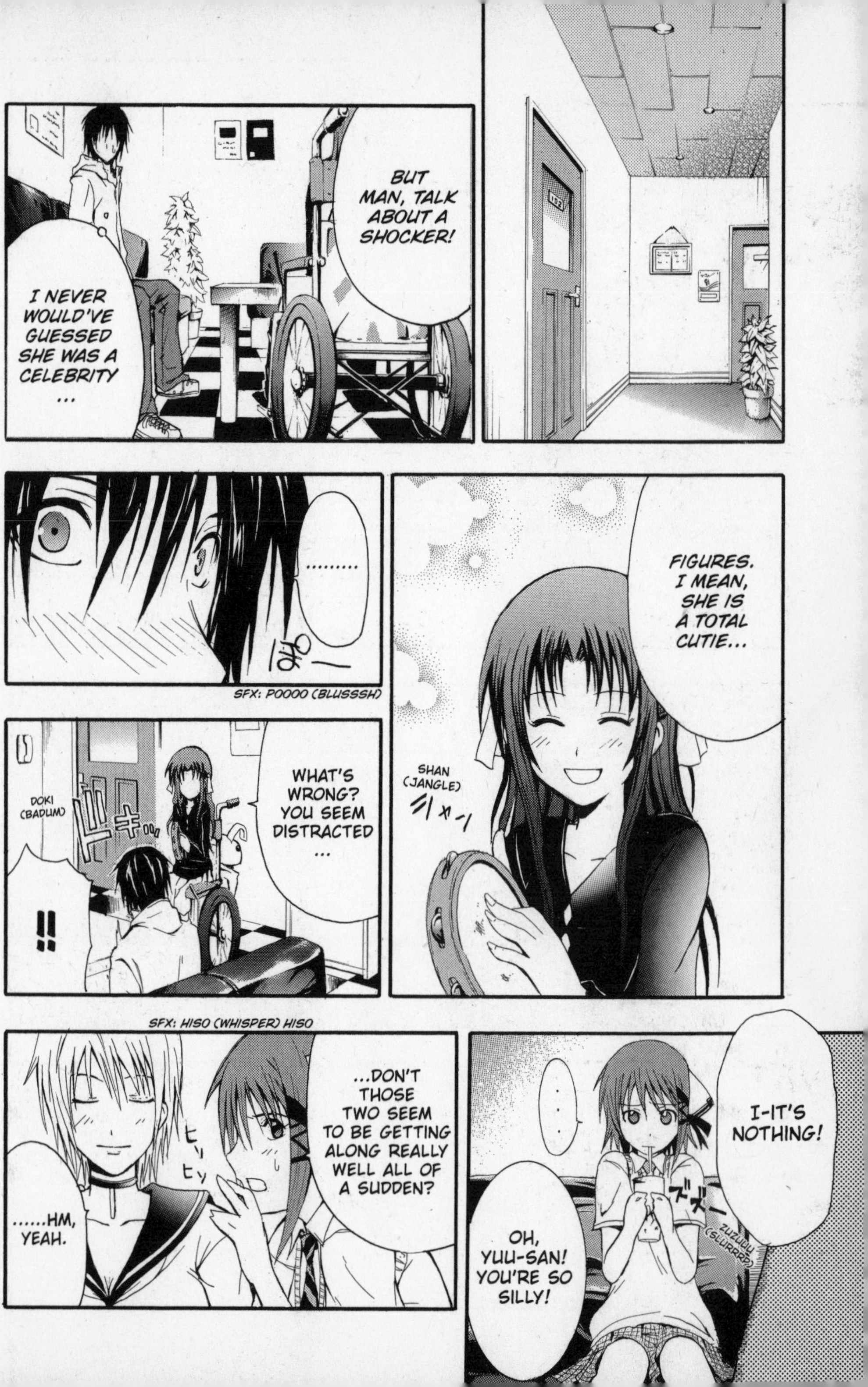
BUT MAN, TALK ABOUT A SHOCKER!
I NEVER WOULD'VE GUESSED SHE WAS A CELEBRITY ...
FIGURES. I MEAN, SHE IS A TOTAL CUTIE...
SHAN (JANGLE)
....
SFX: POOOO (BLUSSSH)
WHAT'S WRONG? YOU SEEM DISTRACTED ...
DOKI (BADUM)
!!
SFX: HISO (WHISPER) HISO
I-IT'S NOTHING!
. . .
ZUZUUU (SLURRRP)
OH, YUU-SAN! YOU'RE SO SILLY!
...DON'T THOSE TWO SEEM TO BE GETTING ALONG REALLY WELL ALL OF A SUDDEN?
......HM, YEAH.

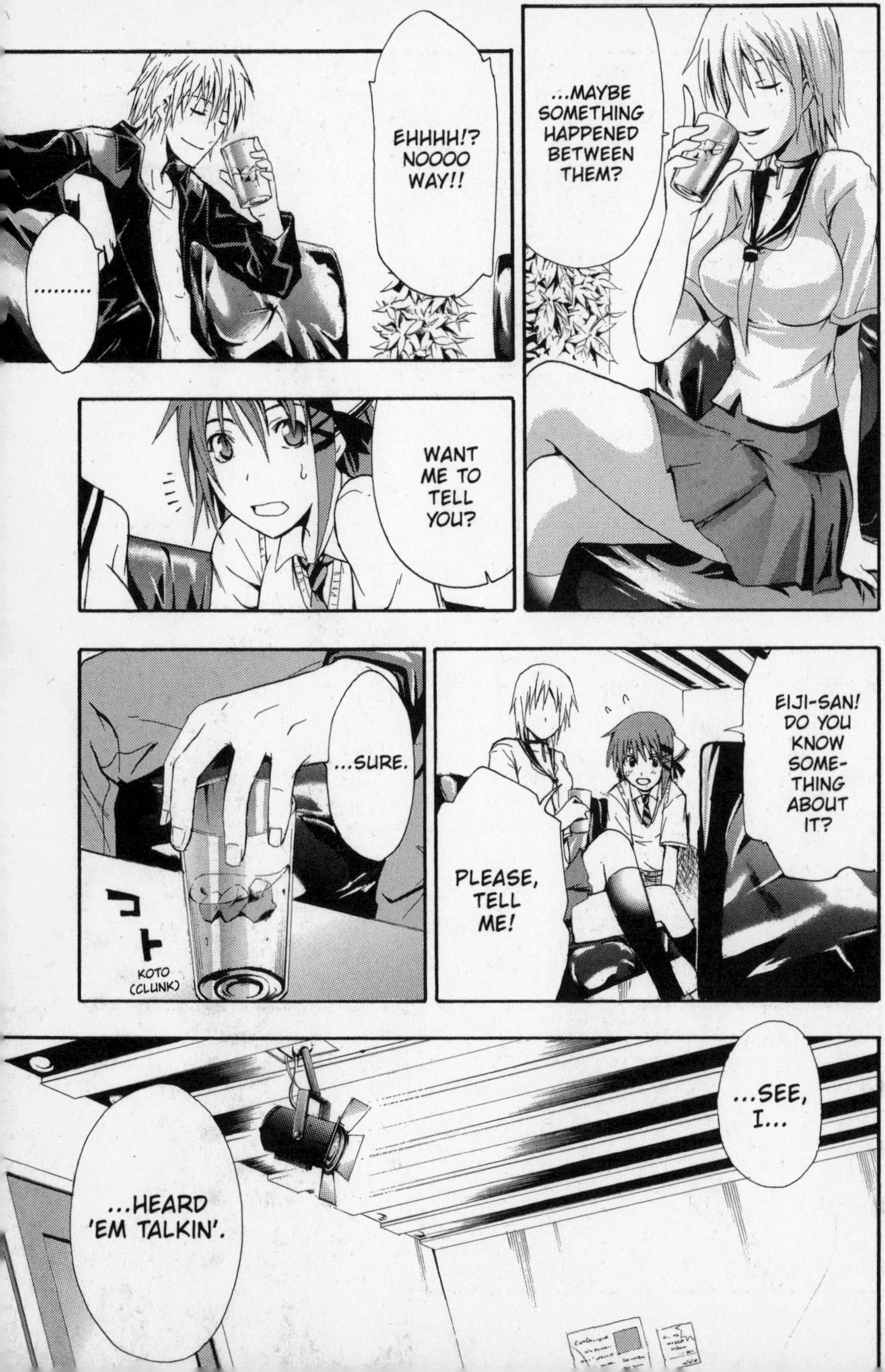
...MAYBE SOMETHING HAPPENED BETWEEN THEM?
EHHHH!? NOOOO WAY!!
....
WANT ME TO TELL YOU?
EIJI-SAN! DO YOU KNOW SOME-THING ABOUT IT?
PLEASE, TELL ME!
...SURE.
コト
KOTO (CLUNK)
...SEE, I...
...HEARD 'EM TALKIN'.

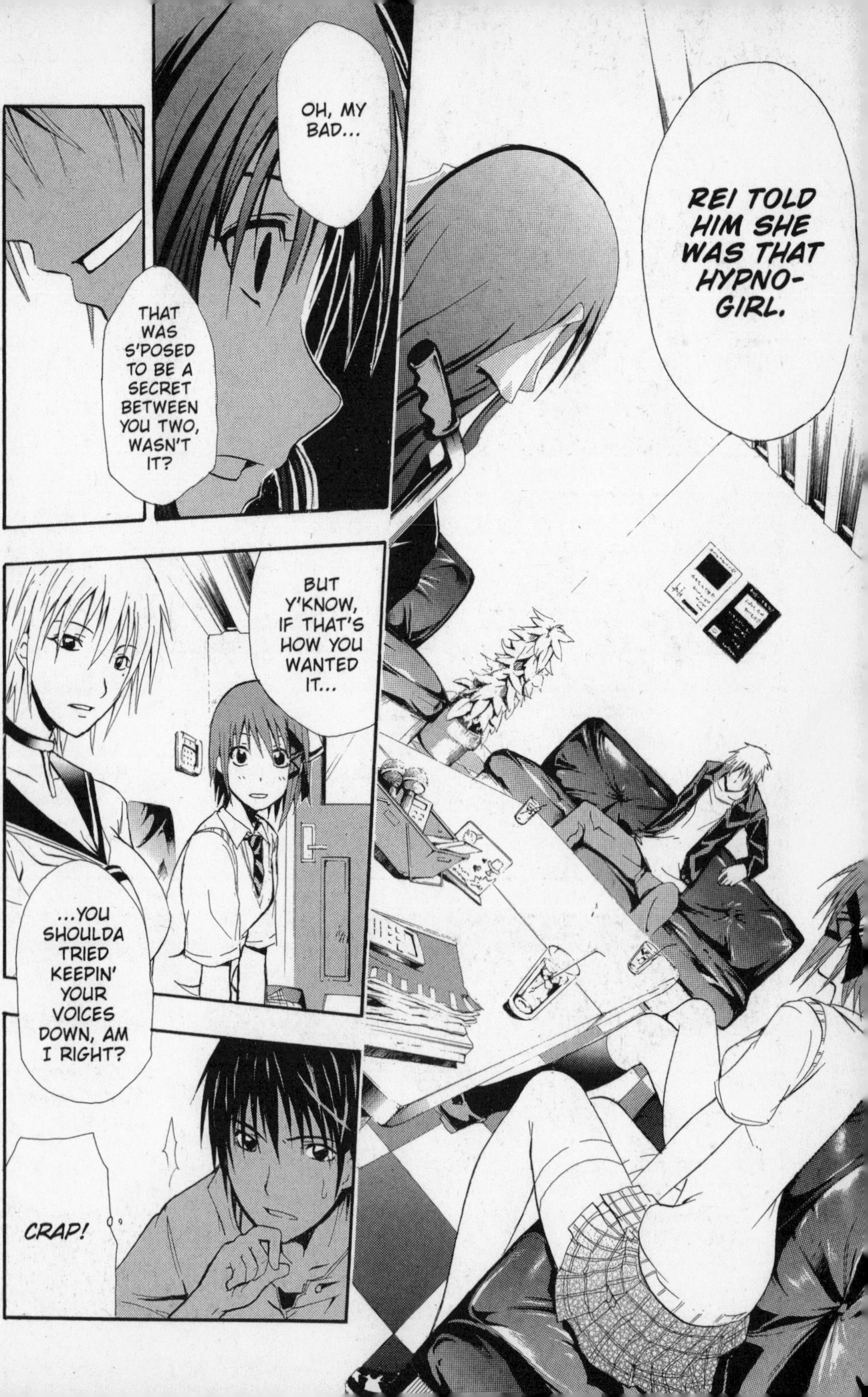
REI TOLD HIM SHE WAS THAT HYPNO-GIRL.
OH, MY BAD...
THAT WAS S'POSED TO BE A SECRET BETWEEN YOU TWO, WASN'T IT?
BUT Y'KNOW, IF THAT'S HOW YOU WANTED IT...
...YOU SHOULDA TRIED KEEPIN' YOUR VOICES DOWN, AM I RIGHT?
CRAP!

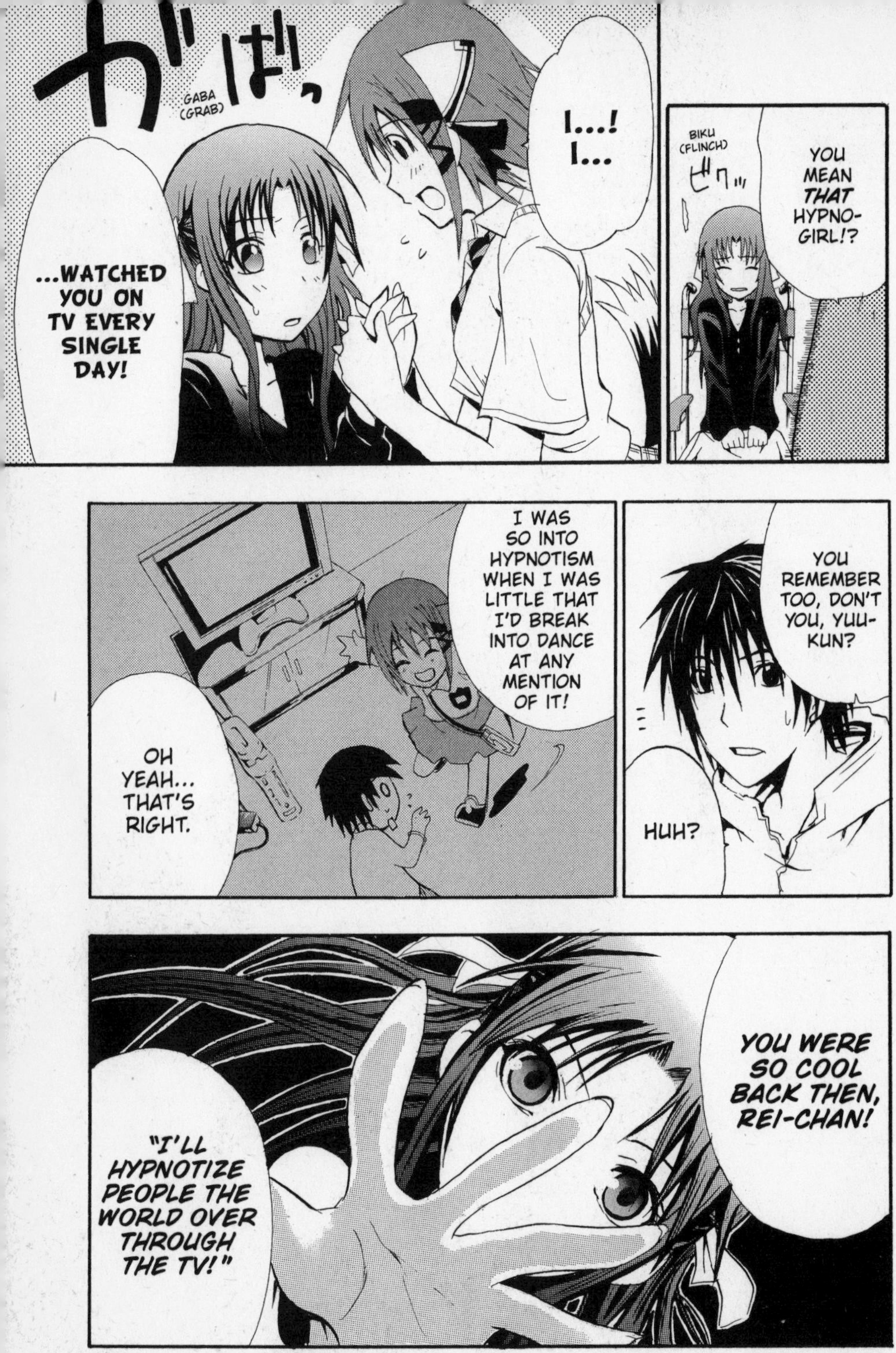
BIKU (FLINCH)
ビクッ
YOU MEAN *THAT* HYPNO-GIRL!?
I...! I...
がばっ
GABA (GRAB)
...WATCHED YOU ON TV EVERY SINGLE DAY!
YOU REMEMBER TOO, DON'T YOU, YUU-KUN?
HUH?
I WAS SO INTO HYPNOTISM WHEN I WAS LITTLE THAT I'D BREAK INTO DANCE AT ANY MENTION OF IT!
OH YEAH... THAT'S RIGHT.
YOU WERE SO COOL BACK THEN, REI-CHAN!
"I'LL HYPNOTIZE PEOPLE THE WORLD OVER THROUGH THE TV!"

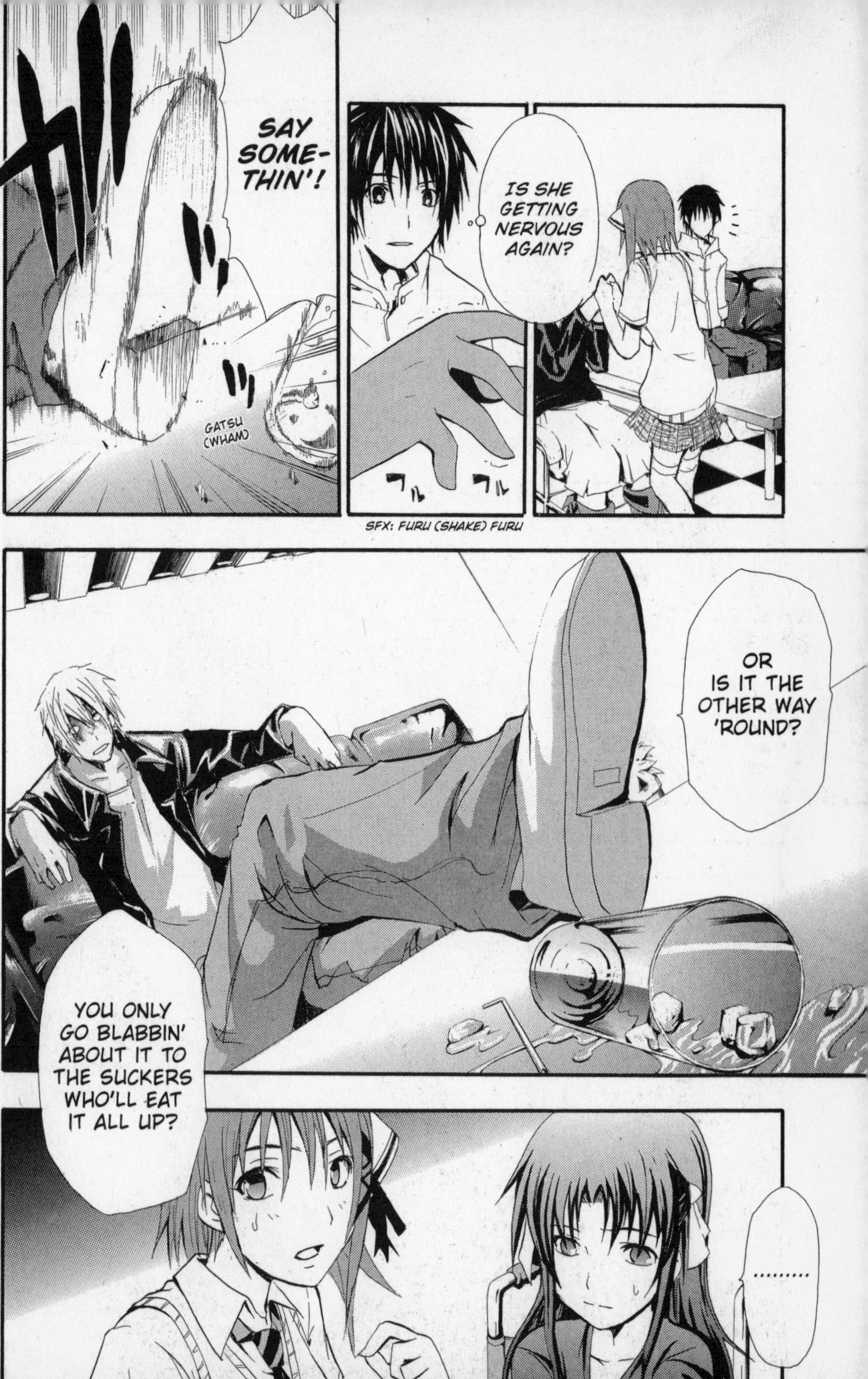
IS SHE GETTING NERVOUS AGAIN?
SAY SOME-THIN'!
GATSU (WHAM)
SFX: FURU (SHAKE) FURU
OR IS IT THE OTHER WAY 'ROUND?
YOU ONLY GO BLABBIN' ABOUT IT TO THE SUCKERS WHO'LL EAT IT ALL UP?
....

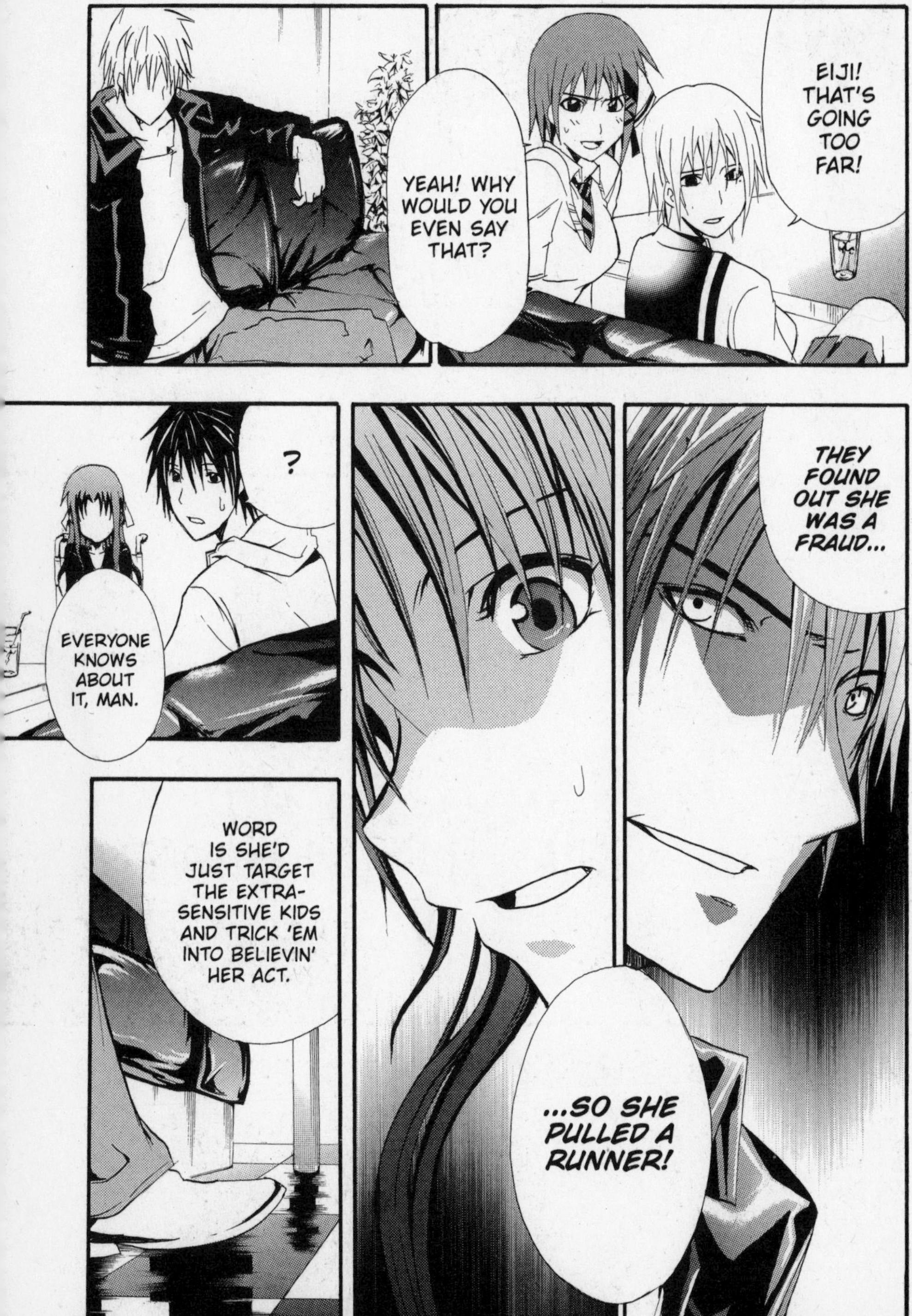
EIJI! THAT'S GOING TOO FAR!
YEAH! WHY WOULD YOU EVEN SAY THAT?
THEY FOUND OUT SHE WAS A FRAUD...
...SO SHE PULLED A RUNNER!
?
EVERYONE KNOWS ABOUT IT, MAN.
WORD IS SHE'D JUST TARGET THE EXTRA-SENSITIVE KIDS AND TRICK 'EM INTO BELIEVIN' HER ACT.

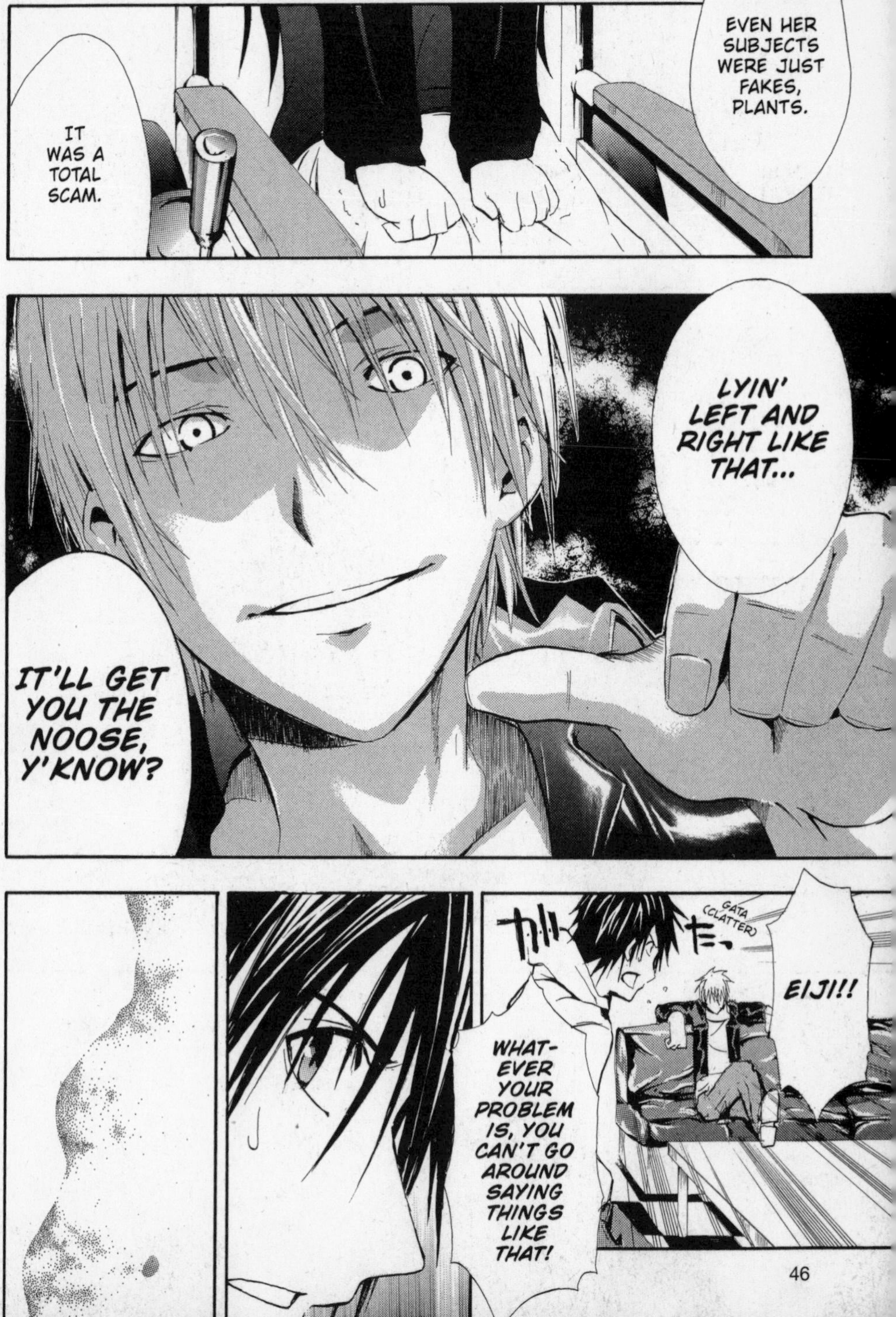
EVEN HER SUBJECTS WERE JUST FAKES, PLANTS.
IT WAS A TOTAL SCAM.
LYIN' LEFT AND RIGHT LIKE THAT...
IT'LL GET YOU THE NOOSE, Y'KNOW?
GATA (CLATTER)
EIJI!!
WHAT-EVER YOUR PROBLEM IS, YOU CAN'T GO AROUND SAYING THINGS LIKE THAT!

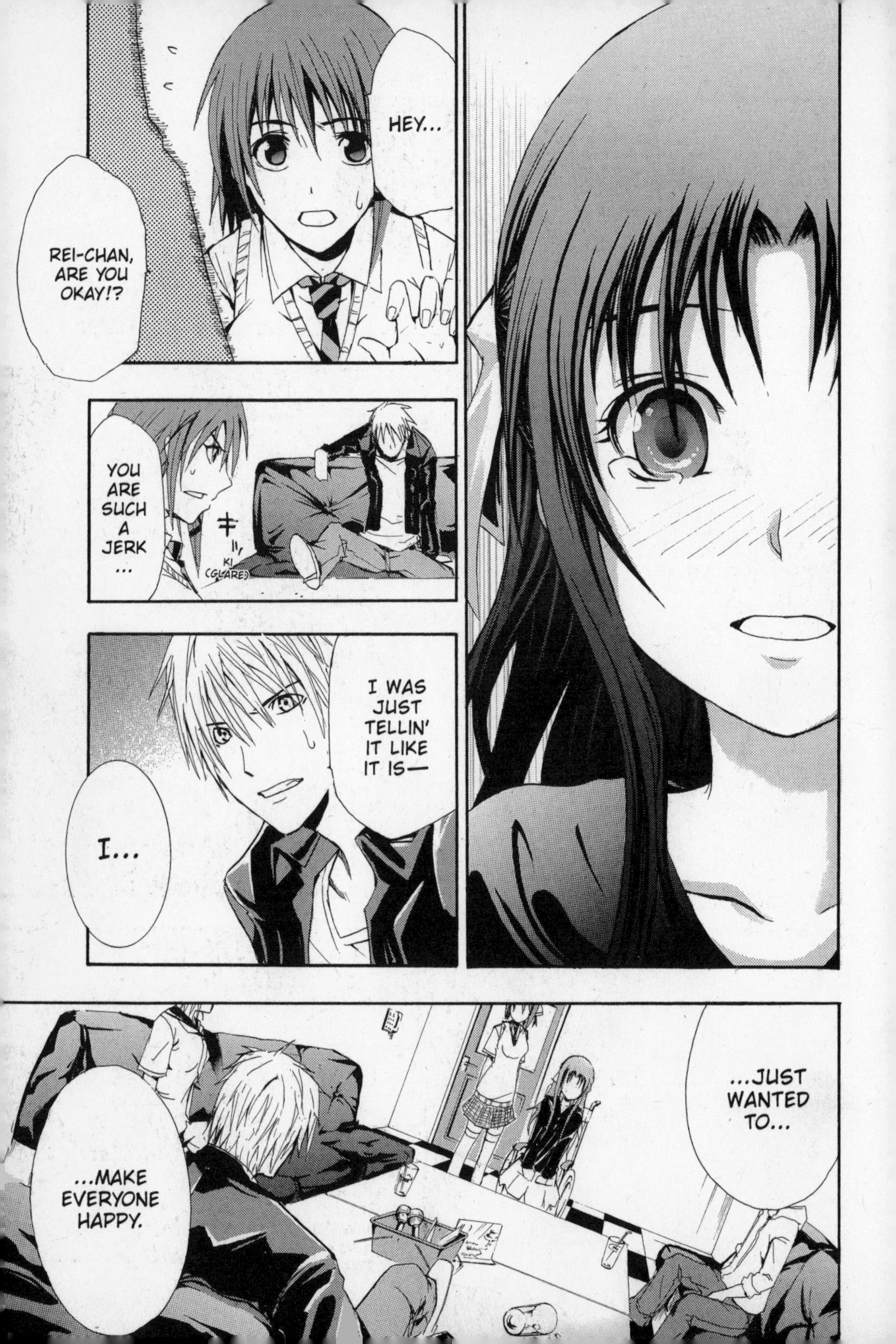
HEY...
REI-CHAN, ARE YOU OKAY!?
YOU ARE SUCH A JERK...
KI (GLARE)
I WAS JUST TELLIN' IT LIKE IT IS—
I...
...JUST WANTED TO...
...MAKE EVERYONE HAPPY.

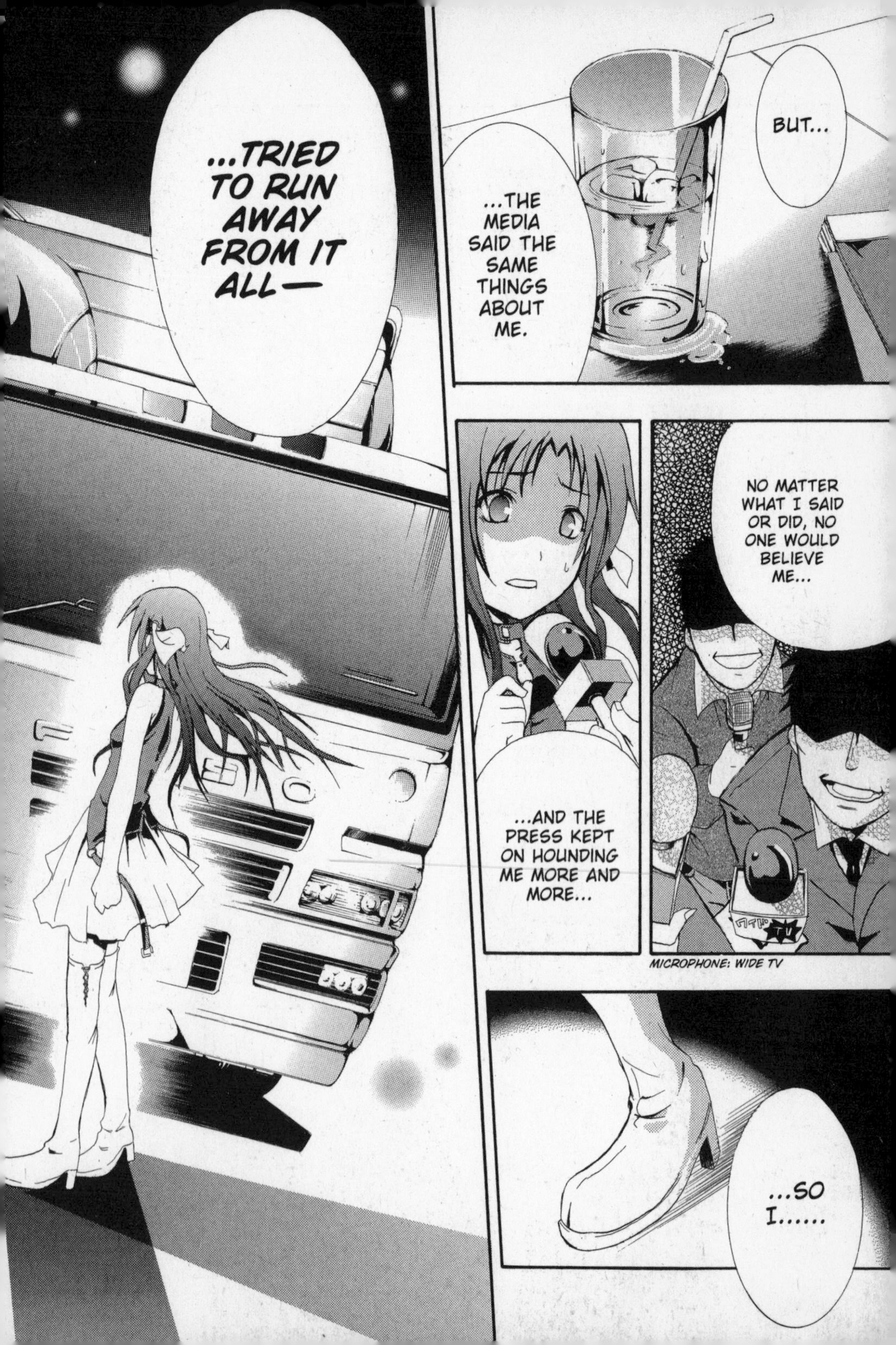
BUT...
...THE MEDIA SAID THE SAME THINGS ABOUT ME.
NO MATTER WHAT I SAID OR DID, NO ONE WOULD BELIEVE ME...
...AND THE PRESS KEPT ON HOUNDING ME MORE AND MORE...
...SO I......
...TRIED TO RUN AWAY FROM IT ALL—
MICROPHONE: WIDE TV

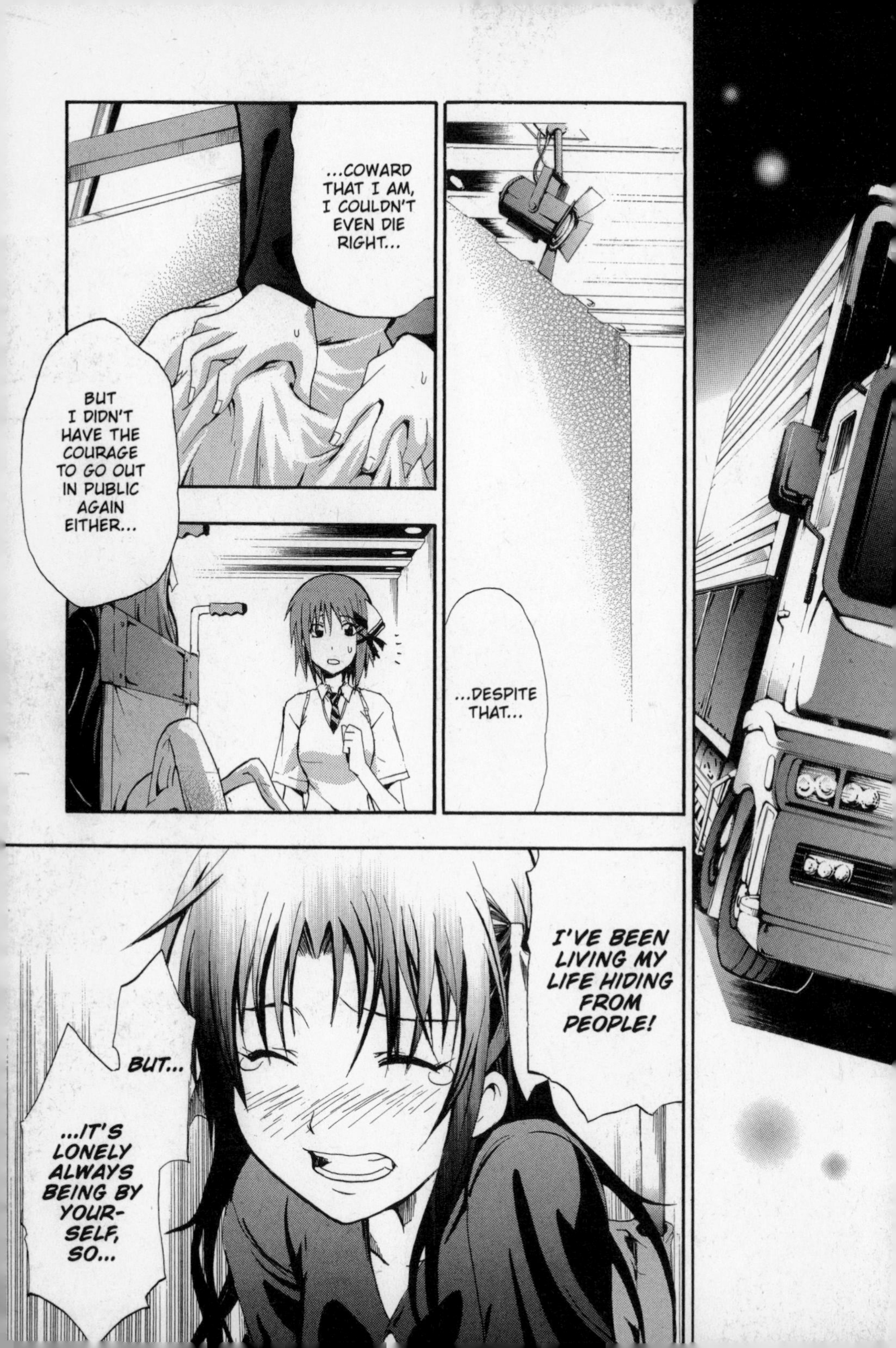
...COWARD THAT I AM, I COULDN'T EVEN DIE RIGHT...
BUT I DIDN'T HAVE THE COURAGE TO GO OUT IN PUBLIC AGAIN EITHER...
...DESPITE THAT...
I'VE BEEN LIVING MY LIFE HIDING FROM PEOPLE!
BUT...
...IT'S LONELY ALWAYS BEING BY YOUR-SELF, SO...

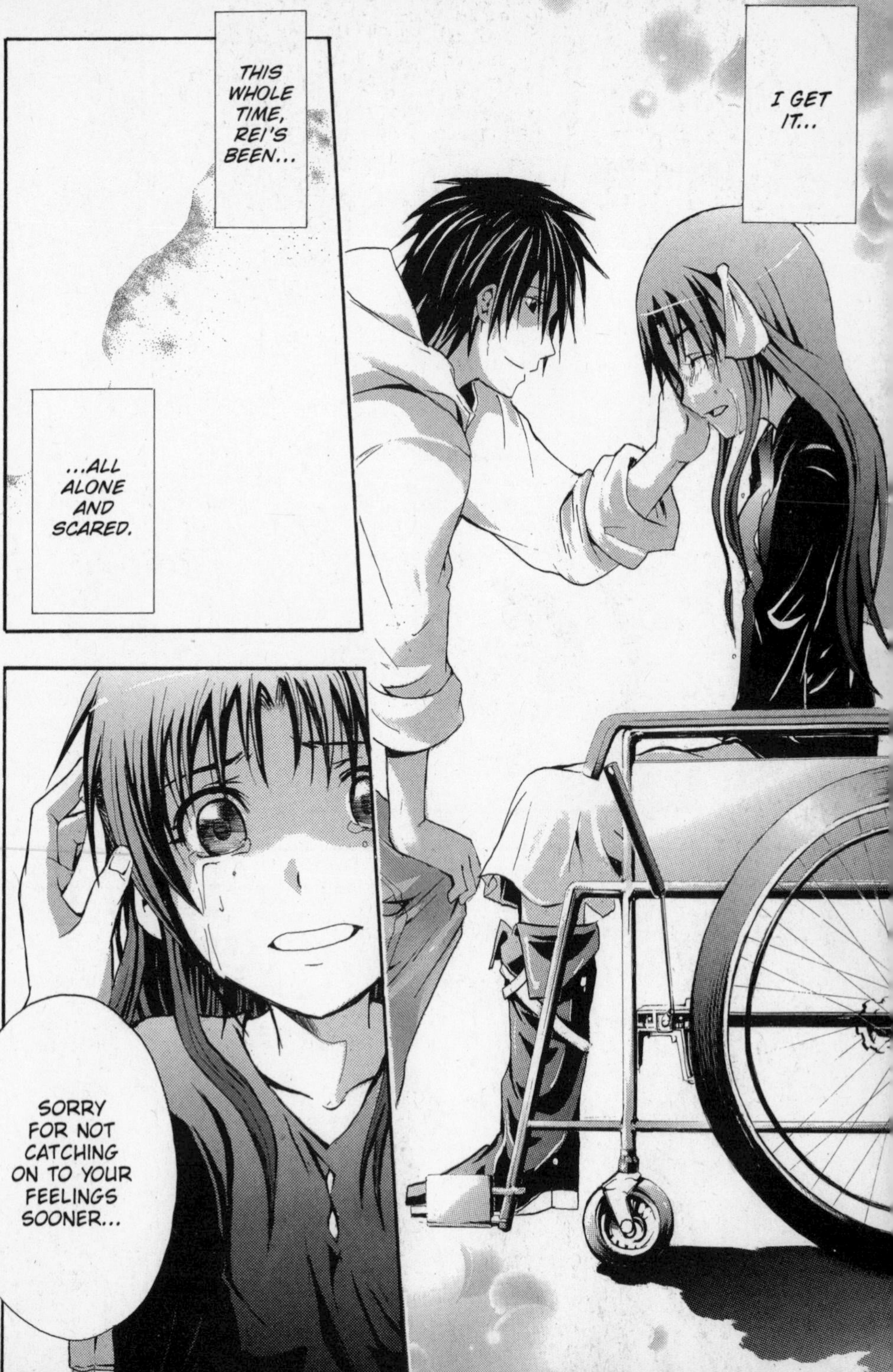
I GET IT...
THIS WHOLE TIME, REI'S BEEN...
...ALL ALONE AND SCARED.
SORRY FOR NOT CATCHING ON TO YOUR FEELINGS SOONER...

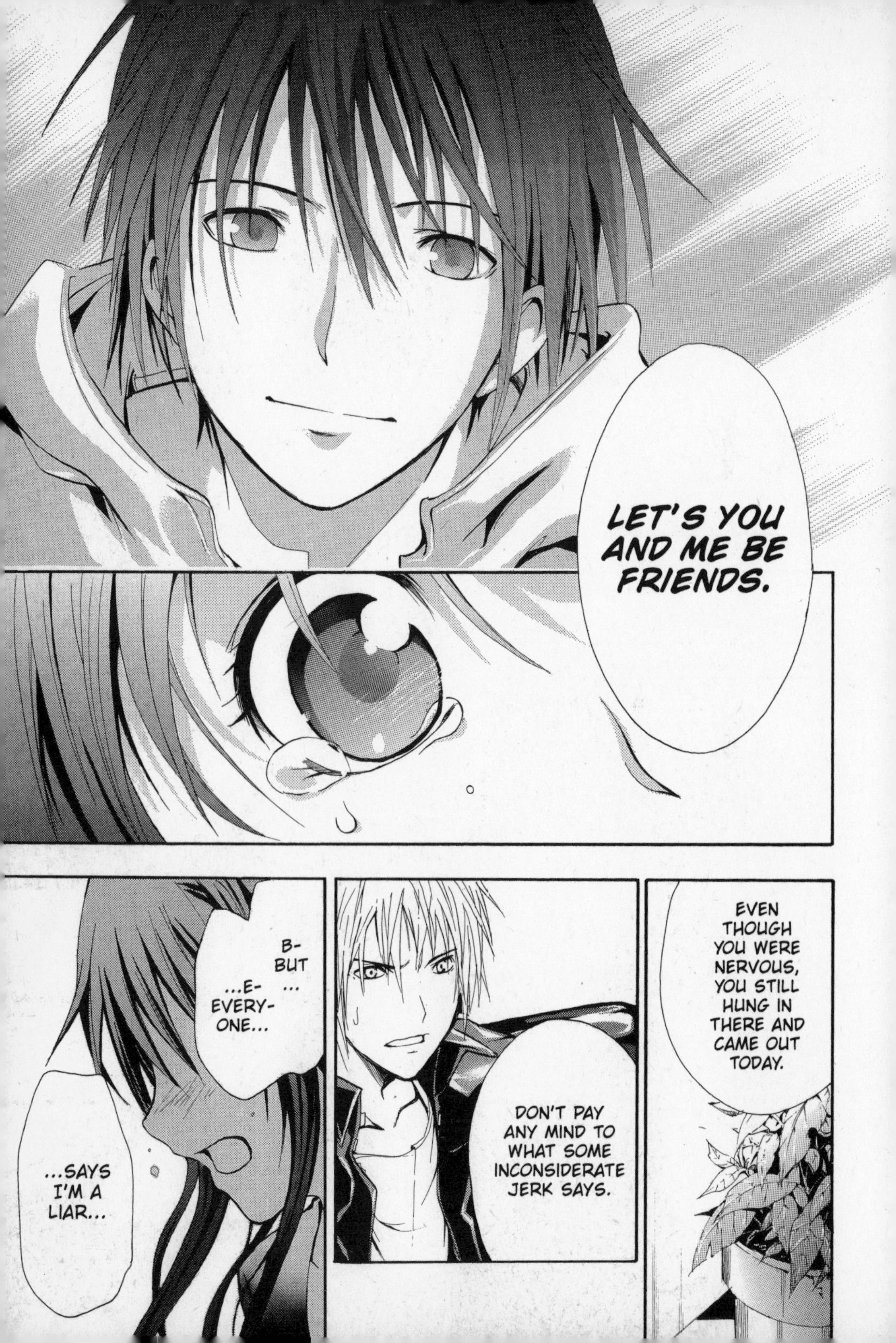
LET'S YOU AND ME BE FRIENDS.
EVEN THOUGH YOU WERE NERVOUS, YOU STILL HUNG IN THERE AND CAME OUT TODAY.
DON'T PAY ANY MIND TO WHAT SOME INCONSIDERATE JERK SAYS.
B-BUT ...
...E-EVERYONE...
...SAYS I'M A LIAR...

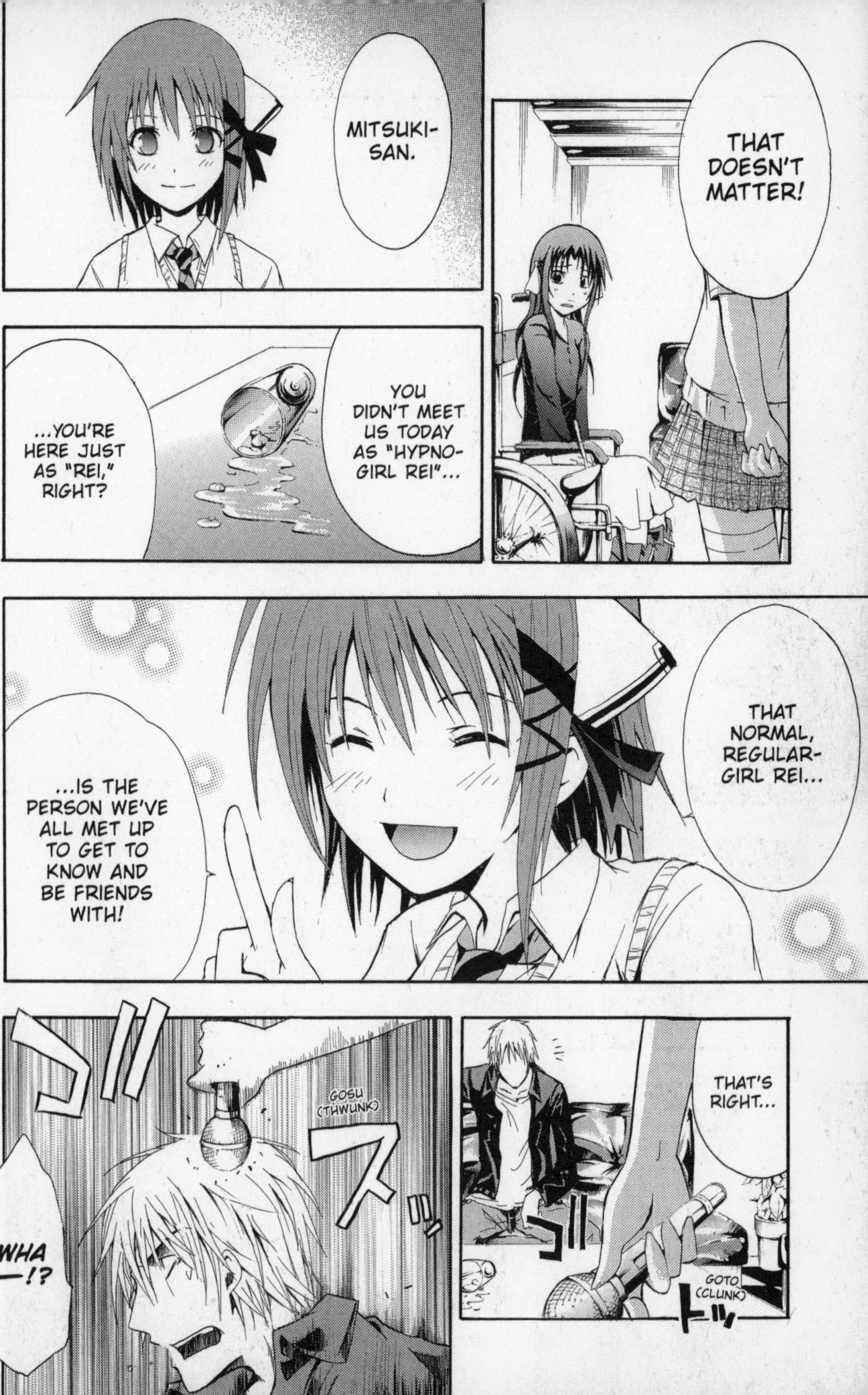
THAT DOESN'T MATTER!
MITSUKI-SAN.
YOU DIDN'T MEET US TODAY AS "HYPNO-GIRL REI"...
...YOU'RE HERE JUST AS "REI," RIGHT?
THAT NORMAL, REGULAR-GIRL REI...
...IS THE PERSON WE'VE ALL MET UP TO GET TO KNOW AND BE FRIENDS WITH!
THAT'S RIGHT...
GOTO (CLUNK)
GOSU (THWUNK)
WHA—!?

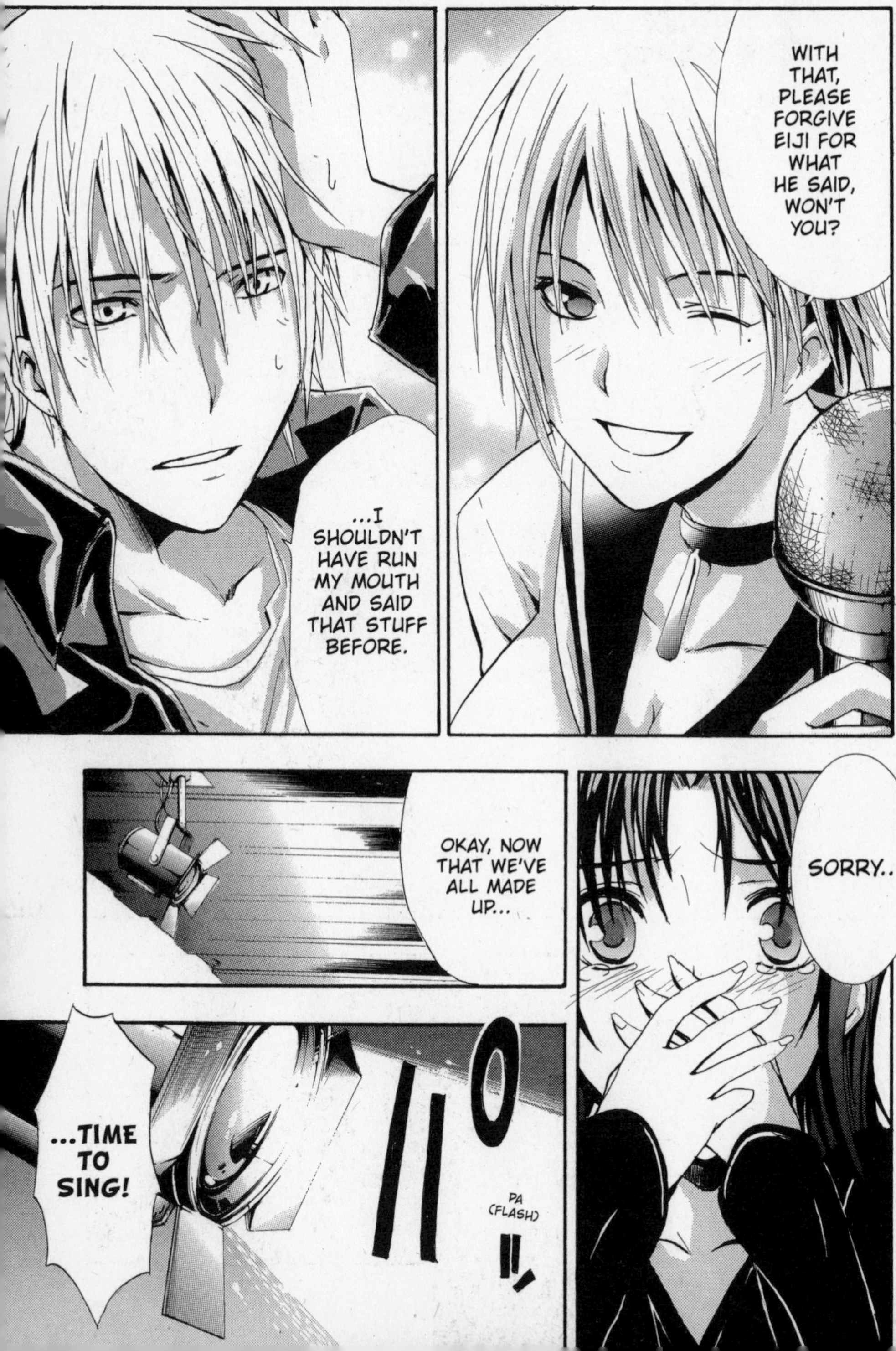
WITH THAT, PLEASE FORGIVE EIJI FOR WHAT HE SAID, WON'T YOU?
...I SHOULDN'T HAVE RUN MY MOUTH AND SAID THAT STUFF BEFORE.
SORRY...
OKAY, NOW THAT WE'VE ALL MADE UP...
...TIME TO SING!
PA (FLASH)

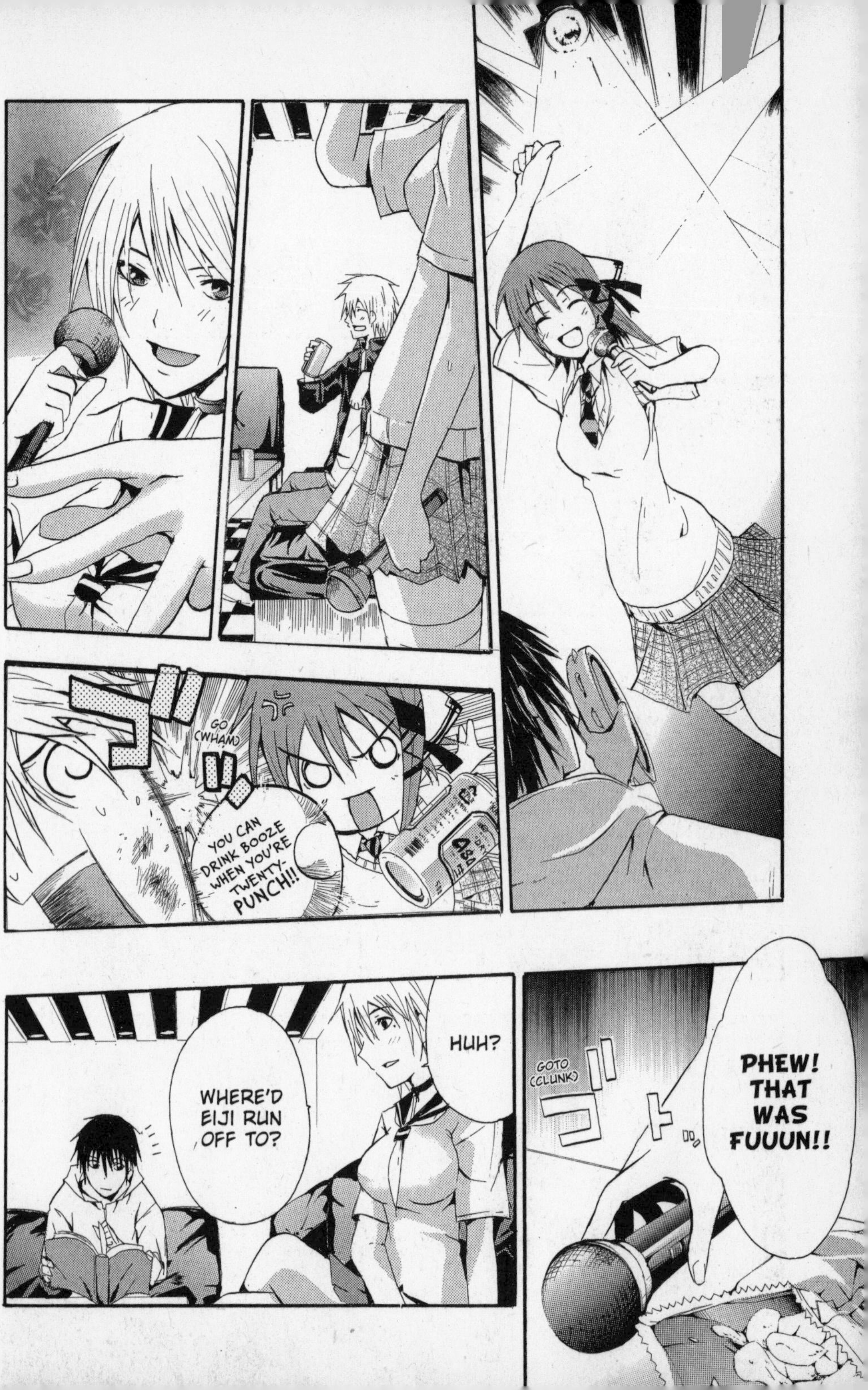
GO (WHAM)
YOU CAN DRINK BOOZE WHEN YOU'RE TWENTY-PUNCH!!
GOTO (CLUNK)
PHEW! THAT WAS FUUUN!!
HUH?
WHERE'D EIJI RUN OFF TO?

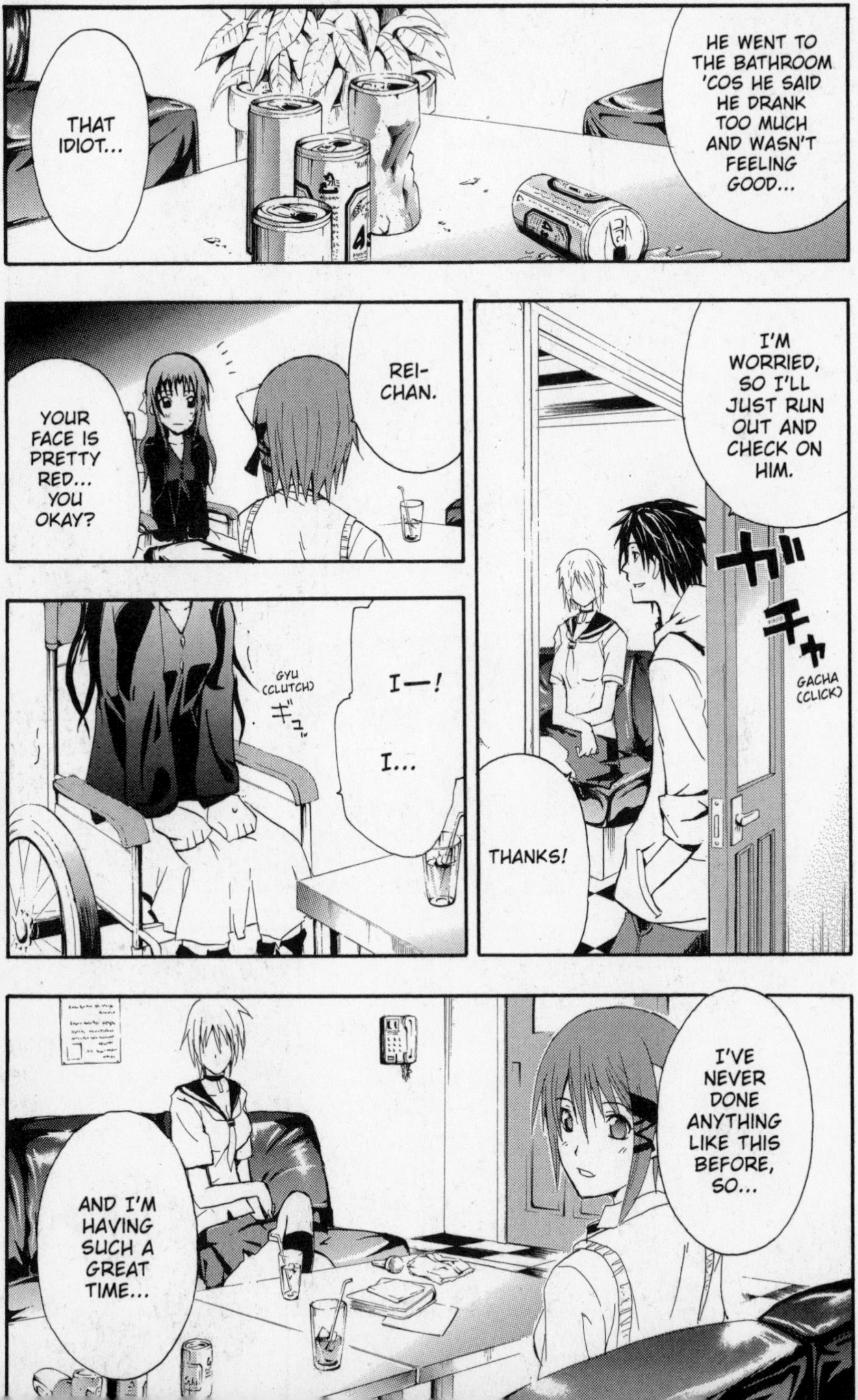
HE WENT TO THE BATHROOM 'COS HE SAID HE DRANK TOO MUCH AND WASN'T FEELING GOOD...
THAT IDIOT...
I'M WORRIED, SO I'LL JUST RUN OUT AND CHECK ON HIM.
ガチャ
GACHA (CLICK)
THANKS!
REI-CHAN.
YOUR FACE IS PRETTY RED... YOU OKAY?
I—!
I...
GYU (CLUTCH)
ギュ
I'VE NEVER DONE ANYTHING LIKE THIS BEFORE, SO...
AND I'M HAVING SUCH A GREAT TIME...

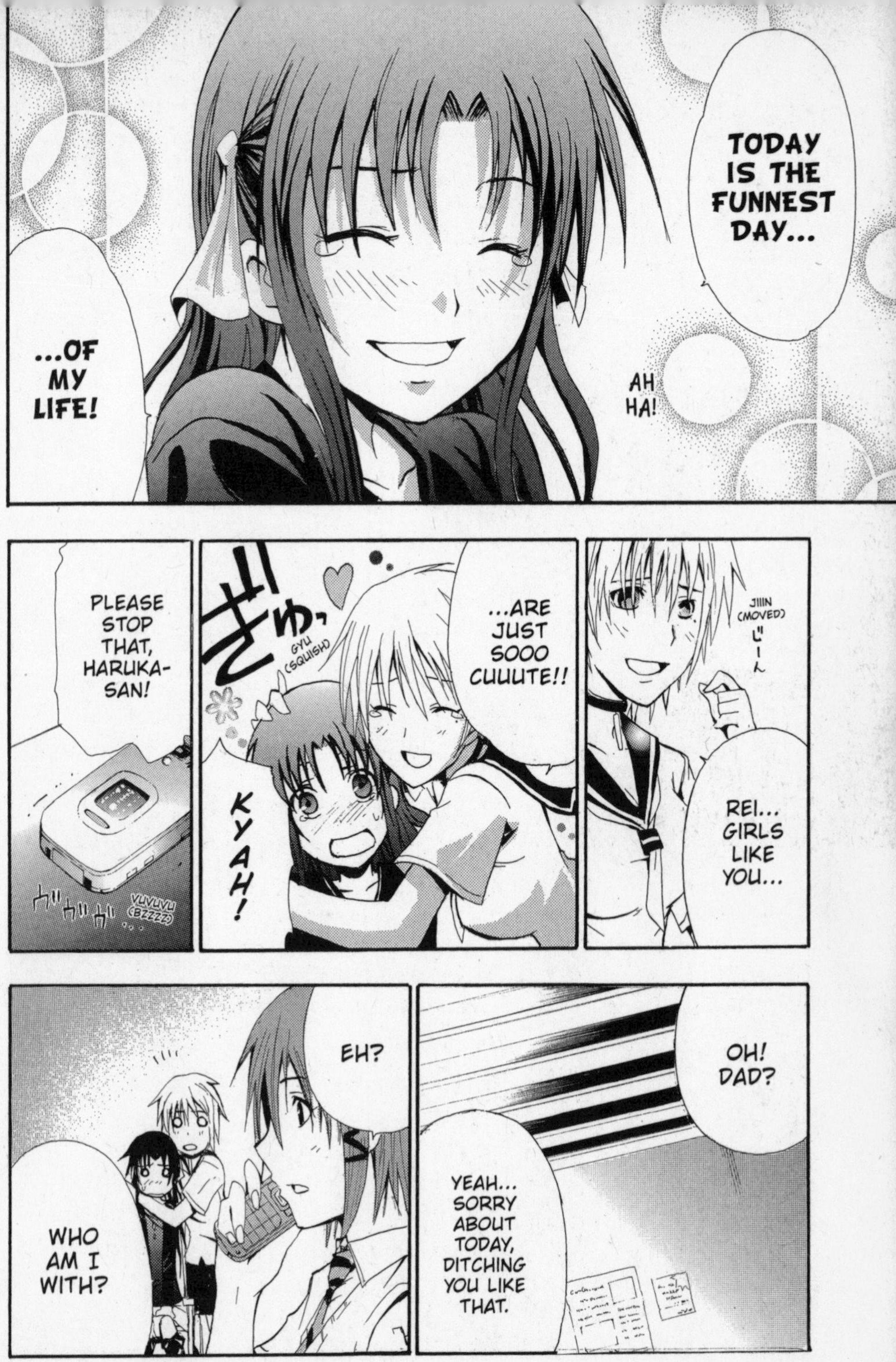
TODAY IS THE FUNNEST DAY...
AH HA!
...OF MY LIFE!
JIIIN (MOVED)
じーん
REI... GIRLS LIKE YOU...
...ARE JUST SOOO CUUUTE!!
ぎゅっ
GYU (SQUISH)
KYAH!
PLEASE STOP THAT, HARUKA-SAN!
ヴヴヴヴ
VUVUVU (BZZZZ)
OH! DAD?
YEAH... SORRY ABOUT TODAY, DITCHING YOU LIKE THAT.
EH?
WHO AM I WITH?

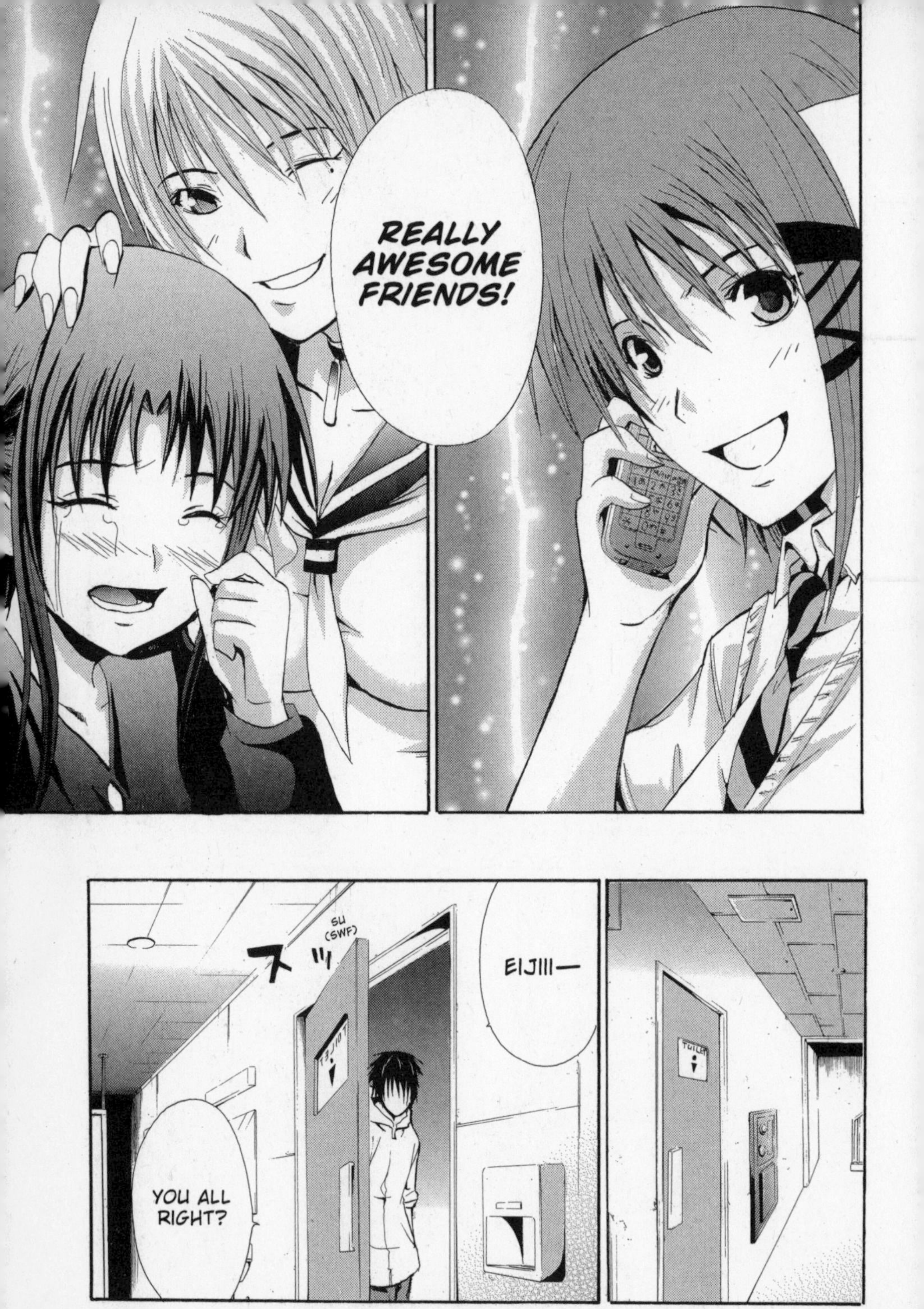
REALLY AWESOME FRIENDS!
EIJIII—
SU (SWF)
YOU ALL RIGHT?

HUH?

コン (KNOCK)
KON

EIJI?

C'MON, JUST ANSWER ME!

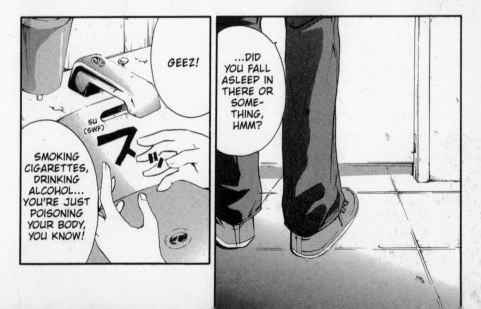

GEEZ!

...DID YOU FALL ASLEEP IN THERE OR SOMETHING, HMM?

ス (SWF)
SU

SMOKING CIGARETTES, DRINKING ALCOHOL... YOU'RE JUST POISONING YOUR BODY, YOU KNOW!

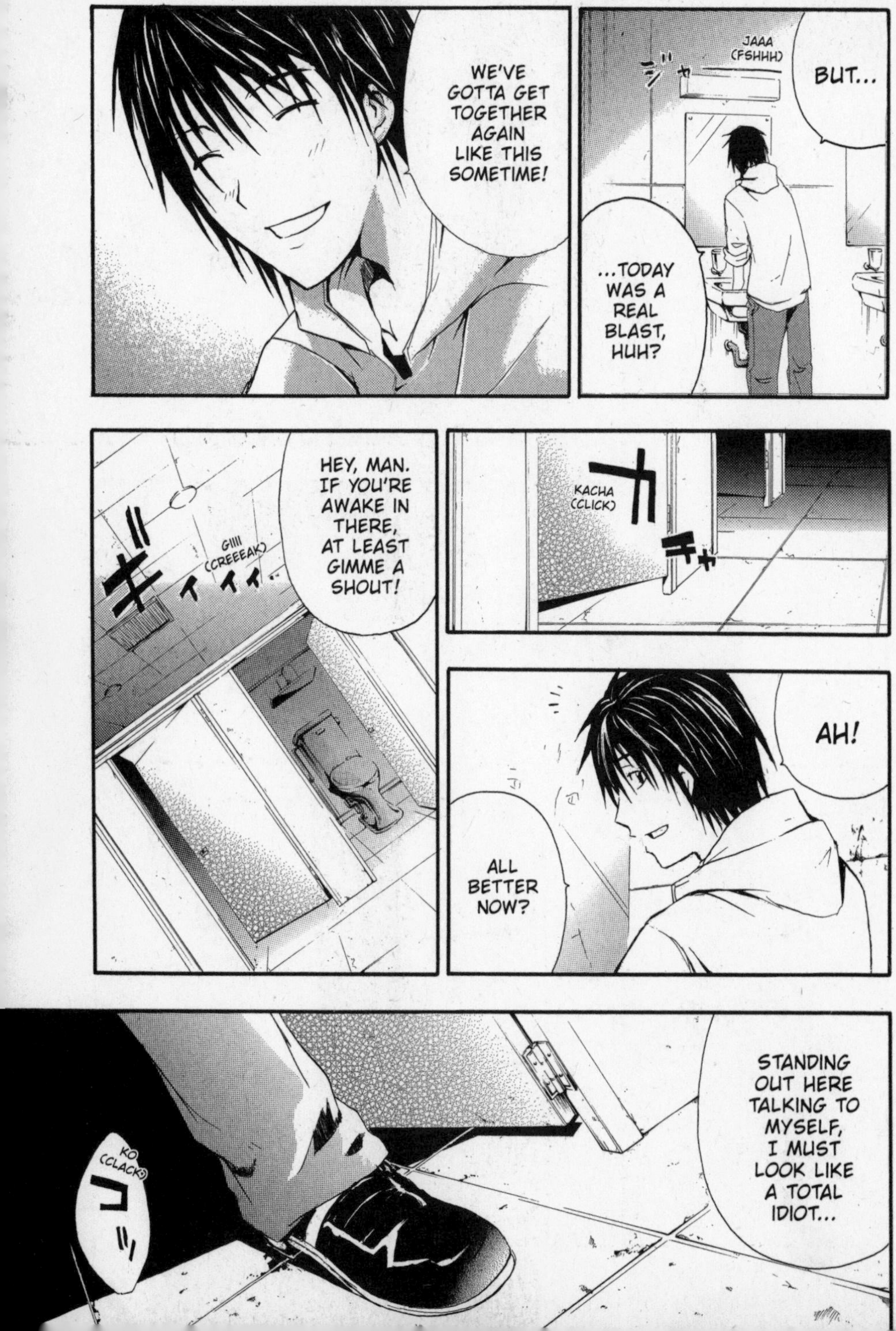
JAAA (FSHHH)
BUT...
...TODAY WAS A REAL BLAST, HUH?
WE'VE GOTTA GET TOGETHER AGAIN LIKE THIS SOMETIME!
KACHA (CLICK)
AH!
ALL BETTER NOW?
GIIII (CREEEAK)
HEY, MAN. IF YOU'RE AWAKE IN THERE, AT LEAST GIMME A SHOUT!
STANDING OUT HERE TALKING TO MYSELF, I MUST LOOK LIKE A TOTAL IDIOT...
KO (CLACK)

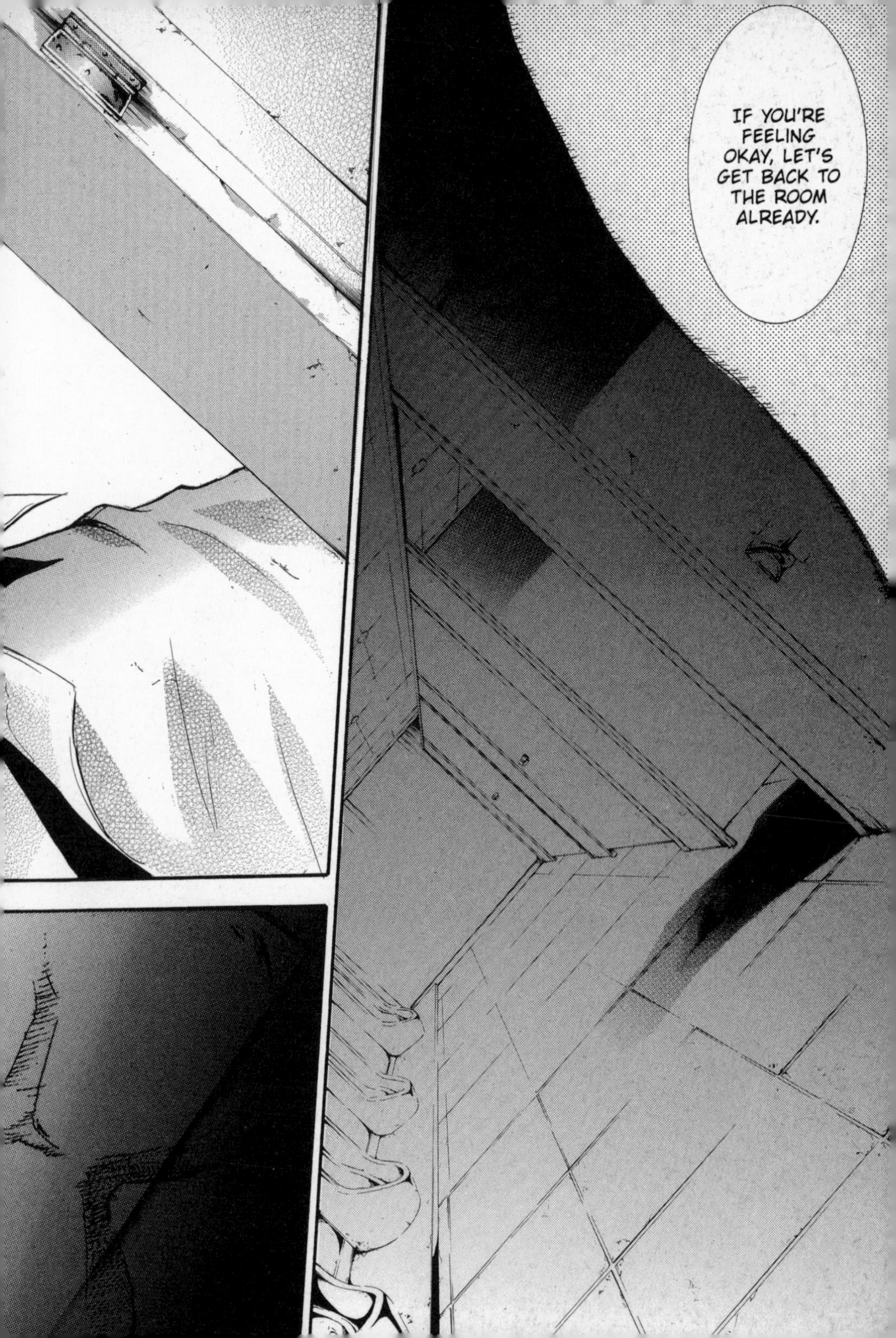
IF YOU'RE FEELING OKAY, LET'S GET BACK TO THE ROOM ALREADY.

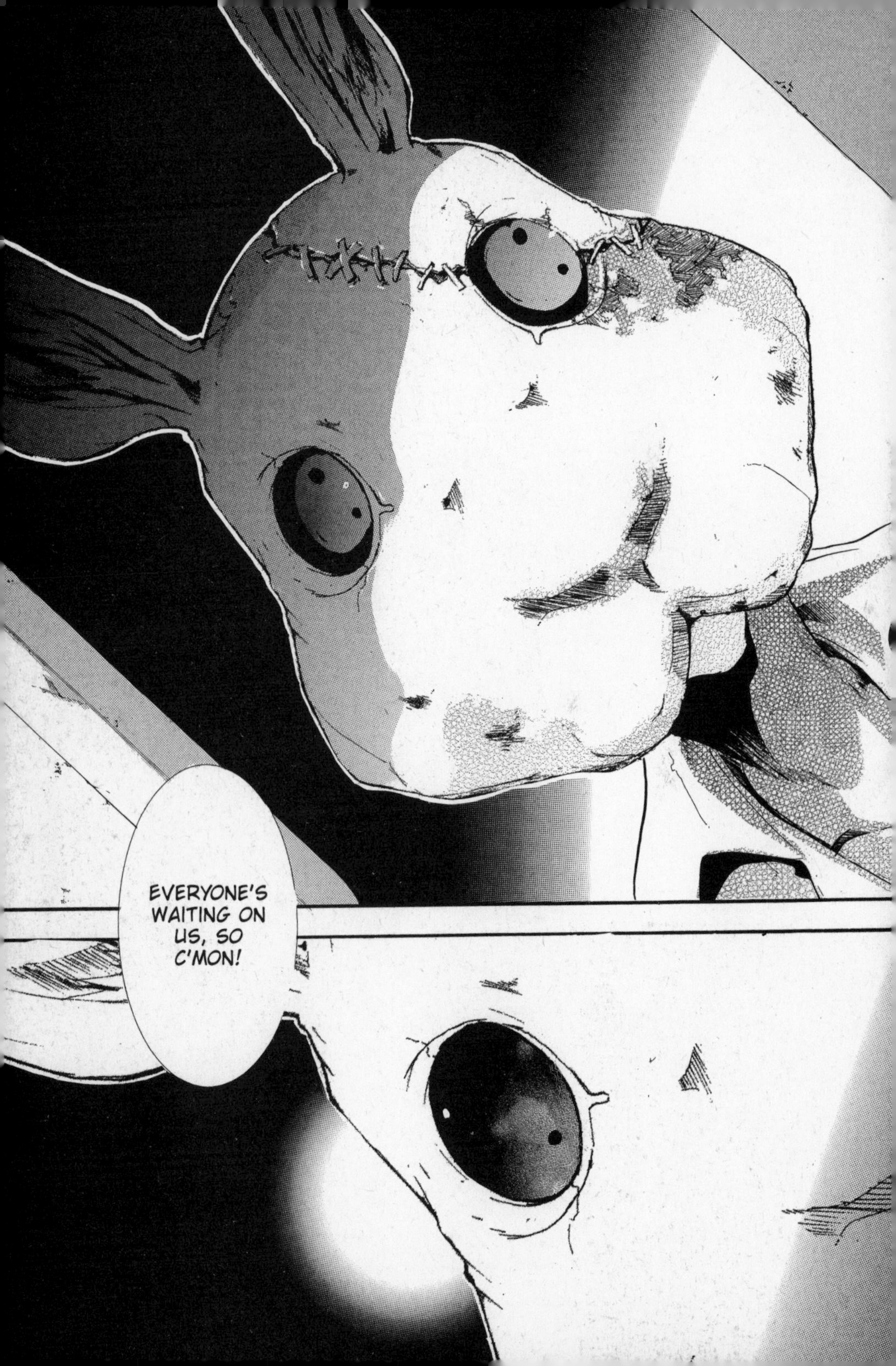
EVERYONE'S WAITING ON US, SO C'MON!

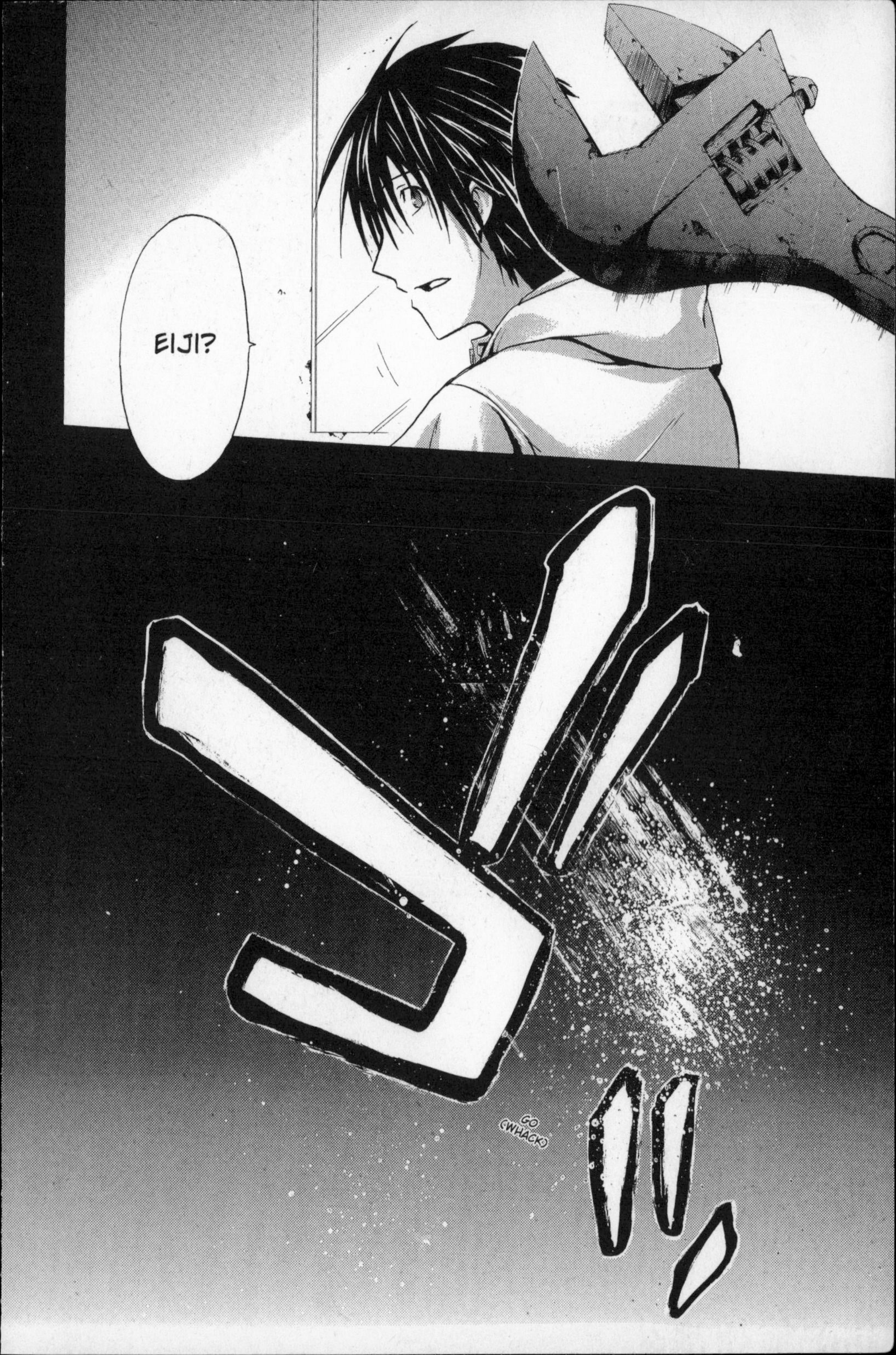
EIJI?
GO (WHACK)

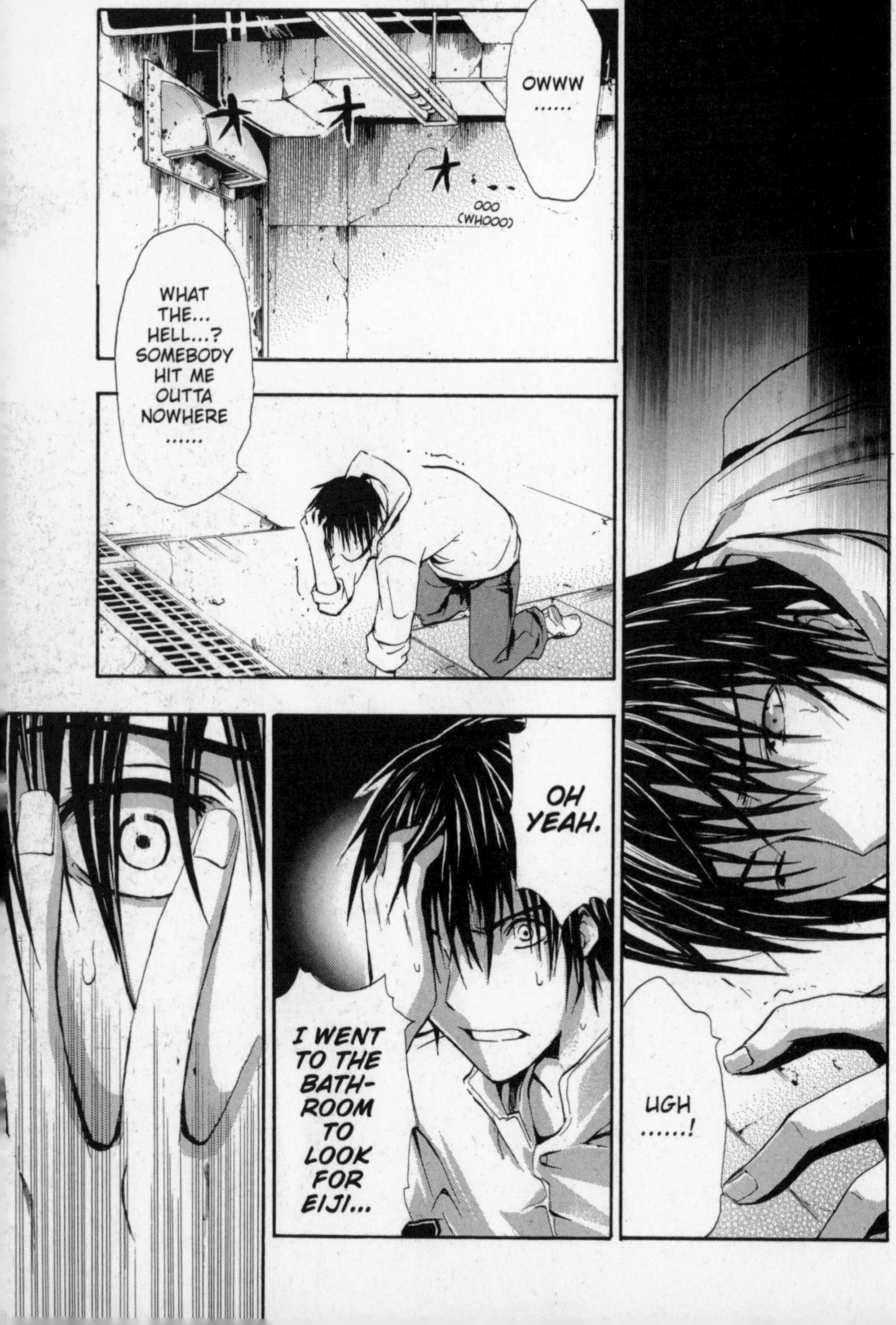
UGH ......!
OWWW ......
OOO (WHOOO)
WHAT THE... HELL...? SOMEBODY HIT ME OUTTA NOWHERE ......
OH YEAH.
I WENT TO THE BATH-ROOM TO LOOK FOR EIJI...

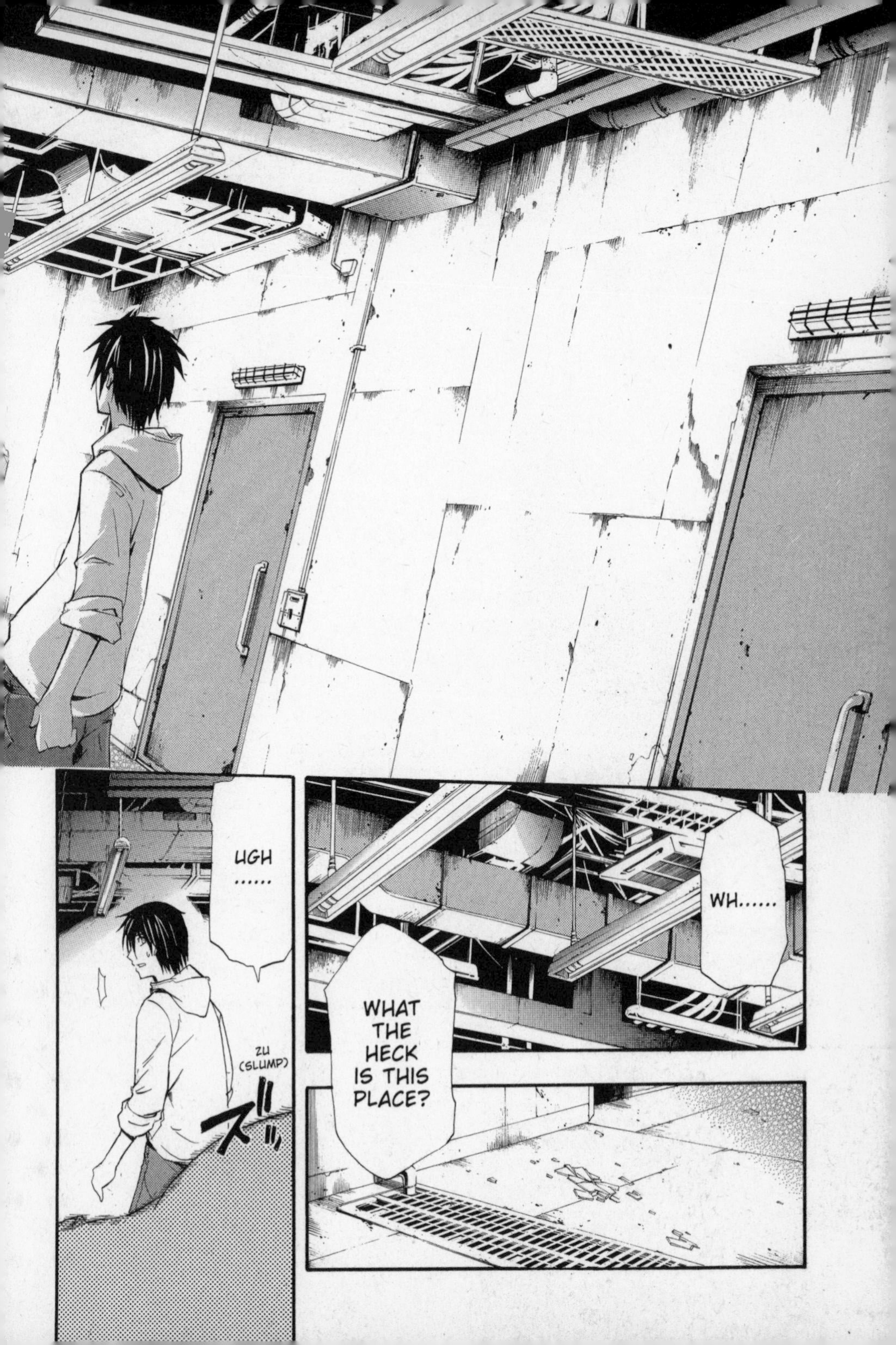
WH......
WHAT THE HECK IS THIS PLACE?
UGH ......
ZU (SLUMP)

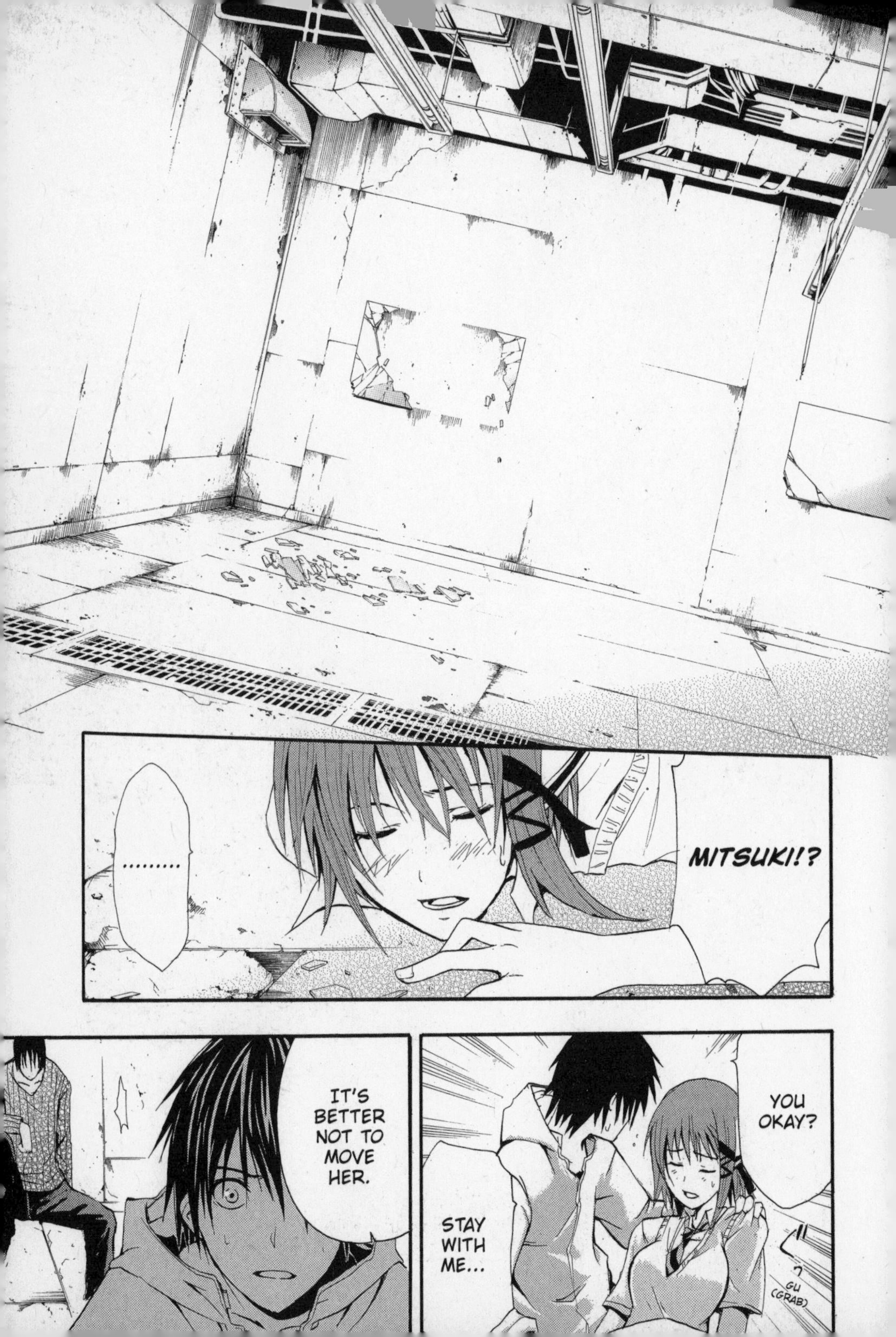
MITSUKI!?
....
YOU OKAY?
STAY WITH ME...
GU (GRAB)
IT'S BETTER NOT TO MOVE HER.

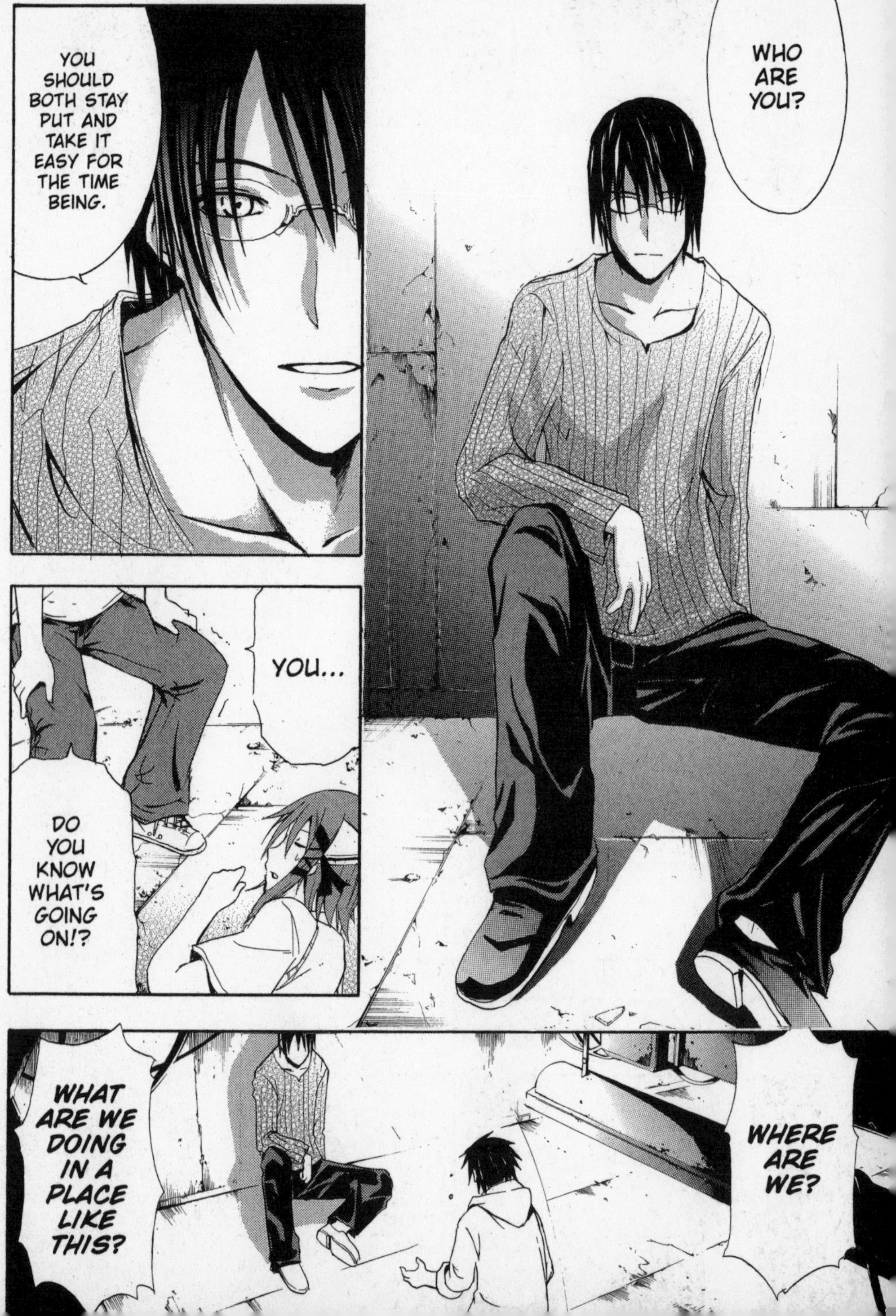
WHO ARE YOU?
YOU SHOULD BOTH STAY PUT AND TAKE IT EASY FOR THE TIME BEING.
YOU...
DO YOU KNOW WHAT'S GOING ON!?
WHERE ARE WE?
WHAT ARE WE DOING IN A PLACE LIKE THIS?

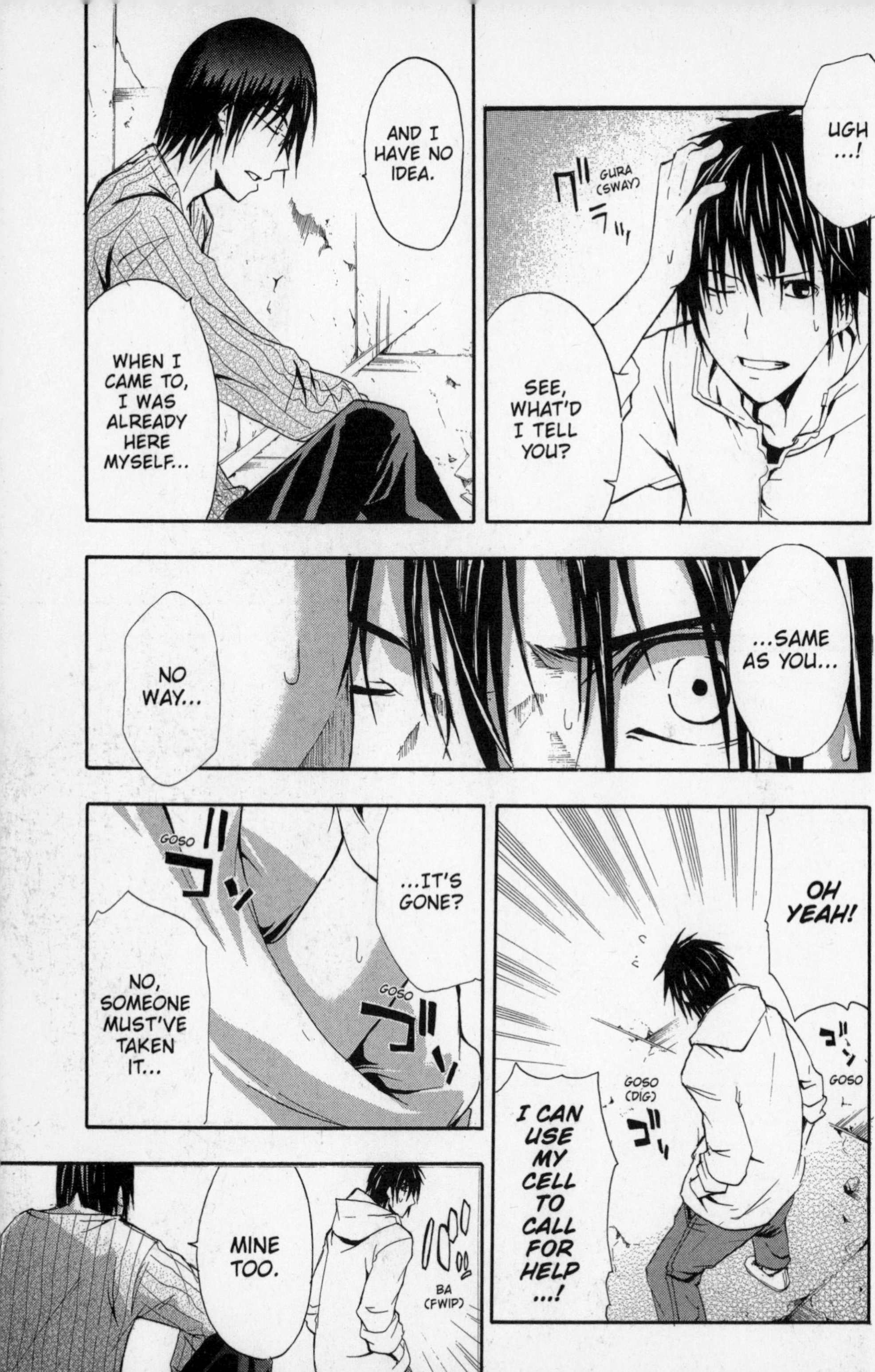
UGH ...!
GURA (SWAY)
SEE, WHAT'D I TELL YOU?
AND I HAVE NO IDEA.
WHEN I CAME TO, I WAS ALREADY HERE MYSELF...
...SAME AS YOU...
NO WAY...
OH YEAH!
GOSO
GOSO (DIG)
I CAN USE MY CELL TO CALL FOR HELP ...!
GOSO
...IT'S GONE?
GOSO
NO, SOMEONE MUST'VE TAKEN IT...
BA (FWIP)
MINE TOO.

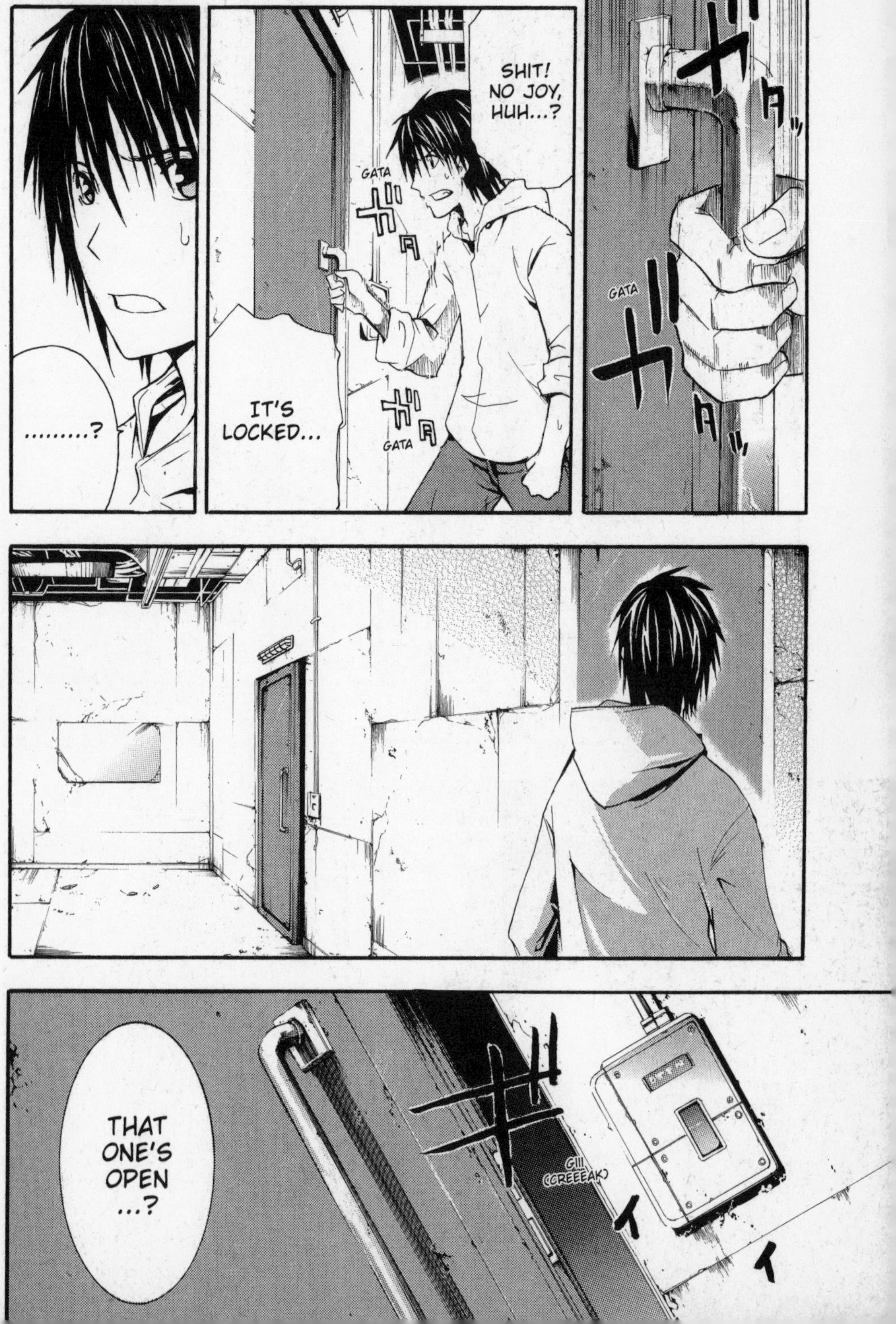
GATA (RATTLE)
GATA
SHIT! NO JOY, HUH...?
GATA
GATA
IT'S LOCKED...
.........?
GIII (CREEEAK)
THAT ONE'S OPEN ...?

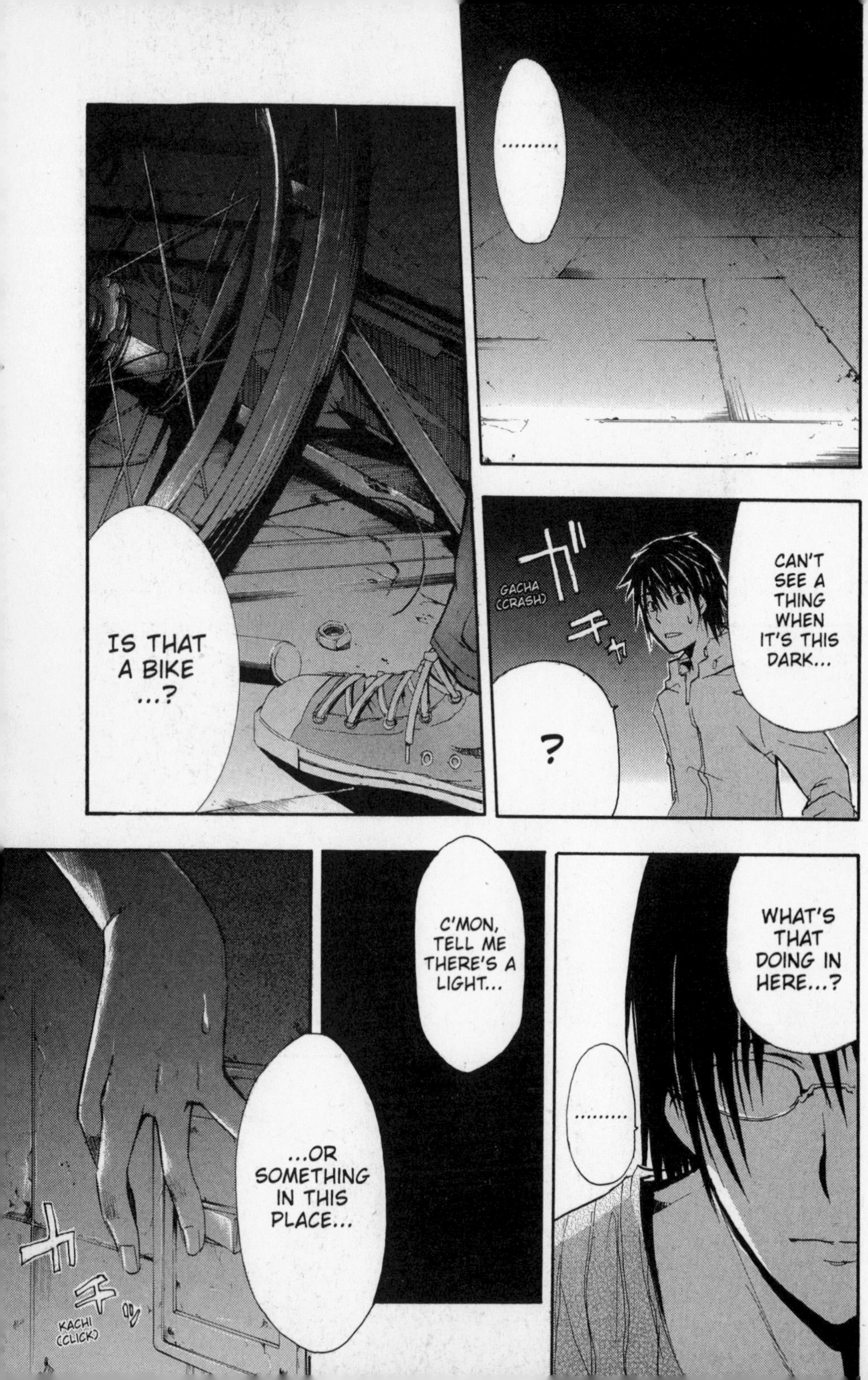
....
CAN'T SEE A THING WHEN IT'S THIS DARK...
ガチャ
GACHA (CRASH)
?
IS THAT A BIKE ...?
WHAT'S THAT DOING IN HERE...?
....
C'MON, TELL ME THERE'S A LIGHT...
...OR SOMETHING IN THIS PLACE...
カチッ
KACHI (CLICK)

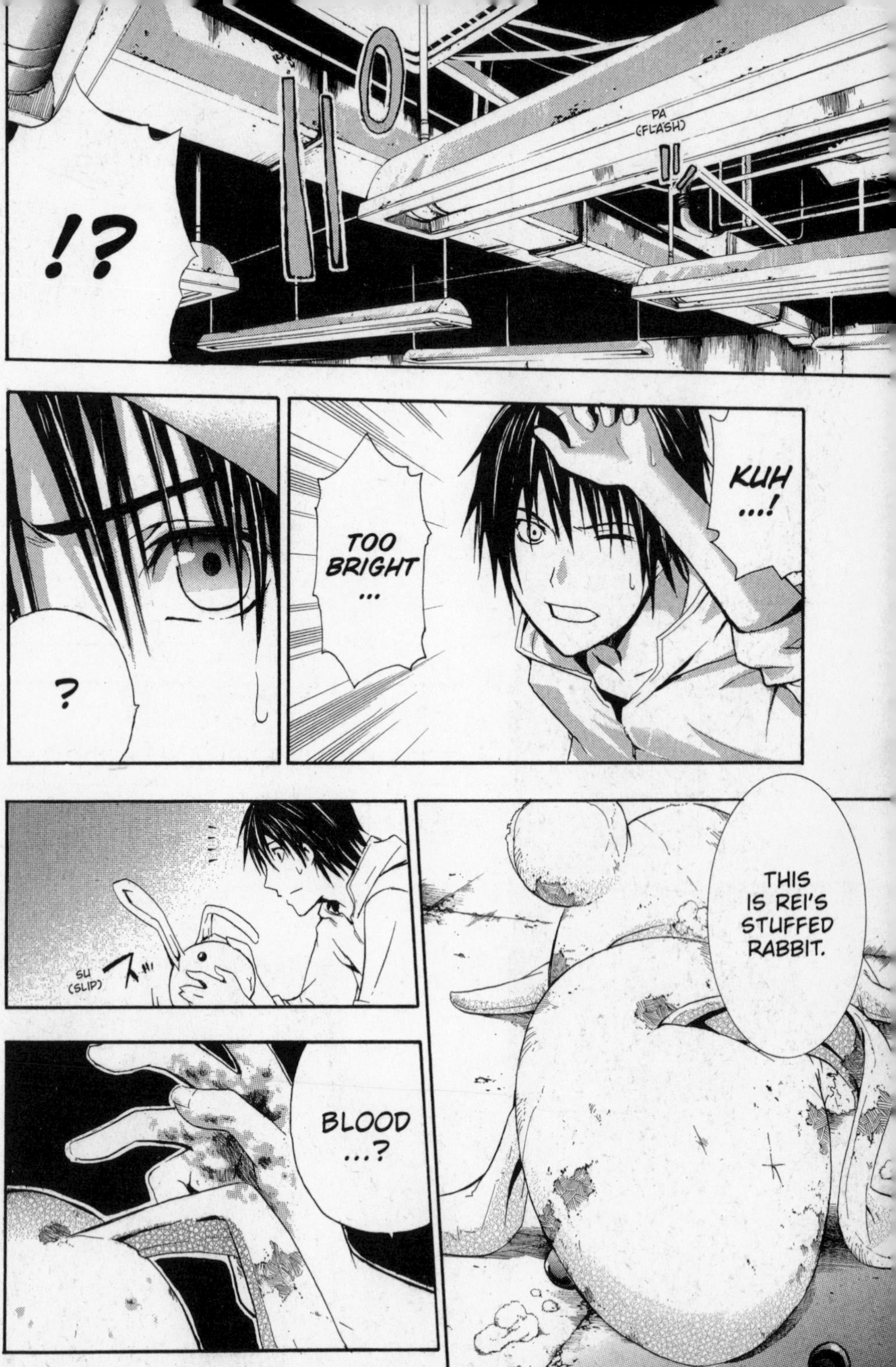
PA (FLASH)
!?
KUH ...!
TOO BRIGHT ...
?
THIS IS REI'S STUFFED RABBIT.
SU (SLIP)
BLOOD ...?

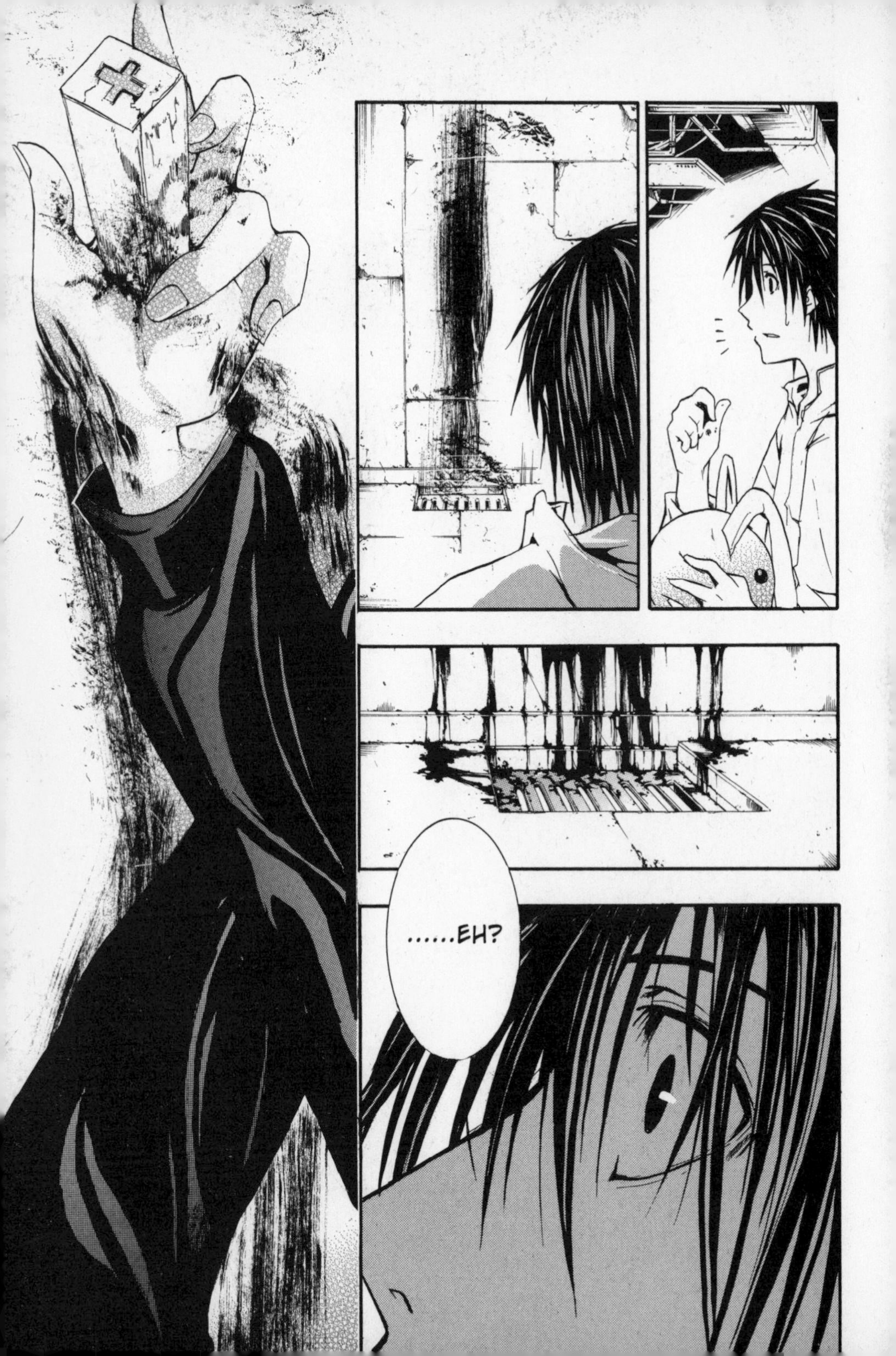
......EH?

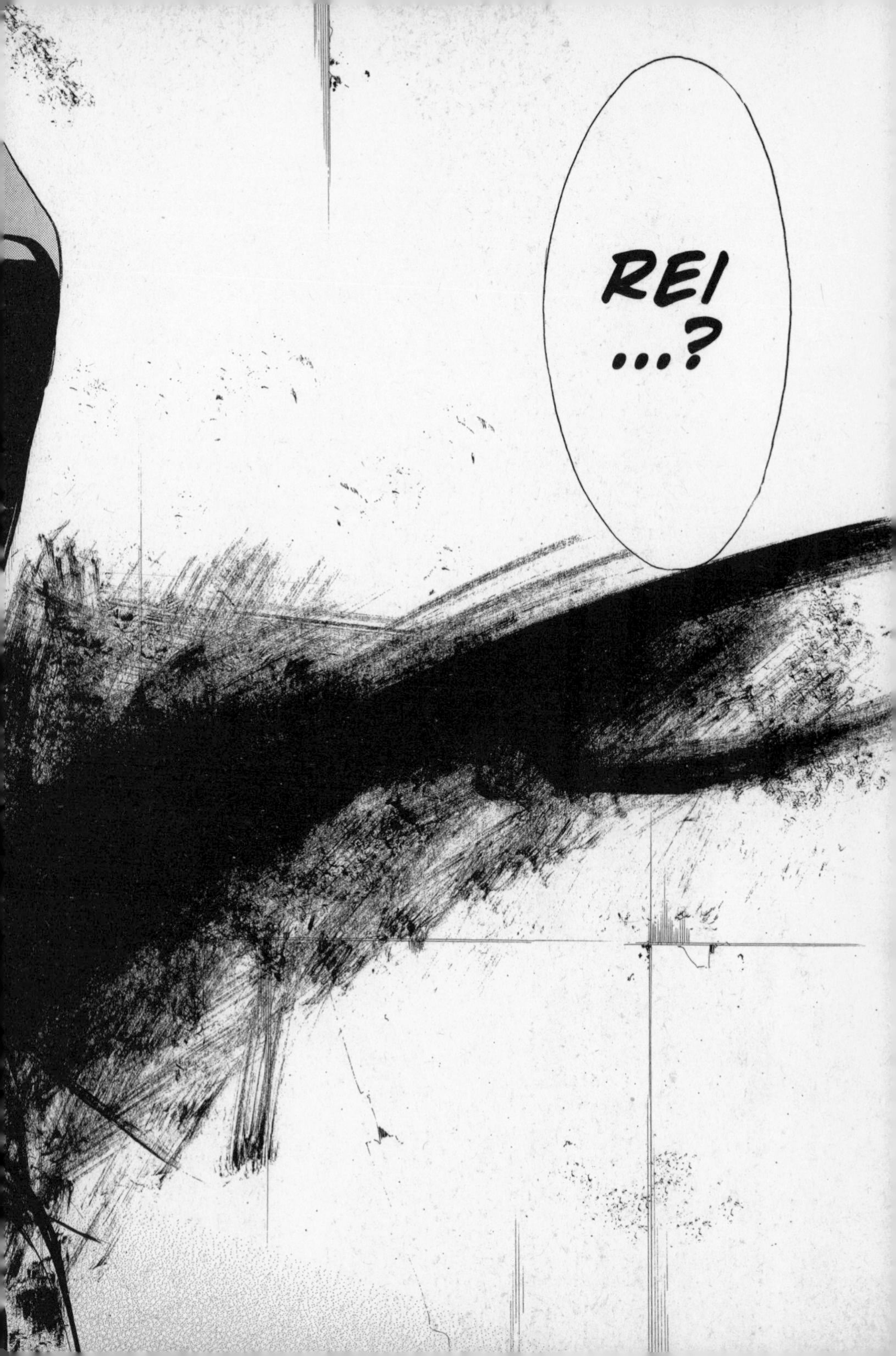
REI
...?

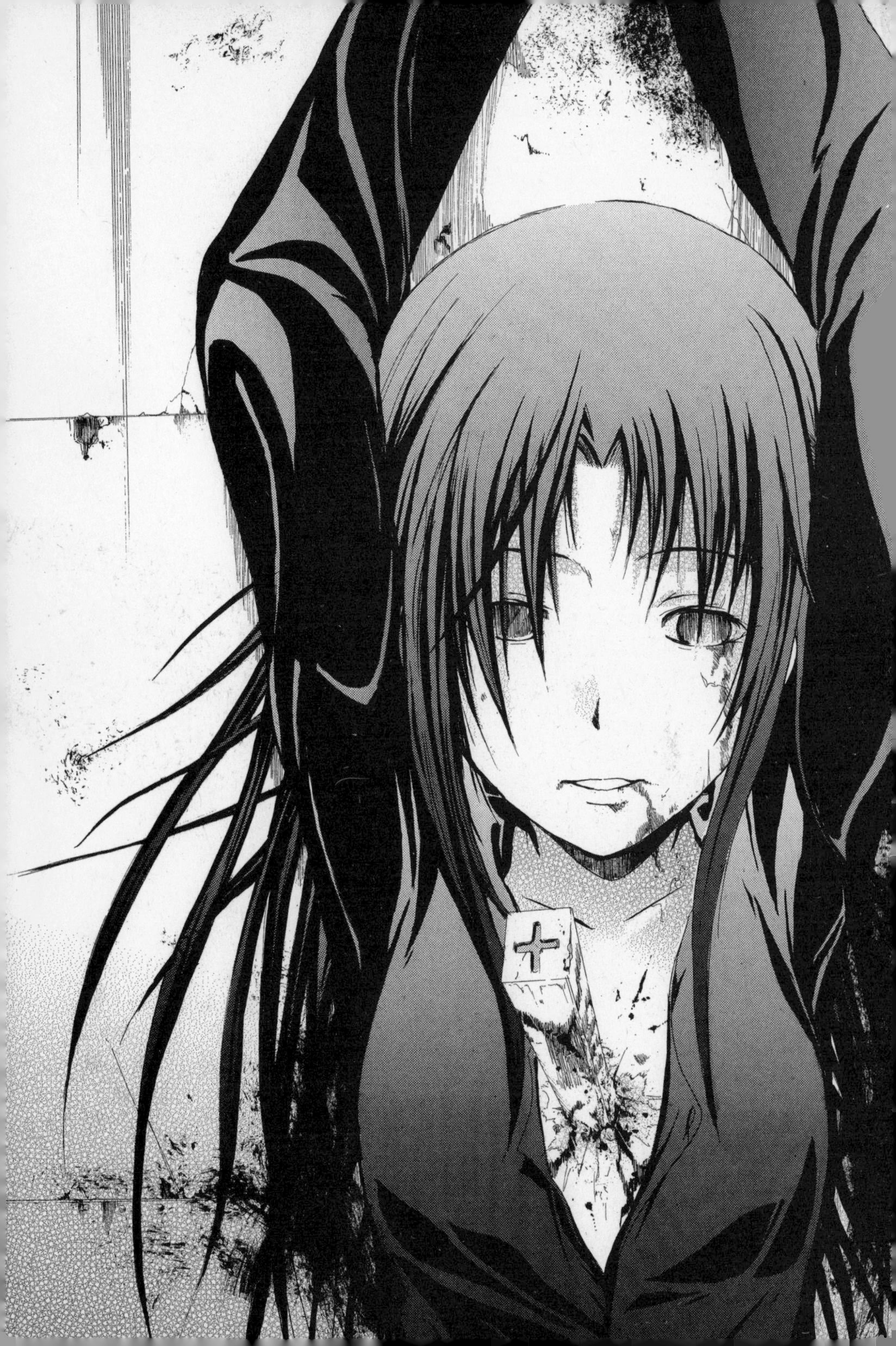

Doubt

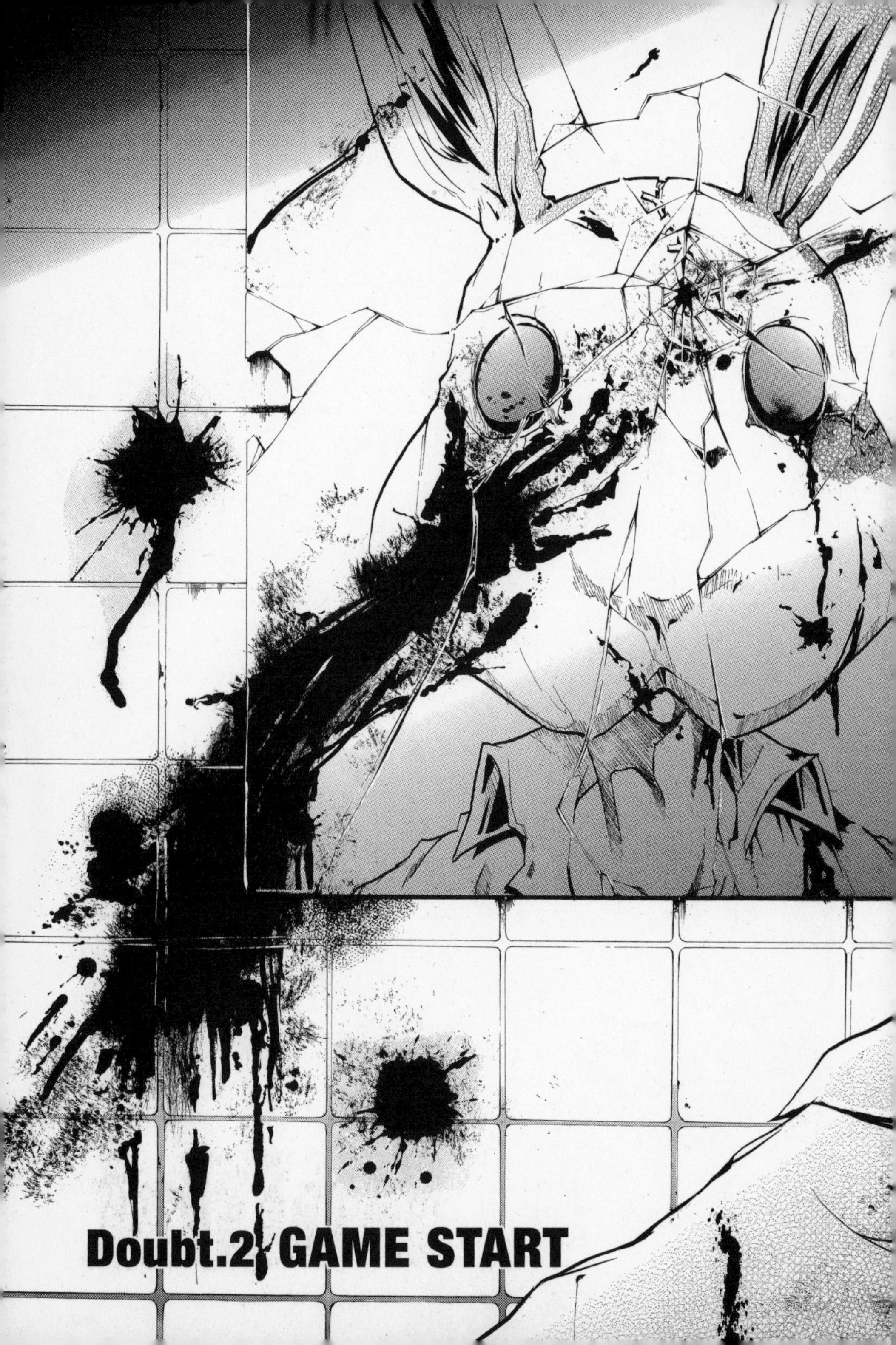
Doubt.2 GAME START

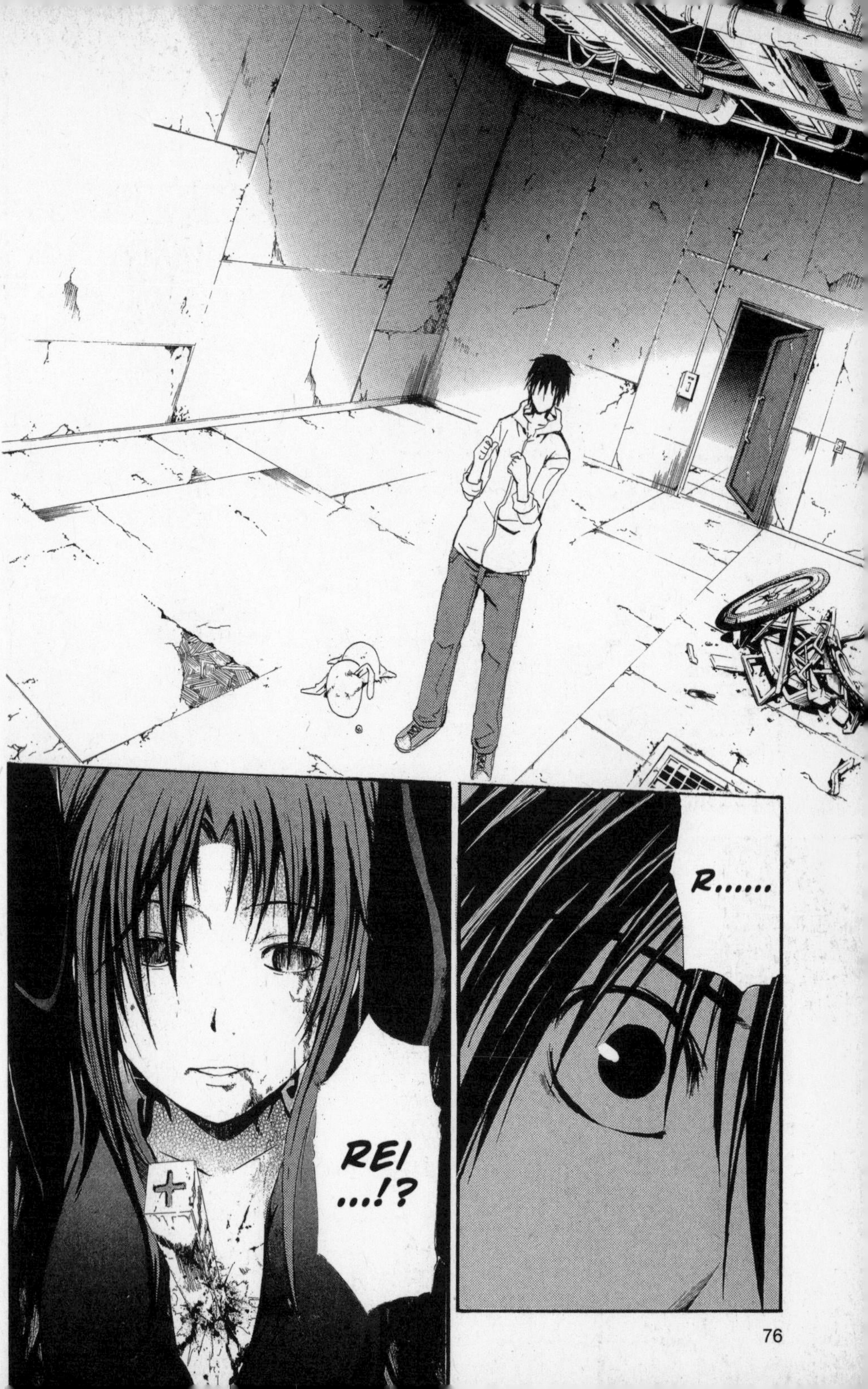
R......
REI
...!?

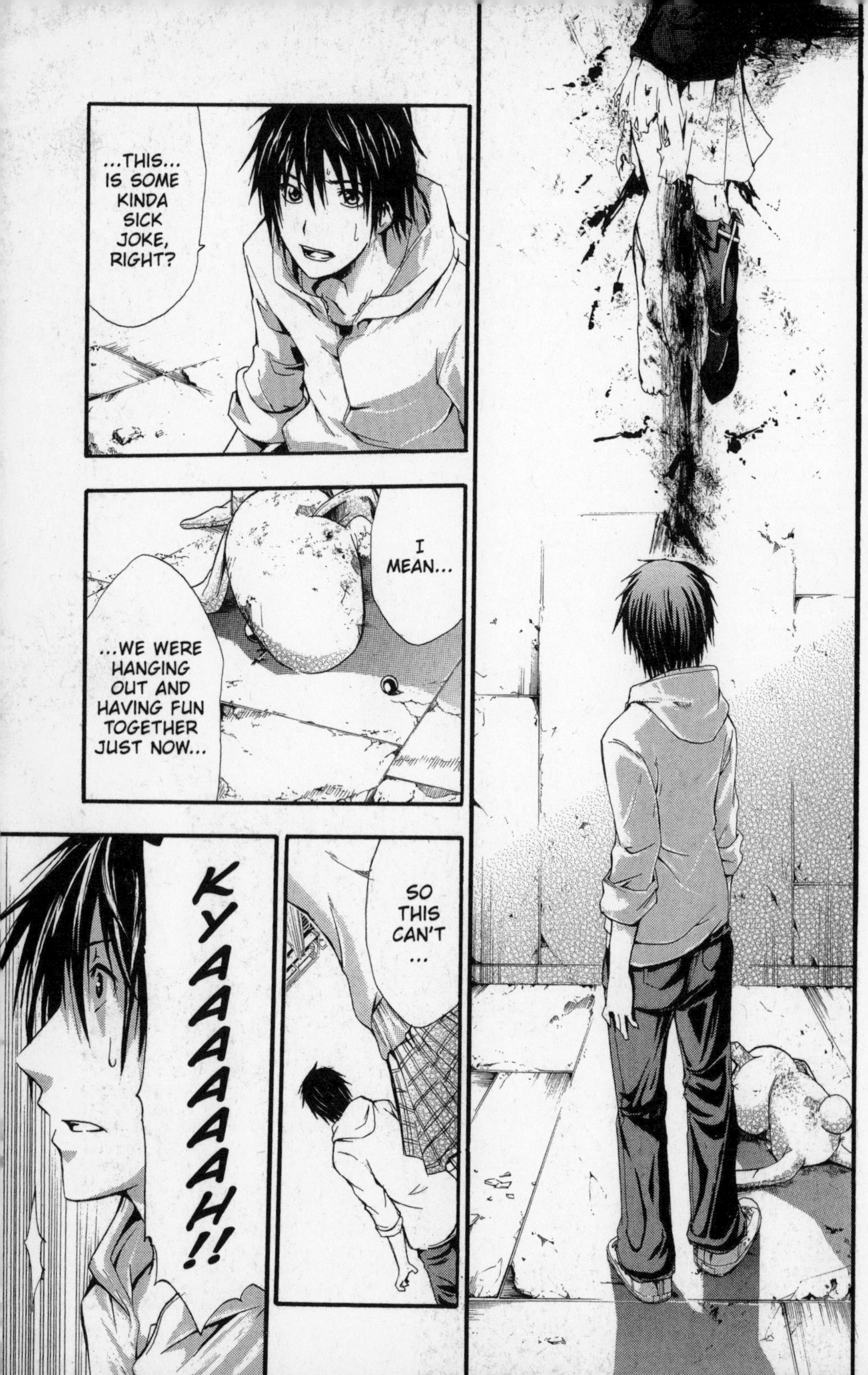

...THIS... IS SOME KINDA SICK JOKE, RIGHT?
I MEAN...
...WE WERE HANGING OUT AND HAVING FUN TOGETHER JUST NOW...
SO THIS CAN'T ...
KYAAAAAAAH!!

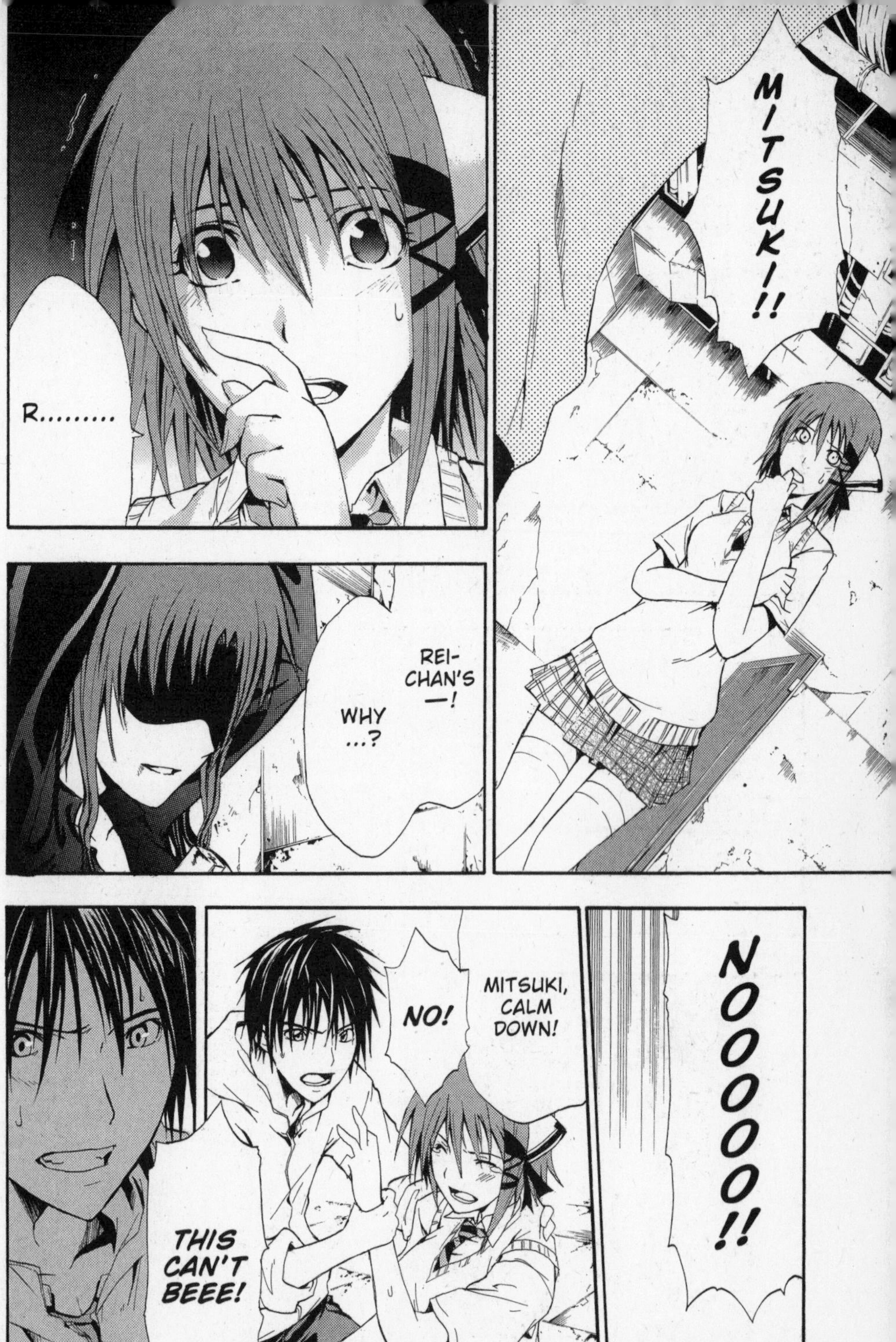
MITSUKI!!
R.........
REI-CHAN'S—!
WHY...?
NOOOOOO!!
MITSUKI, CALM DOWN!
NO!
THIS CAN'T BEEE!

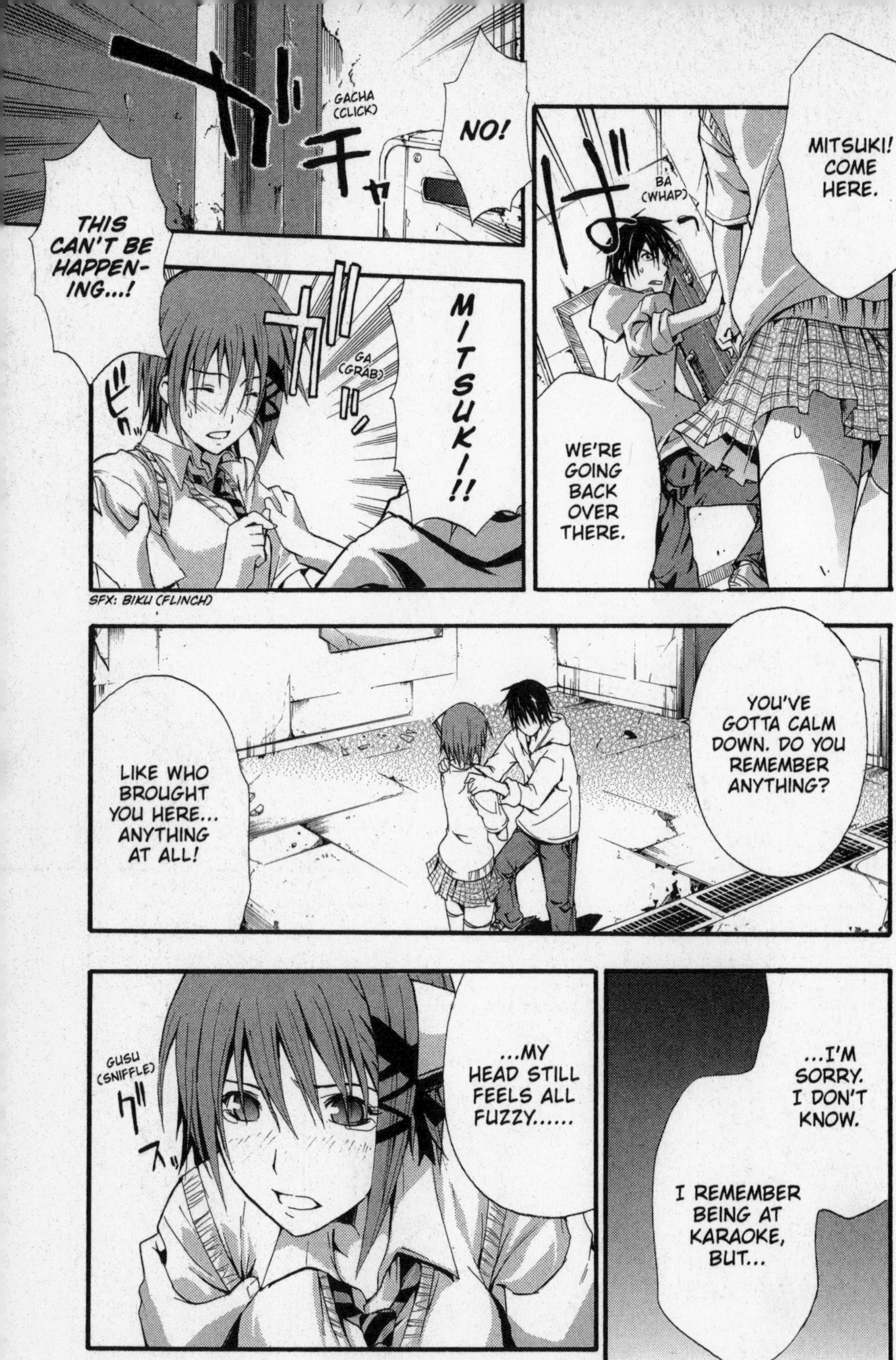
MITSUKI! COME HERE.
BA (WHAP)
WE'RE GOING BACK OVER THERE.
NO!
GACHA (CLICK)
THIS CAN'T BE HAPPEN-ING...!
MITSUKI!!
GA (GRAB)
SFX: BIKU (FLINCH)
YOU'VE GOTTA CALM DOWN. DO YOU REMEMBER ANYTHING?
LIKE WHO BROUGHT YOU HERE... ANYTHING AT ALL!
...I'M SORRY. I DON'T KNOW.
I REMEMBER BEING AT KARAOKE, BUT...
...MY HEAD STILL FEELS ALL FUZZY......
GUSU (SNIFFLE)

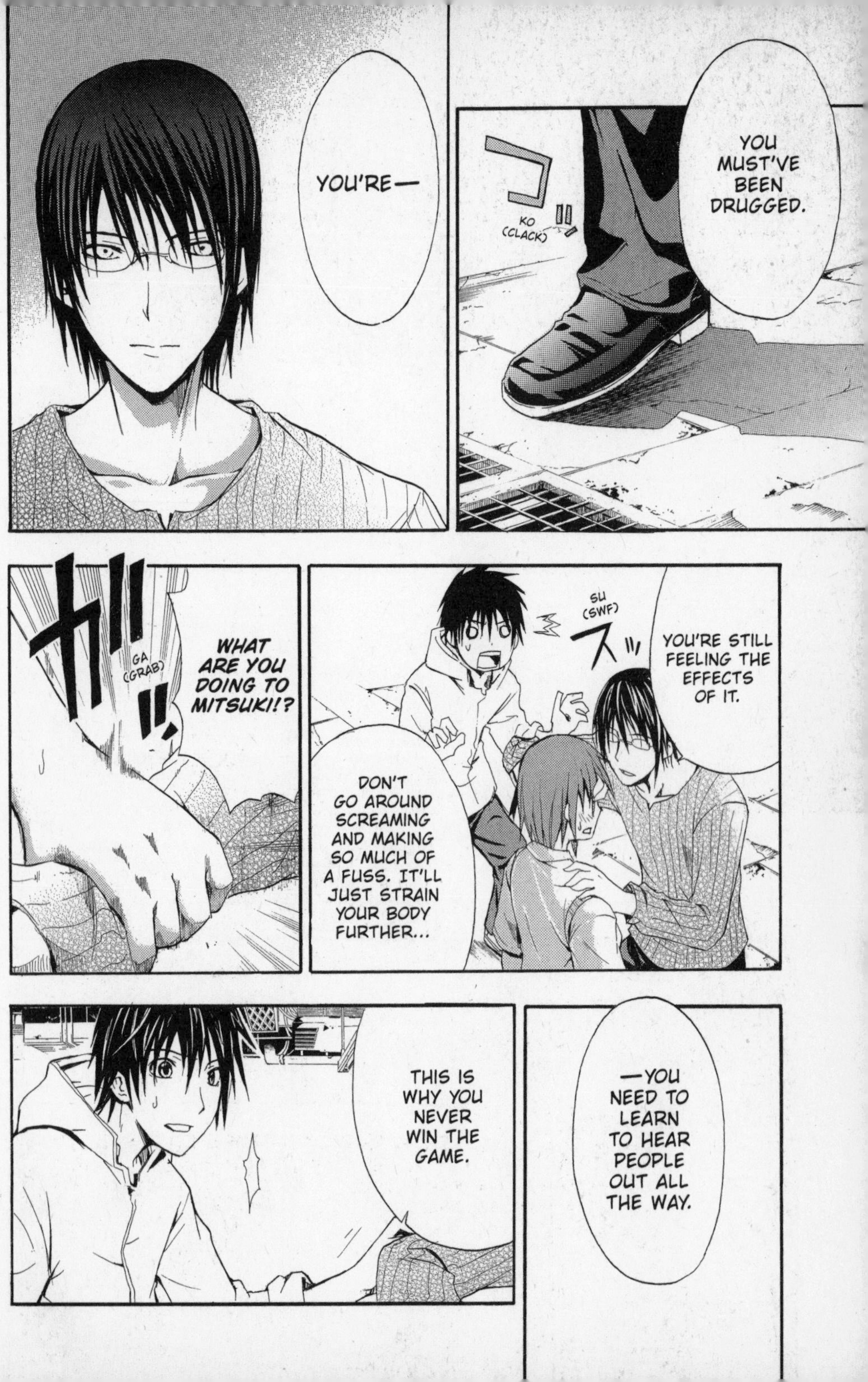
YOU MUST'VE BEEN DRUGGED.
KO (CLACK)
YOU'RE—
SU (SWF)
YOU'RE STILL FEELING THE EFFECTS OF IT.
DON'T GO AROUND SCREAMING AND MAKING SO MUCH OF A FUSS. IT'LL JUST STRAIN YOUR BODY FURTHER...
GA (GRAB)
WHAT ARE YOU DOING TO MITSUKI!?
—YOU NEED TO LEARN TO HEAR PEOPLE OUT ALL THE WAY.
THIS IS WHY YOU NEVER WIN THE GAME.

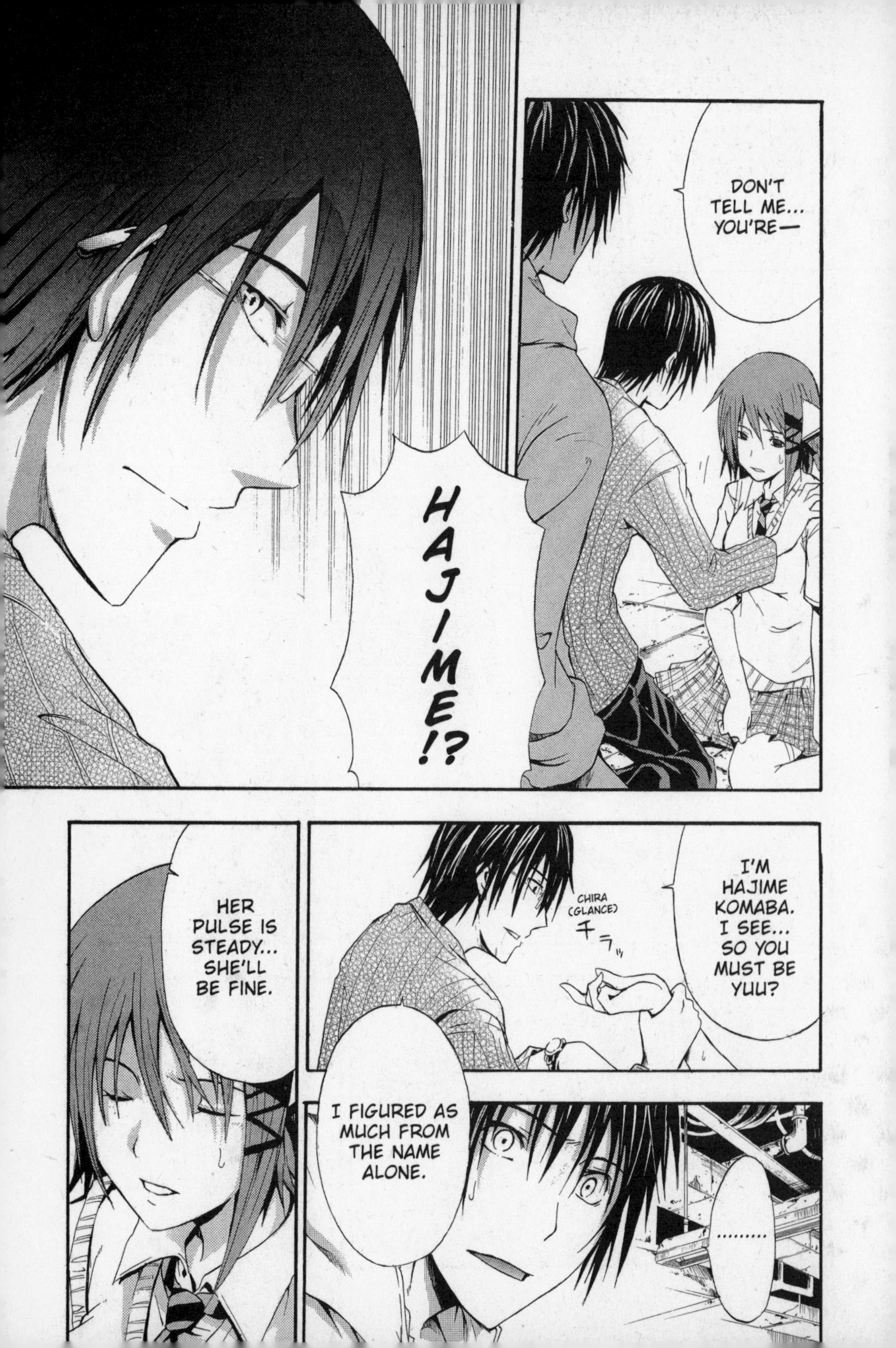
DON'T TELL ME... YOU'RE—
HAJIME!?
I'M HAJIME KOMABA. I SEE... SO YOU MUST BE YUU?
CHIRA (GLANCE)
チラッ
I FIGURED AS MUCH FROM THE NAME ALONE.
....
HER PULSE IS STEADY... SHE'LL BE FINE.

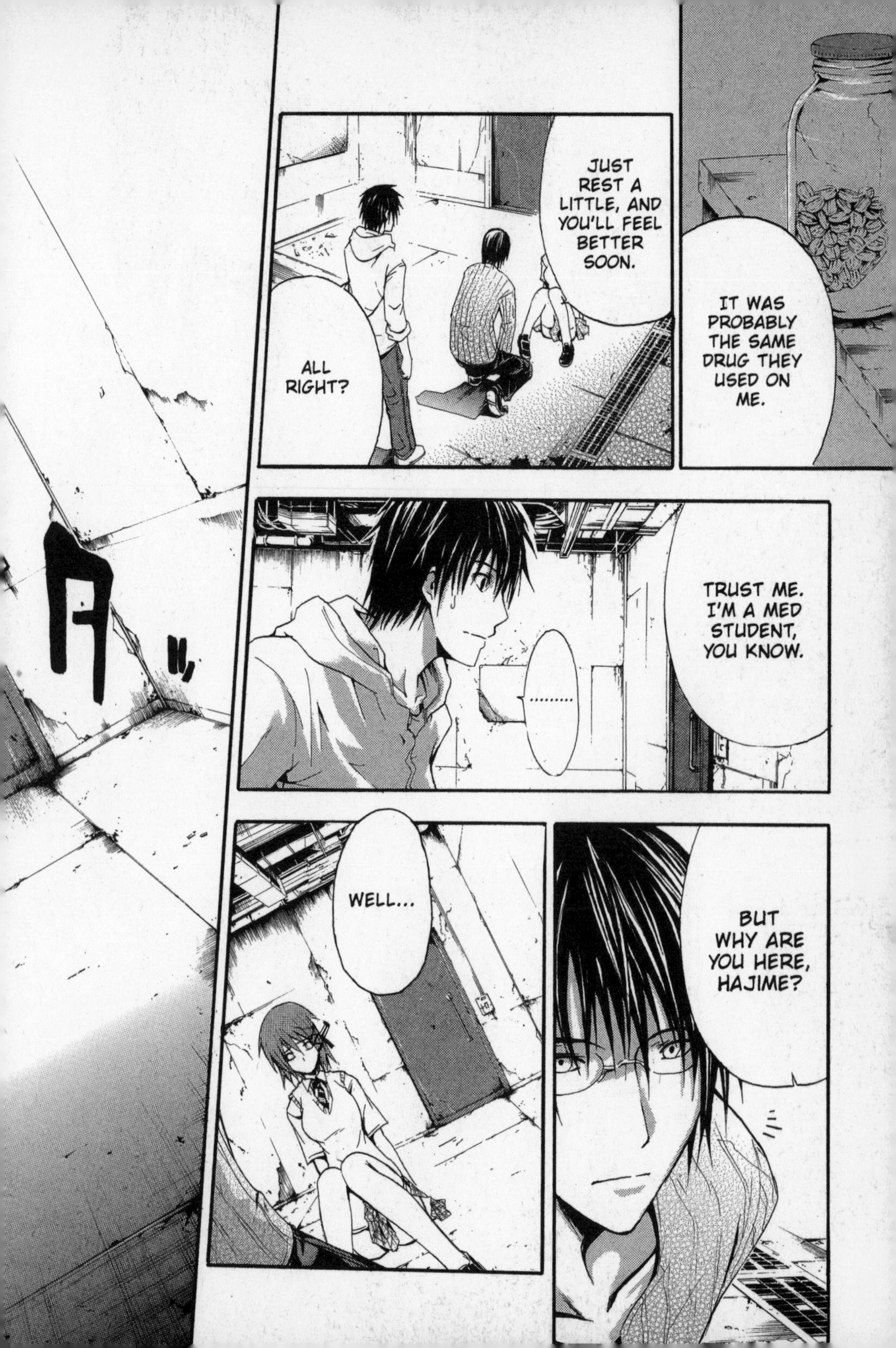
IT WAS PROBABLY THE SAME DRUG THEY USED ON ME.
JUST REST A LITTLE, AND YOU'LL FEEL BETTER SOON.
ALL RIGHT?
TRUST ME. I'M A MED STUDENT, YOU KNOW.
....
BUT WHY ARE YOU HERE, HAJIME?
WELL...

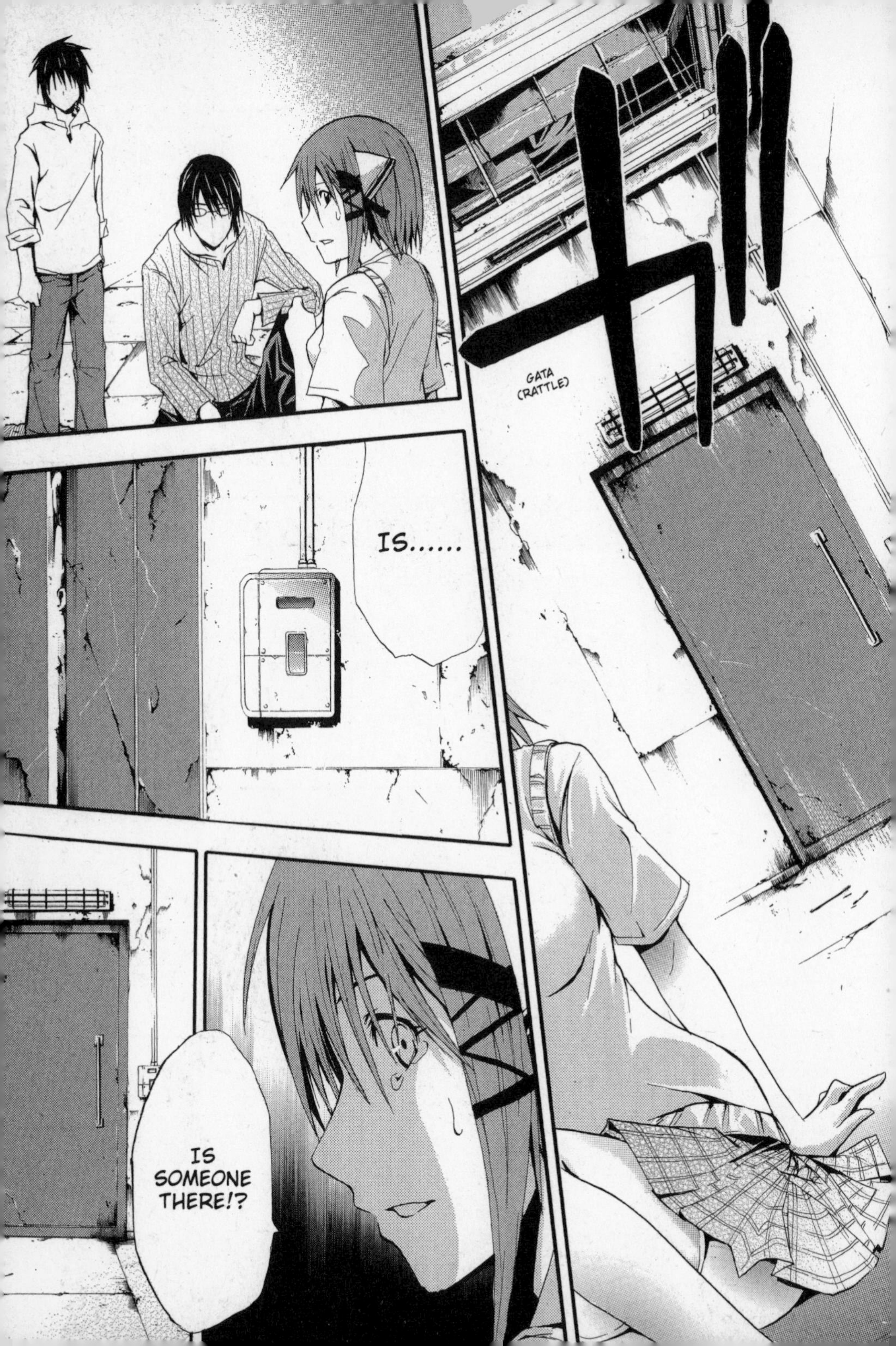
GATA (RATTLE)
IS......
IS SOMEONE THERE!?

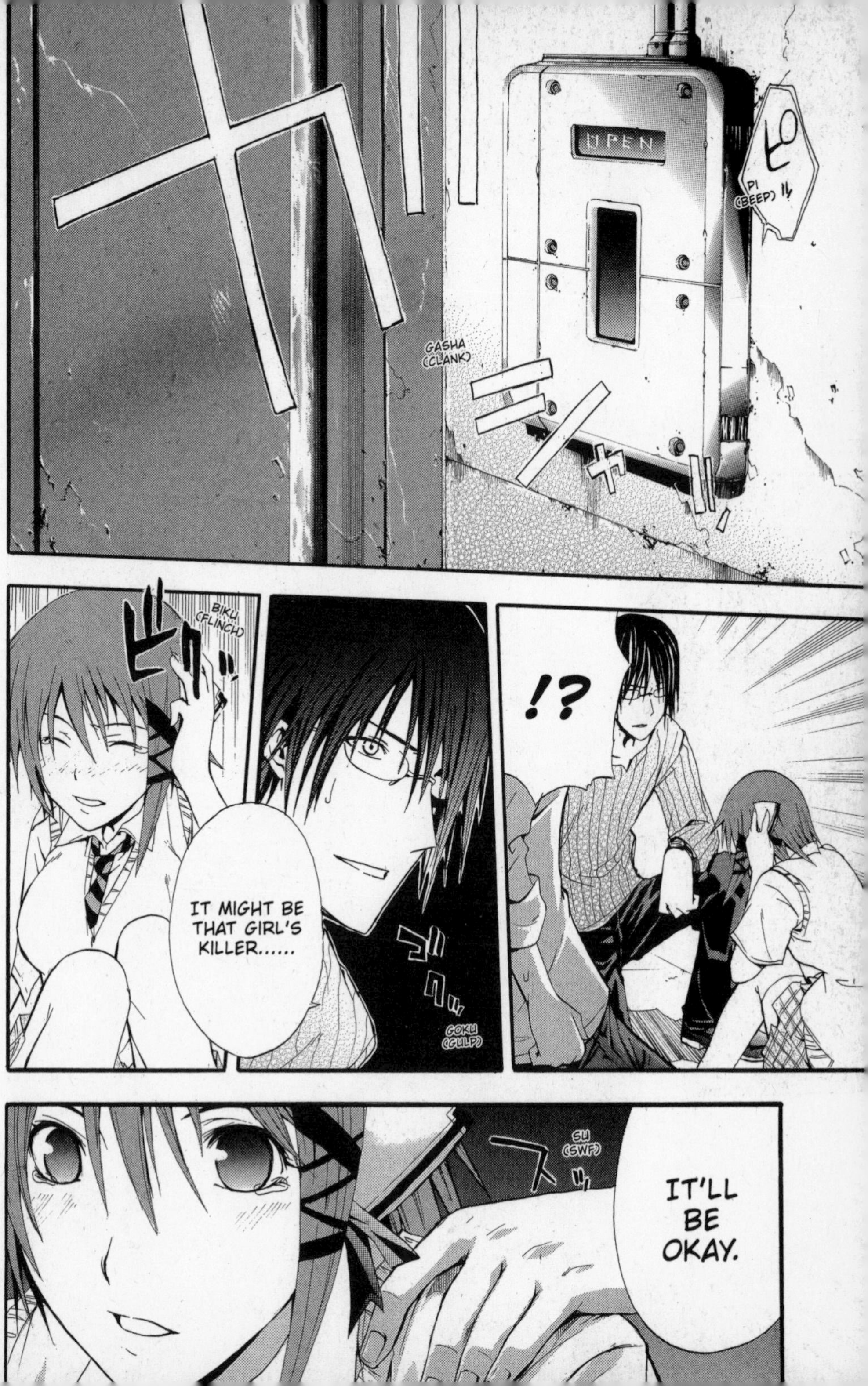
PI (BEEP)
GASHA (CLANK)
BIKU (FLINCH)
!?
GOKU (GULP)
IT MIGHT BE THAT GIRL'S KILLER......
IT'LL BE OKAY.
SU (SWF)

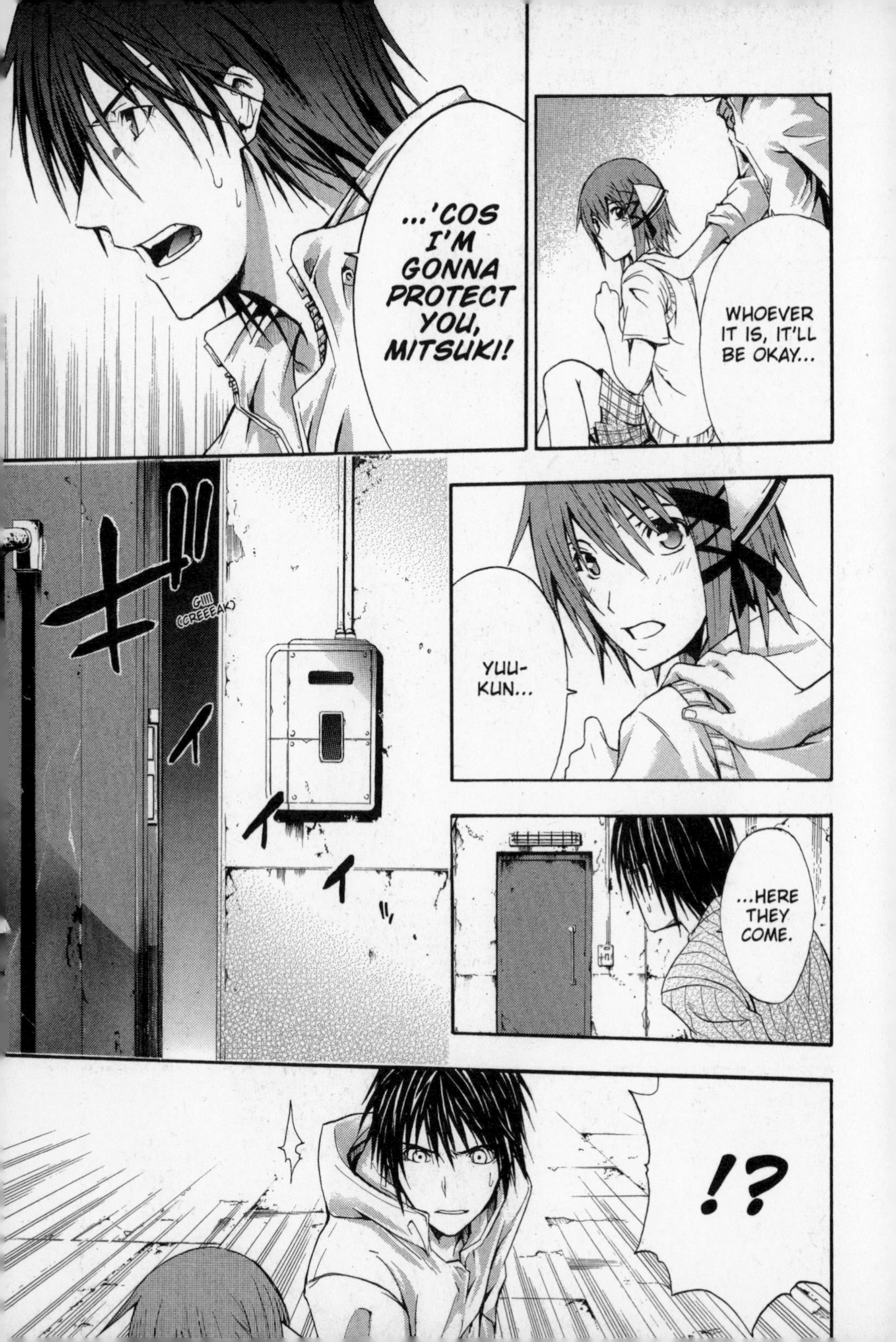
WHOEVER IT IS, IT'LL BE OKAY...
...'COS I'M GONNA PROTECT YOU, MITSUKI!
YUU-KUN...
...HERE THEY COME.
GIIII (CREEEAK)
!?

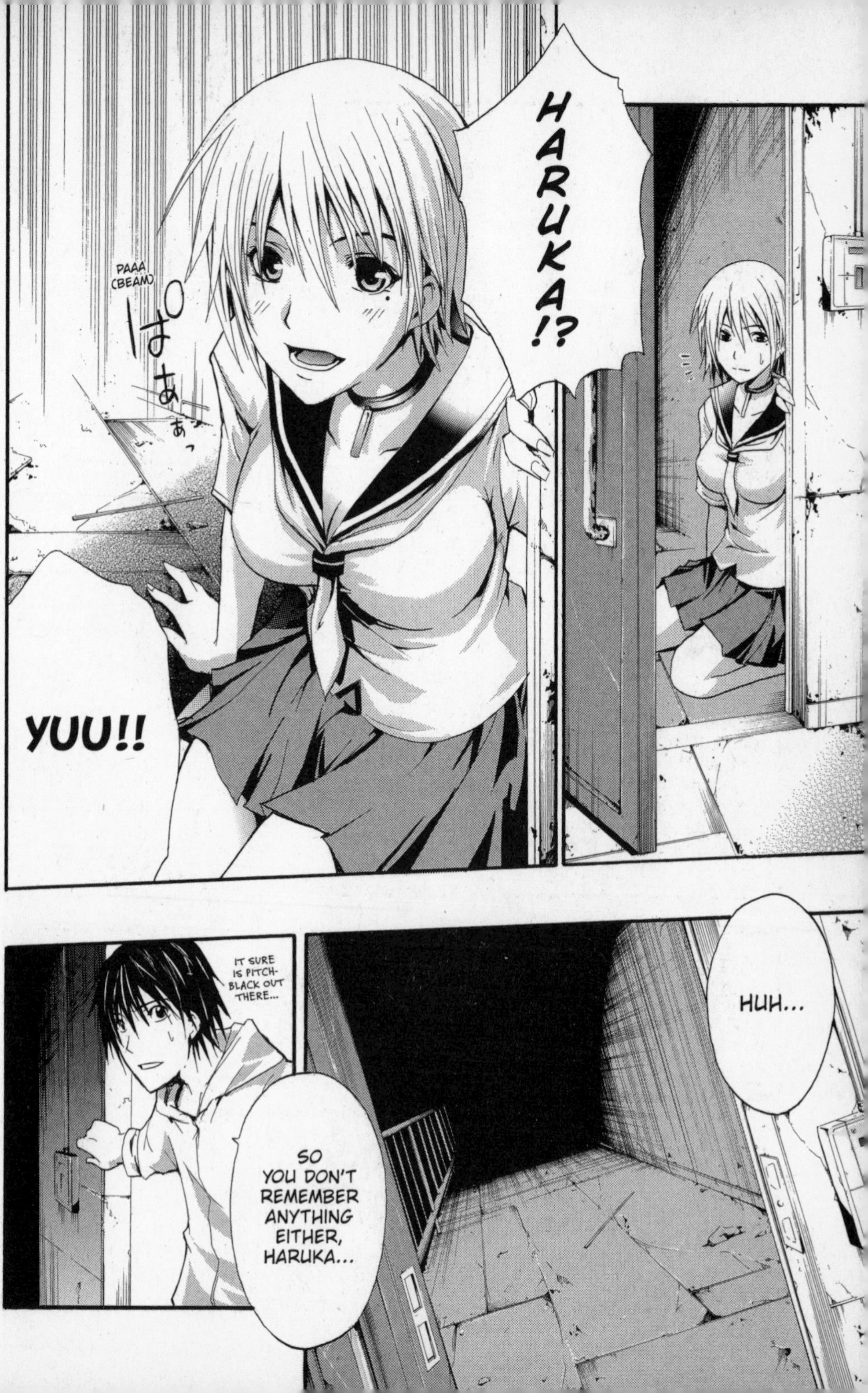
HARUKA!?
PAAA (BEAM)
ぱあぁっ
YUU!!
HUH...
IT SURE IS PITCH-BLACK OUT THERE...
SO YOU DON'T REMEMBER ANYTHING EITHER, HARUKA...

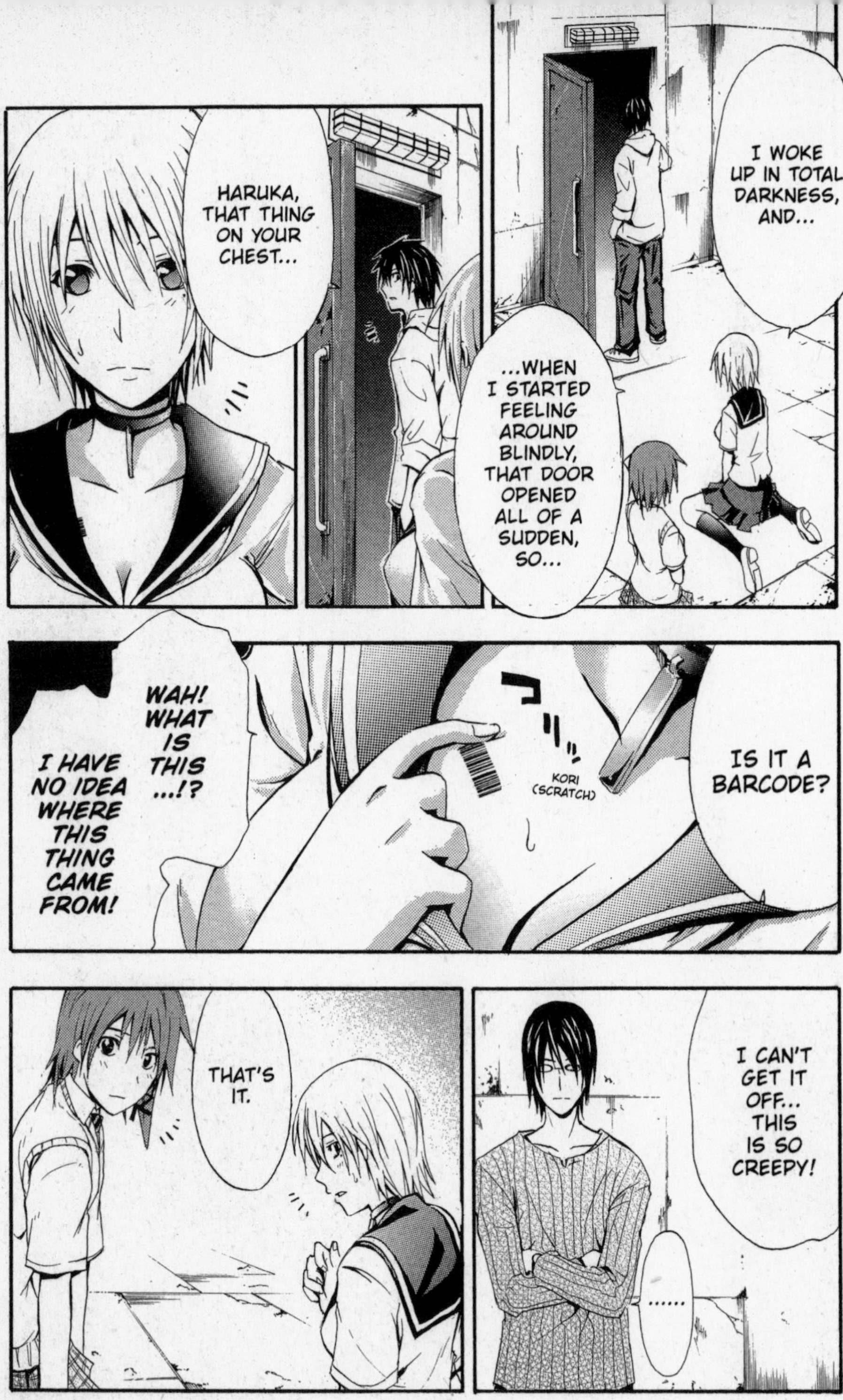
I WOKE UP IN TOTAL DARKNESS, AND...
...WHEN I STARTED FEELING AROUND BLINDLY, THAT DOOR OPENED ALL OF A SUDDEN, SO...
HARUKA, THAT THING ON YOUR CHEST...
IS IT A BARCODE?
KORI (SCRATCH)
WAH! WHAT IS THIS ...!?
I HAVE NO IDEA WHERE THIS THING CAME FROM!
I CAN'T GET IT OFF... THIS IS SO CREEPY!
......
THAT'S IT.

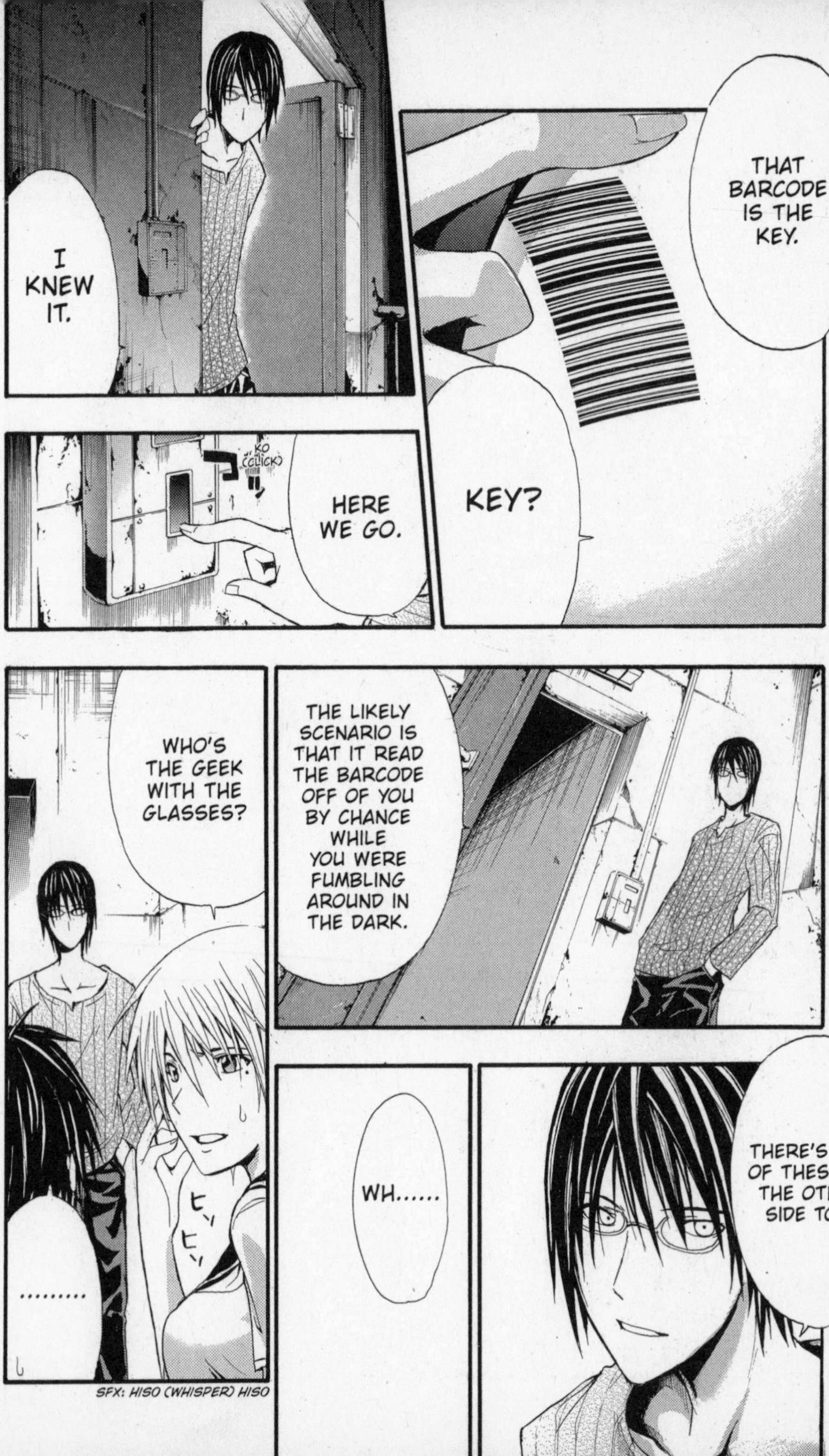
THAT BARCODE IS THE KEY.
KEY?
I KNEW IT.
KO (CLICK)
HERE WE GO.
THE LIKELY SCENARIO IS THAT IT READ THE BARCODE OFF OF YOU BY CHANCE WHILE YOU WERE FUMBLING AROUND IN THE DARK.
THERE'S ONE OF THESE ON THE OTHER SIDE TOO.
WH......
WHO'S THE GEEK WITH THE GLASSES?
....
SFX: HISO (WHISPER) HISO

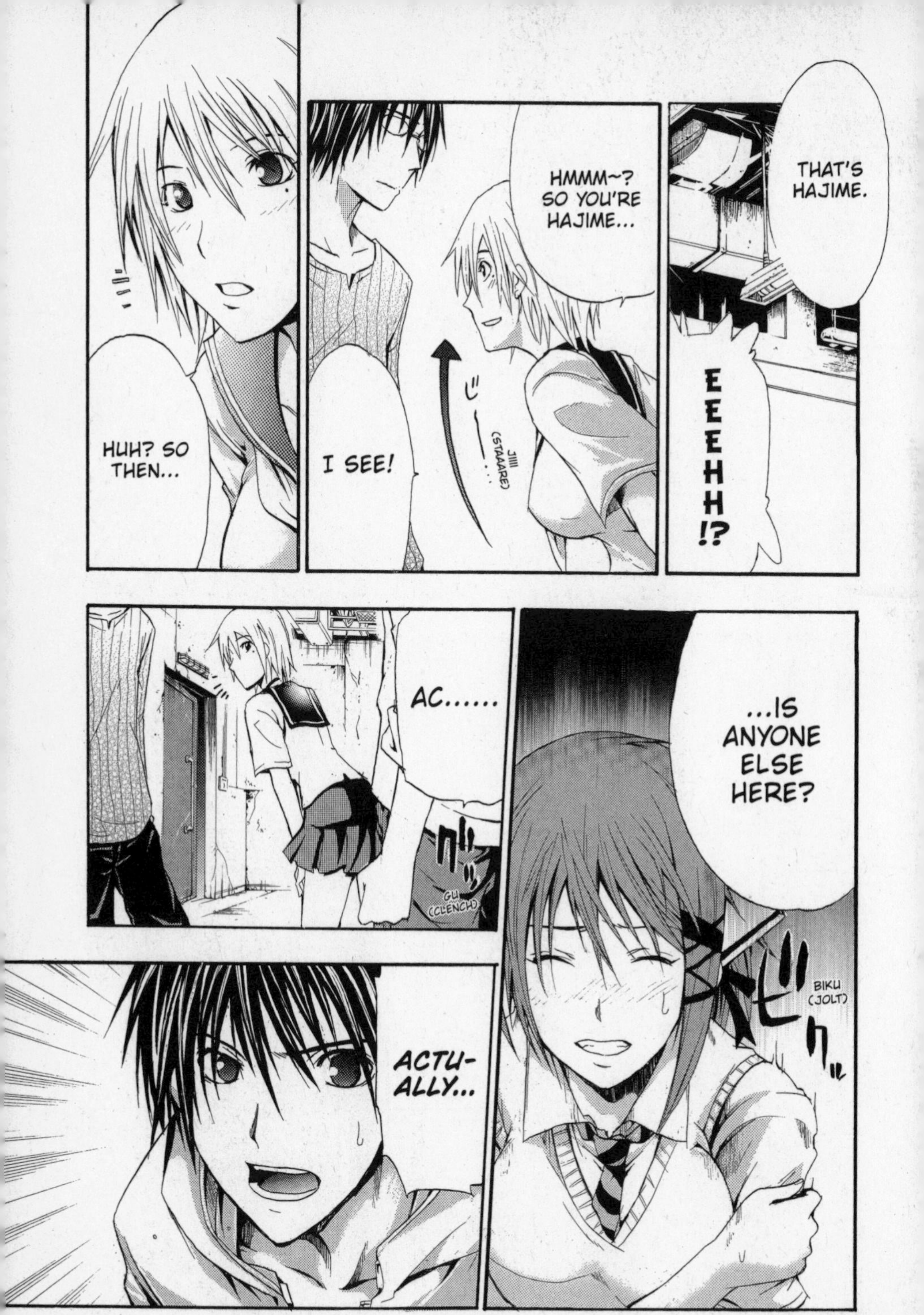
THAT'S HAJIME.
EEEHH!?
HMMM~? SO YOU'RE HAJIME...
I SEE!
JIIII (STAARE)
HUH? SO THEN...
...IS ANYONE ELSE HERE?
BIKU (JOLT)
AC......
GU (CLENCH)
ACTU-ALLY...

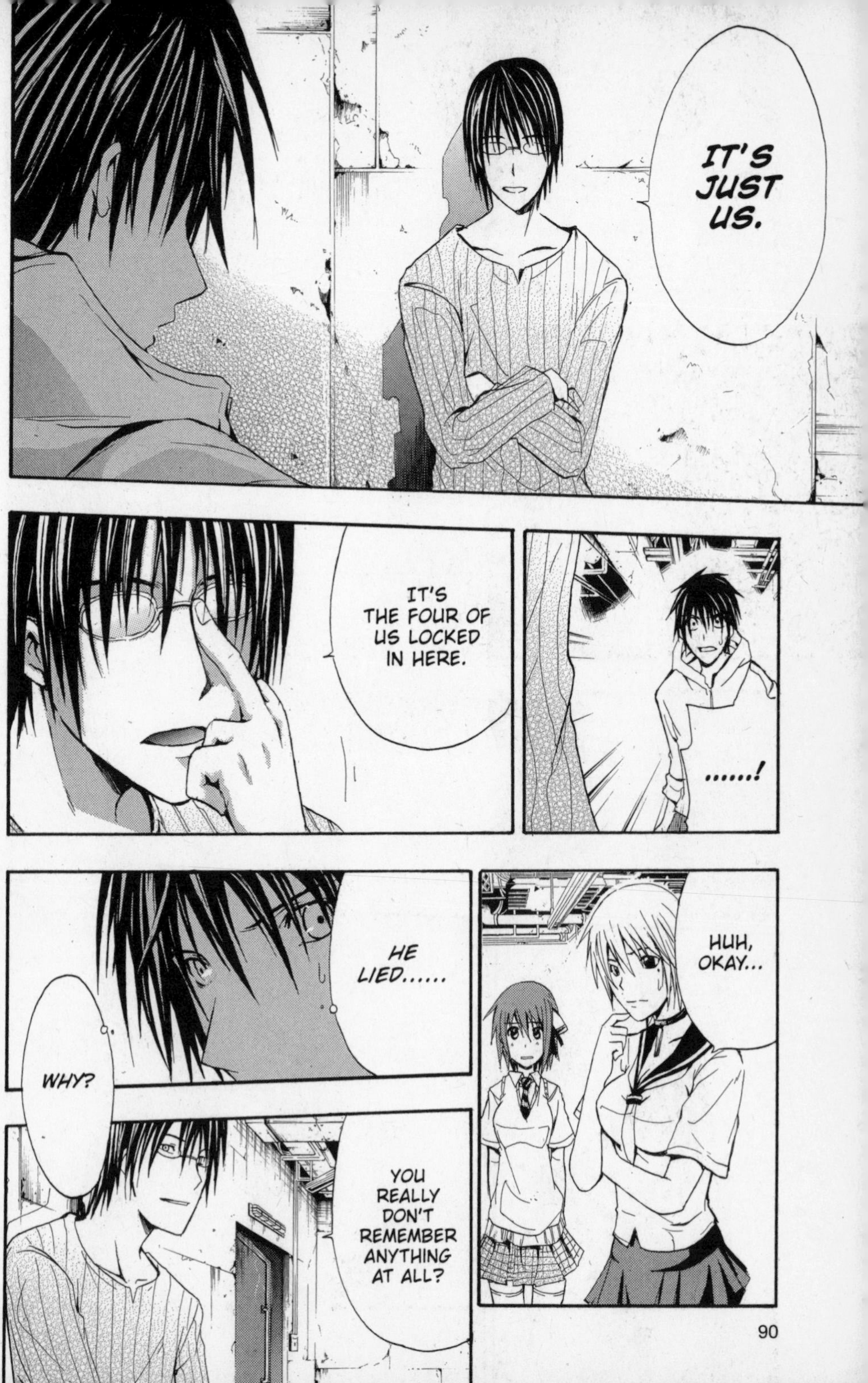
IT'S JUST US.
......!
IT'S THE FOUR OF US LOCKED IN HERE.
HUH, OKAY...
HE LIED......
WHY?
YOU REALLY DON'T REMEMBER ANYTHING AT ALL?

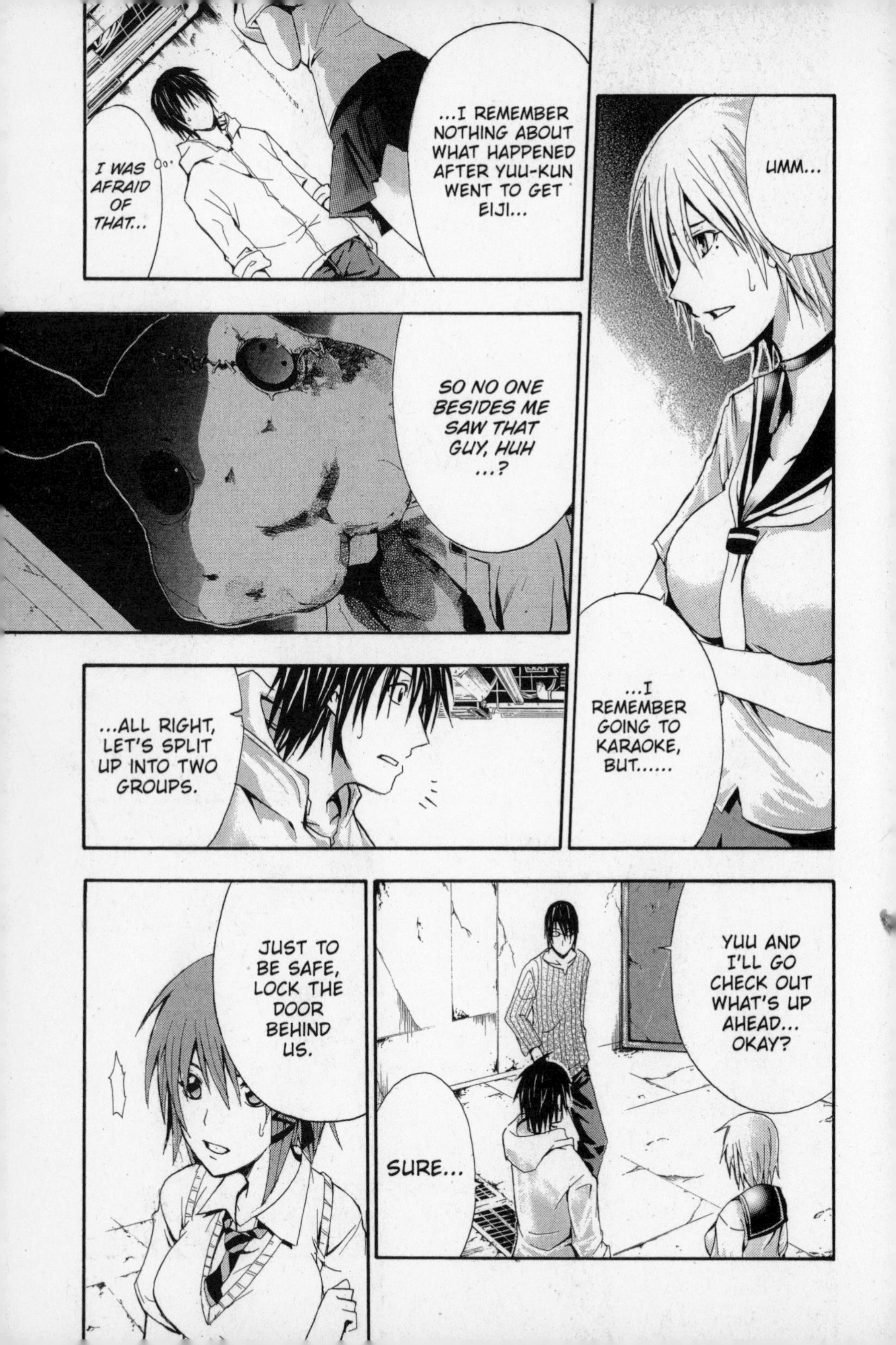
UMM...
...I REMEMBER GOING TO KARAOKE, BUT......
...I REMEMBER NOTHING ABOUT WHAT HAPPENED AFTER YUU-KUN WENT TO GET EIJI...
I WAS AFRAID OF THAT...
SO NO ONE BESIDES ME SAW THAT GUY, HUH ...?
...ALL RIGHT, LET'S SPLIT UP INTO TWO GROUPS.
YUU AND I'LL GO CHECK OUT WHAT'S UP AHEAD... OKAY?
SURE...
JUST TO BE SAFE, LOCK THE DOOR BEHIND US.

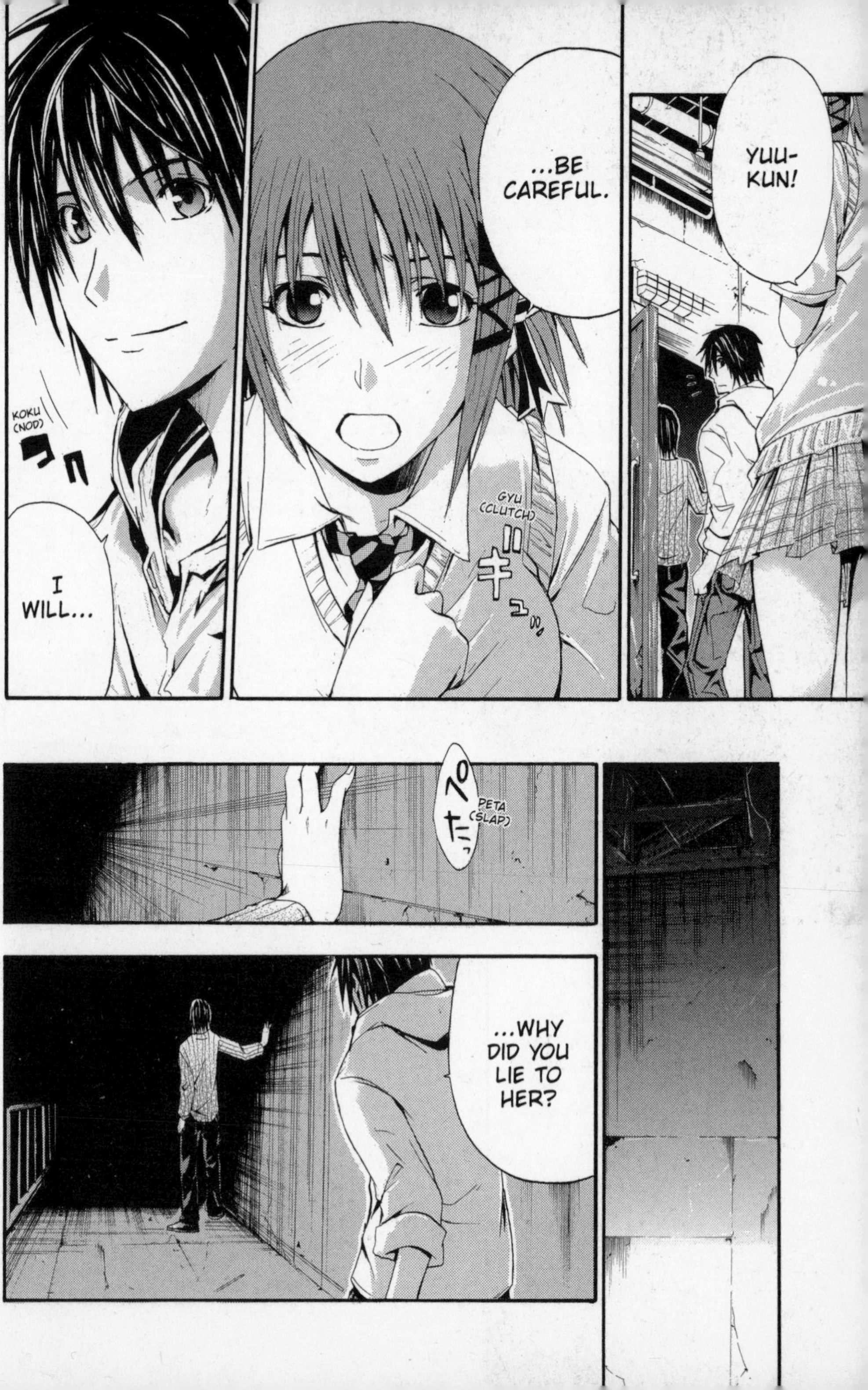
YUU-KUN!
...BE CAREFUL.
GYU (CLUTCH)
KOKU (NOD)
I WILL...
PETA (SLAP)
...WHY DID YOU LIE TO HER?

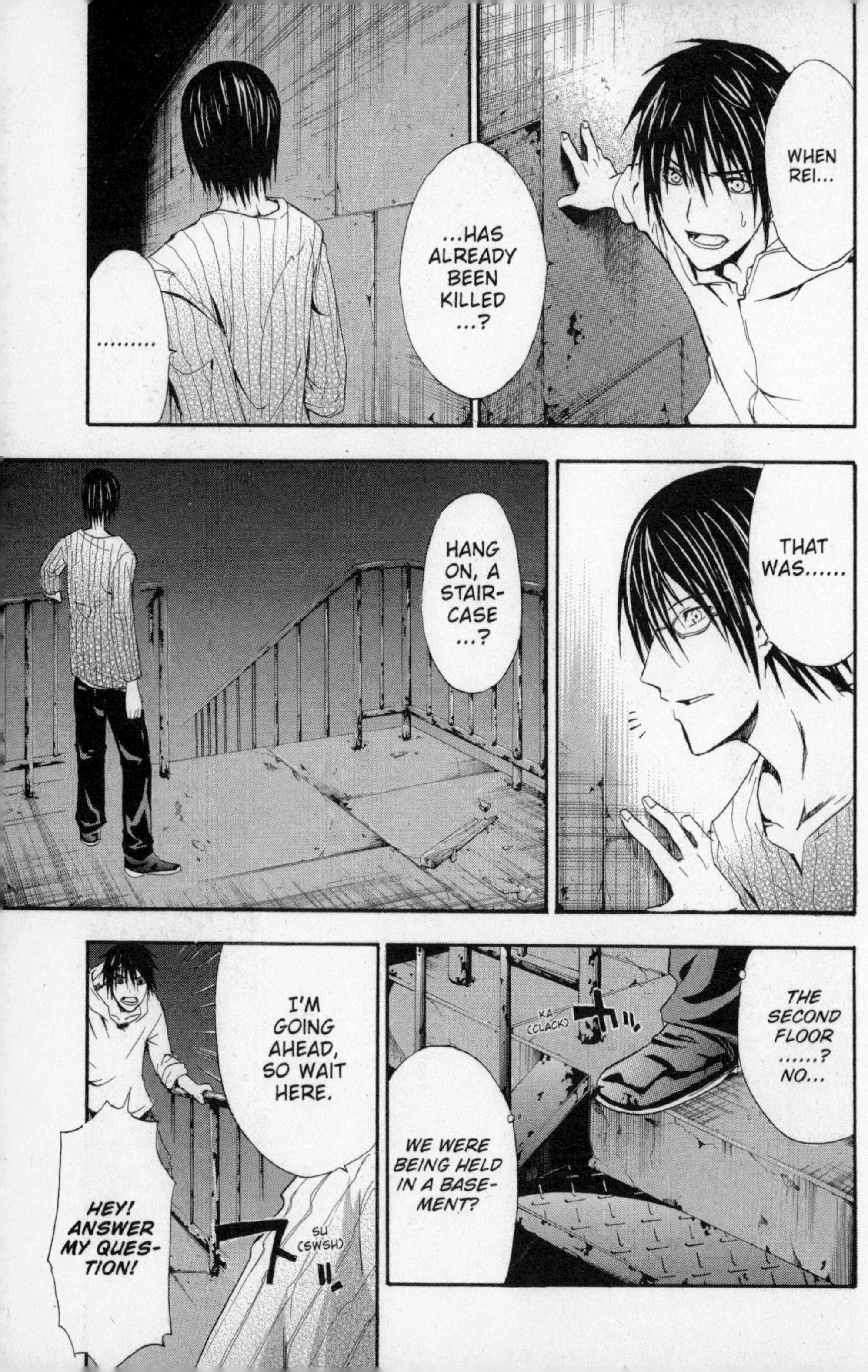
WHEN REI...
...HAS ALREADY BEEN KILLED ...?
....
THAT WAS......
HANG ON, A STAIR-CASE ...?
THE SECOND FLOOR ......? NO...
KA (CLACK)
WE WERE BEING HELD IN A BASE-MENT?
I'M GOING AHEAD, SO WAIT HERE.
SU (SWSH)
HEY! ANSWER MY QUES-TION!

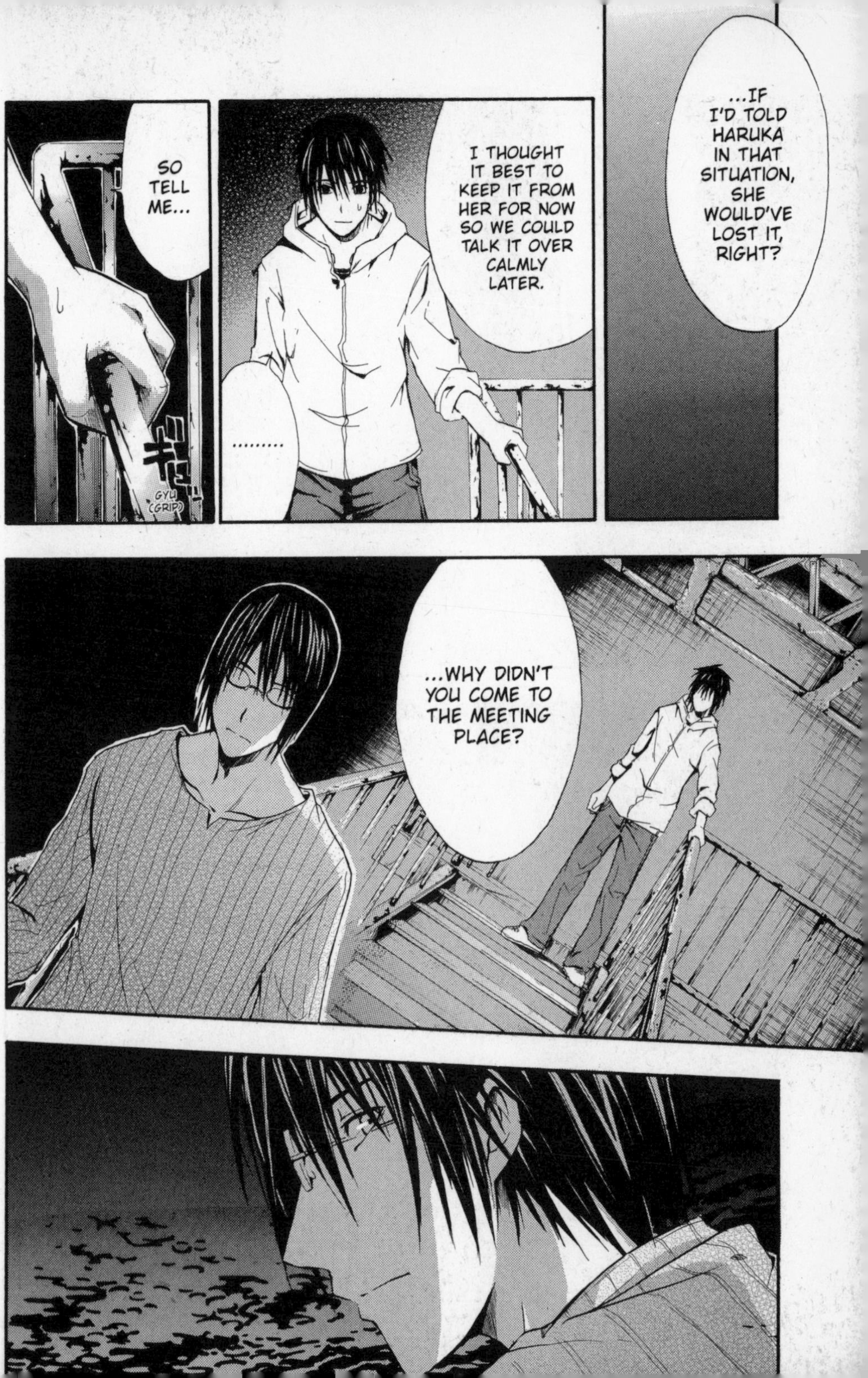
...IF I'D TOLD HARUKA IN THAT SITUATION, SHE WOULD'VE LOST IT, RIGHT?
I THOUGHT IT BEST TO KEEP IT FROM HER FOR NOW SO WE COULD TALK IT OVER CALMLY LATER.
....
SO TELL ME...
GYU (GRIP)
...WHY DIDN'T YOU COME TO THE MEETING PLACE?

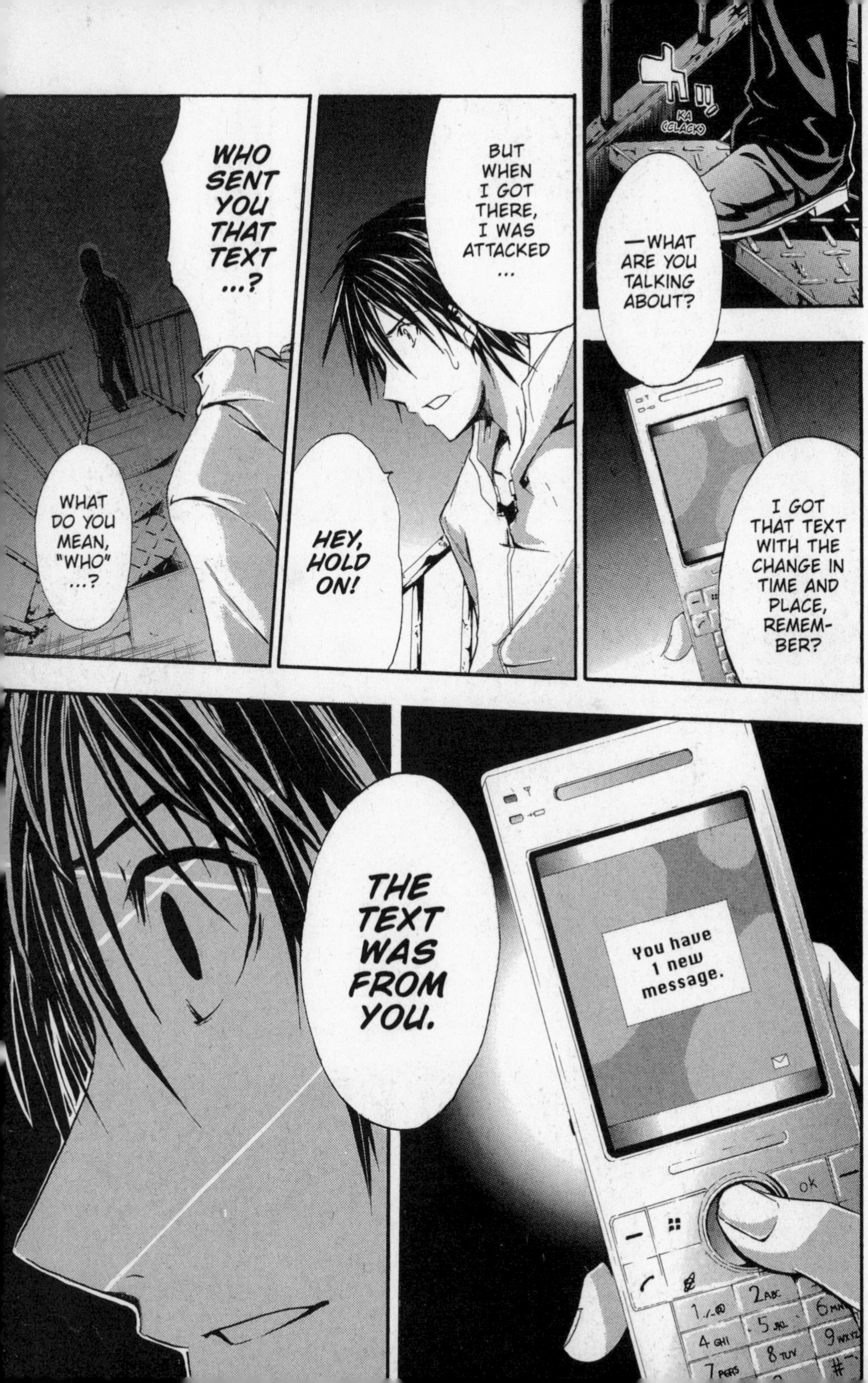
KA (CLACK)
—WHAT ARE YOU TALKING ABOUT?
I GOT THAT TEXT WITH THE CHANGE IN TIME AND PLACE, REMEMBER?
BUT WHEN I GOT THERE, I WAS ATTACKED ...
HEY, HOLD ON!
WHO SENT YOU THAT TEXT ...?
WHAT DO YOU MEAN, "WHO" ...?
You have 1 new message.
THE TEXT WAS FROM YOU.

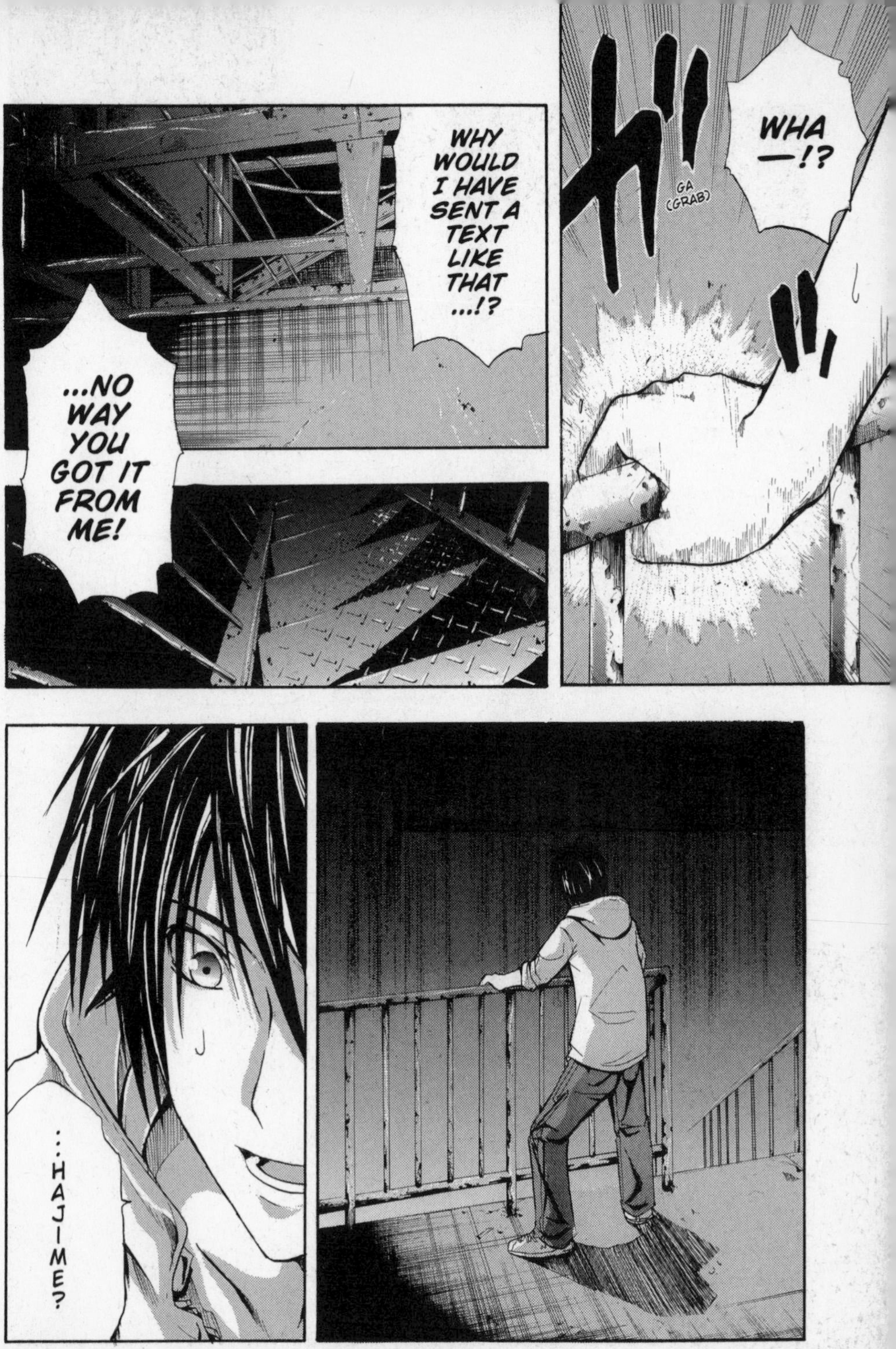
WHA—!?
GA (GRAB)
WHY WOULD I HAVE SENT A TEXT LIKE THAT ...!?
...NO WAY YOU GOT IT FROM ME!
...HAJIME?

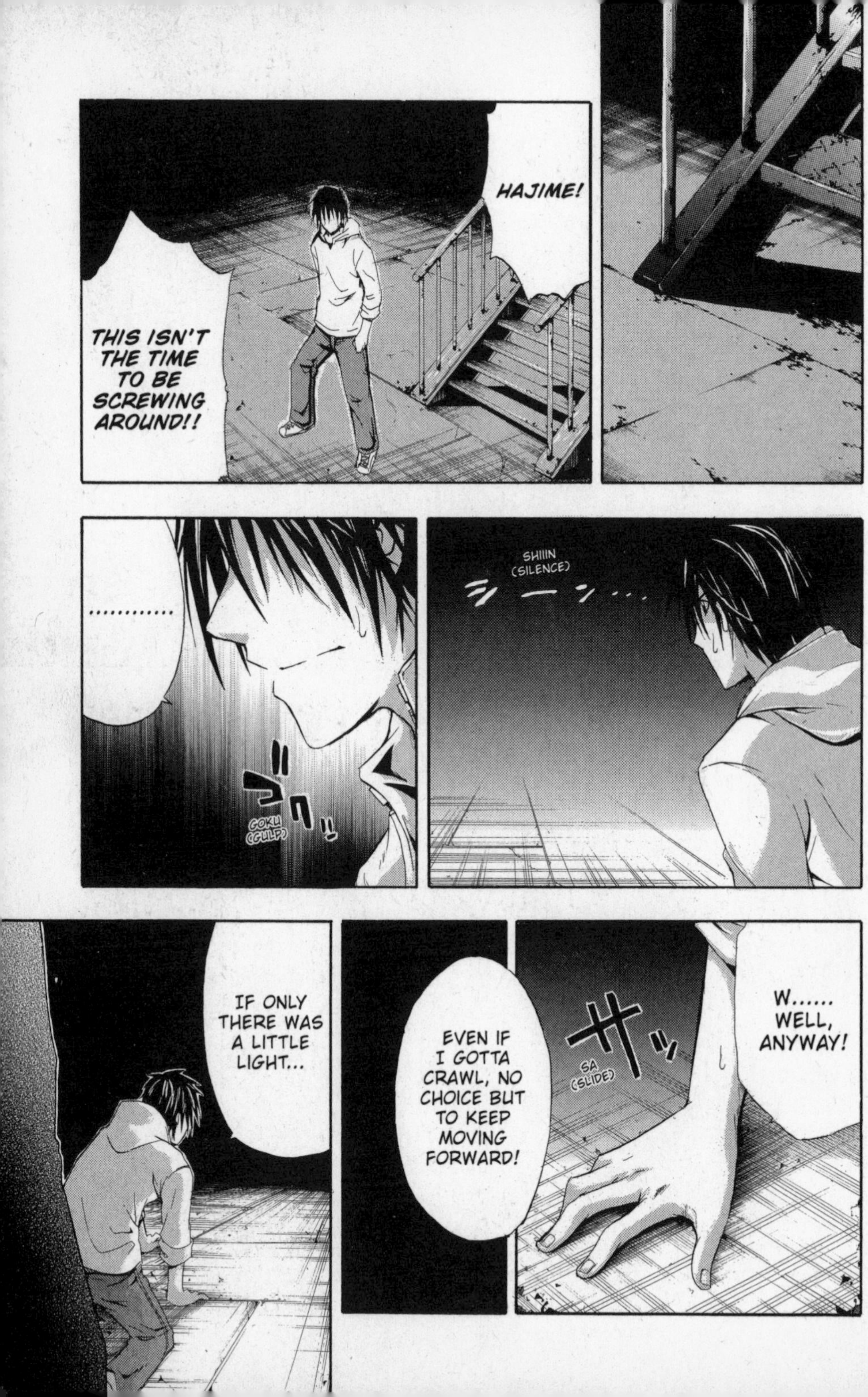

HAJIME!
THIS ISN'T THE TIME TO BE SCREWING AROUND!!
SHIIN (SILENCE)
....
GOKU (GULP)
W...... WELL, ANYWAY!
SA (SLIDE)
EVEN IF I GOTTA CRAWL, NO CHOICE BUT TO KEEP MOVING FORWARD!
IF ONLY THERE WAS A LITTLE LIGHT...

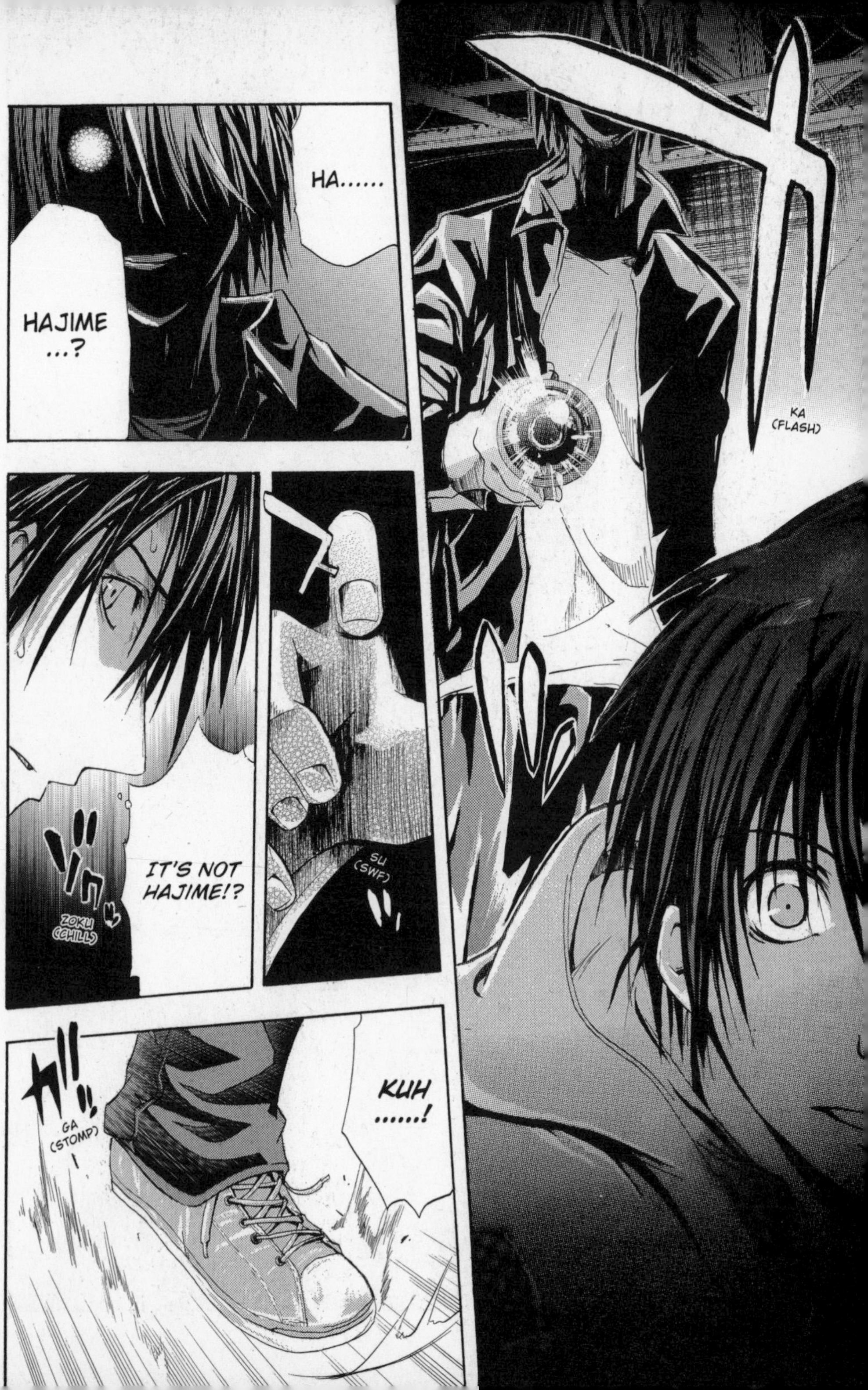
KA (FLASH)
HA......
HAJIME ...?
SU (SWF)
IT'S NOT HAJIME!?
ZOKU (CHILL)
KUH ......!
GA (STOMP)

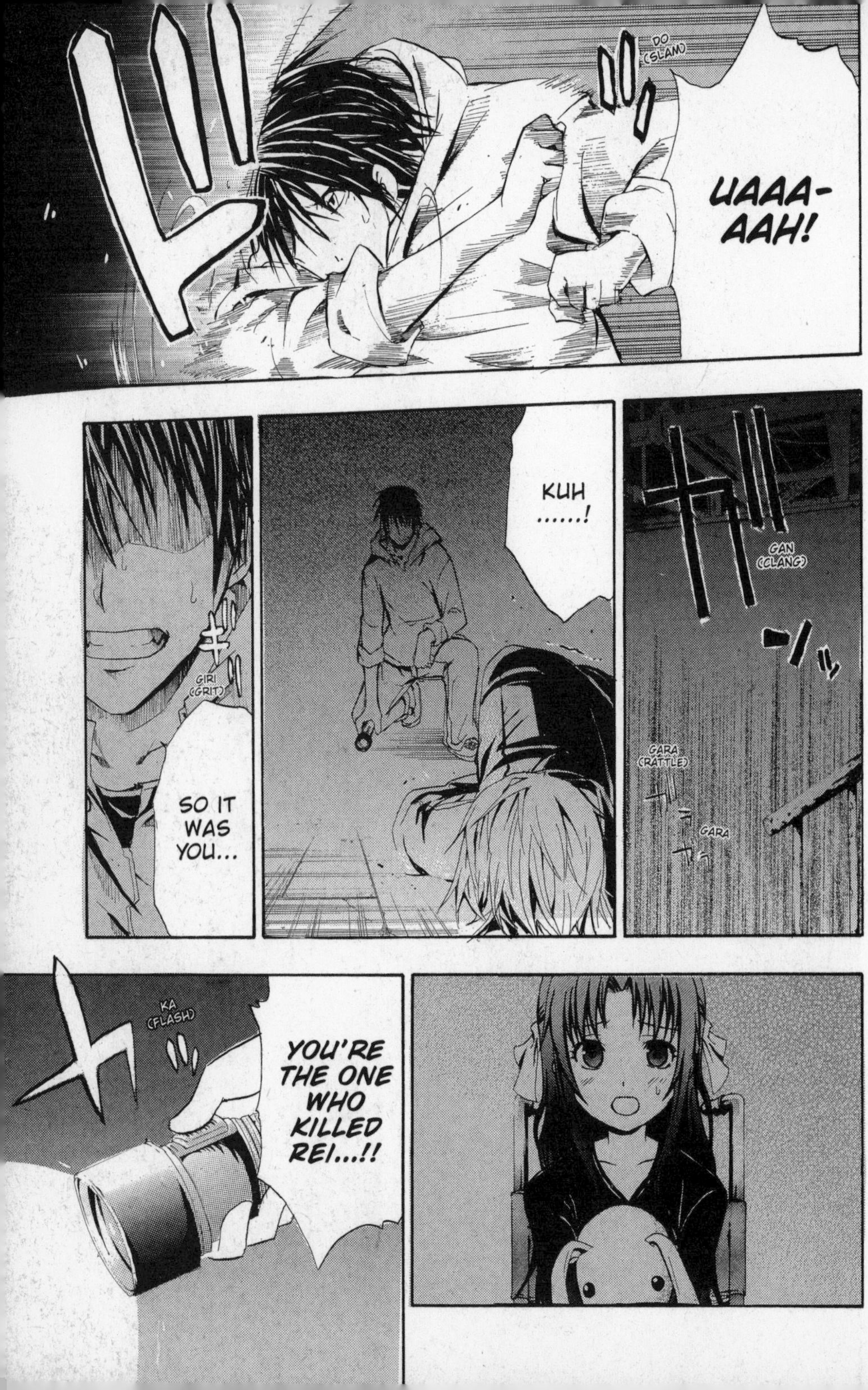
DO
(SLAM)
UAAAA-
AAH!
GAN
(CLANG)
GARA
(RATTLE)
GARA
KUH
......!
GIRI
(GRIT)
SO IT
WAS
YOU...
KA
(FLASH)
YOU'RE
THE ONE
WHO
KILLED
REI...!!

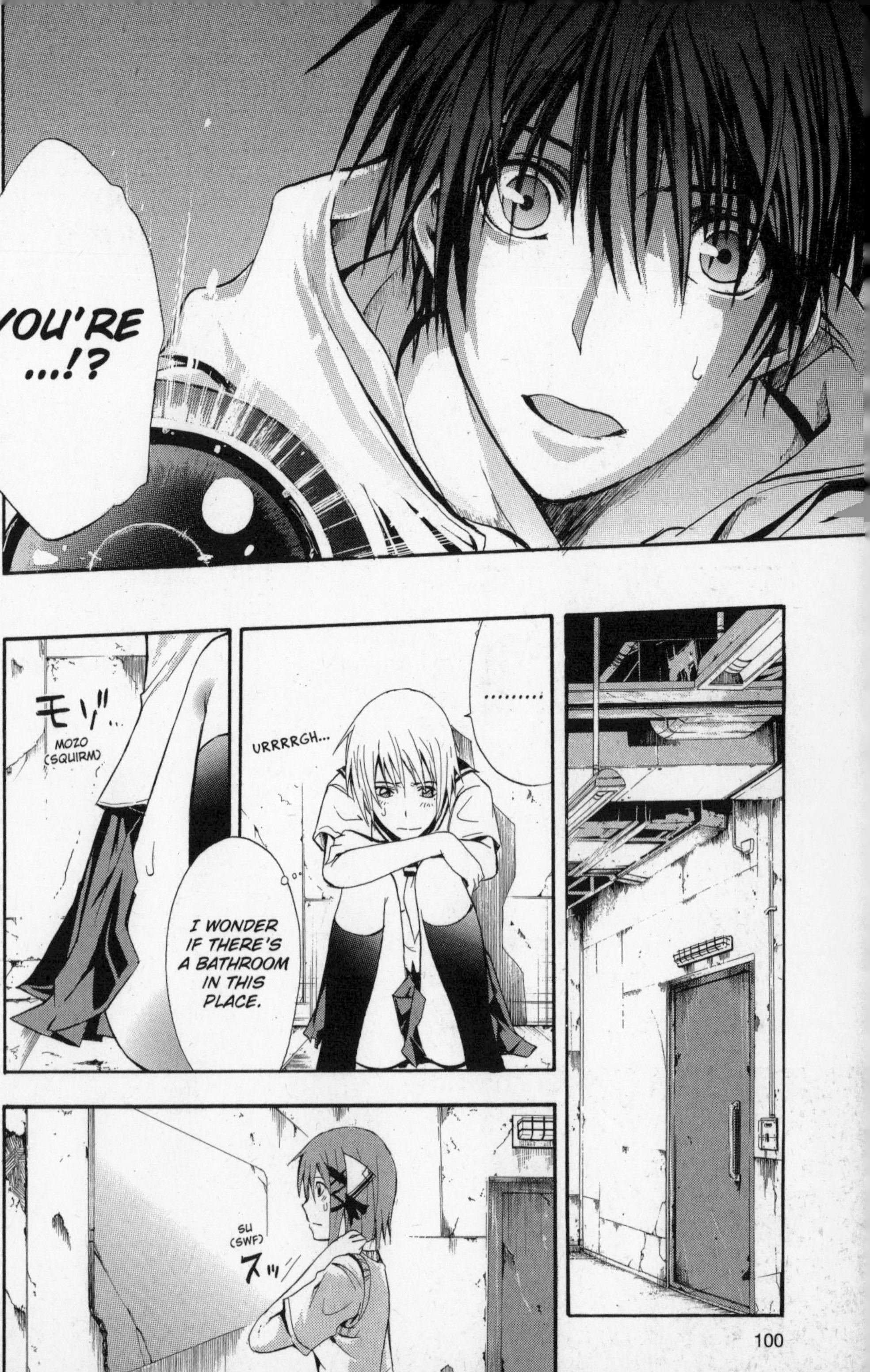

YOU'RE ...!?
....
URRRRGH...
I WONDER IF THERE'S A BATHROOM IN THIS PLACE.
モゾ..
MOZO (SQUIRM)
SU (SWF)
スッ

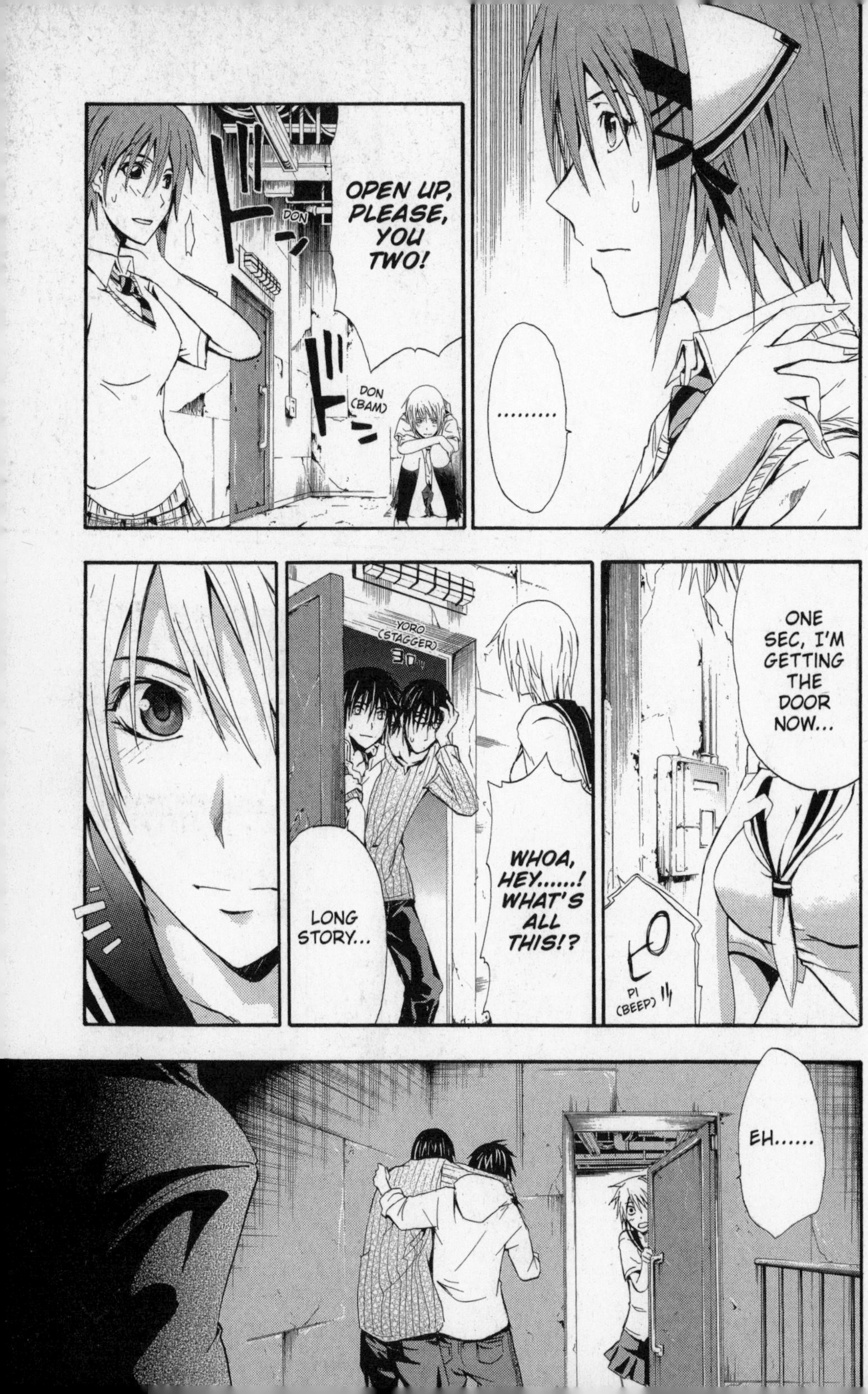
....
OPEN UP, PLEASE, YOU TWO!
DON
DON (BAM)
ONE SEC, I'M GETTING THE DOOR NOW...
PI (BEEP)
YORO (STAGGER)
WHOA, HEY......! WHAT'S ALL THIS!?
LONG STORY...
EH......

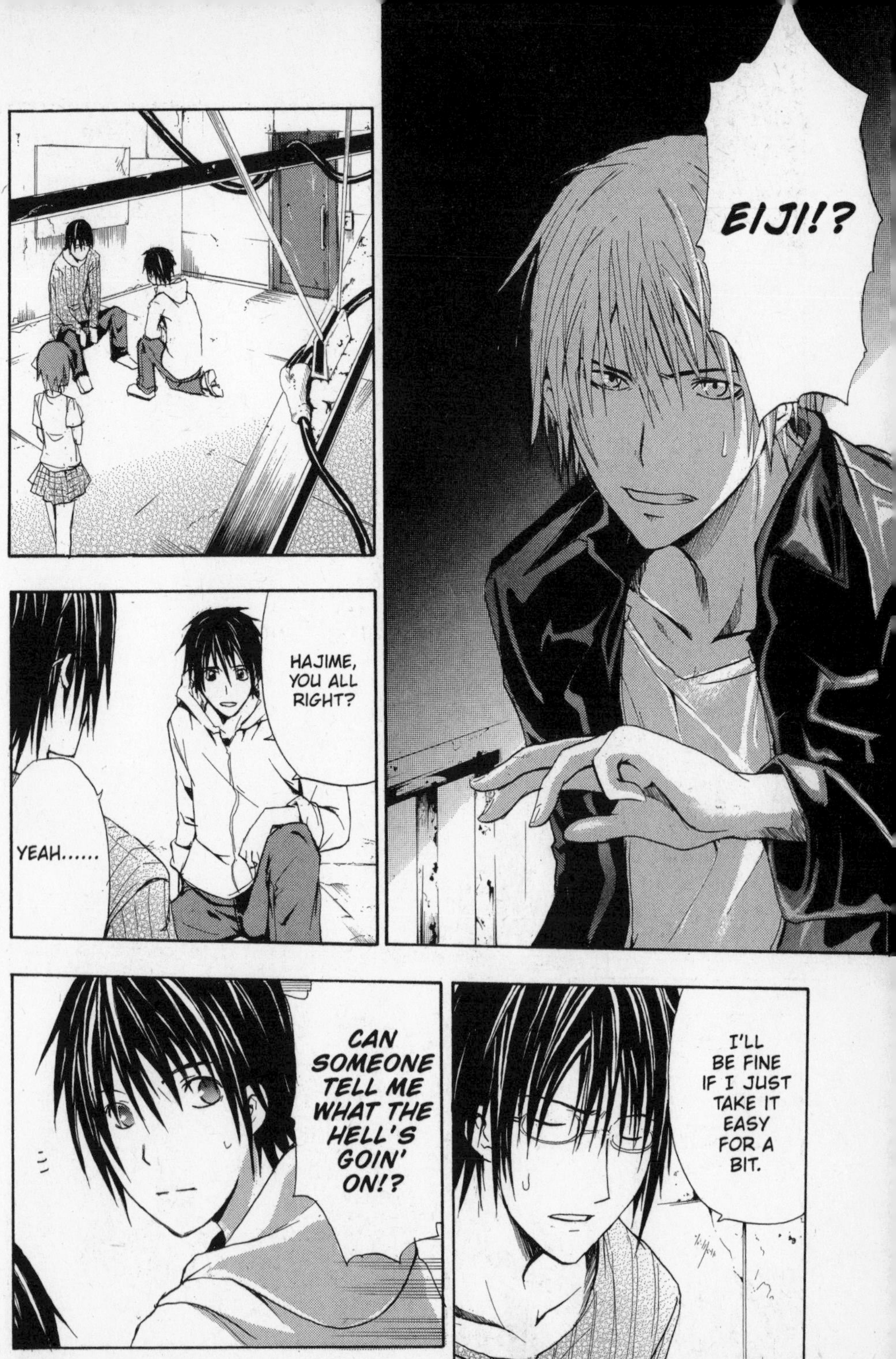
EIJI!?
HAJIME, YOU ALL RIGHT?
YEAH......
I'LL BE FINE IF I JUST TAKE IT EASY FOR A BIT.
CAN SOMEONE TELL ME WHAT THE HELL'S GOIN' ON!?

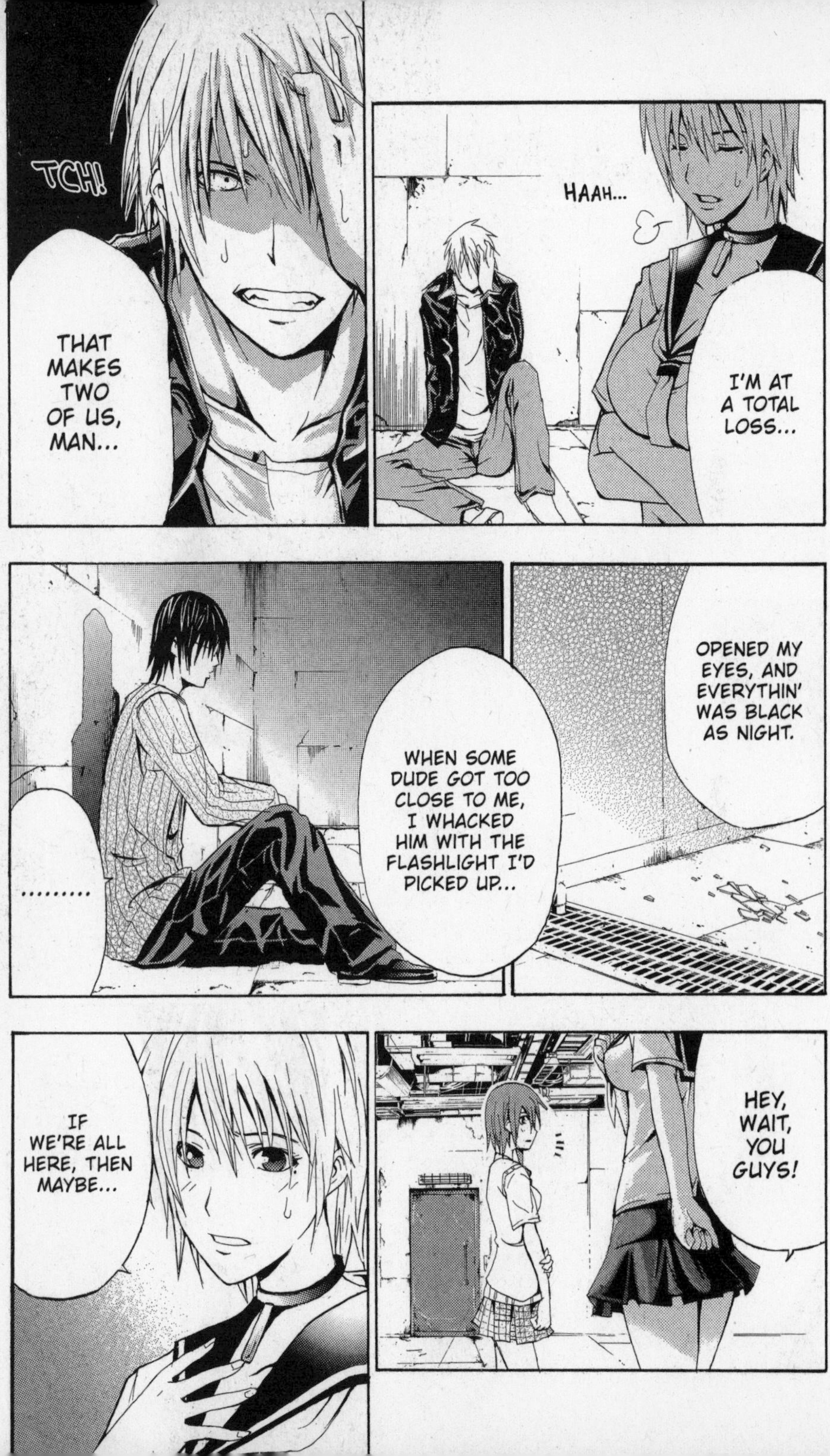
HAAH...
I'M AT A TOTAL LOSS...
TCH!
THAT MAKES TWO OF US, MAN...
OPENED MY EYES, AND EVERYTHIN' WAS BLACK AS NIGHT.
WHEN SOME DUDE GOT TOO CLOSE TO ME, I WHACKED HIM WITH THE FLASHLIGHT I'D PICKED UP...
....
HEY, WAIT, YOU GUYS!
IF WE'RE ALL HERE, THEN MAYBE...

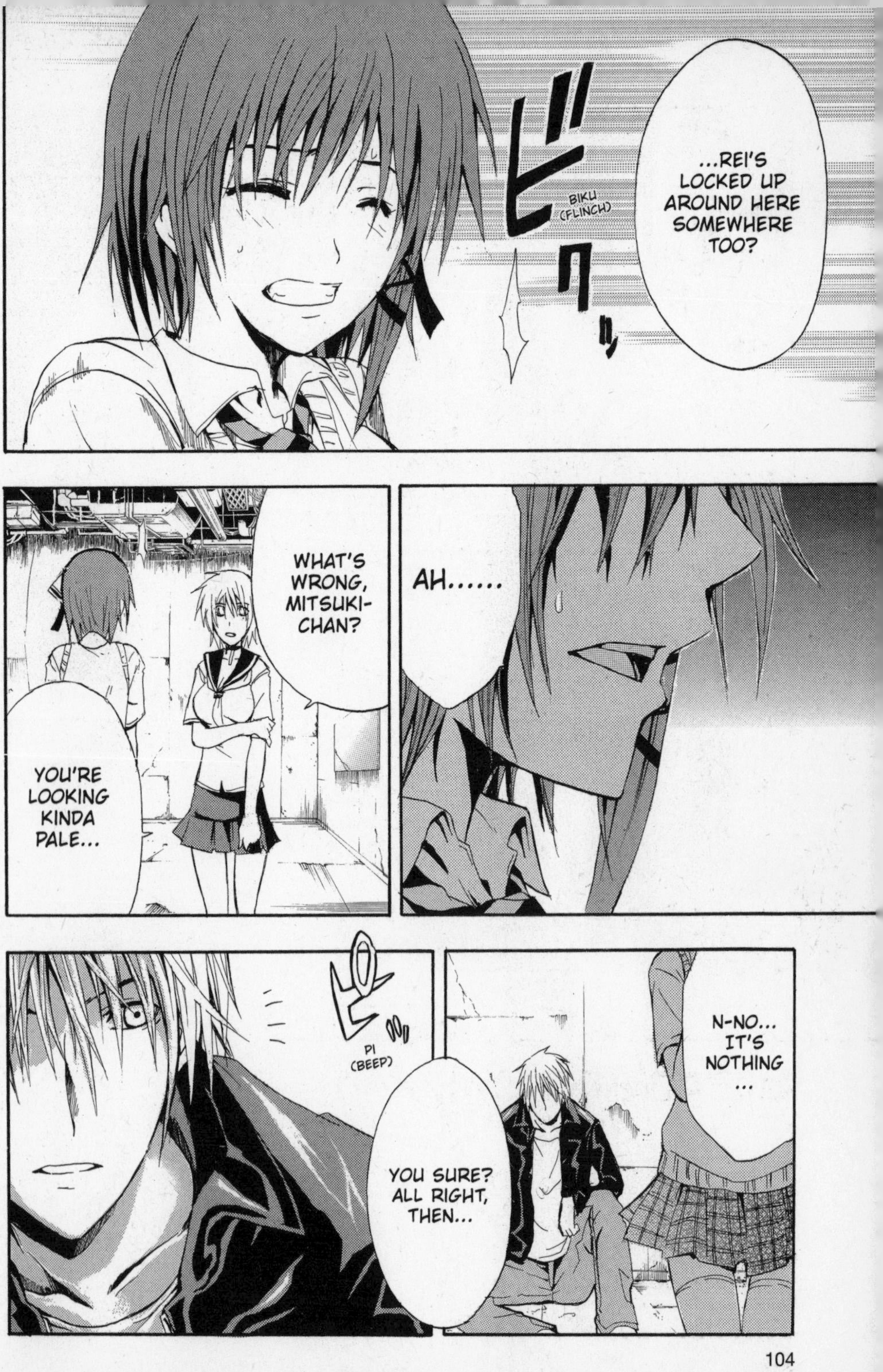
...REI'S LOCKED UP AROUND HERE SOMEWHERE TOO?
BIKU (FLINCH)
AH......
WHAT'S WRONG, MITSUKI-CHAN?
YOU'RE LOOKING KINDA PALE...
N-NO... IT'S NOTHING ...
YOU SURE? ALL RIGHT, THEN...
PI (BEEP)

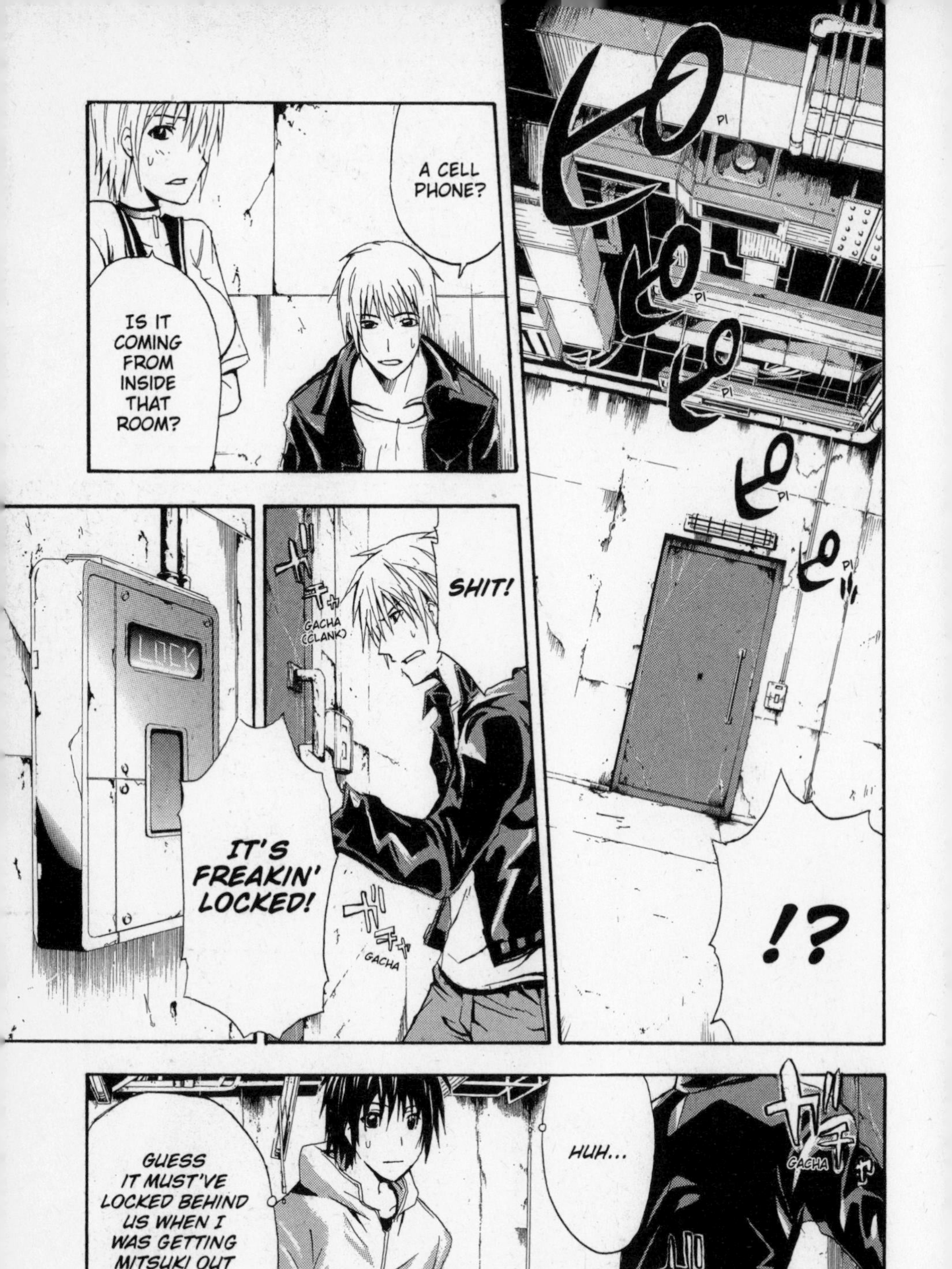
PI
PI
PI
PI
PI
!?
A CELL PHONE?
IS IT COMING FROM INSIDE THAT ROOM?
SHIT!
GACHA (CLANK)
IT'S FREAKIN' LOCKED!
GACHA
GACHA
HUH...
GACHA
GUESS IT MUST'VE LOCKED BEHIND US WHEN I WAS GETTING MITSUKI OUT OF THERE.

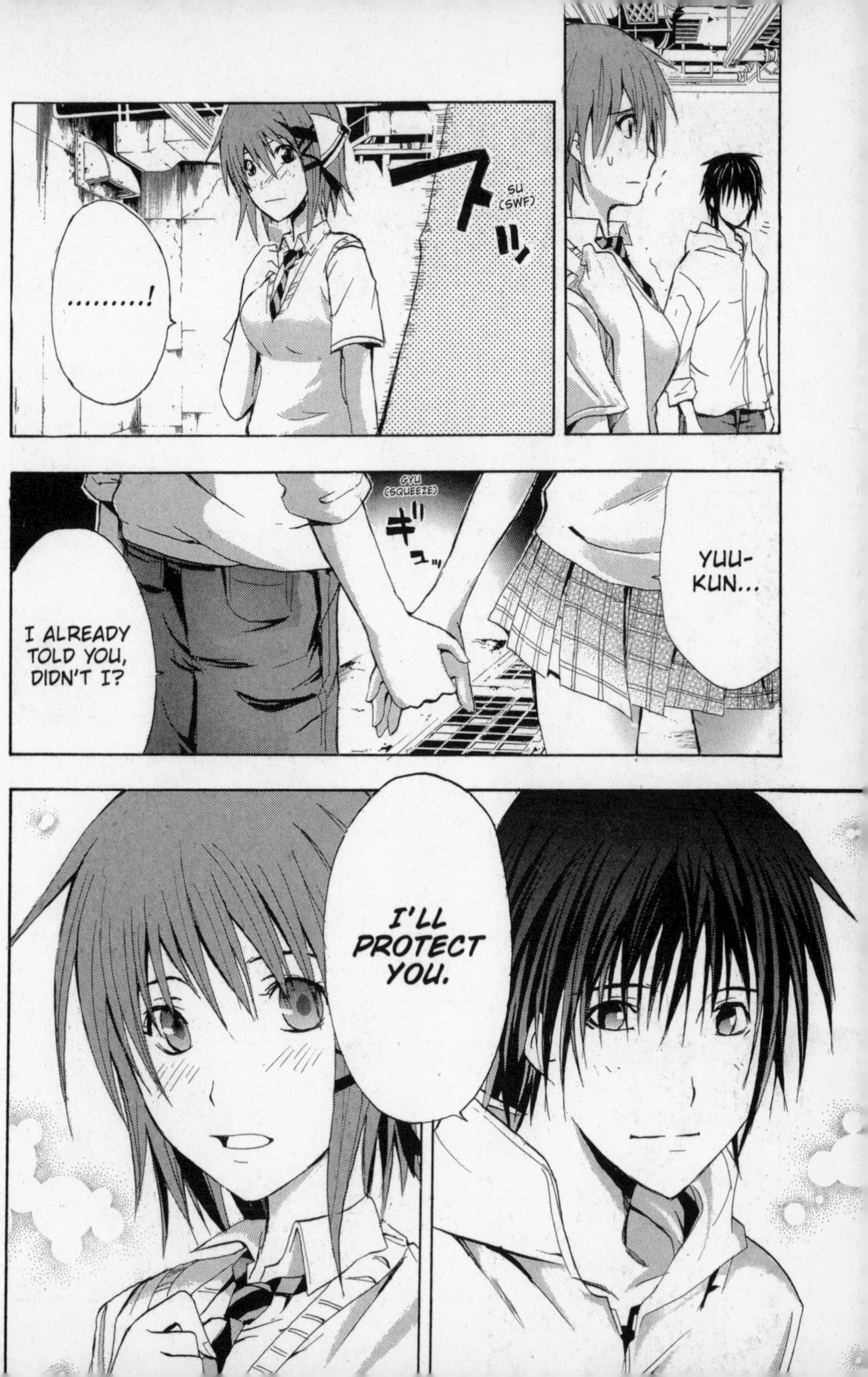

SU (SWF)
スッ
.........!
YUU-KUN...
GYU (SQUEEZE)
ギュッ
I ALREADY TOLD YOU, DIDN'T I?
I'LL PROTECT YOU.

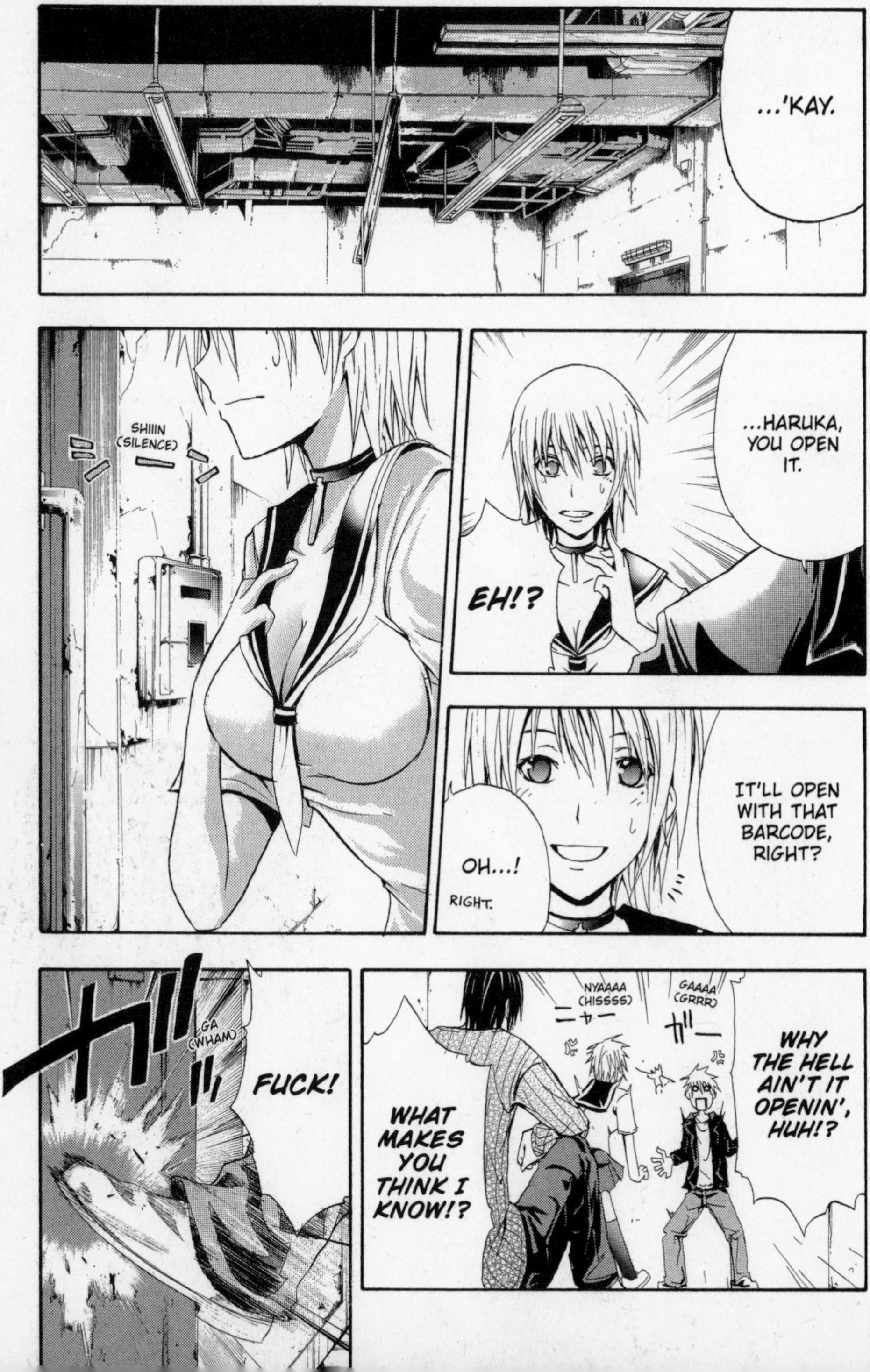
...'KAY.
...HARUKA, YOU OPEN IT.
EH!?
IT'LL OPEN WITH THAT BARCODE, RIGHT?
OH...!
RIGHT.
SHIIIN (SILENCE)
GAAAA (GRRR)
ガー
WHY THE HELL AIN'T IT OPENIN', HUH!?
NYAAAA (HISSSS)
ニャー
WHAT MAKES YOU THINK I KNOW!?
GA (WHAM)
FUCK!

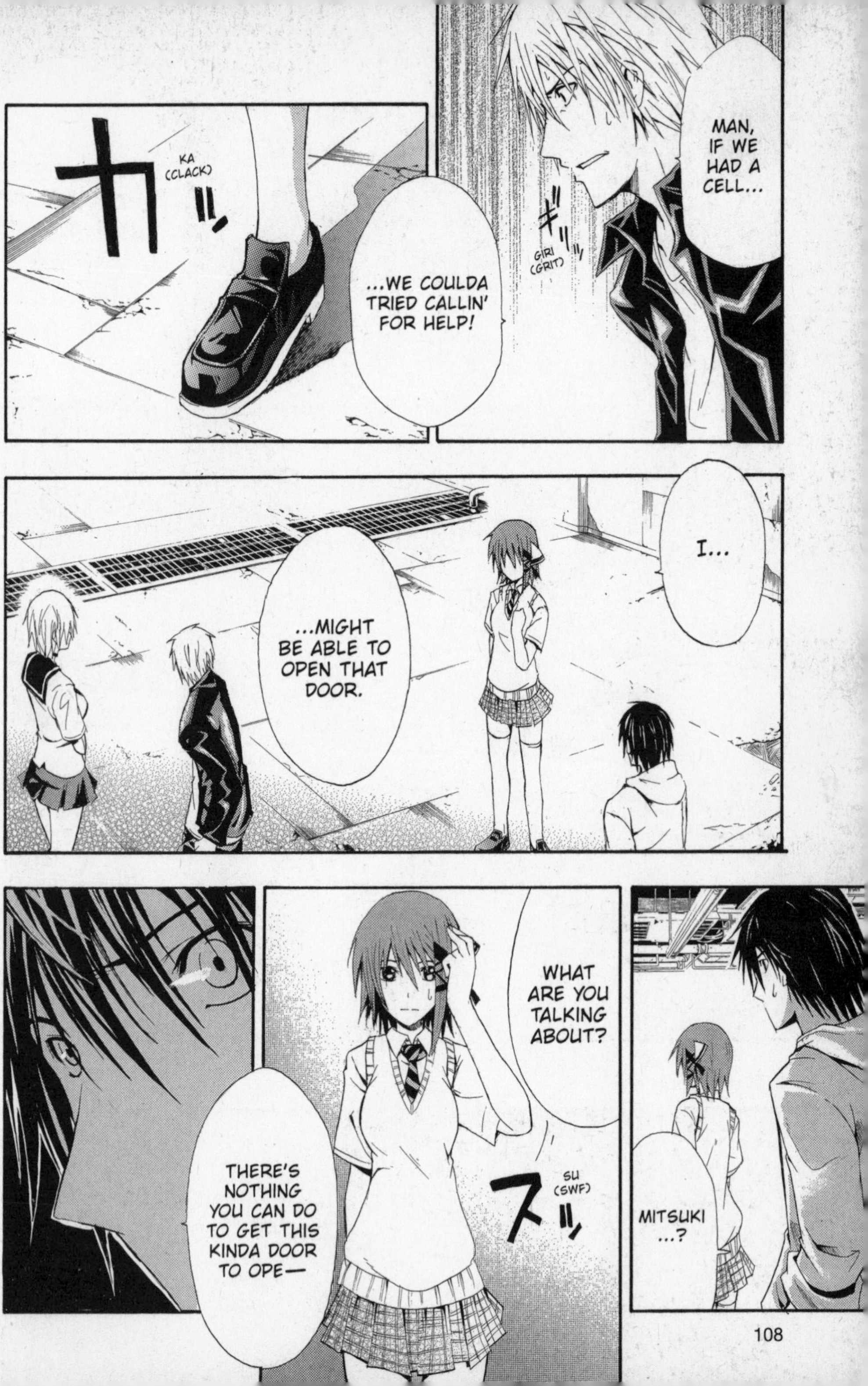
MAN, IF WE HAD A CELL...
GIRI (GRIT)
KA (CLACK)
...WE COULDA TRIED CALLIN' FOR HELP!
I...
...MIGHT BE ABLE TO OPEN THAT DOOR.
MITSUKI ...?
WHAT ARE YOU TALKING ABOUT?
THERE'S NOTHING YOU CAN DO TO GET THIS KINDA DOOR TO OPE—
SU (SWF)

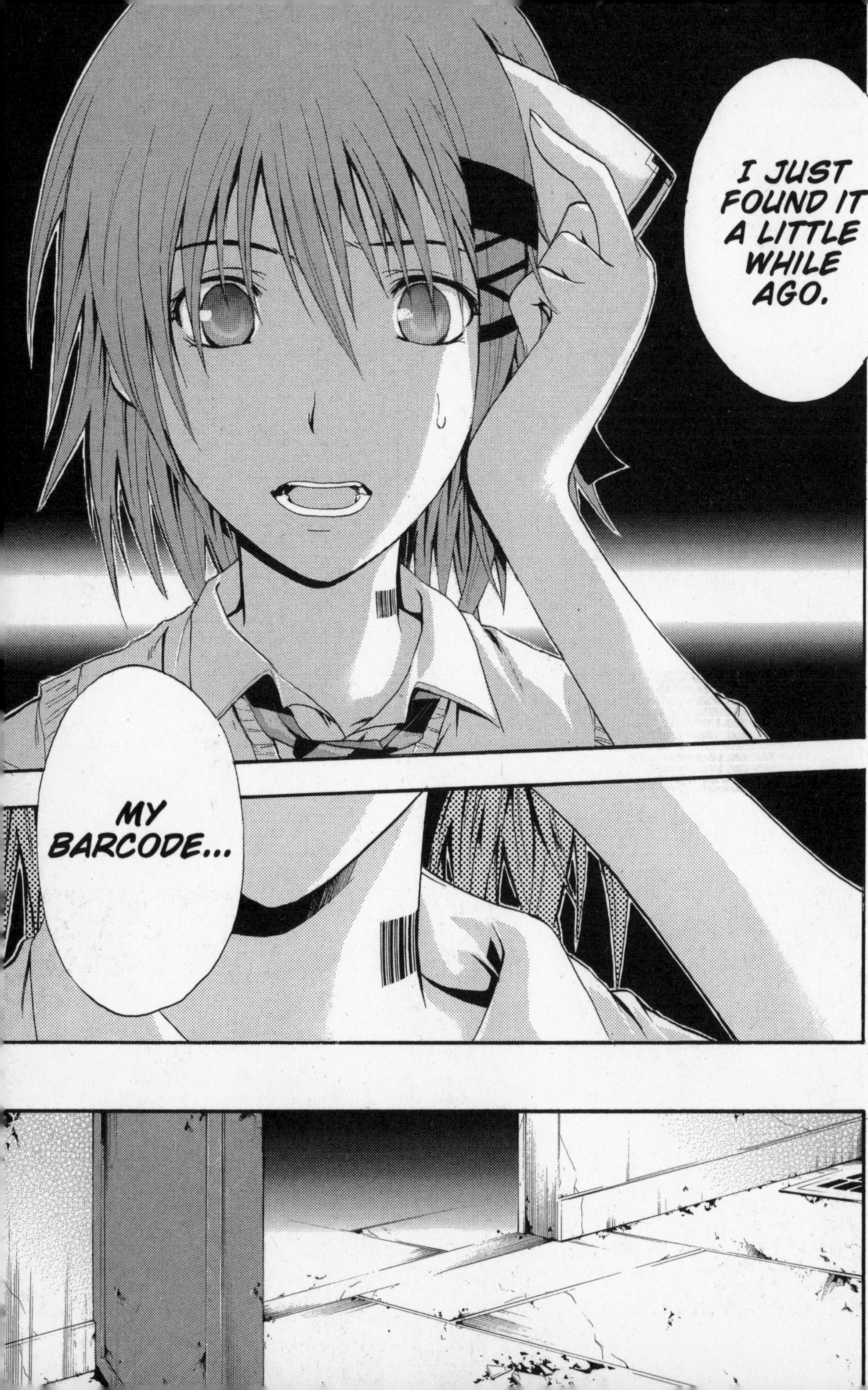
I JUST FOUND IT A LITTLE WHILE AGO.
MY BARCODE...

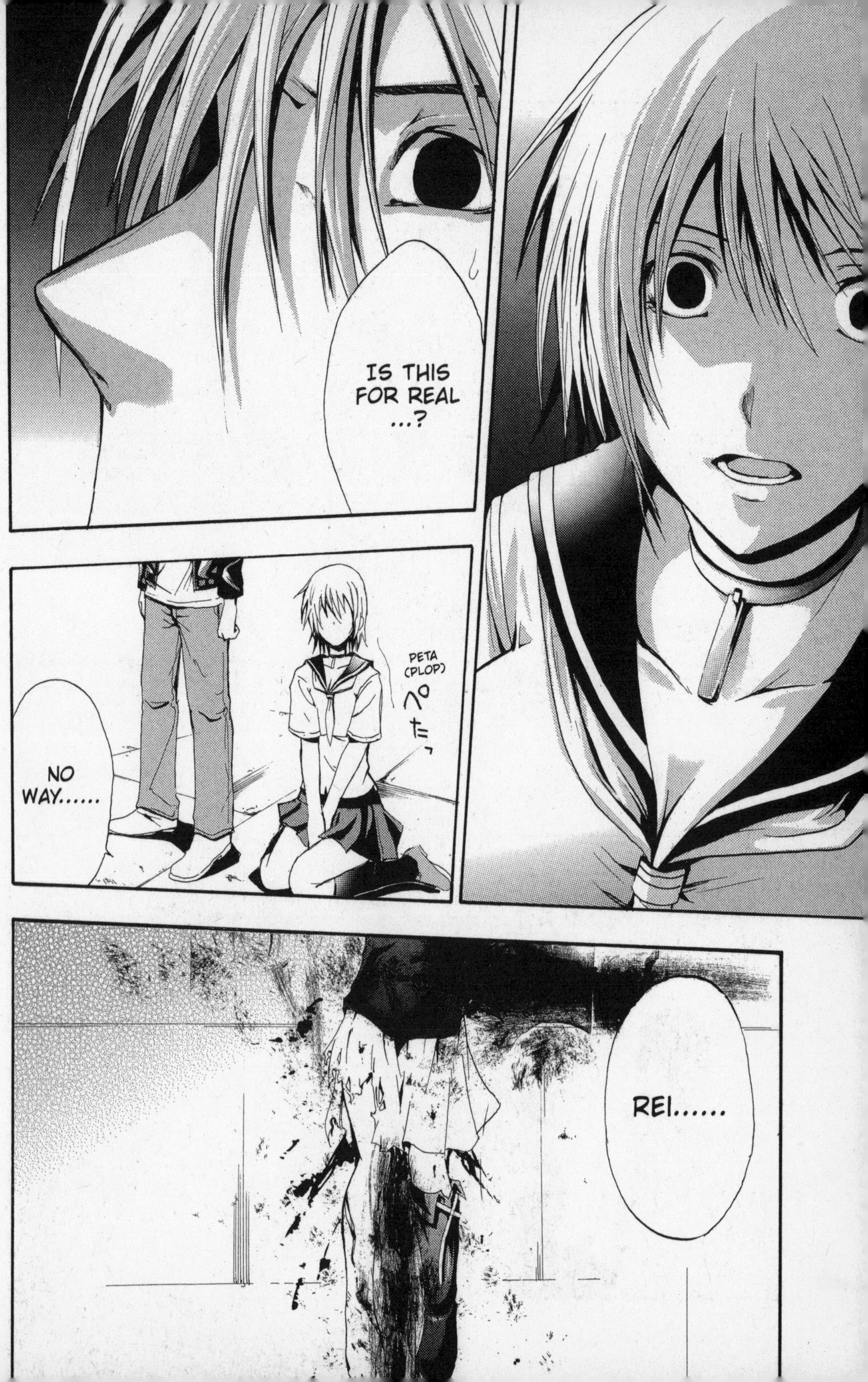
IS THIS FOR REAL ...?
PETA (PLOP)
ぺた
NO WAY......
REI......

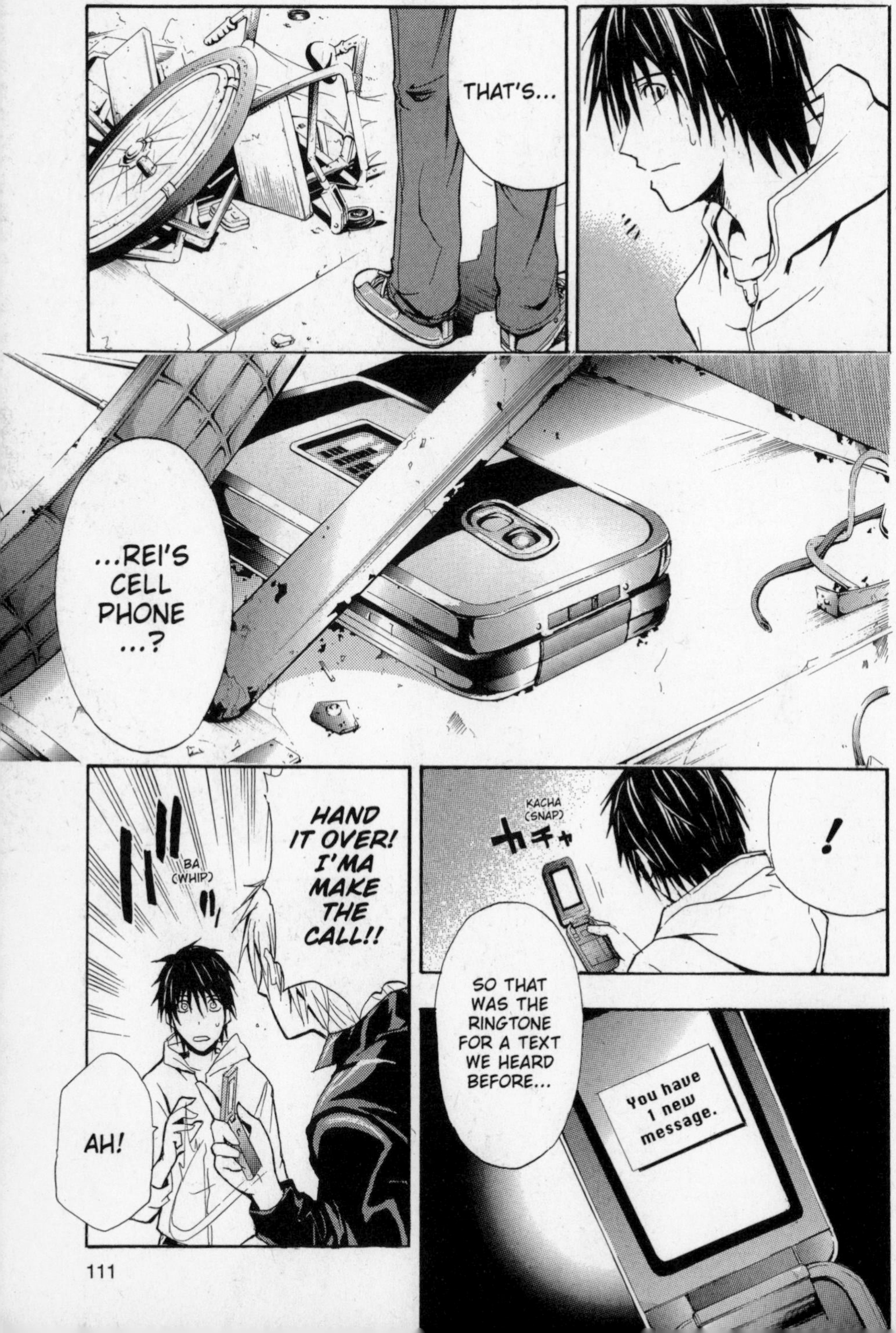
THAT'S...
...REI'S CELL PHONE ...?
KACHA (SNAP)
!
SO THAT WAS THE RINGTONE FOR A TEXT WE HEARD BEFORE...
You have 1 new message.
HAND IT OVER! I'MA MAKE THE CALL!!
BA (WHIP)
AH!

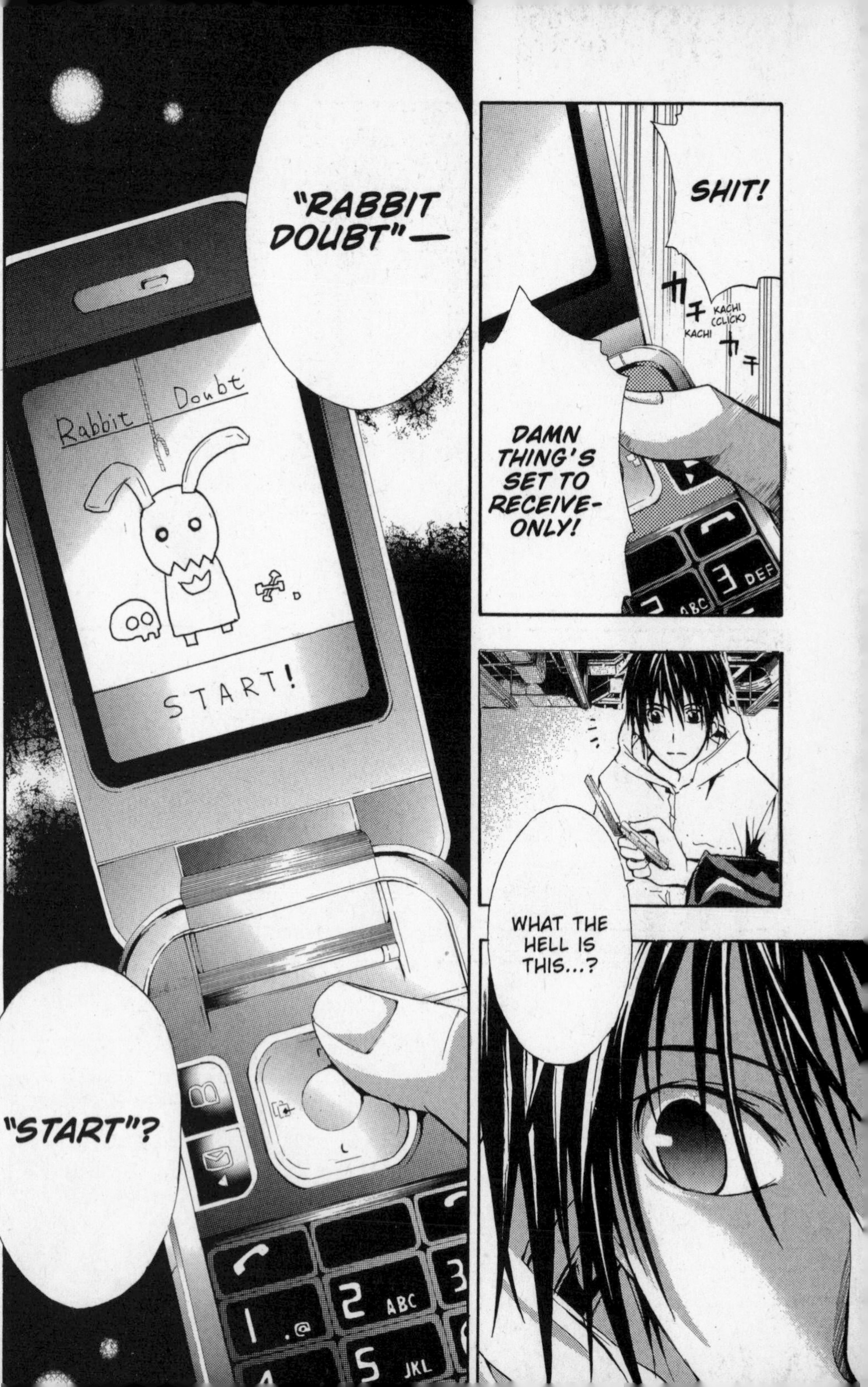
SHIT!
カチ
KACHI (CLICK)
KACHI
カチ
DAMN THING'S SET TO RECEIVE-ONLY!
WHAT THE HELL IS THIS...?
"RABBIT DOUBT"—
Rabbit Doubt
START!
"START"?

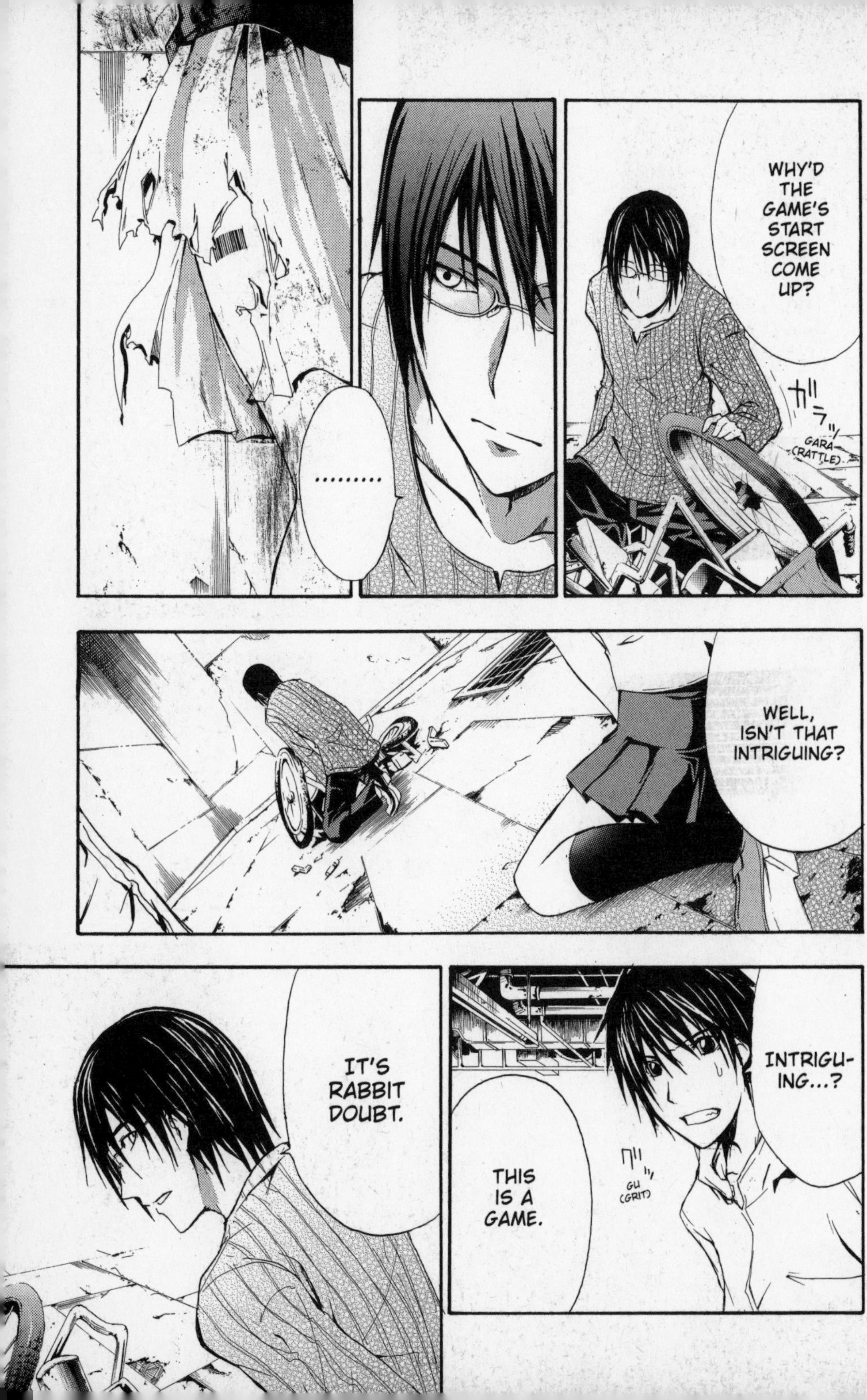
WHY'D THE GAME'S START SCREEN COME UP?
ガラ
GARA (RATTLE)
....
WELL, ISN'T THAT INTRIGUING?
INTRIGU-ING...?
グッ
GU (GRIT)
THIS IS A GAME.
IT'S RABBIT DOUBT.

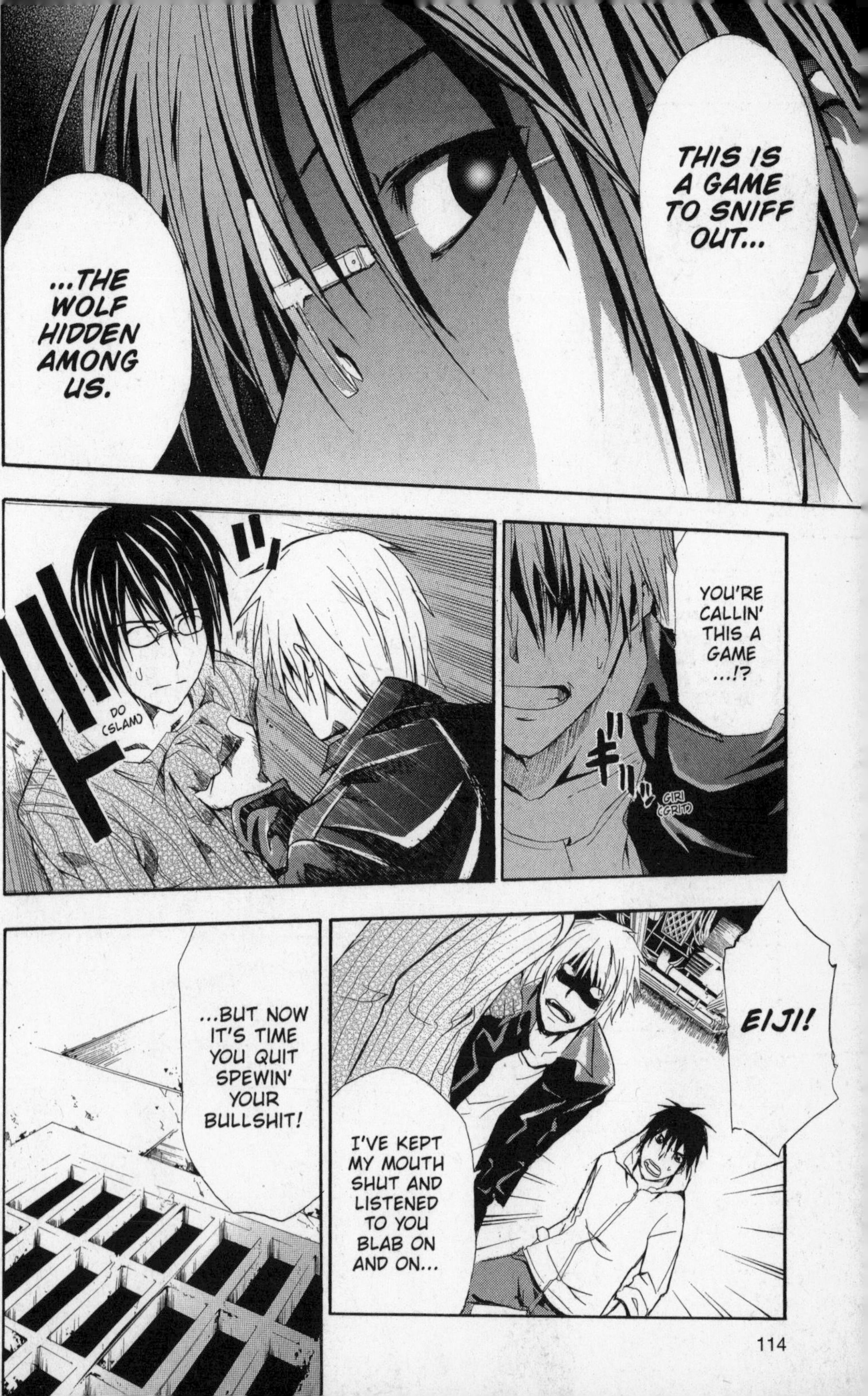
THIS IS A GAME TO SNIFF OUT...
...THE WOLF HIDDEN AMONG US.
YOU'RE CALLIN' THIS A GAME ...!?
GIRI (GRIT)
DO (SLAM)
EIJI!
I'VE KEPT MY MOUTH SHUT AND LISTENED TO YOU BLAB ON AND ON...
...BUT NOW IT'S TIME YOU QUIT SPEWIN' YOUR BULLSHIT!

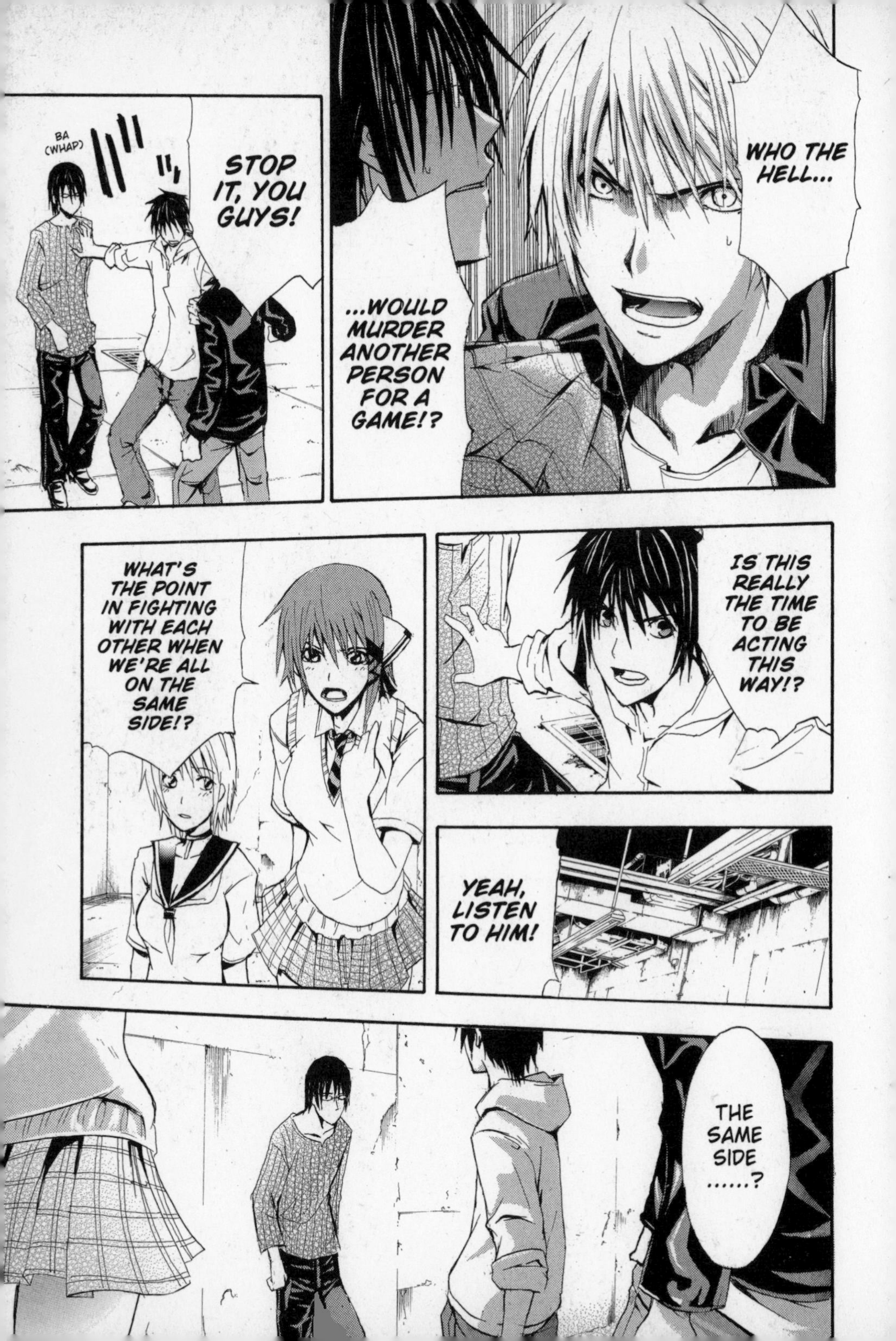
WHO THE HELL...
...WOULD MURDER ANOTHER PERSON FOR A GAME!?
BA (WHAP)
STOP IT, YOU GUYS!
IS THIS REALLY THE TIME TO BE ACTING THIS WAY!?
YEAH, LISTEN TO HIM!
WHAT'S THE POINT IN FIGHTING WITH EACH OTHER WHEN WE'RE ALL ON THE SAME SIDE!?
THE SAME SIDE ......?

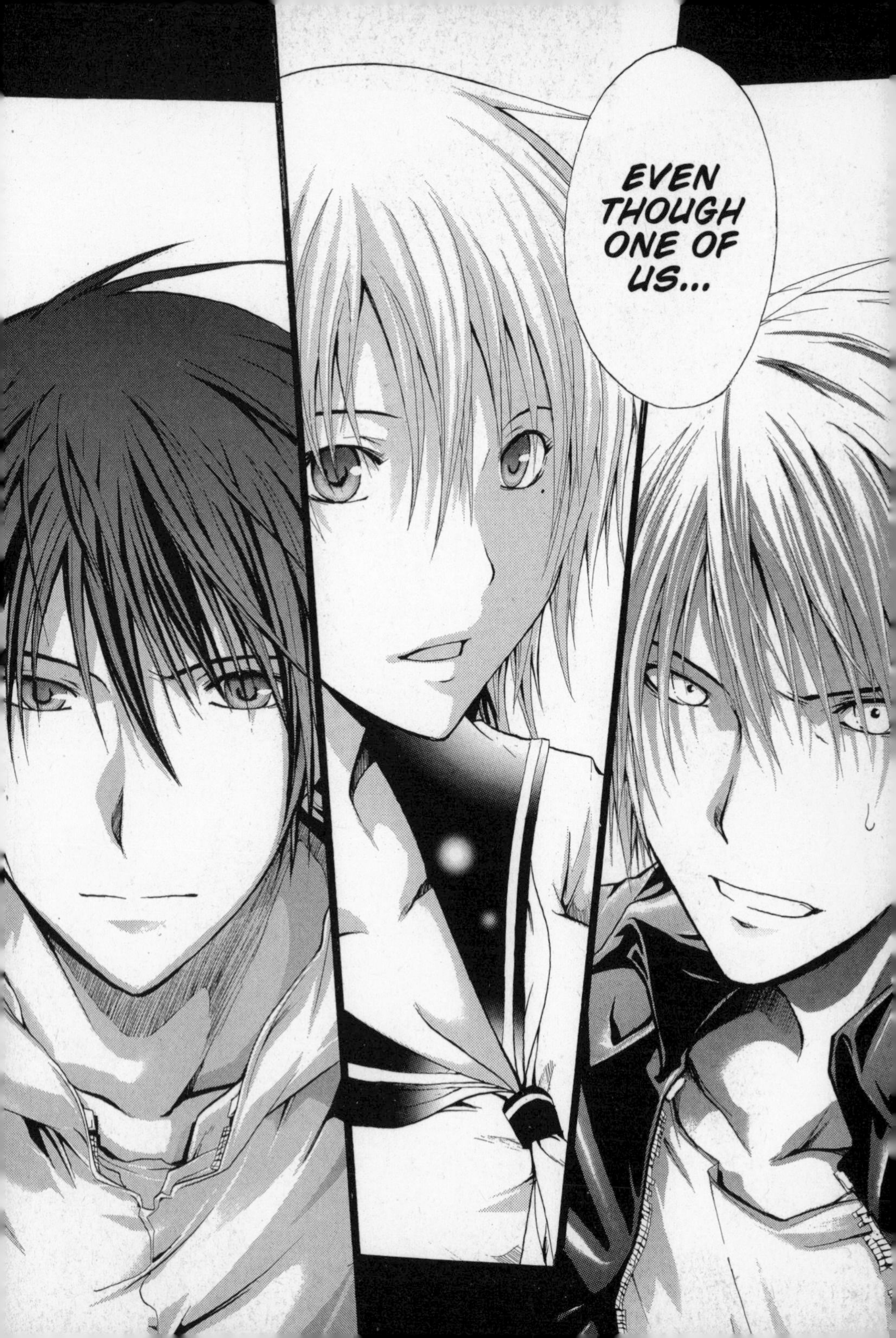
EVEN THOUGH ONE OF US...

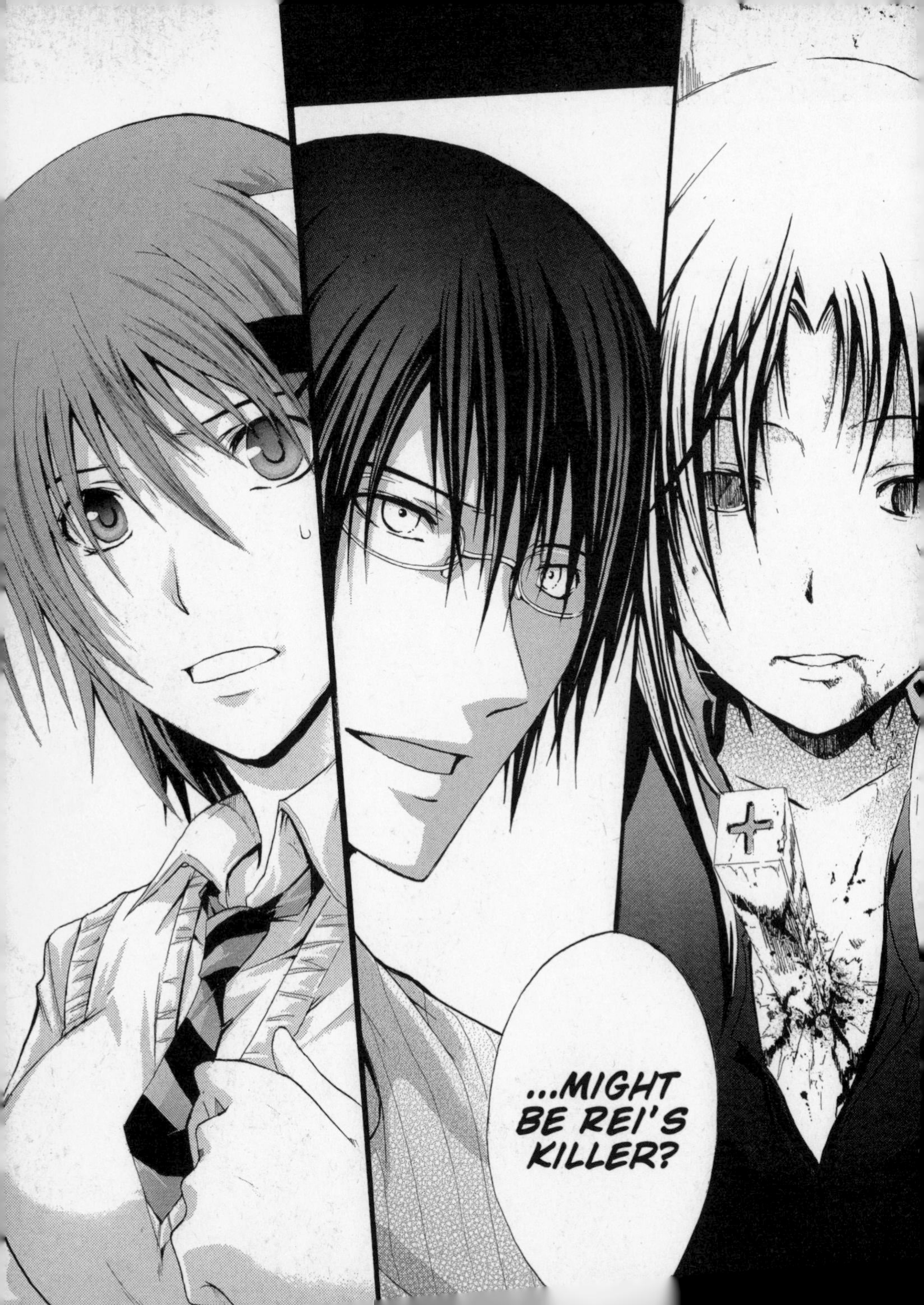
...MIGHT BE REI'S KILLER?

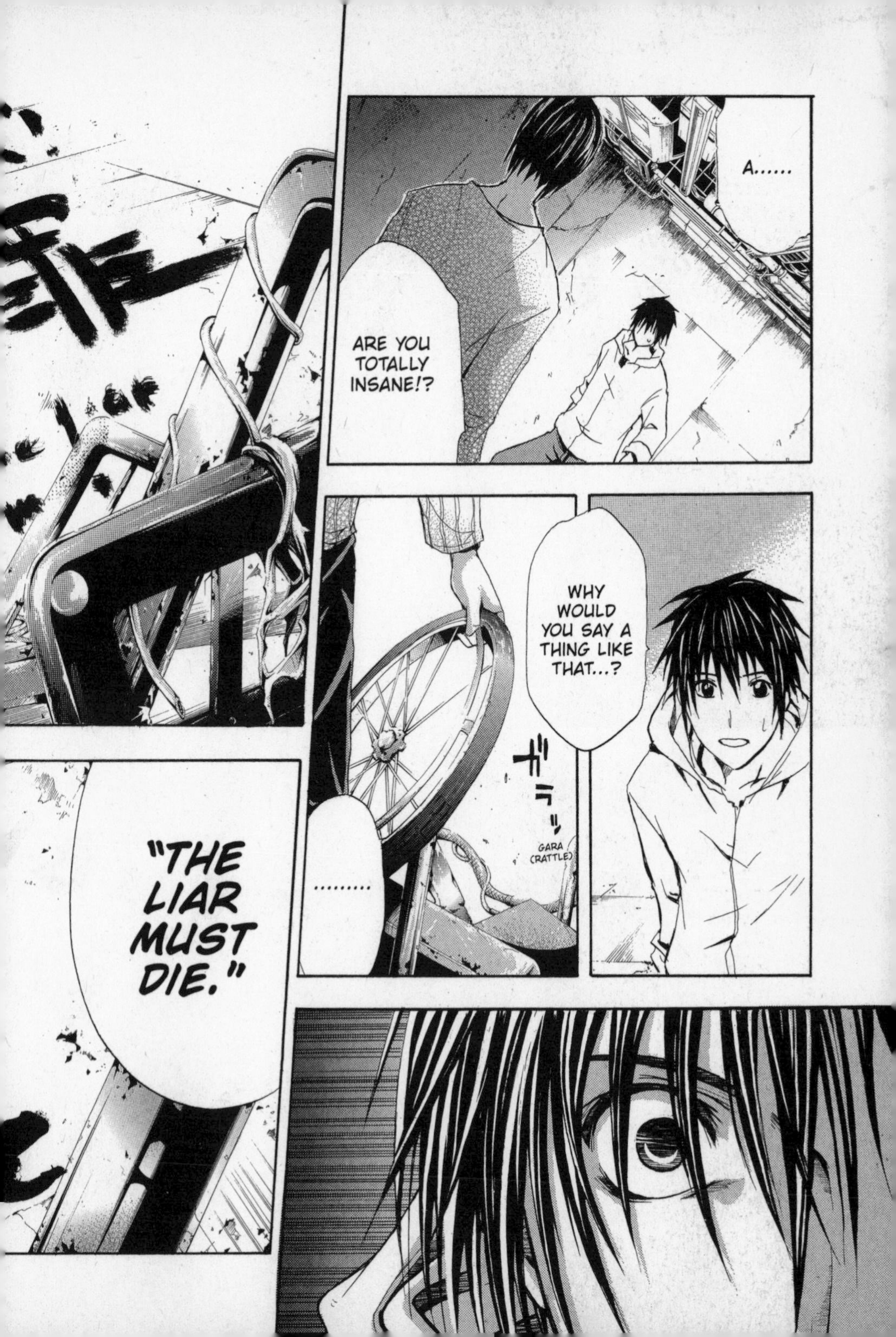
A......
ARE YOU TOTALLY INSANE!?
WHY WOULD YOU SAY A THING LIKE THAT...?
GARA (RATTLE)
....
"THE LIAR MUST DIE."

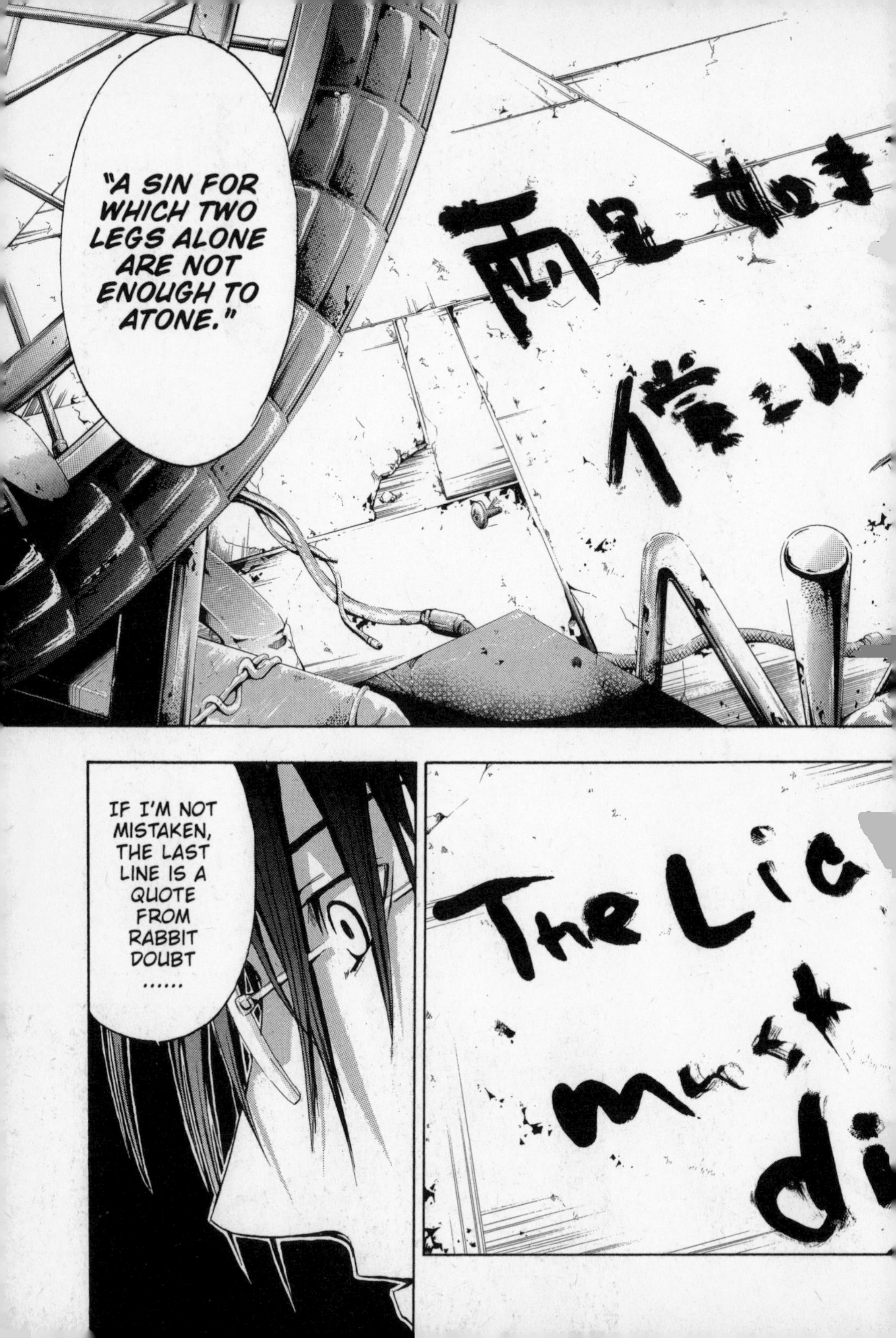
"A SIN FOR WHICH TWO LEGS ALONE ARE NOT ENOUGH TO ATONE."
The Lie must di
IF I'M NOT MISTAKEN, THE LAST LINE IS A QUOTE FROM RABBIT DOUBT ......

YOU GET IT NOW, DON'T YOU?

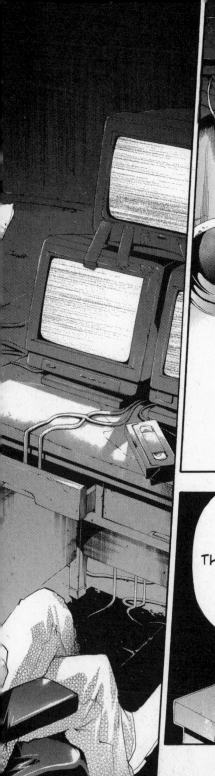

THAT...

JI (SST)
JI

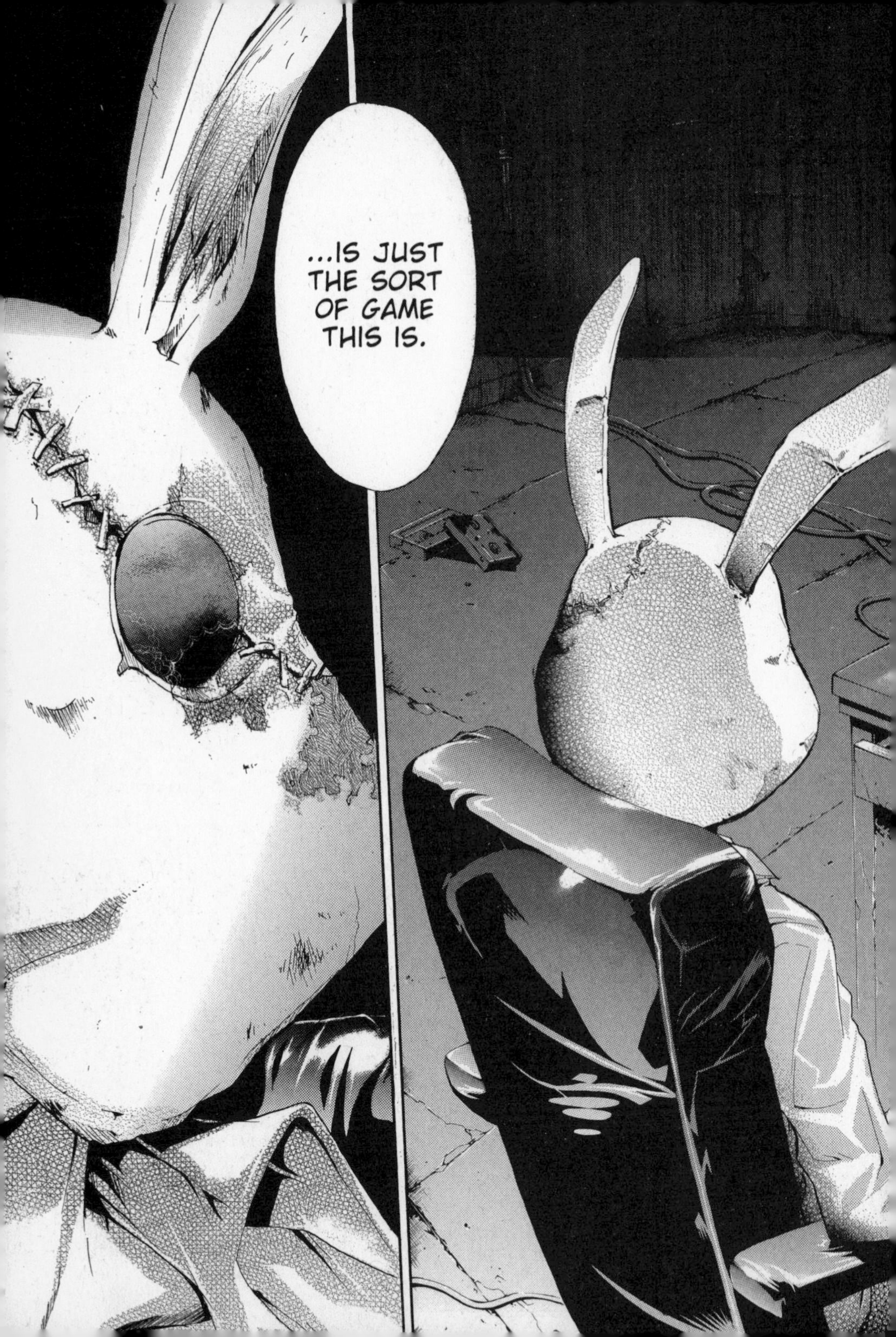
...IS JUST THE SORT OF GAME THIS IS.

Doubt

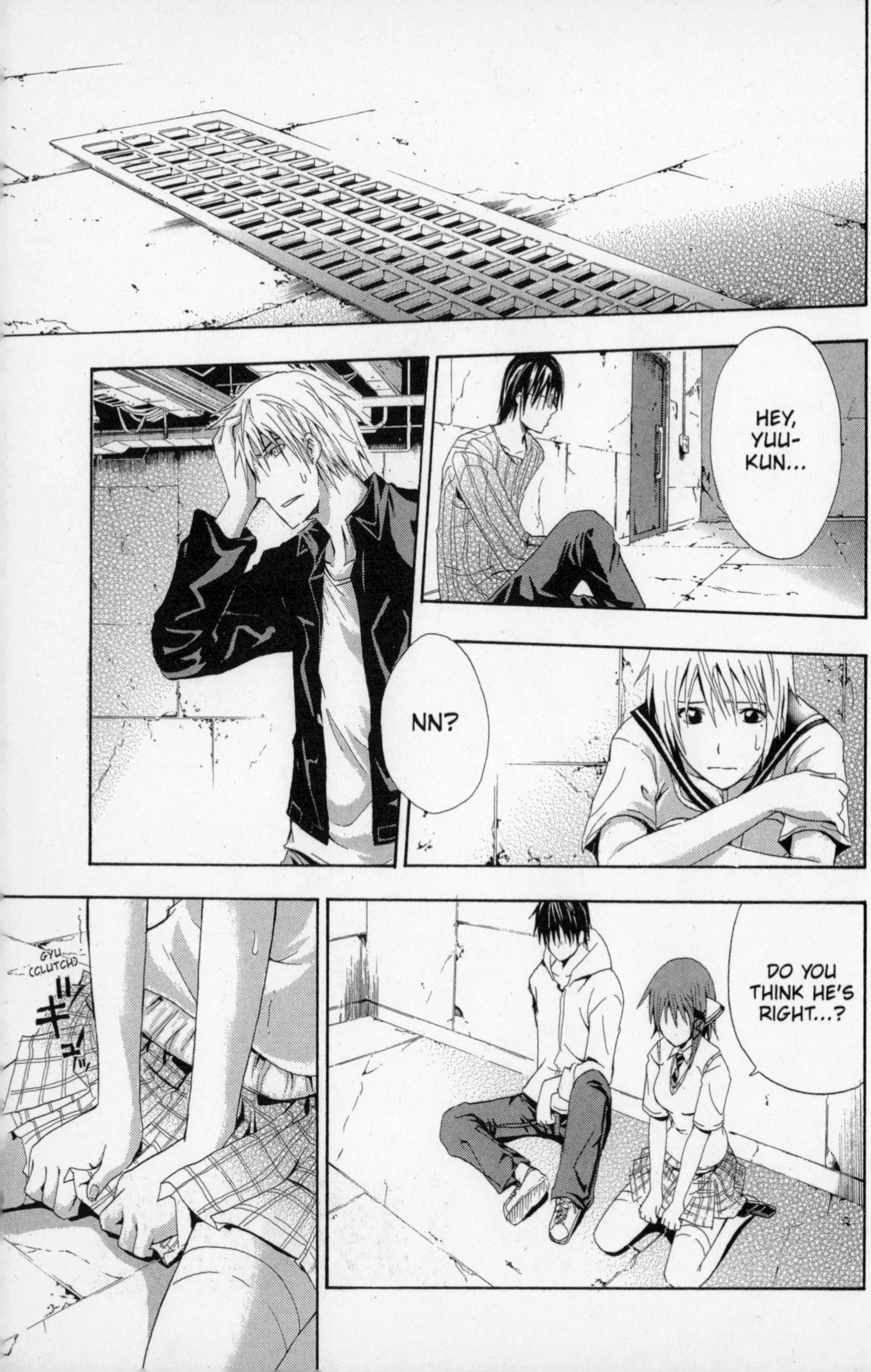
HEY, YUU-KUN...
NN?
DO YOU THINK HE'S RIGHT...?
GYU (CLUTCH)
ギュッ

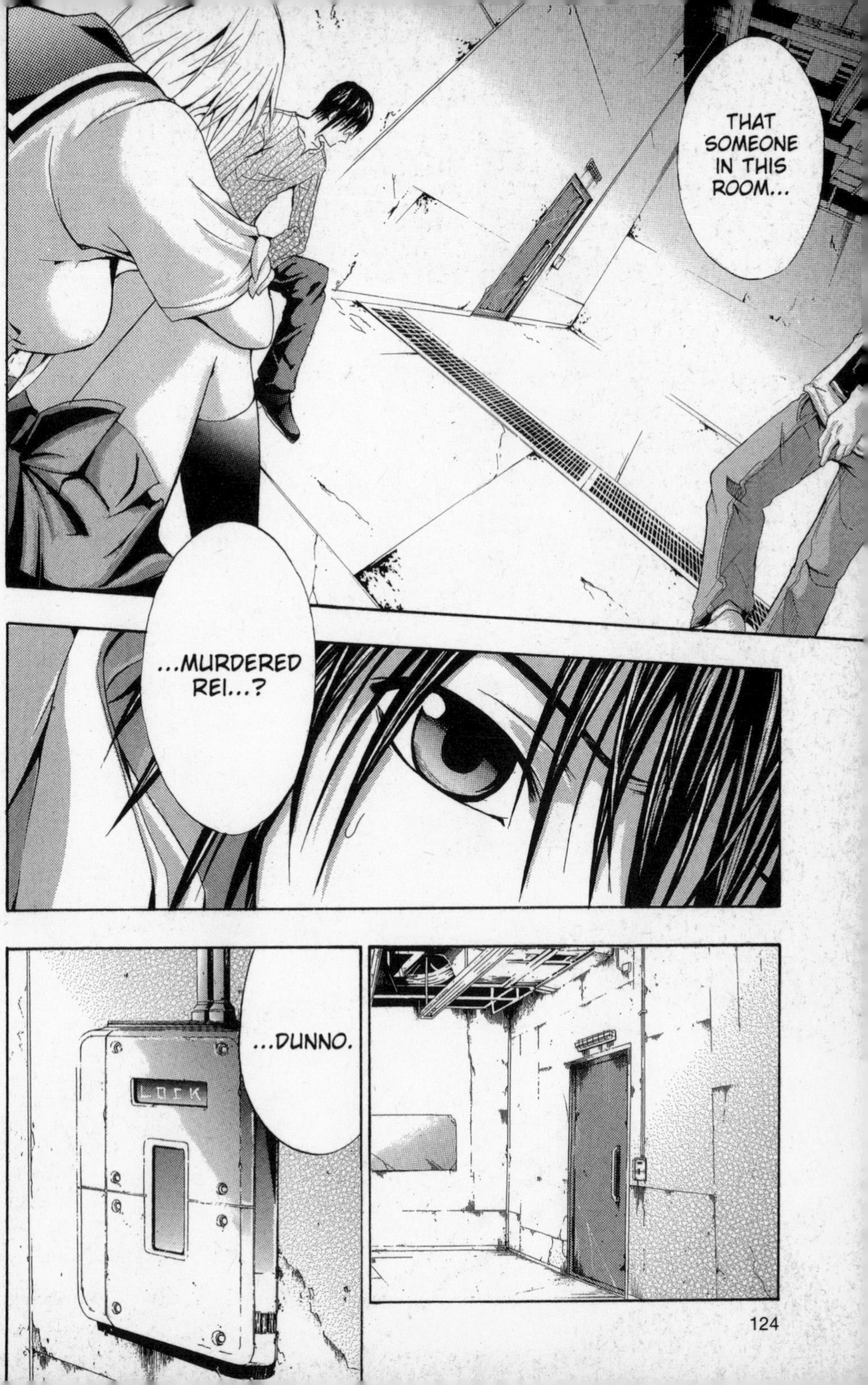
THAT SOMEONE IN THIS ROOM...
...MURDERED REI...?
...DUNNO.
LOCK

Doubt.3 KEY ITEM

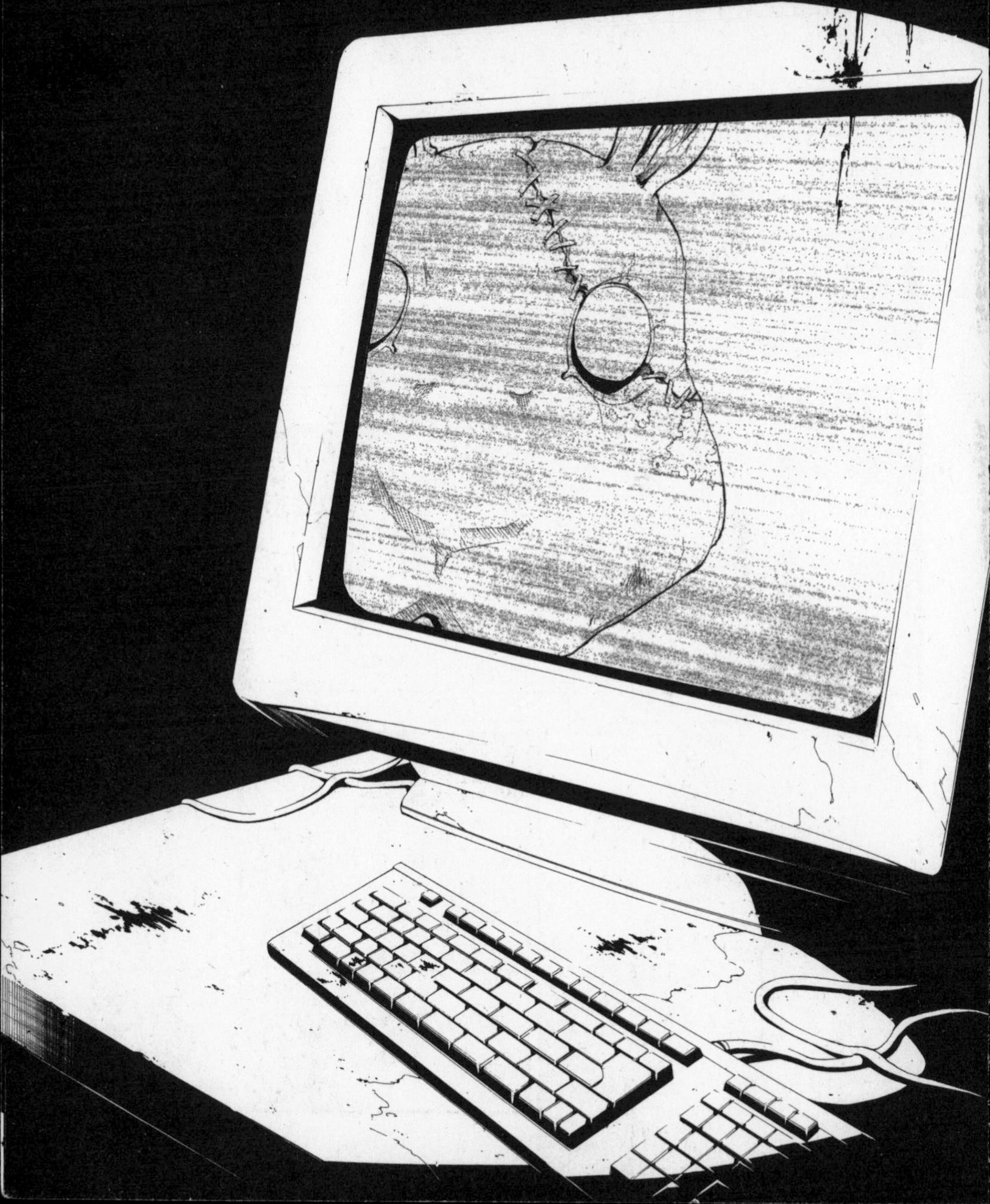

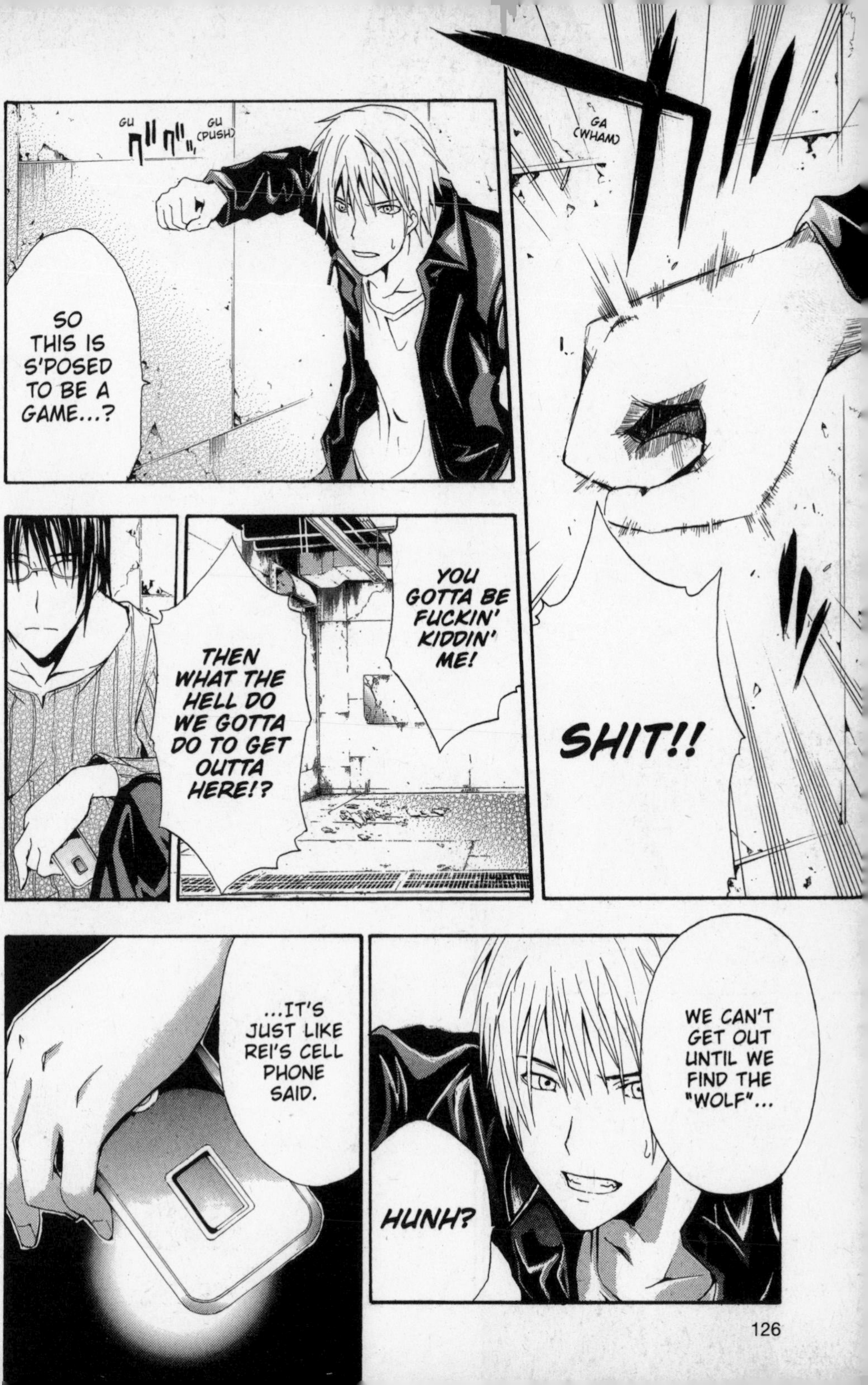

GA (WHAM)
SHIT!!
GU GU (PUSH)
SO THIS IS S'POSED TO BE A GAME...?
YOU GOTTA BE FUCKIN' KIDDIN' ME!
THEN WHAT THE HELL DO WE GOTTA DO TO GET OUTTA HERE!?
WE CAN'T GET OUT UNTIL WE FIND THE "WOLF"...
HUNH?
...IT'S JUST LIKE REI'S CELL PHONE SAID.

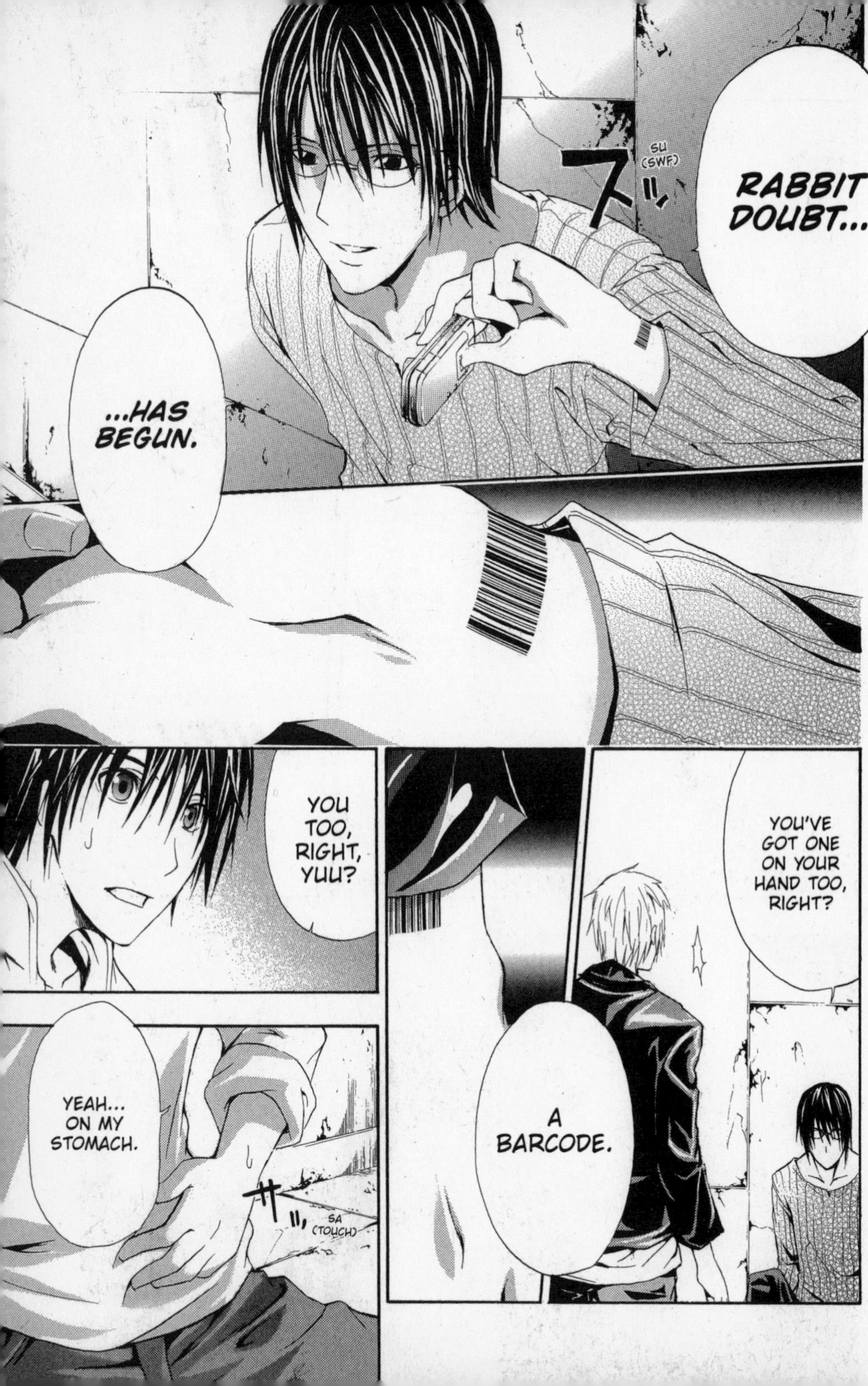
RABBIT DOUBT...
SU (SWF)
...HAS BEGUN.
YOU'VE GOT ONE ON YOUR HAND TOO, RIGHT?
A BARCODE.
YOU TOO, RIGHT, YUU?
YEAH... ON MY STOMACH.
SA (TOUCH)

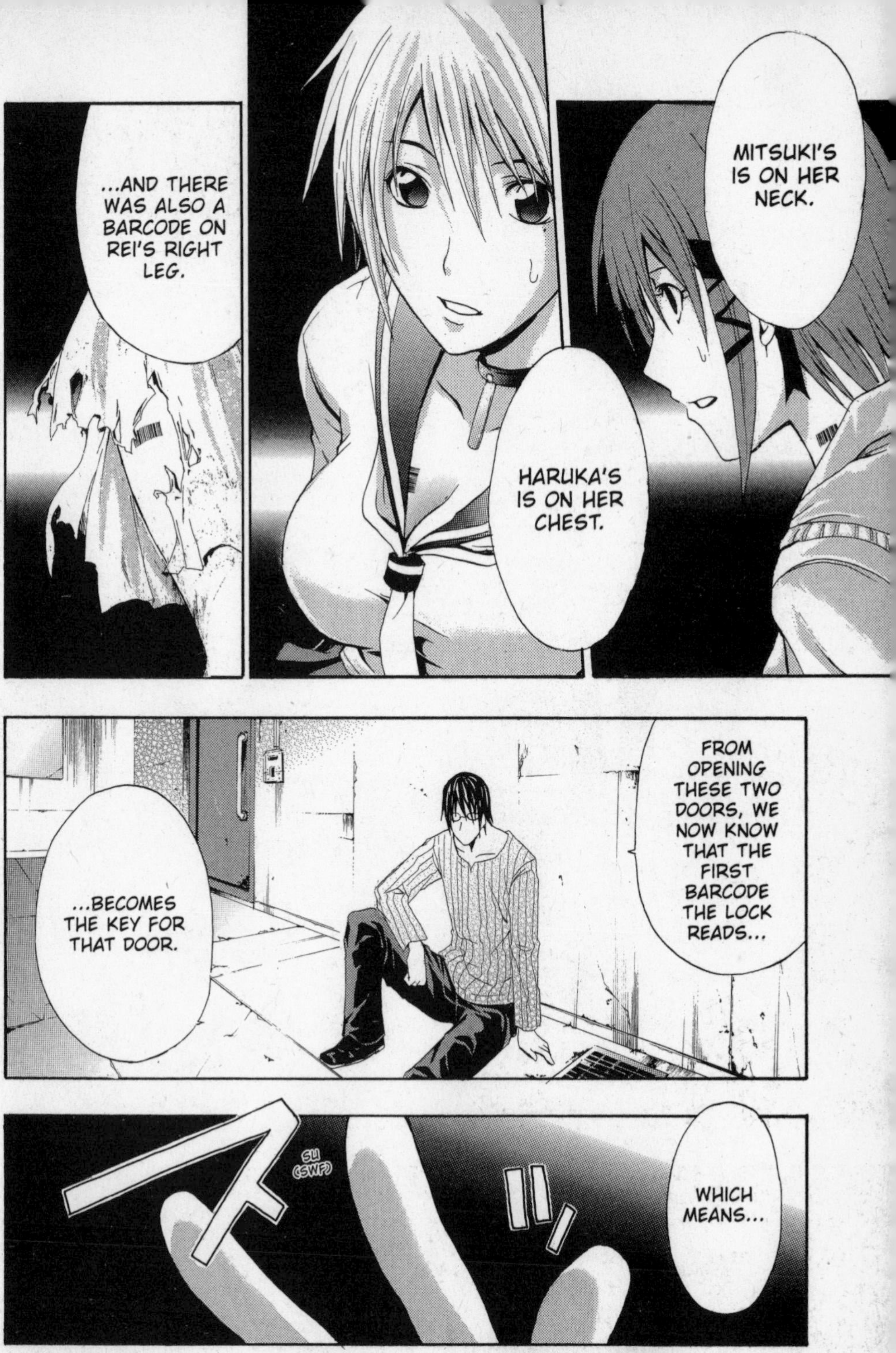
MITSUKI'S IS ON HER NECK.
HARUKA'S IS ON HER CHEST.
...AND THERE WAS ALSO A BARCODE ON REI'S RIGHT LEG.
FROM OPENING THESE TWO DOORS, WE NOW KNOW THAT THE FIRST BARCODE THE LOCK READS...
...BECOMES THE KEY FOR THAT DOOR.
WHICH MEANS...
SU (SWF)

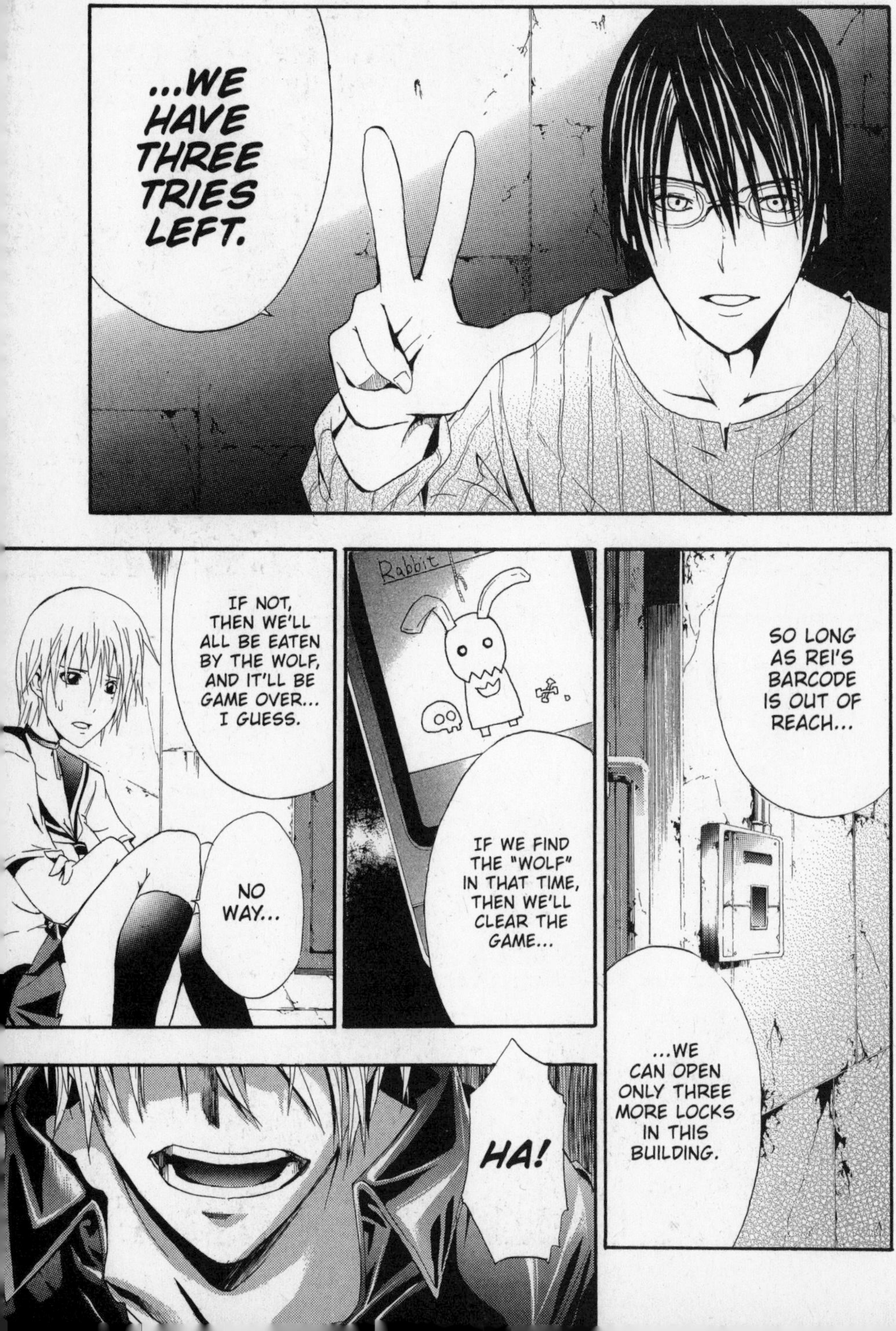
...WE HAVE THREE TRIES LEFT.
SO LONG AS REI'S BARCODE IS OUT OF REACH...
...WE CAN OPEN ONLY THREE MORE LOCKS IN THIS BUILDING.
Rabbit
IF WE FIND THE "WOLF" IN THAT TIME, THEN WE'LL CLEAR THE GAME...
IF NOT, THEN WE'LL ALL BE EATEN BY THE WOLF, AND IT'LL BE GAME OVER... I GUESS.
NO WAY...
HA!

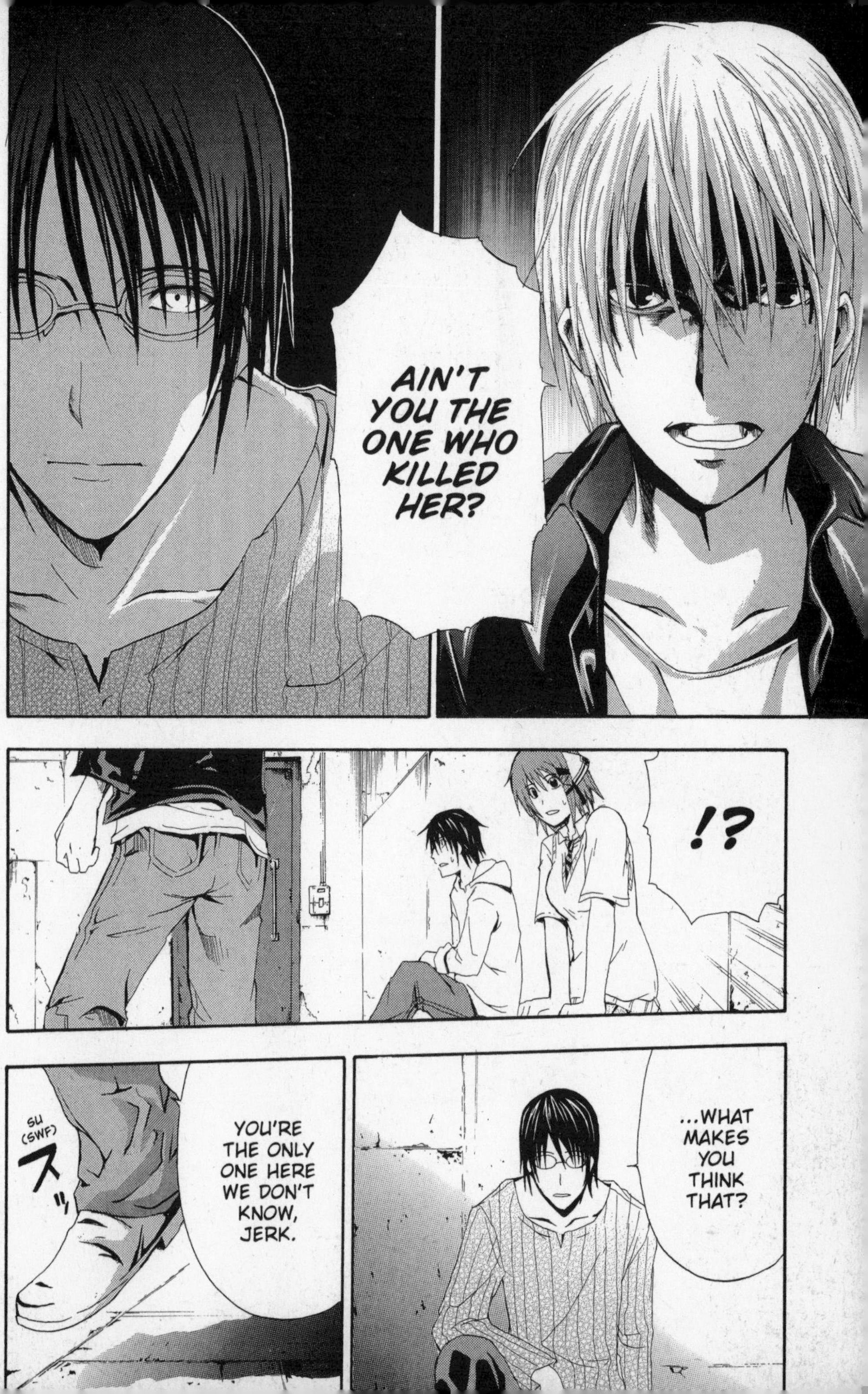
AIN'T YOU THE ONE WHO KILLED HER?
!?
...WHAT MAKES YOU THINK THAT?
YOU'RE THE ONLY ONE HERE WE DON'T KNOW, JERK.
SU (SWF)

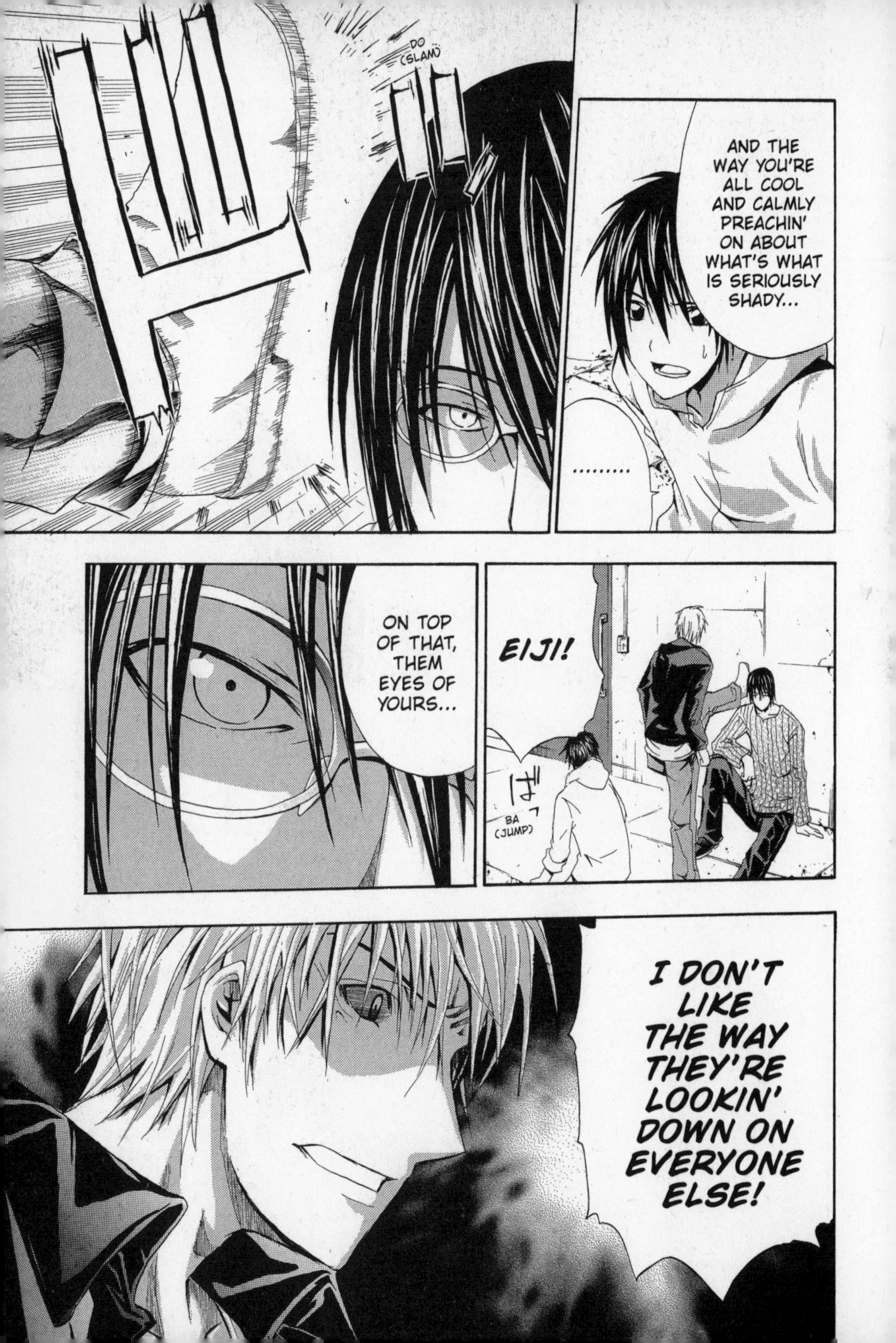
DO (SLAM)
AND THE WAY YOU'RE ALL COOL AND CALMLY PREACHIN' ON ABOUT WHAT'S WHAT IS SERIOUSLY SHADY...
....
EIJI!
ばっ
BA (JUMP)
ON TOP OF THAT, THEM EYES OF YOURS...
I DON'T LIKE THE WAY THEY'RE LOOKIN' DOWN ON EVERYONE ELSE!

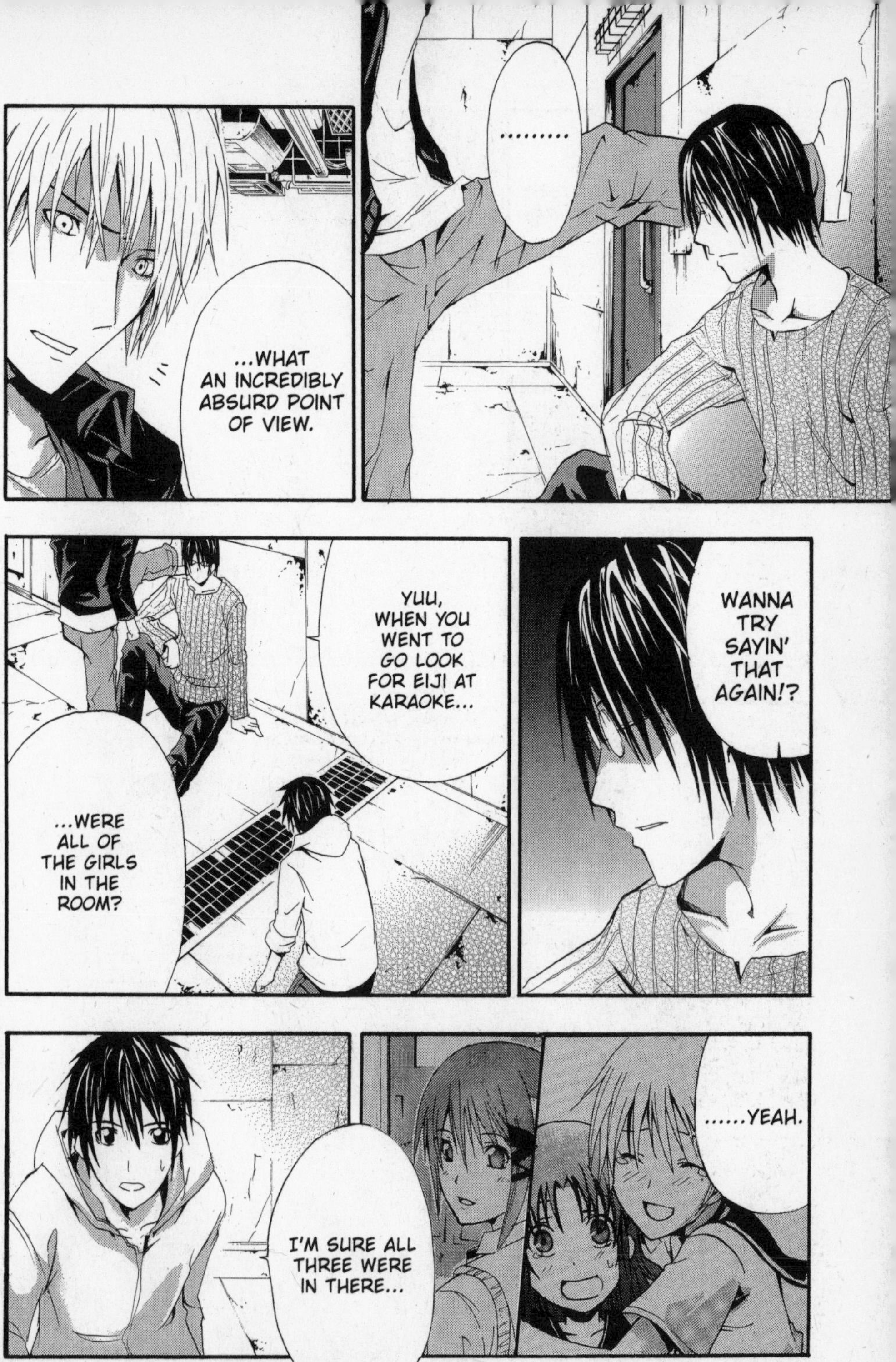
....
...WHAT AN INCREDIBLY ABSURD POINT OF VIEW.
WANNA TRY SAYIN' THAT AGAIN!?
YUU, WHEN YOU WENT TO GO LOOK FOR EIJI AT KARAOKE...
...WERE ALL OF THE GIRLS IN THE ROOM?
......YEAH.
I'M SURE ALL THREE WERE IN THERE...

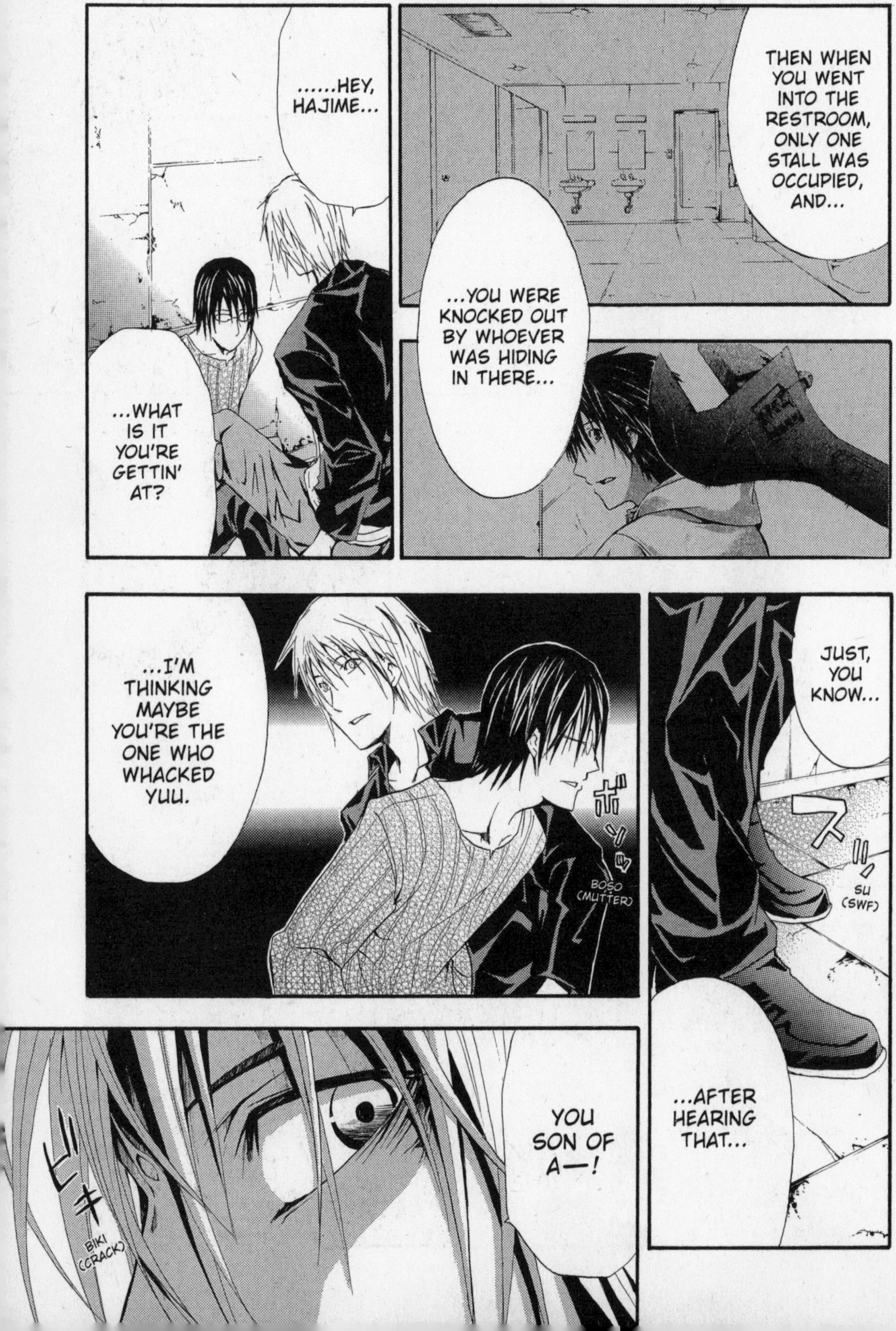
THEN WHEN YOU WENT INTO THE RESTROOM, ONLY ONE STALL WAS OCCUPIED, AND...
...YOU WERE KNOCKED OUT BY WHOEVER WAS HIDING IN THERE...
......HEY, HAJIME...
...WHAT IS IT YOU'RE GETTIN' AT?
JUST, YOU KNOW...
SU (SWF)
...AFTER HEARING THAT...
...I'M THINKING MAYBE YOU'RE THE ONE WHO WHACKED YUU.
BOSO (MUTTER)
YOU SON OF A—!
BIKI (CRACK)

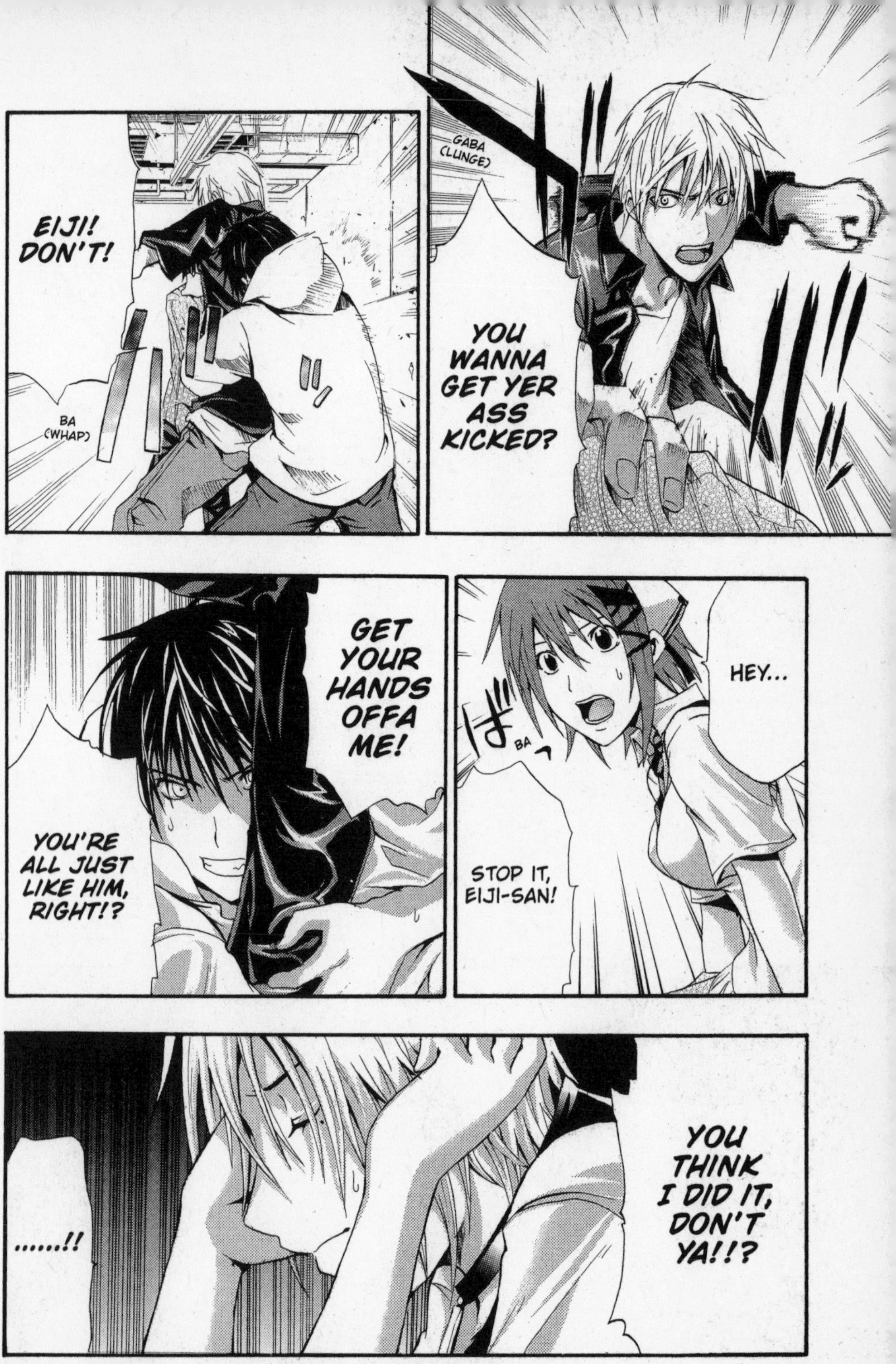
GABA (LUNGE)
YOU WANNA GET YER ASS KICKED?
EIJI! DON'T!
BA (WHAP)
HEY...
ば BA
STOP IT, EIJI-SAN!
GET YOUR HANDS OFFA ME!
YOU'RE ALL JUST LIKE HIM, RIGHT!?
YOU THINK I DID IT, DON'T YA!!?
......!!

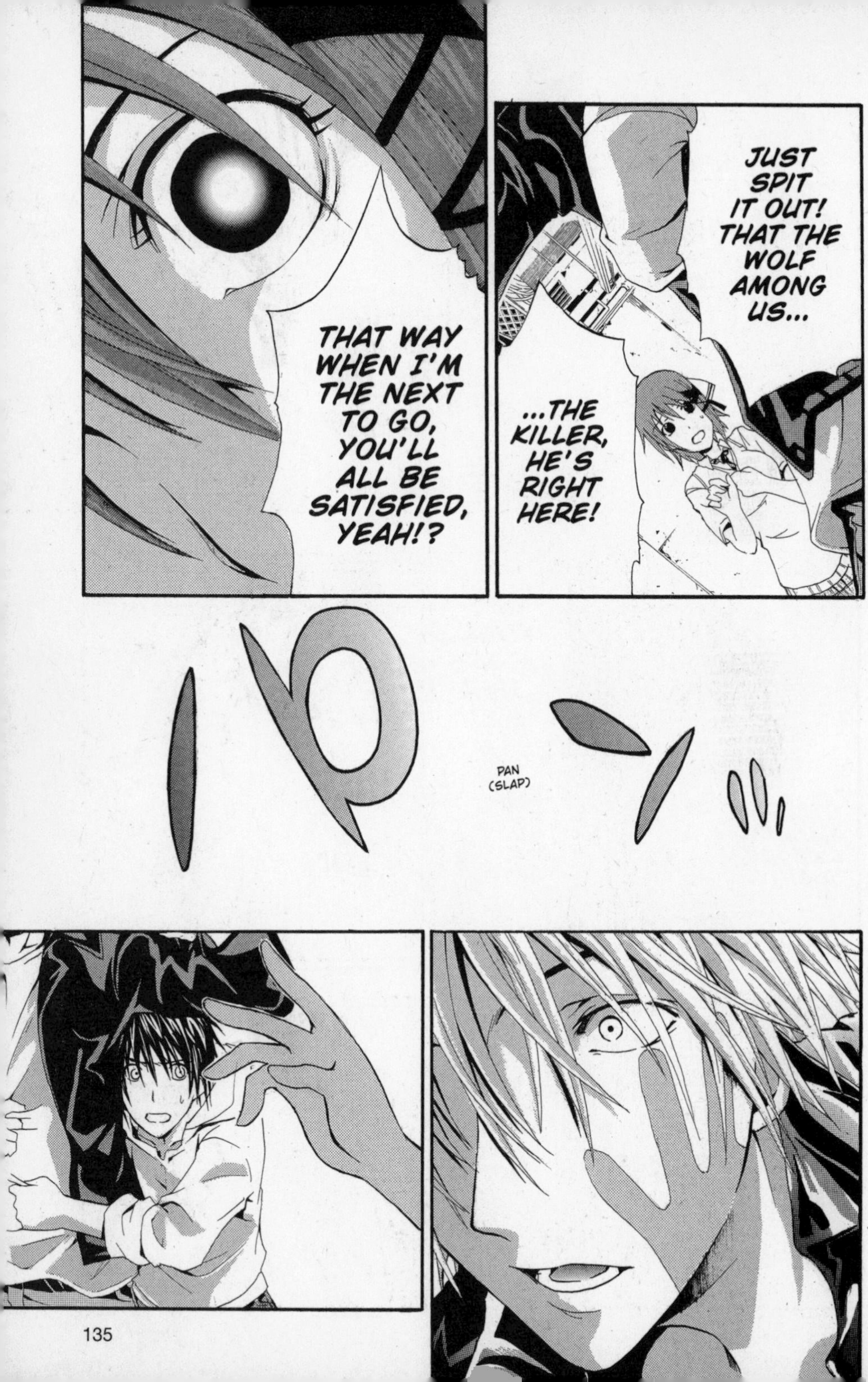
JUST SPIT IT OUT! THAT THE WOLF AMONG US...
...THE KILLER, HE'S RIGHT HERE!
THAT WAY WHEN I'M THE NEXT TO GO, YOU'LL ALL BE SATISFIED, YEAH!?
PAN (SLAP)

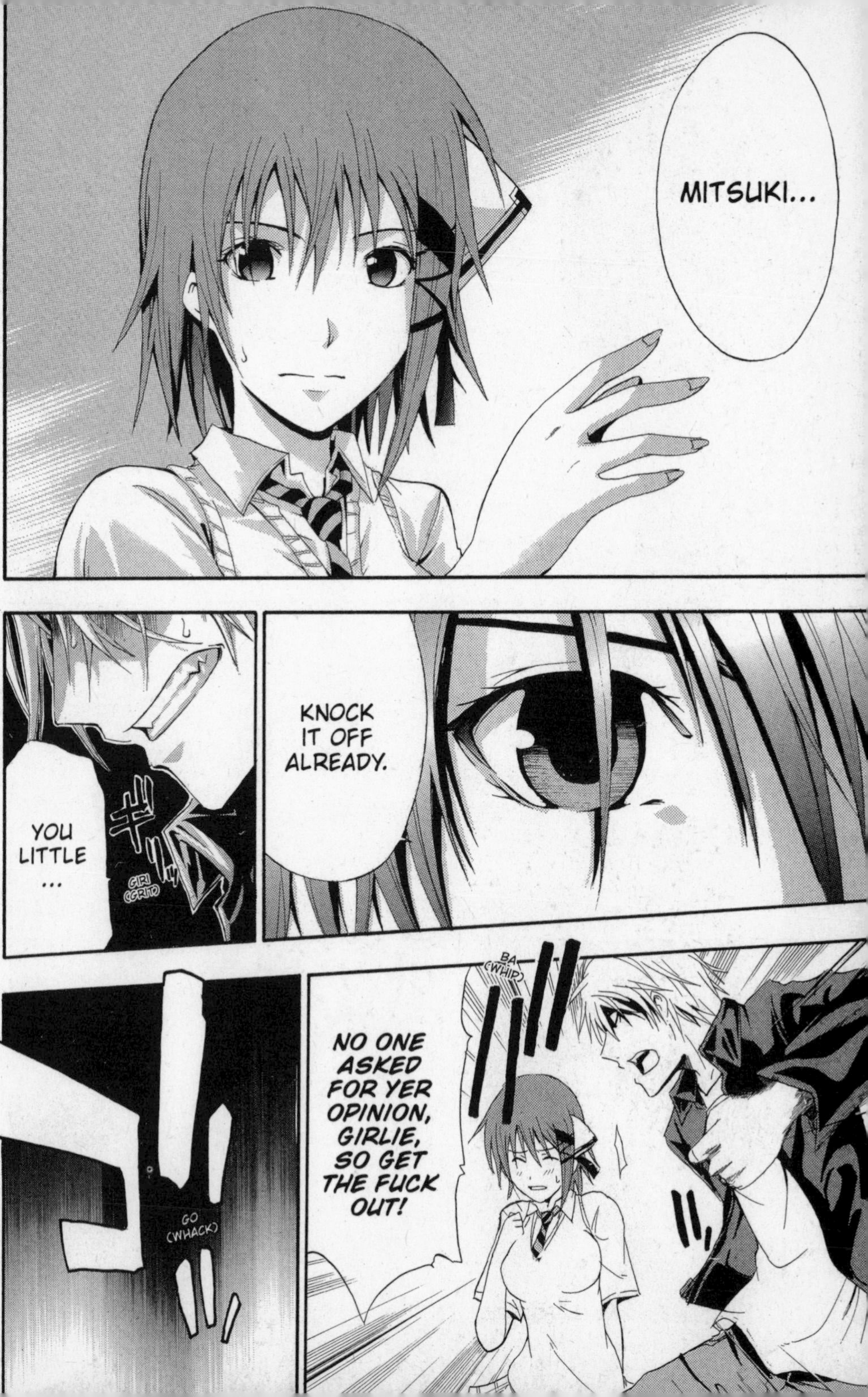
MITSUKI...
KNOCK IT OFF ALREADY.
YOU LITTLE ...
GIRI (GRIT)
BA (WHIP)
NO ONE ASKED FOR YER OPINION, GIRLIE, SO GET THE FUCK OUT!
GO (WHACK)

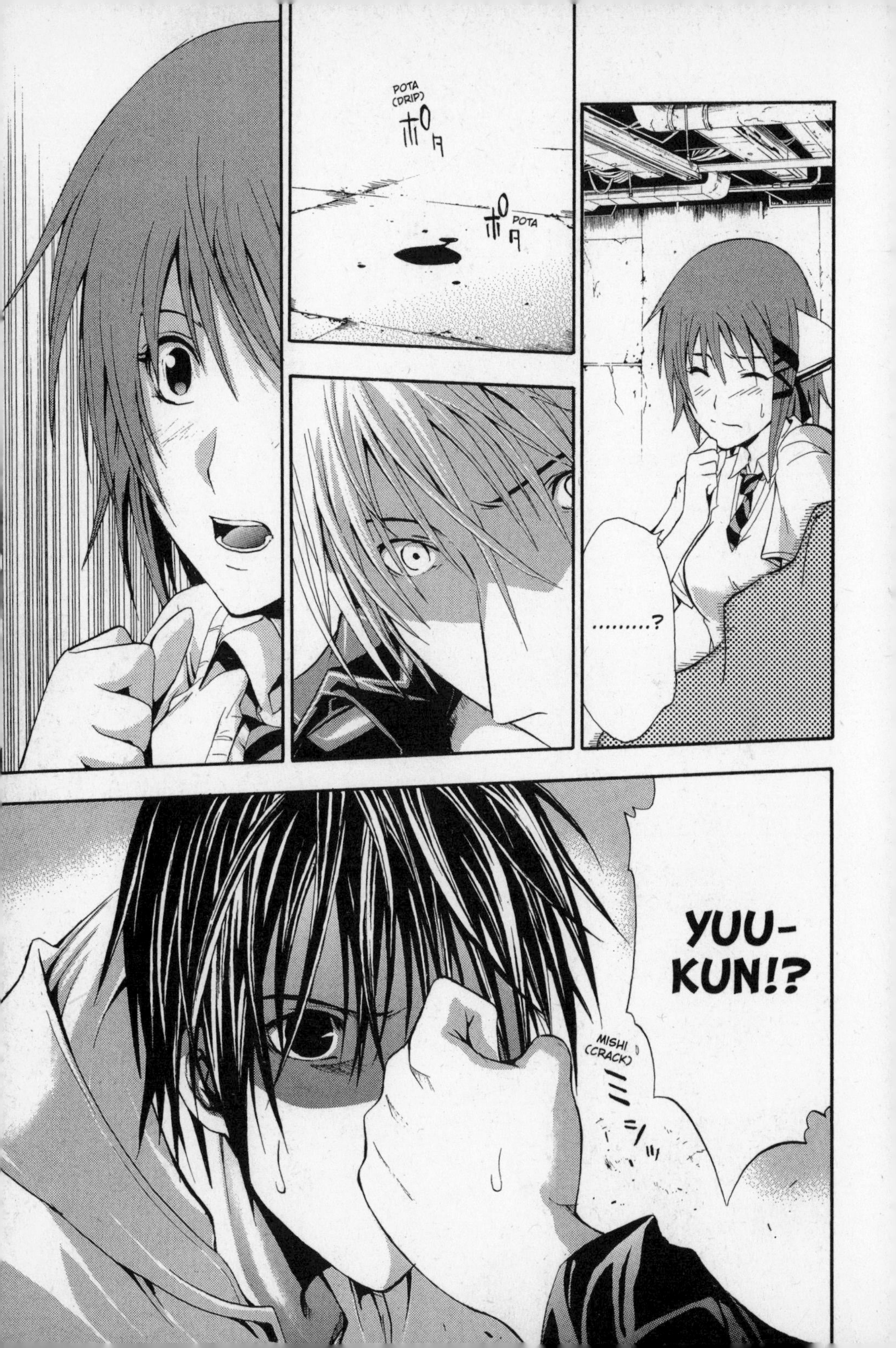
..........?
POTA (DRIP)
POTA
YUU-KUN!?
MISHI (CRACK)

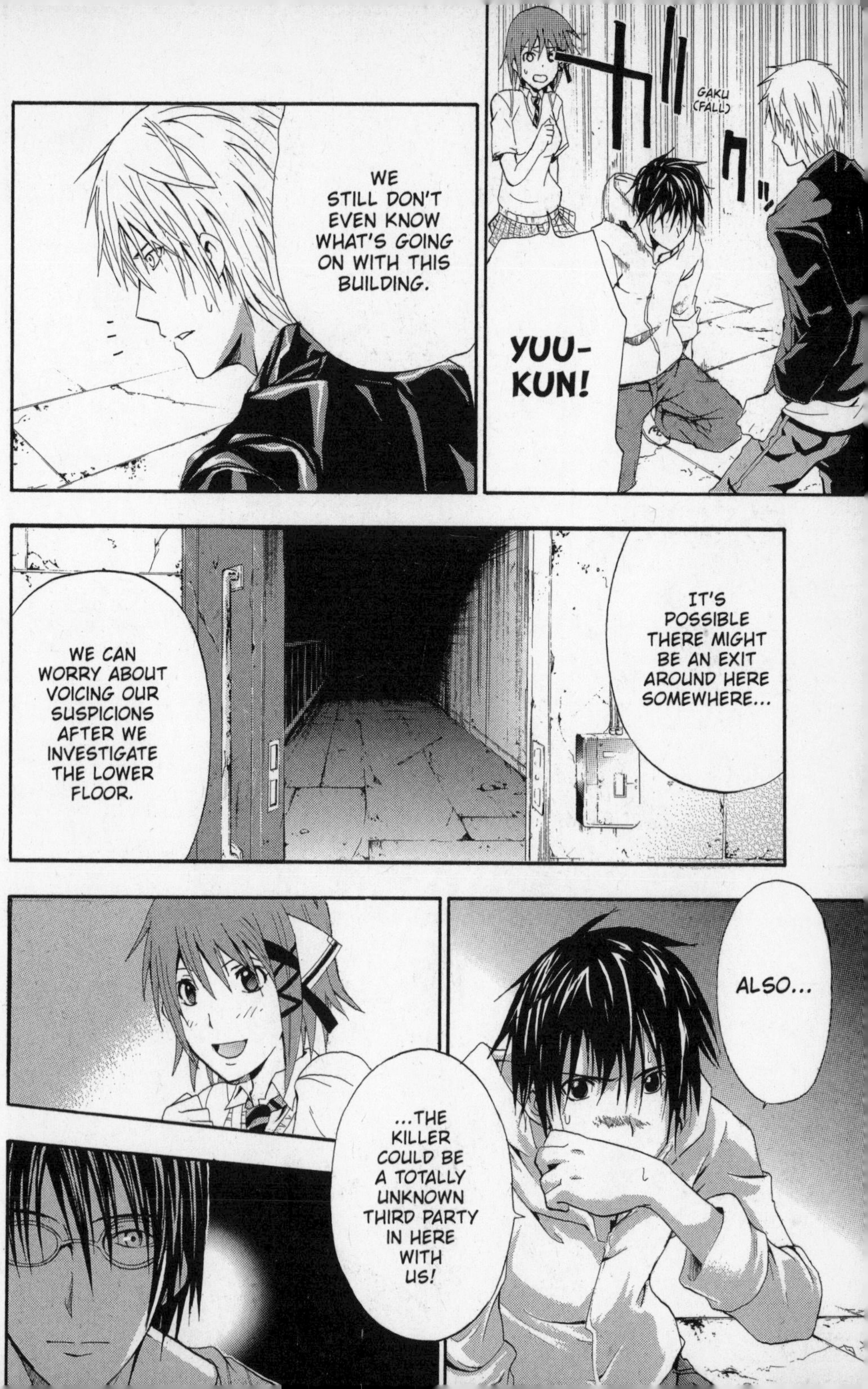
GAKU (FALL)
YUU-KUN!
WE STILL DON'T EVEN KNOW WHAT'S GOING ON WITH THIS BUILDING.
IT'S POSSIBLE THERE MIGHT BE AN EXIT AROUND HERE SOMEWHERE...
WE CAN WORRY ABOUT VOICING OUR SUSPICIONS AFTER WE INVESTIGATE THE LOWER FLOOR.
ALSO...
...THE KILLER COULD BE A TOTALLY UNKNOWN THIRD PARTY IN HERE WITH US!

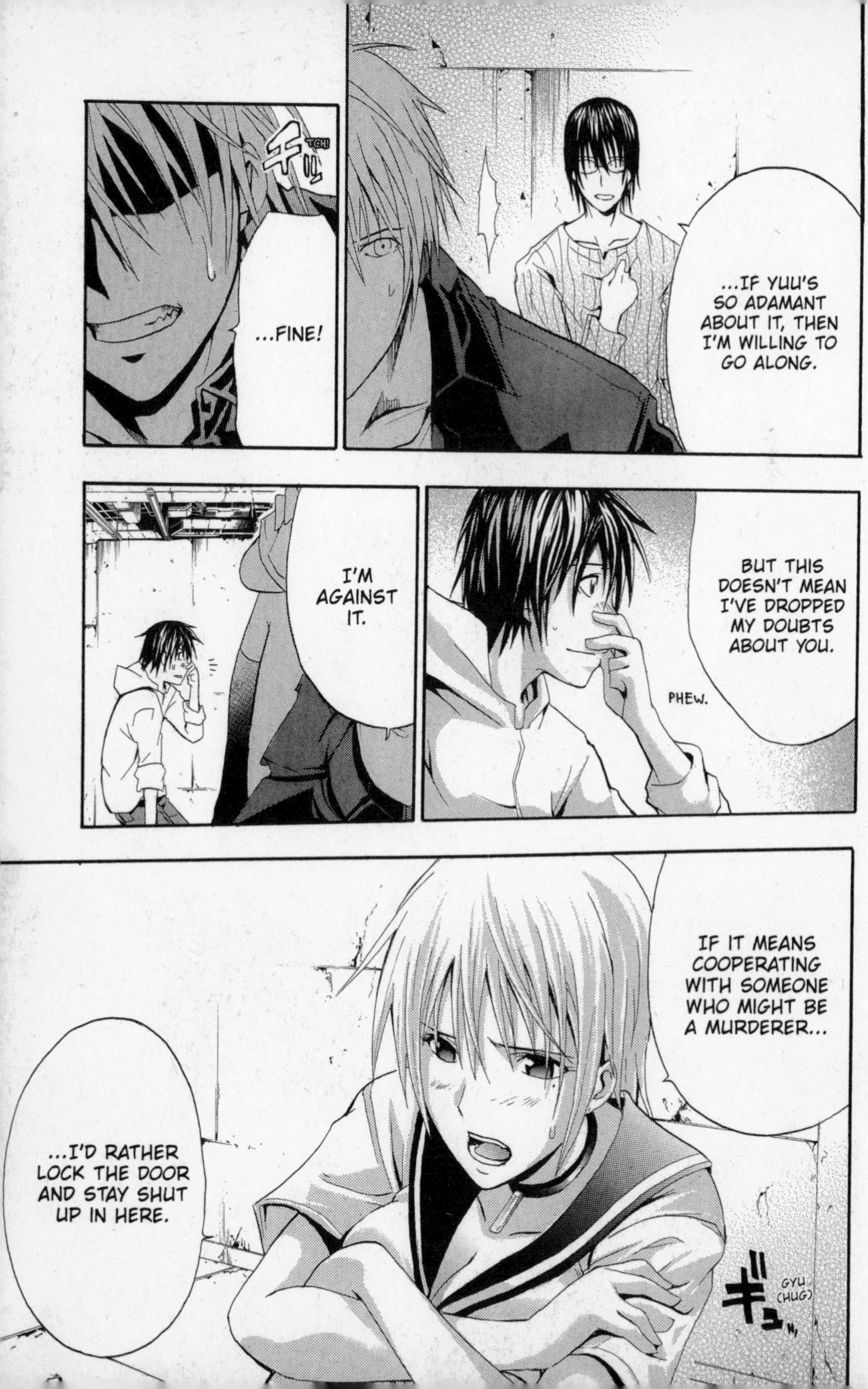
...IF YUU'S SO ADAMANT ABOUT IT, THEN I'M WILLING TO GO ALONG.
TCH!
...FINE!
BUT THIS DOESN'T MEAN I'VE DROPPED MY DOUBTS ABOUT YOU.
PHEW.
I'M AGAINST IT.
IF IT MEANS COOPERATING WITH SOMEONE WHO MIGHT BE A MURDERER...
...I'D RATHER LOCK THE DOOR AND STAY SHUT UP IN HERE.
GYU (HUG)

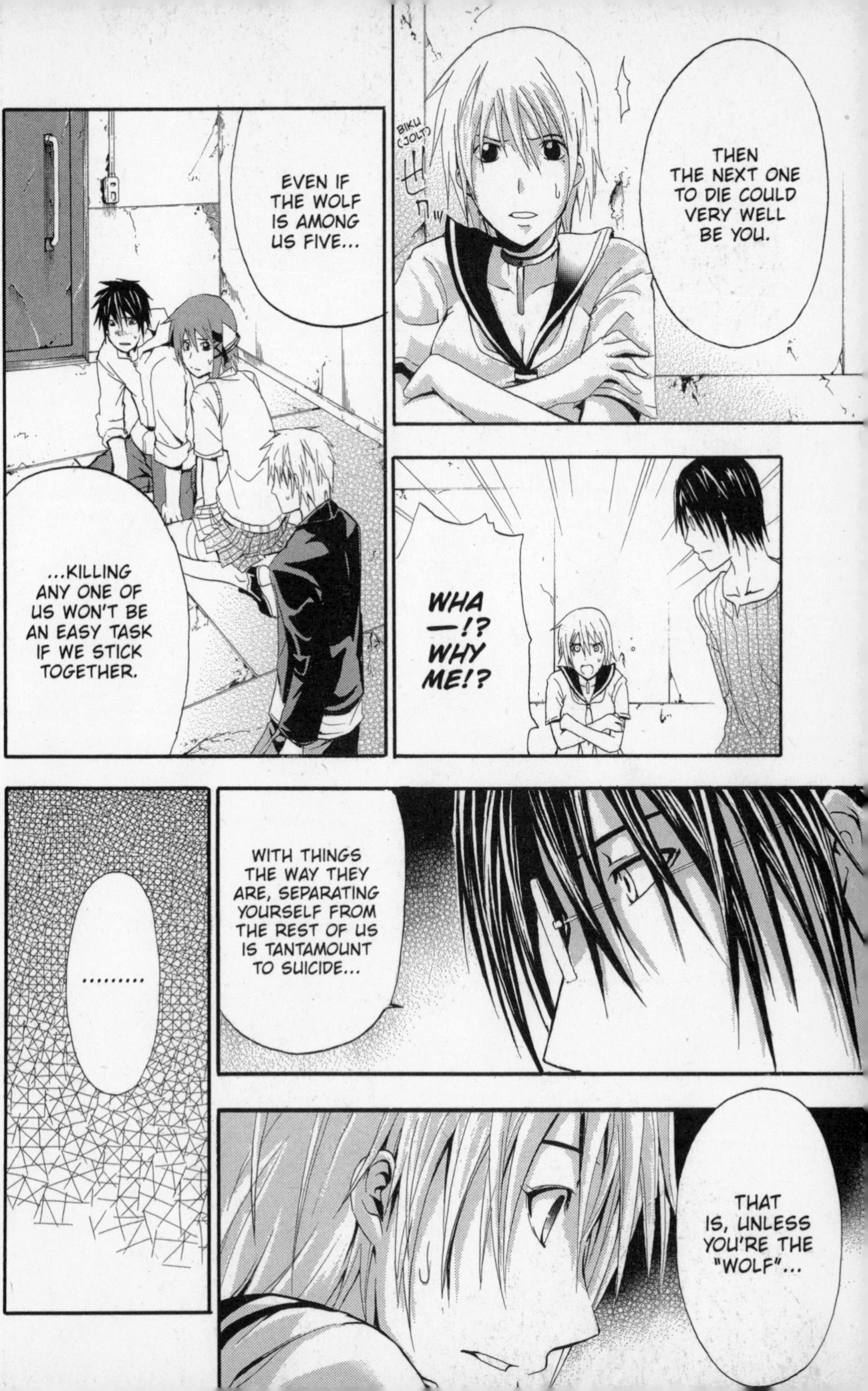
BIKU (JOLT)
THEN THE NEXT ONE TO DIE COULD VERY WELL BE YOU.
WHA—!? WHY ME!?
EVEN IF THE WOLF IS AMONG US FIVE...
...KILLING ANY ONE OF US WON'T BE AN EASY TASK IF WE STICK TOGETHER.
WITH THINGS THE WAY THEY ARE, SEPARATING YOURSELF FROM THE REST OF US IS TANTAMOUNT TO SUICIDE...
THAT IS, UNLESS YOU'RE THE "WOLF"...
....

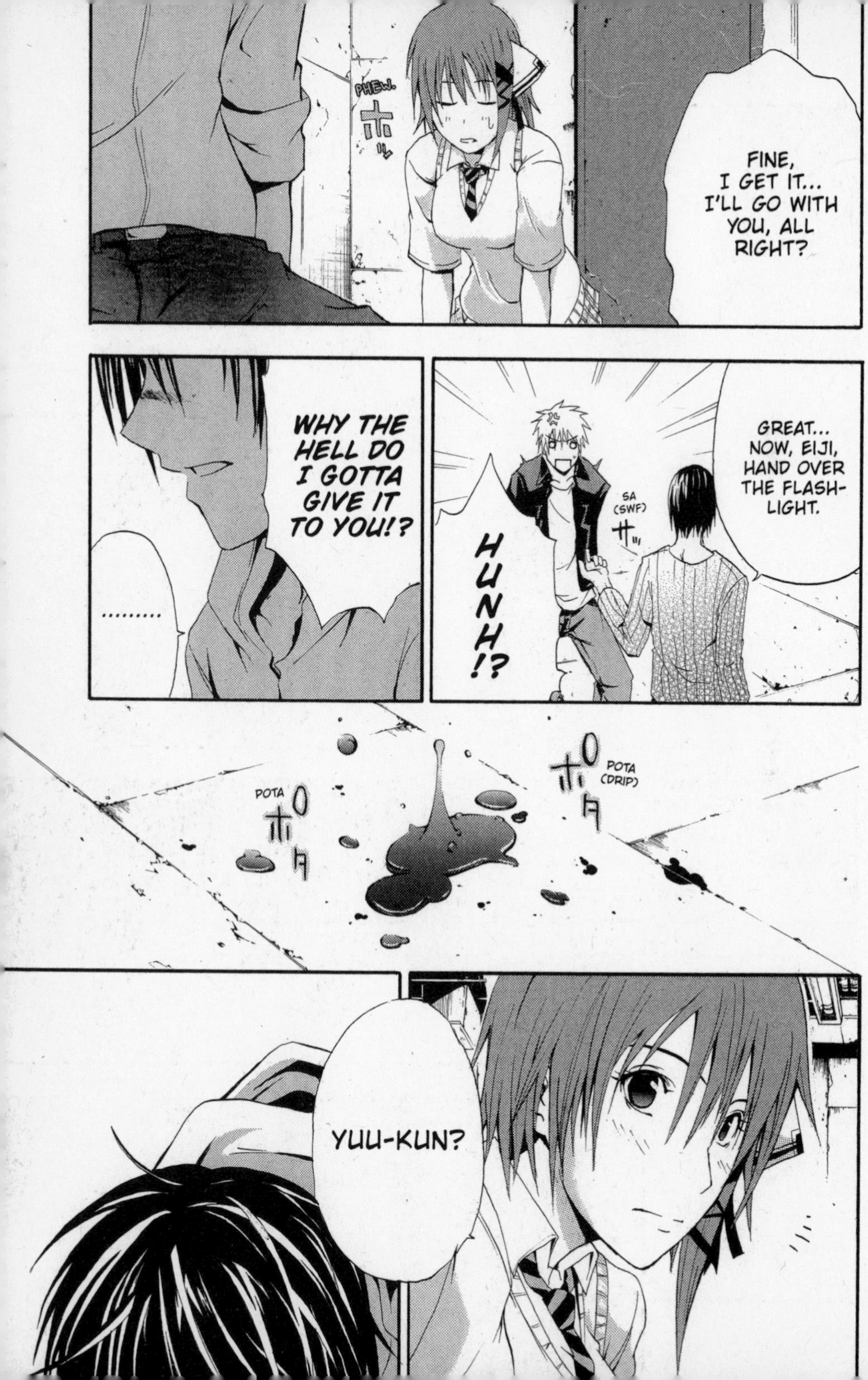
FINE, I GET IT... I'LL GO WITH YOU, ALL RIGHT?
PHEW.
GREAT... NOW, EIJI, HAND OVER THE FLASH-LIGHT.
SA (SWF)
HUNH!?
WHY THE HELL DO I GOTTA GIVE IT TO YOU!?
....
POTA (DRIP)
POTA
YUU-KUN?

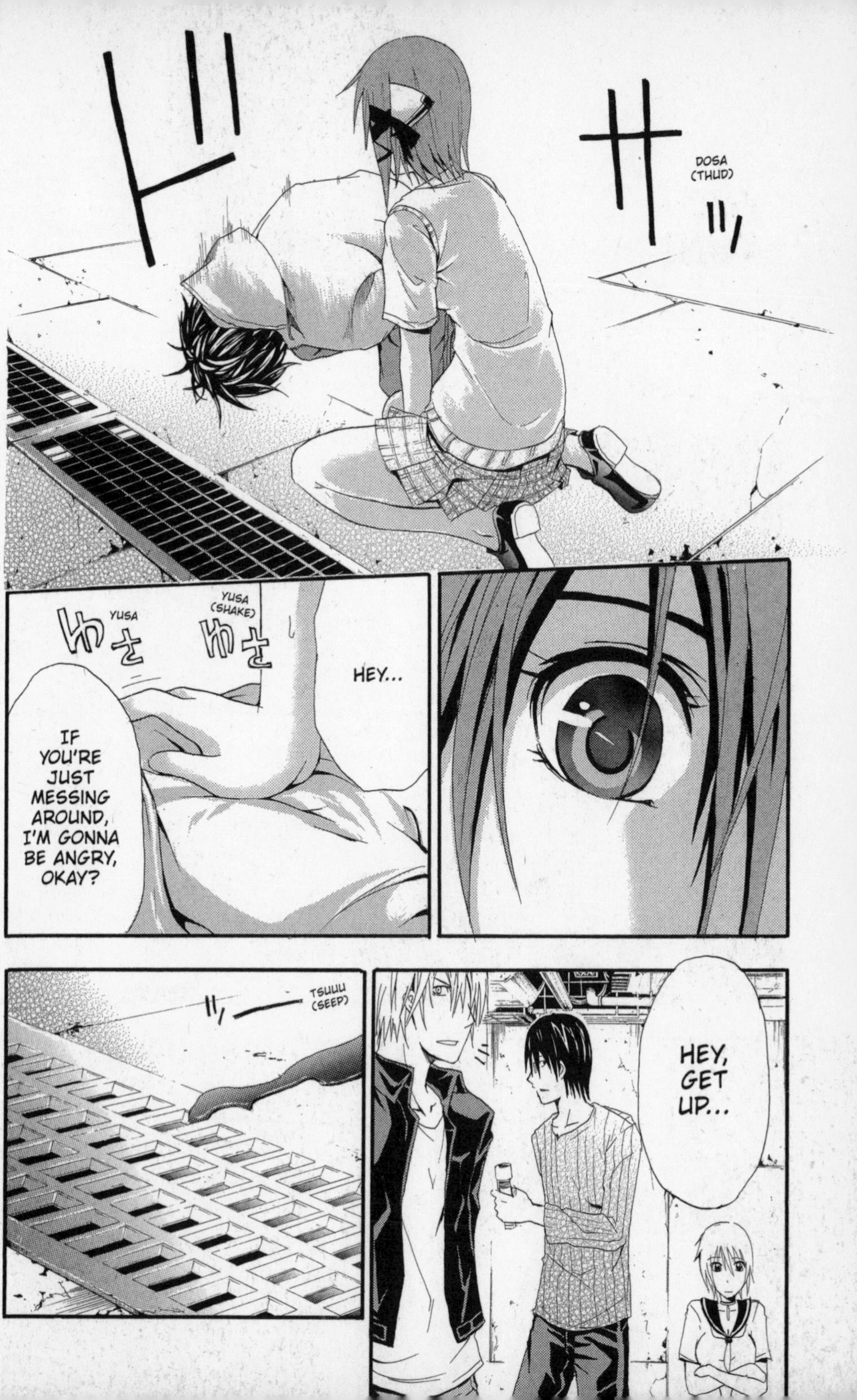
ドサッ
DOSA (THUD)
ゆさ ゆさ
YUSA (SHAKE)
YUSA
HEY...
IF YOU'RE JUST MESSING AROUND, I'M GONNA BE ANGRY, OKAY?
HEY, GET UP...
ツー
TSUUU (SEEP)

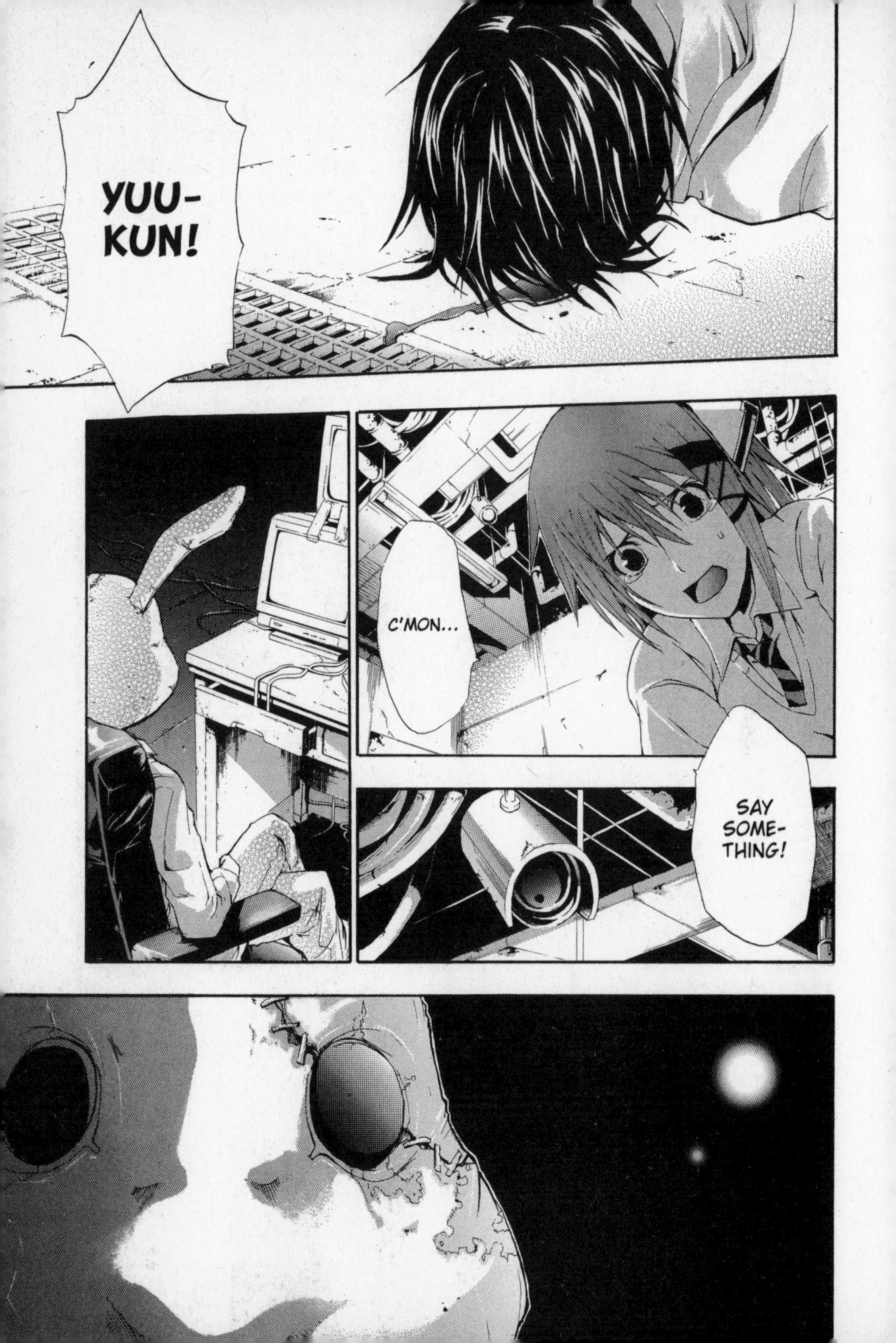
YUU-KUN!
C'MON...
SAY SOMETHING!

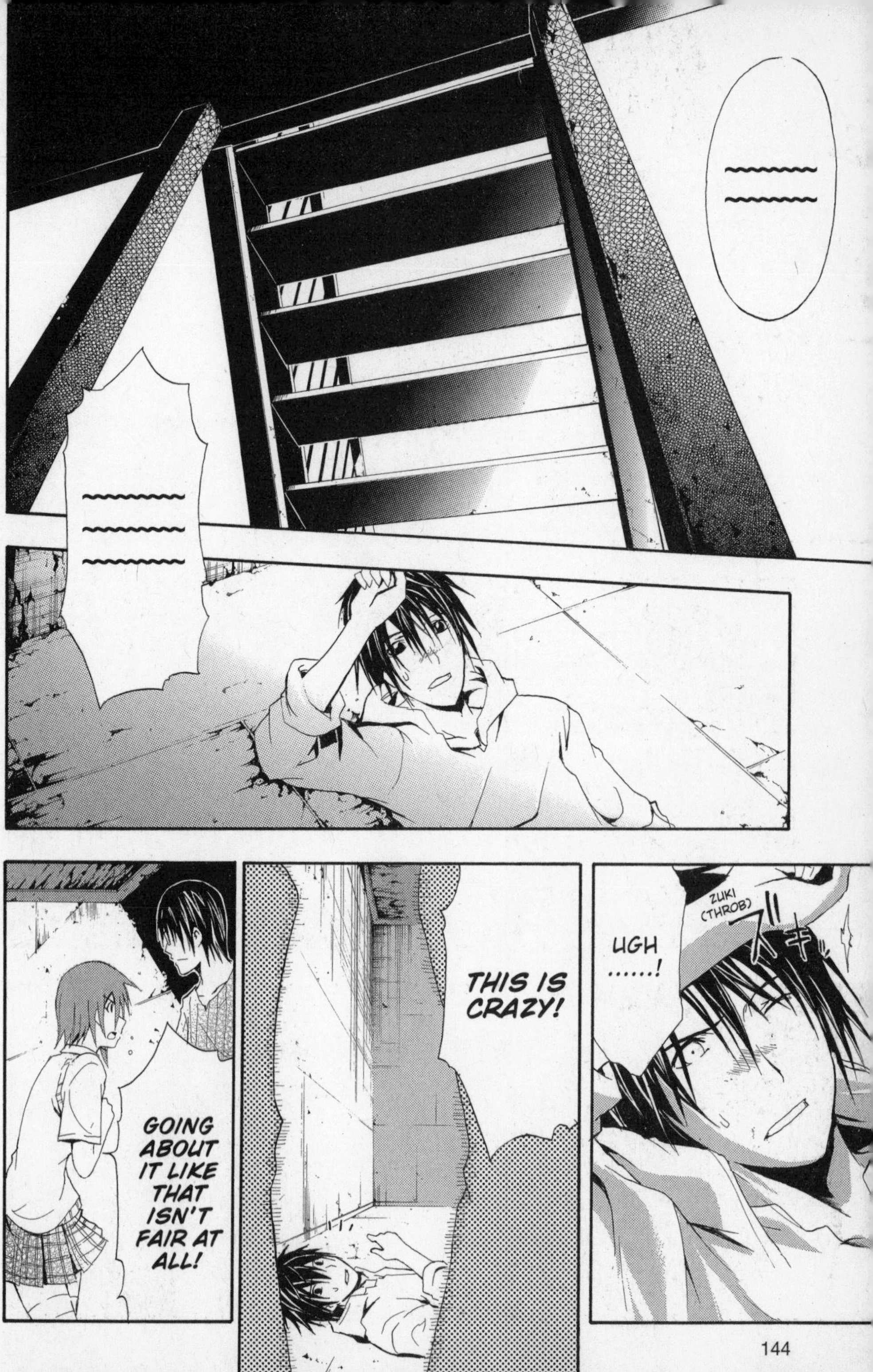
ZUKI (THROB)
UGH ......!
THIS IS CRAZY!
GOING ABOUT IT LIKE THAT ISN'T FAIR AT ALL!

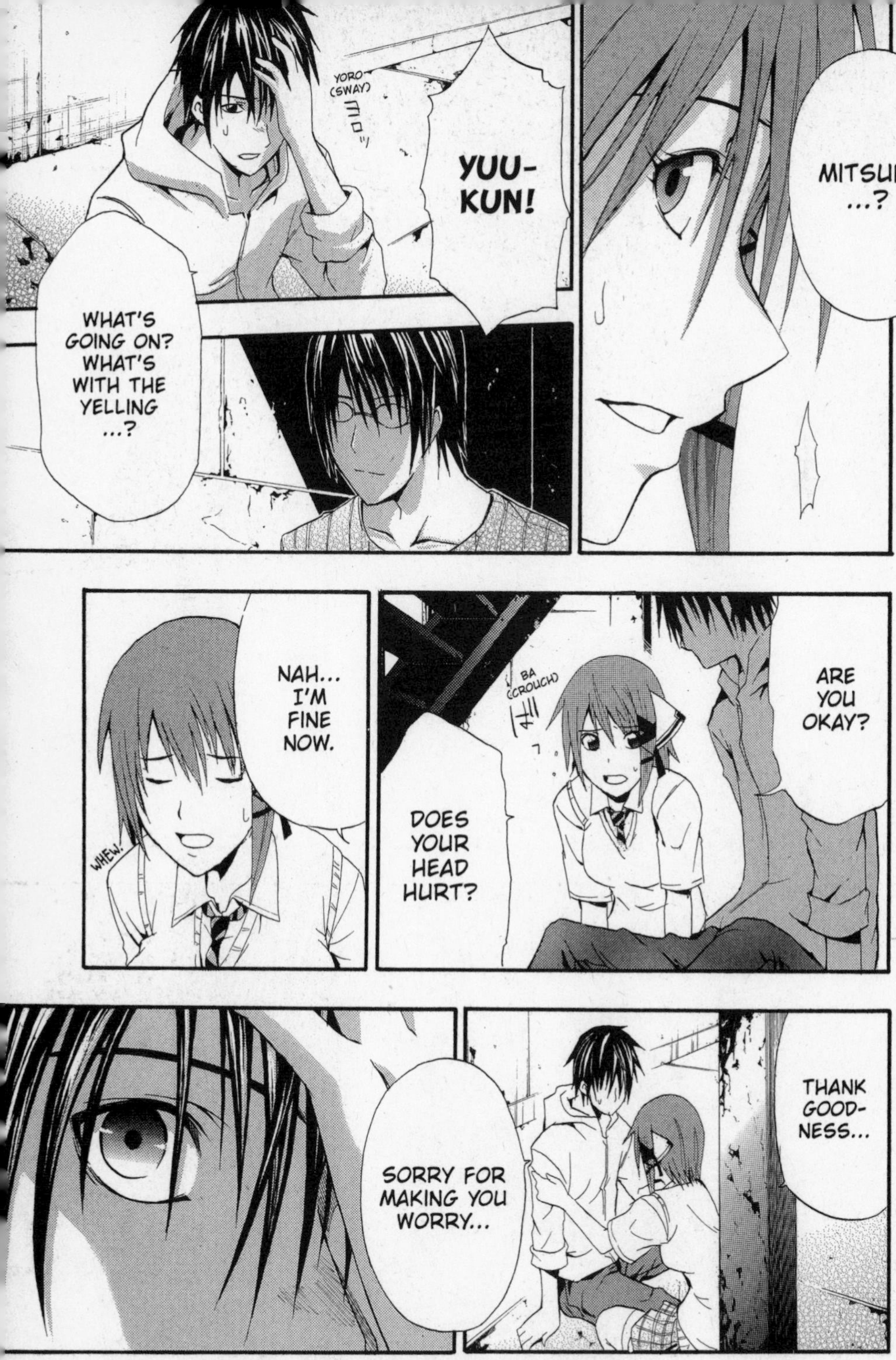
MITSUKI ...?
YORO (SWAY)
YUU-KUN!
WHAT'S GOING ON? WHAT'S WITH THE YELLING ...?
ARE YOU OKAY?
BA (CROUCH)
DOES YOUR HEAD HURT?
NAH... I'M FINE NOW.
WHEW!
THANK GOOD-NESS...
SORRY FOR MAKING YOU WORRY...

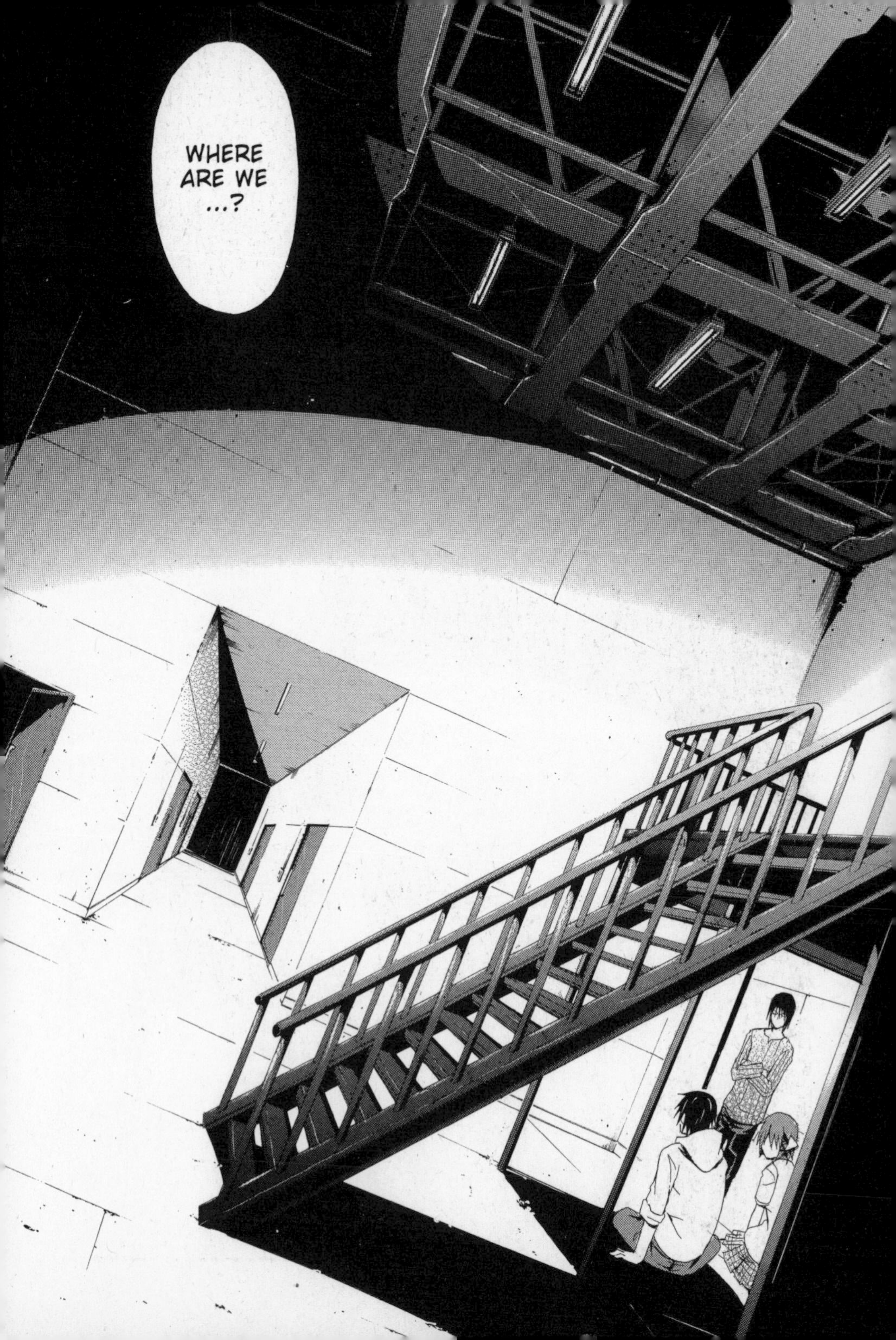
WHERE ARE WE ...?

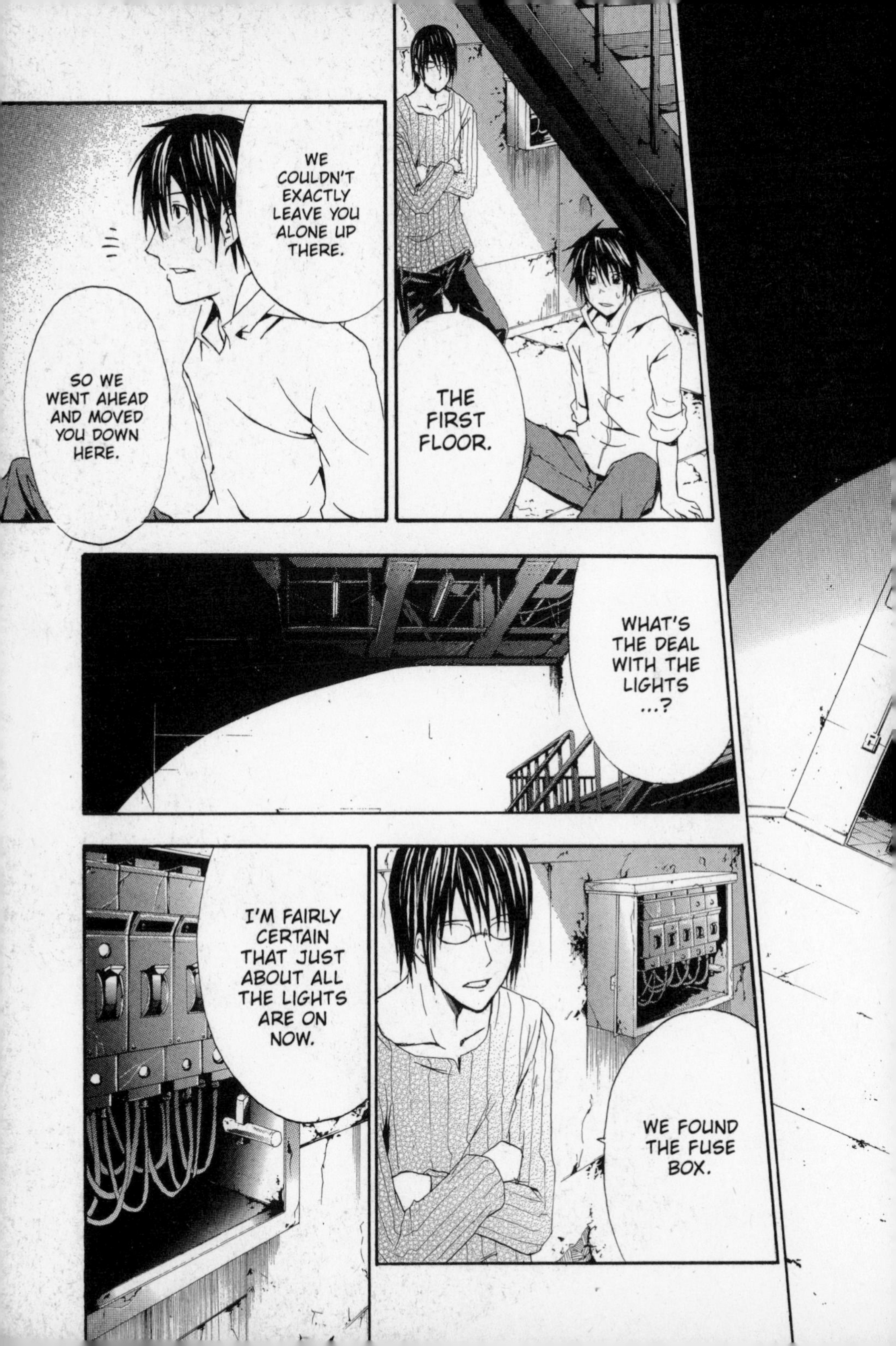
THE FIRST FLOOR.
WE COULDN'T EXACTLY LEAVE YOU ALONE UP THERE.
SO WE WENT AHEAD AND MOVED YOU DOWN HERE.
WHAT'S THE DEAL WITH THE LIGHTS ...?
WE FOUND THE FUSE BOX.
I'M FAIRLY CERTAIN THAT JUST ABOUT ALL THE LIGHTS ARE ON NOW.

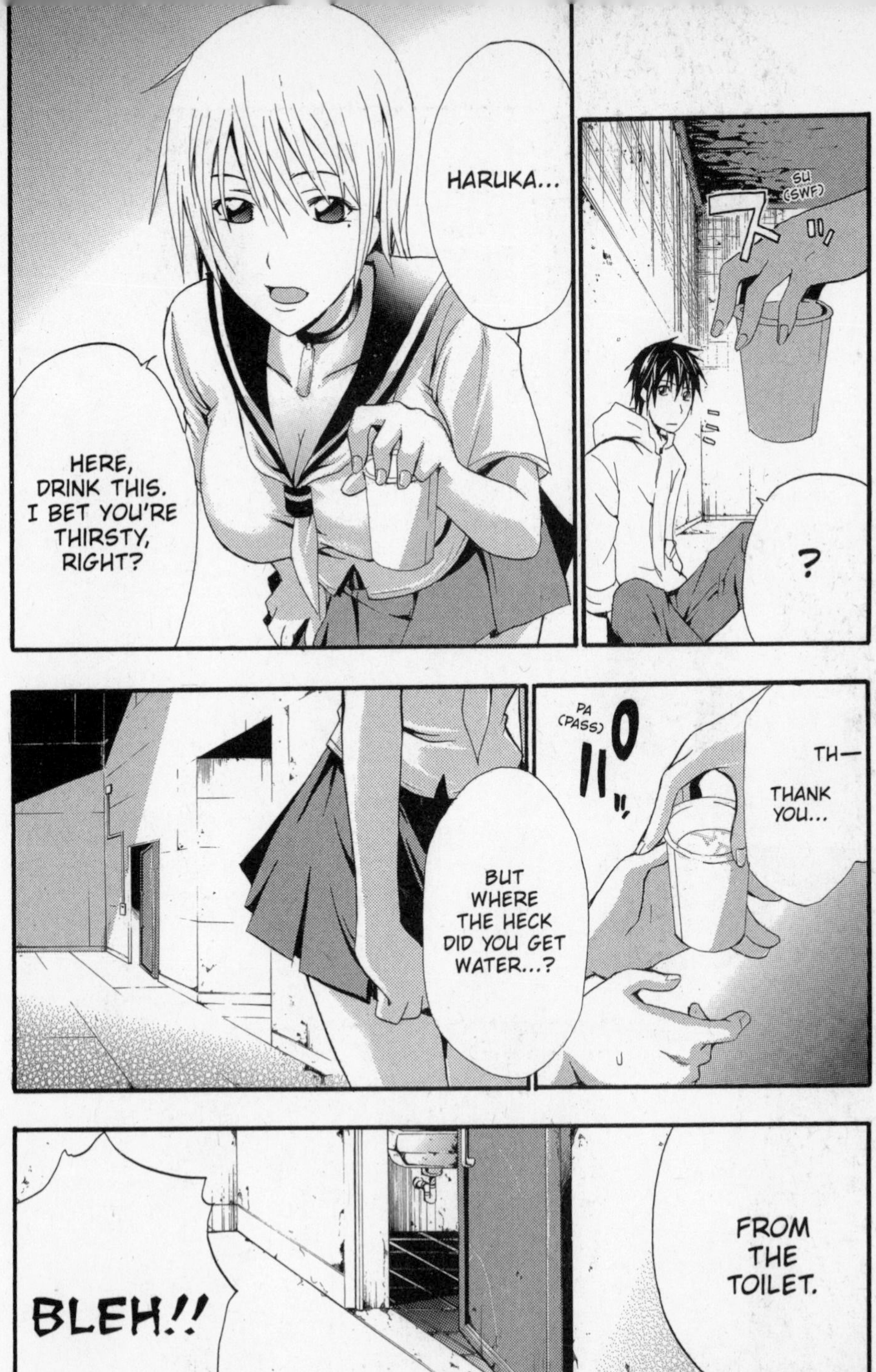
SU (SWF)
?
HARUKA...
HERE, DRINK THIS. I BET YOU'RE THIRSTY, RIGHT?
PA (PASS)
TH— THANK YOU...
BUT WHERE THE HECK DID YOU GET WATER...?
FROM THE TOILET.
BLEH!!

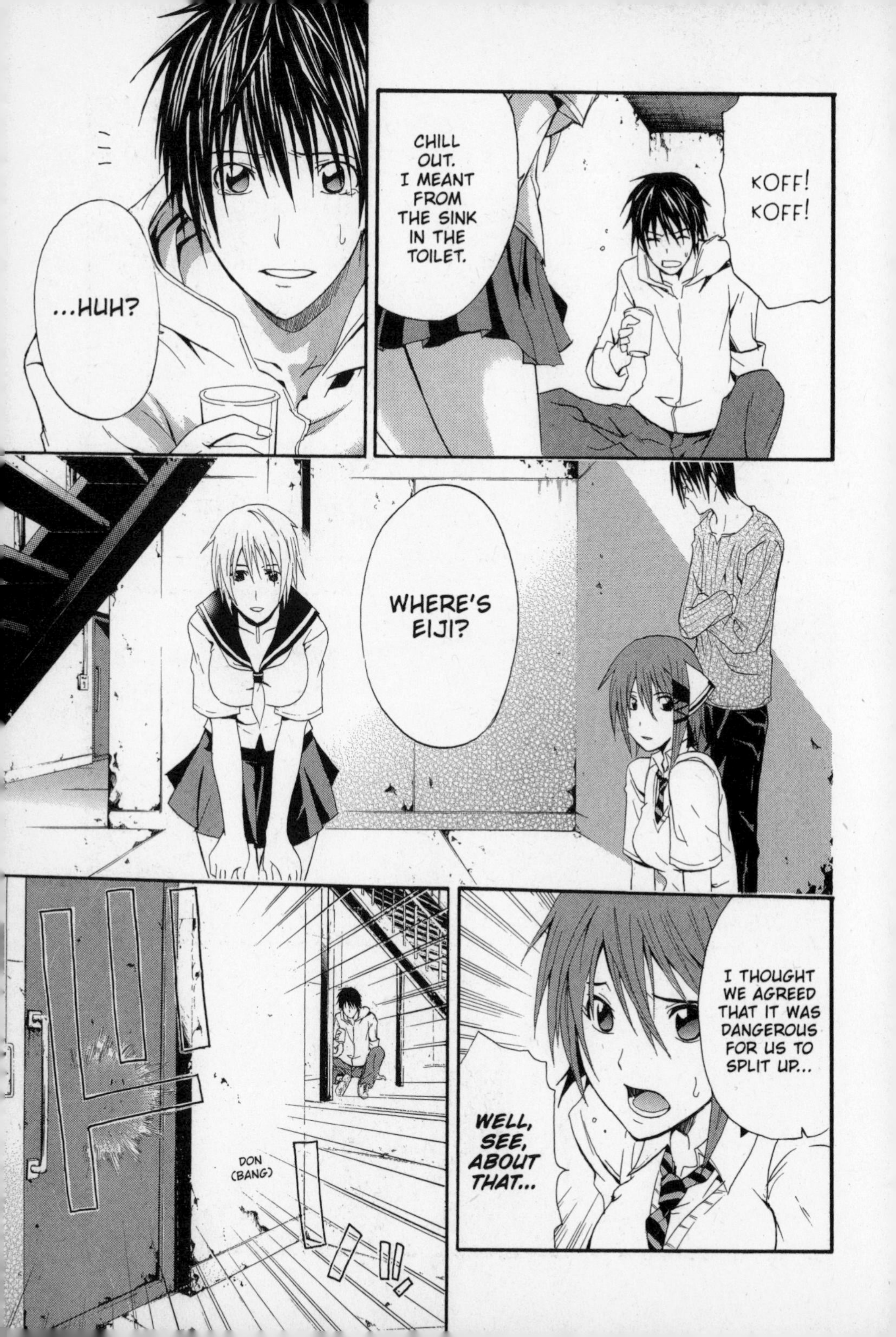
KOFF! KOFF!
CHILL OUT. I MEANT FROM THE SINK IN THE TOILET.
...HUH?
WHERE'S EIJI?
I THOUGHT WE AGREED THAT IT WAS DANGEROUS FOR US TO SPLIT UP...
WELL, SEE, ABOUT THAT...
DON (BANG)

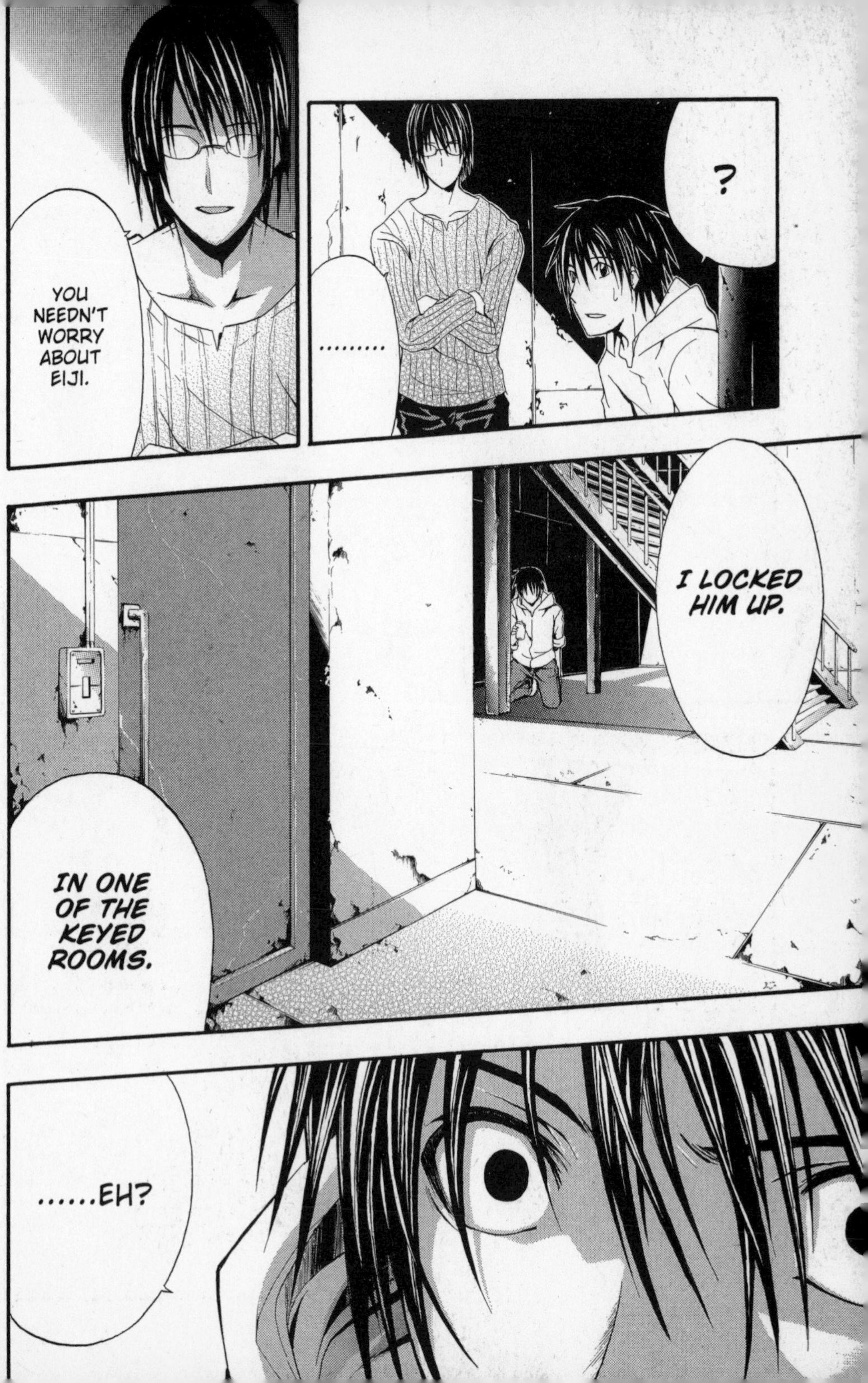
?
....
YOU NEEDN'T WORRY ABOUT EIJI.
I LOCKED HIM UP.
IN ONE OF THE KEYED ROOMS.
......EH?

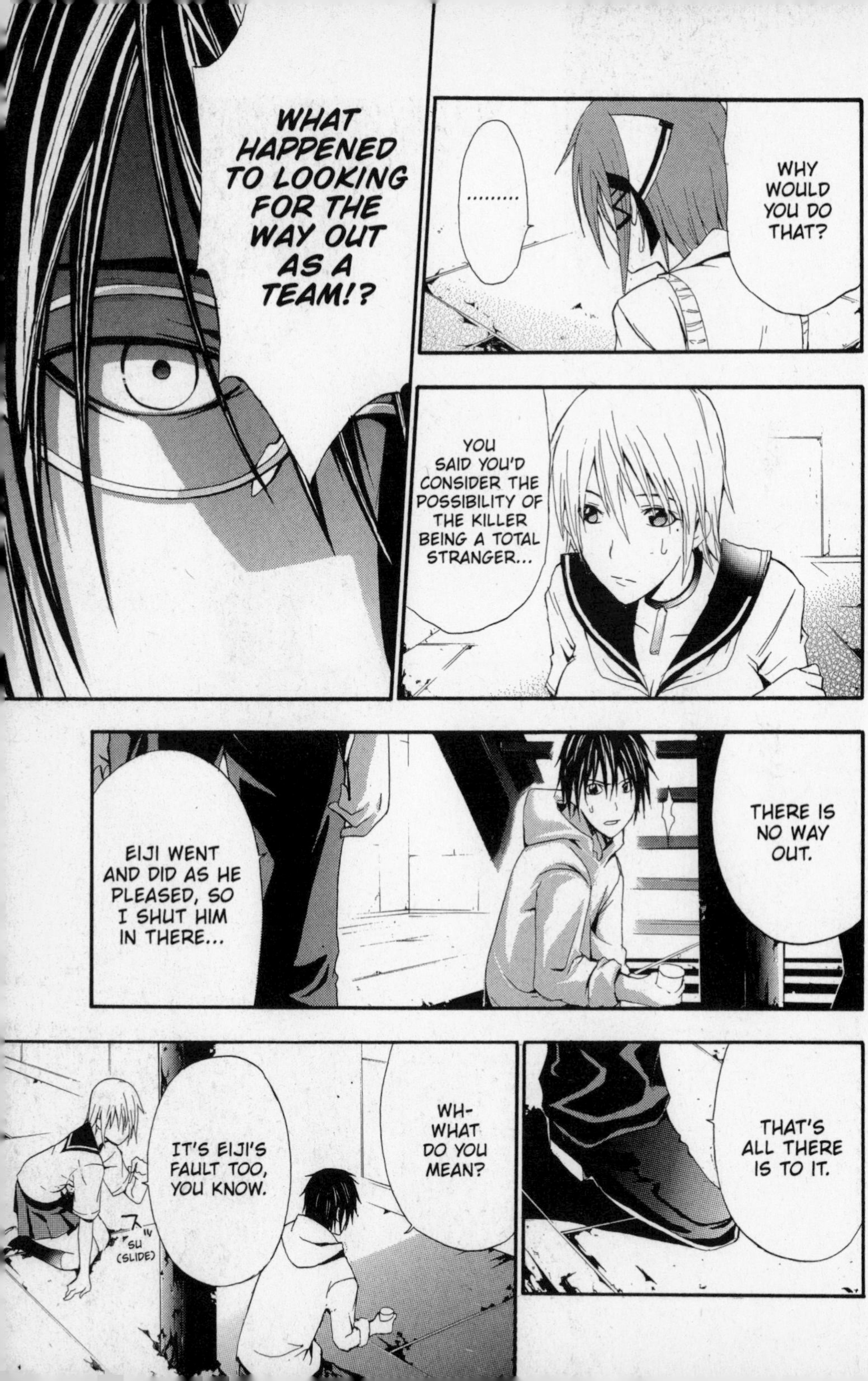
WHY WOULD YOU DO THAT?
....
YOU SAID YOU'D CONSIDER THE POSSIBILITY OF THE KILLER BEING A TOTAL STRANGER...
WHAT HAPPENED TO LOOKING FOR THE WAY OUT AS A TEAM!?
THERE IS NO WAY OUT.
EIJI WENT AND DID AS HE PLEASED, SO I SHUT HIM IN THERE...
THAT'S ALL THERE IS TO IT.
WH-WHAT DO YOU MEAN?
IT'S EIJI'S FAULT TOO, YOU KNOW.
SU (SLIDE)

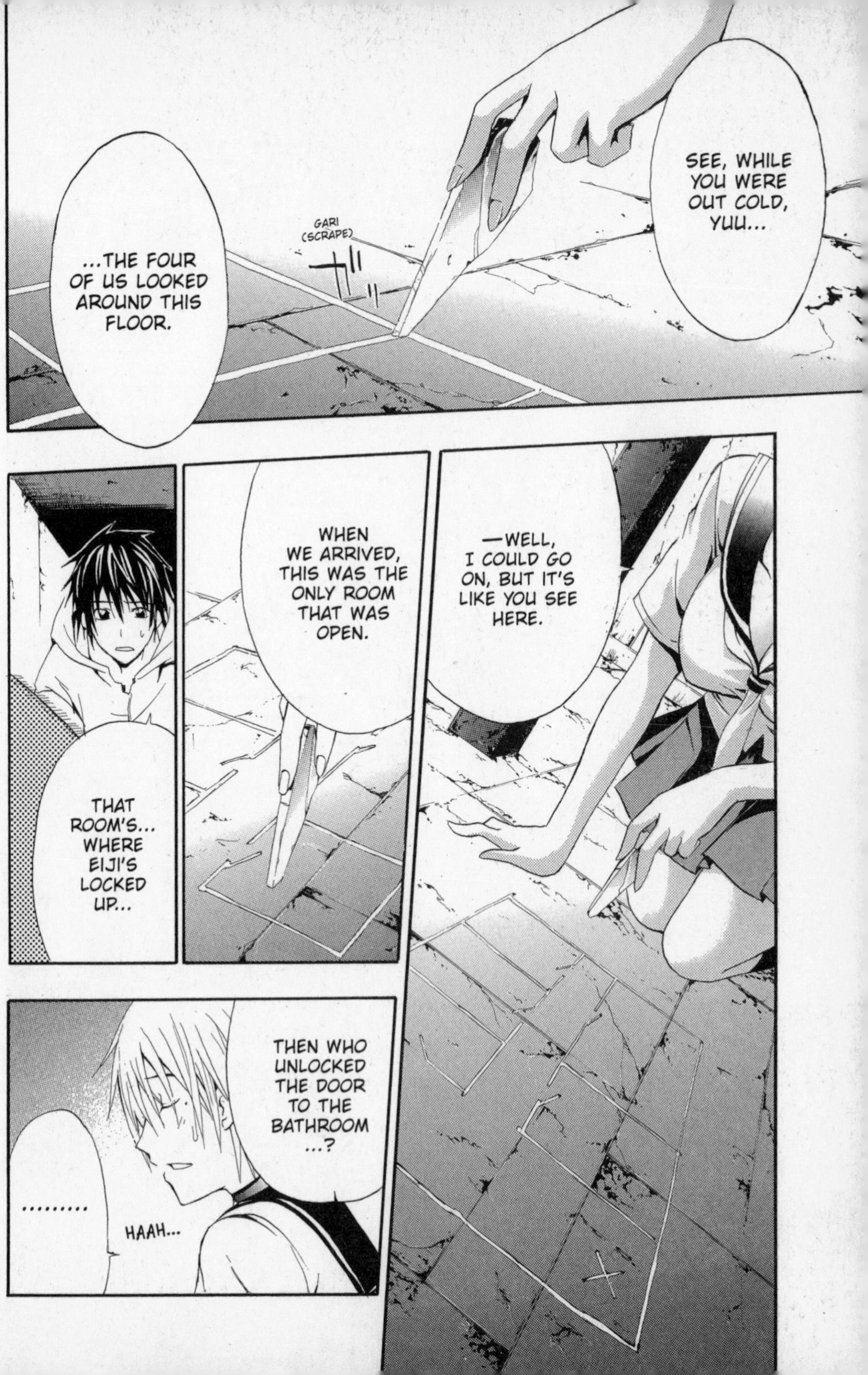
SEE, WHILE YOU WERE OUT COLD, YUU...
GARI (SCRAPE)
...THE FOUR OF US LOOKED AROUND THIS FLOOR.
—WELL, I COULD GO ON, BUT IT'S LIKE YOU SEE HERE.
WHEN WE ARRIVED, THIS WAS THE ONLY ROOM THAT WAS OPEN.
THAT ROOM'S... WHERE EIJI'S LOCKED UP...
THEN WHO UNLOCKED THE DOOR TO THE BATHROOM ...?
....
HAAH...

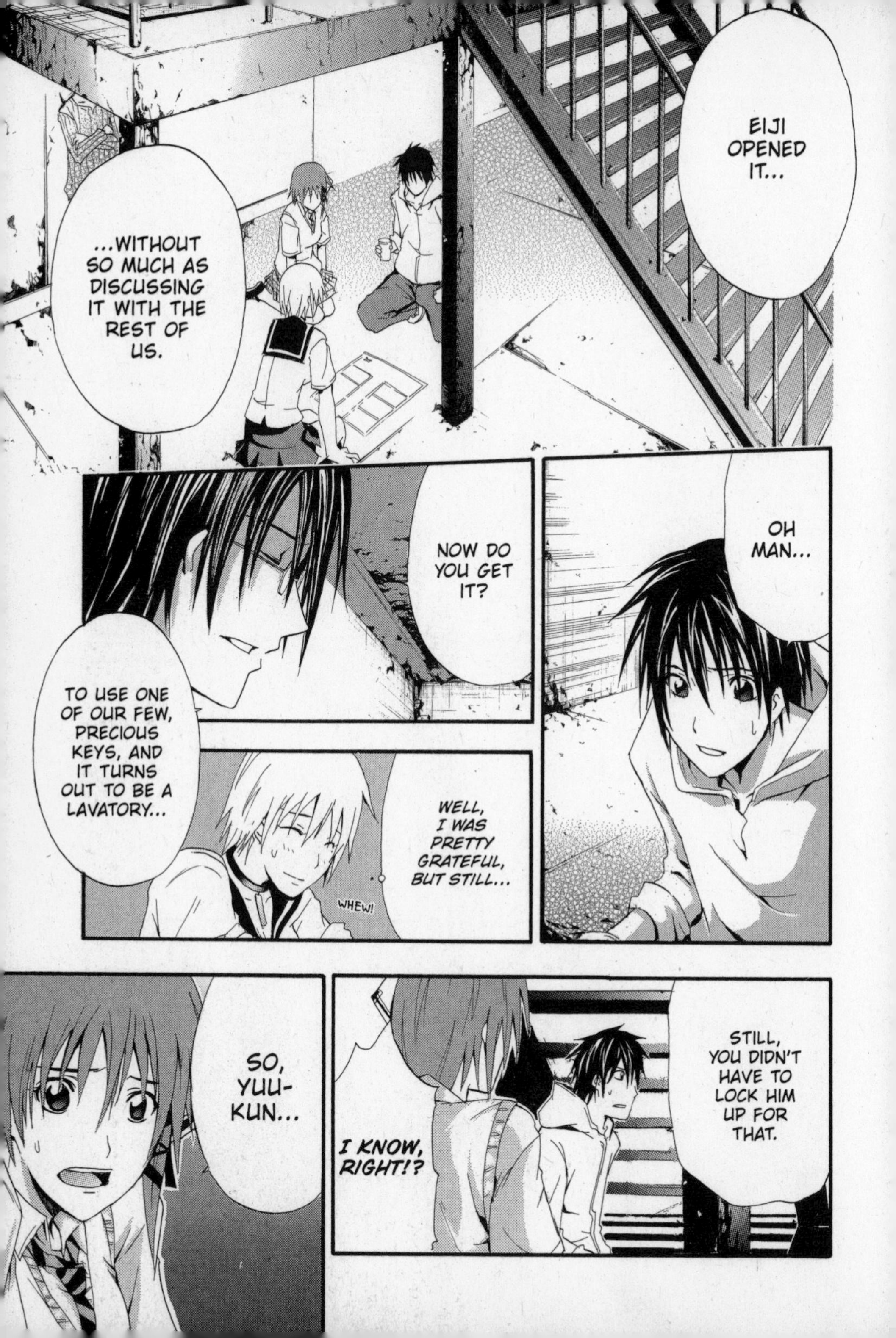

EIJI OPENED IT...
...WITHOUT SO MUCH AS DISCUSSING IT WITH THE REST OF US.
OH MAN...
NOW DO YOU GET IT?
TO USE ONE OF OUR FEW, PRECIOUS KEYS, AND IT TURNS OUT TO BE A LAVATORY...
WELL, I WAS PRETTY GRATEFUL, BUT STILL...
WHEW!
STILL, YOU DIDN'T HAVE TO LOCK HIM UP FOR THAT.
I KNOW, RIGHT!?
SO, YUU-KUN...

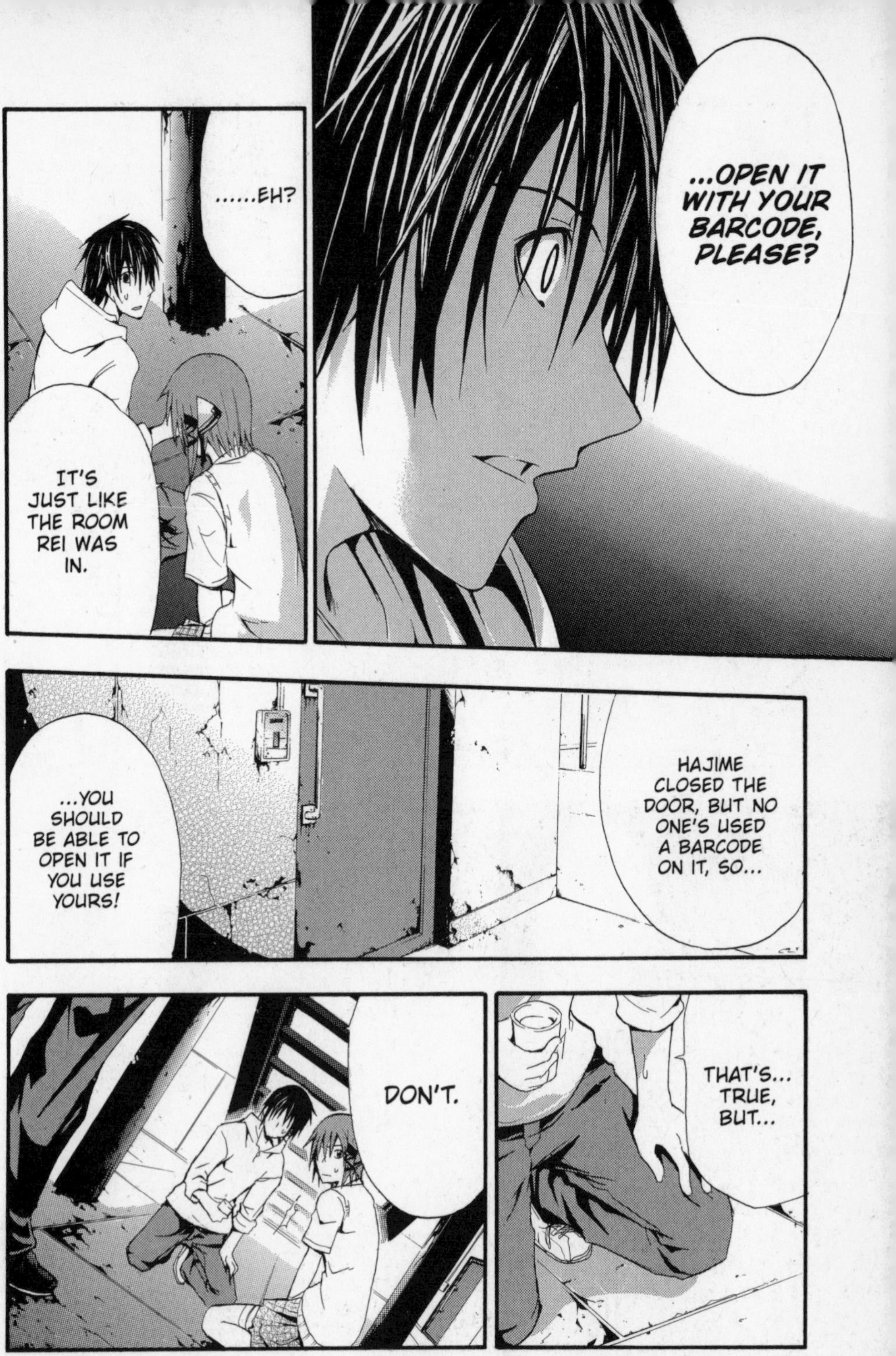
...OPEN IT WITH YOUR BARCODE, PLEASE?
......EH?
IT'S JUST LIKE THE ROOM REI WAS IN.
HAJIME CLOSED THE DOOR, BUT NO ONE'S USED A BARCODE ON IT, SO...
...YOU SHOULD BE ABLE TO OPEN IT IF YOU USE YOURS!
THAT'S... TRUE, BUT...
DON'T.

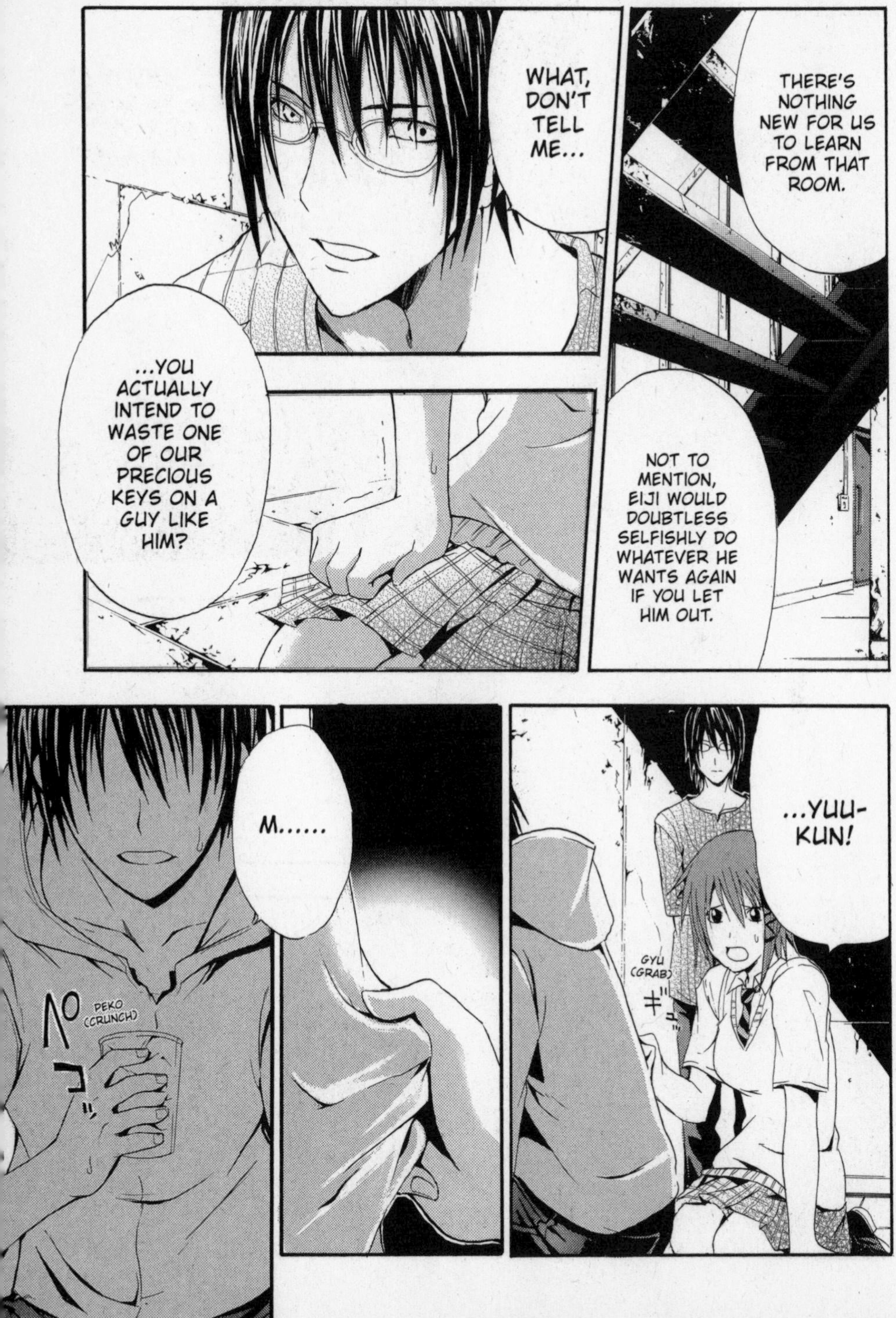
THERE'S NOTHING NEW FOR US TO LEARN FROM THAT ROOM.
NOT TO MENTION, EIJI WOULD DOUBTLESS SELFISHLY DO WHATEVER HE WANTS AGAIN IF YOU LET HIM OUT.
WHAT, DON'T TELL ME...
...YOU ACTUALLY INTEND TO WASTE ONE OF OUR PRECIOUS KEYS ON A GUY LIKE HIM?
...YUU-KUN!
GYU (GRAB)
M......
PEKO (CRUNCH)

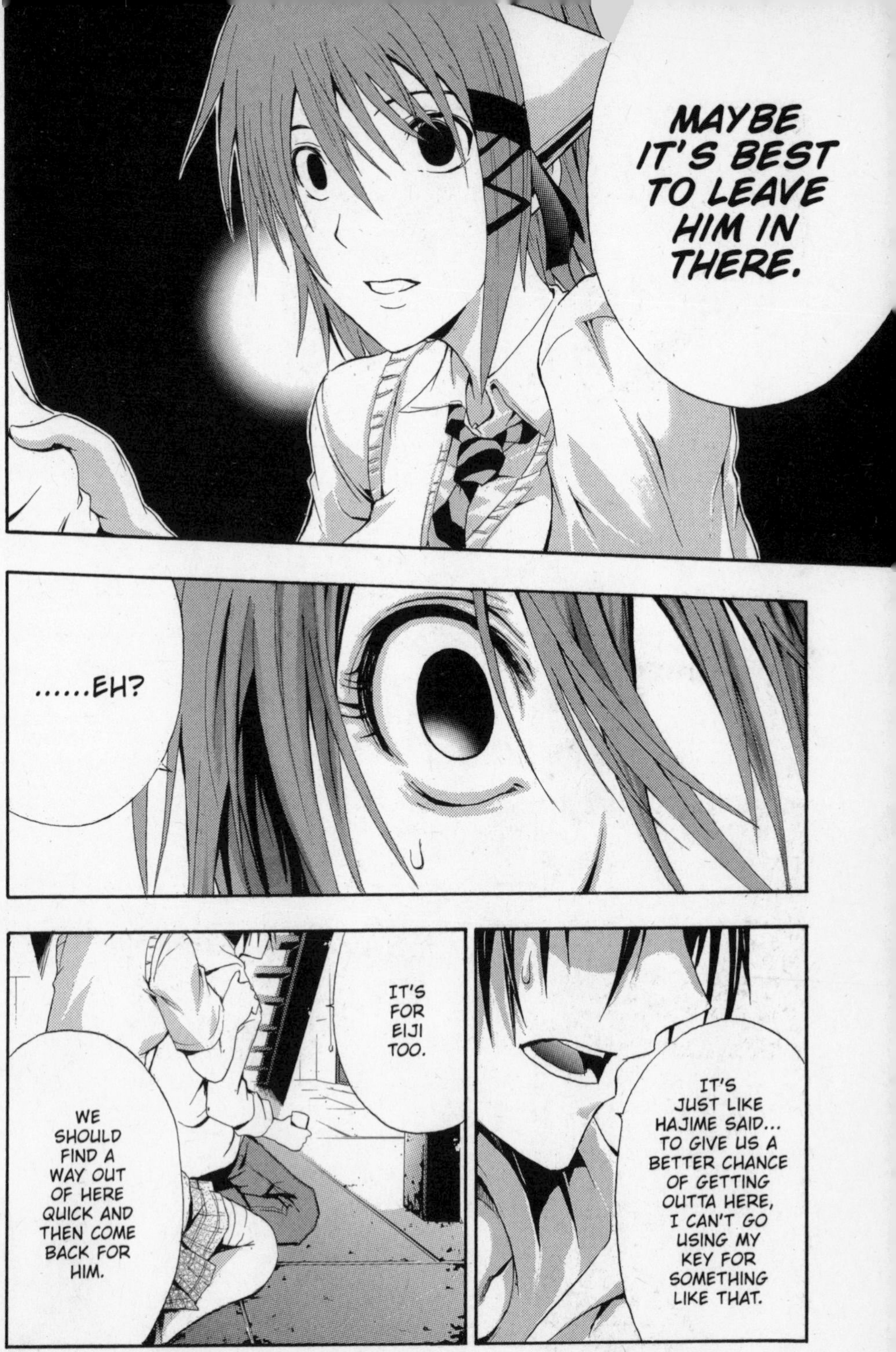
MAYBE IT'S BEST TO LEAVE HIM IN THERE.
......EH?
IT'S JUST LIKE HAJIME SAID... TO GIVE US A BETTER CHANCE OF GETTING OUTTA HERE, I CAN'T GO USING MY KEY FOR SOMETHING LIKE THAT.
IT'S FOR EIJI TOO.
WE SHOULD FIND A WAY OUT OF HERE QUICK AND THEN COME BACK FOR HIM.

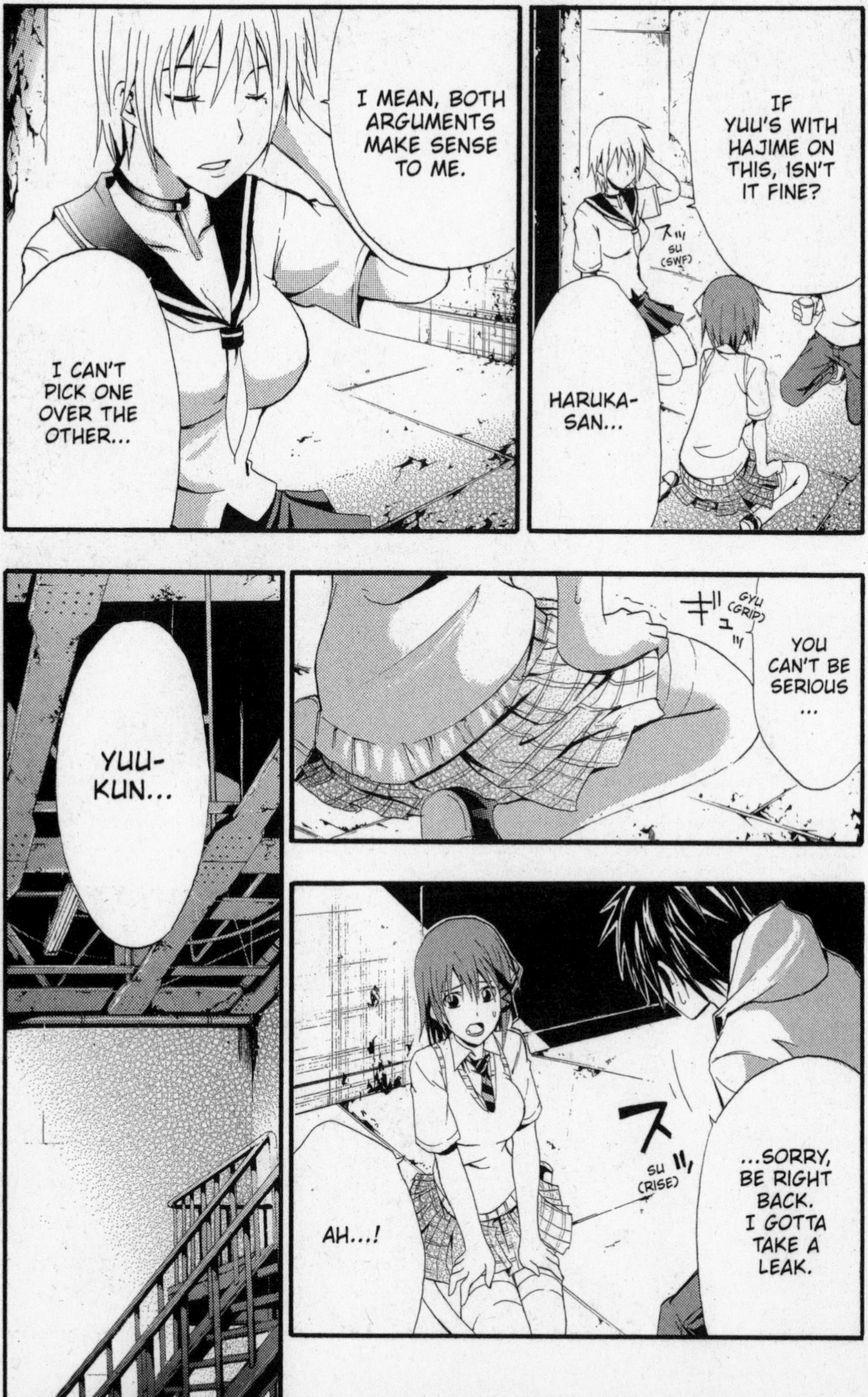
IF YUU'S WITH HAJIME ON THIS, ISN'T IT FINE?
スッ SU (SWF)
HARUKA-SAN...
I MEAN, BOTH ARGUMENTS MAKE SENSE TO ME.
I CAN'T PICK ONE OVER THE OTHER...
ギュッ GYU (GRIP)
YOU CAN'T BE SERIOUS ...
...SORRY, BE RIGHT BACK. I GOTTA TAKE A LEAK.
スッ SU (RISE)
AH...!
YUU-KUN...

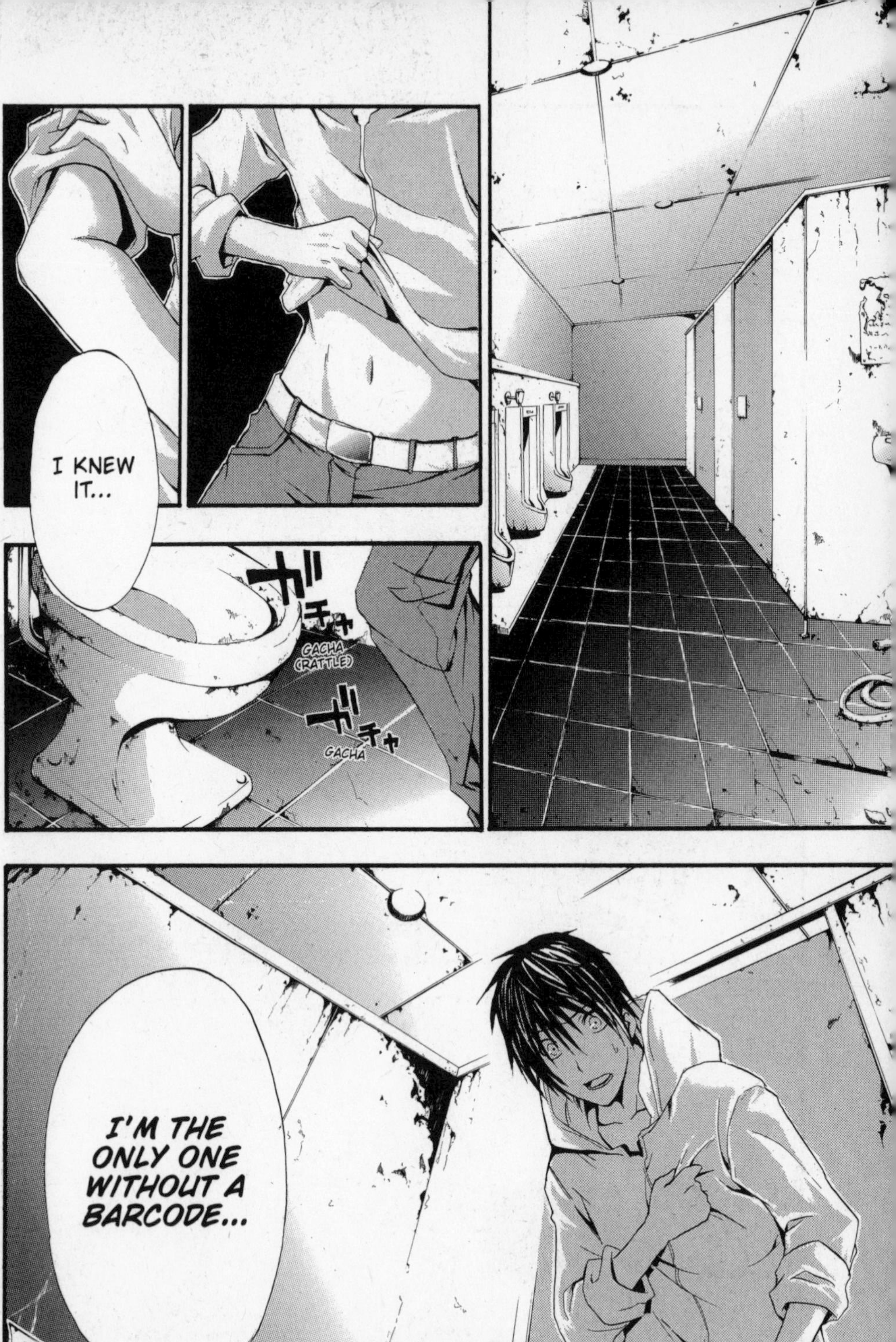
I KNEW IT...
ガチャ
GACHA (RATTLE)
ガチャ
GACHA
I'M THE ONLY ONE WITHOUT A BARCODE...

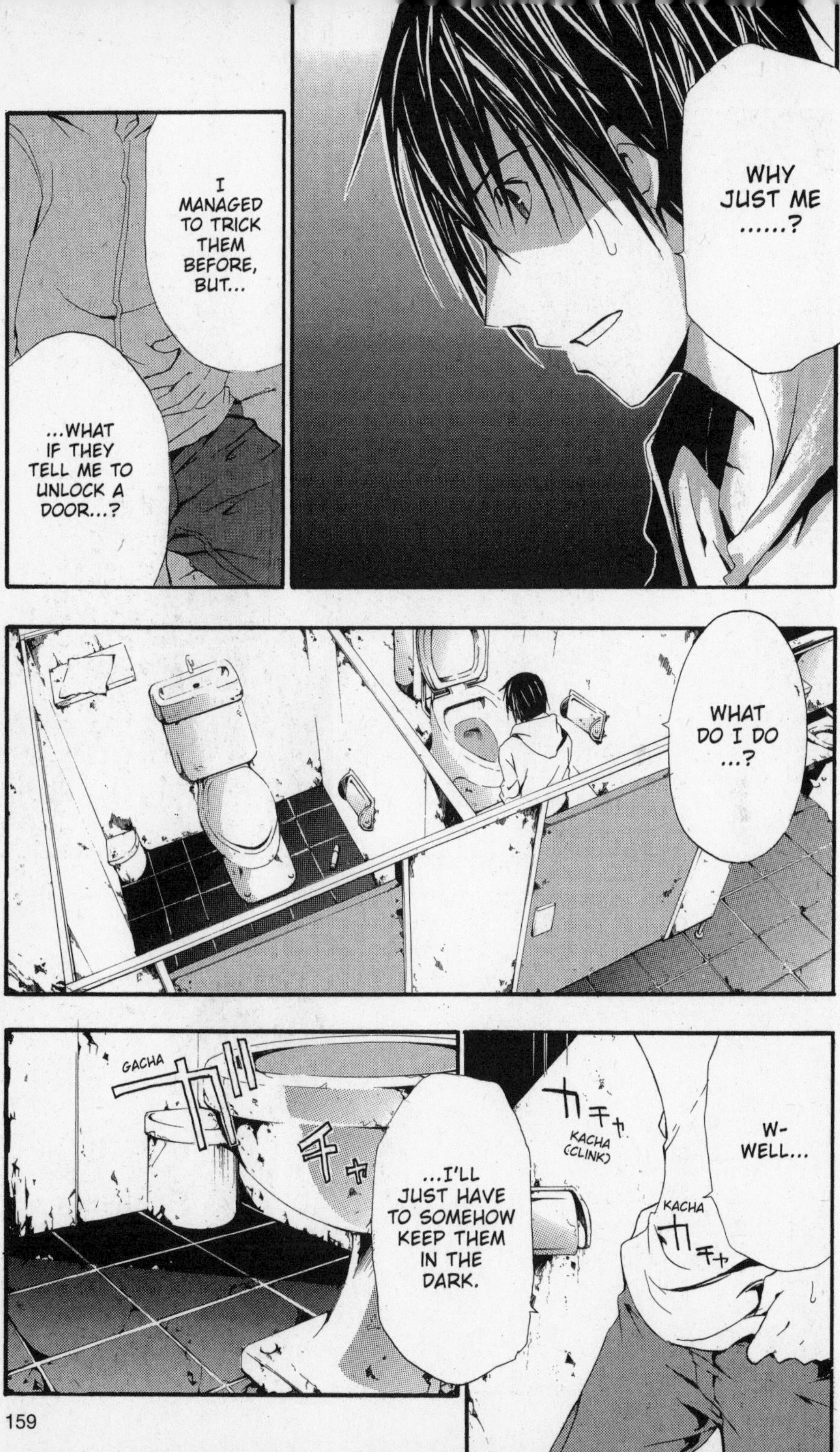
WHY JUST ME ......?
I MANAGED TO TRICK THEM BEFORE, BUT...
...WHAT IF THEY TELL ME TO UNLOCK A DOOR...?
WHAT DO I DO ...?
W-WELL...
カチャ
KACHA (CLINK)
カチャ
KACHA
...I'LL JUST HAVE TO SOMEHOW KEEP THEM IN THE DARK.
ガチャ
GACHA

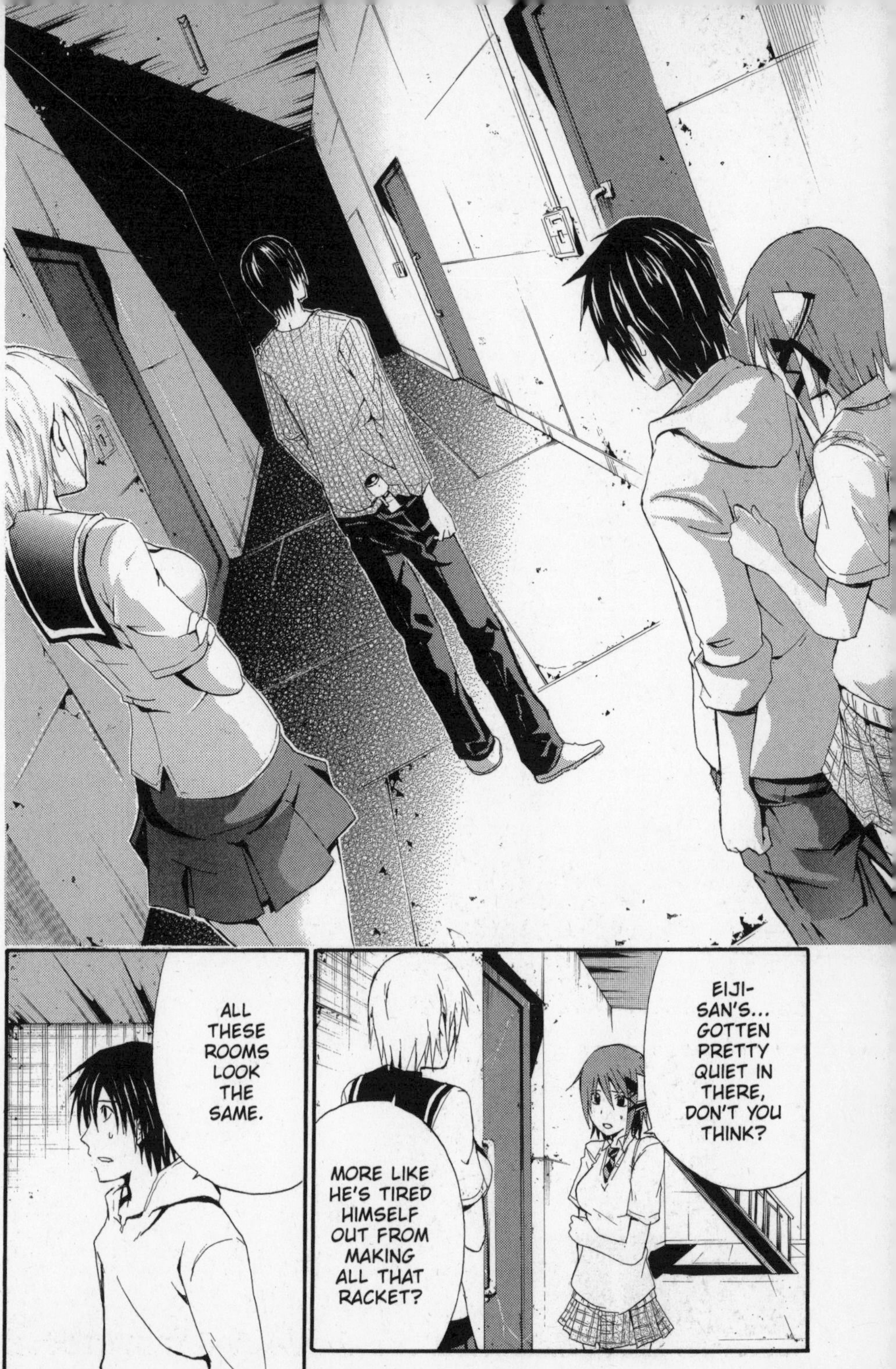
EIJI-SAN'S... GOTTEN PRETTY QUIET IN THERE, DON'T YOU THINK?
MORE LIKE HE'S TIRED HIMSELF OUT FROM MAKING ALL THAT RACKET?
ALL THESE ROOMS LOOK THE SAME.

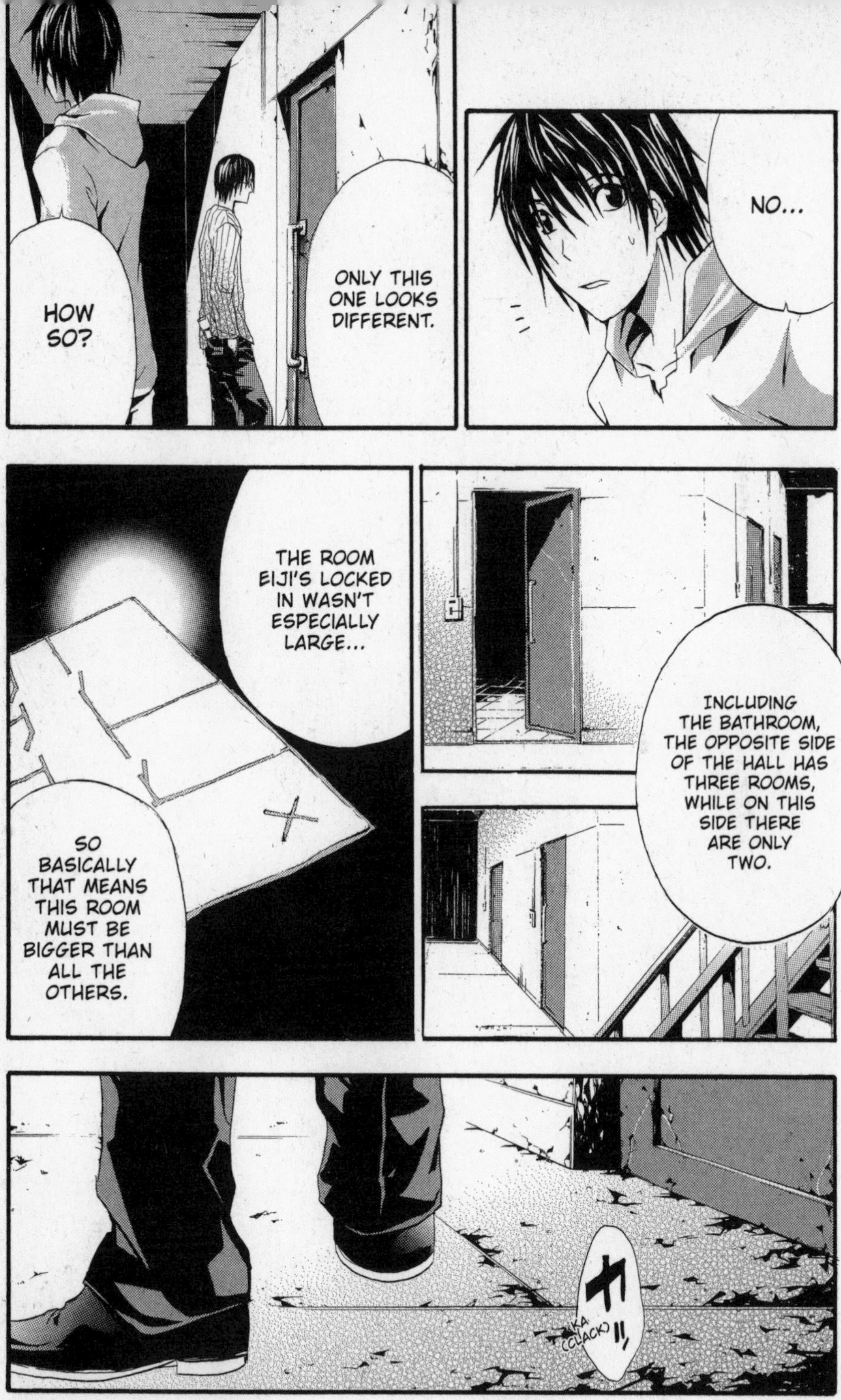
NO...
ONLY THIS ONE LOOKS DIFFERENT.
HOW SO?
INCLUDING THE BATHROOM, THE OPPOSITE SIDE OF THE HALL HAS THREE ROOMS, WHILE ON THIS SIDE THERE ARE ONLY TWO.
THE ROOM EIJI'S LOCKED IN WASN'T ESPECIALLY LARGE...
SO BASICALLY THAT MEANS THIS ROOM MUST BE BIGGER THAN ALL THE OTHERS.
KA (CLACK)

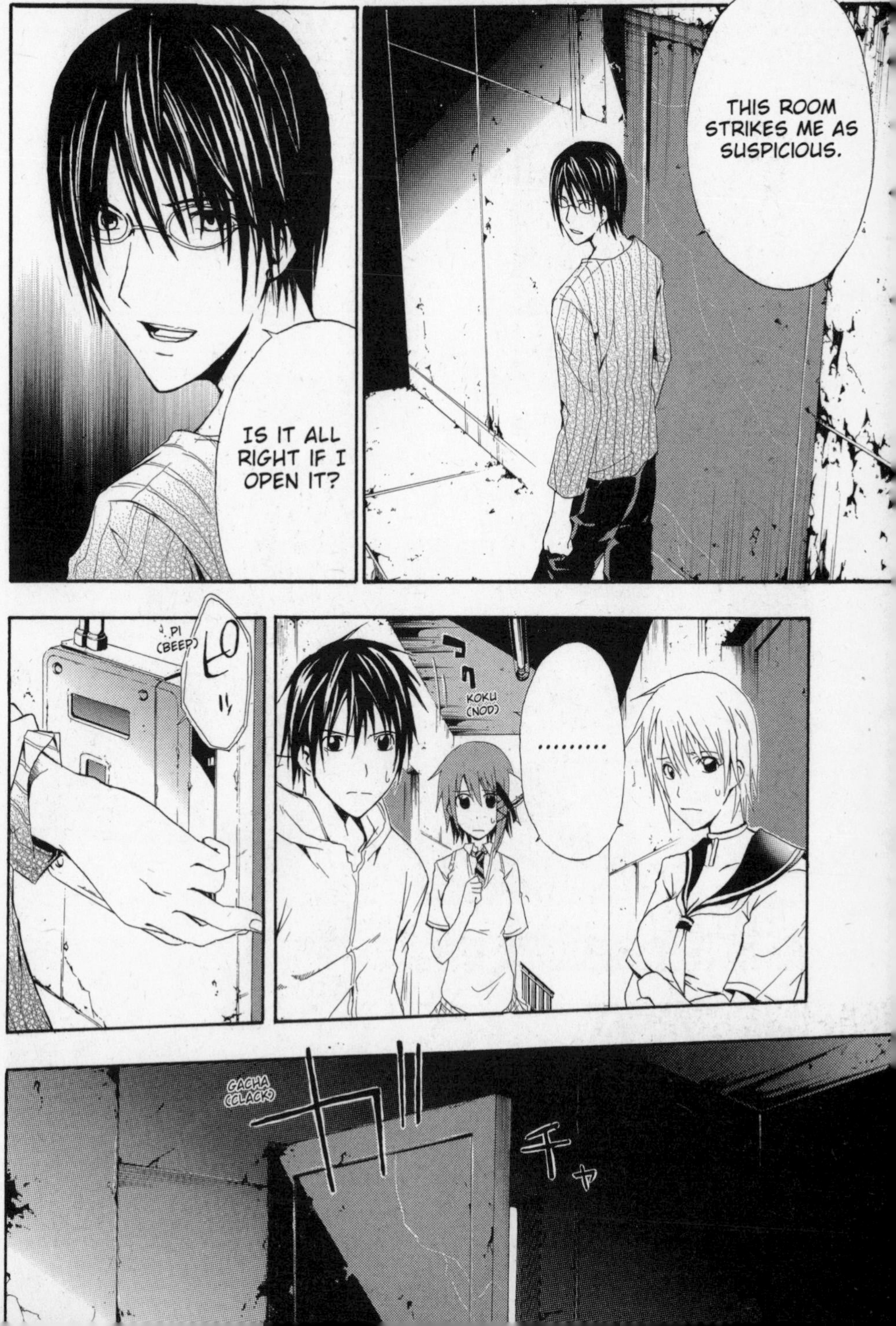
THIS ROOM STRIKES ME AS SUSPICIOUS.
IS IT ALL RIGHT IF I OPEN IT?
KOKU (NOD)
....
PI (BEEP)
GACHA (CLACK)

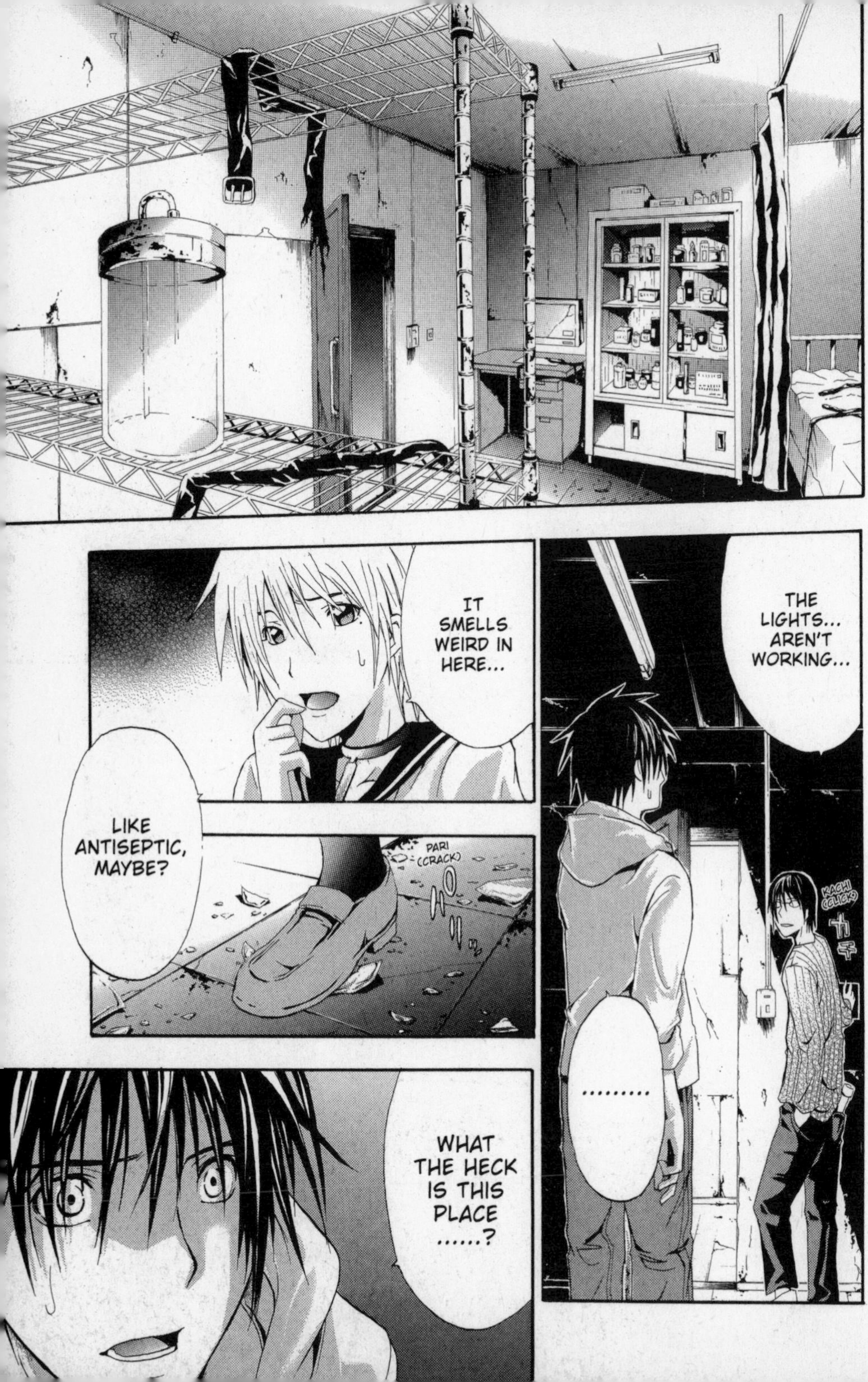
THE LIGHTS... AREN'T WORKING...
KACHI (CLICK)
....
IT SMELLS WEIRD IN HERE...
LIKE ANTISEPTIC, MAYBE?
PARI (CRACK)
WHAT THE HECK IS THIS PLACE ......?

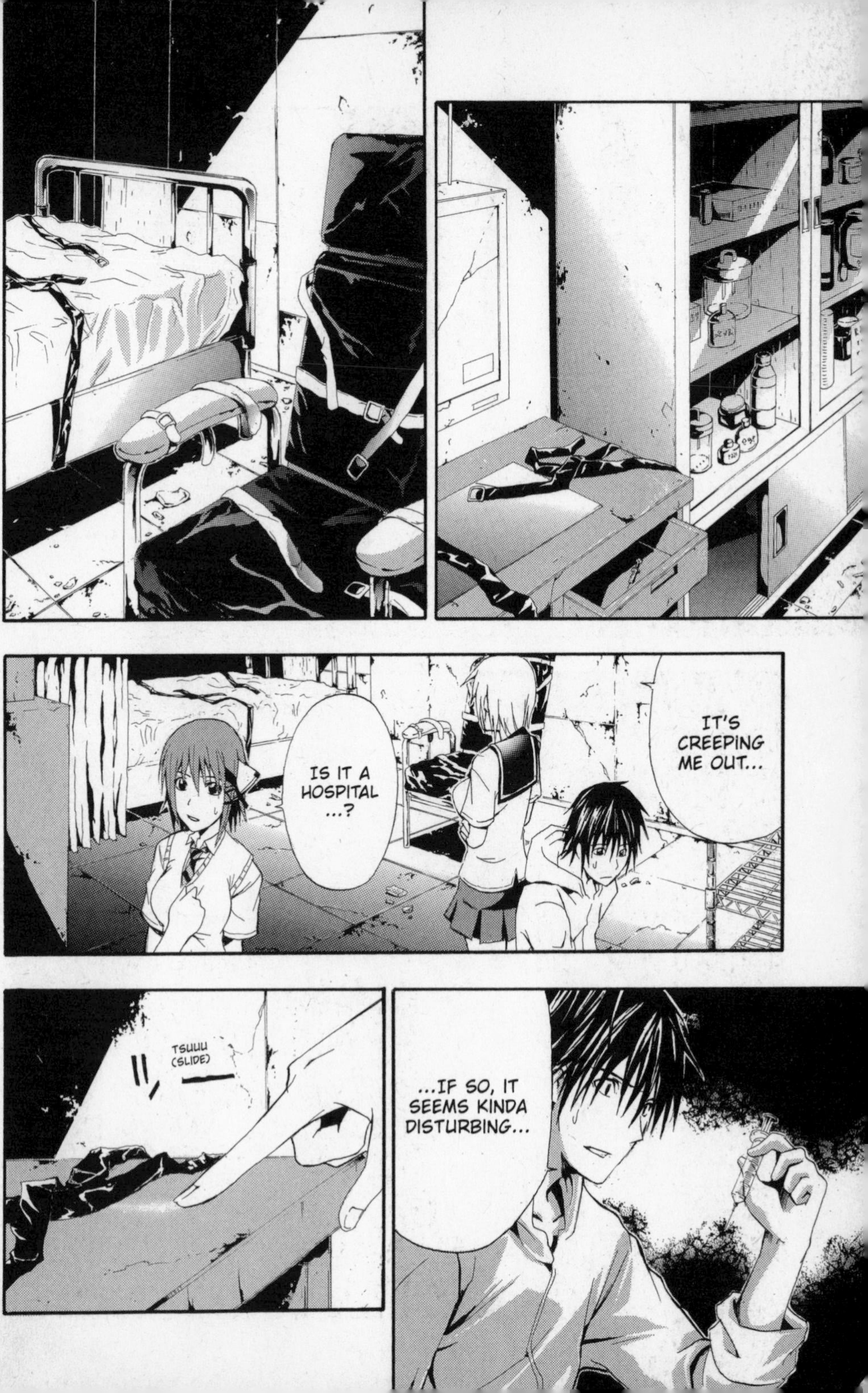
IT'S CREEPING ME OUT...
IS IT A HOSPITAL ...?
...IF SO, IT SEEMS KINDA DISTURBING...
TSUUU (SLIDE)

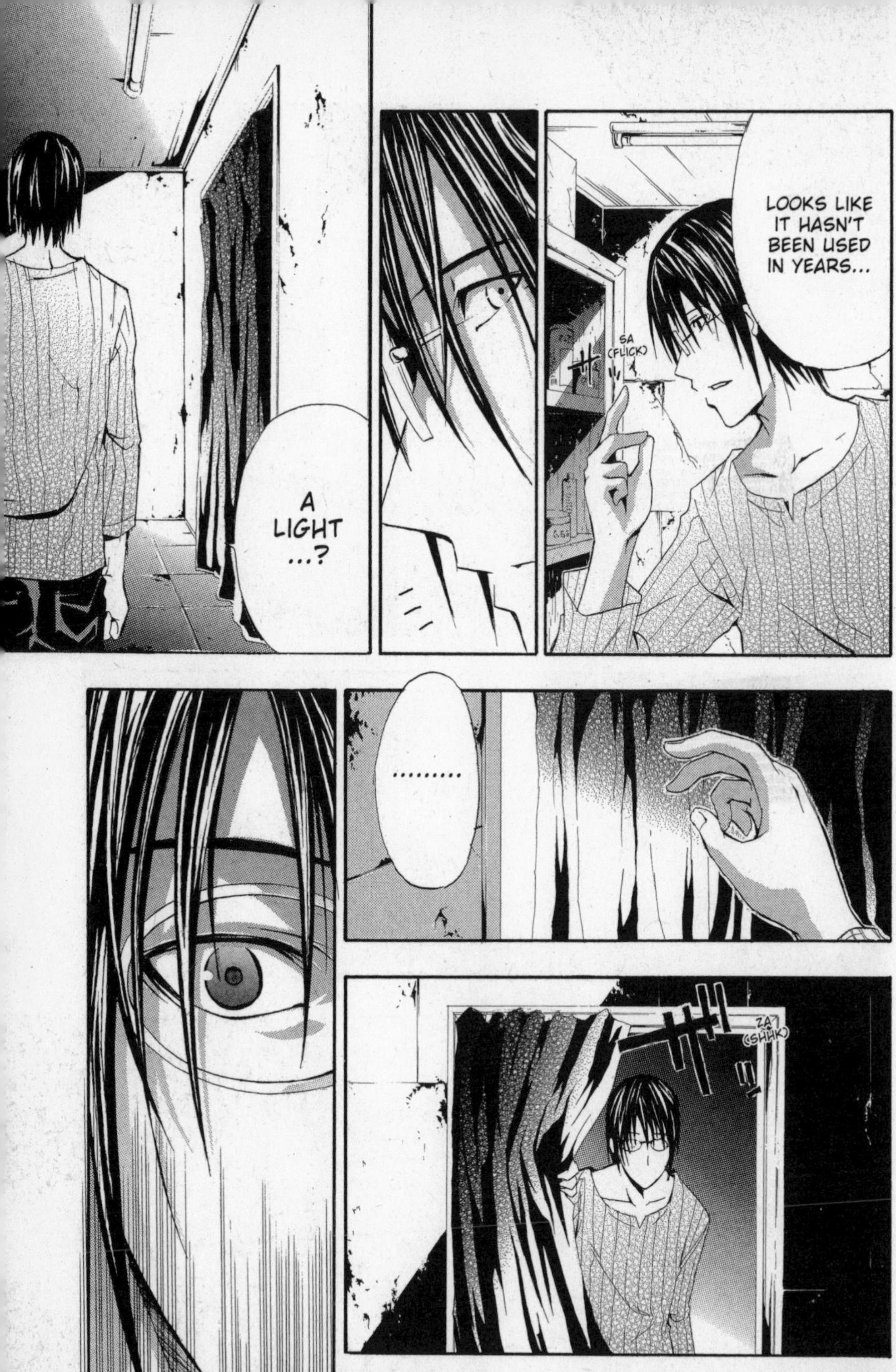
LOOKS LIKE IT HASN'T BEEN USED IN YEARS...
SA (FLICK)
A LIGHT ...?
....
ZA (SHHK)

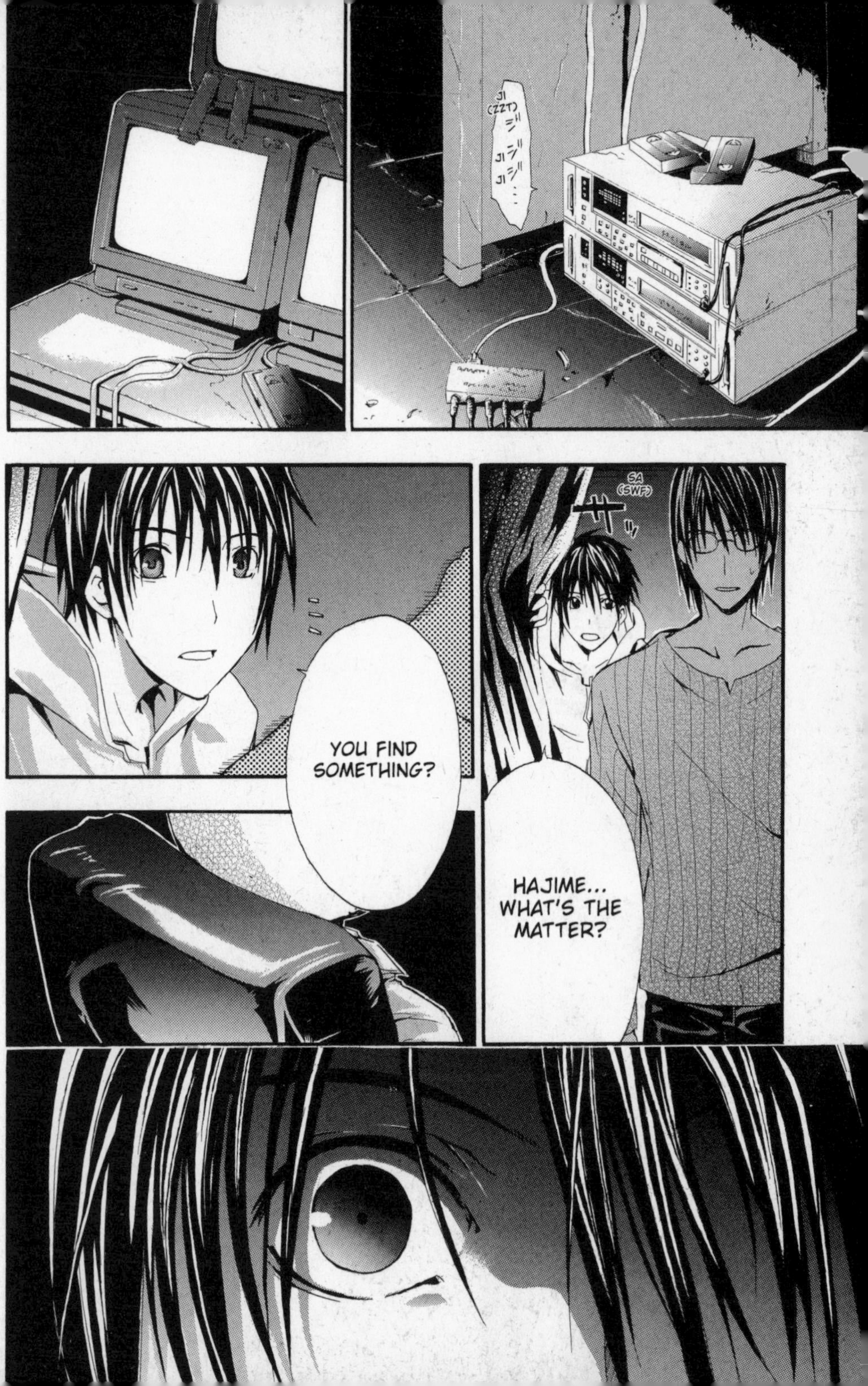
JI (ZZT) JI JI
SA (SWF)
HAJIME... WHAT'S THE MATTER?
YOU FIND SOMETHING?

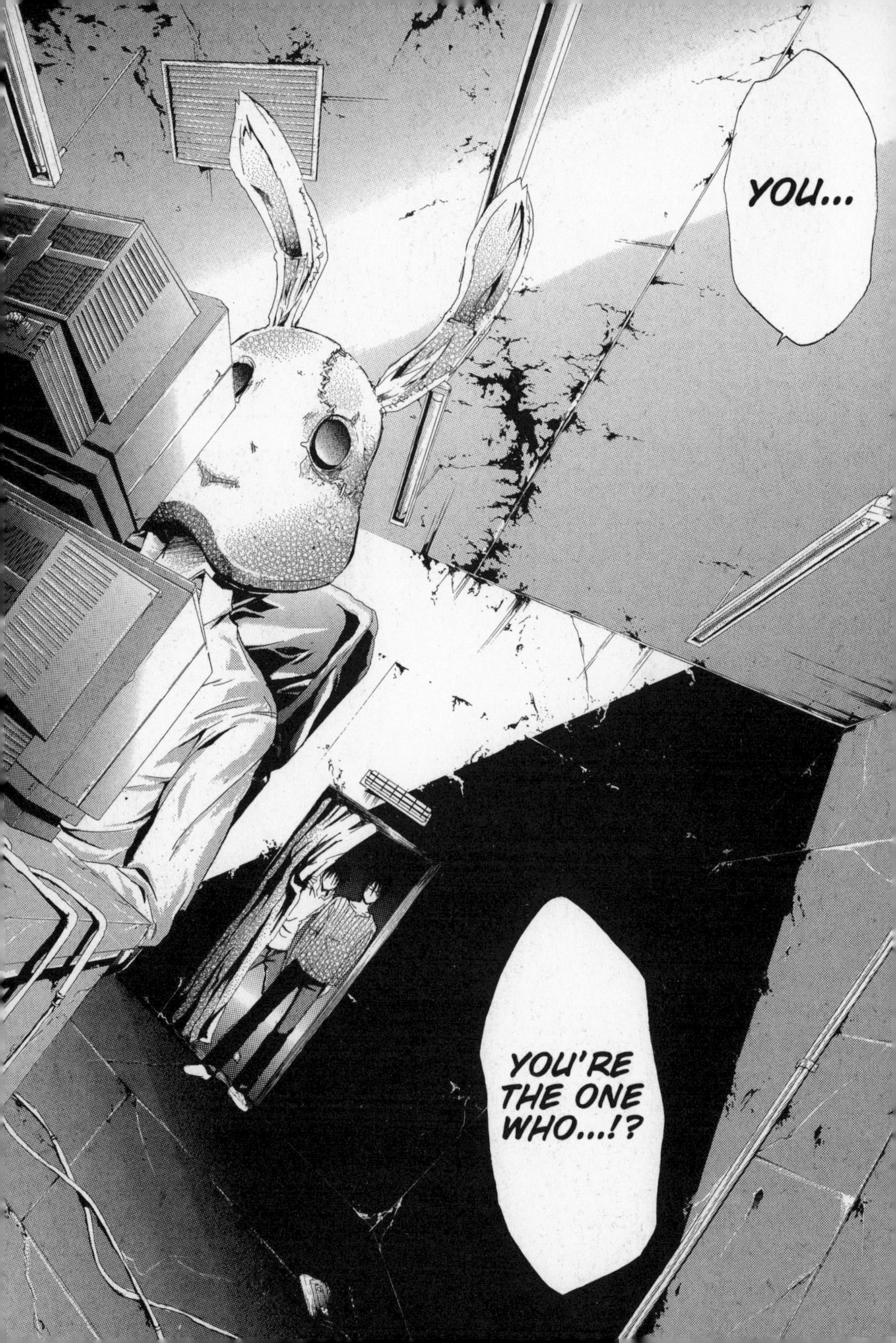
YOU...
YOU'RE THE ONE WHO...!?

Doubt

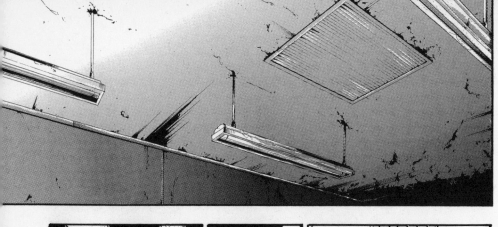

...IT'S HIM.

GYU
(GRIP)

HE'S THE ONE WHO KILLED REI...

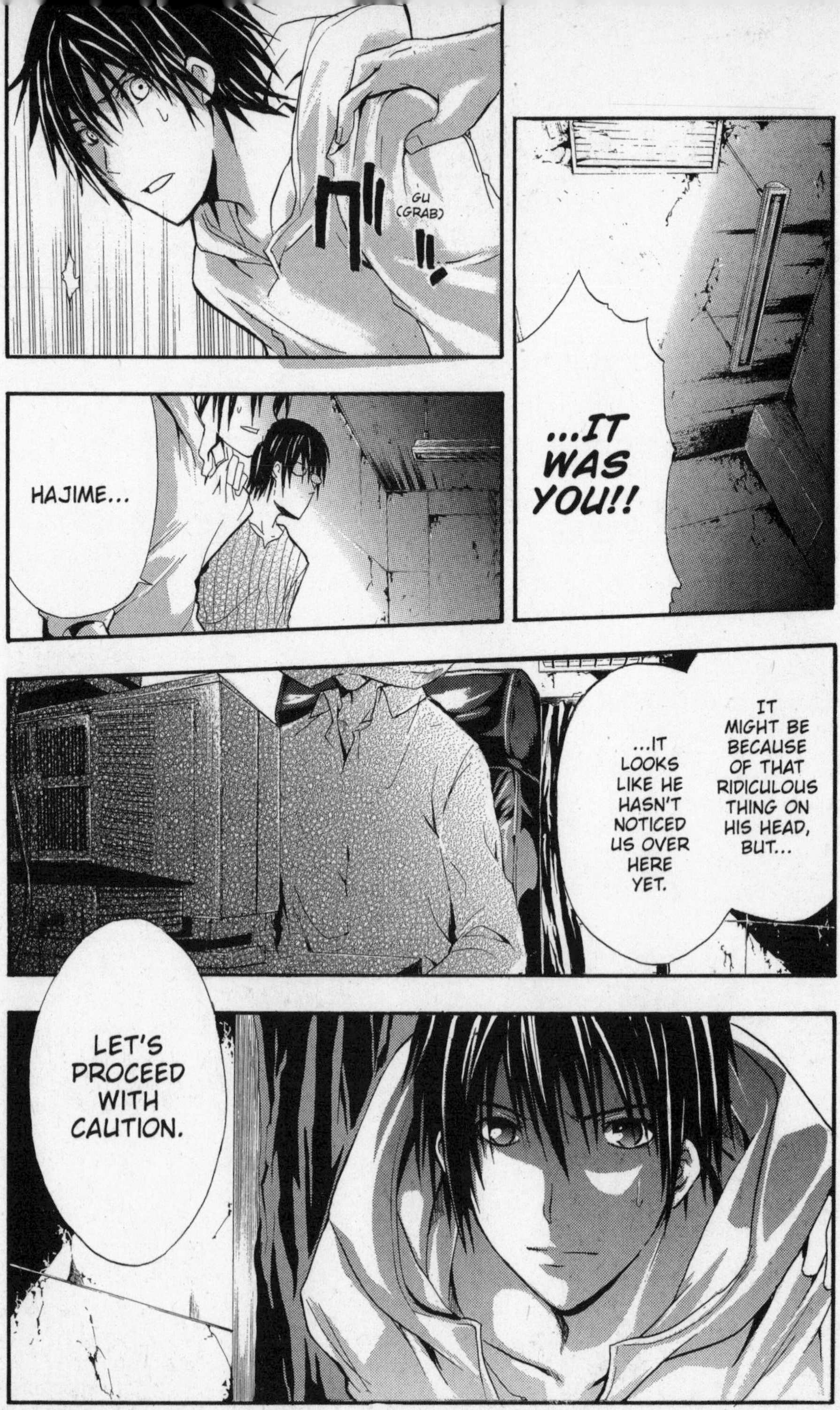
...IT WAS YOU!!
GU (GRAB)
HAJIME...
...IT LOOKS LIKE HE HASN'T NOTICED US OVER HERE YET.
IT MIGHT BE BECAUSE OF THAT RIDICULOUS THING ON HIS HEAD, BUT...
LET'S PROCEED WITH CAUTION.

Doubt.4 GO ON

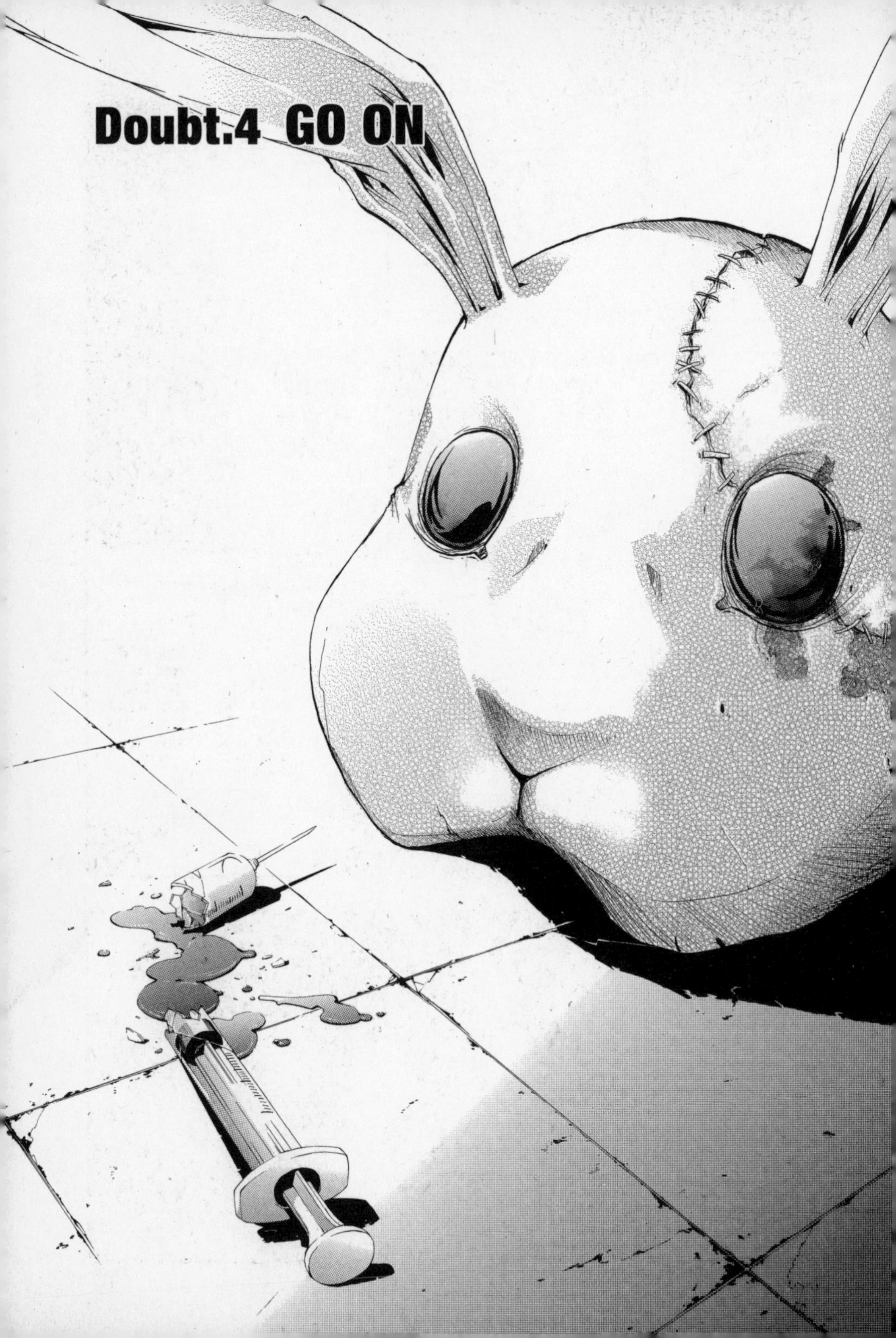

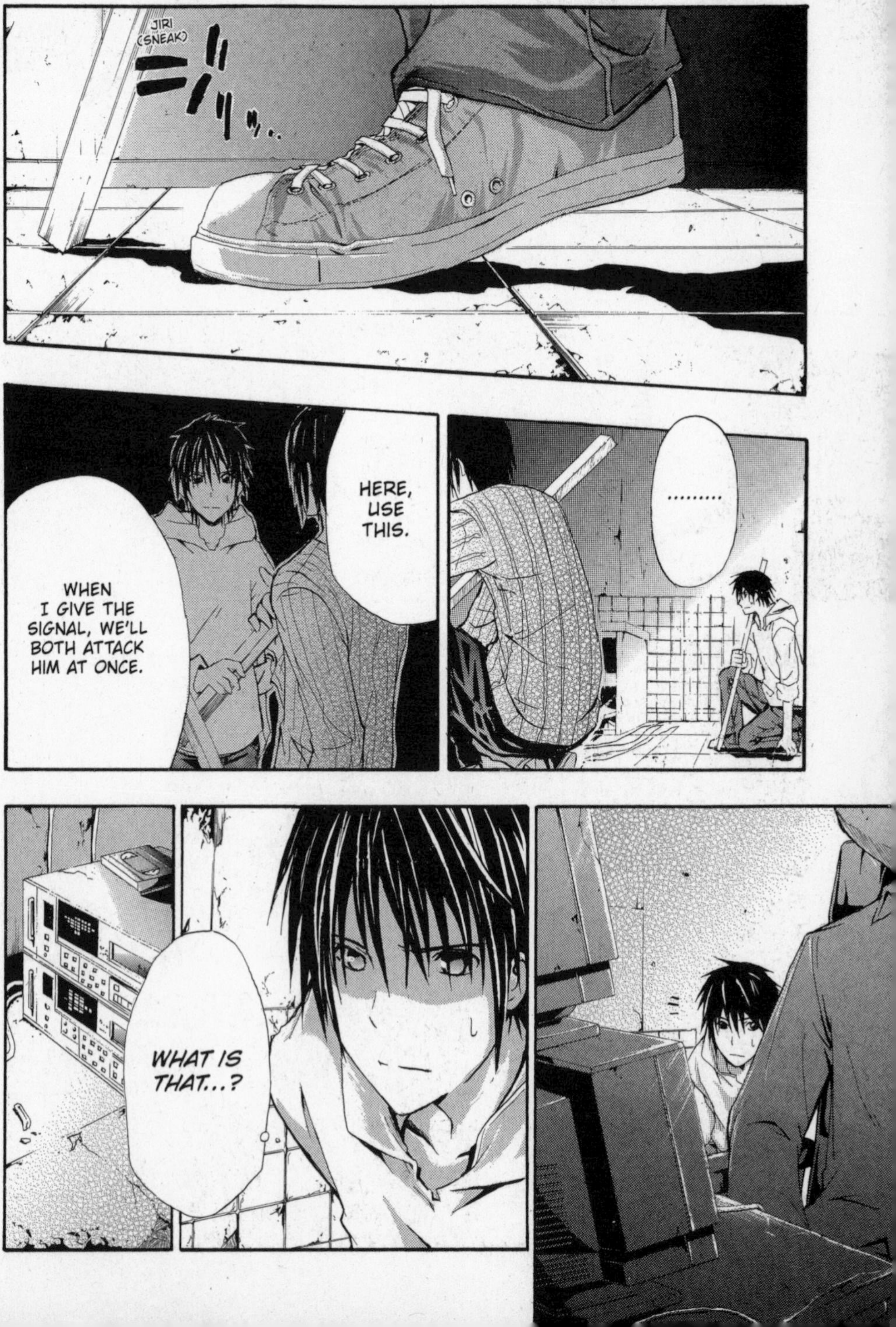
JIRI (SNEAK)
....
HERE, USE THIS.
WHEN I GIVE THE SIGNAL, WE'LL BOTH ATTACK HIM AT ONCE.
WHAT IS THAT...?

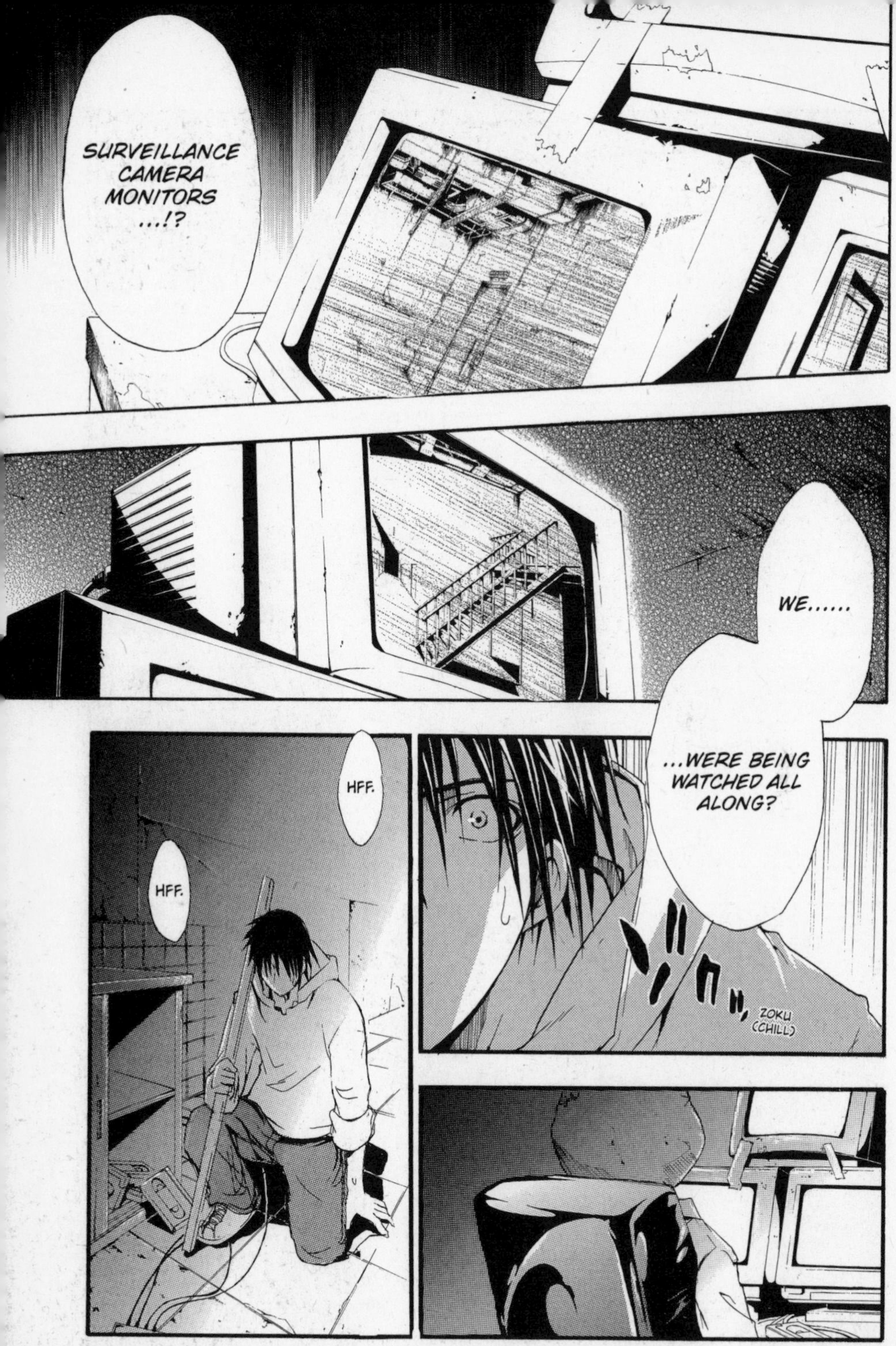
SURVEILLANCE CAMERA MONITORS ...!?
WE......
...WERE BEING WATCHED ALL ALONG?
ZOKU (CHILL)
HFF.
HFF.

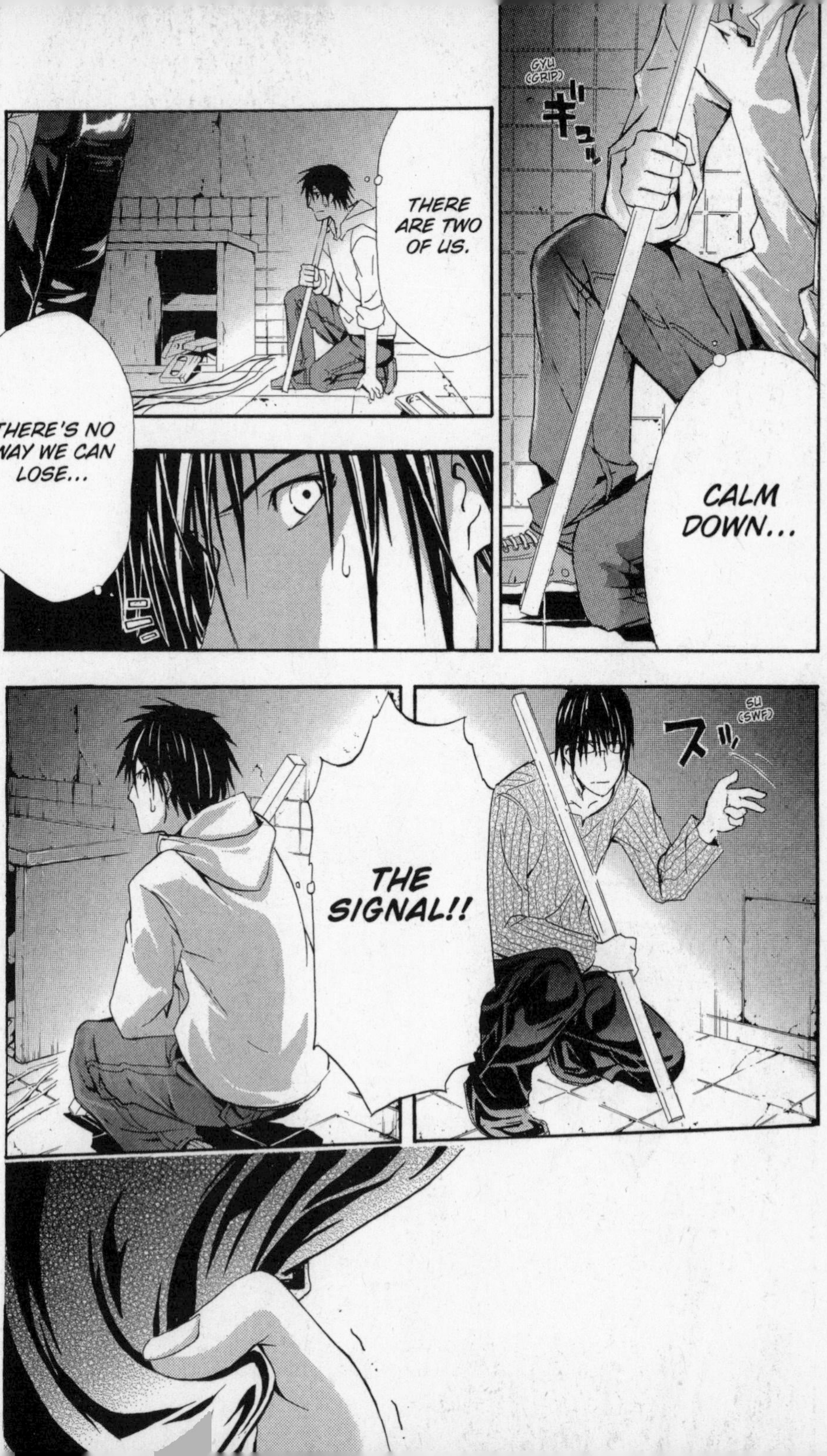
GYU (GRIP)
ギュッ
CALM DOWN...
THERE ARE TWO OF US.
THERE'S NO WAY WE CAN LOSE...
SU (SWF)
ズッ
THE SIGNAL!!

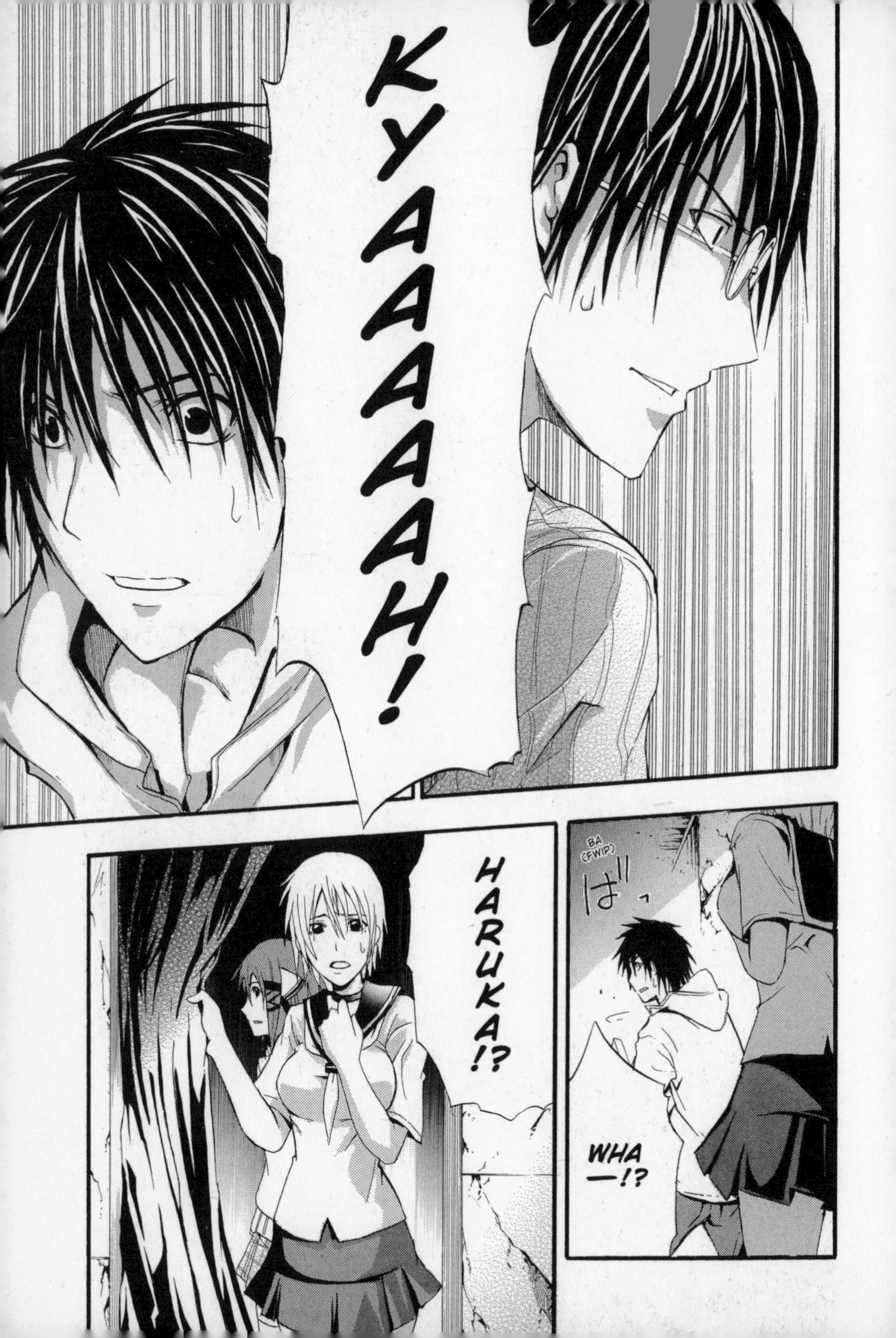
KYAAAAAH!
BA (FWIP)
ば"っ
WHA—!?
HARUKA!?

......!!

TCH!

ギュッ GYU (GRIP)

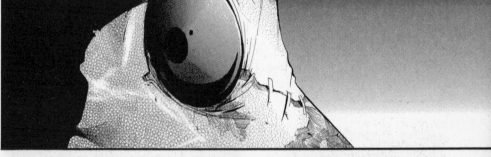

.........?

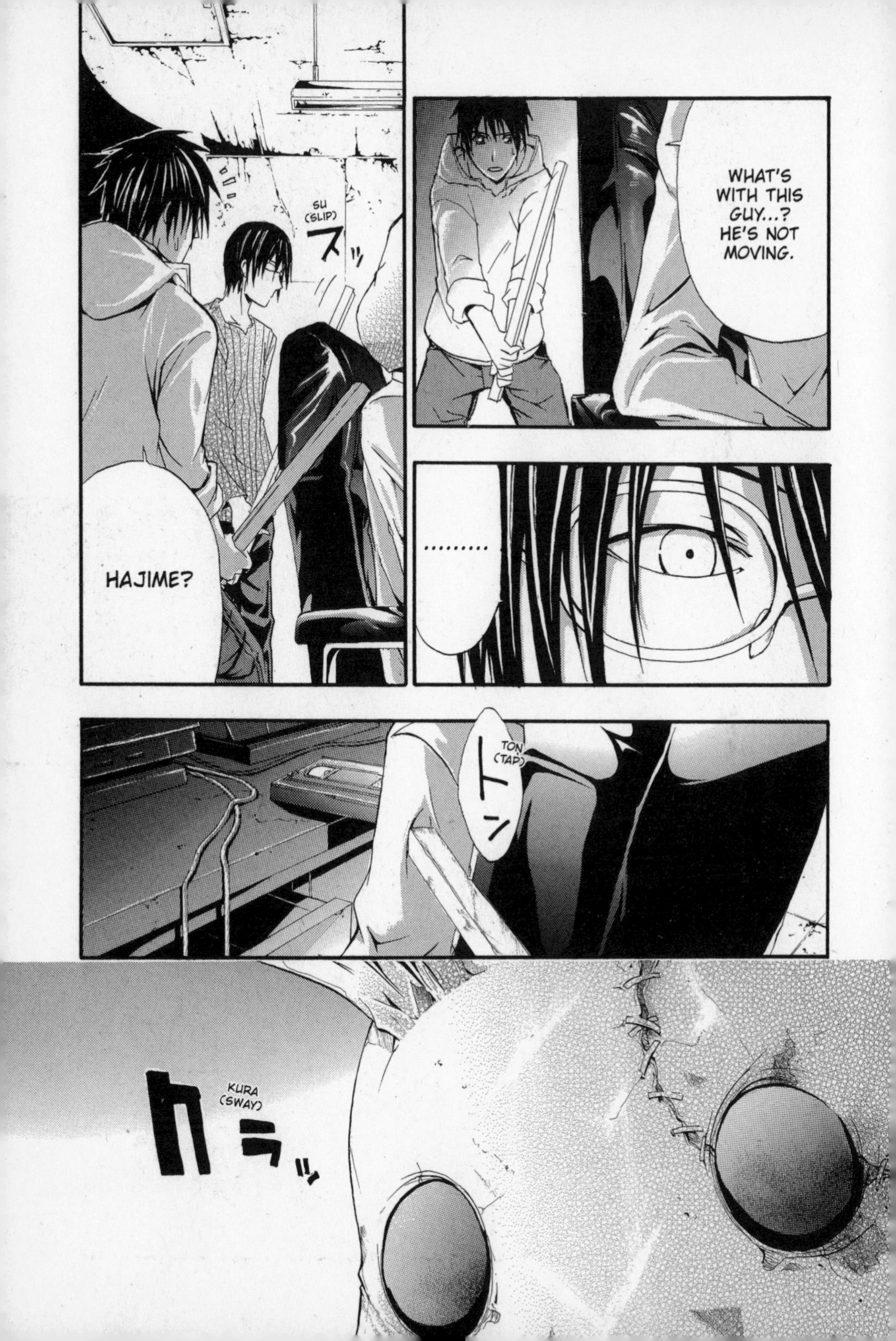
WHAT'S WITH THIS GUY...? HE'S NOT MOVING.
....
SU (SLIP)
ズッ
HAJIME?
TON (TAP)
トン
KURA (SWAY)

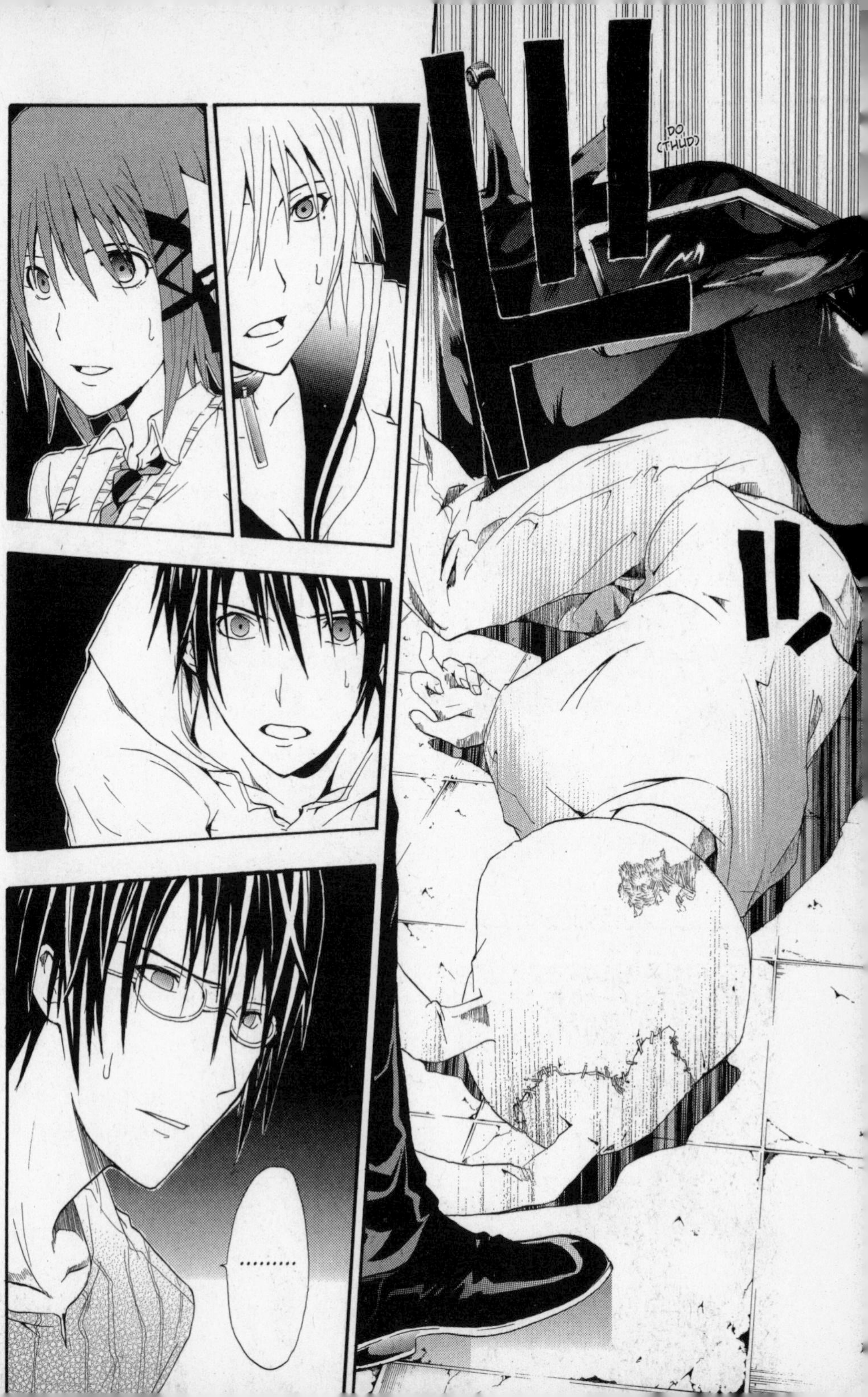
DO
(THUD)
....

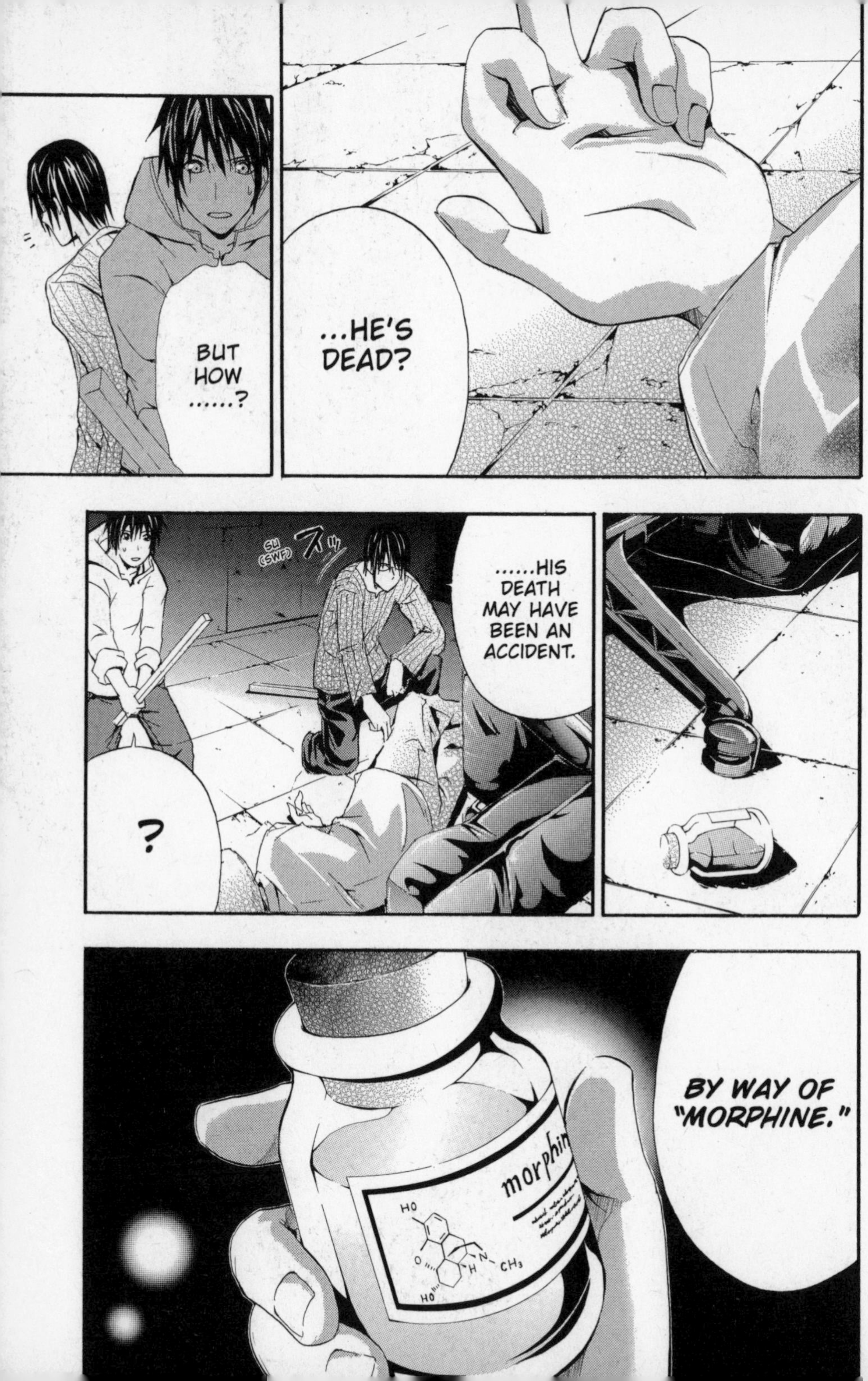
...HE'S DEAD?
BUT HOW ......?
......HIS DEATH MAY HAVE BEEN AN ACCIDENT.
SU (SWF)
?
BY WAY OF "MORPHINE."
morphin

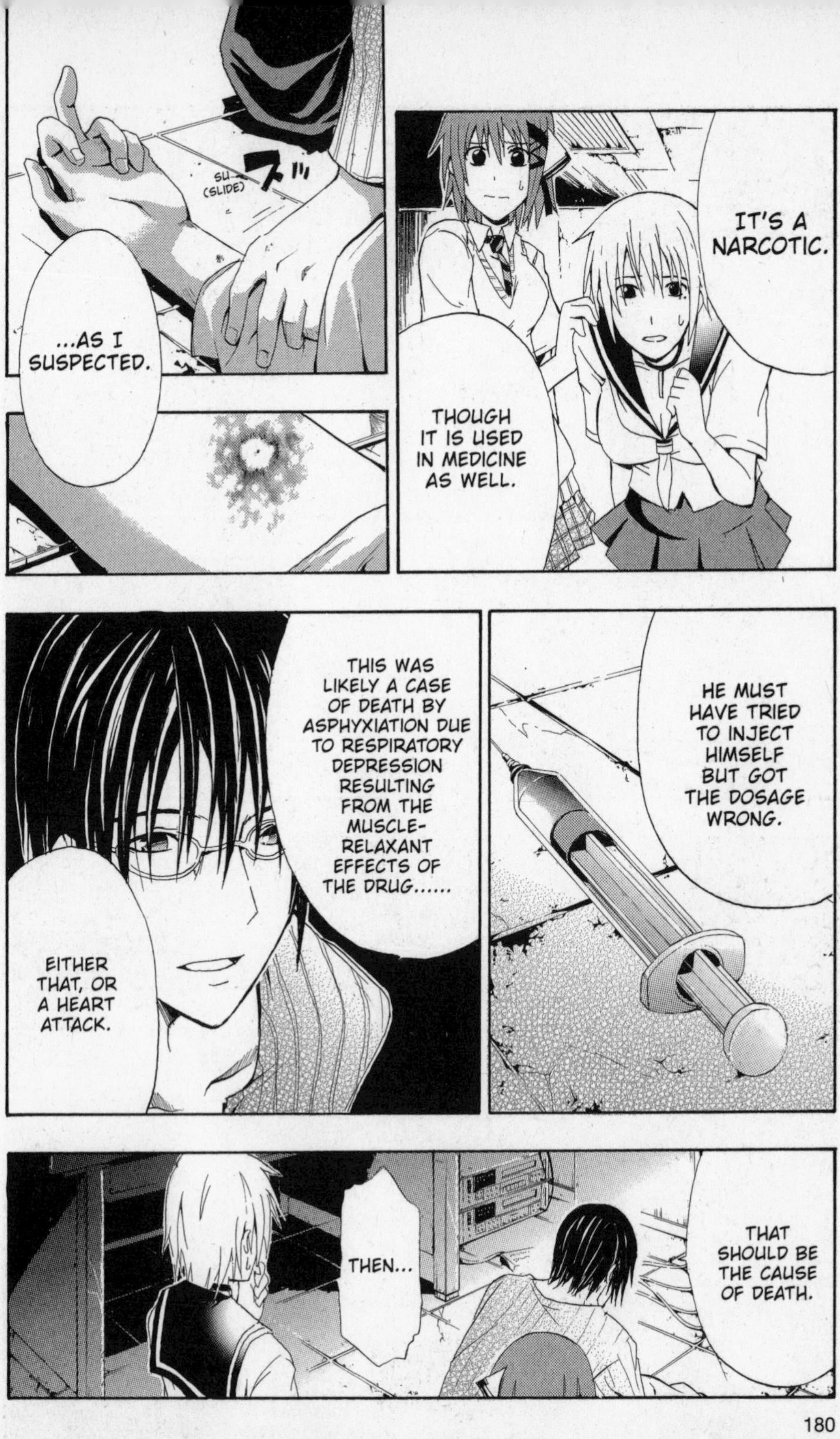
IT'S A NARCOTIC.
THOUGH IT IS USED IN MEDICINE AS WELL.
SU (SLIDE)
...AS I SUSPECTED.
HE MUST HAVE TRIED TO INJECT HIMSELF BUT GOT THE DOSAGE WRONG.
THIS WAS LIKELY A CASE OF DEATH BY ASPHYXIATION DUE TO RESPIRATORY DEPRESSION RESULTING FROM THE MUSCLE-RELAXANT EFFECTS OF THE DRUG......
EITHER THAT, OR A HEART ATTACK.
THAT SHOULD BE THE CAUSE OF DEATH.
THEN...

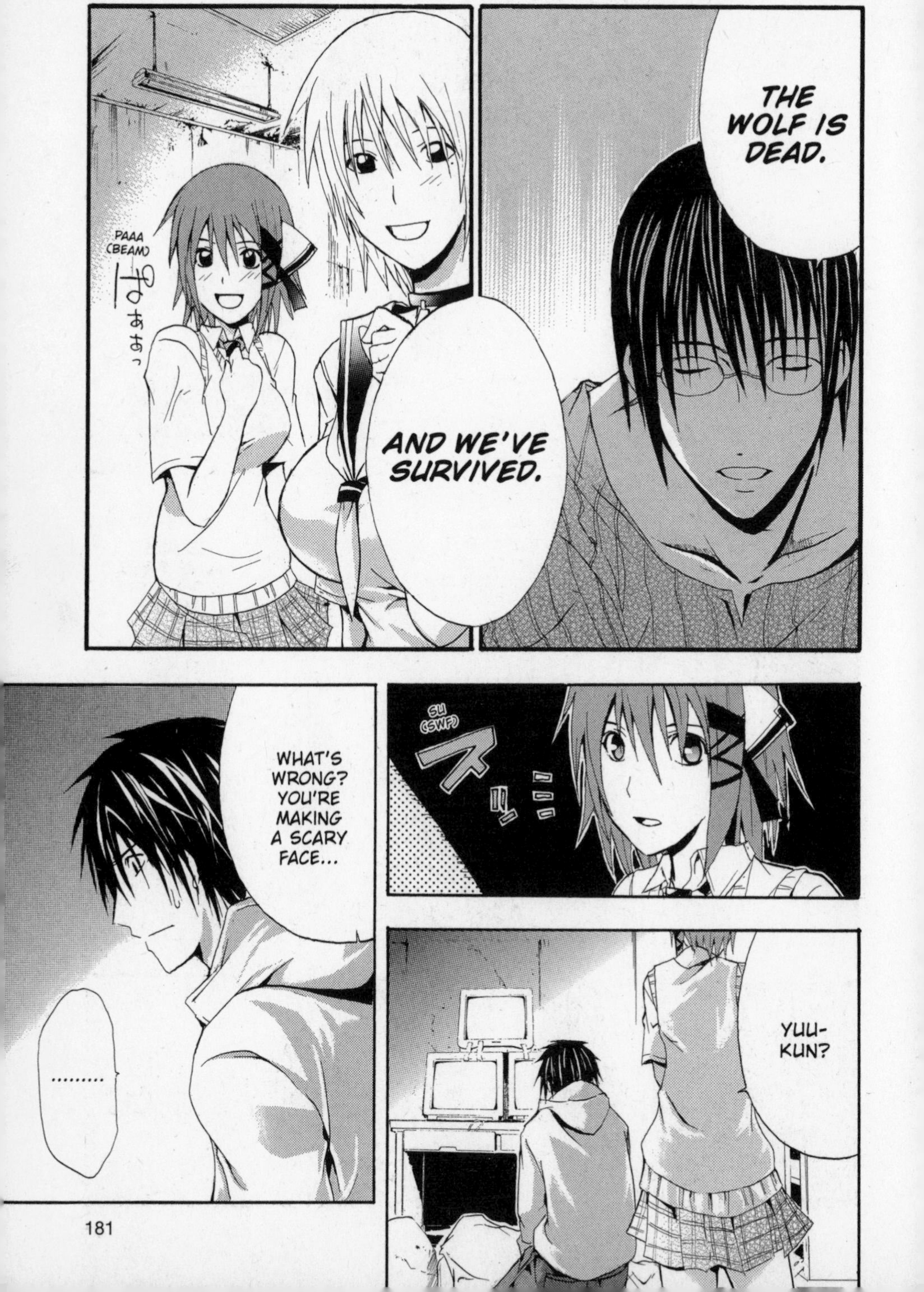
THE WOLF IS DEAD.
AND WE'VE SURVIVED.
PAAA (BEAM)
SU (SWF)
YUU-KUN?
WHAT'S WRONG? YOU'RE MAKING A SCARY FACE...
....

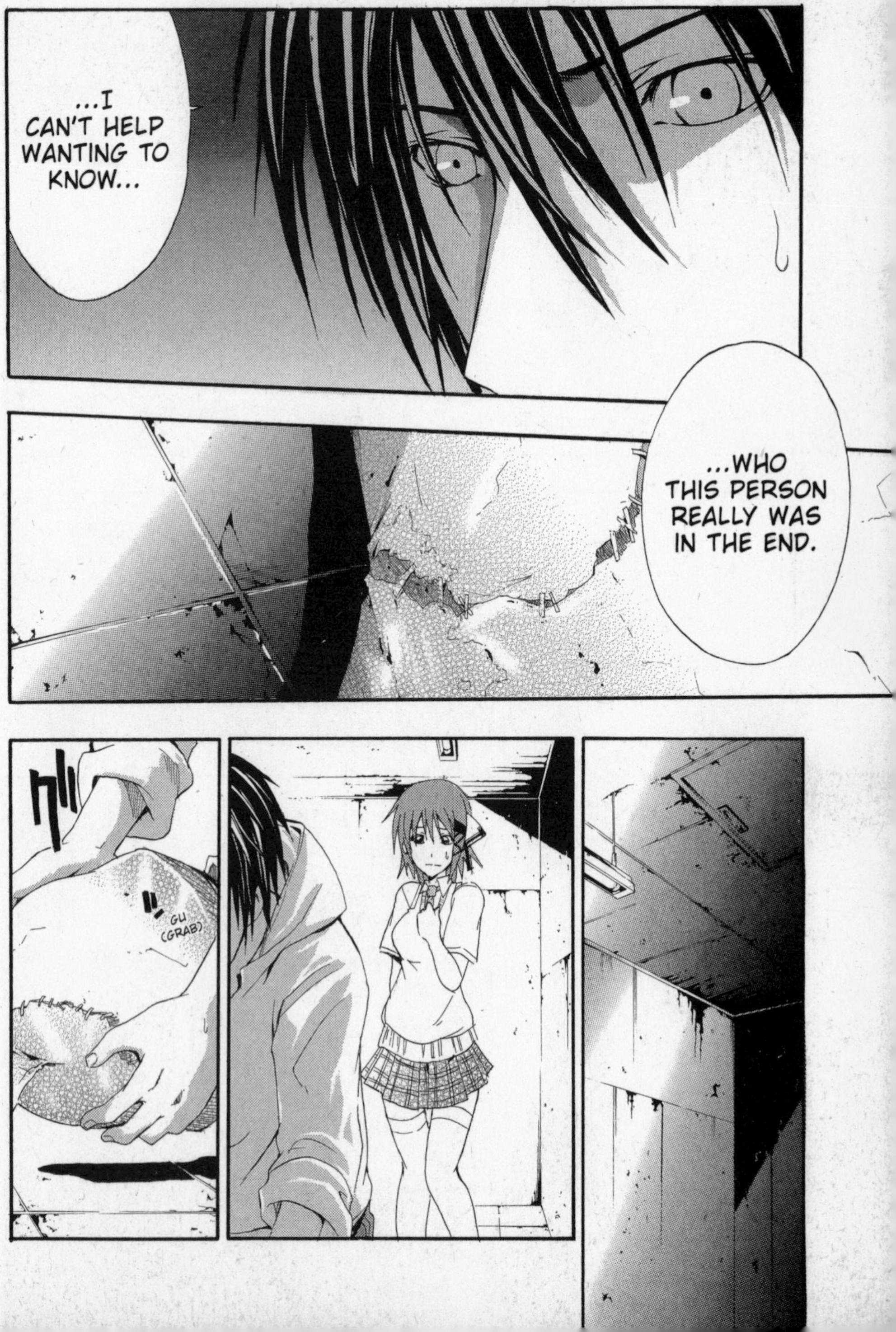
...I CAN'T HELP WANTING TO KNOW...
...WHO THIS PERSON REALLY WAS IN THE END.
GU (GRAB)

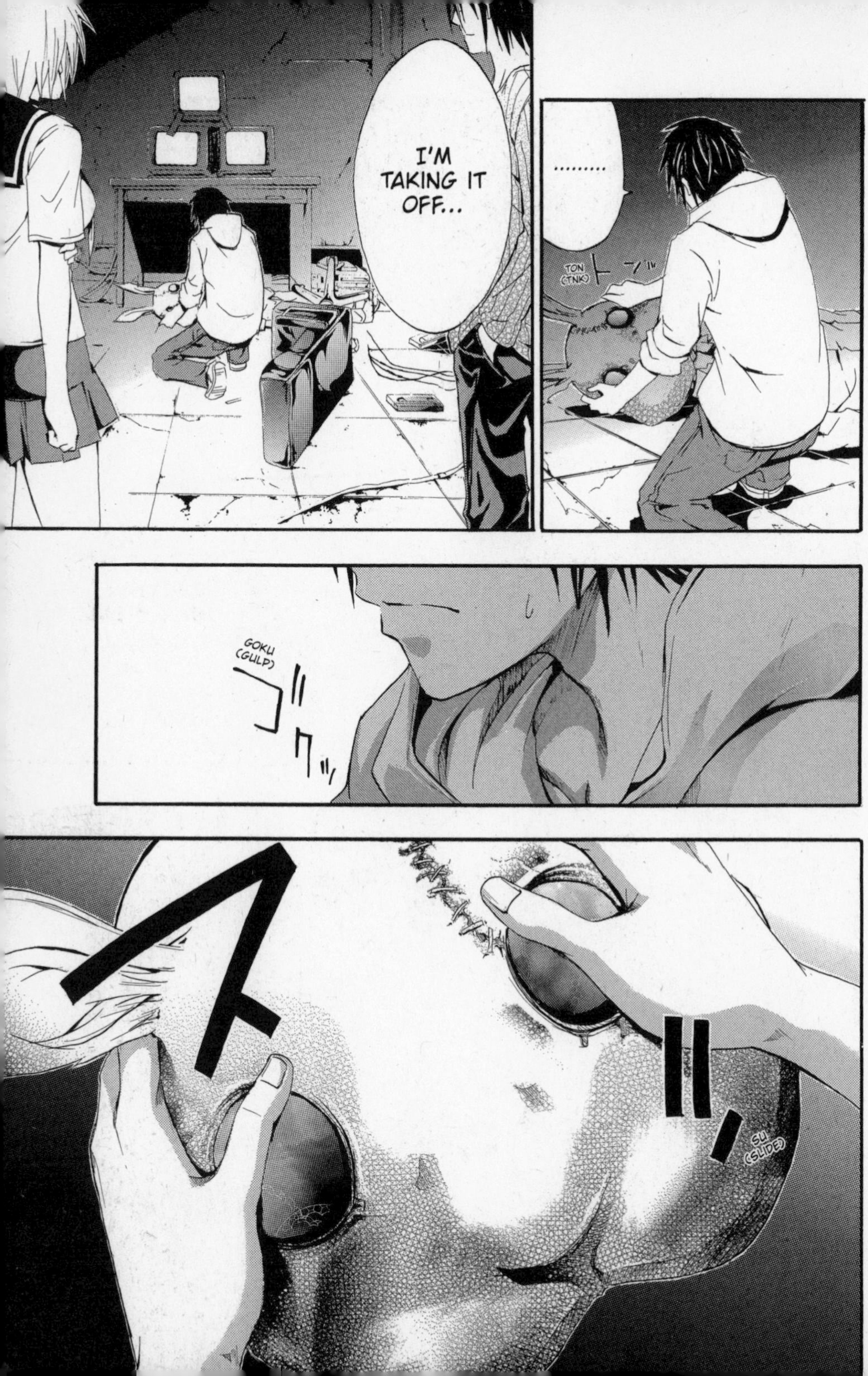
....
TON (TNK)
I'M TAKING IT OFF...
GOKU (GULP)
SU (SLIDE)

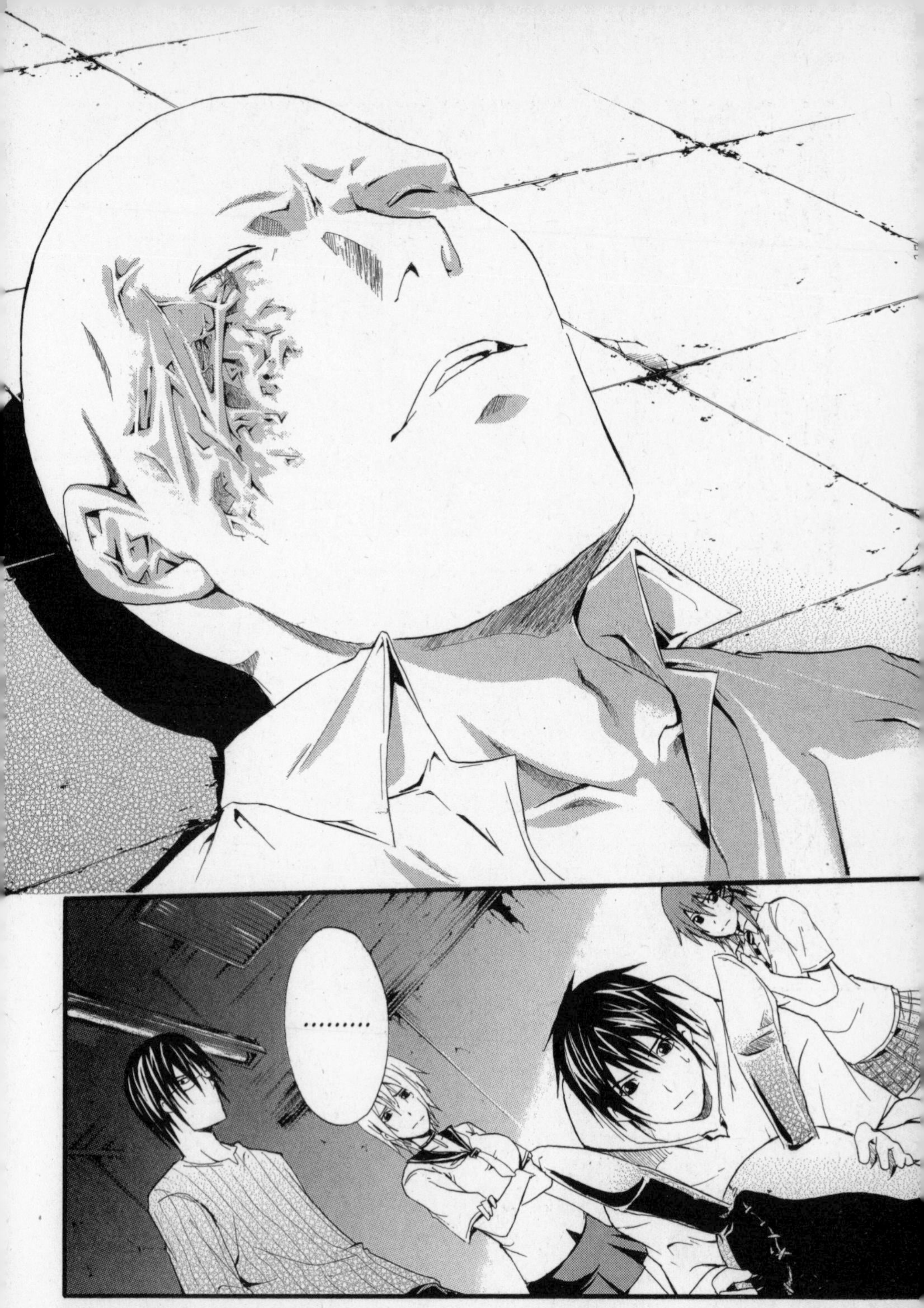
....

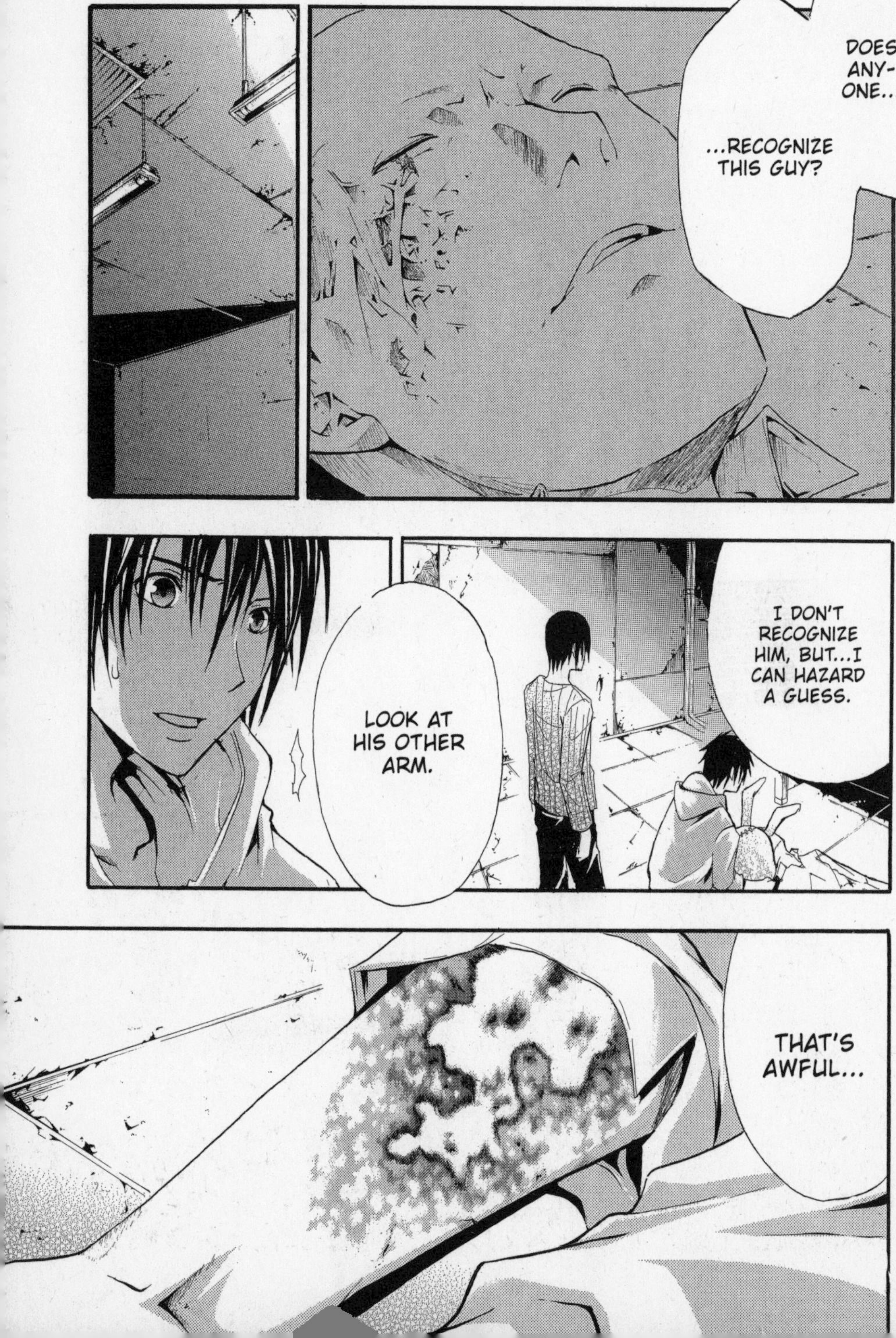
DOES ANY-ONE...
...RECOGNIZE THIS GUY?
I DON'T RECOGNIZE HIM, BUT...I CAN HAZARD A GUESS.
LOOK AT HIS OTHER ARM.
THAT'S AWFUL...

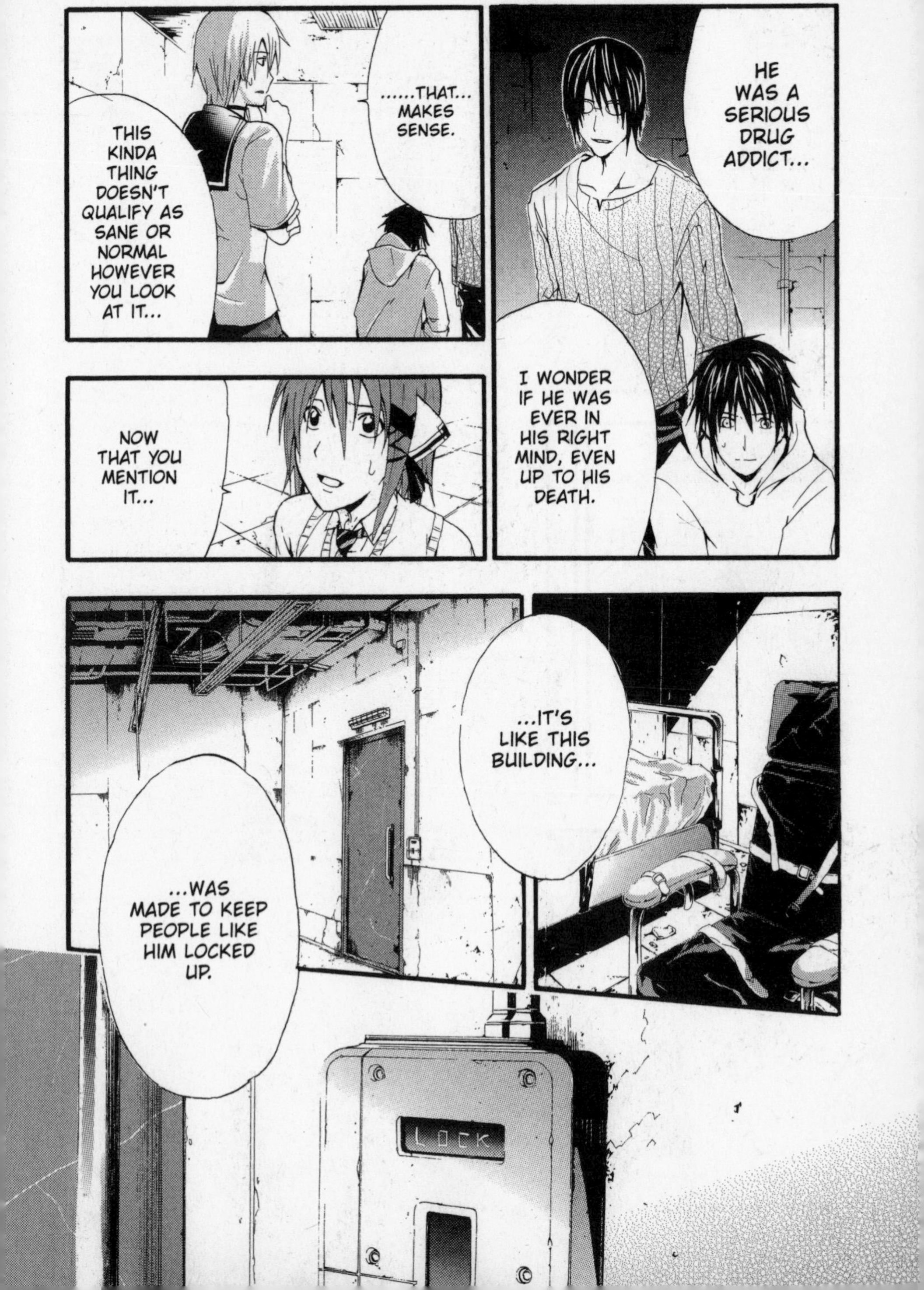
HE WAS A SERIOUS DRUG ADDICT...
I WONDER IF HE WAS EVER IN HIS RIGHT MIND, EVEN UP TO HIS DEATH.
......THAT... MAKES SENSE.
THIS KINDA THING DOESN'T QUALIFY AS SANE OR NORMAL HOWEVER YOU LOOK AT IT...
NOW THAT YOU MENTION IT...
...IT'S LIKE THIS BUILDING...
...WAS MADE TO KEEP PEOPLE LIKE HIM LOCKED UP.
LOCK

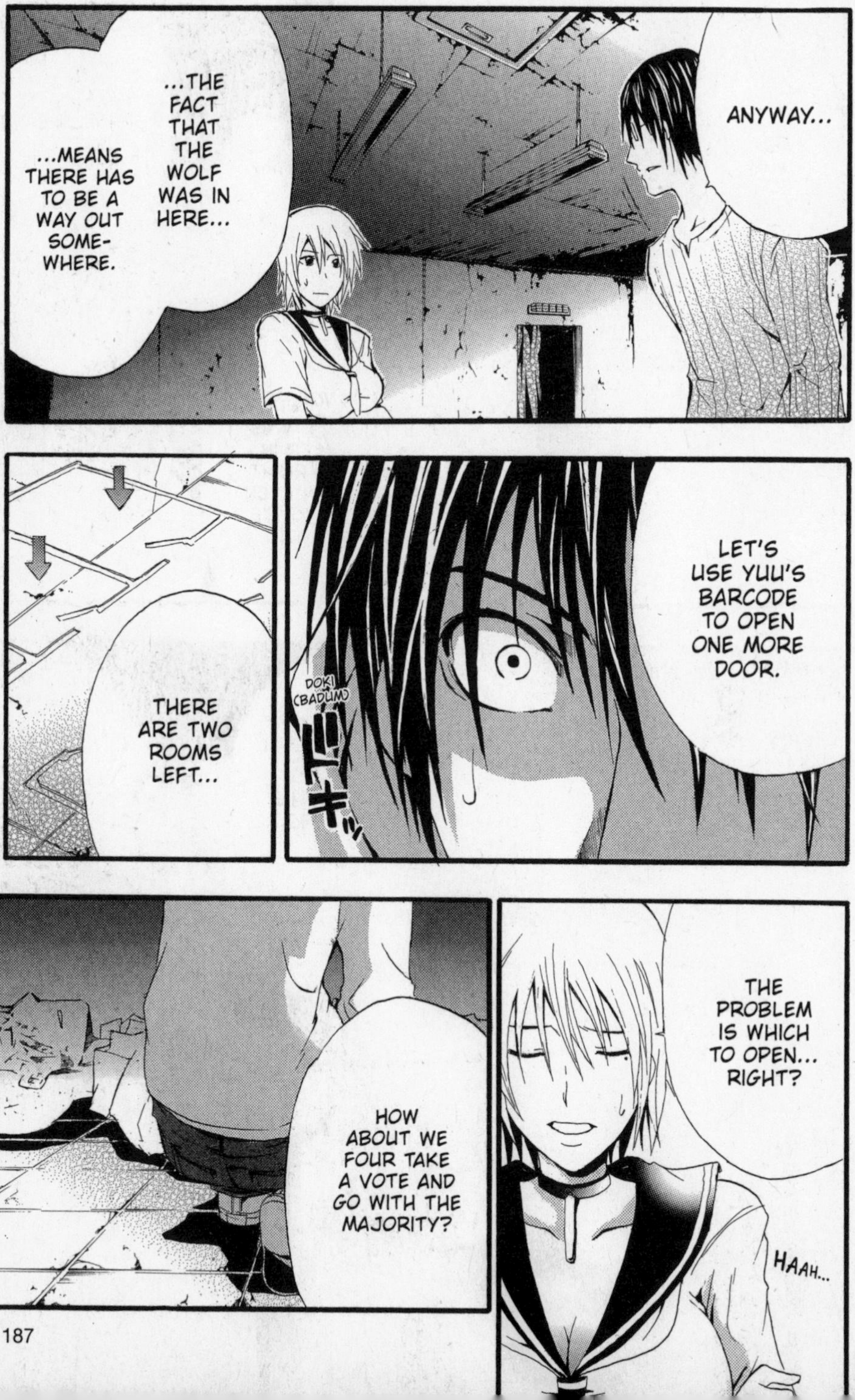
ANYWAY...
...THE FACT THAT THE WOLF WAS IN HERE...
...MEANS THERE HAS TO BE A WAY OUT SOME-WHERE.
LET'S USE YUU'S BARCODE TO OPEN ONE MORE DOOR.
DOKI (BADUM)
THERE ARE TWO ROOMS LEFT...
THE PROBLEM IS WHICH TO OPEN... RIGHT?
HAAH...
HOW ABOUT WE FOUR TAKE A VOTE AND GO WITH THE MAJORITY?

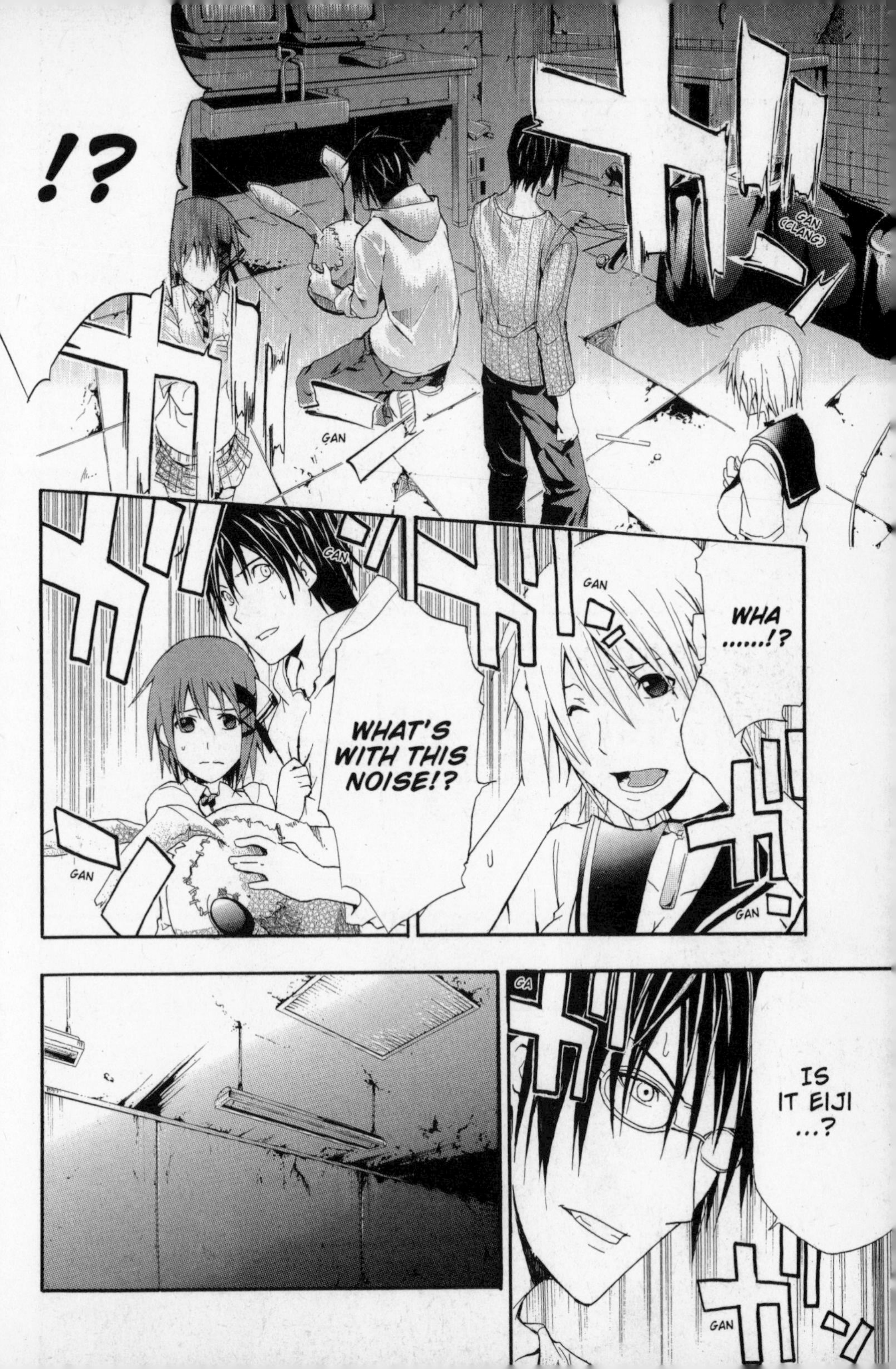
GAN (CLANG)
!?
GAN
GAN
WHA ......!?
GAN
GAN
WHAT'S WITH THIS NOISE!?
GAN
GA
IS IT EIJI ...?
GAN

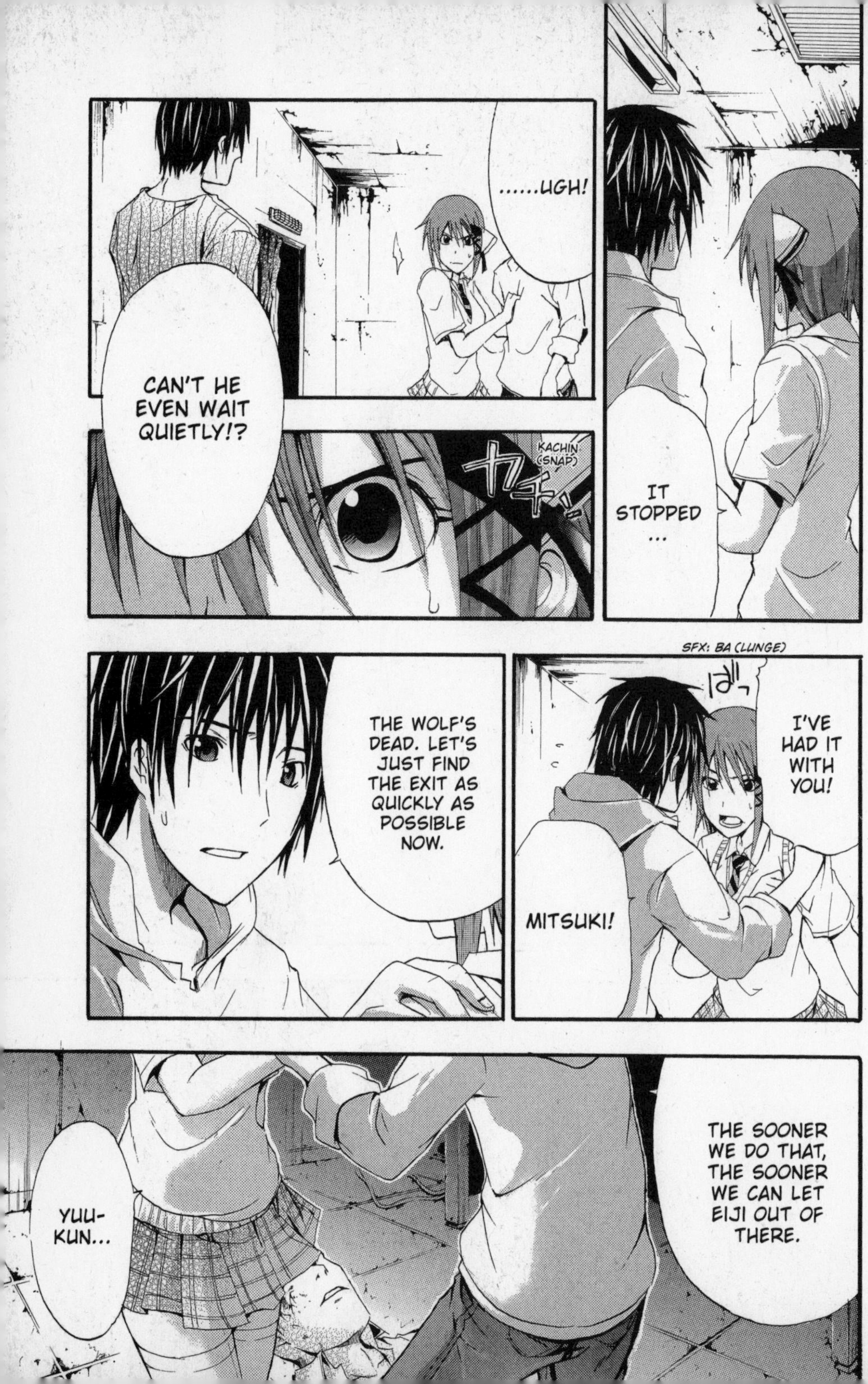
IT STOPPED ...
......UGH!
CAN'T HE EVEN WAIT QUIETLY!?
KACHIN (SNAP)
SFX: BA (LUNGE)
I'VE HAD IT WITH YOU!
MITSUKI!
THE WOLF'S DEAD. LET'S JUST FIND THE EXIT AS QUICKLY AS POSSIBLE NOW.
THE SOONER WE DO THAT, THE SOONER WE CAN LET EIJI OUT OF THERE.
YUU-KUN...

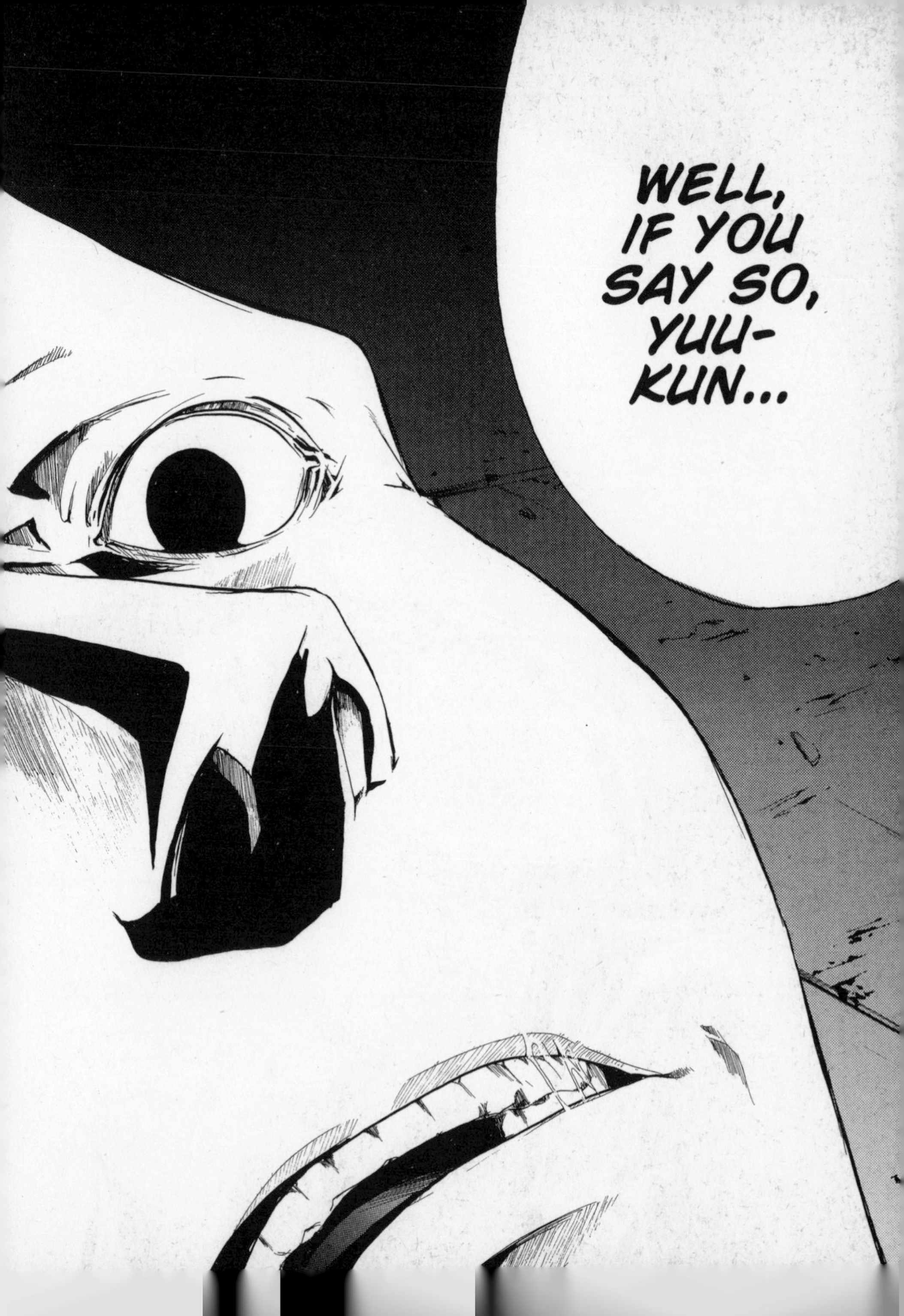
WELL, IF YOU SAY SO, YUU-KUN...

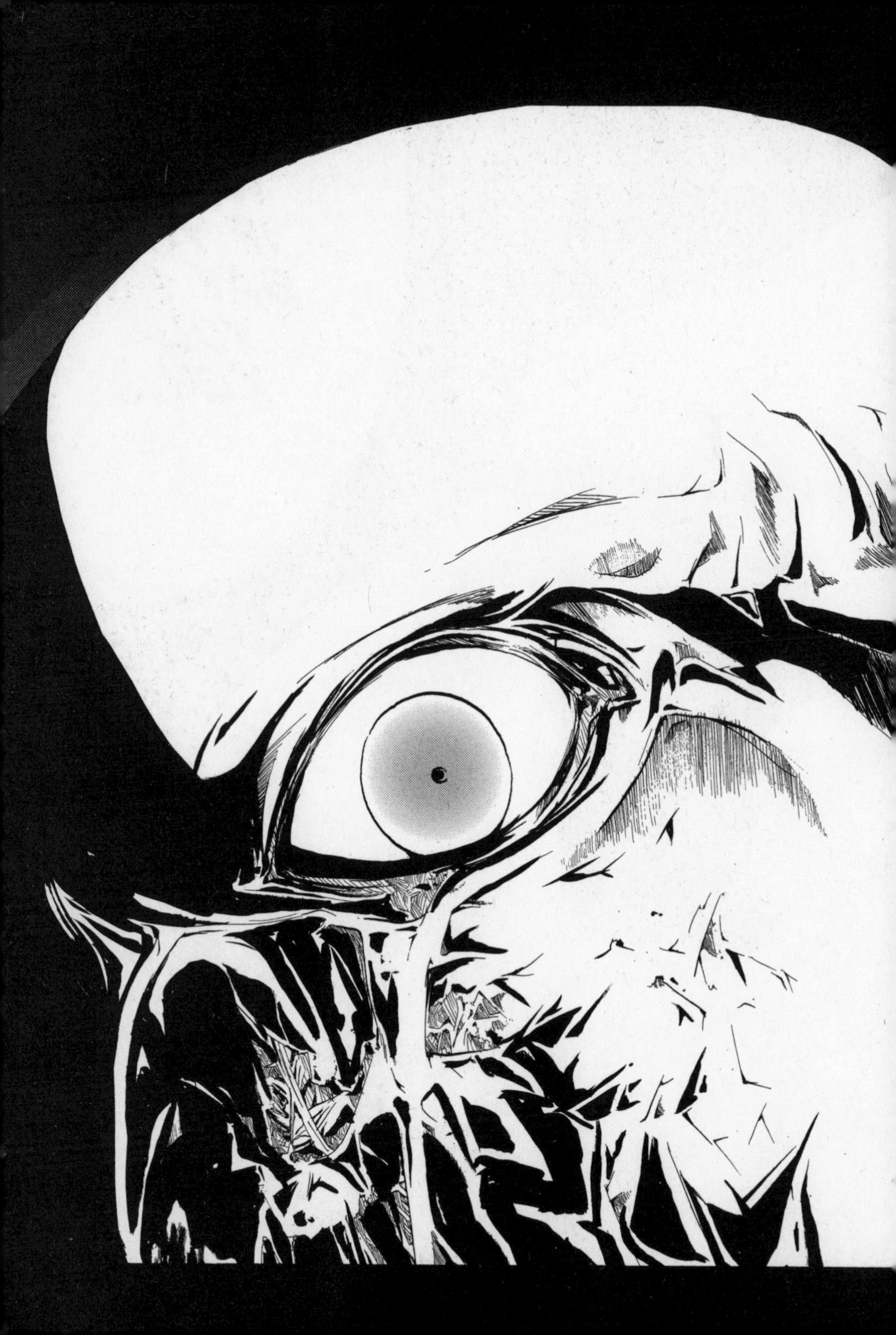

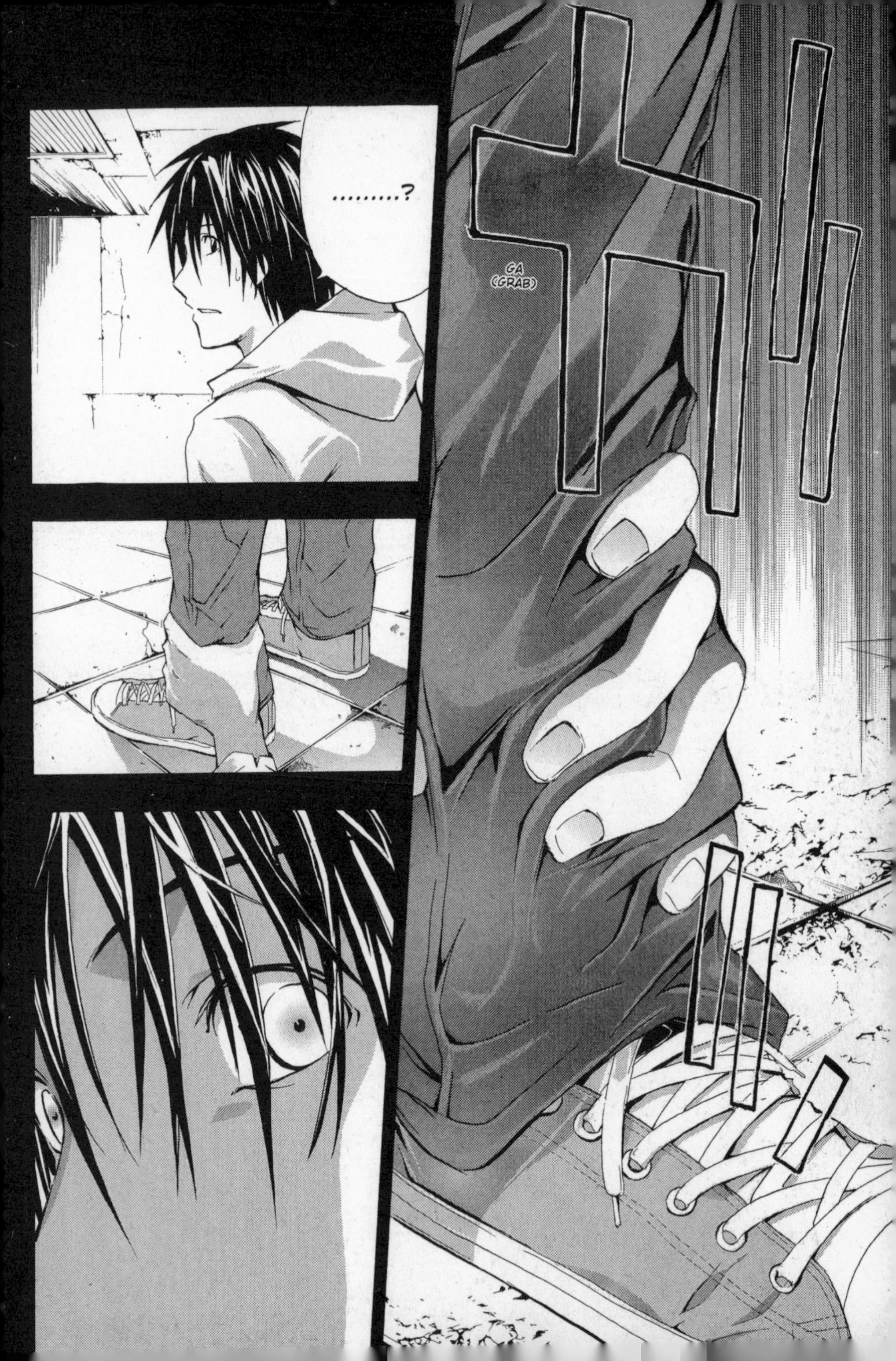
GA (GRAB)
.........?

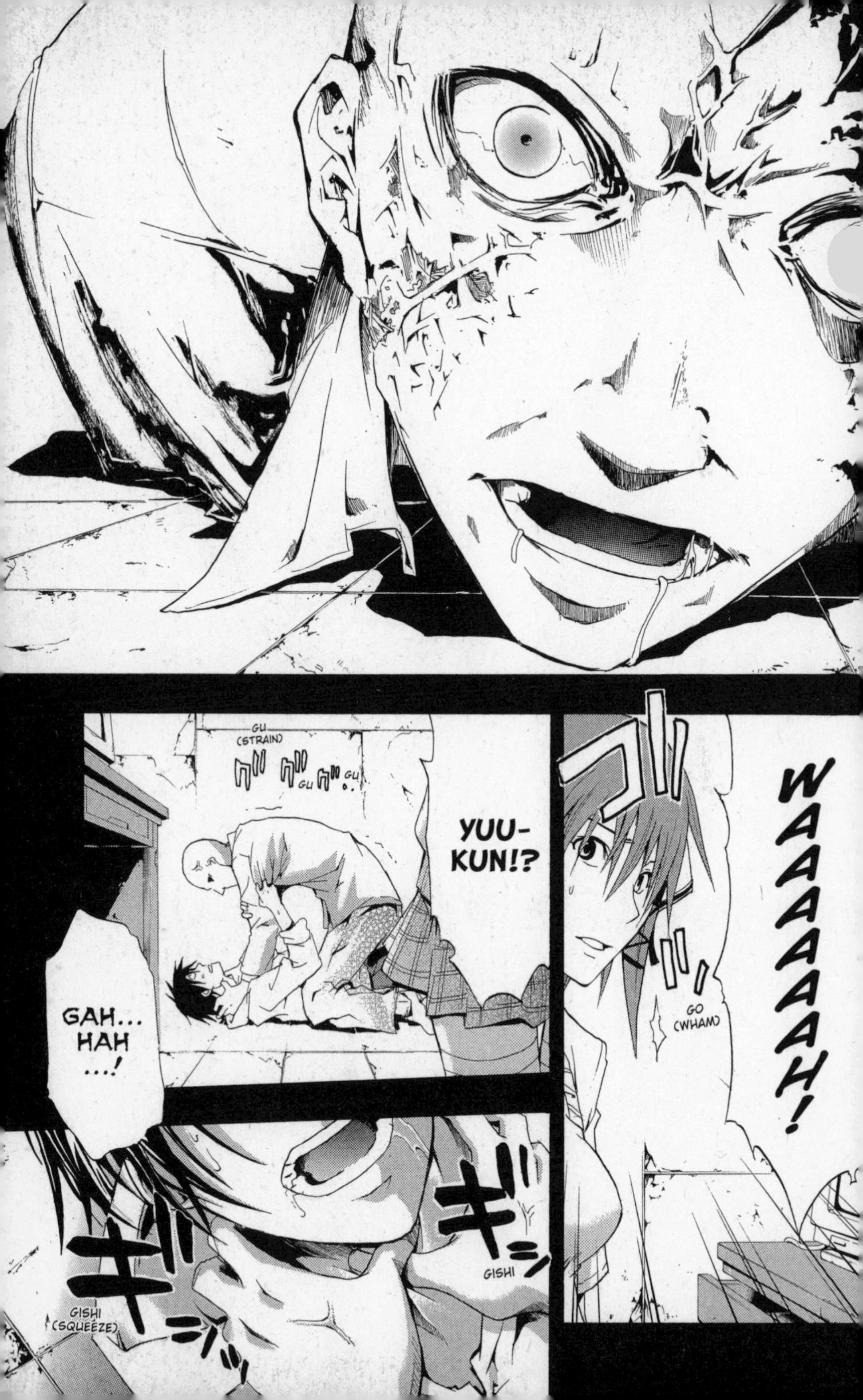
WAAAAAAAAH!
GO (WHAM)
GU (STRAIN)
GU
GU
YUU-KUN!?
GAH... HAH ...!
GISHI
GISHI (SQUEEZE)

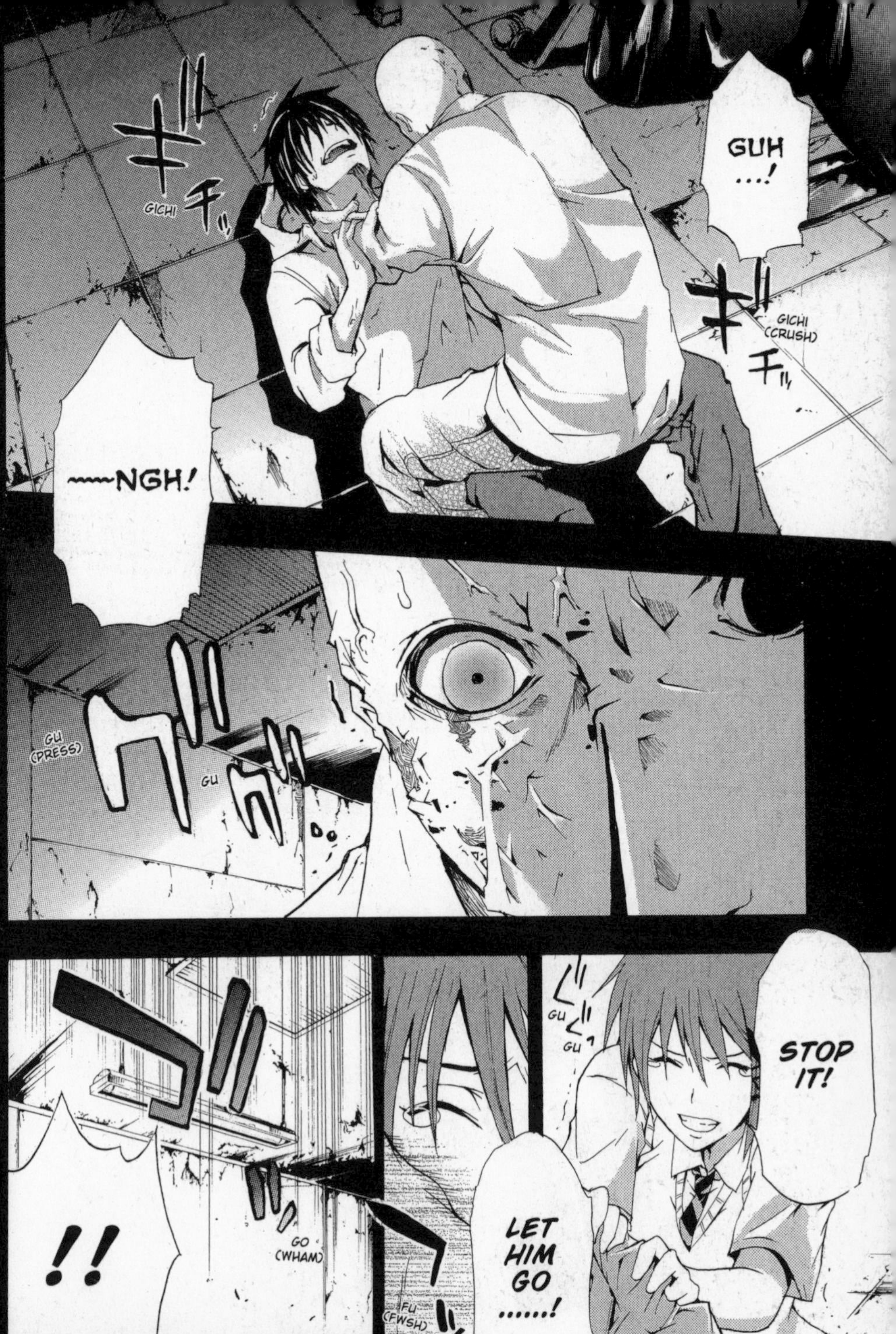
GUH ...!
GICHI
GICHI (CRUSH)
——NGH!
GU (PRESS)
GU
STOP IT!
GU
GU
LET HIM GO ......!
FU (FWSH)
GO (WHAM)
!!

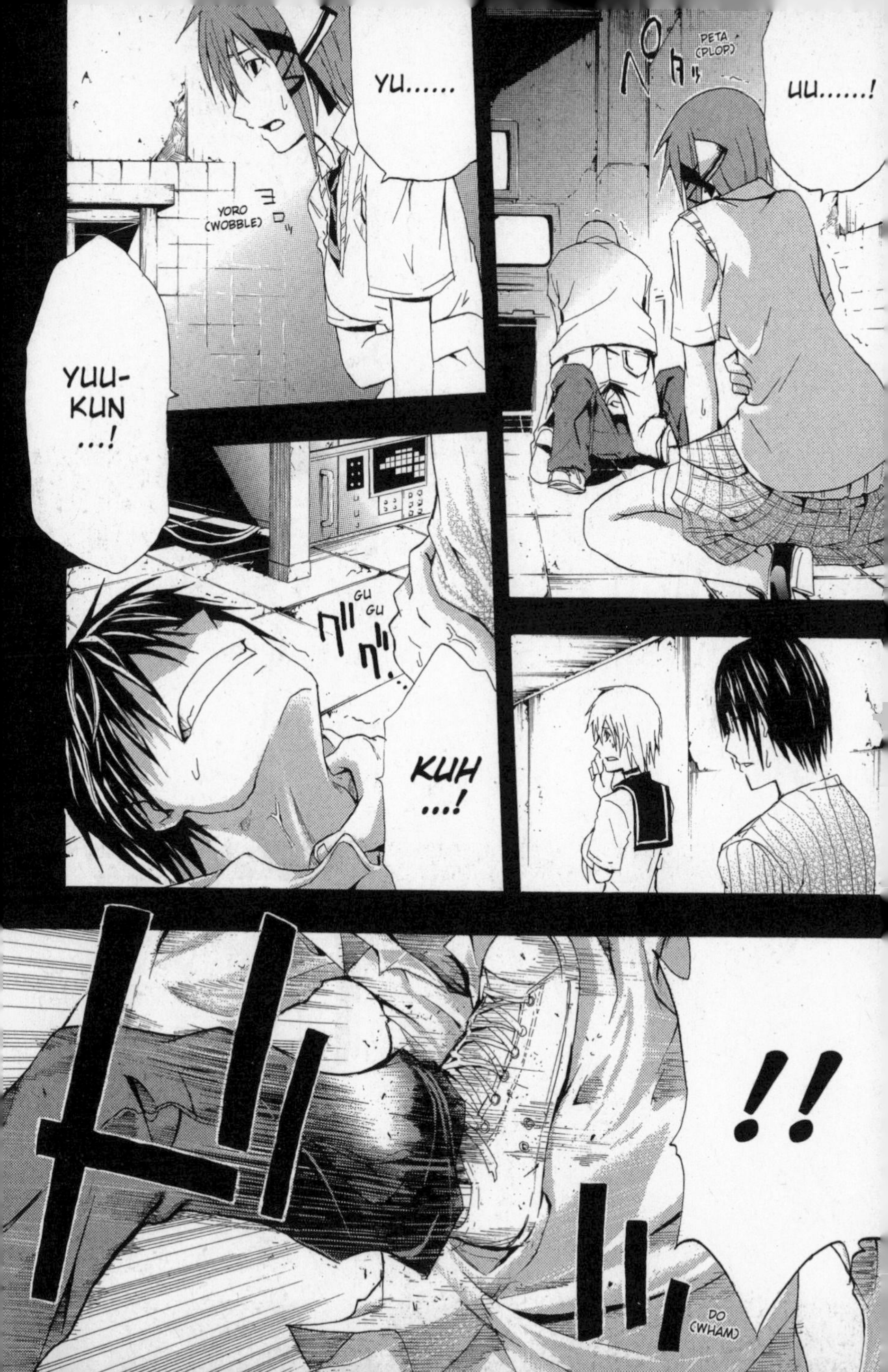
PETA (PLOP)
UU......!
YU......
YORO (WOBBLE)
YUU-KUN...!
GU GU
KUH...!
!!
DO (WHAM)

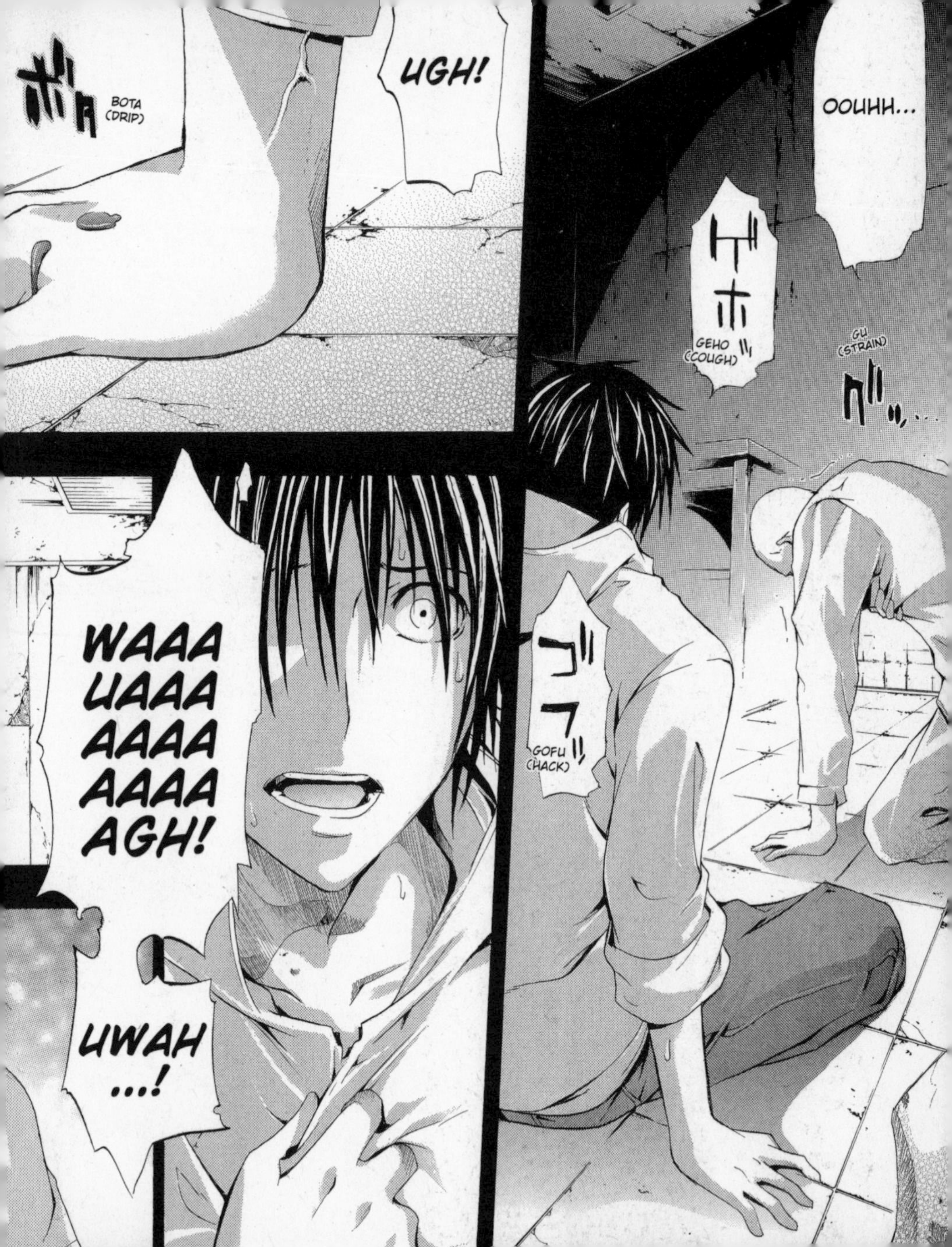
OOUHH...
ゲホッ
GEHO (COUGH)
グッ...
GU (STRAIN)
ゴフッ
GOFU (HACK)
UGH!
ボタ
BOTA (DRIP)
WAAA UAAA AAAA AAAA AGH!
UWAH ...!

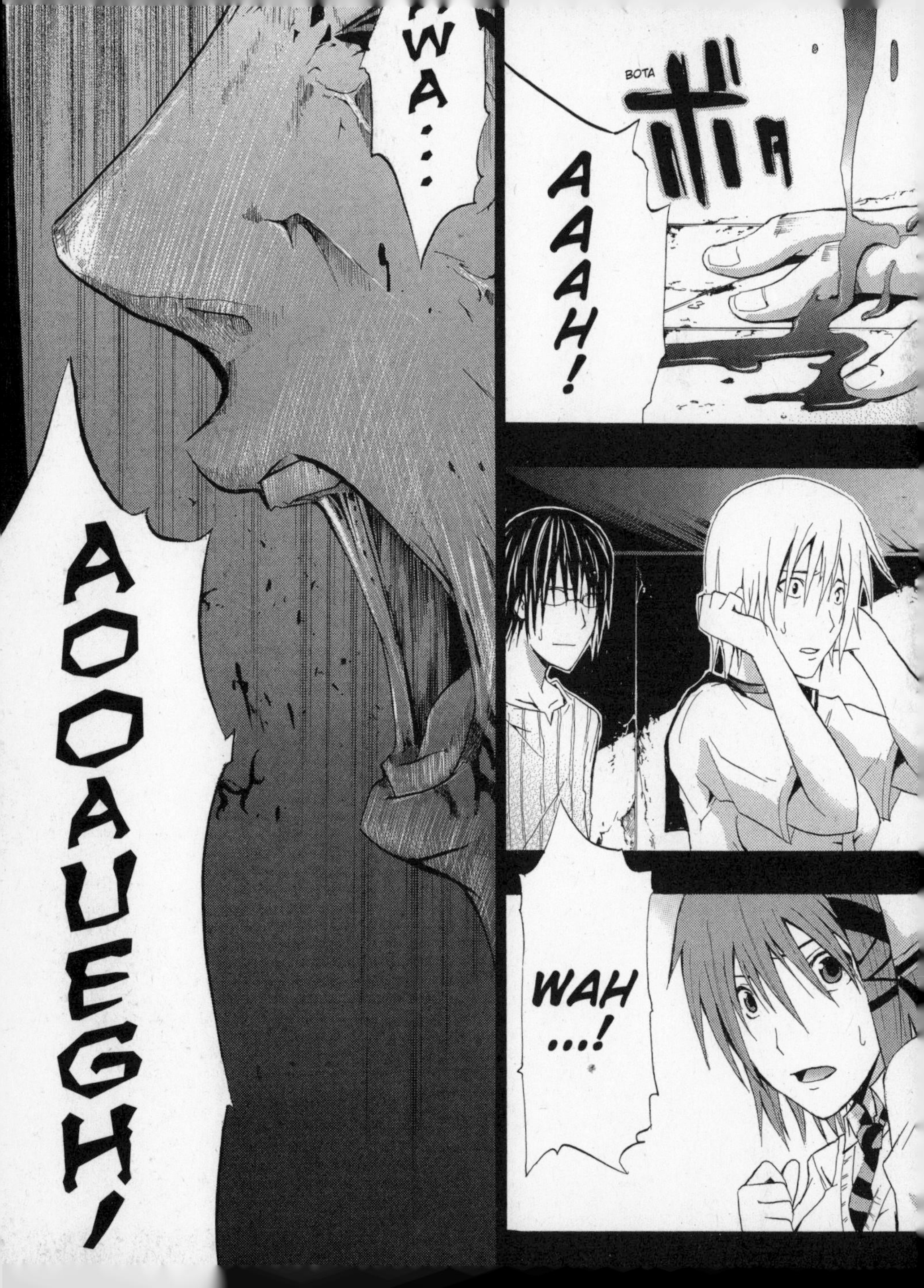
BOTA
ボタ
AAAAH!
WAH ...!
WA...
AOOAUEGH!

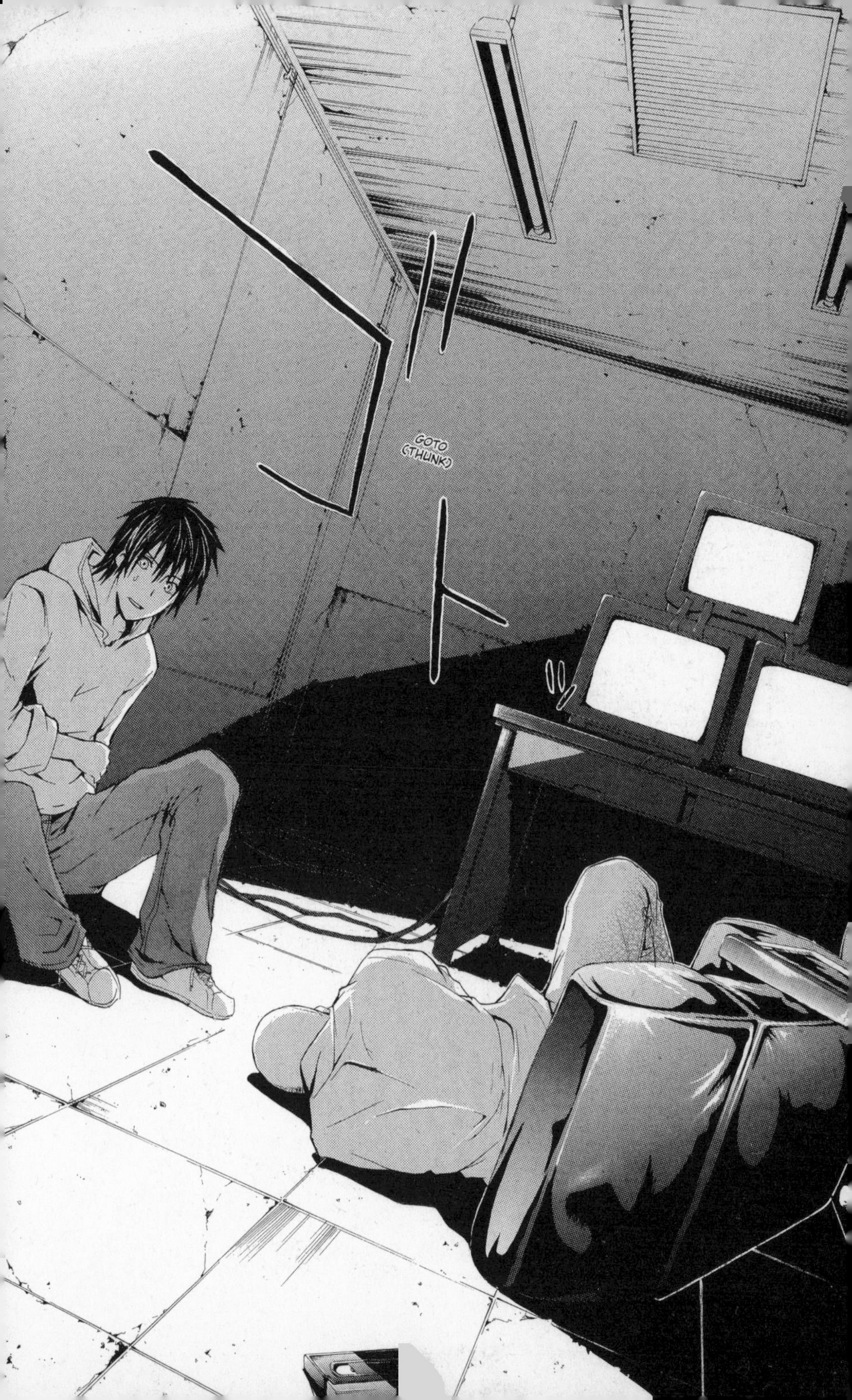
GOTO (THUNK)

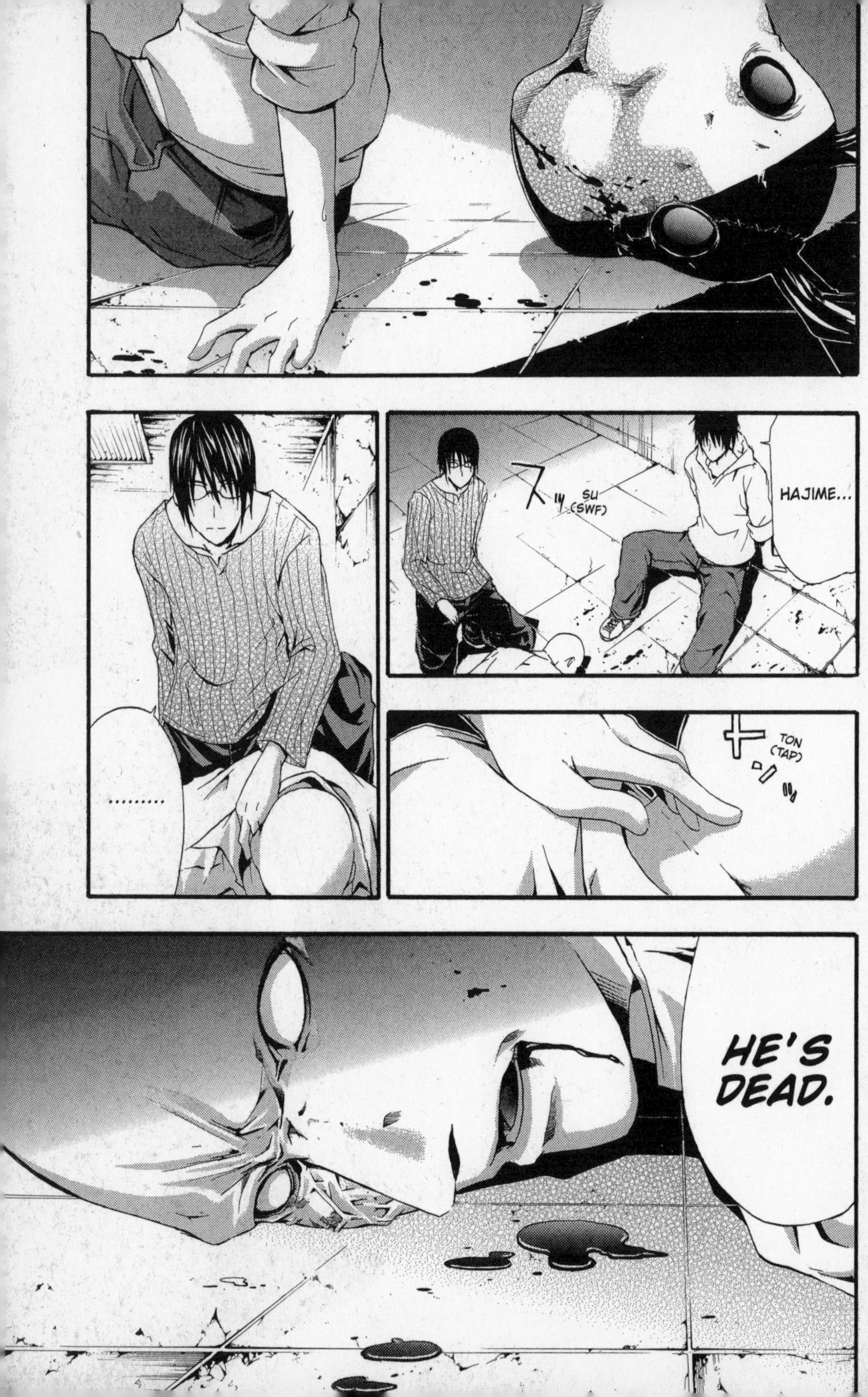
HAJIME...
SU (SWF)
TON (TAP)
....
HE'S DEAD.

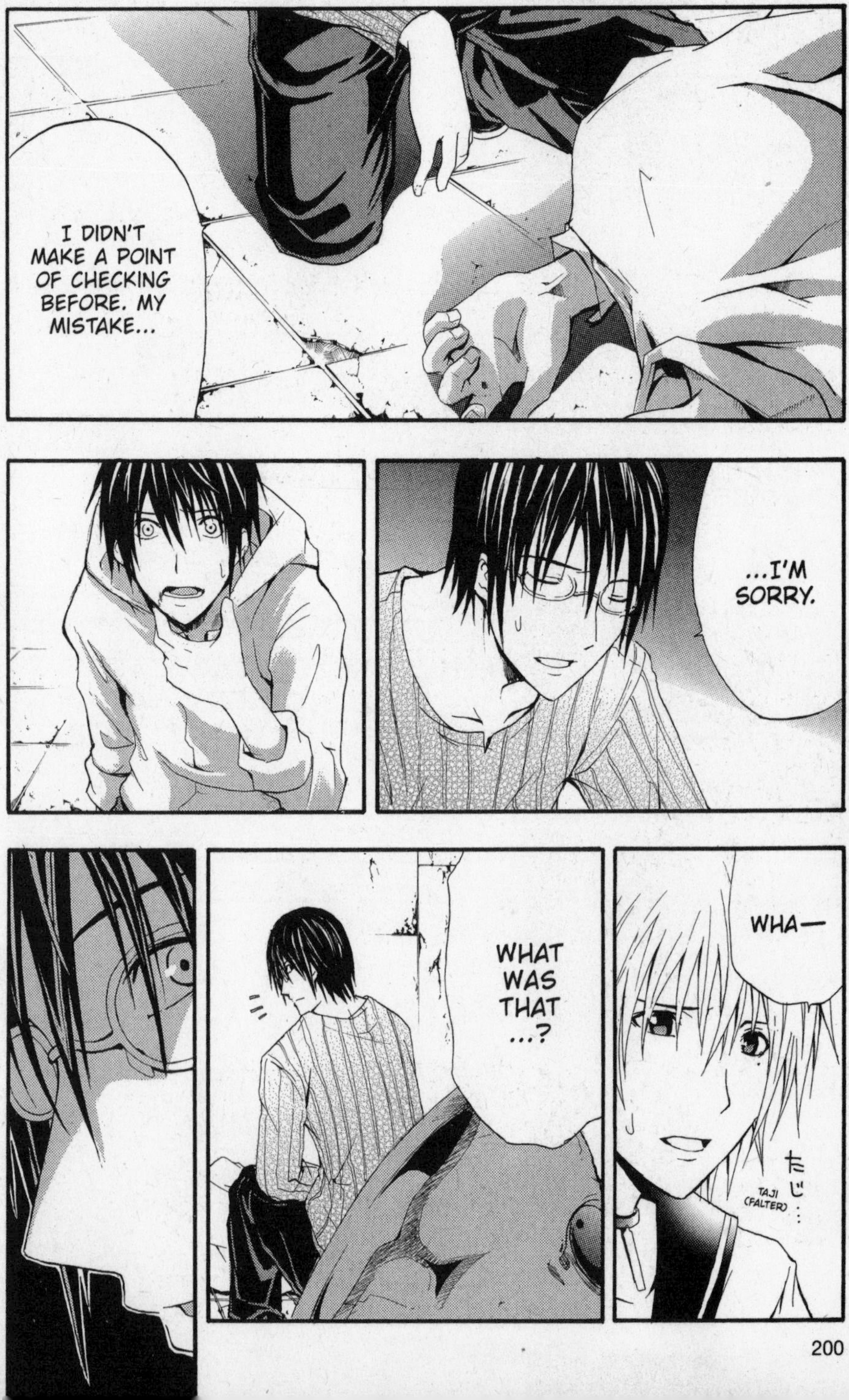
I DIDN'T MAKE A POINT OF CHECKING BEFORE. MY MISTAKE...
...I'M SORRY.
WHA—
たじ…
TAJI (FALTER)
WHAT WAS THAT ...?

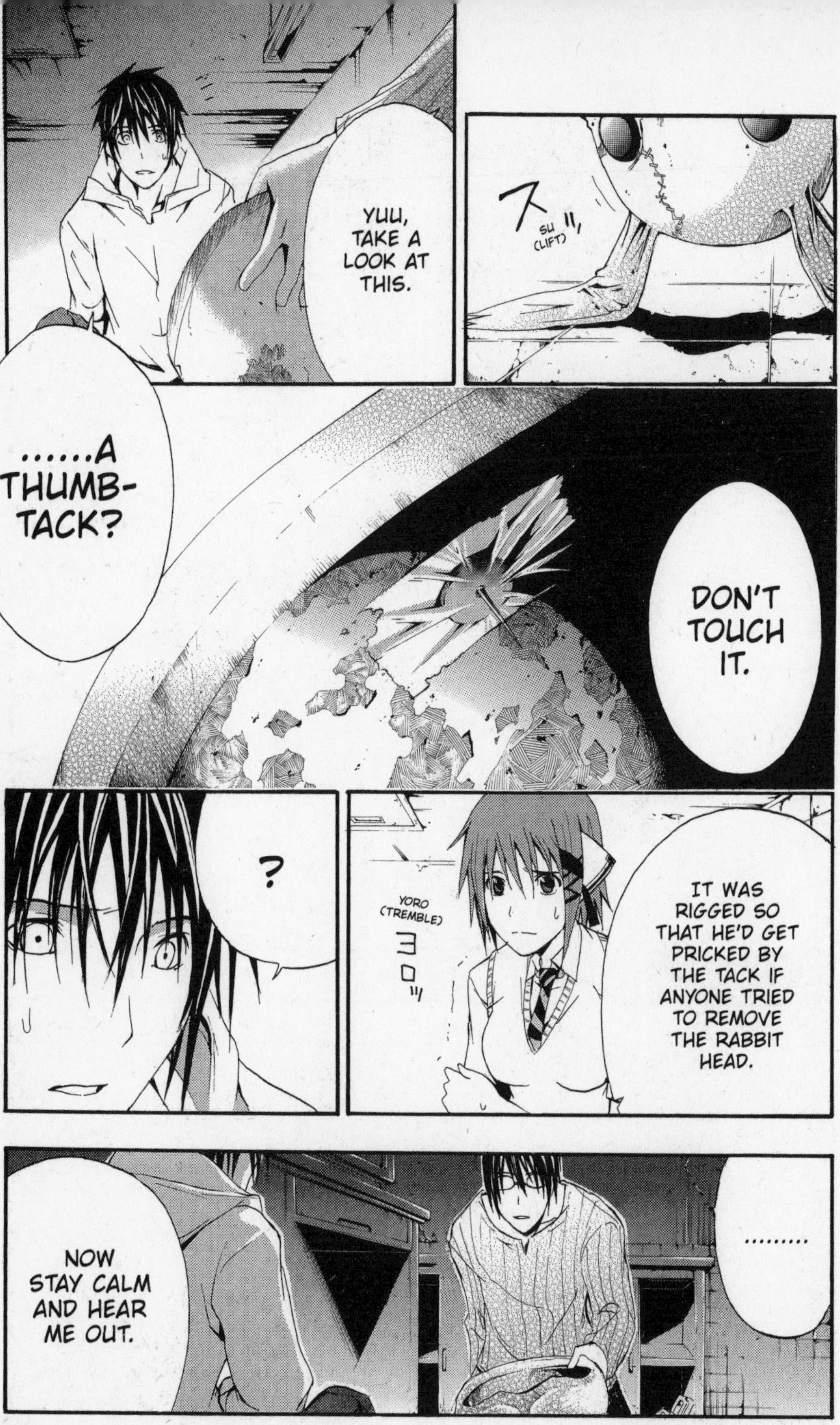
ス
SU (LIFT)
YUU, TAKE A LOOK AT THIS.
......A THUMB-TACK?
DON'T TOUCH IT.
YORO (TREMBLE)
ヨロッ
IT WAS RIGGED SO THAT HE'D GET PRICKED BY THE TACK IF ANYONE TRIED TO REMOVE THE RABBIT HEAD.
?
....
NOW STAY CALM AND HEAR ME OUT.

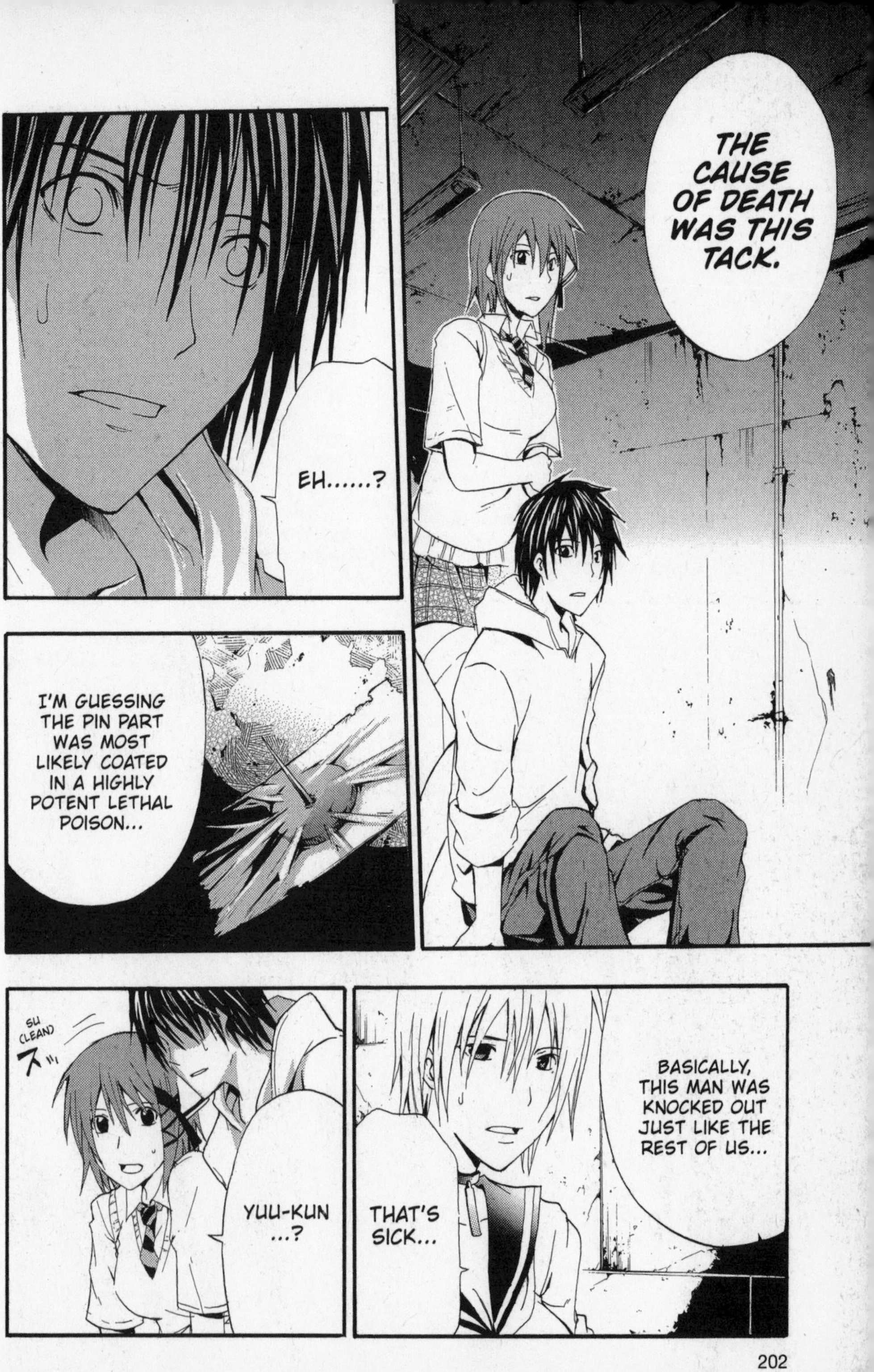
THE CAUSE OF DEATH WAS THIS TACK.
EH......?
I'M GUESSING THE PIN PART WAS MOST LIKELY COATED IN A HIGHLY POTENT LETHAL POISON...
BASICALLY, THIS MAN WAS KNOCKED OUT JUST LIKE THE REST OF US...
THAT'S SICK...
SU CLEAND
ス
YUU-KUN ...?

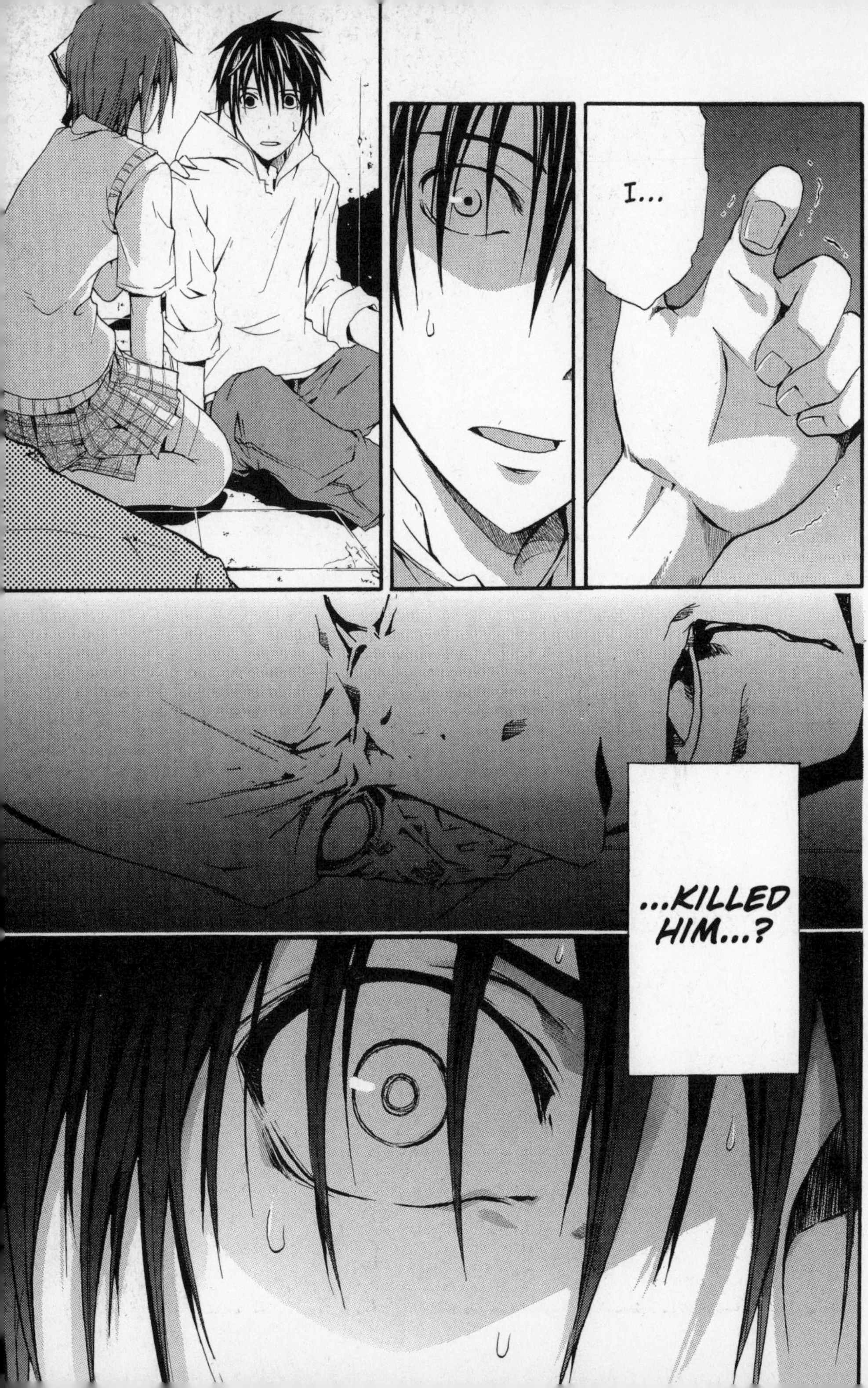
I...
...KILLED HIM...?

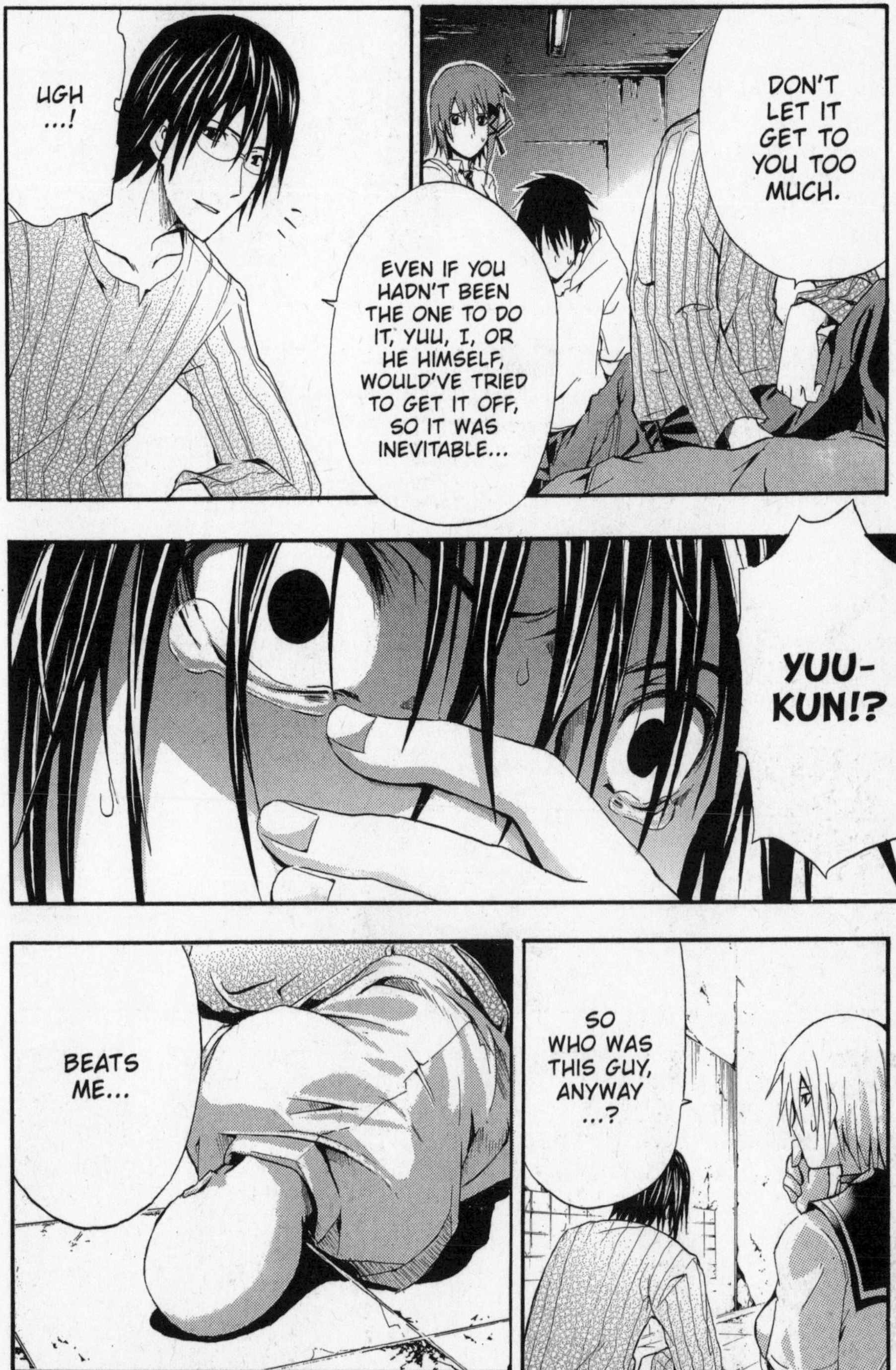
DON'T LET IT GET TO YOU TOO MUCH.
EVEN IF YOU HADN'T BEEN THE ONE TO DO IT, YUU, I, OR HE HIMSELF, WOULD'VE TRIED TO GET IT OFF, SO IT WAS INEVITABLE...
UGH ...!
YUU-KUN!?
SO WHO WAS THIS GUY, ANYWAY ...?
BEATS ME...

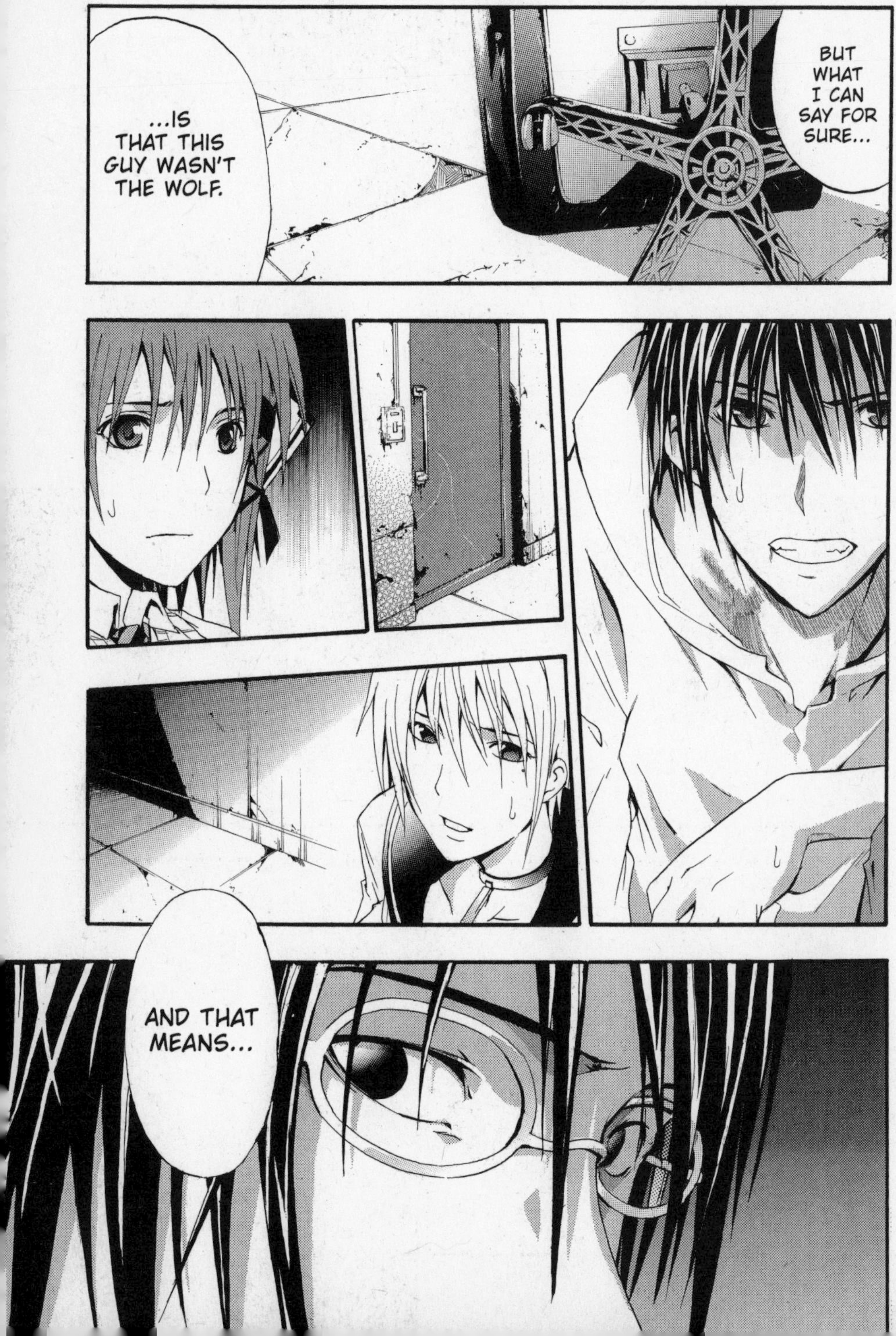
BUT WHAT I CAN SAY FOR SURE...
...IS THAT THIS GUY WASN'T THE WOLF.
AND THAT MEANS...

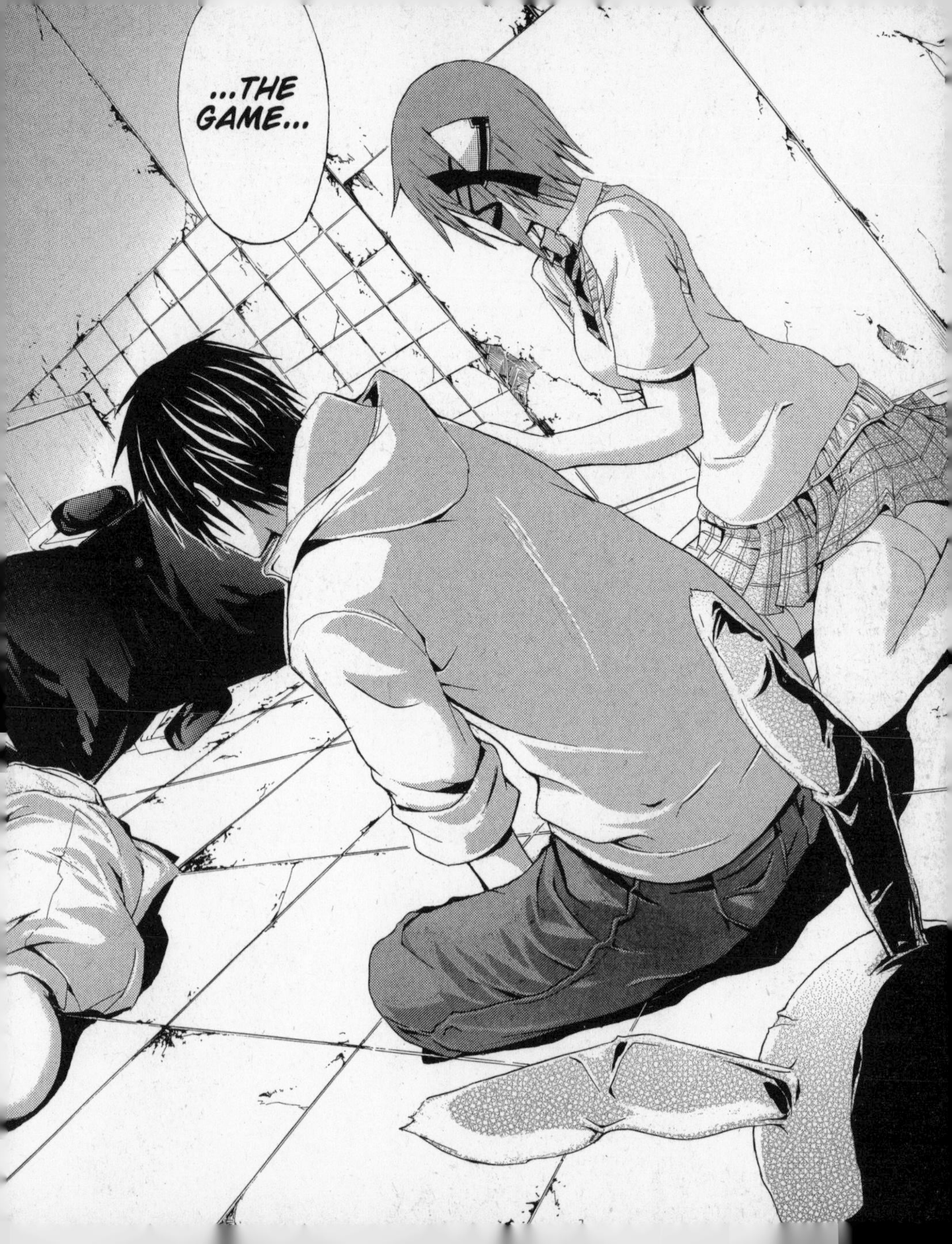
...THE GAME...

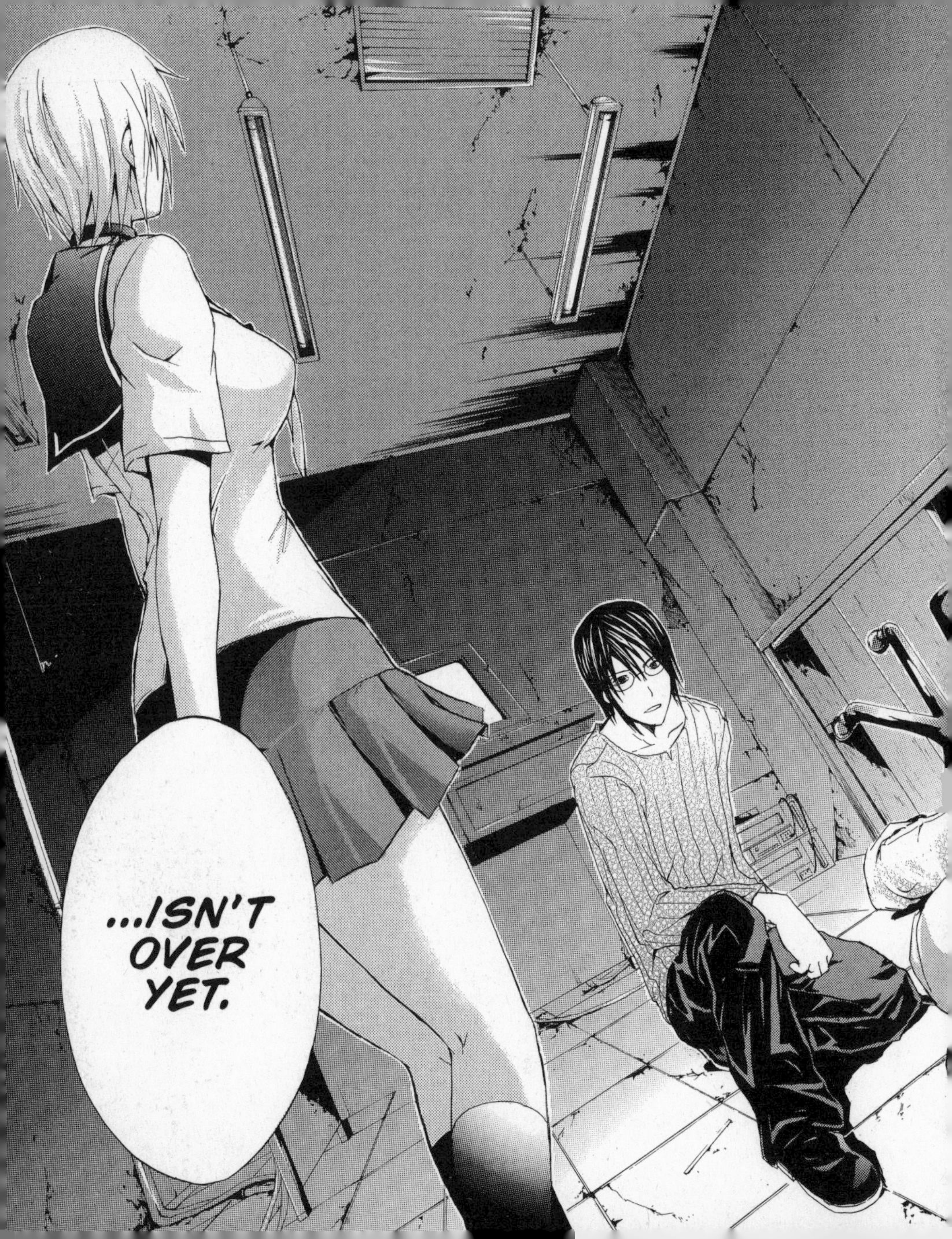
...ISN'T OVER YET.

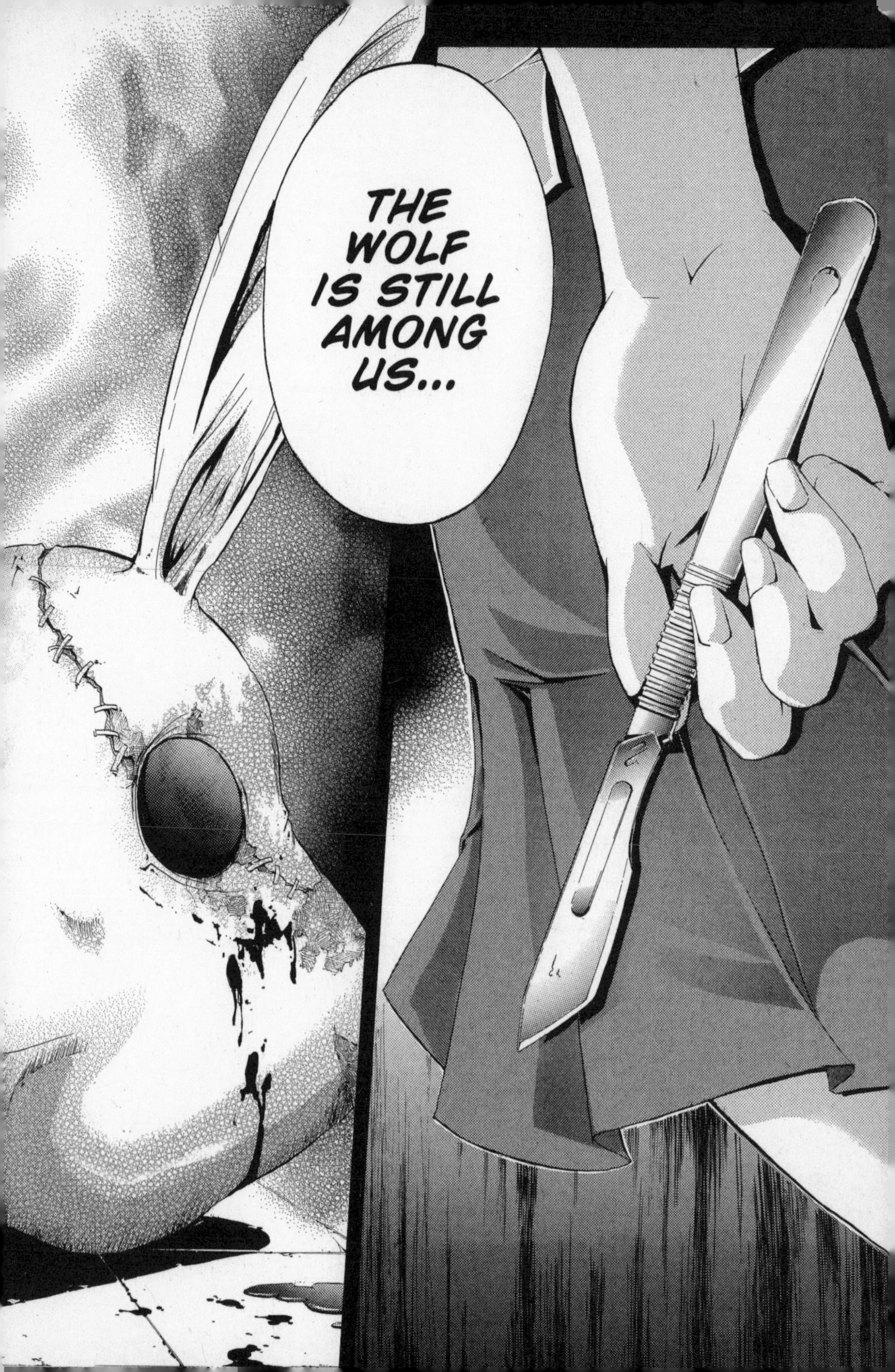
THE WOLF IS STILL AMONG US...

Doubt

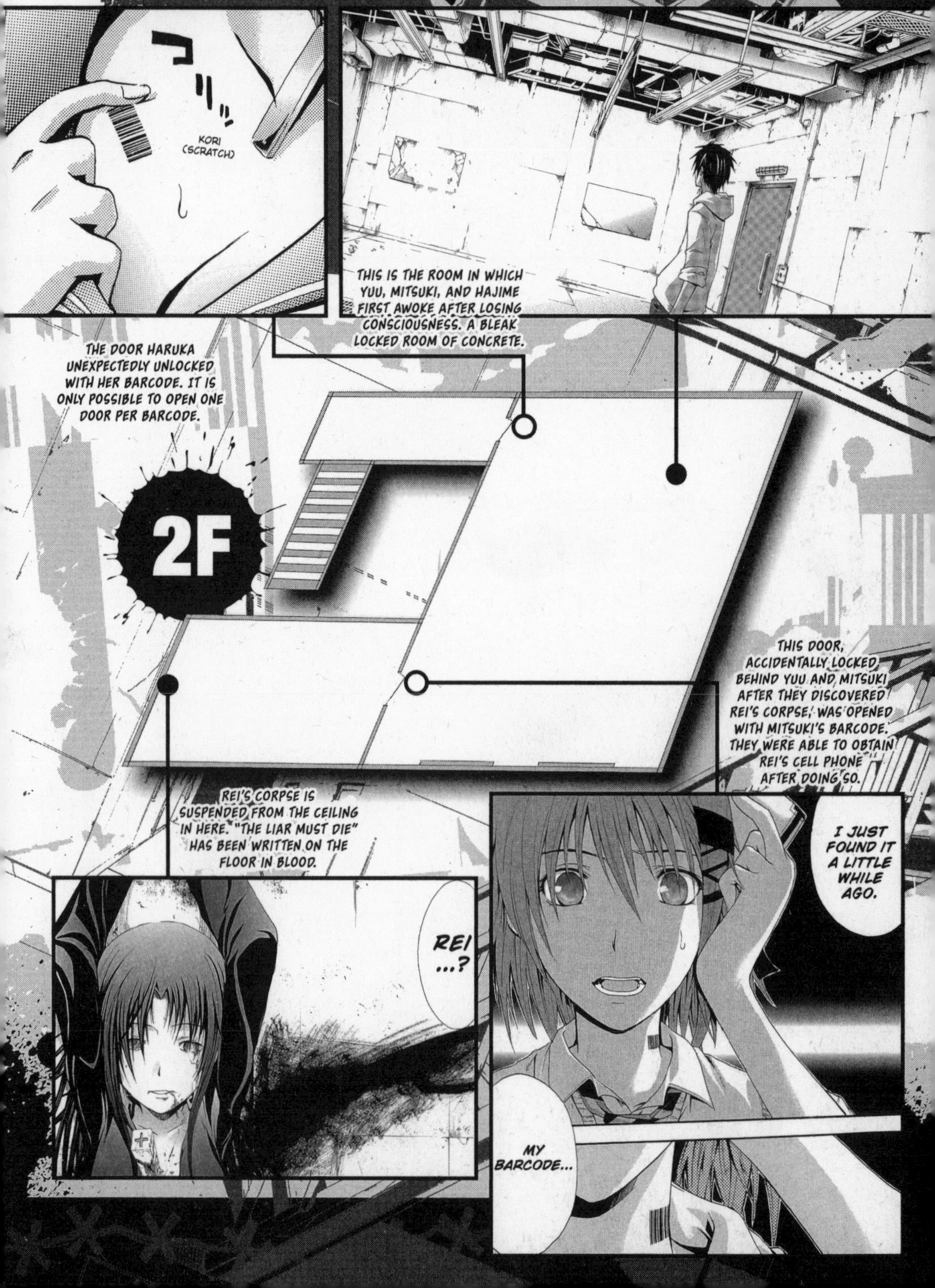
THIS IS THE ROOM IN WHICH YUU, MITSUKI, AND HAJIME FIRST AWOKE AFTER LOSING CONSCIOUSNESS. A BLEAK LOCKED ROOM OF CONCRETE.
コリッ
KORI (SCRATCH)
THE DOOR HARUKA UNEXPECTEDLY UNLOCKED WITH HER BARCODE. IT IS ONLY POSSIBLE TO OPEN ONE DOOR PER BARCODE.
2F
THIS DOOR, ACCIDENTALLY LOCKED BEHIND YUU AND MITSUKI AFTER THEY DISCOVERED REI'S CORPSE, WAS OPENED WITH MITSUKI'S BARCODE. THEY WERE ABLE TO OBTAIN REI'S CELL PHONE AFTER DOING SO.
REI'S CORPSE IS SUSPENDED FROM THE CEILING IN HERE. "THE LIAR MUST DIE" HAS BEEN WRITTEN ON THE FLOOR IN BLOOD.
I JUST FOUND IT A LITTLE WHILE AGO.
MY BARCODE...
REI ...?

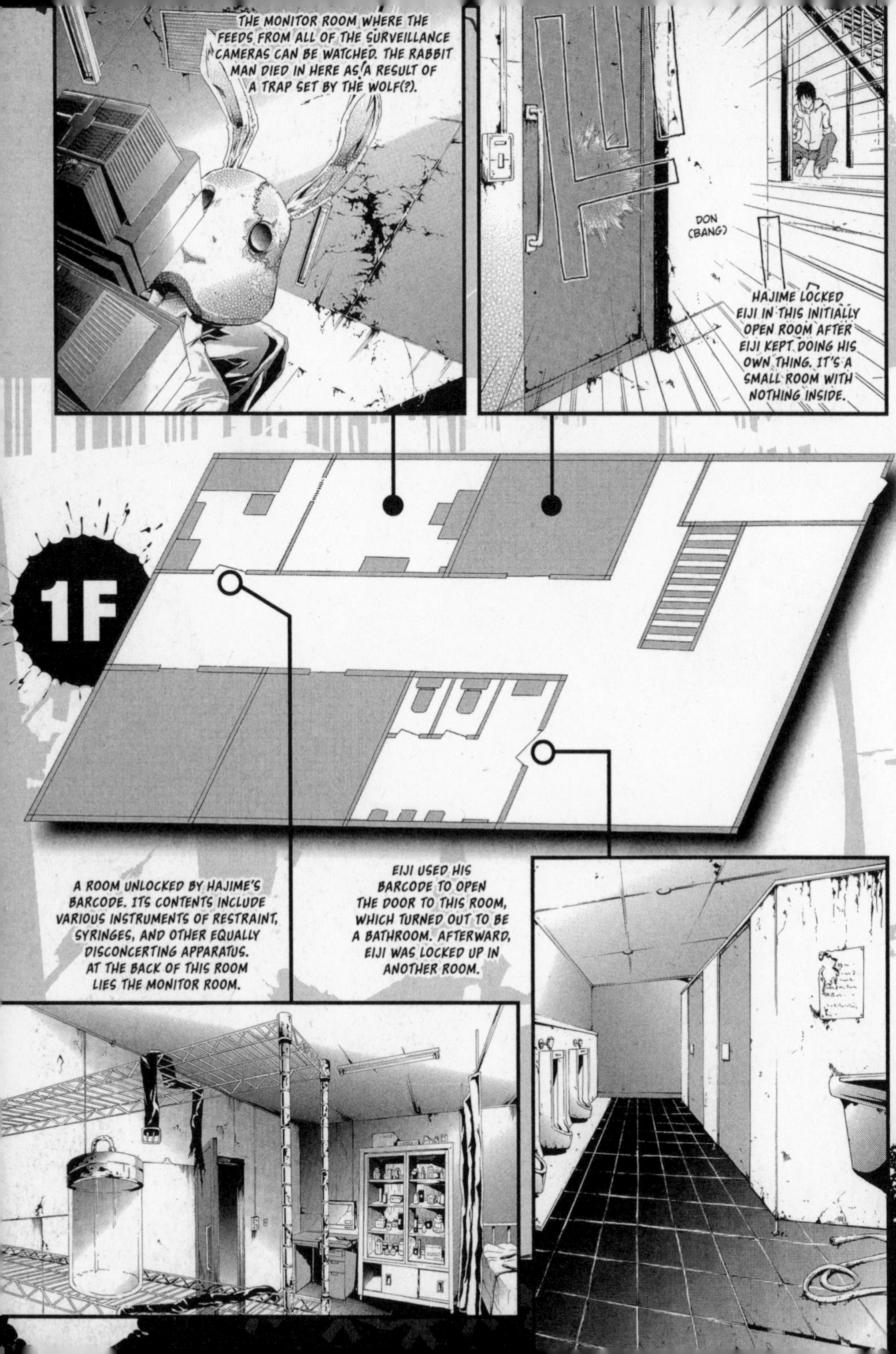
DON (BANG)
HAJIME LOCKED EIJI IN THIS INITIALLY OPEN ROOM AFTER EIJI KEPT DOING HIS OWN THING. IT'S A SMALL ROOM WITH NOTHING INSIDE.
THE MONITOR ROOM WHERE THE FEEDS FROM ALL OF THE SURVEILLANCE CAMERAS CAN BE WATCHED. THE RABBIT MAN DIED IN HERE AS A RESULT OF A TRAP SET BY THE WOLF(?).
1F
EIJI USED HIS BARCODE TO OPEN THE DOOR TO THIS ROOM, WHICH TURNED OUT TO BE A BATHROOM. AFTERWARD, EIJI WAS LOCKED UP IN ANOTHER ROOM.
A ROOM UNLOCKED BY HAJIME'S BARCODE. ITS CONTENTS INCLUDE VARIOUS INSTRUMENTS OF RESTRAINT, SYRINGES, AND OTHER EQUALLY DISCONCERTING APPARATUS. AT THE BACK OF THIS ROOM LIES THE MONITOR ROOM.

Doubt

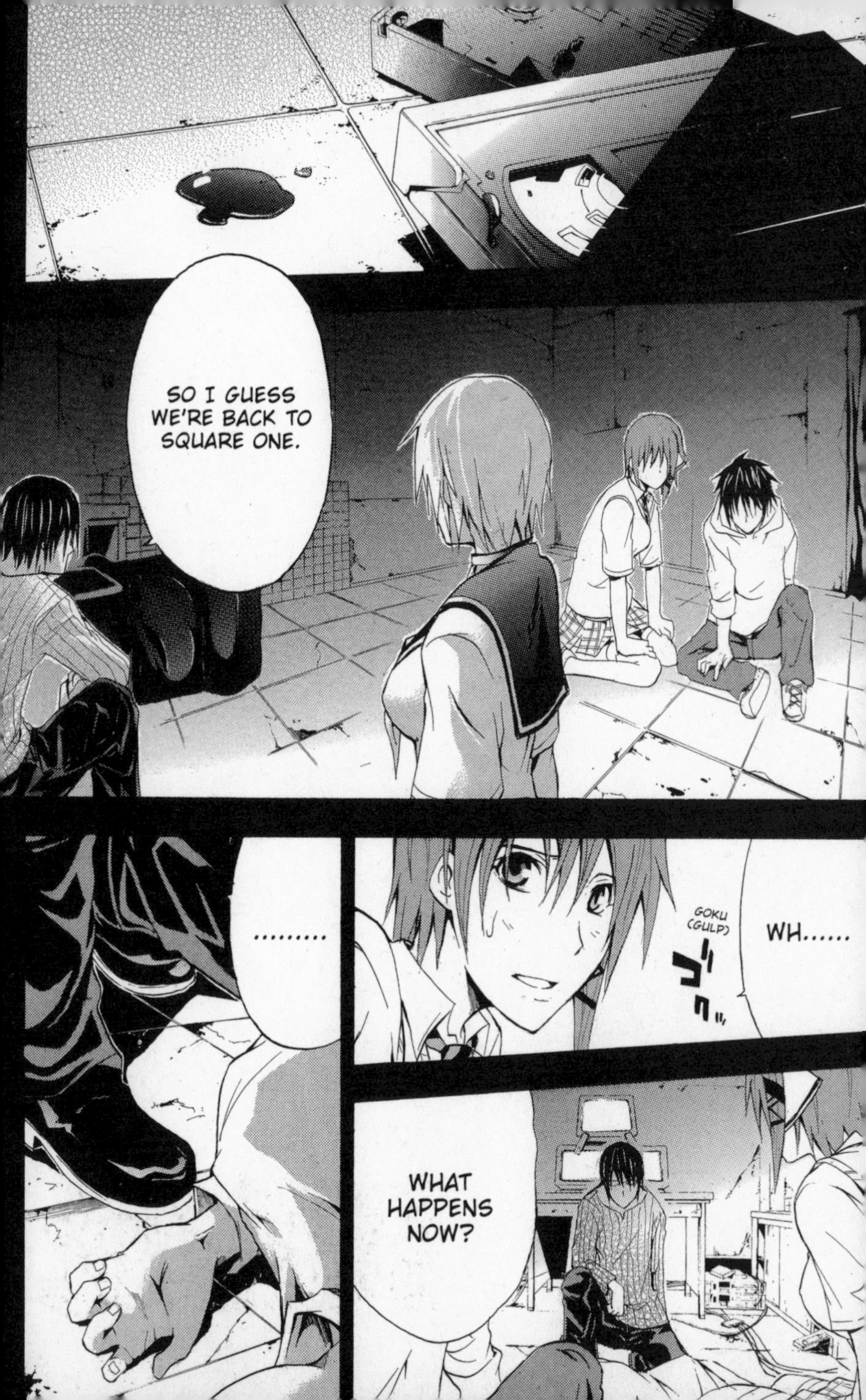
SO I GUESS WE'RE BACK TO SQUARE ONE.
WH......
GOKU (GULP)
WHAT HAPPENS NOW?
....

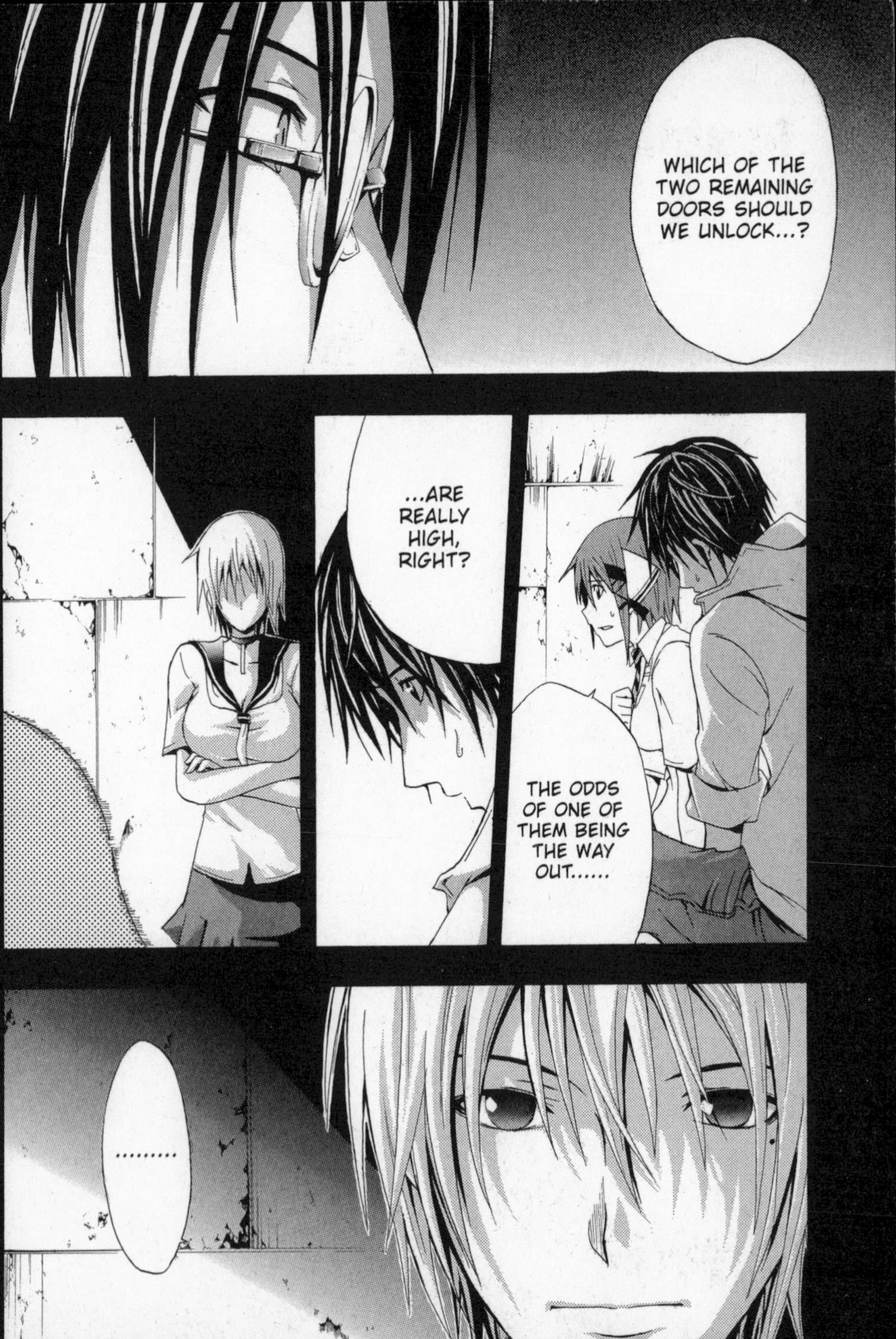
WHICH OF THE TWO REMAINING DOORS SHOULD WE UNLOCK...?
THE ODDS OF ONE OF THEM BEING THE WAY OUT......
...ARE REALLY HIGH, RIGHT?
....

Doubt.5 FILE

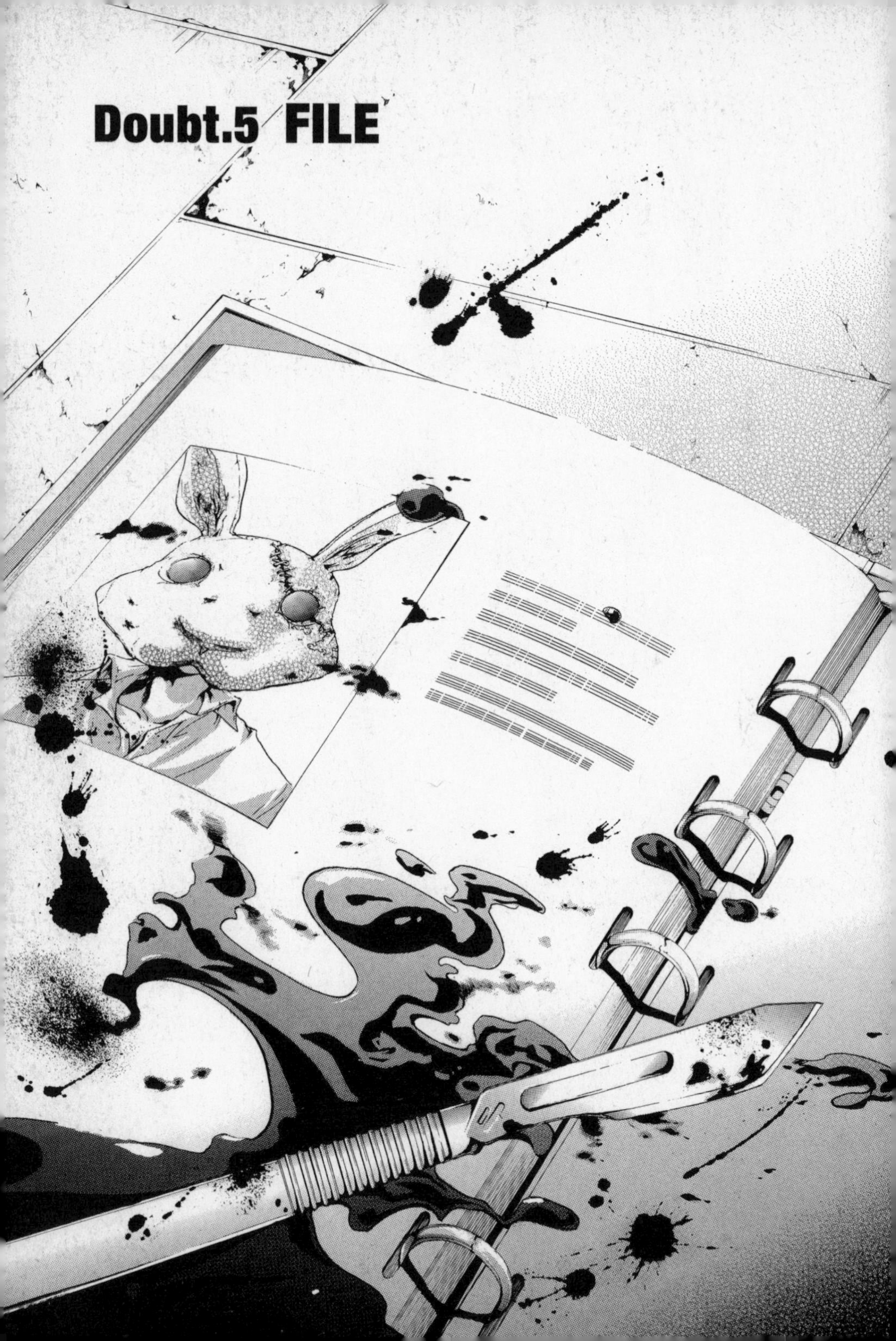

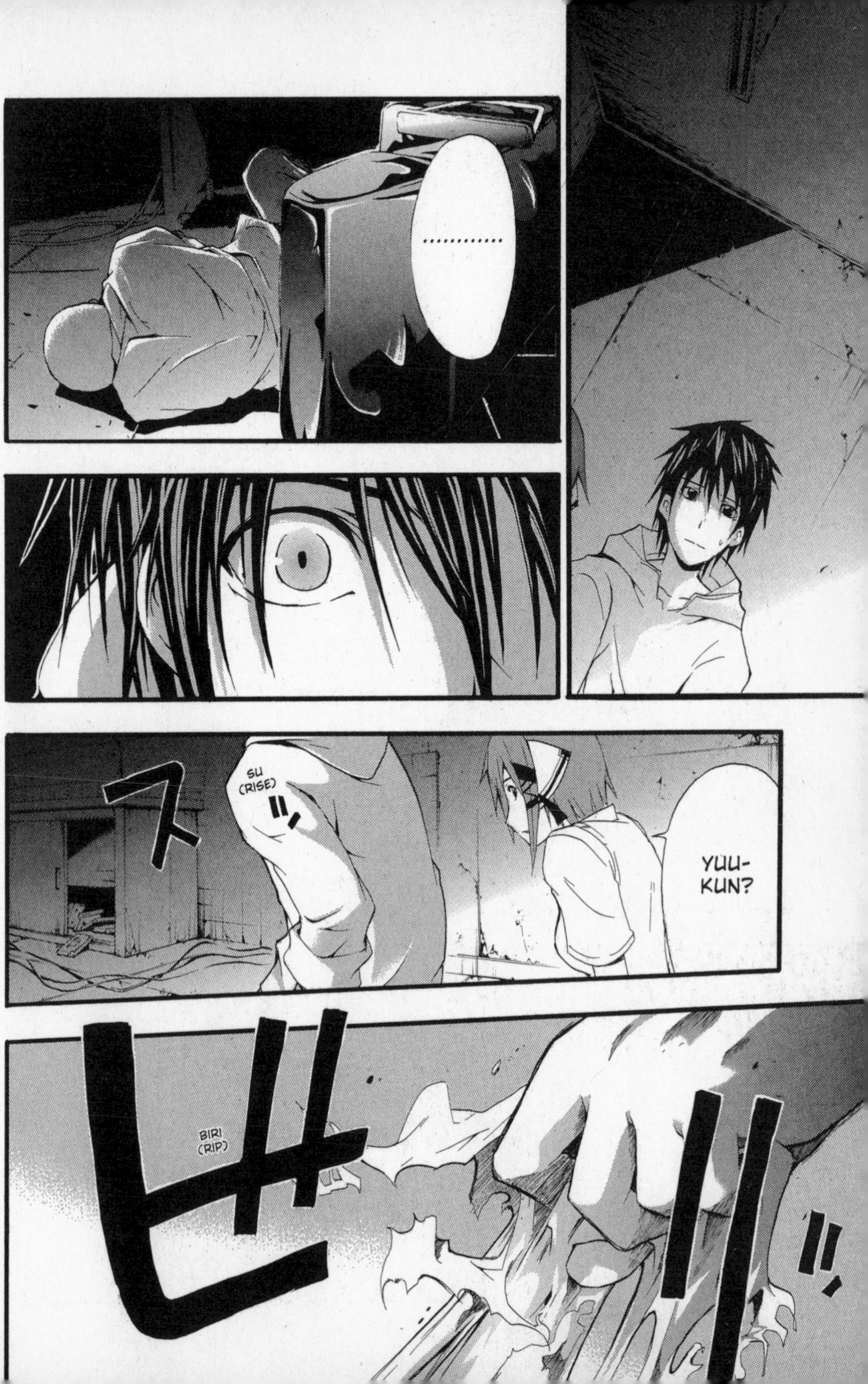
....
YUU-
KUN?
SU
(RISE)
BIRI
(RIP)

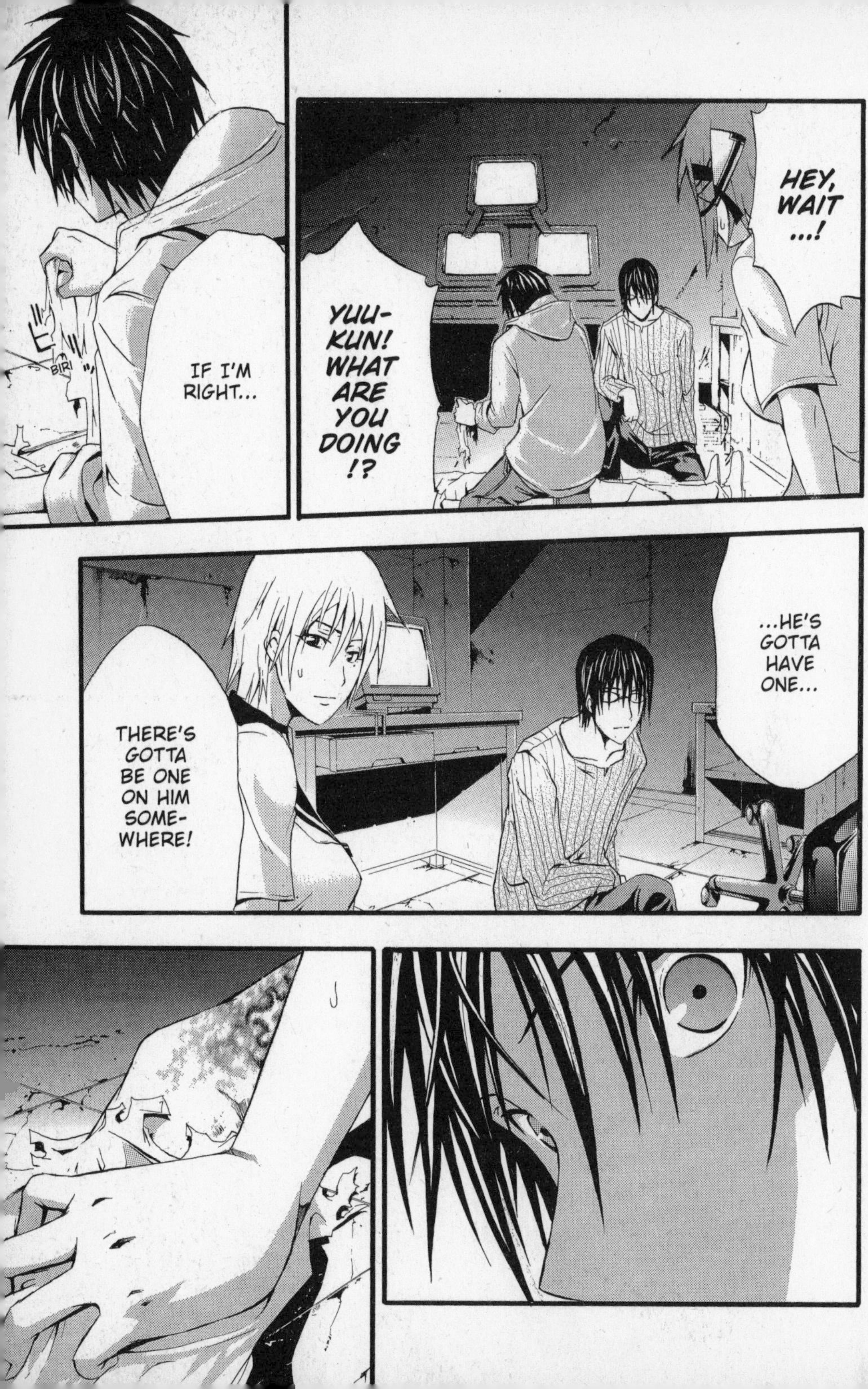
HEY, WAIT ...!
YUU-KUN! WHAT ARE YOU DOING!?
BIRI
IF I'M RIGHT...
...HE'S GOTTA HAVE ONE...
THERE'S GOTTA BE ONE ON HIM SOME-WHERE!

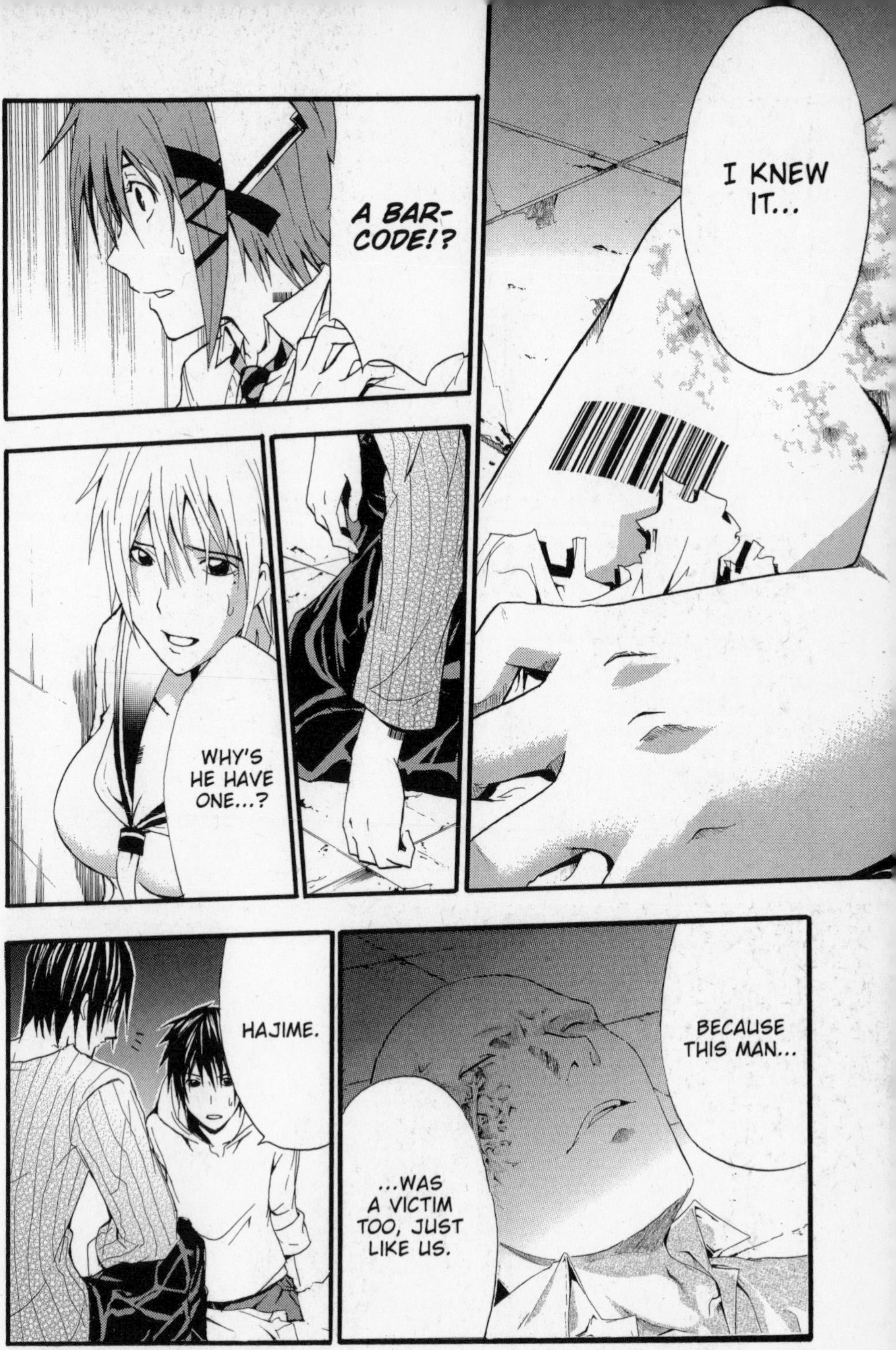
I KNEW IT...
A BAR-CODE!?
WHY'S HE HAVE ONE...?
BECAUSE THIS MAN...
...WAS A VICTIM TOO, JUST LIKE US.
HAJIME.

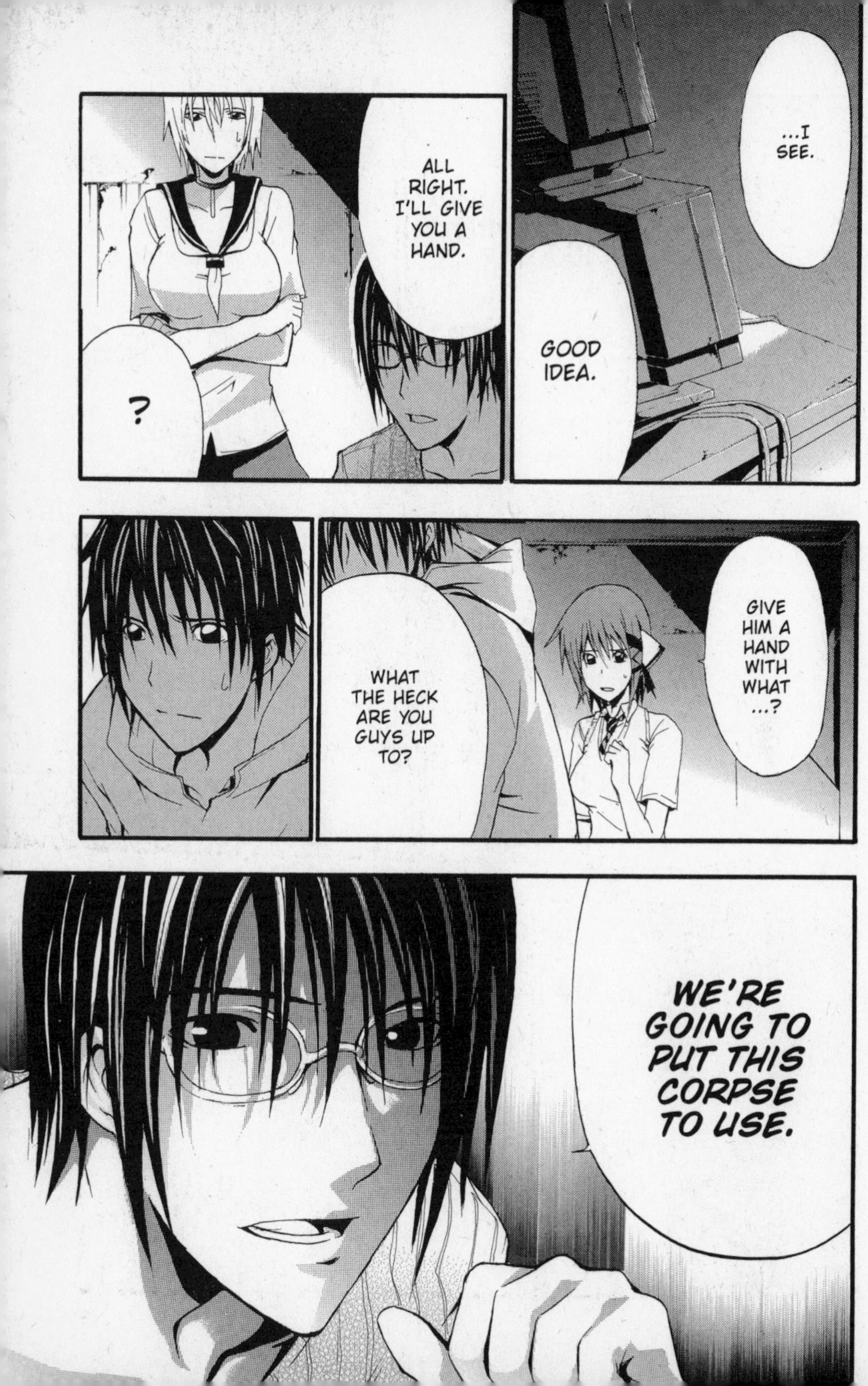
...I SEE.
GOOD IDEA.
ALL RIGHT. I'LL GIVE YOU A HAND.
?
GIVE HIM A HAND WITH WHAT ...?
WHAT THE HECK ARE YOU GUYS UP TO?
WE'RE GOING TO PUT THIS CORPSE TO USE.

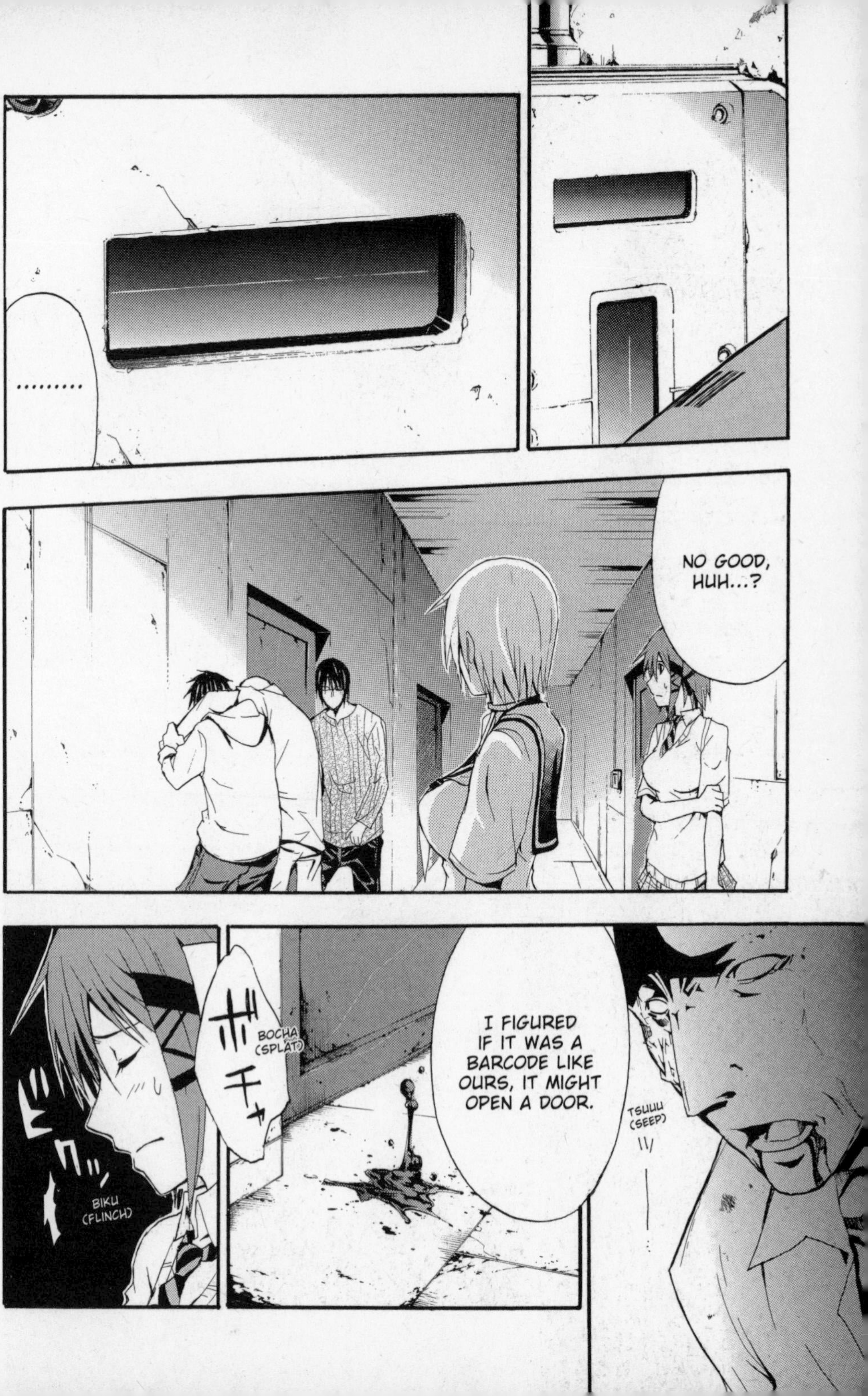
....
NO GOOD, HUH...?
I FIGURED IF IT WAS A BARCODE LIKE OURS, IT MIGHT OPEN A DOOR.
TSUUU (SEEP)
BOCHA (SPLAT)
BIKU (FLINCH)

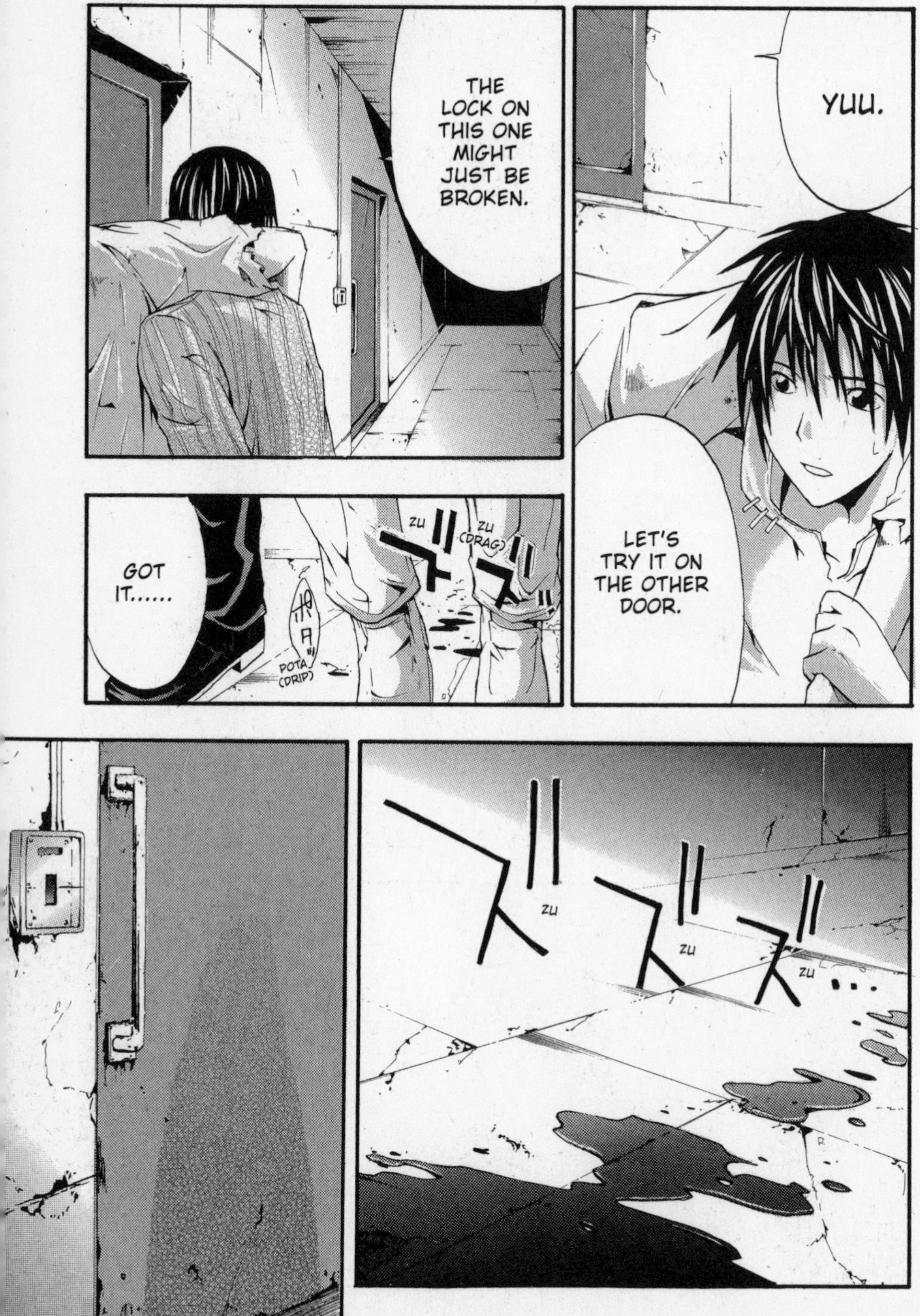
YUU.
LET'S TRY IT ON THE OTHER DOOR.
THE LOCK ON THIS ONE MIGHT JUST BE BROKEN.
ZU
ZU (DRAG)
GOT IT......
POTA (DRIP)
ZU
ZU
ZU...

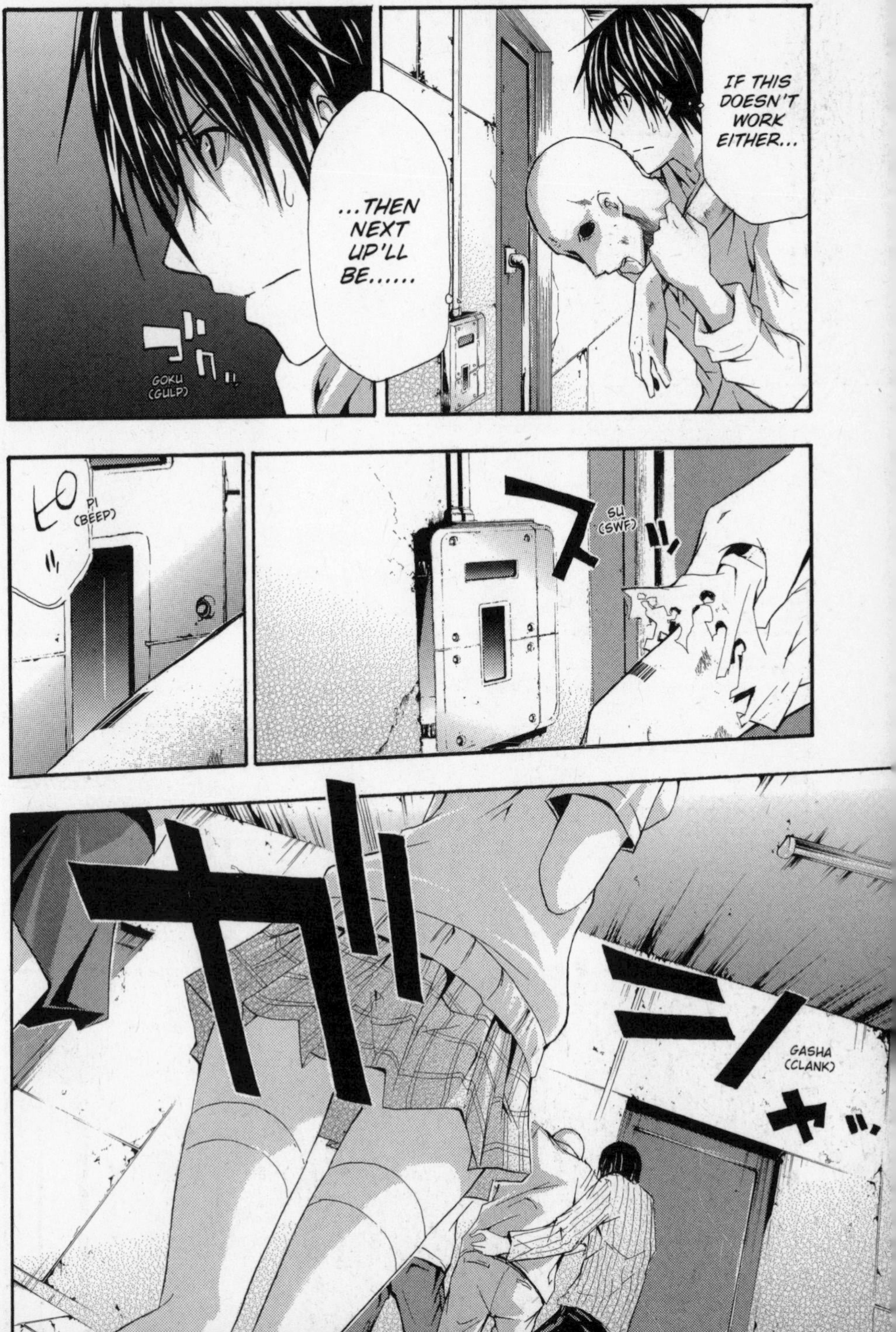
IF THIS DOESN'T WORK EITHER...
...THEN NEXT UP'LL BE......
GOKU (GULP)
SU (SWF)
PI (BEEP)
GASHA (CLANK)

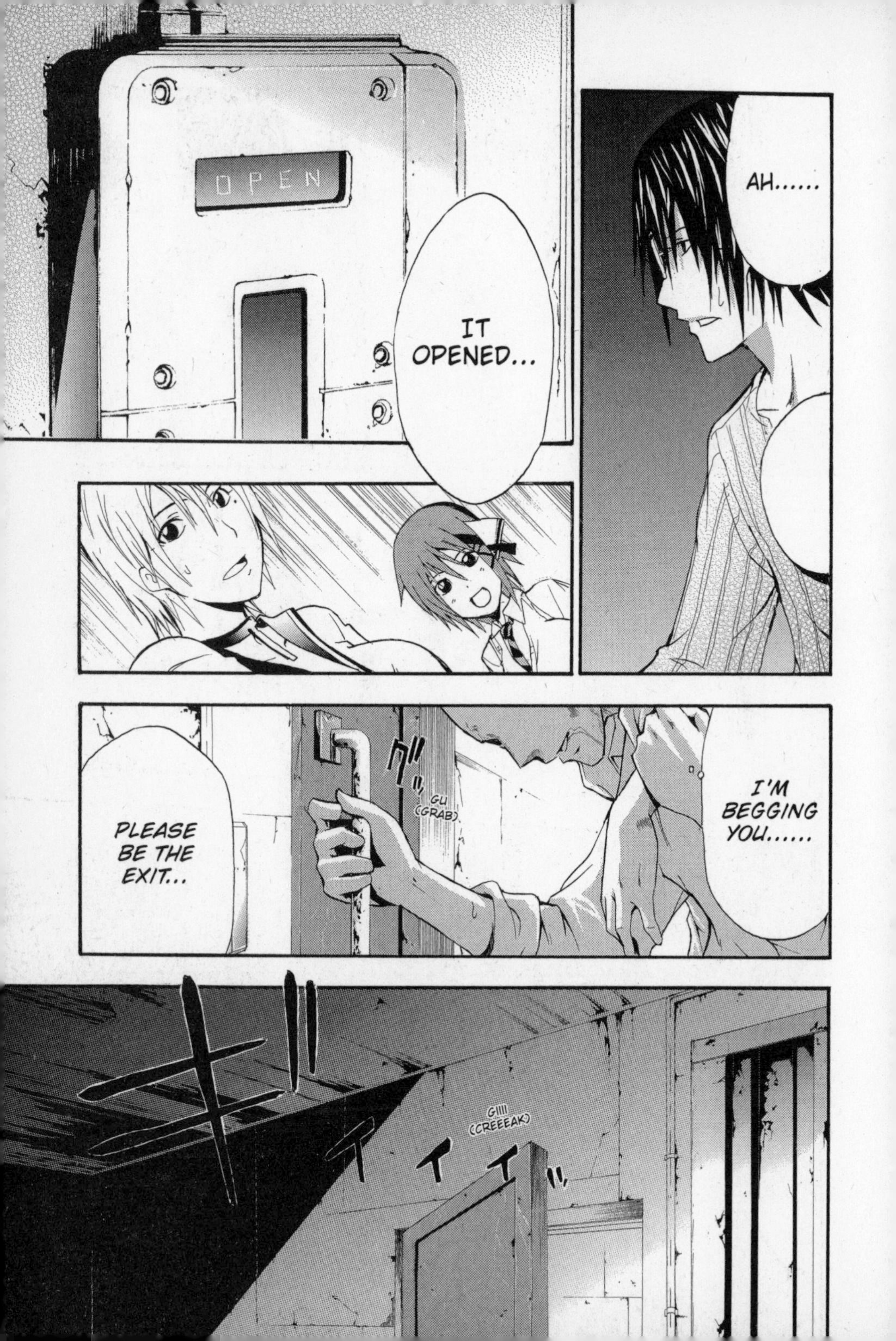
AH......
OPEN
IT OPENED...
I'M BEGGING YOU......
GU (GRAB)
PLEASE BE THE EXIT...
GIIII (CREEEAK)

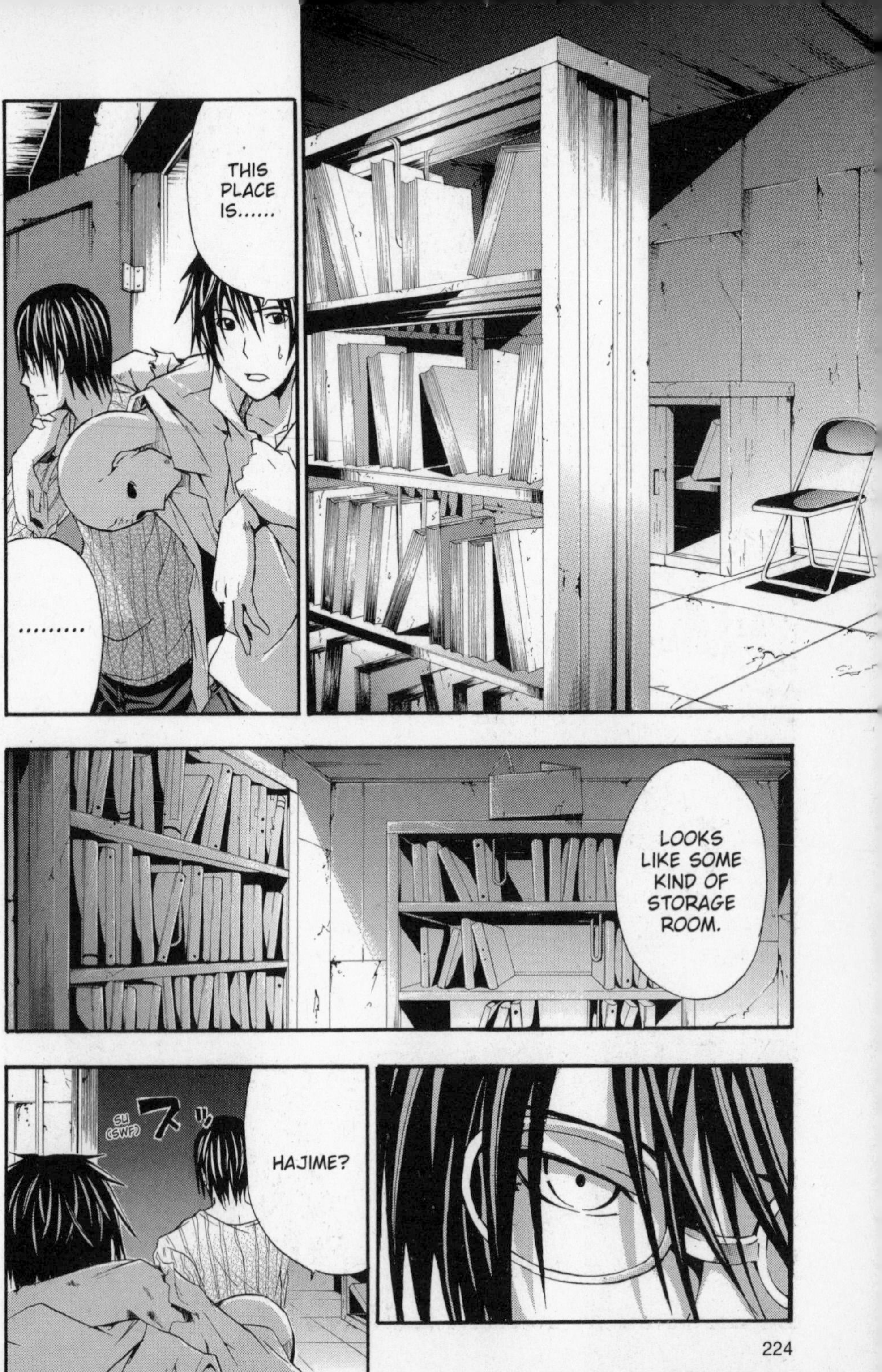
THIS PLACE IS......
....
LOOKS LIKE SOME KIND OF STORAGE ROOM.
SU (SWF)
HAJIME?

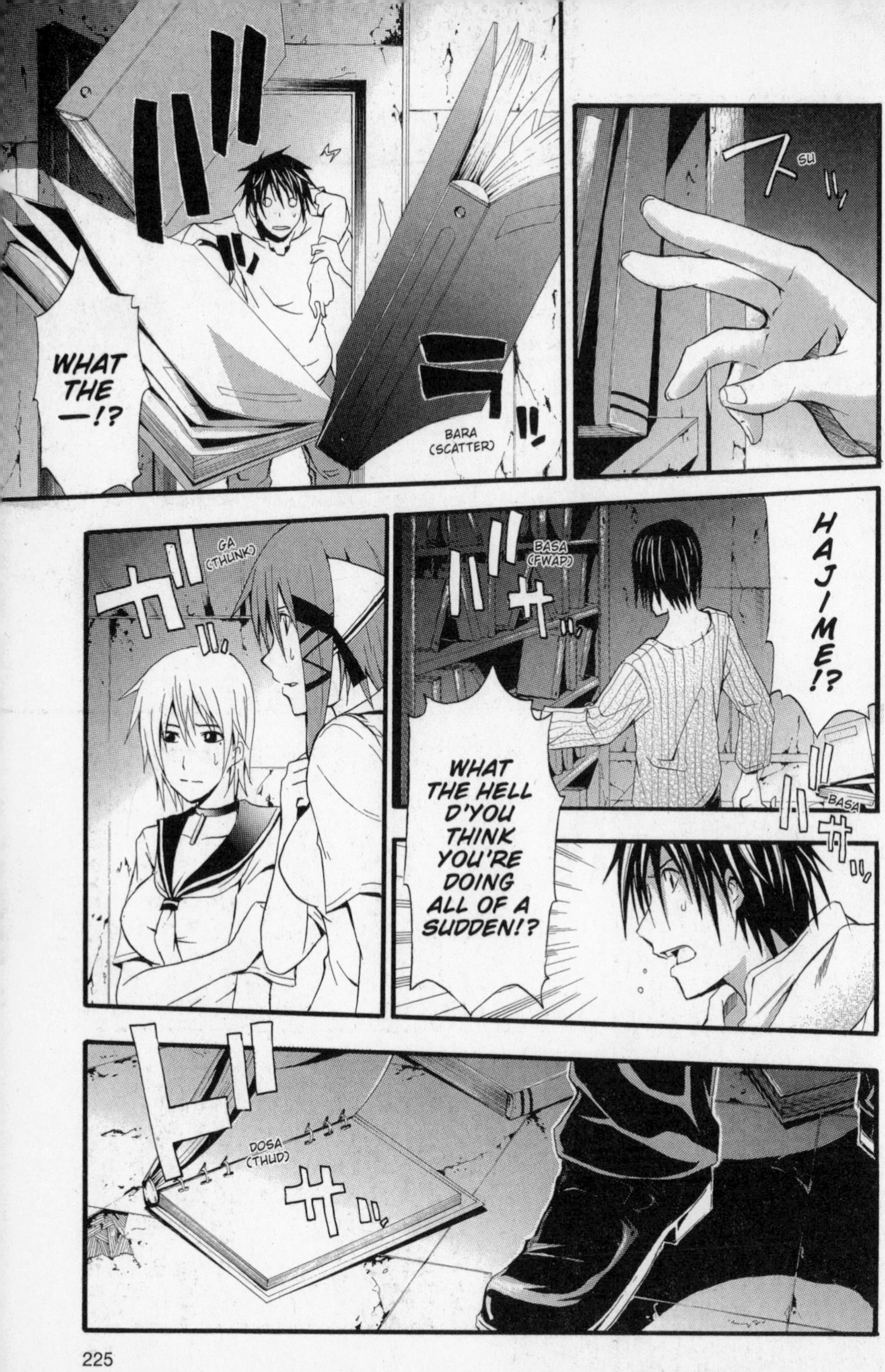
SU
WHAT THE—!?
BARA (SCATTER)
HAJIME!?
BASA (FWAP)
BASA
WHAT THE HELL D'YOU THINK YOU'RE DOING ALL OF A SUDDEN!?
GA (THUNK)
DOSA (THUD)

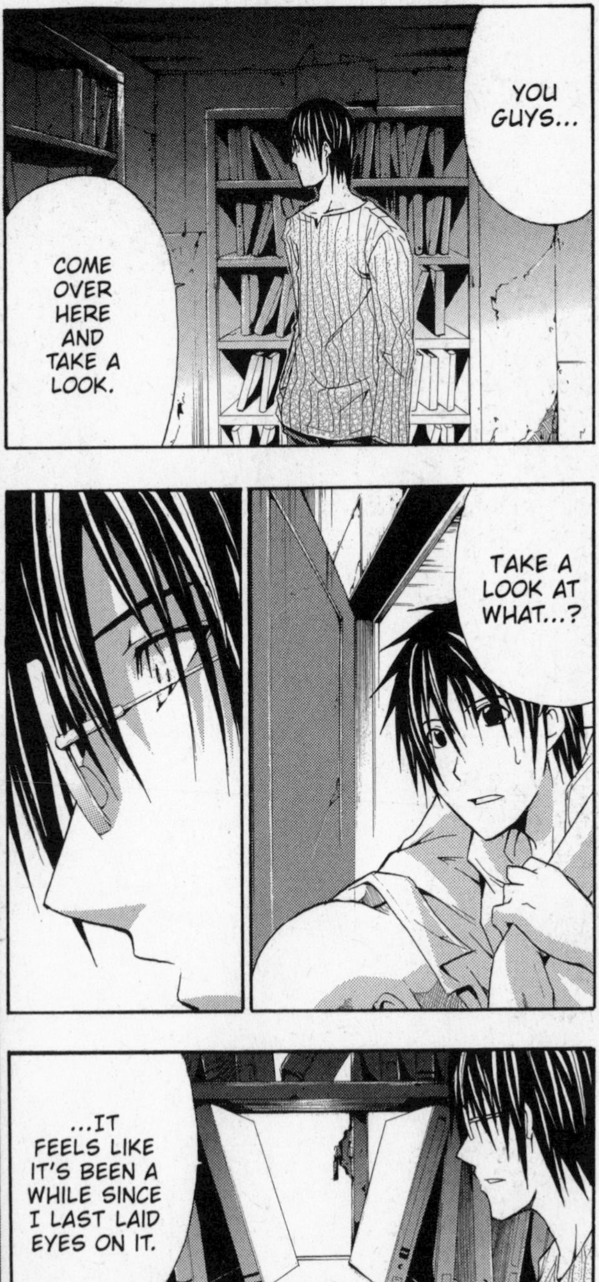
YOU GUYS...
COME OVER HERE AND TAKE A LOOK.
TAKE A LOOK AT WHAT...?
...IT FEELS LIKE IT'S BEEN A WHILE SINCE I LAST LAID EYES ON IT.
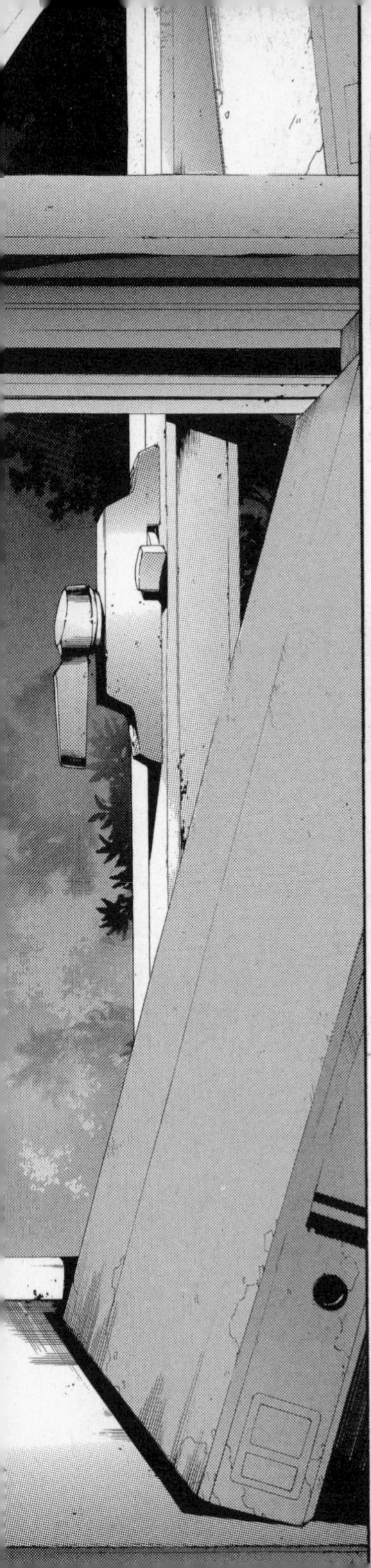

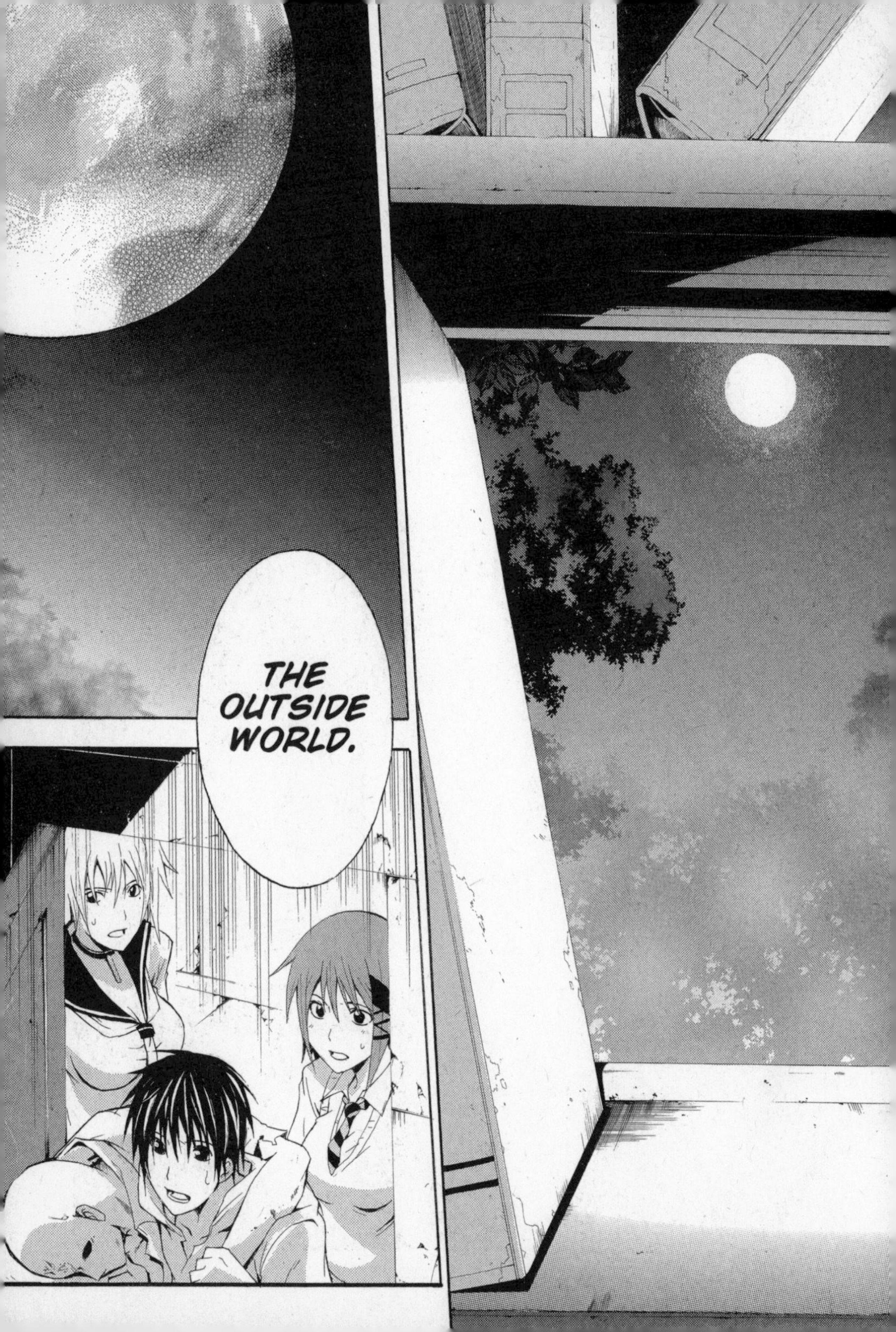
THE OUTSIDE WORLD.

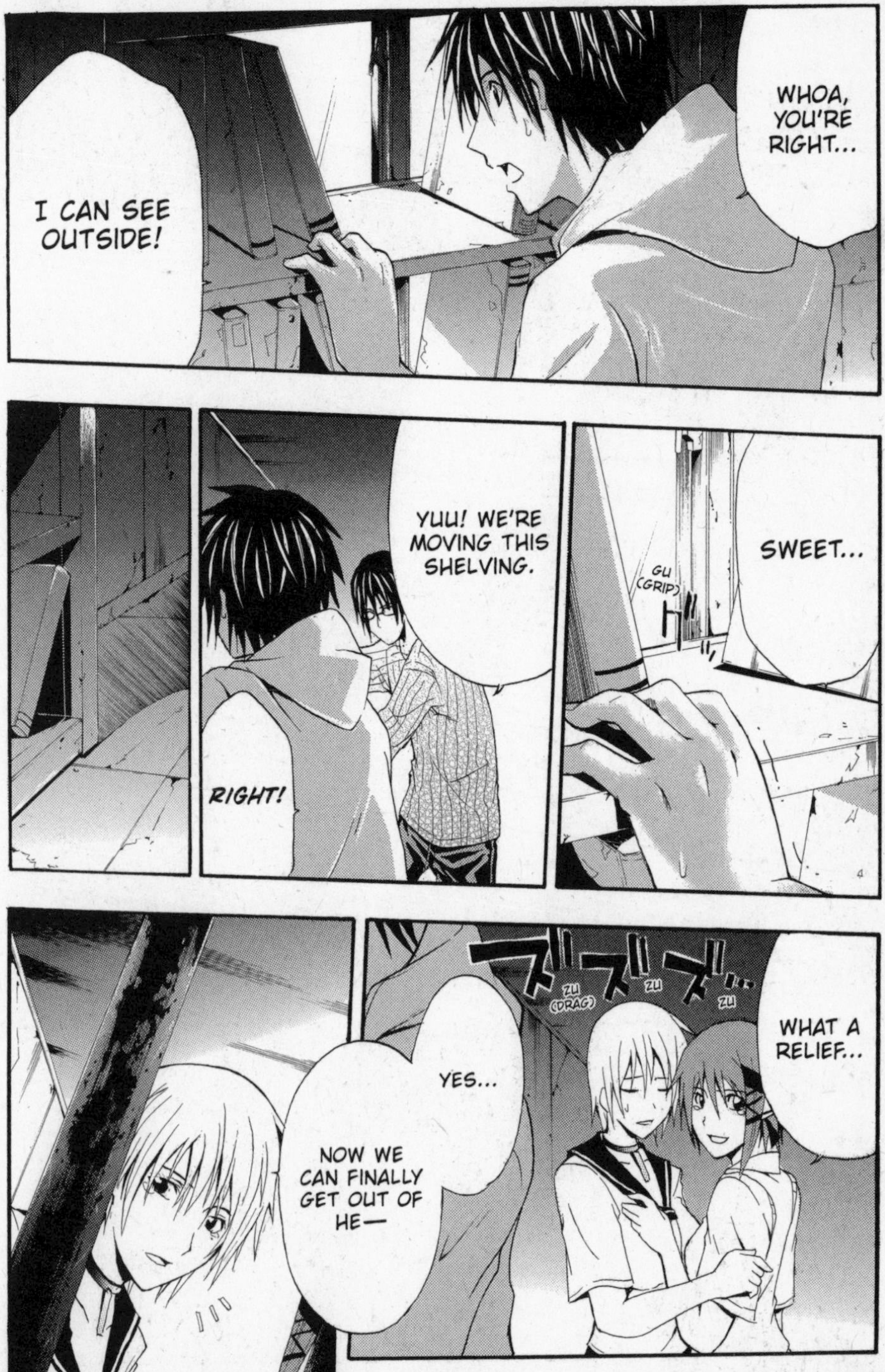
WHOA, YOU'RE RIGHT...
I CAN SEE OUTSIDE!
SWEET...
GU (GRIP)
YUU! WE'RE MOVING THIS SHELVING.
RIGHT!
ZU (DRAG) ZU ZU
WHAT A RELIEF...
YES...
NOW WE CAN FINALLY GET OUT OF HE—

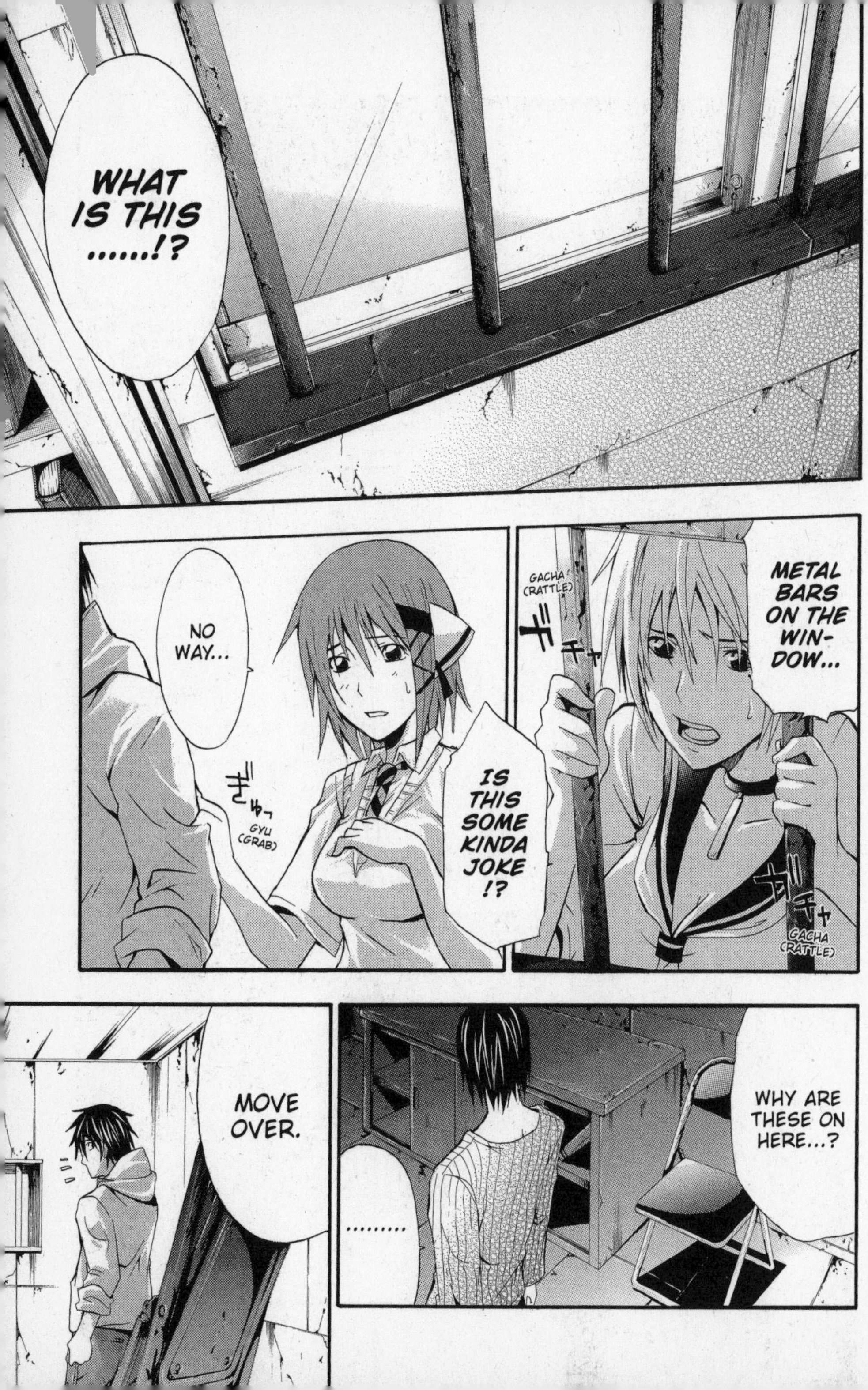
WHAT IS THIS ......!?
METAL BARS ON THE WIN-DOW...
GACHA (RATTLE)
GACHA (RATTLE)
NO WAY...
IS THIS SOME KINDA JOKE!?
GYU (GRAB)
WHY ARE THESE ON HERE...?
....
MOVE OVER.

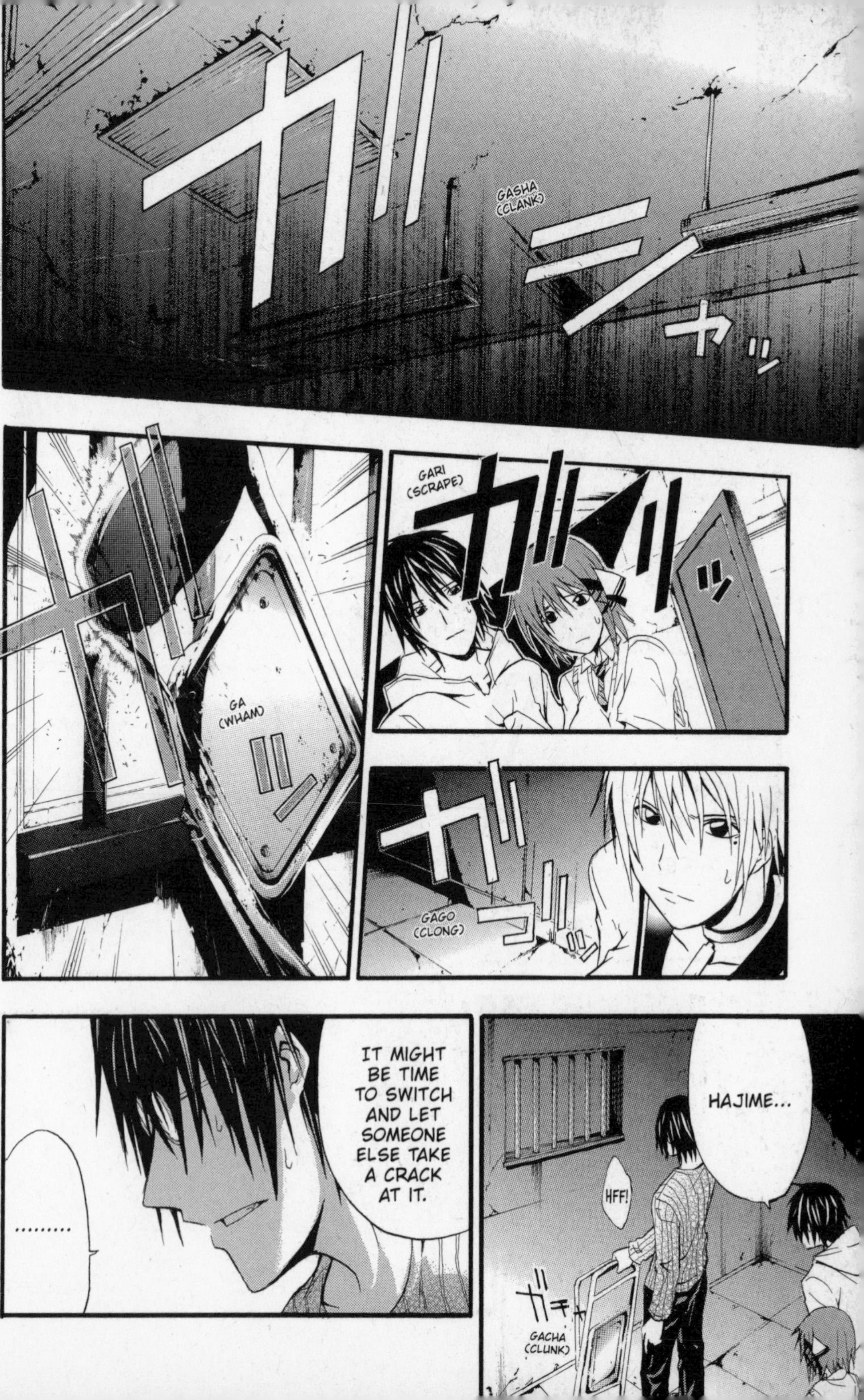
GASHA (CLANK)
GARI (SCRAPE)
GAGO (CLONG)
GA (WHAM)
HAJIME...
HFF!
GACHA (CLUNK)
IT MIGHT BE TIME TO SWITCH AND LET SOMEONE ELSE TAKE A CRACK AT IT.
....

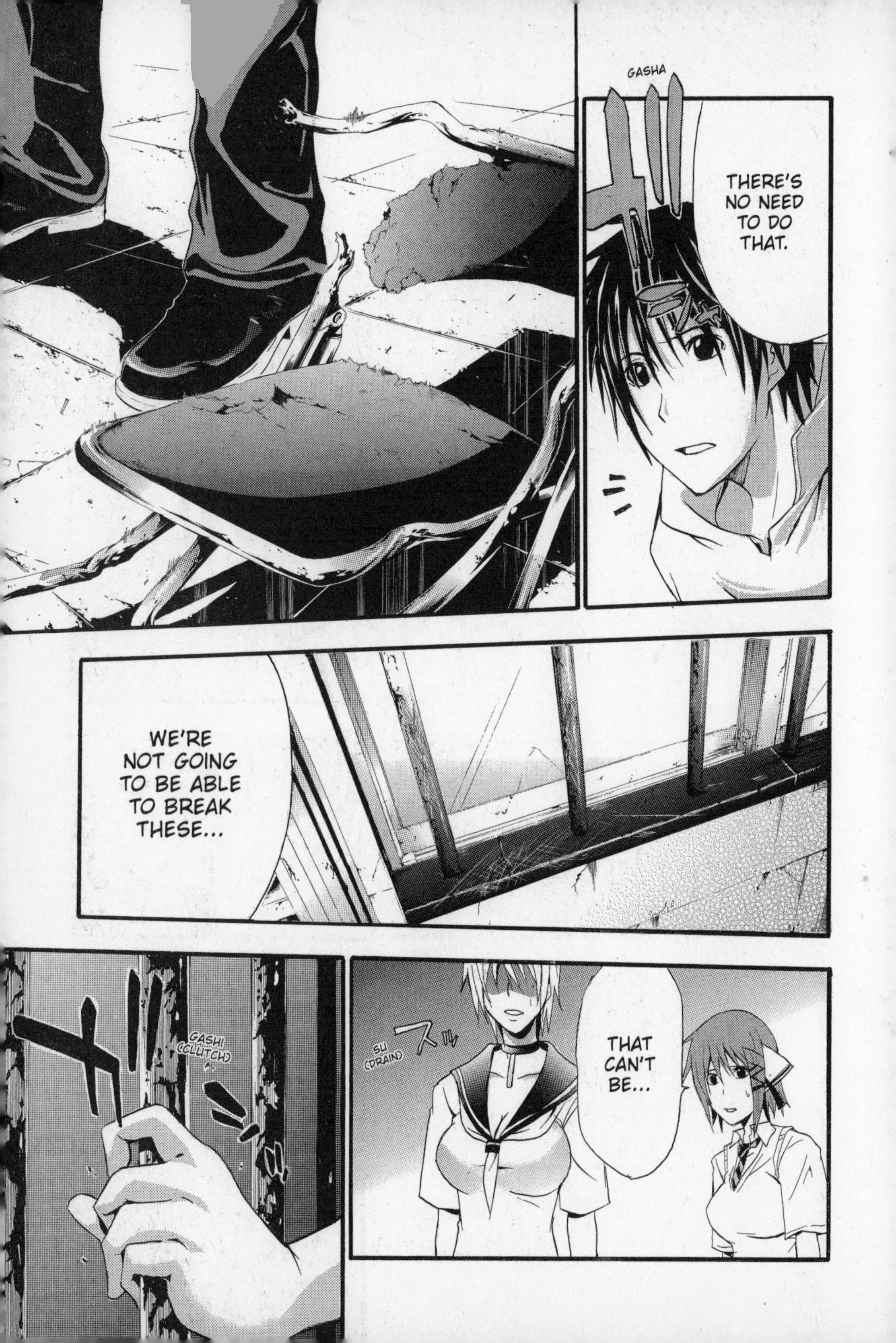
GASHA
THERE'S NO NEED TO DO THAT.
WE'RE NOT GOING TO BE ABLE TO BREAK THESE...
SU (DRAIN)
THAT CAN'T BE...
GASHI (CLUTCH)

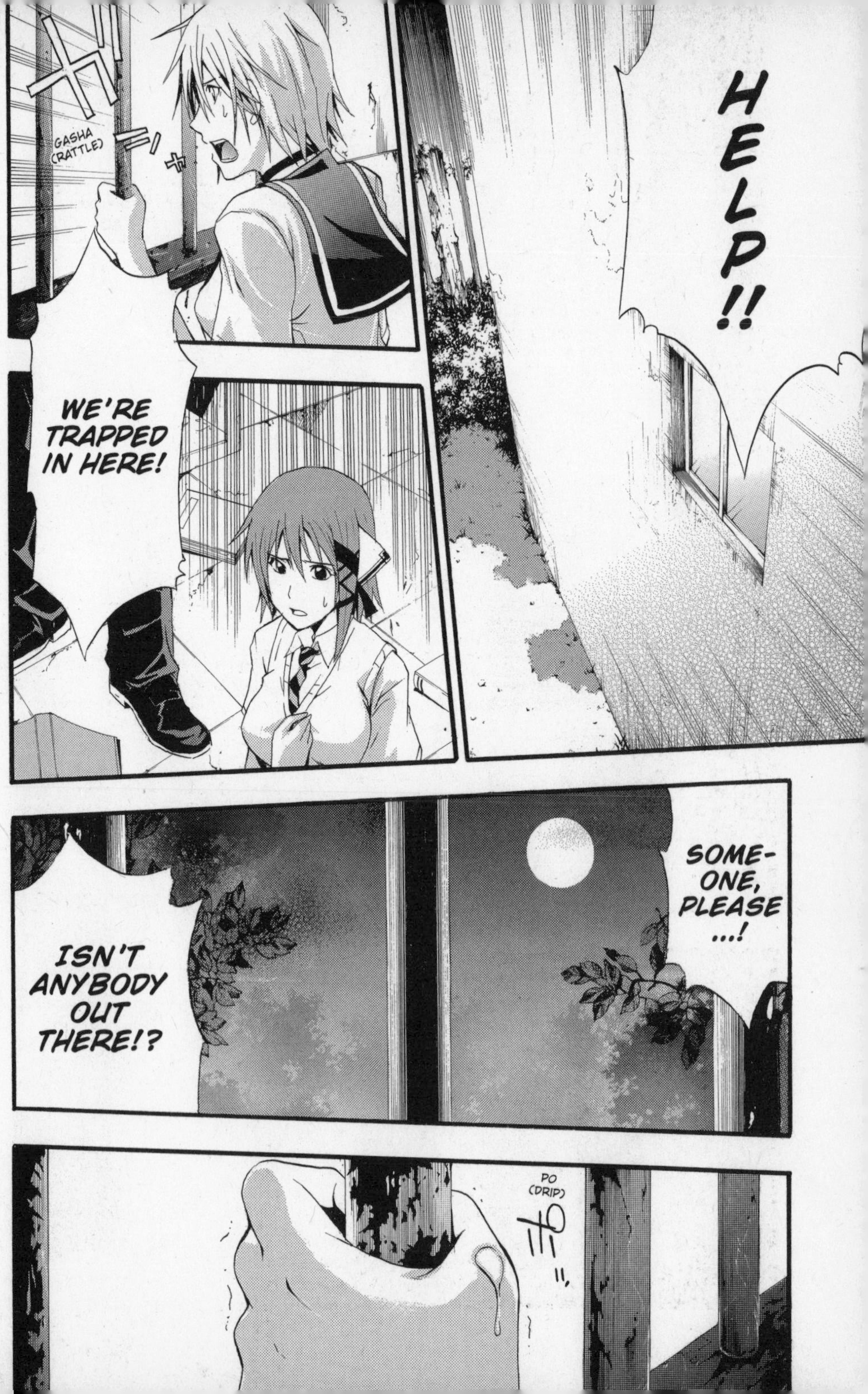
HELP!!
GASHA (RATTLE)
WE'RE TRAPPED IN HERE!
SOME-ONE, PLEASE ...!
ISN'T ANYBODY OUT THERE!?
PO (DRIP)

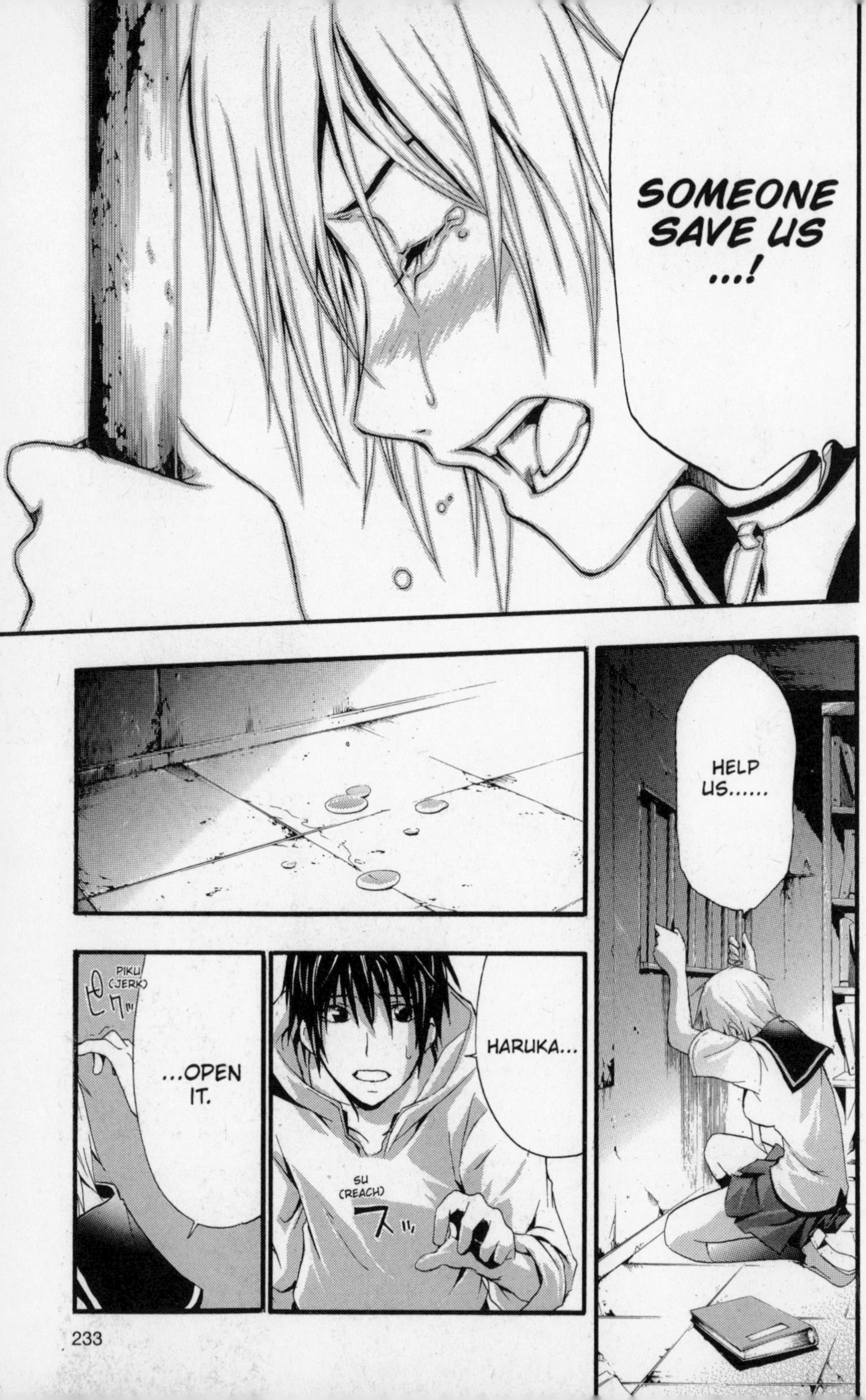
SOMEONE SAVE US ...!
HELP US......
HARUKA...
SU (REACH)
PIKU (JERK)
...OPEN IT.

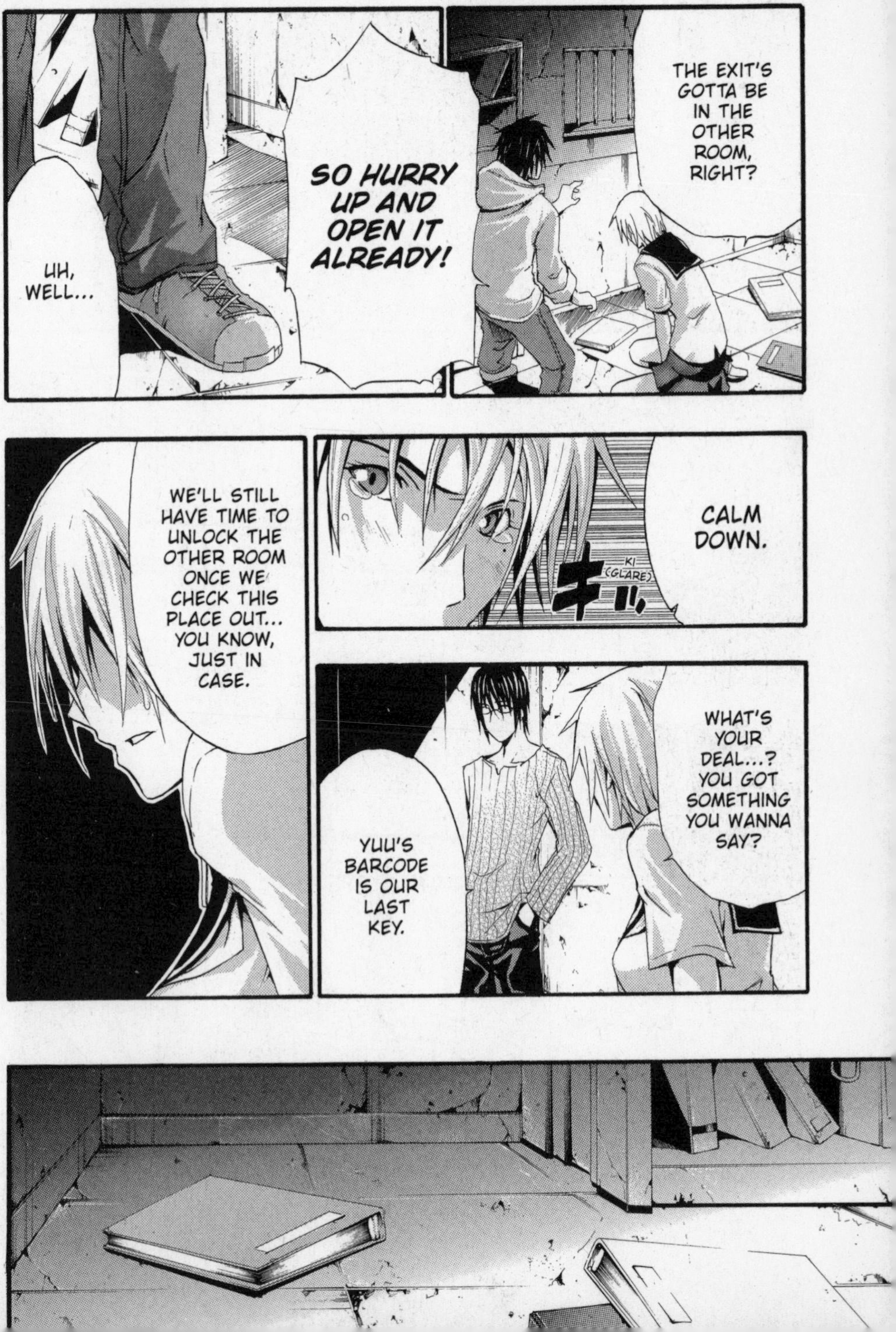
THE EXIT'S GOTTA BE IN THE OTHER ROOM, RIGHT?
SO HURRY UP AND OPEN IT ALREADY!
UH, WELL...
CALM DOWN.
キッ
KI (GLARE)
WHAT'S YOUR DEAL...? YOU GOT SOMETHING YOU WANNA SAY?
YUU'S BARCODE IS OUR LAST KEY.
WE'LL STILL HAVE TIME TO UNLOCK THE OTHER ROOM ONCE WE CHECK THIS PLACE OUT... YOU KNOW, JUST IN CASE.

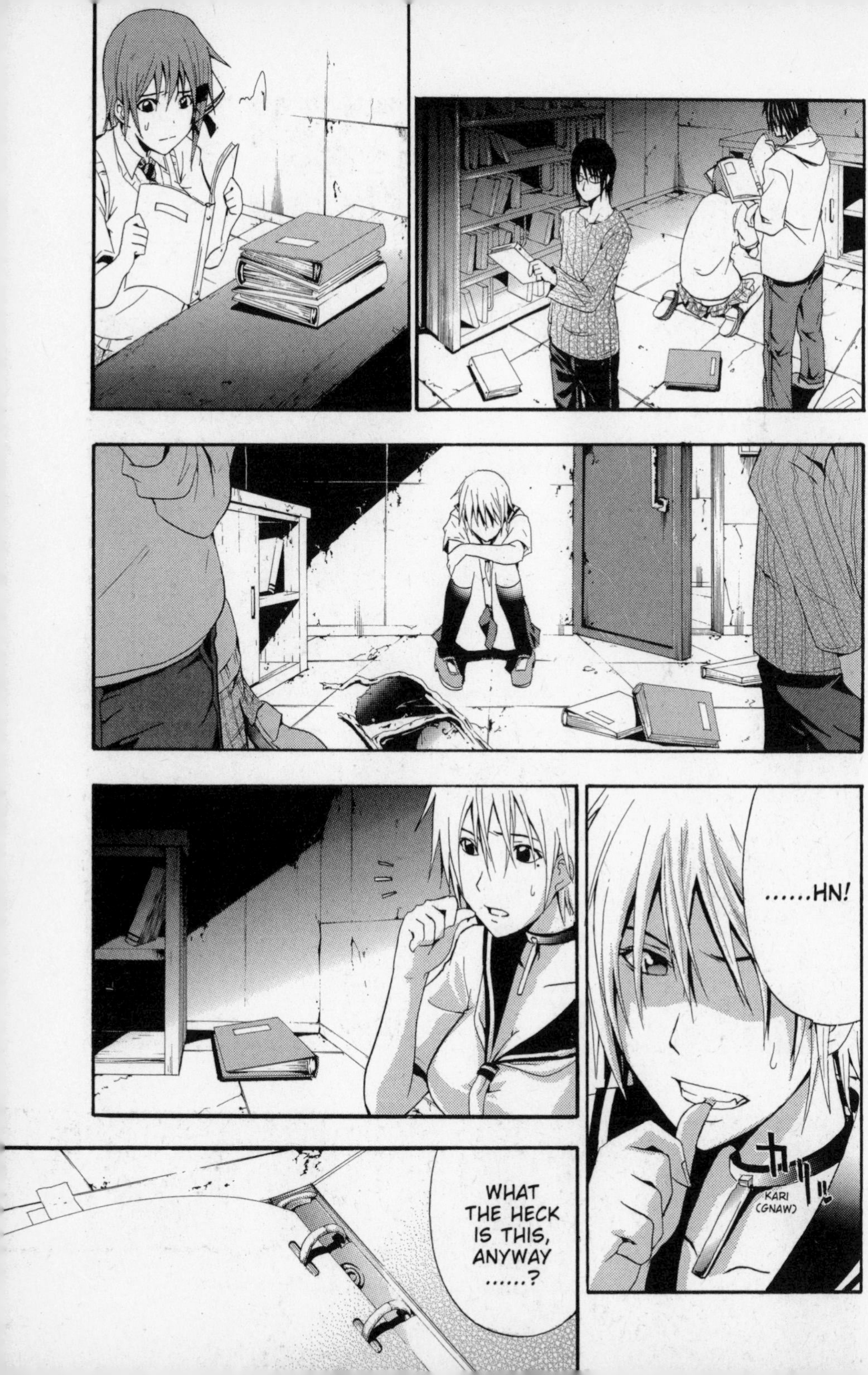
......HN!
KARI (GNAW)
WHAT THE HECK IS THIS, ANYWAY ......?

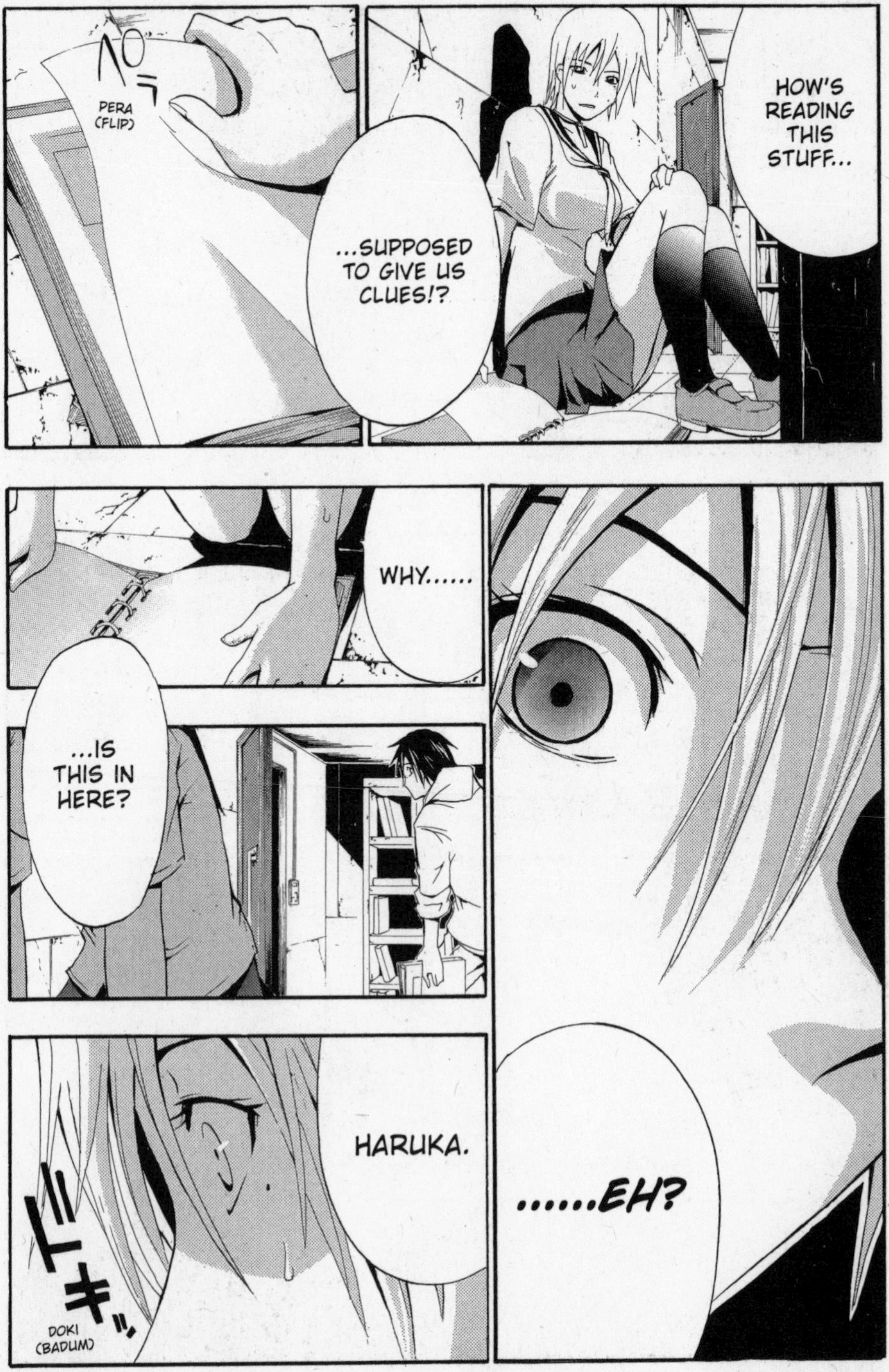
HOW'S READING THIS STUFF...
...SUPPOSED TO GIVE US CLUES!?
ペラ
PERA (FLIP)
......EH?
WHY......
...IS THIS IN HERE?
HARUKA.
ドキッ
DOKI (BADUM)

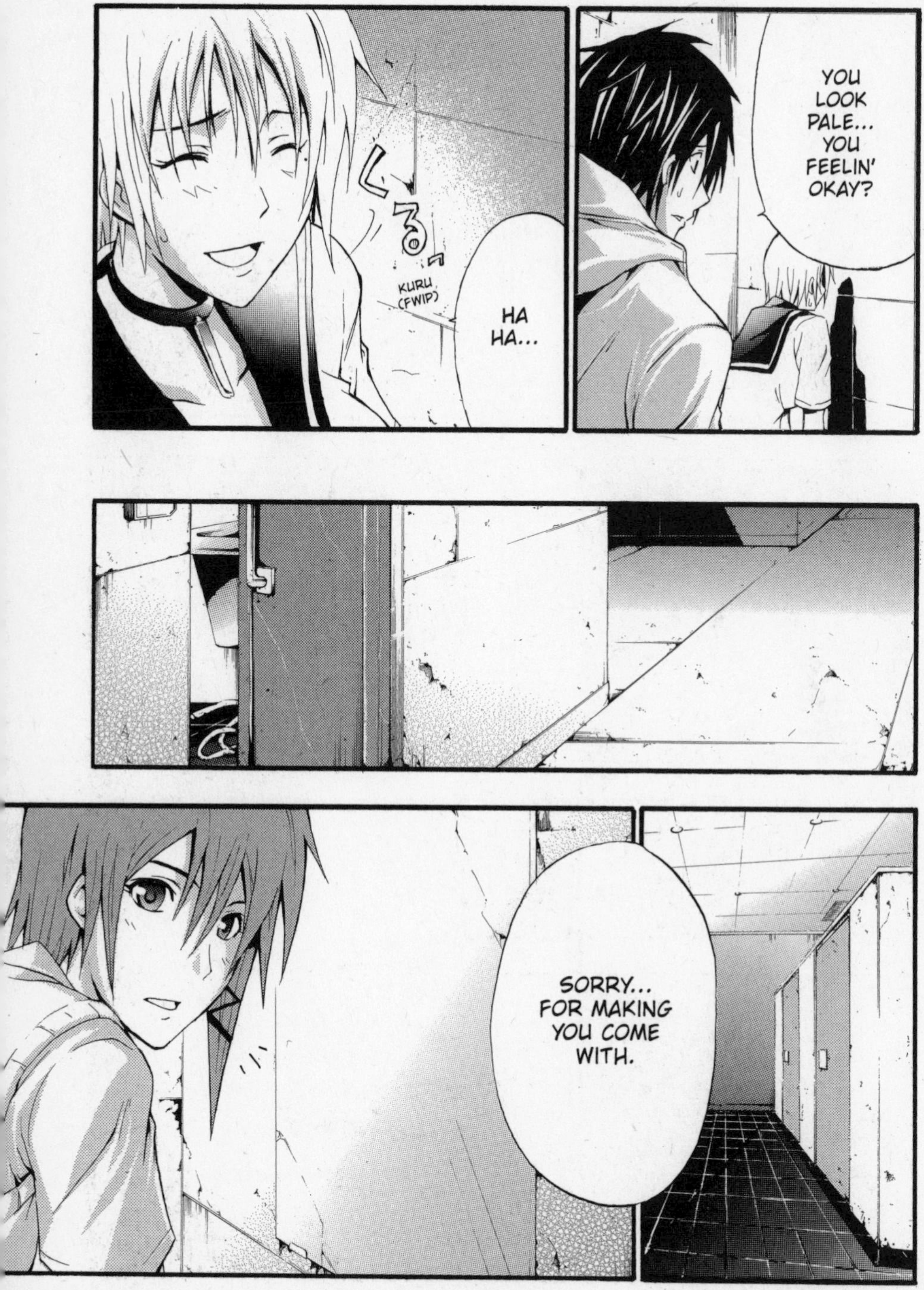
YOU LOOK PALE... YOU FEELIN' OKAY?
くる
KURU (FWIP)
HA HA...
SORRY... FOR MAKING YOU COME WITH.

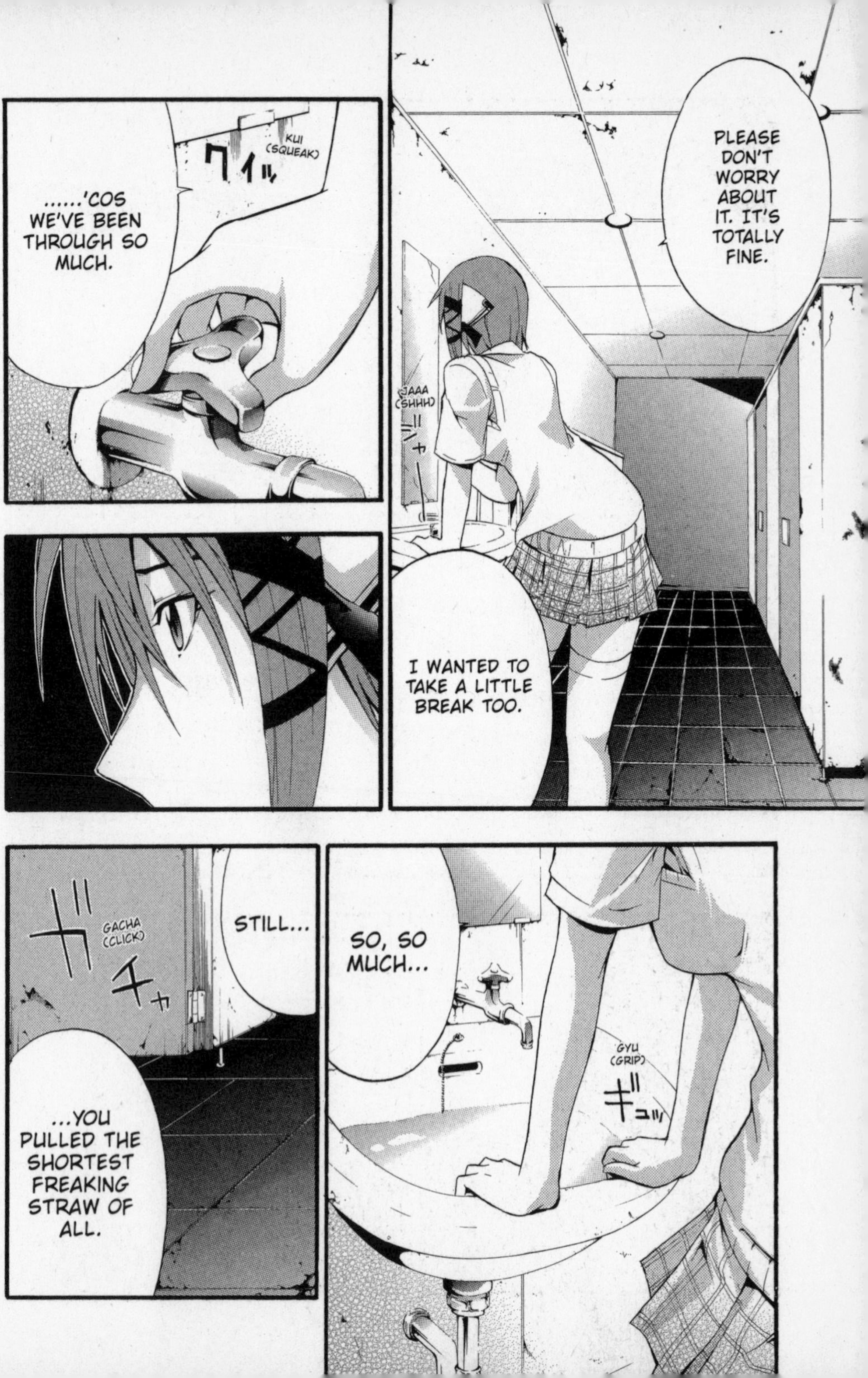
PLEASE DON'T WORRY ABOUT IT. IT'S TOTALLY FINE.
JAAA (SHHH)
I WANTED TO TAKE A LITTLE BREAK TOO.
KUI (SQUEAK)
......'COS WE'VE BEEN THROUGH SO MUCH.
SO, SO MUCH...
GYU (GRIP)
STILL...
GACHA (CLICK)
...YOU PULLED THE SHORTEST FREAKING STRAW OF ALL.

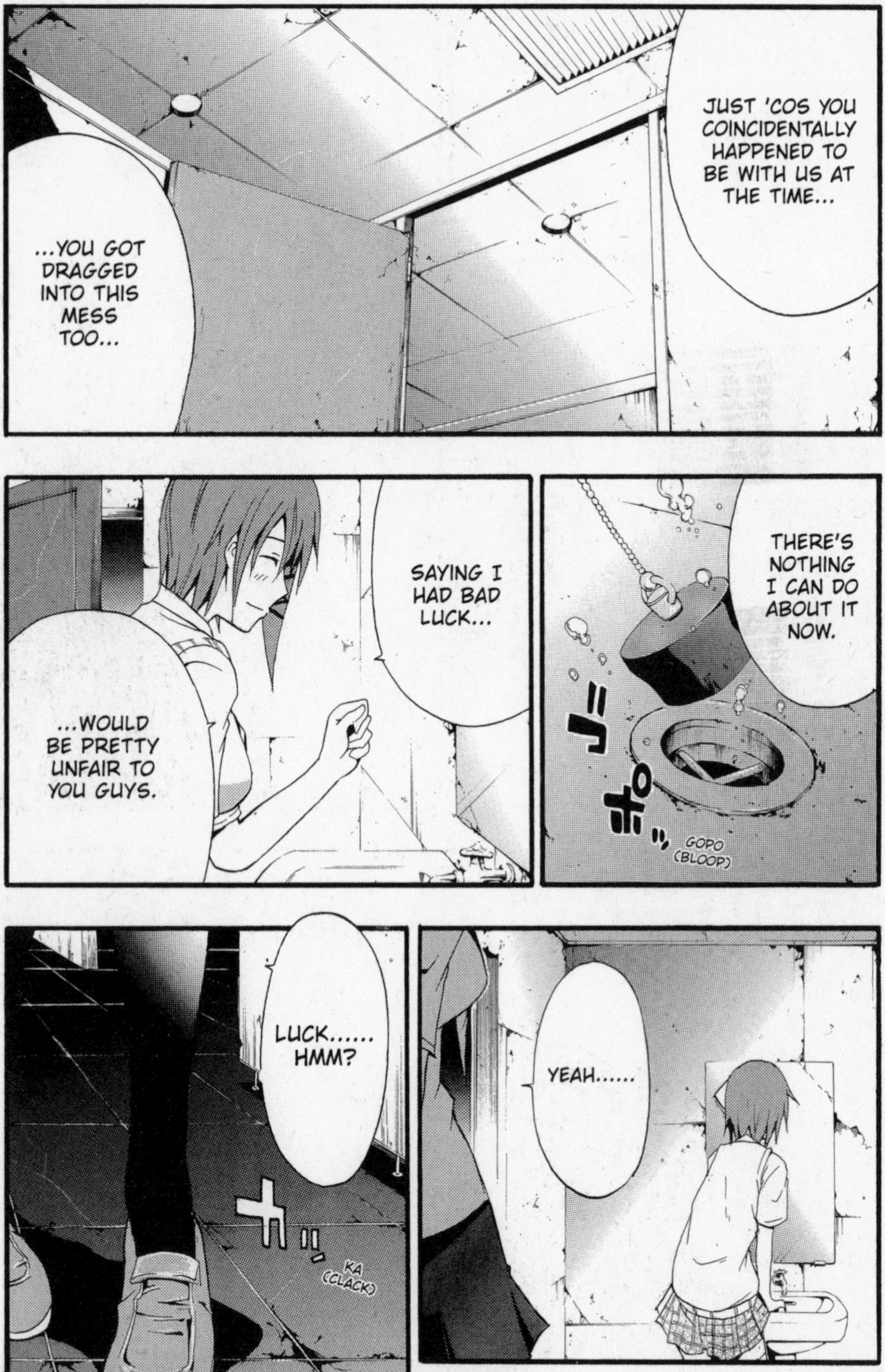
JUST 'COS YOU COINCIDENTALLY HAPPENED TO BE WITH US AT THE TIME...
...YOU GOT DRAGGED INTO THIS MESS TOO...
THERE'S NOTHING I CAN DO ABOUT IT NOW.
GOPO (BLOOP)
SAYING I HAD BAD LUCK...
...WOULD BE PRETTY UNFAIR TO YOU GUYS.
YEAH......
LUCK...... HMM?
KA (CLACK)

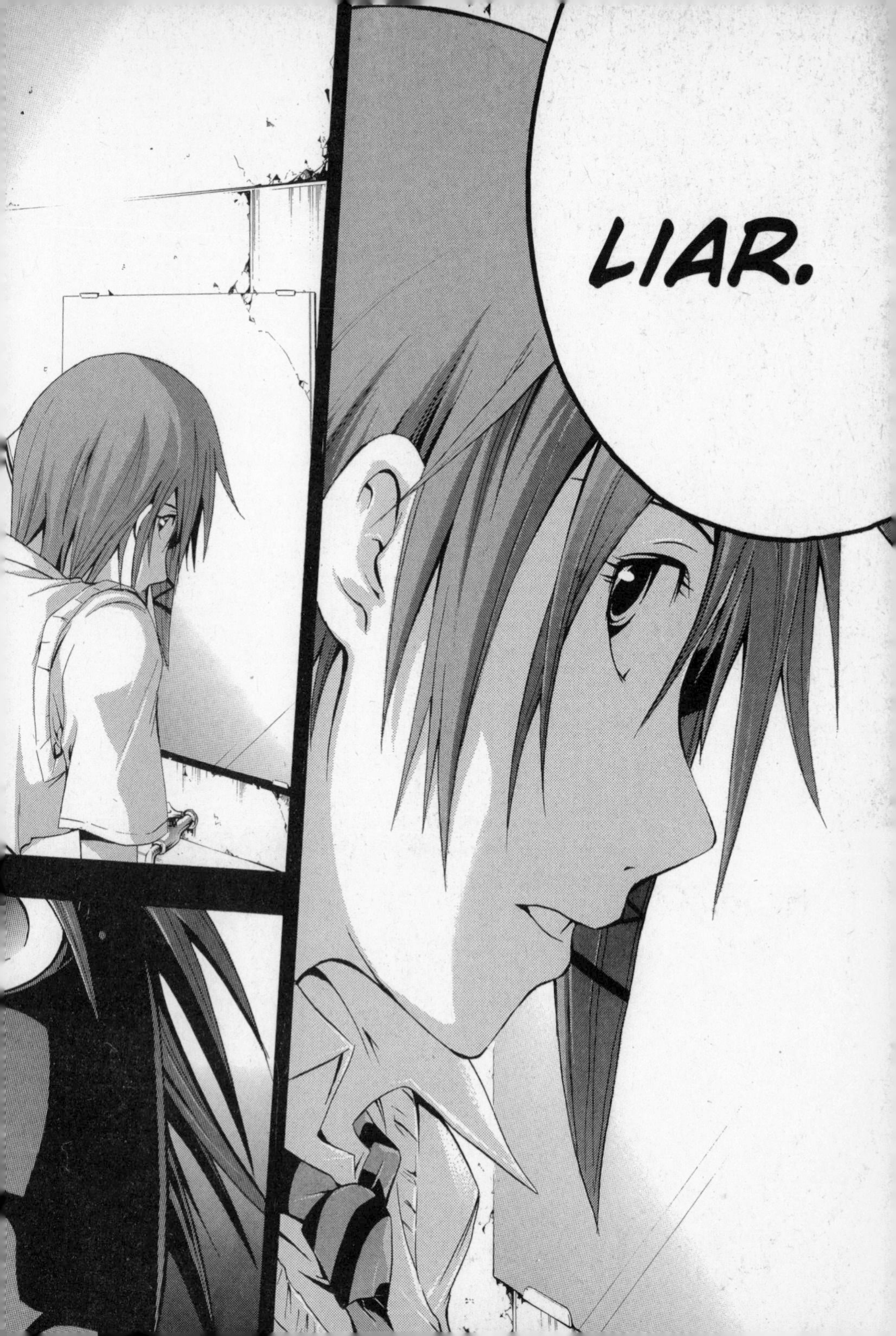
LIAR.

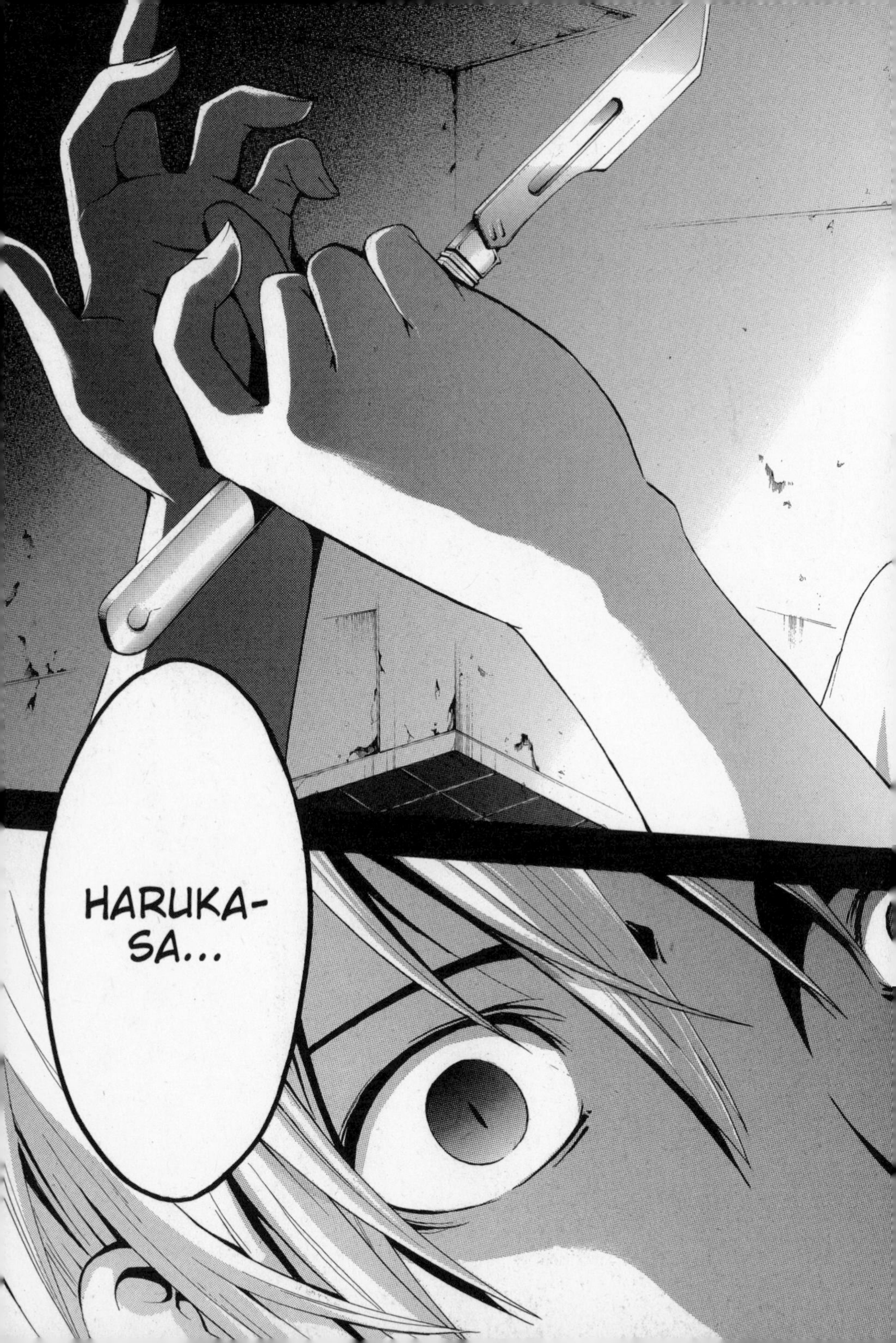
HARUKA-SA...

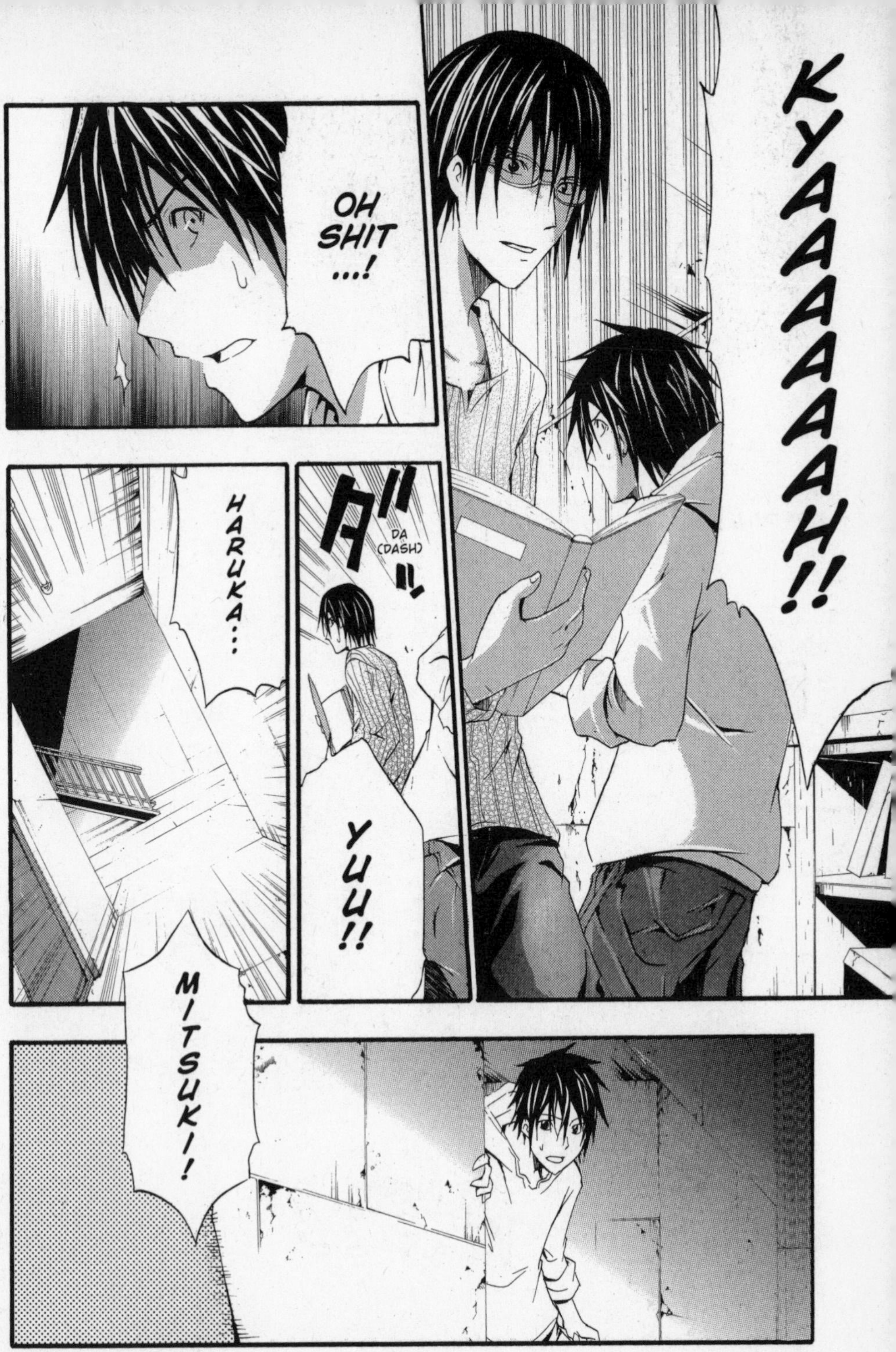
KYAAAAAAH!!
OH SHIT ...!
ダッ
DA (DASH)
YUU!!
HARUKA...
MITSUKI!

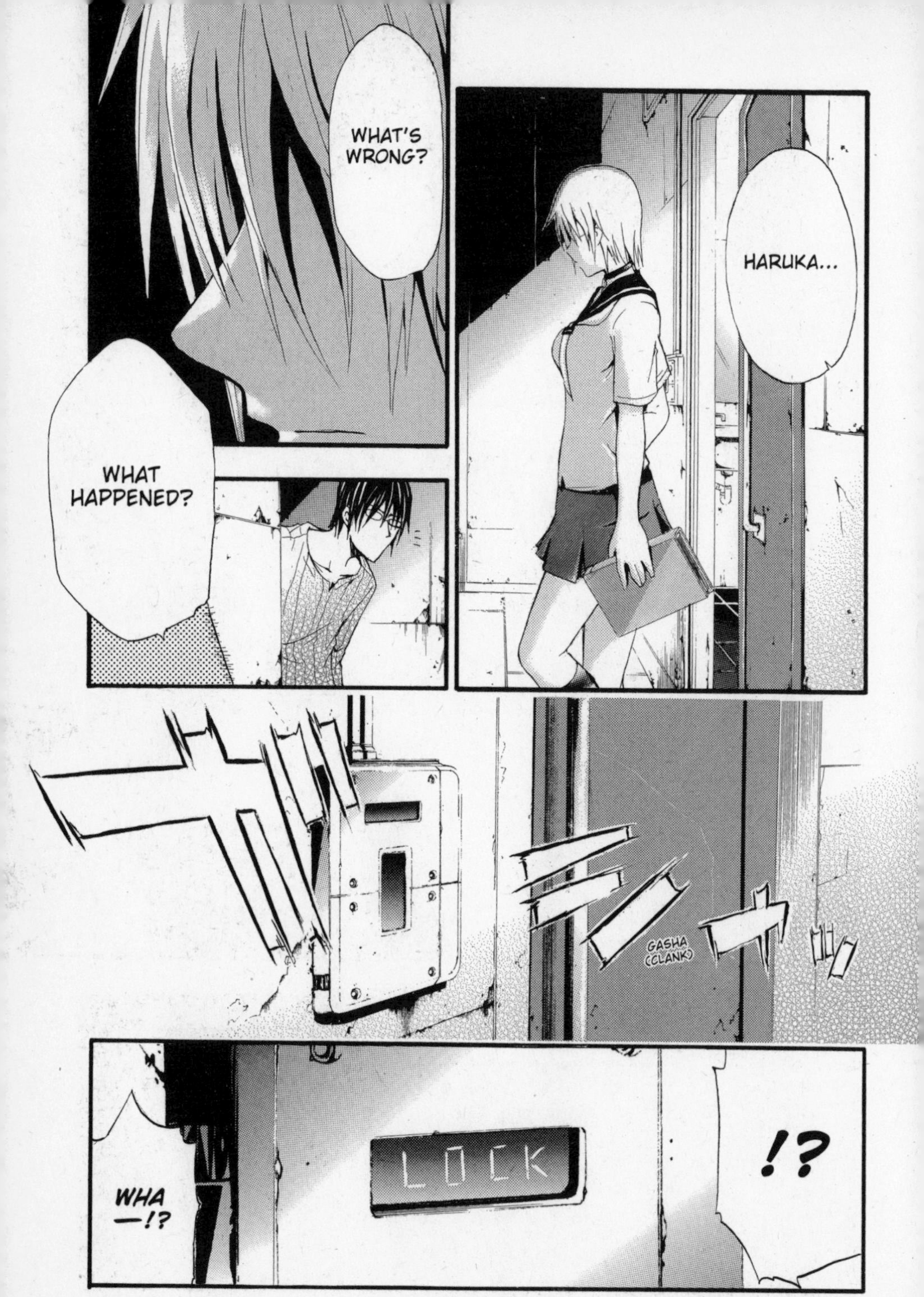
HARUKA...
WHAT'S WRONG?
WHAT HAPPENED?
GASHA (CLANK)
!?
LOCK
WHA—!?

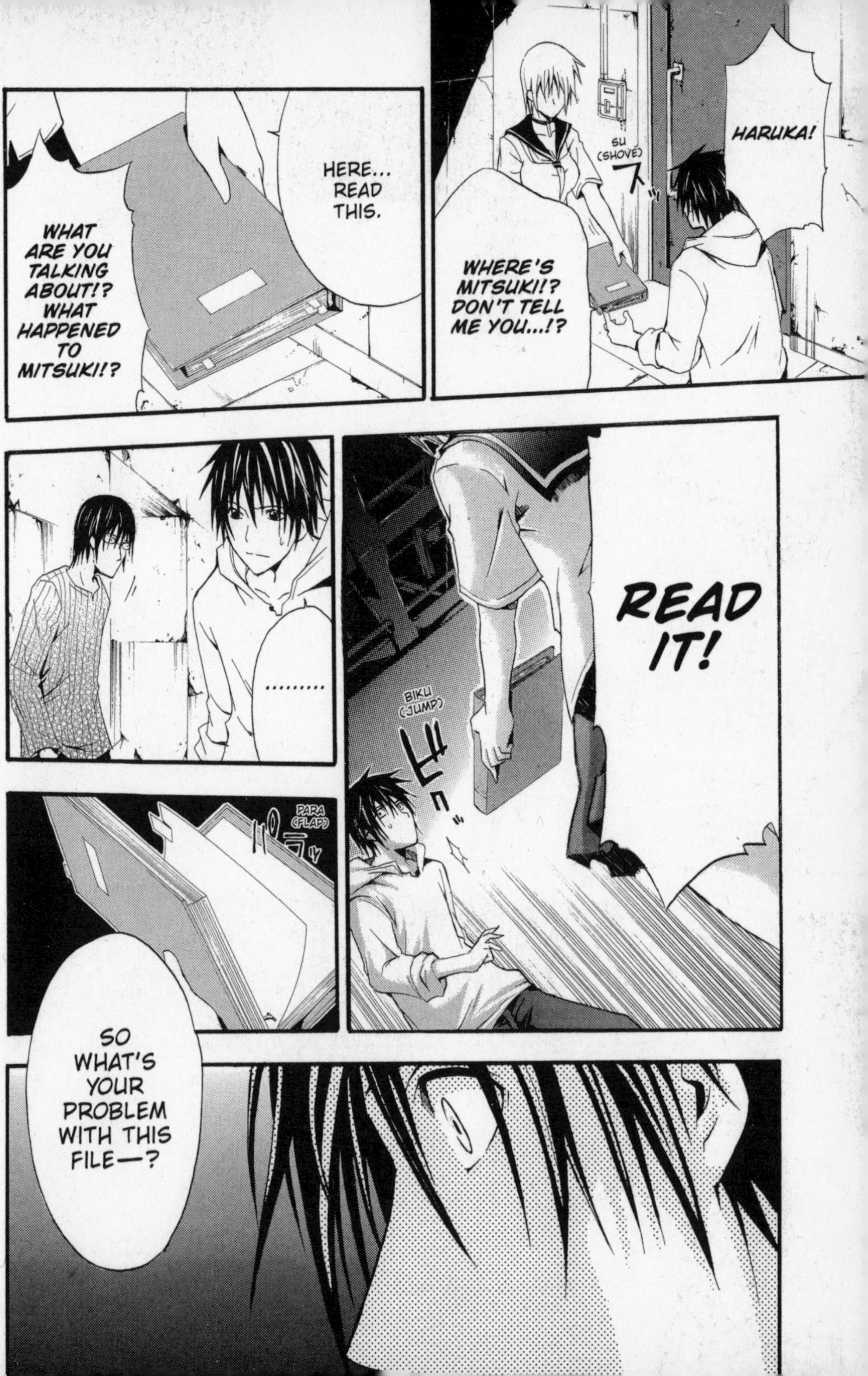

HARUKA!
SU (SHOVE)
WHERE'S MITSUKI!? DON'T TELL ME YOU...!?
HERE... READ THIS.
WHAT ARE YOU TALKING ABOUT!? WHAT HAPPENED TO MITSUKI!?
READ IT!
BIKU (JUMP)
....
PARA (FLAP)
SO WHAT'S YOUR PROBLEM WITH THIS FILE—?

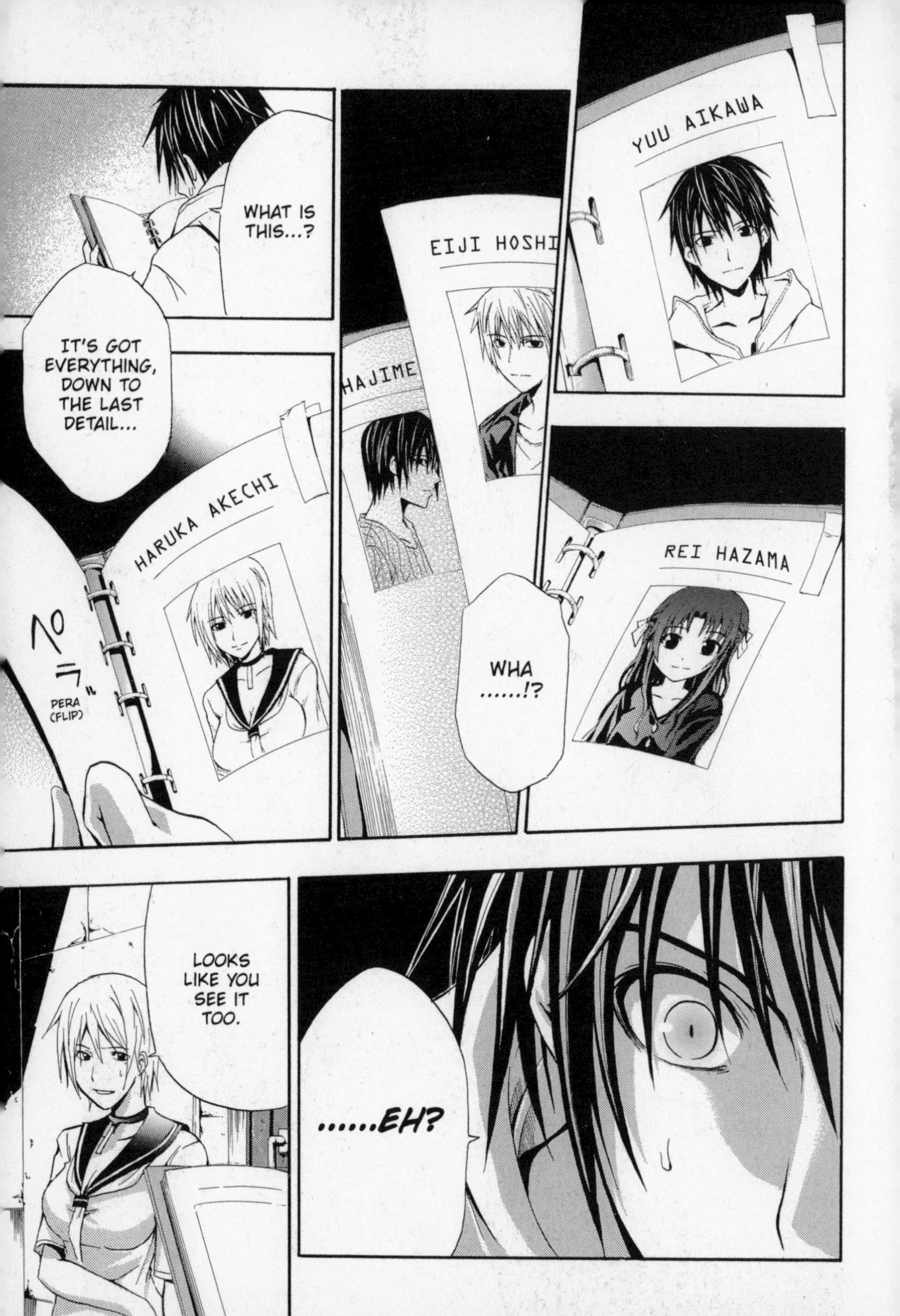
YUU AIKAWA
REI HAZAMA
WHA ......!?
EIJI HOSHI
HAJIME
WHAT IS THIS...?
IT'S GOT EVERYTHING, DOWN TO THE LAST DETAIL...
HARUKA AKECHI
ペラ
PERA (FLIP)
......EH?
LOOKS LIKE YOU SEE IT TOO.

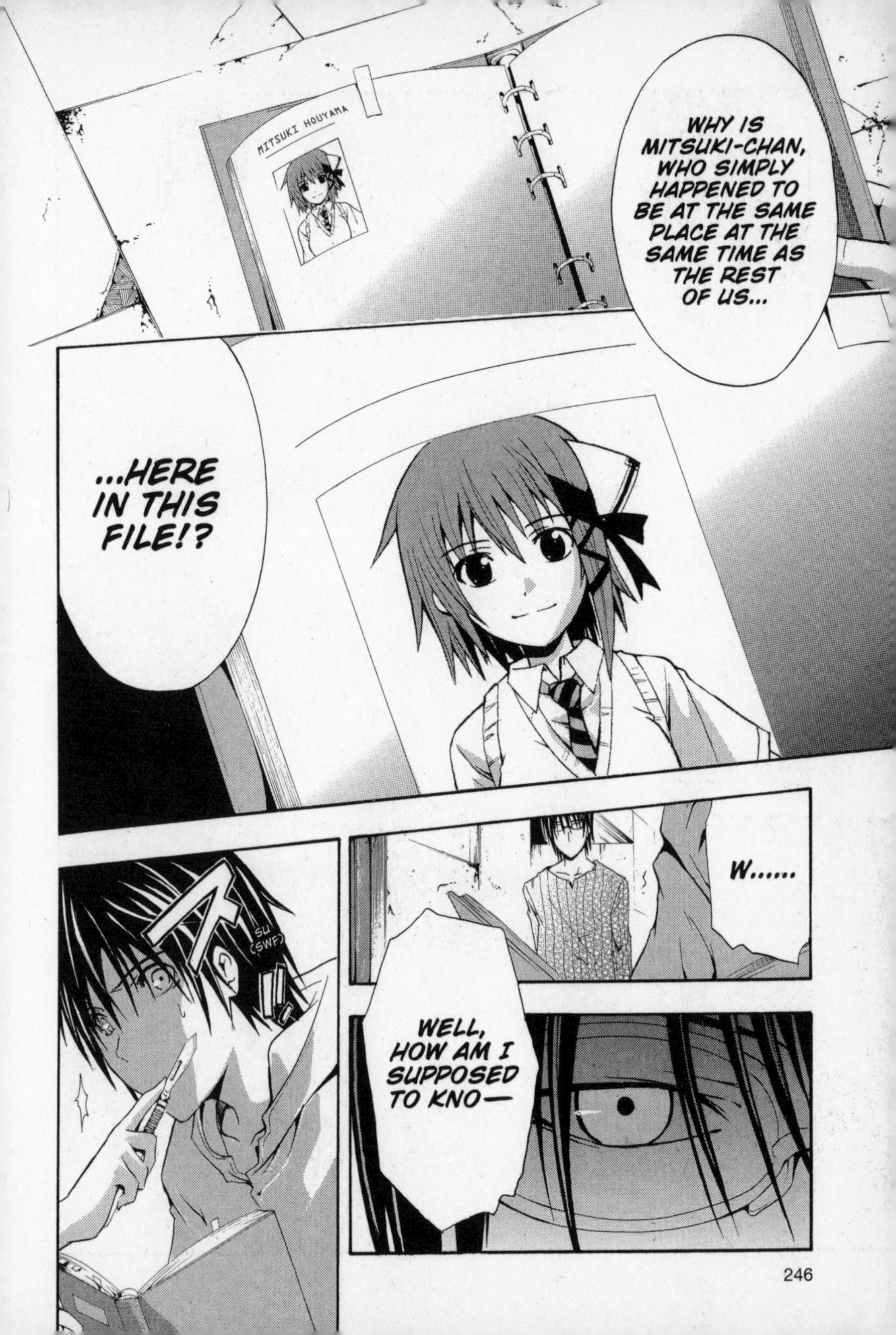
MITSUKI HOUYAMA
WHY IS MITSUKI-CHAN, WHO SIMPLY HAPPENED TO BE AT THE SAME PLACE AT THE SAME TIME AS THE REST OF US...
...HERE IN THIS FILE!?
W......
WELL, HOW AM I SUPPOSED TO KNO—
SU (SWF)

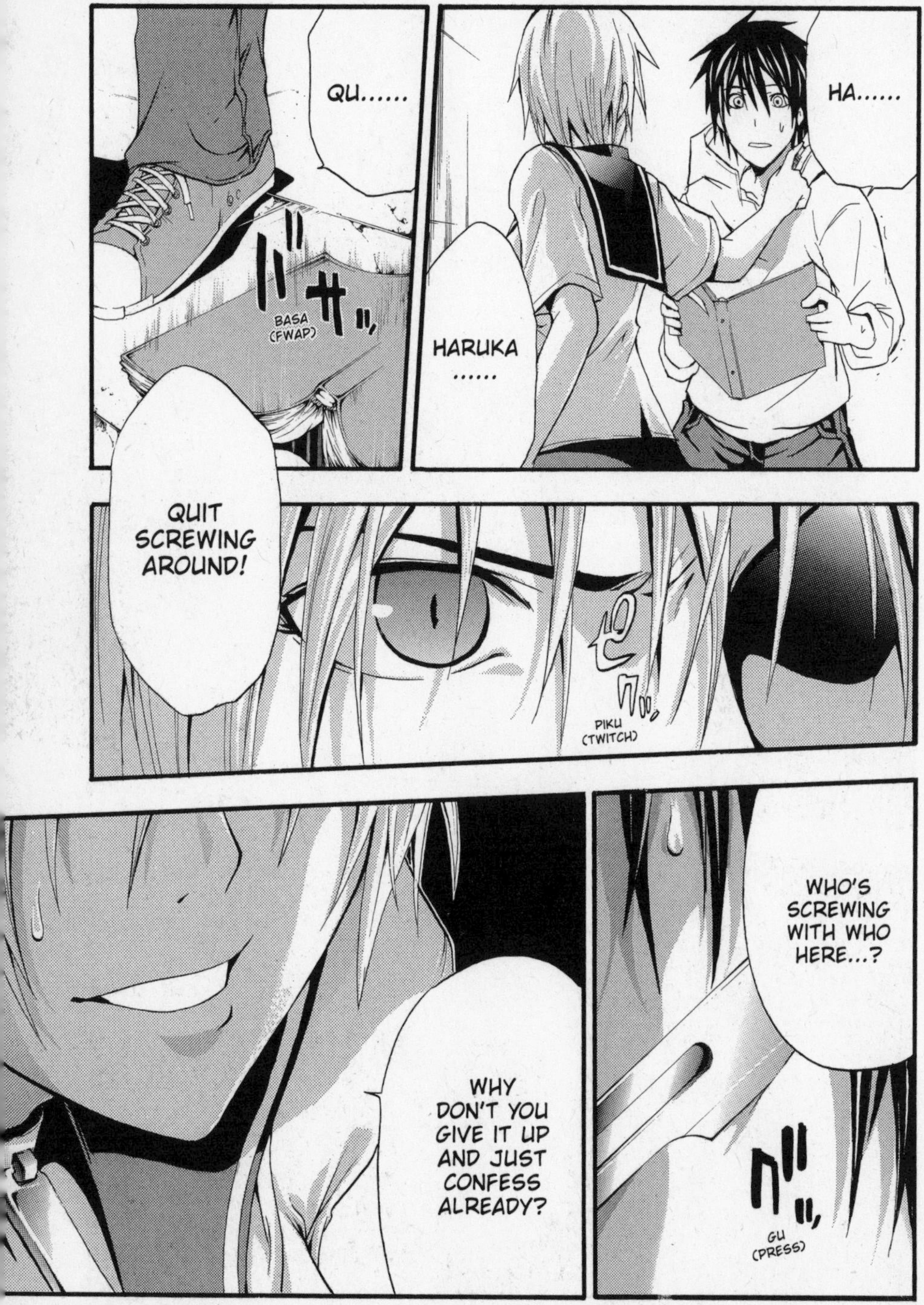
HA......
HARUKA ......
QU......
BASA (FWAP)
QUIT SCREWING AROUND!
PIKU (TWITCH)
WHO'S SCREWING WITH WHO HERE...?
GU (PRESS)
WHY DON'T YOU GIVE IT UP AND JUST CONFESS ALREADY?

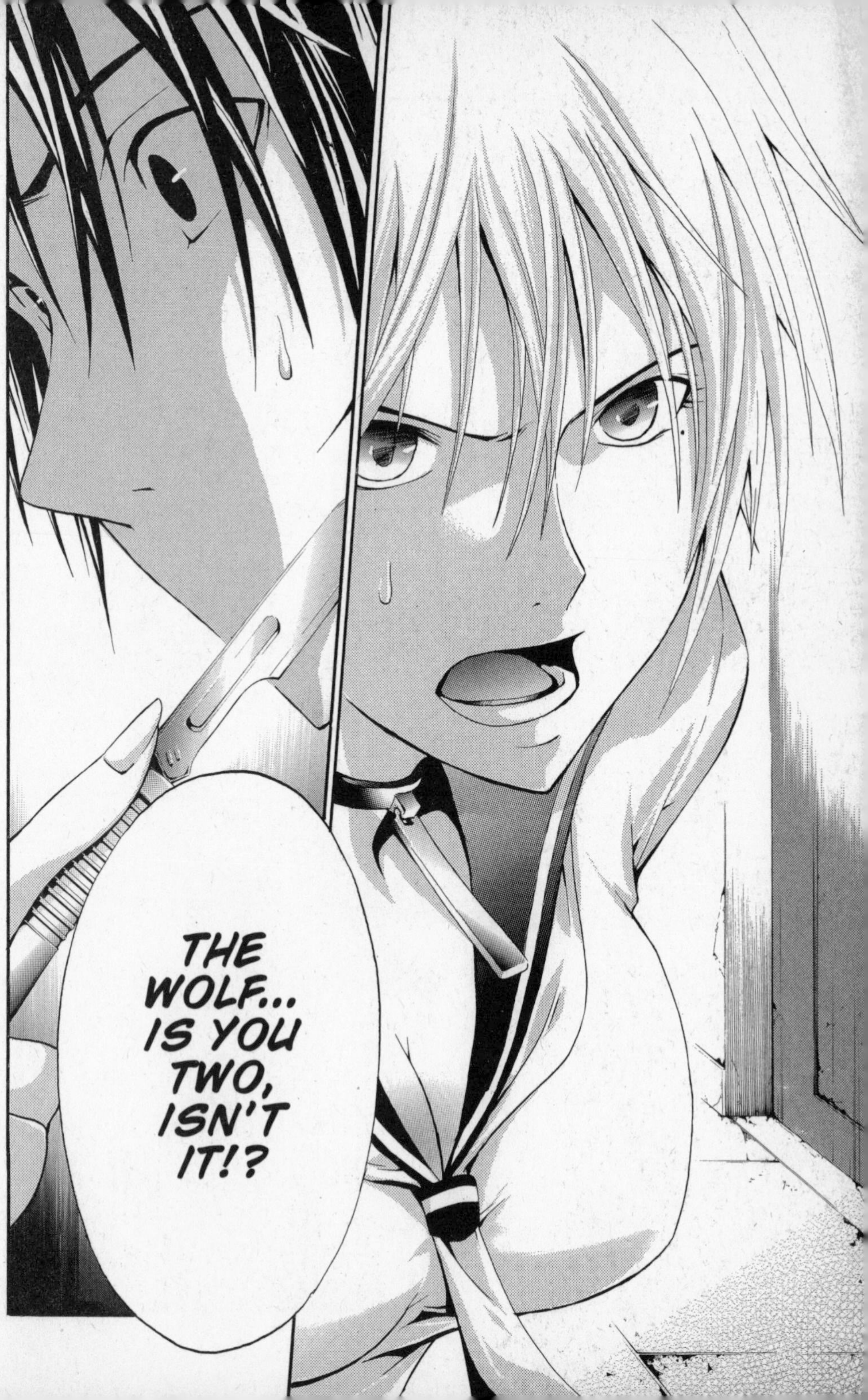
THE WOLF... IS YOU TWO, ISN'T IT!?

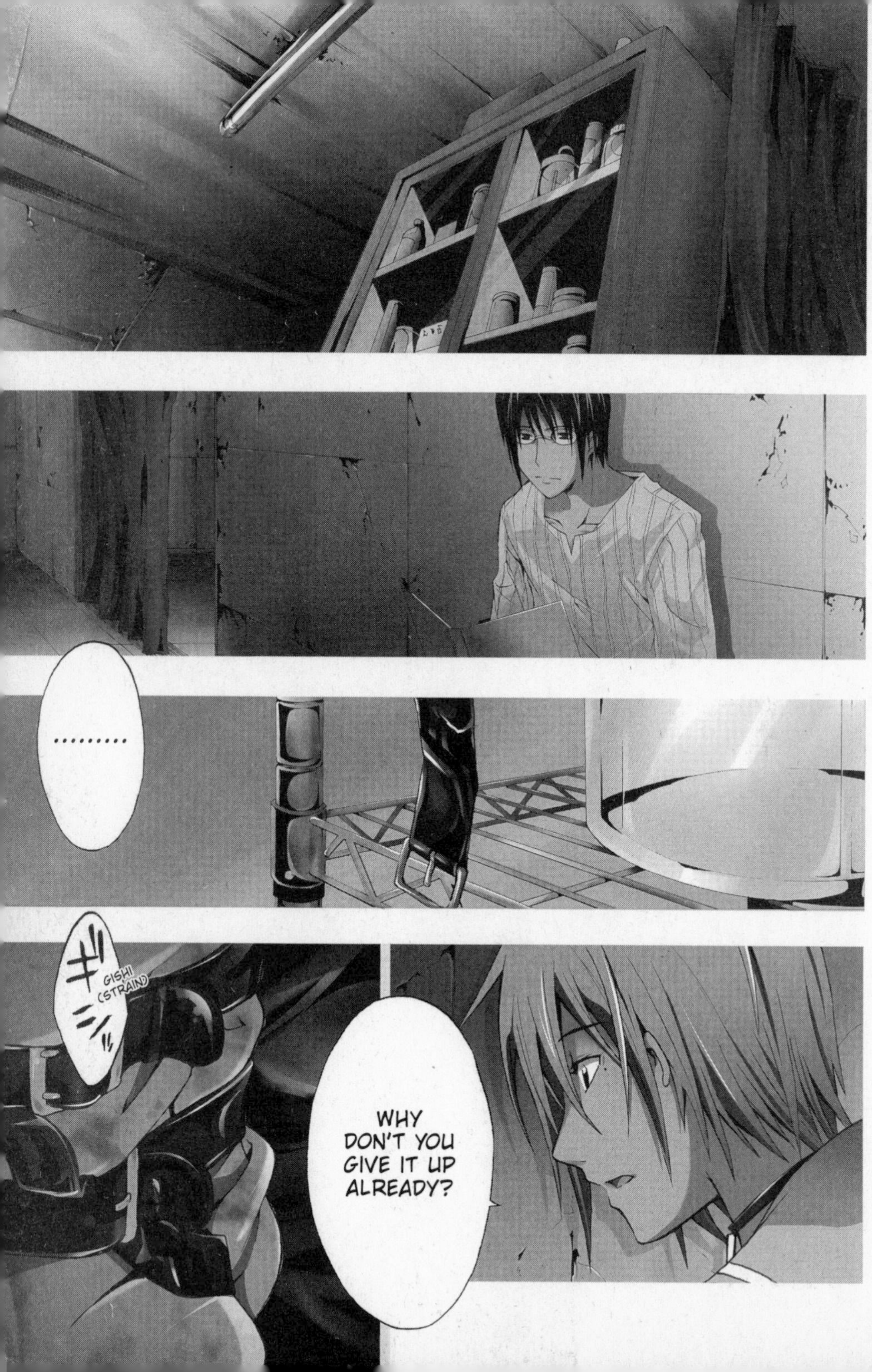
....
GISHI (STRAIN)
WHY DON'T YOU GIVE IT UP ALREADY?

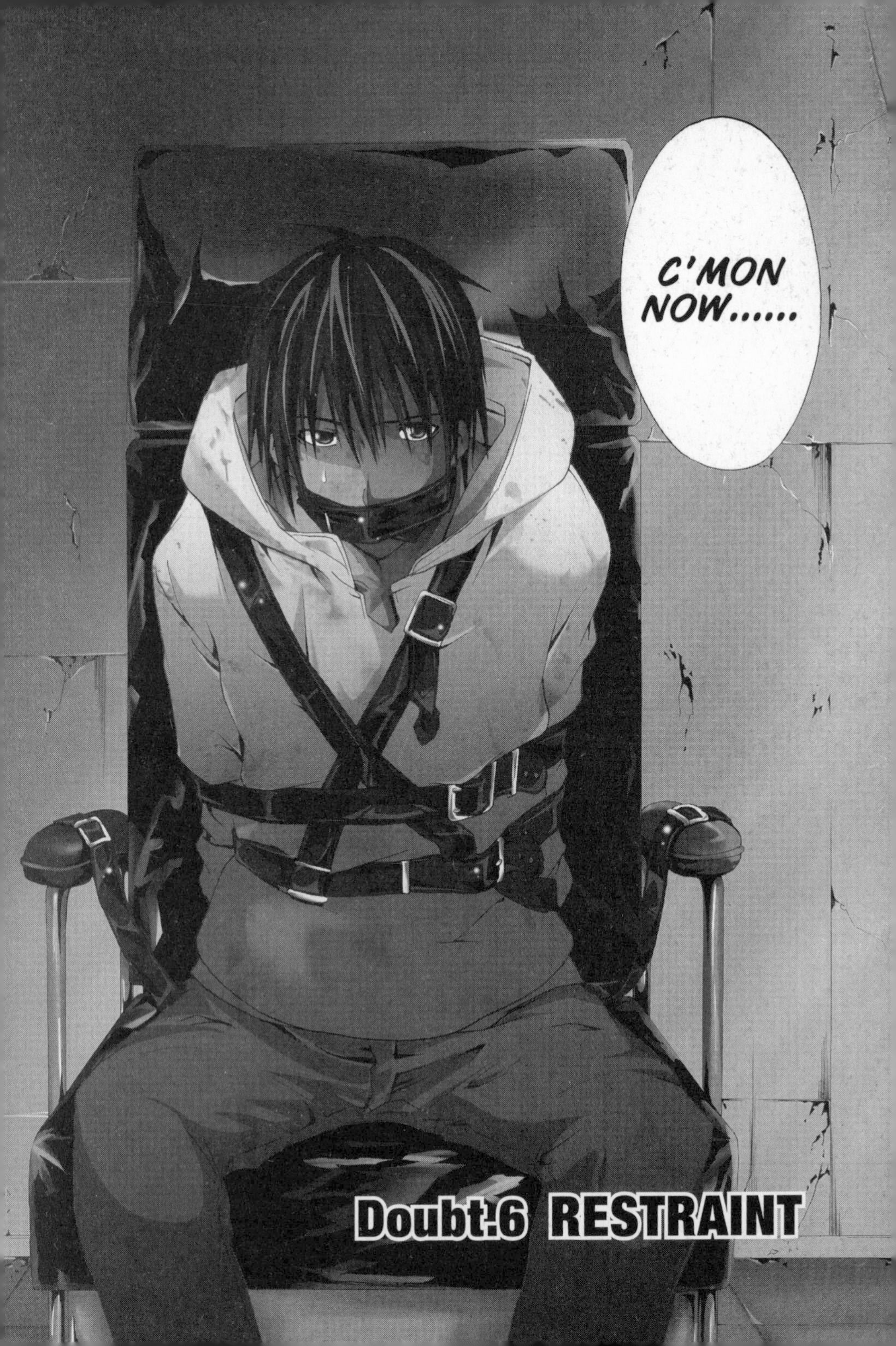
C'MON NOW......
Doubt.6 RESTRAINT

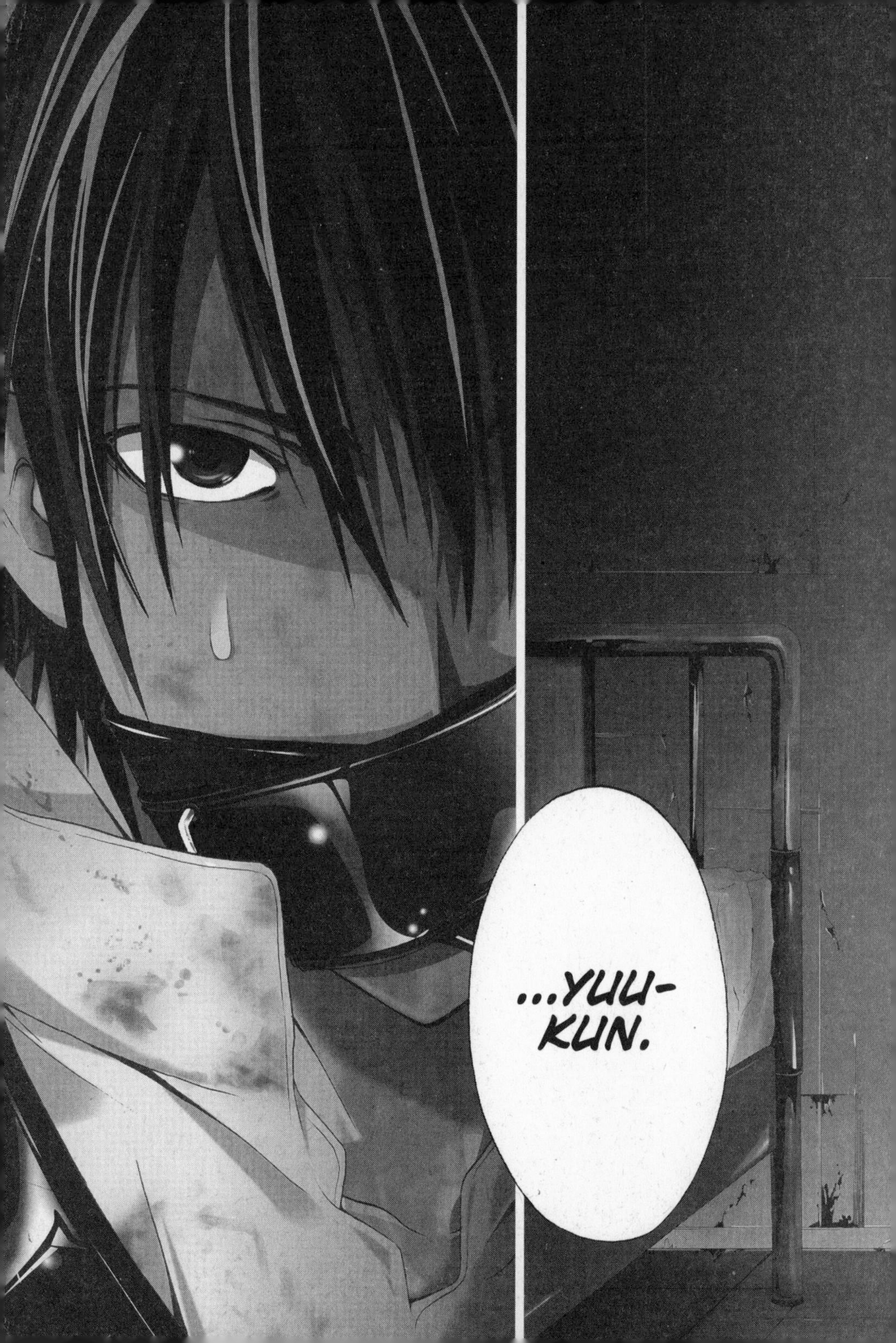
...YUU-KUN.

Doubt

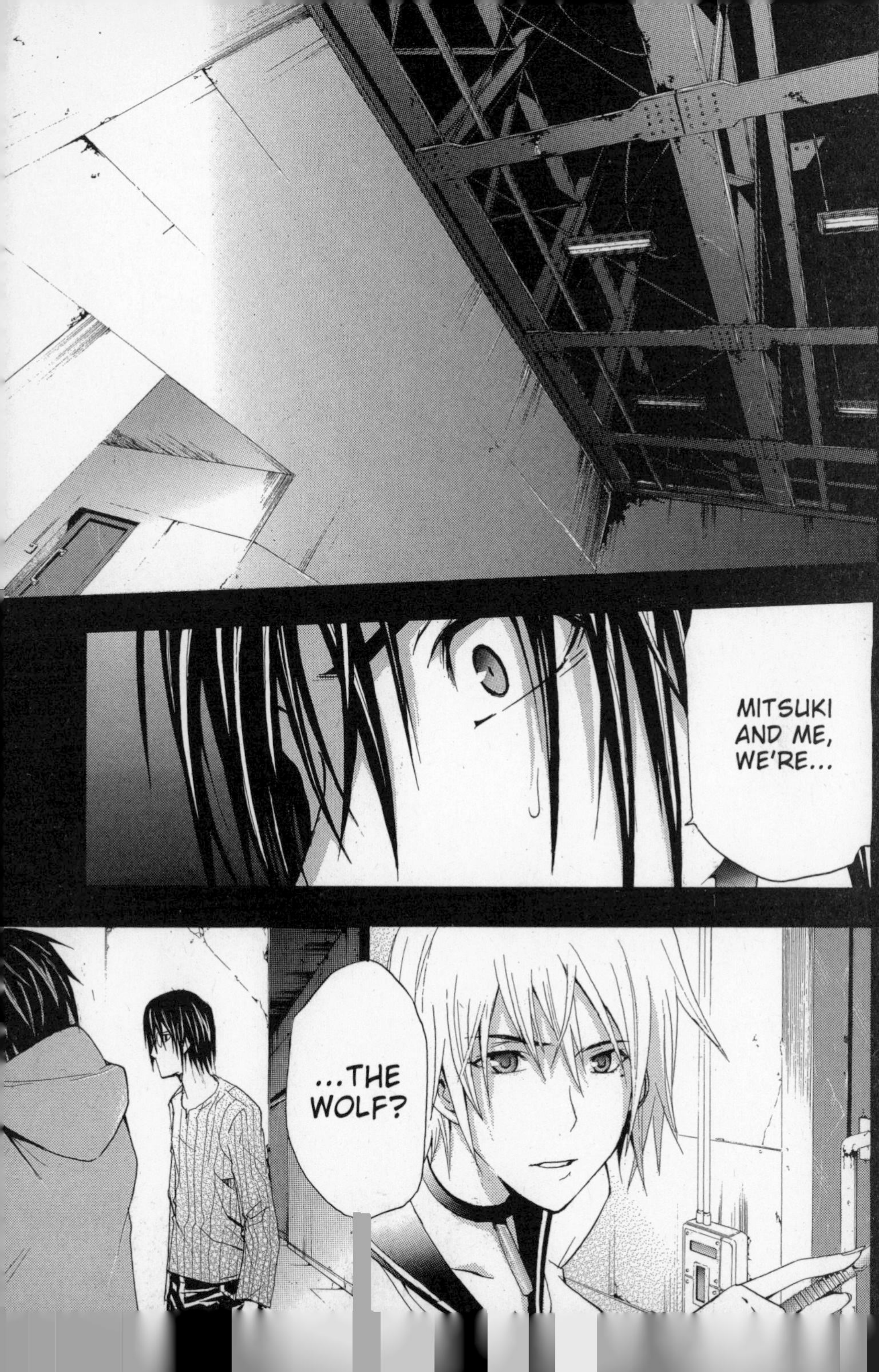
MITSUKI AND ME, WE'RE...
...THE WOLF?

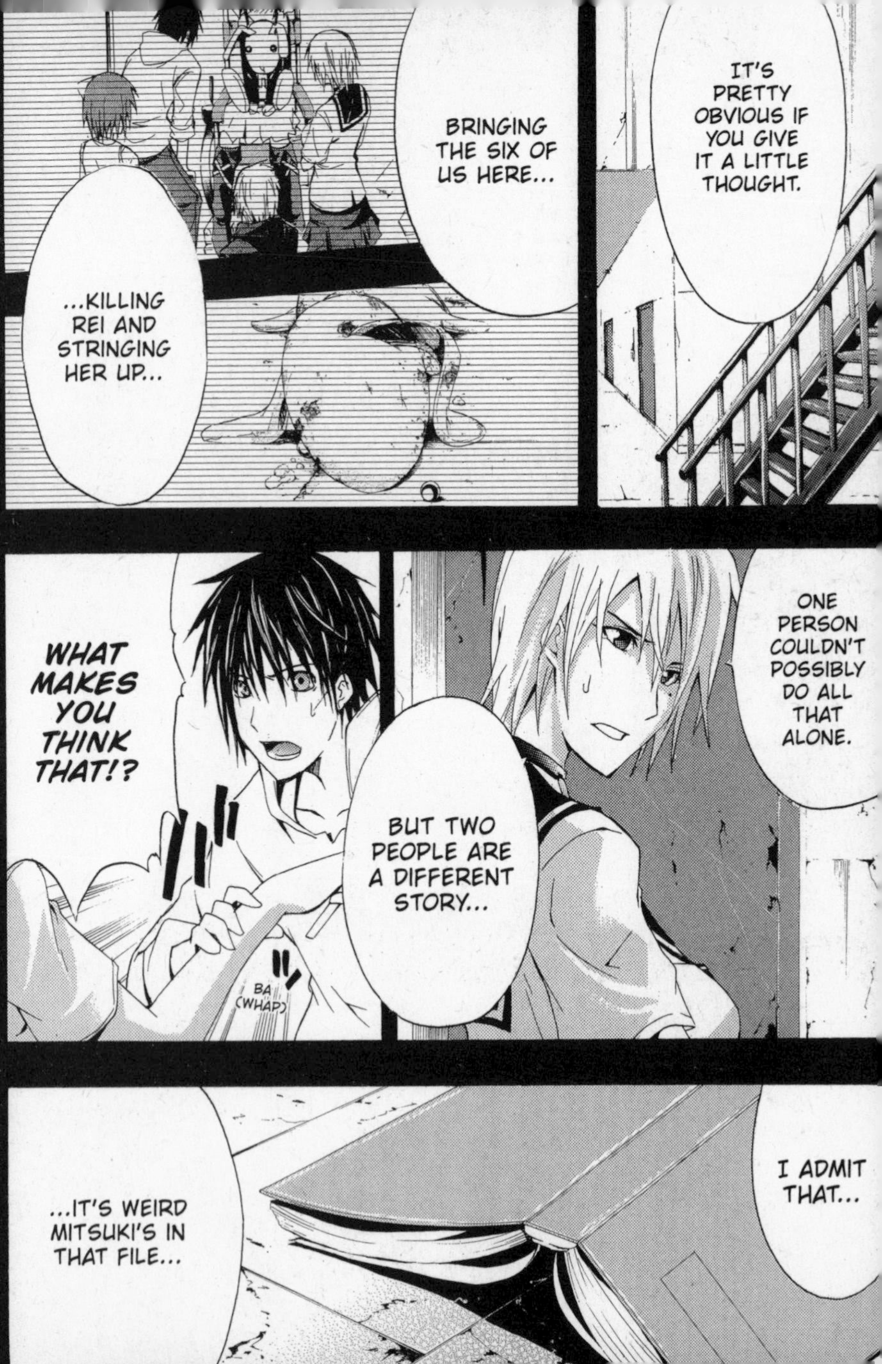
IT'S PRETTY OBVIOUS IF YOU GIVE IT A LITTLE THOUGHT.
BRINGING THE SIX OF US HERE...
...KILLING REI AND STRINGING HER UP...
ONE PERSON COULDN'T POSSIBLY DO ALL THAT ALONE.
BUT TWO PEOPLE ARE A DIFFERENT STORY...
WHAT MAKES YOU THINK THAT!?
BA (WHAP)
I ADMIT THAT...
...IT'S WEIRD MITSUKI'S IN THAT FILE...

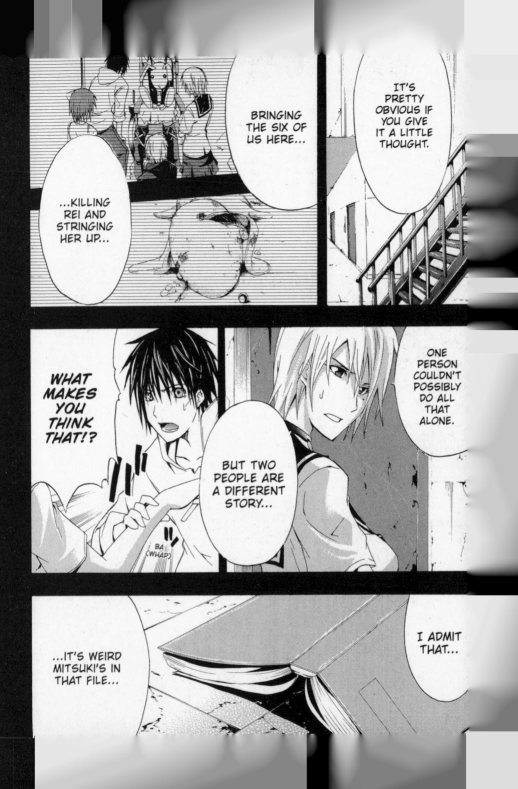

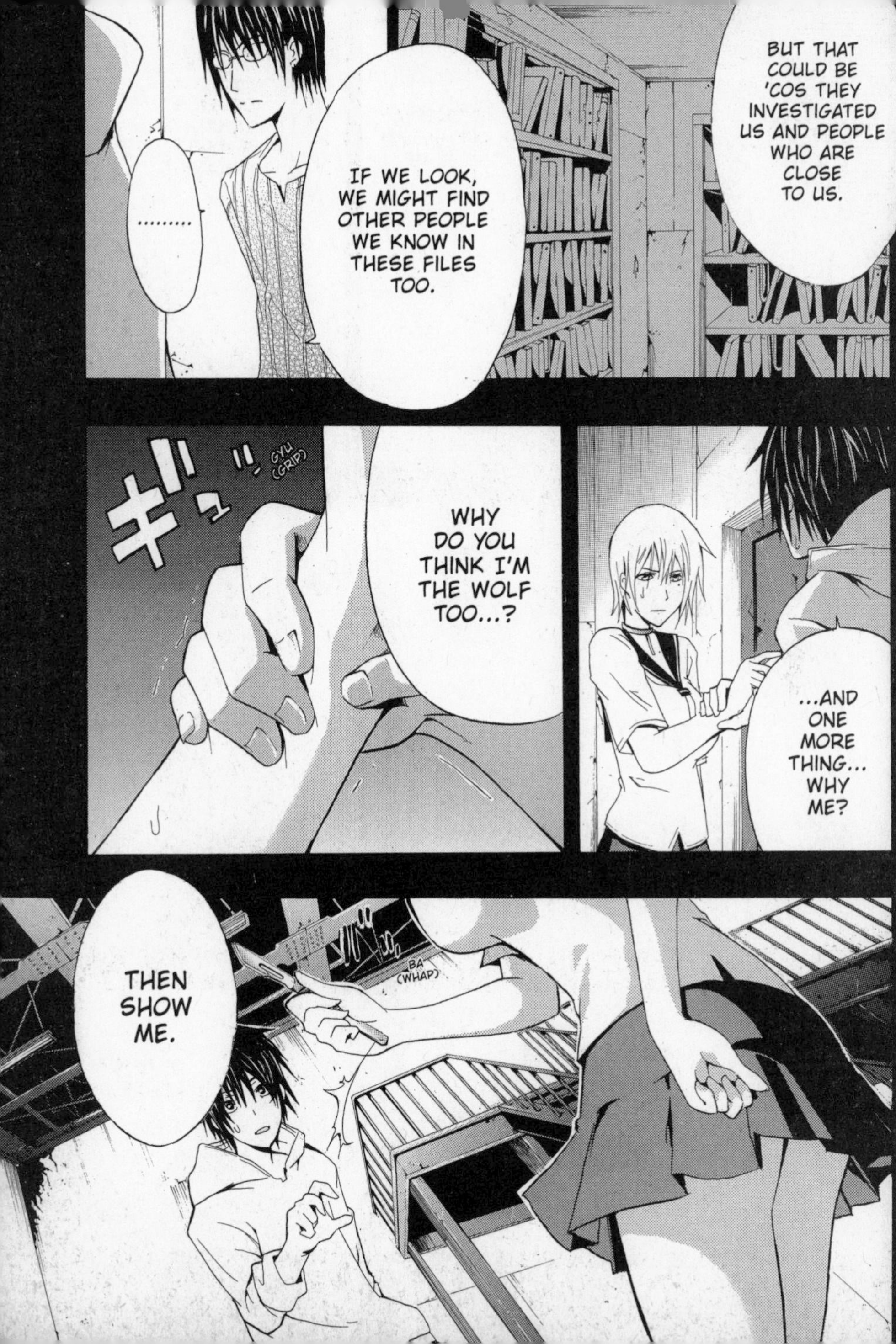

BUT THAT COULD BE 'COS THEY INVESTIGATED US AND PEOPLE WHO ARE CLOSE TO US.
IF WE LOOK, WE MIGHT FIND OTHER PEOPLE WE KNOW IN THESE FILES TOO.
....
...AND ONE MORE THING... WHY ME?
GYU (GRIP)
WHY DO YOU THINK I'M THE WOLF TOO...?
BA (WHAP)
THEN SHOW ME.

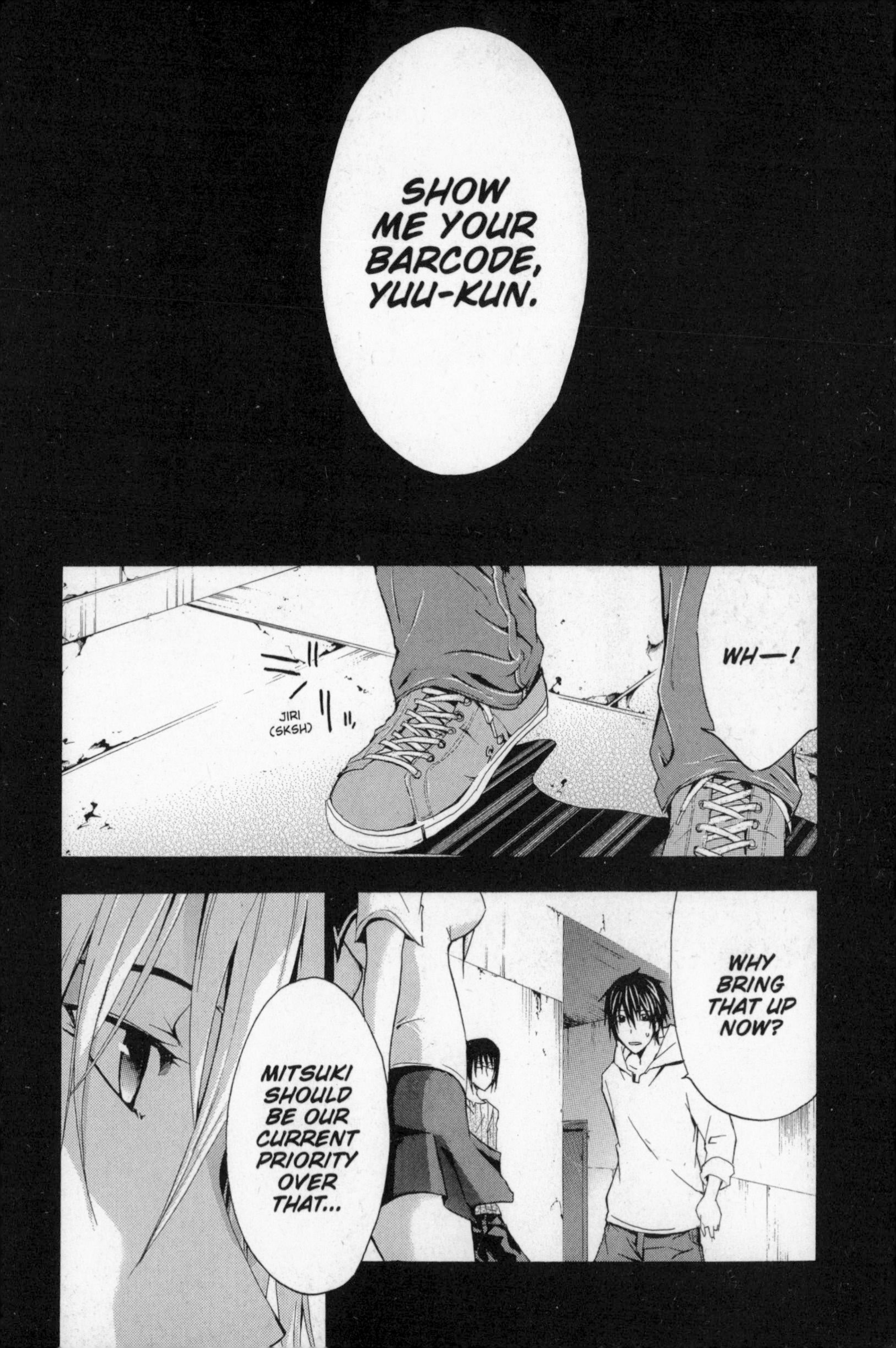
SHOW ME YOUR BARCODE, YUU-KUN.
WH—!
JIRI (SKSH)
WHY BRING THAT UP NOW?
MITSUKI SHOULD BE OUR CURRENT PRIORITY OVER THAT...

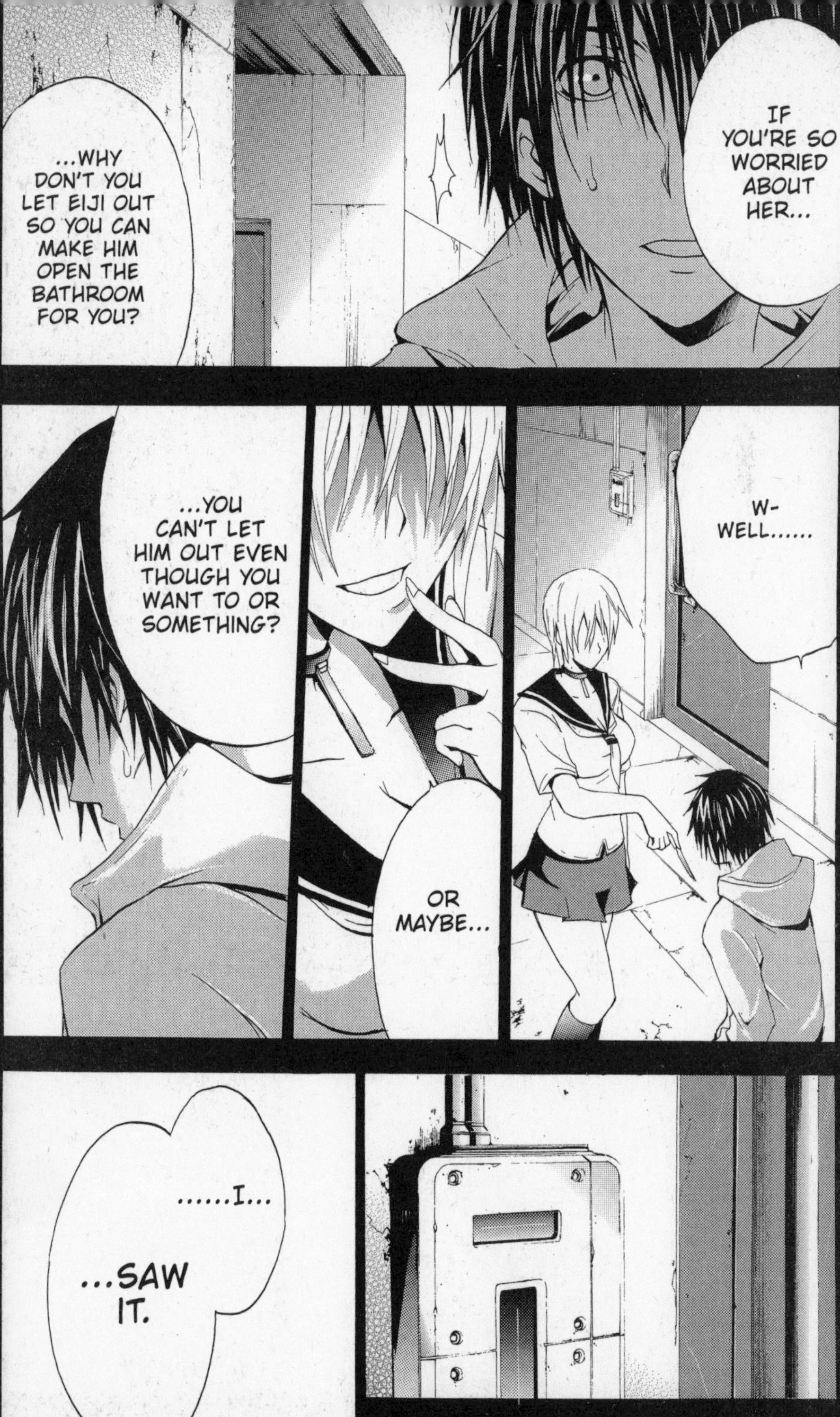
IF YOU'RE SO WORRIED ABOUT HER...
...WHY DON'T YOU LET EIJI OUT SO YOU CAN MAKE HIM OPEN THE BATHROOM FOR YOU?
W-WELL......
OR MAYBE...
...YOU CAN'T LET HIM OUT EVEN THOUGH YOU WANT TO OR SOMETHING?
......I...
...SAW IT.

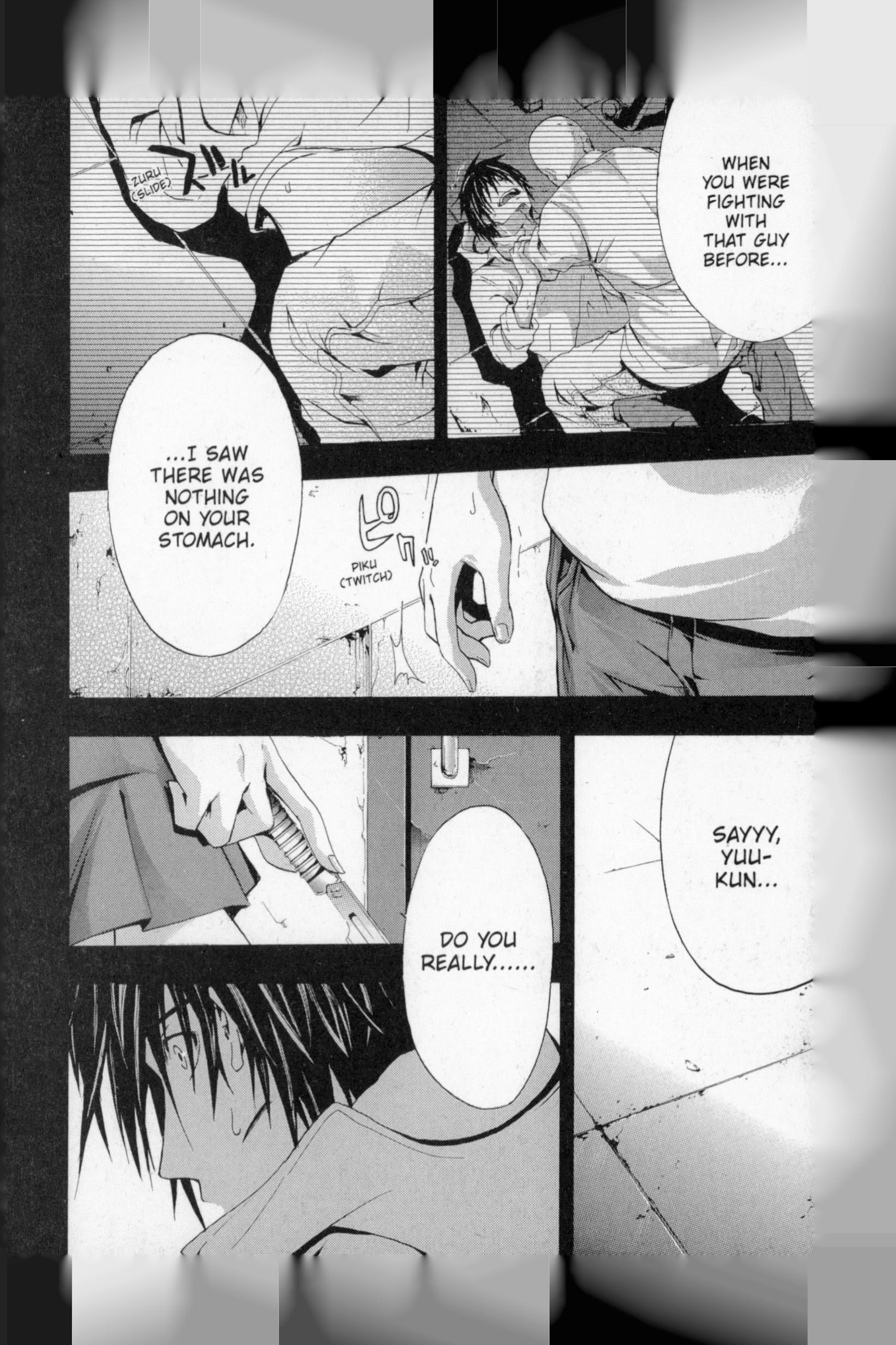
WHEN YOU WERE FIGHTING WITH THAT GUY BEFORE...
ZURU (SLIDE)
...I SAW THERE WAS NOTHING ON YOUR STOMACH.
PIKU (TWITCH)
SAYYY, YUU-KUN...
DO YOU REALLY......

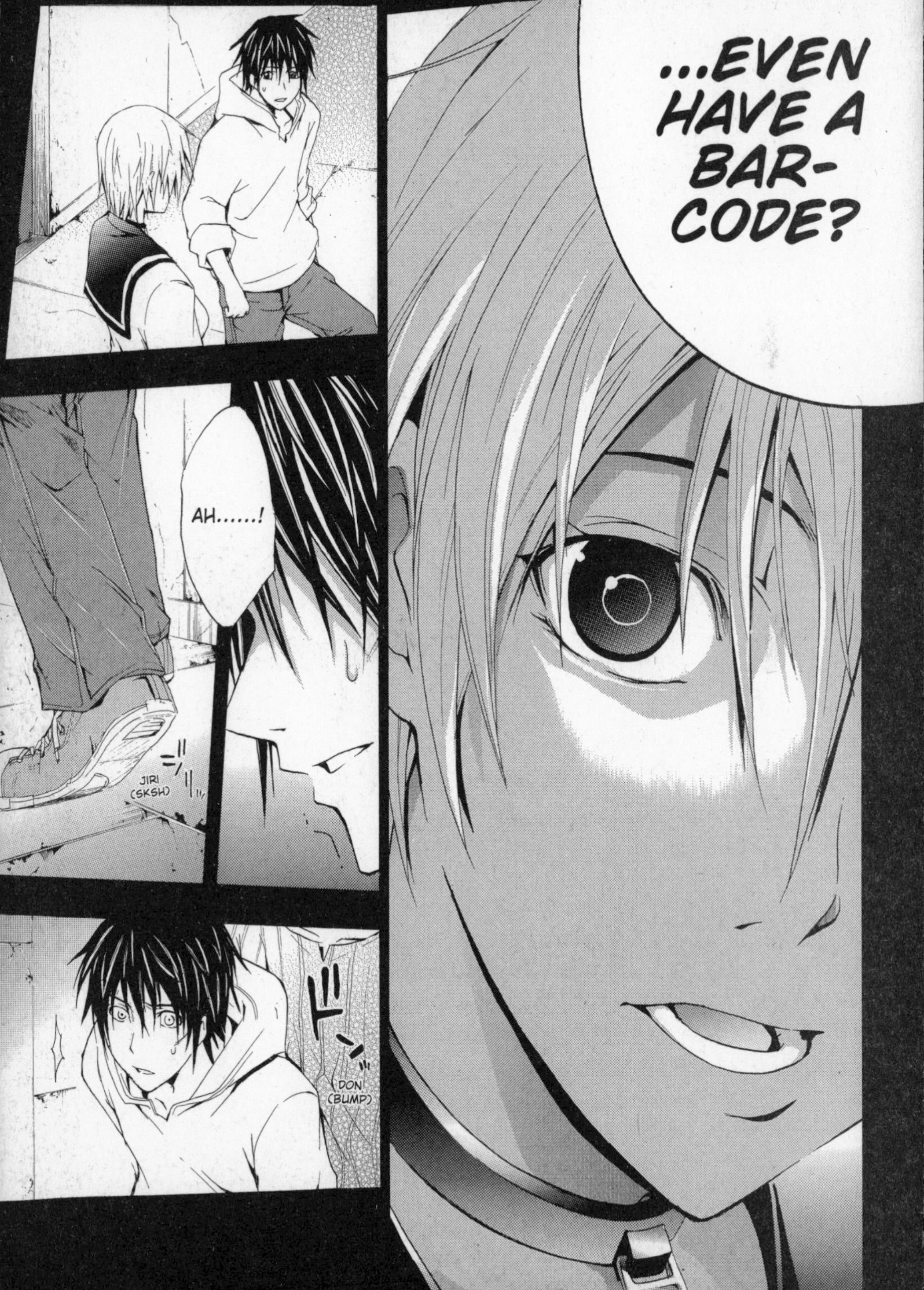

...EVEN HAVE A BAR-CODE?
AH......!
JIRI (SKSH)
DON (BUMP)

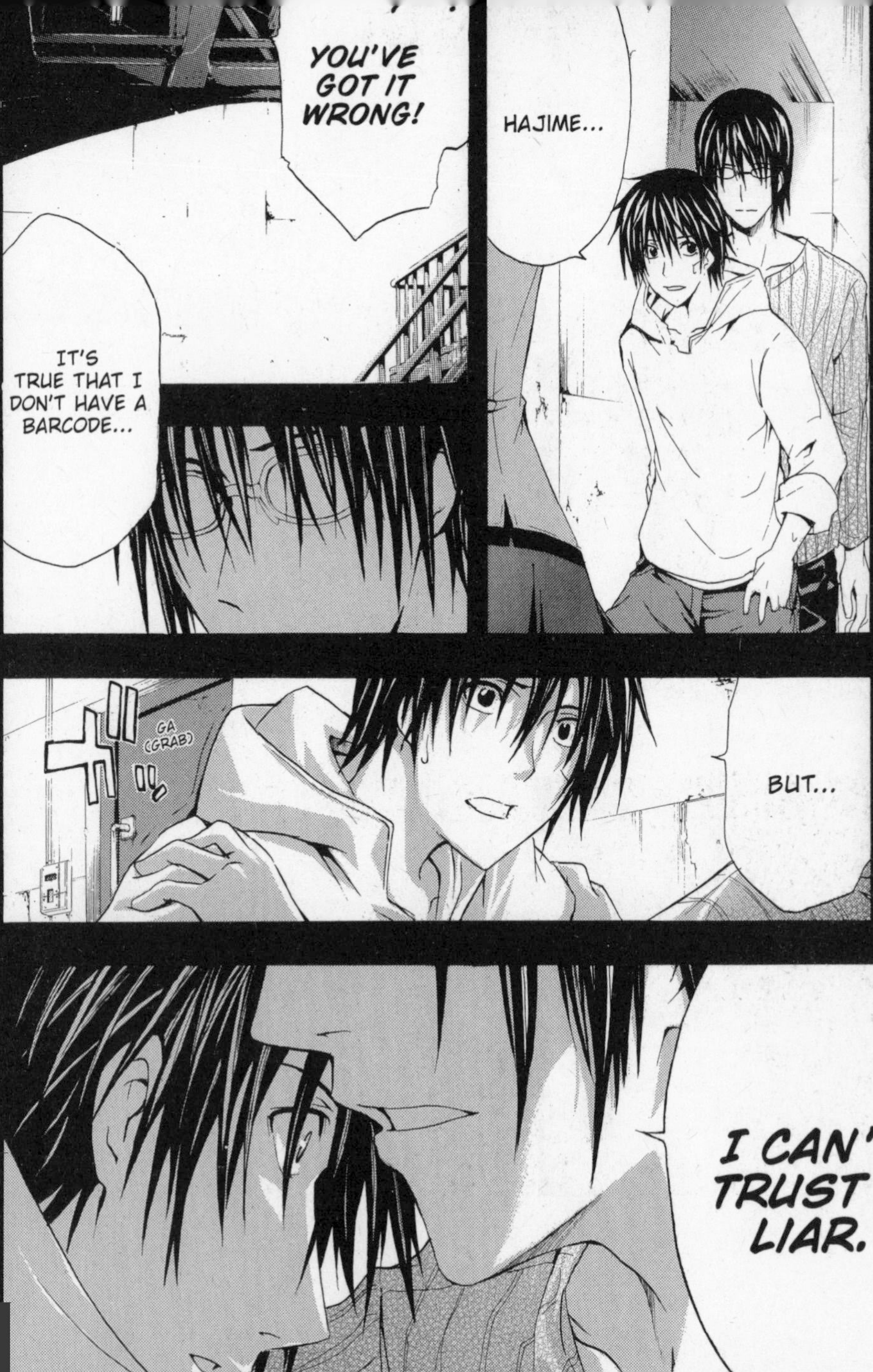
HAJIME...
YOU'VE GOT IT WRONG!
IT'S TRUE THAT I DON'T HAVE A BARCODE...
BUT...
GA (GRAB)
I CAN'T TRUST A LIAR.

ALL
'COS...

...I
LIED...

GAKU
(SLUMP)

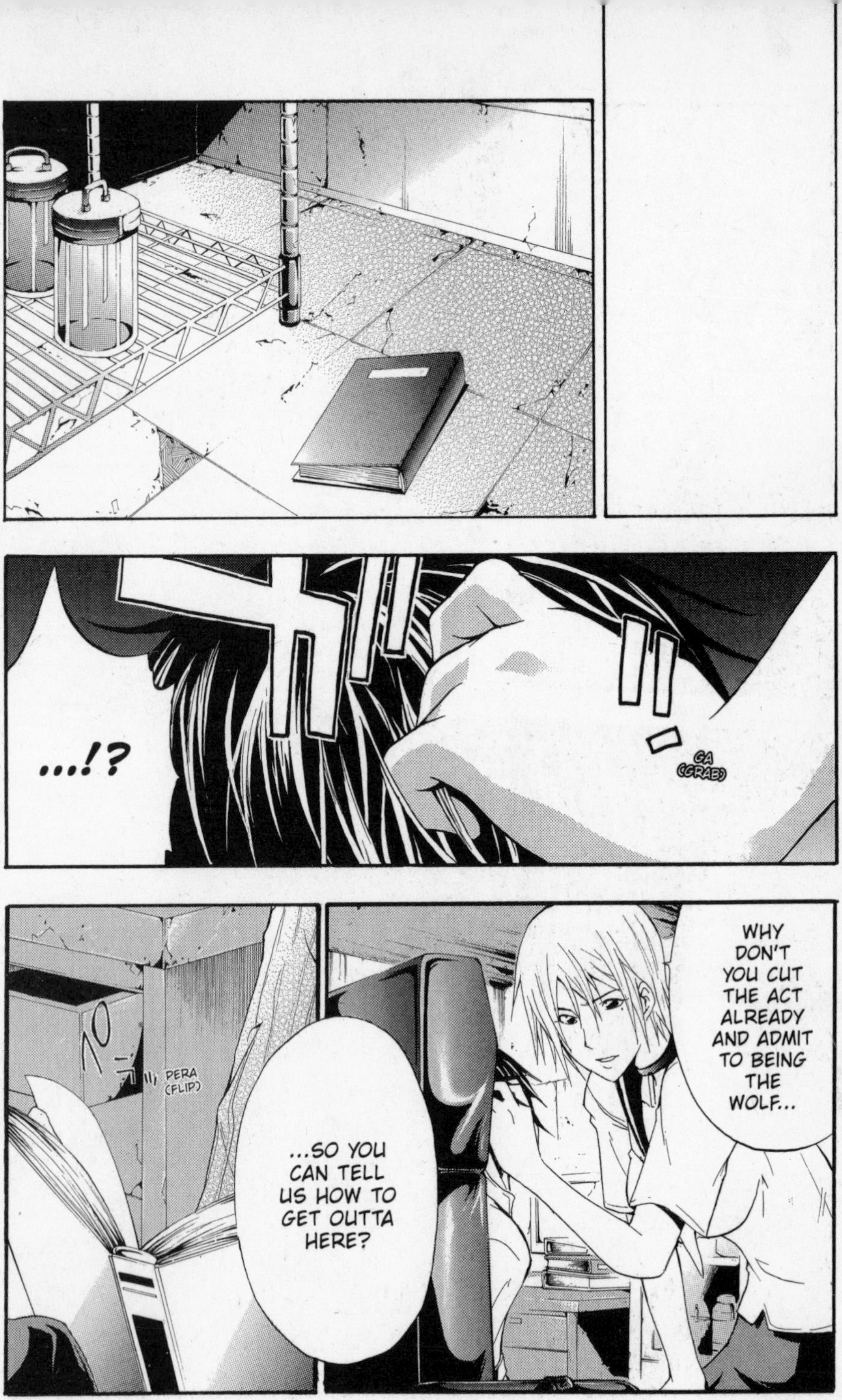
GA (GRAB)
...!?
WHY DON'T YOU CUT THE ACT ALREADY AND ADMIT TO BEING THE WOLF...
...SO YOU CAN TELL US HOW TO GET OUTTA HERE?
PERA (FLIP)

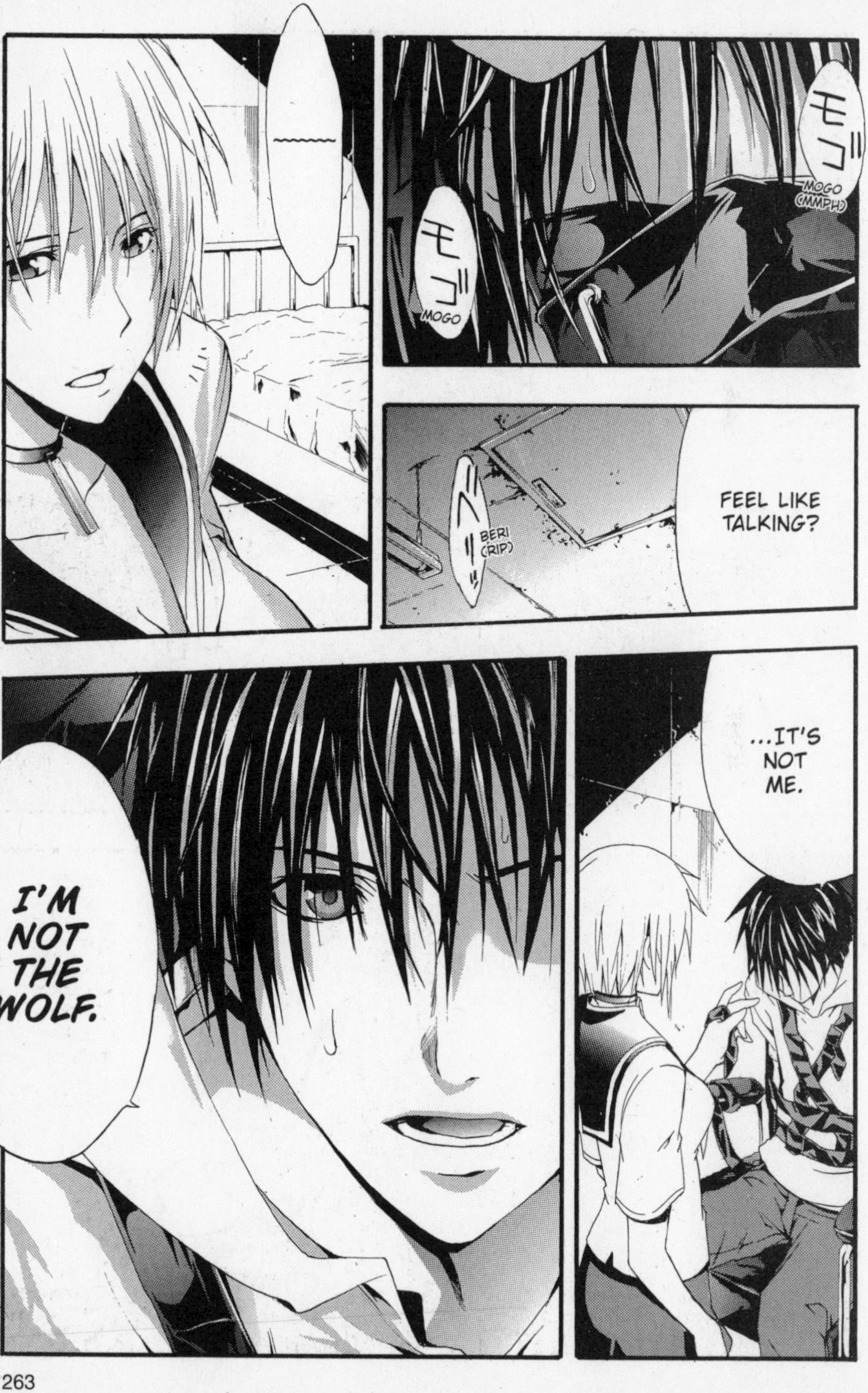

モゴ
MOGO (MMPH)
モゴ
MOGO
FEEL LIKE TALKING?
ベリッ!!
BERI (RIP)
~~~~~
...IT'S NOT ME.
I'M NOT THE WOLF.
~~~~~

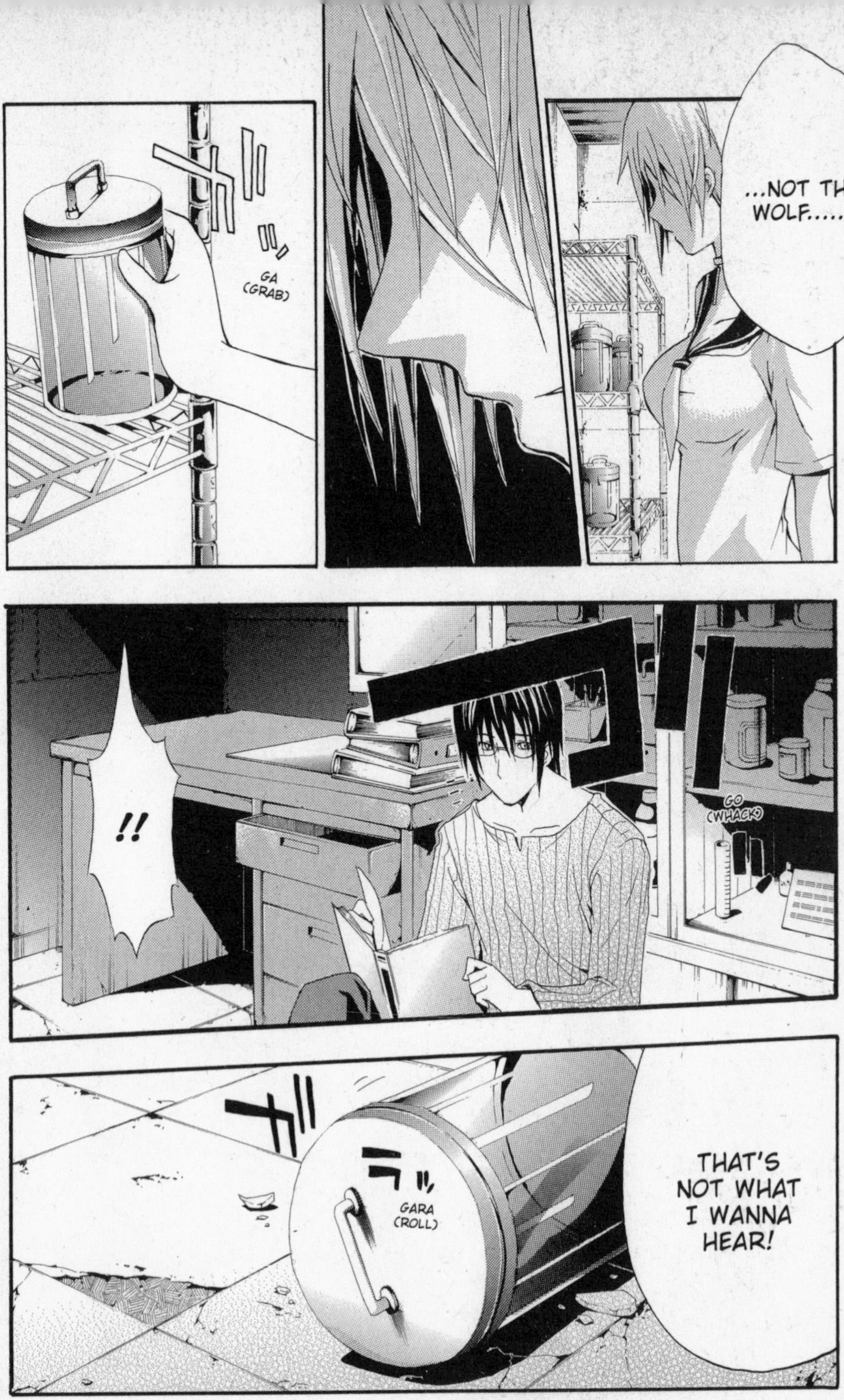
...NOT THE WOLF......
GA (GRAB)
GO (WHACK)
!!
THAT'S NOT WHAT I WANNA HEAR!
GARA (ROLL)

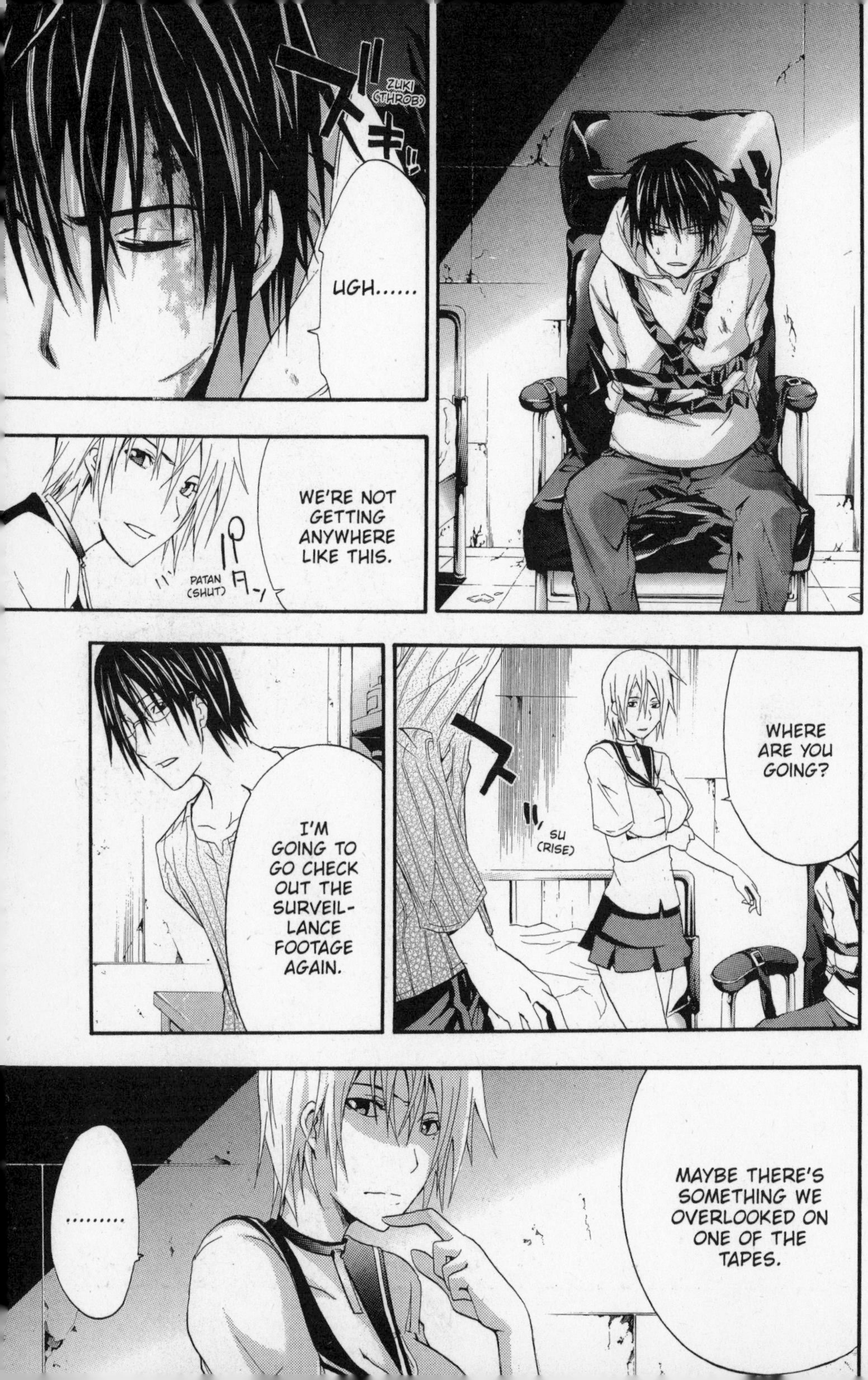
ZUKI (THROB)
UGH......
WE'RE NOT GETTING ANYWHERE LIKE THIS.
PATAN (SHUT)
WHERE ARE YOU GOING?
SU (RISE)
I'M GOING TO GO CHECK OUT THE SURVEIL-LANCE FOOTAGE AGAIN.
MAYBE THERE'S SOMETHING WE OVERLOOKED ON ONE OF THE TAPES.
....

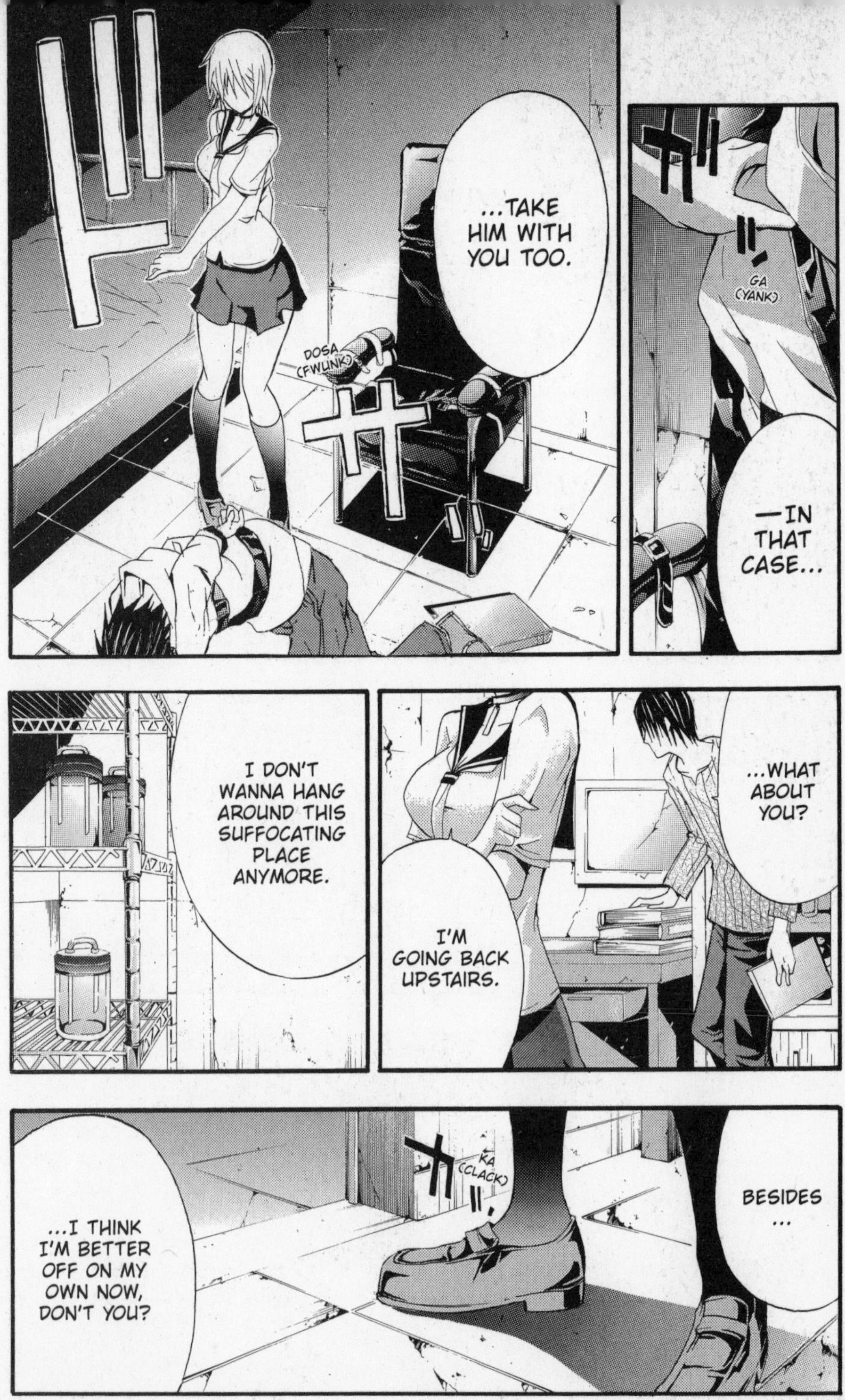
GA (YANK)
—IN THAT CASE...
...TAKE HIM WITH YOU TOO.
DOSA (FWUNK)
...WHAT ABOUT YOU?
I'M GOING BACK UPSTAIRS.
I DON'T WANNA HANG AROUND THIS SUFFOCATING PLACE ANYMORE.
BESIDES...
KA (CLACK)
...I THINK I'M BETTER OFF ON MY OWN NOW, DON'T YOU?

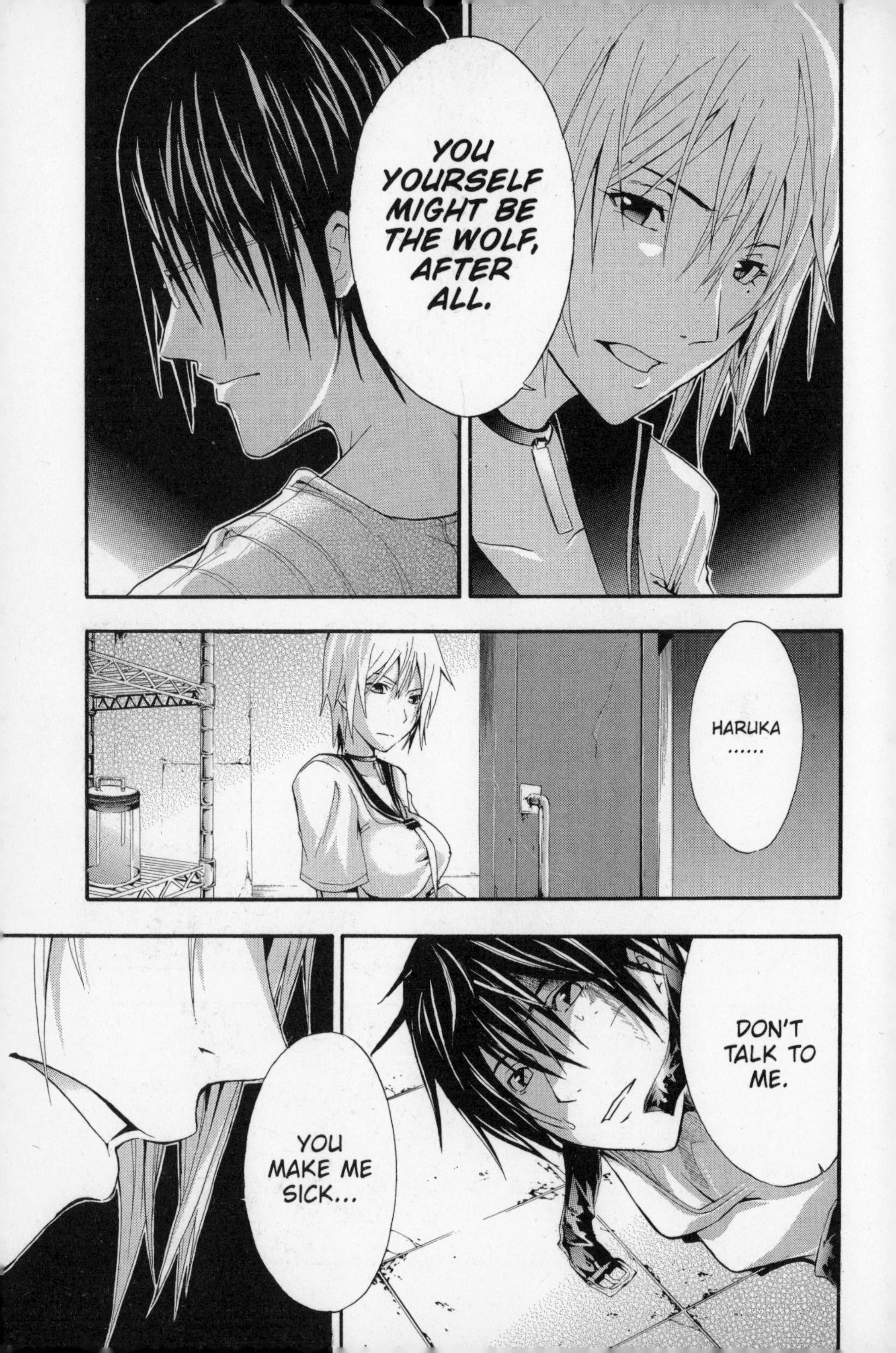
YOU YOURSELF MIGHT BE THE WOLF, AFTER ALL.
HARUKA ......
DON'T TALK TO ME.
YOU MAKE ME SICK...

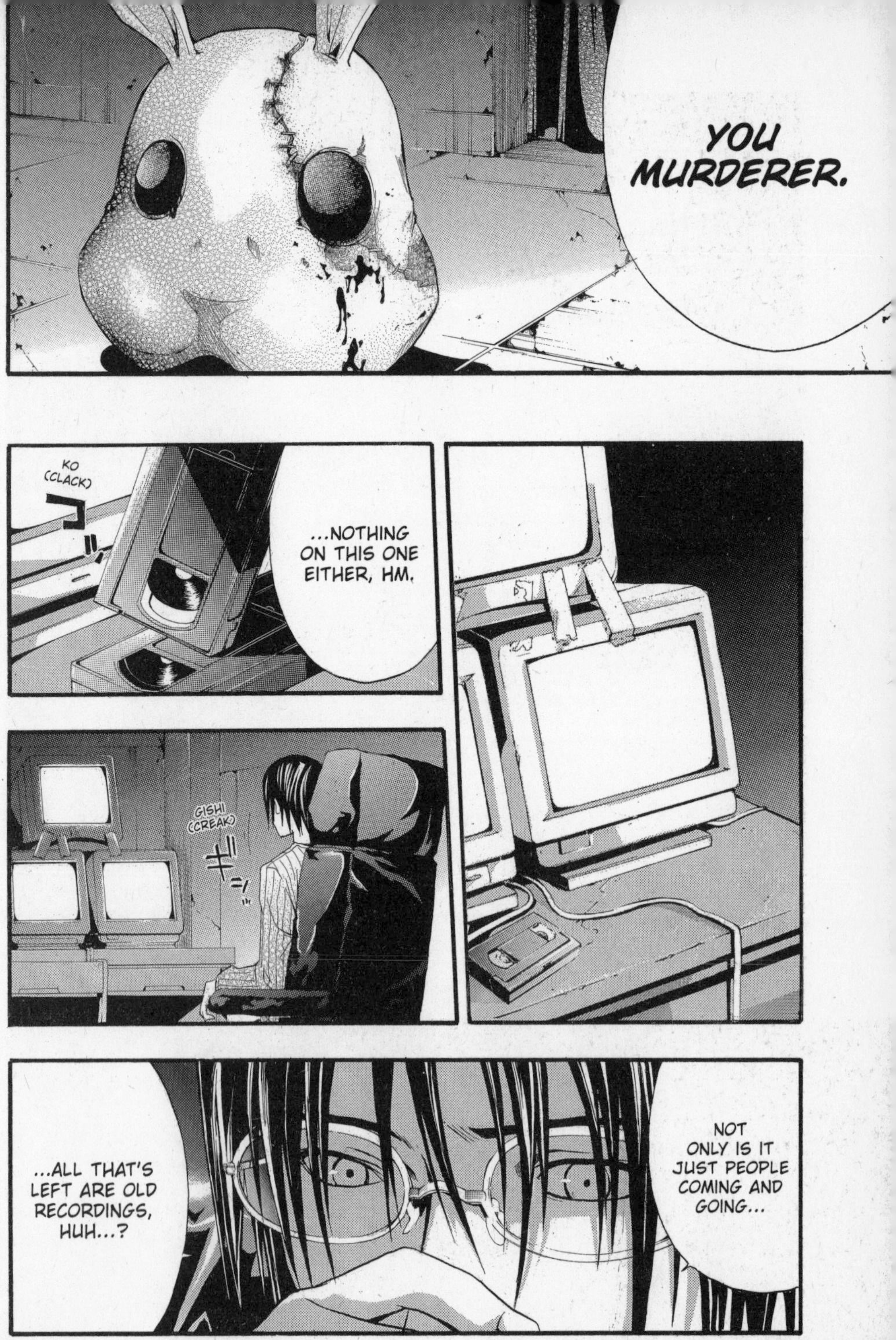
YOU MURDERER.
...NOTHING ON THIS ONE EITHER, HM.
KO (CLACK)
GISHI (CREAK)
NOT ONLY IS IT JUST PEOPLE COMING AND GOING...
...ALL THAT'S LEFT ARE OLD RECORDINGS, HUH...?

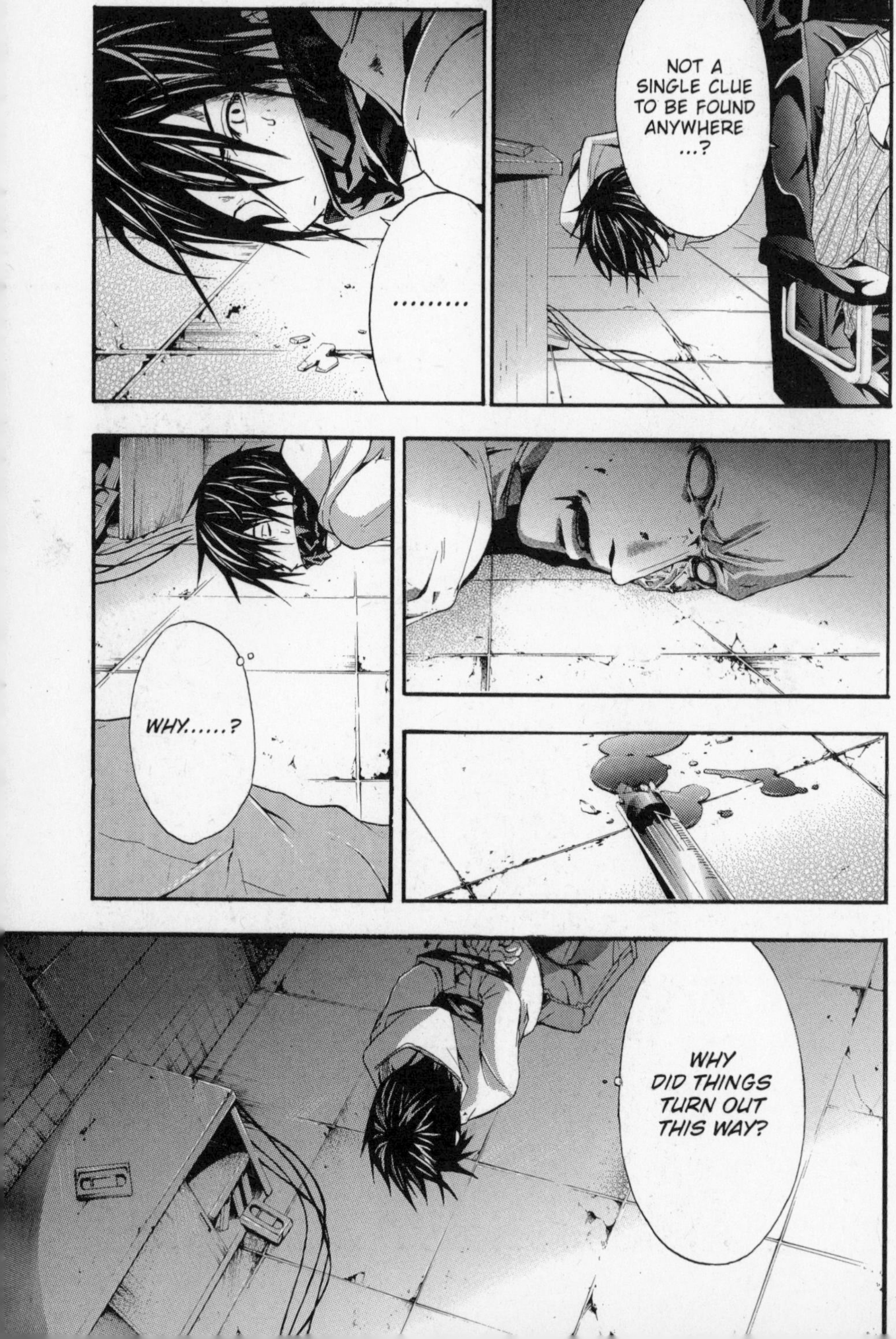
NOT A SINGLE CLUE TO BE FOUND ANYWHERE ...?
....
WHY......?
WHY DID THINGS TURN OUT THIS WAY?

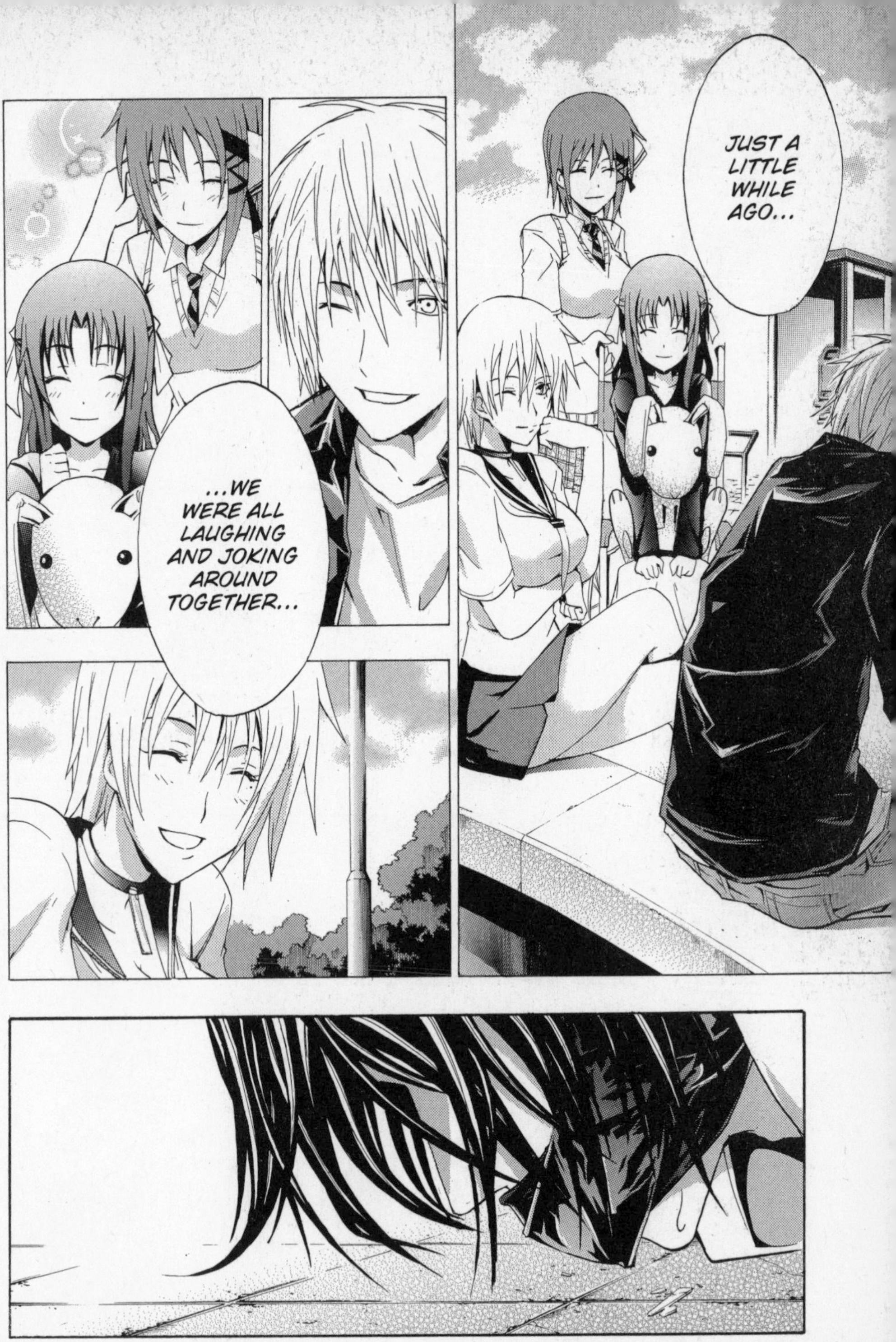
JUST A LITTLE WHILE AGO...
...WE WERE ALL LAUGHING AND JOKING AROUND TOGETHER...

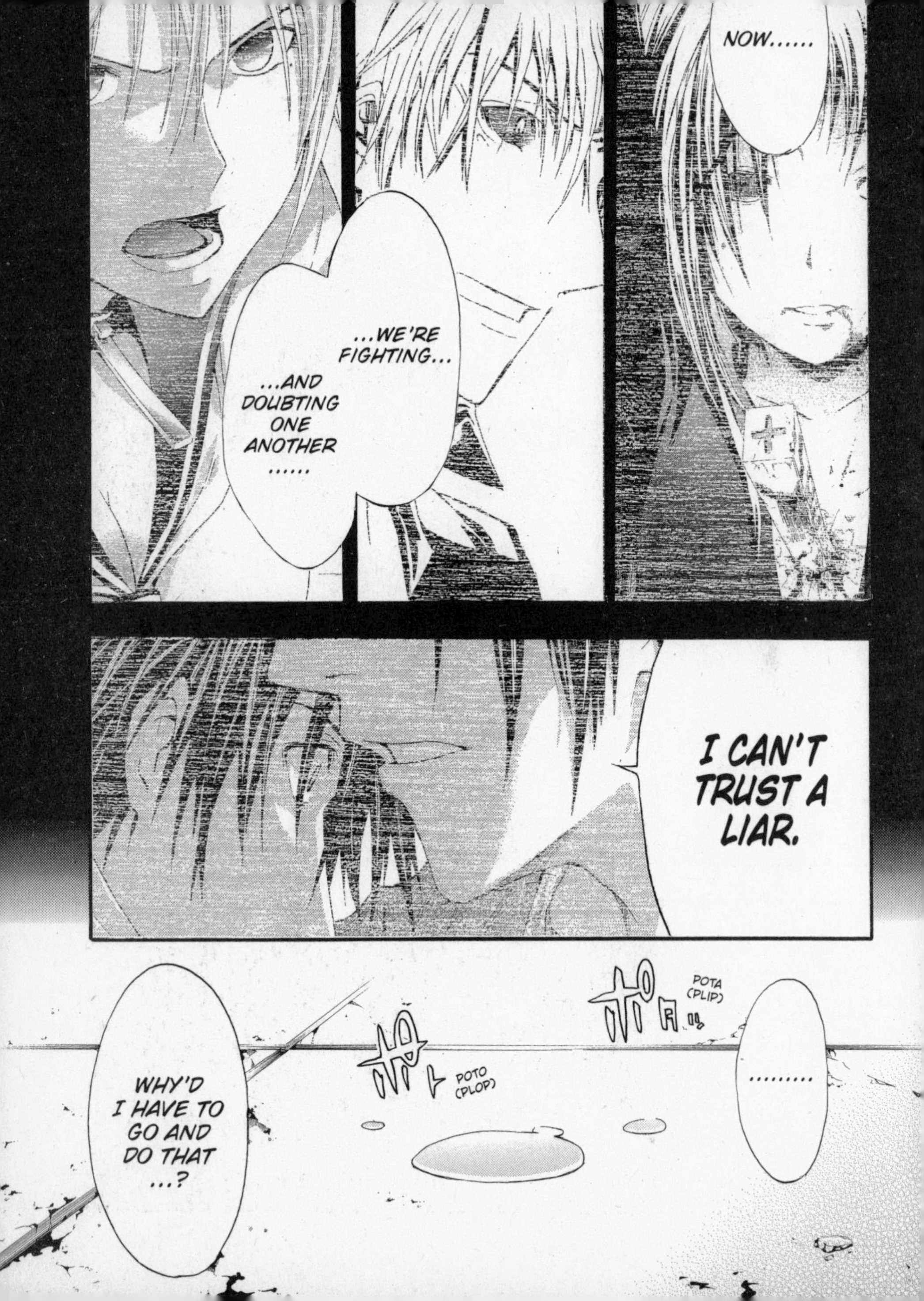
NOW......
...WE'RE FIGHTING...
...AND DOUBTING ONE ANOTHER ......
I CAN'T TRUST A LIAR.
....
POTA (PLIP)
POTO (PLOP)
WHY'D I HAVE TO GO AND DO THAT ...?

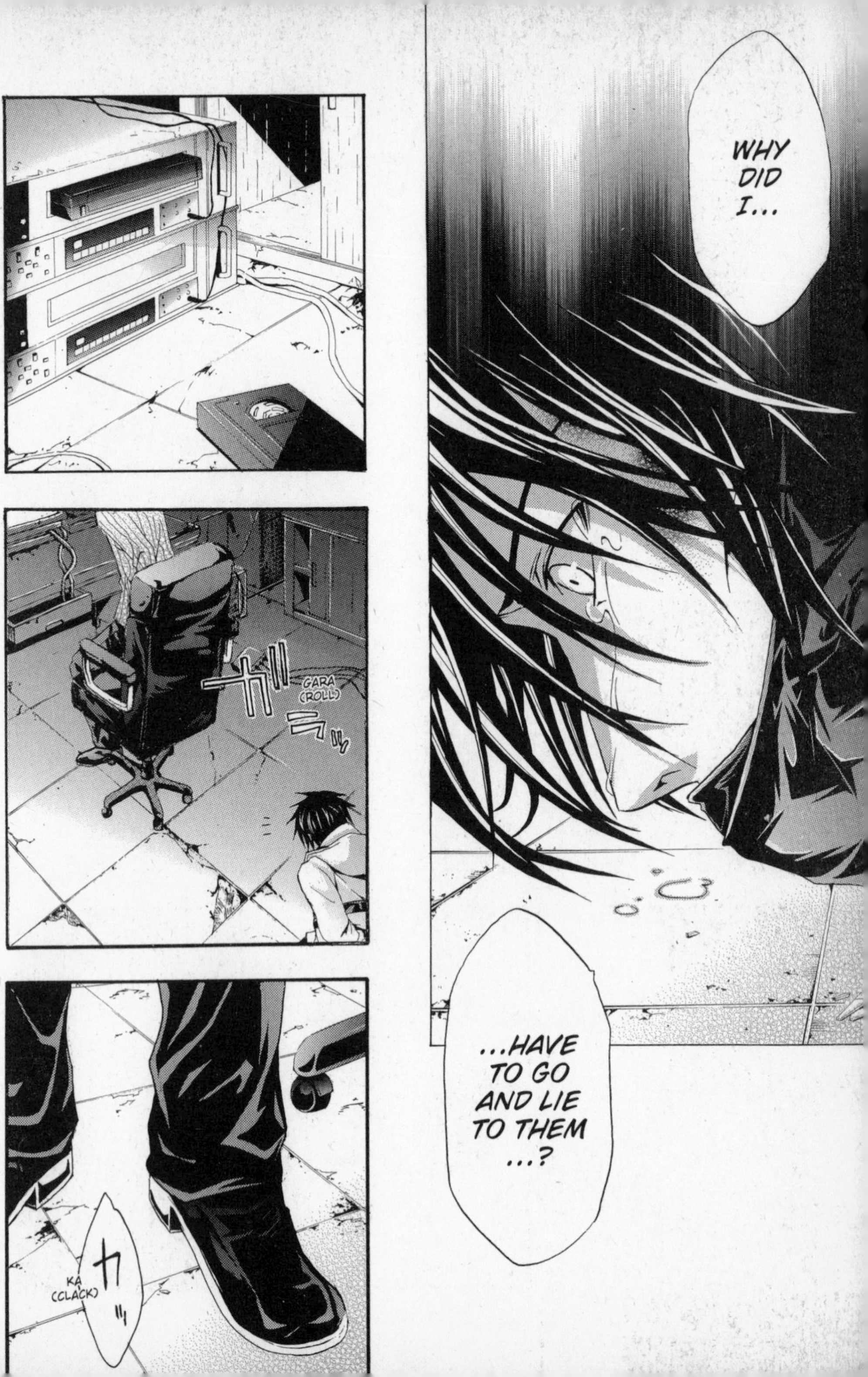
WHY DID I...
...HAVE TO GO AND LIE TO THEM ...?
ガラッ
GARA (ROLL)
カッ
KA (CLACK)

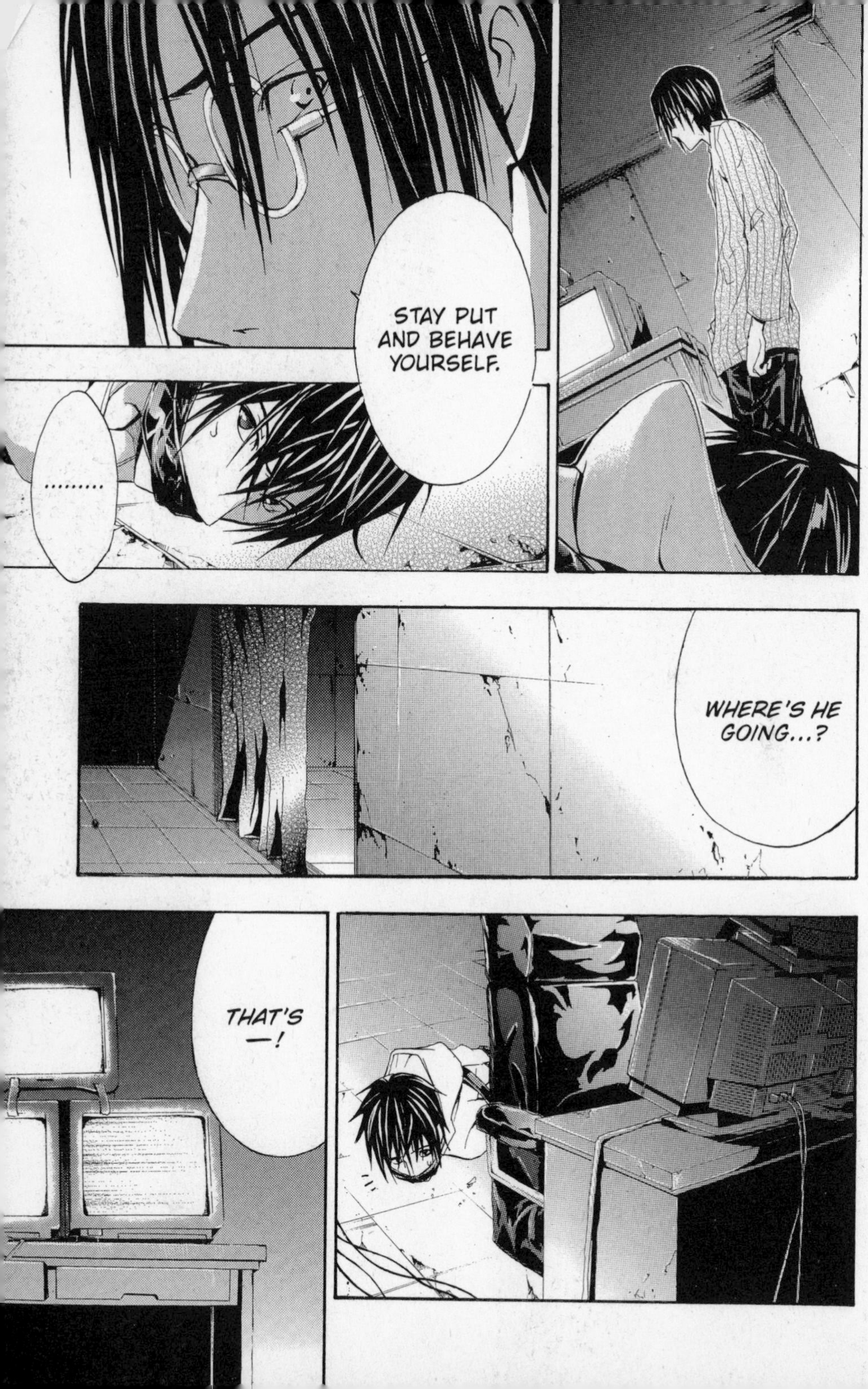
STAY PUT AND BEHAVE YOURSELF.
....
WHERE'S HE GOING...?
THAT'S —!

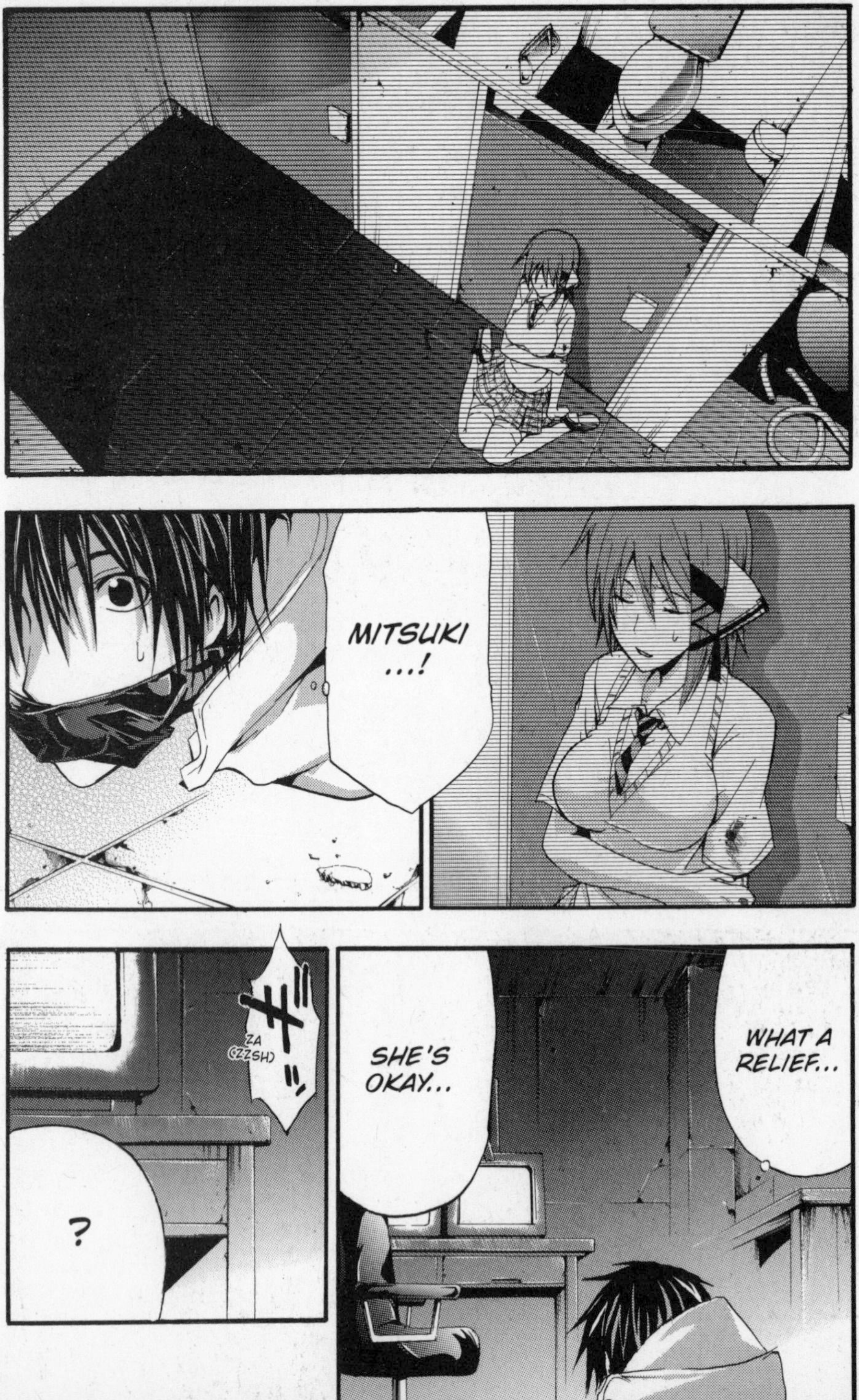
MITSUKI ...!
WHAT A RELIEF...
SHE'S OKAY...
ZA (ZZSH)
?

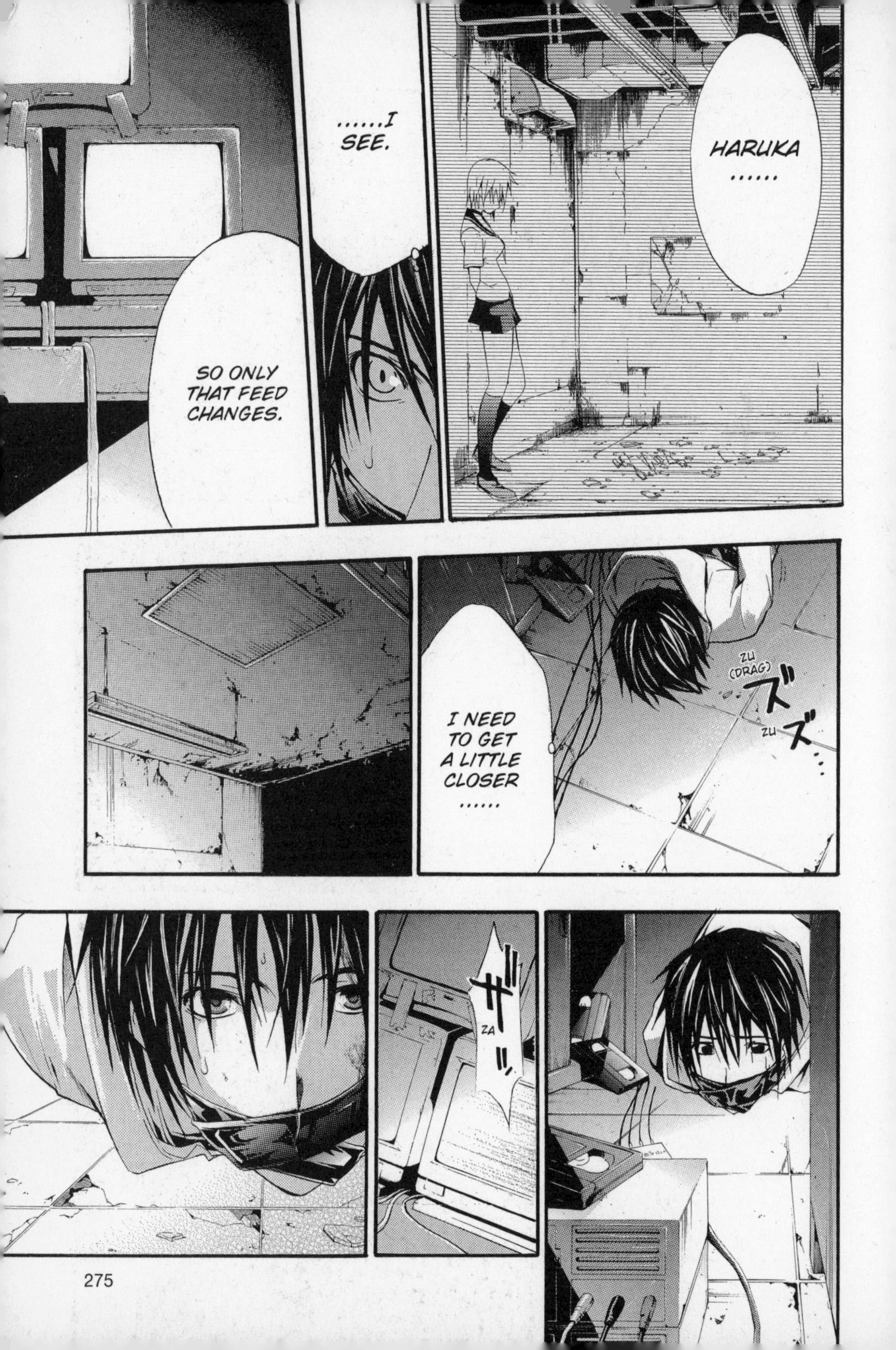
HARUKA ......
......I SEE.
SO ONLY THAT FEED CHANGES.
I NEED TO GET A LITTLE CLOSER ......
ZU (DRAG)
ズ
ZU
ズ...
ザ
ZA

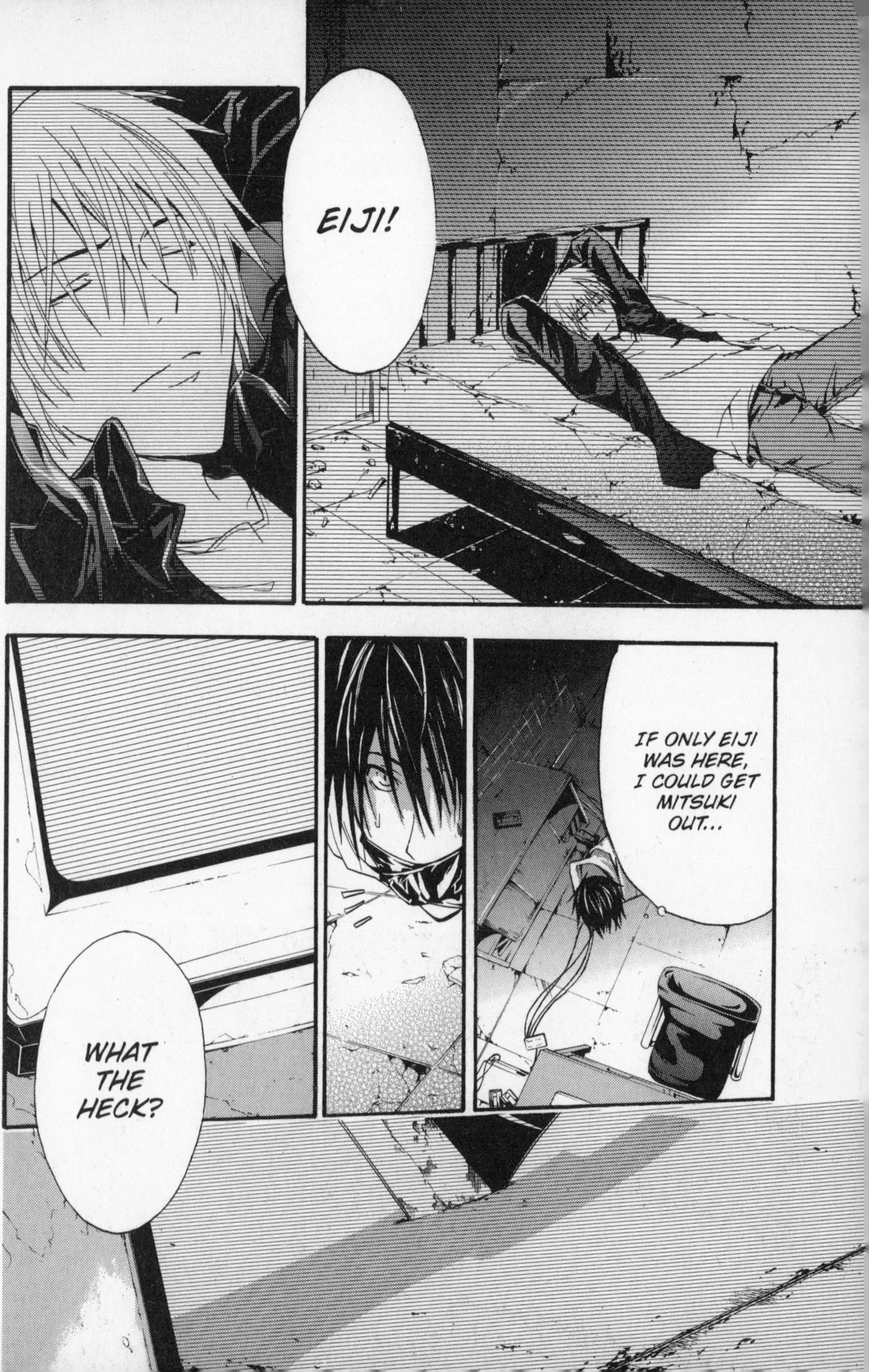
EIJI!
IF ONLY EIJI WAS HERE, I COULD GET MITSUKI OUT...
WHAT THE HECK?

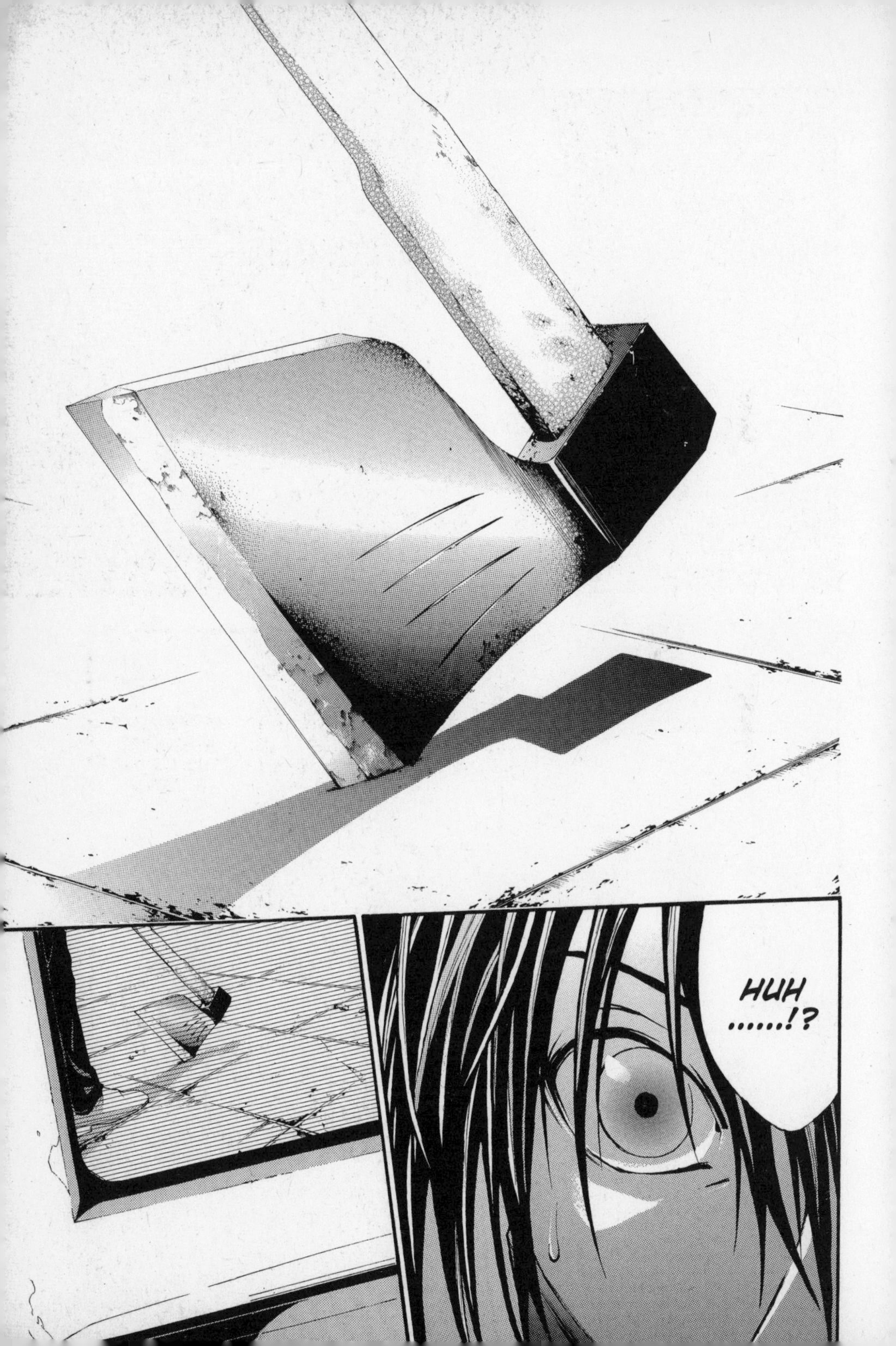
HUH ......!?

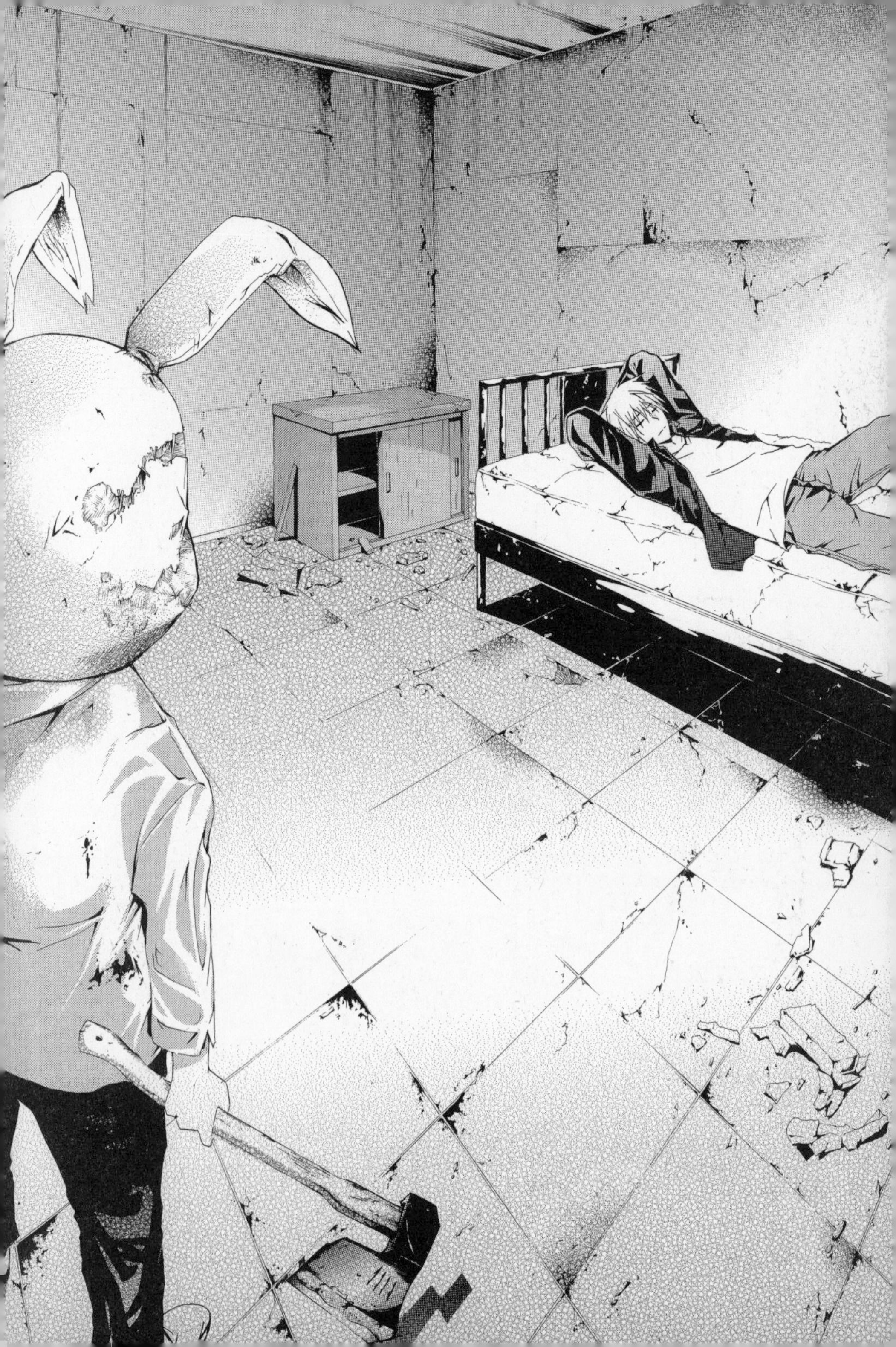

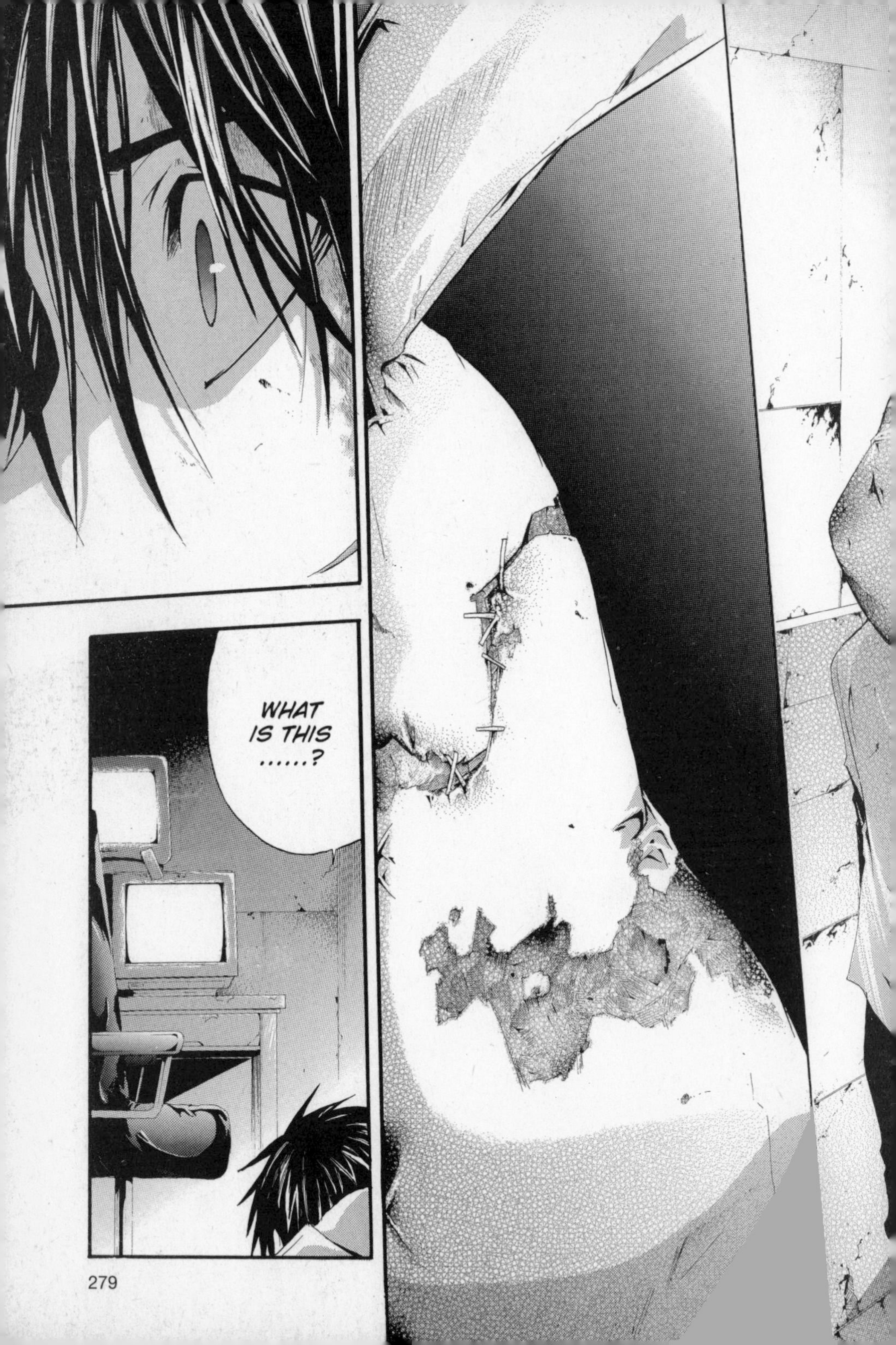
WHAT IS THIS ......?

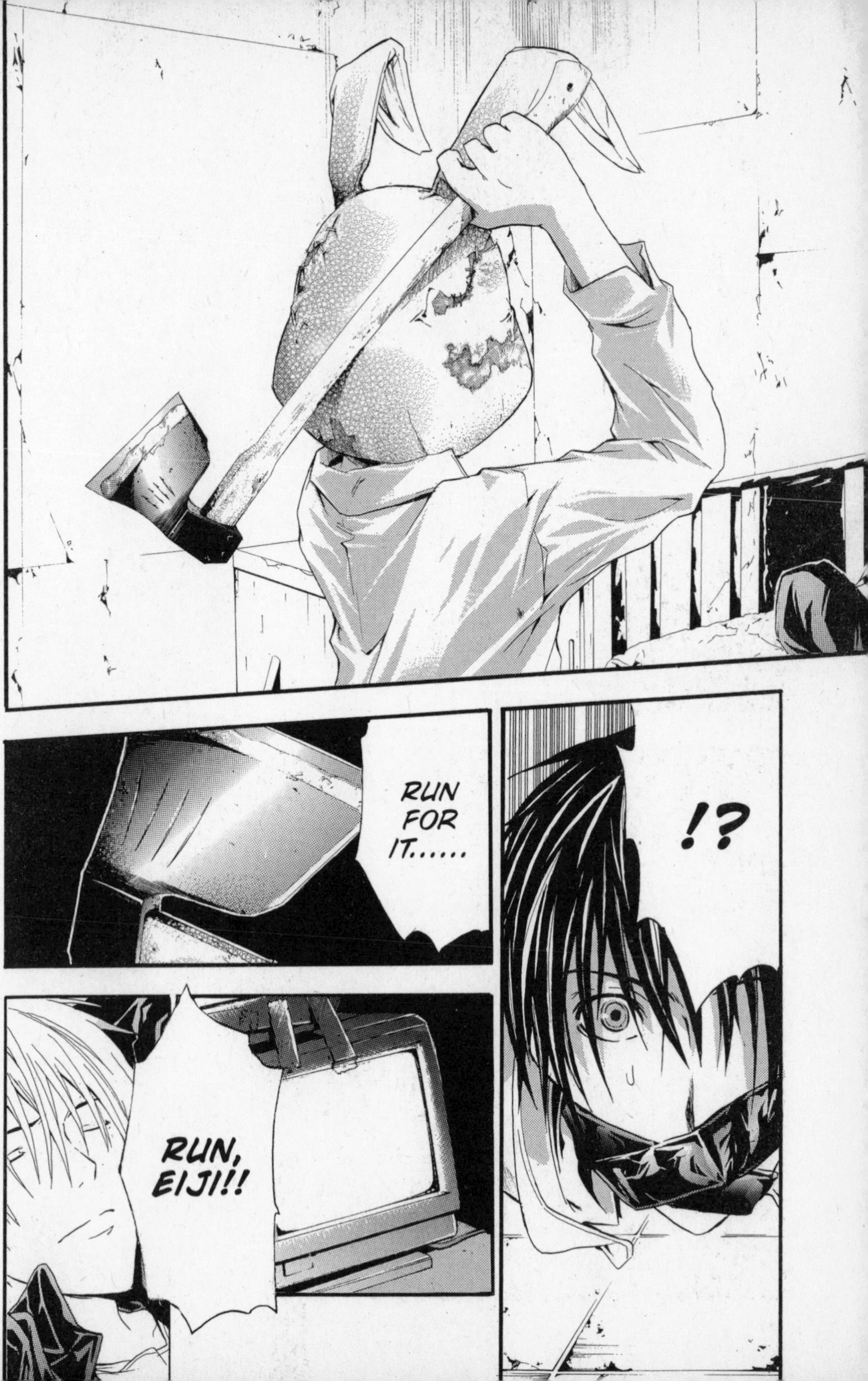
!?
RUN FOR IT......
RUN, EIJI!!

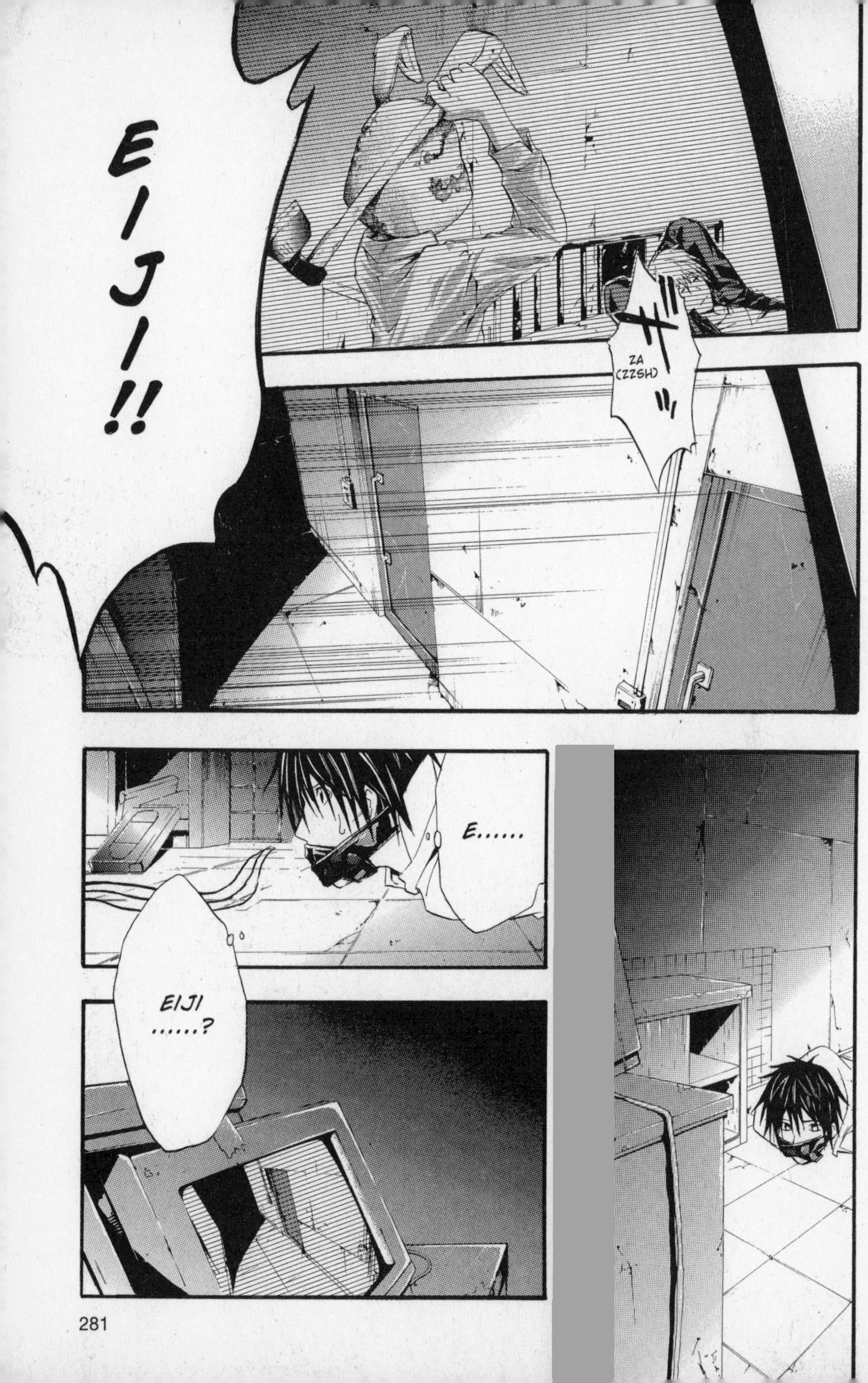
EIJI!!
ZA (ZZSH)
E......
EIJI ......?

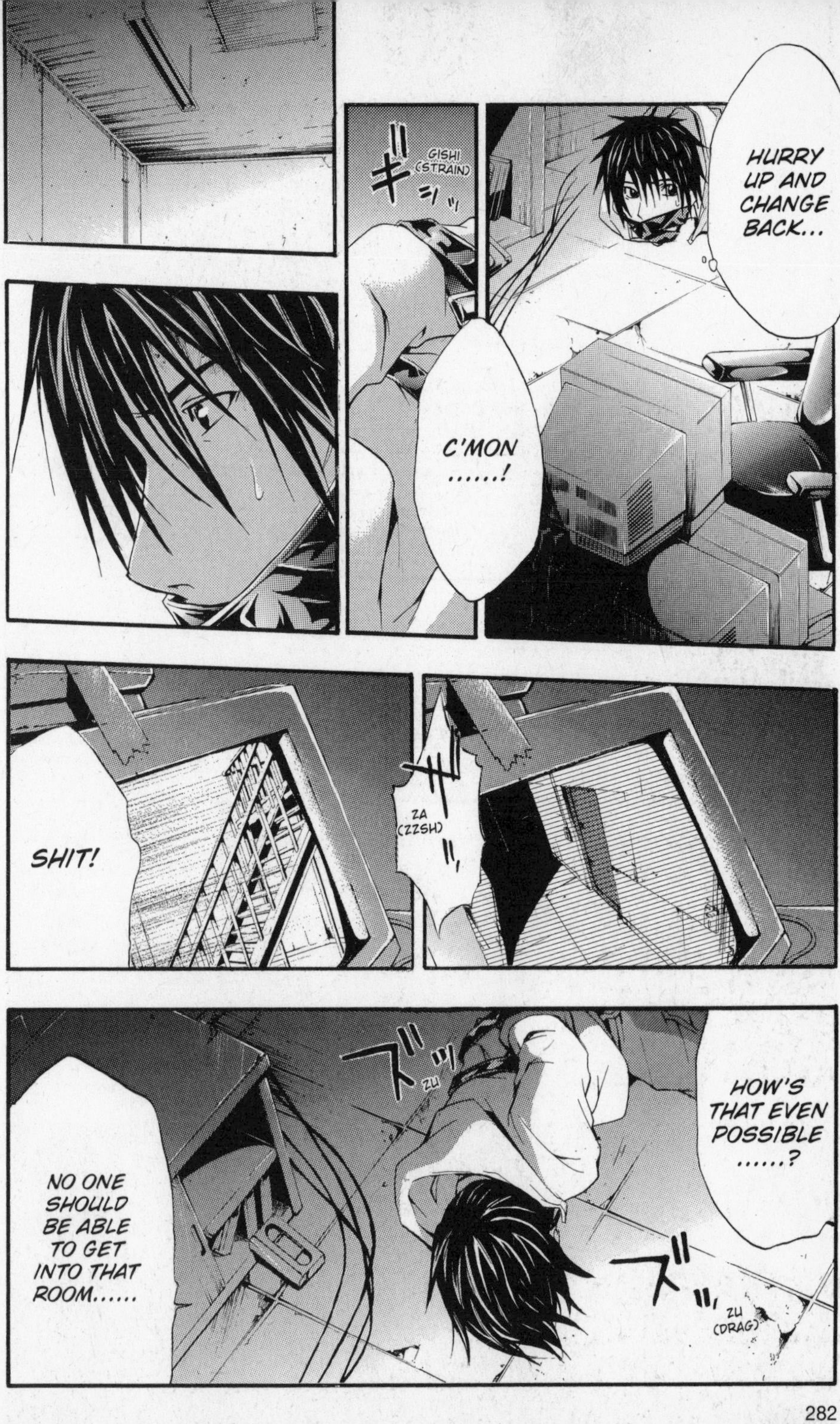
HURRY UP AND CHANGE BACK...
GISHI (STRAIN)
C'MON ......!
ZA (ZZSH)
SHIT!
ZU
HOW'S THAT EVEN POSSIBLE ......?
ZU (DRAG)
NO ONE SHOULD BE ABLE TO GET INTO THAT ROOM......

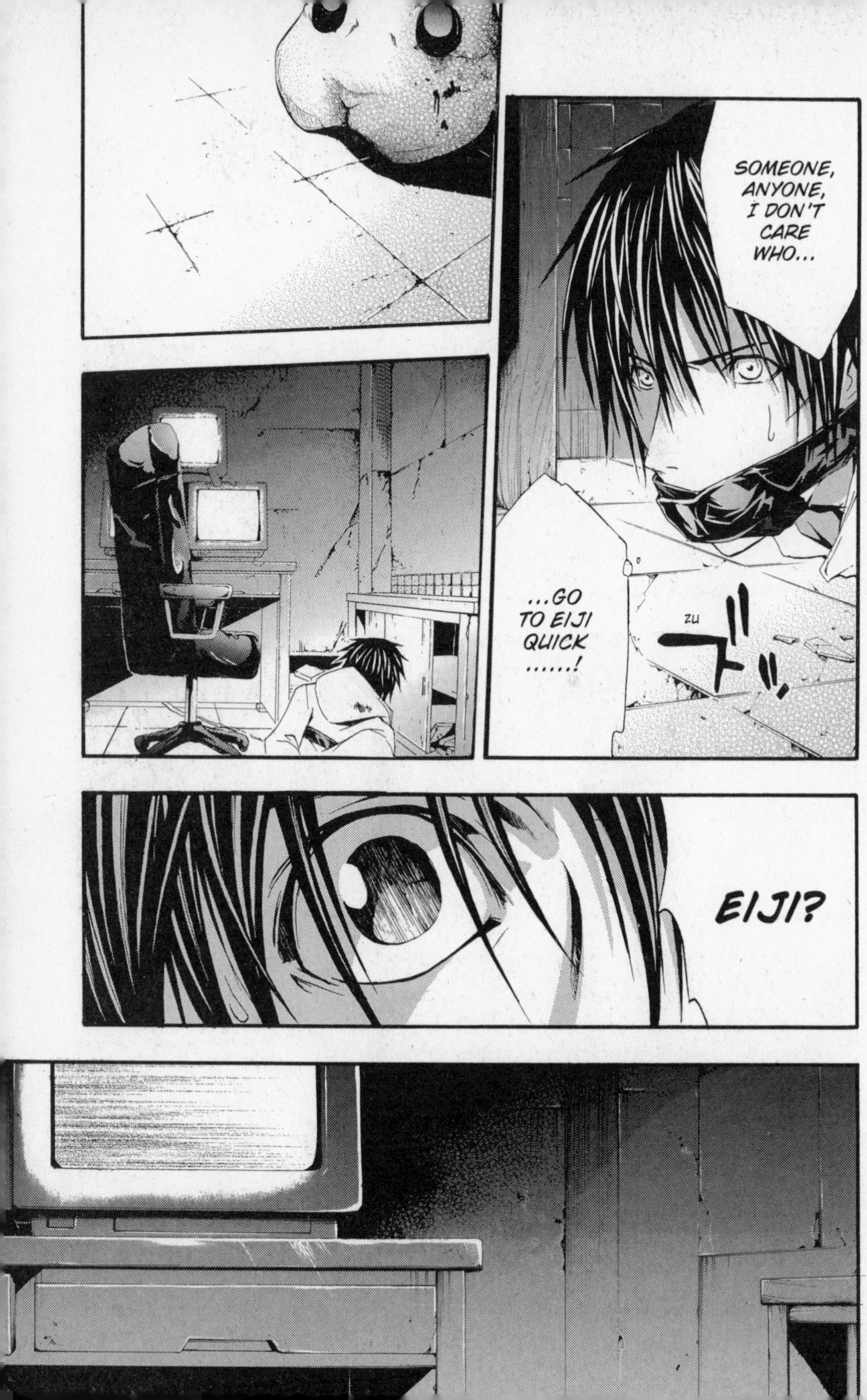
SOMEONE, ANYONE, I DON'T CARE WHO...
...GO TO EIJI QUICK ......!
zu
EIJI?

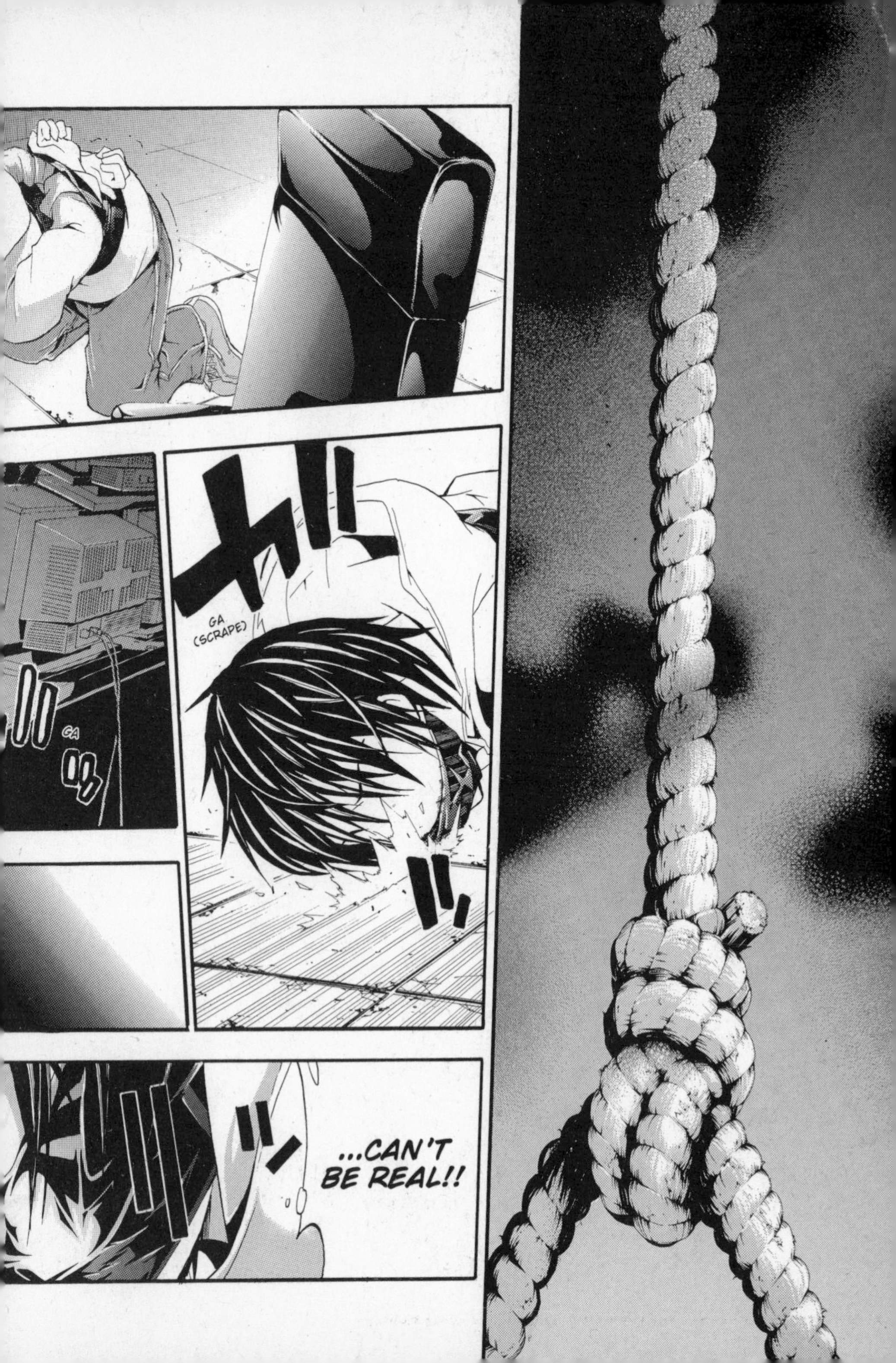
GA
(SCRAPE)
GA
...CAN'T
BE REAL!!

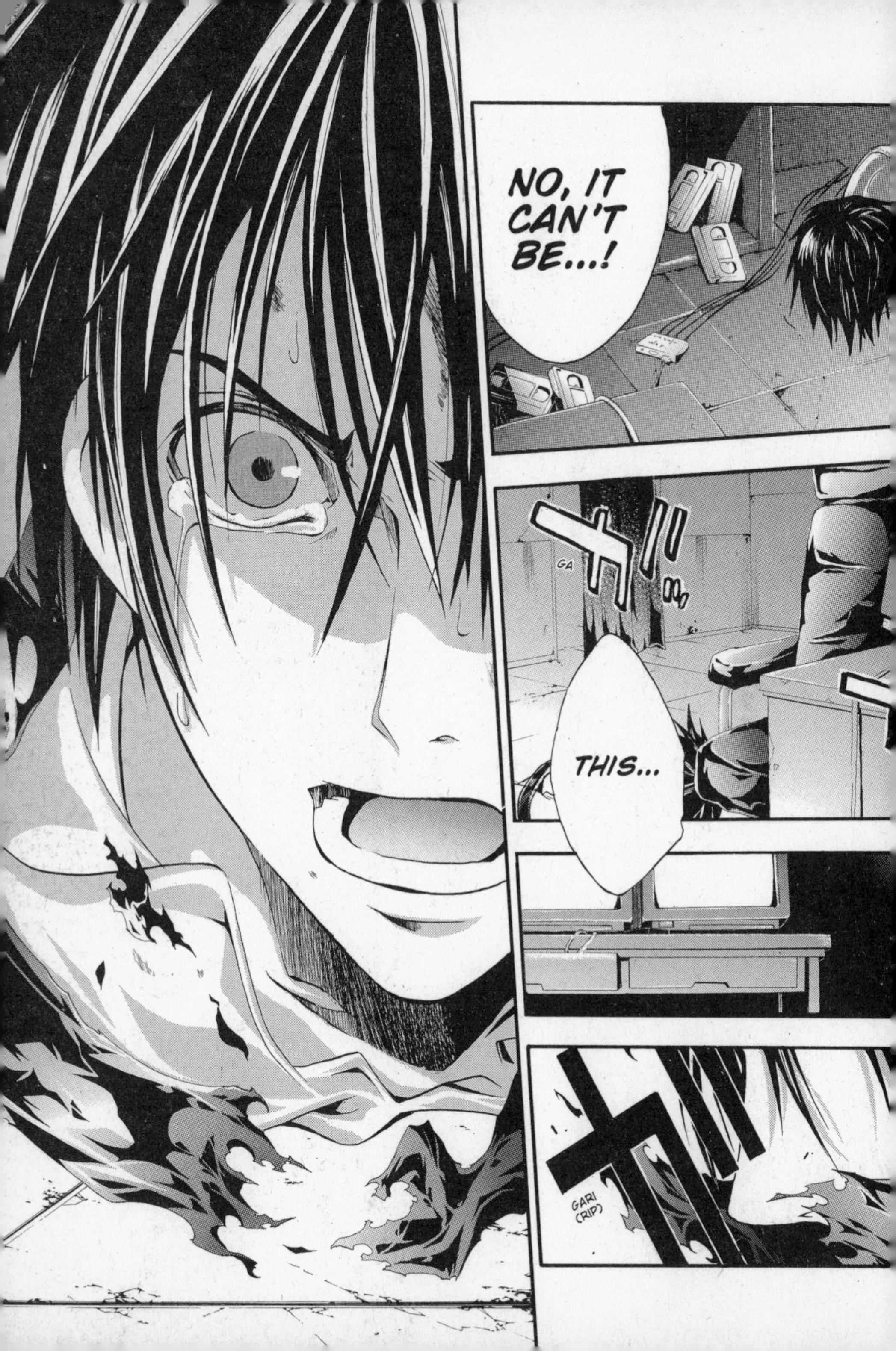
NO, IT CAN'T BE...!
GA
THIS...
GARI (RIP)

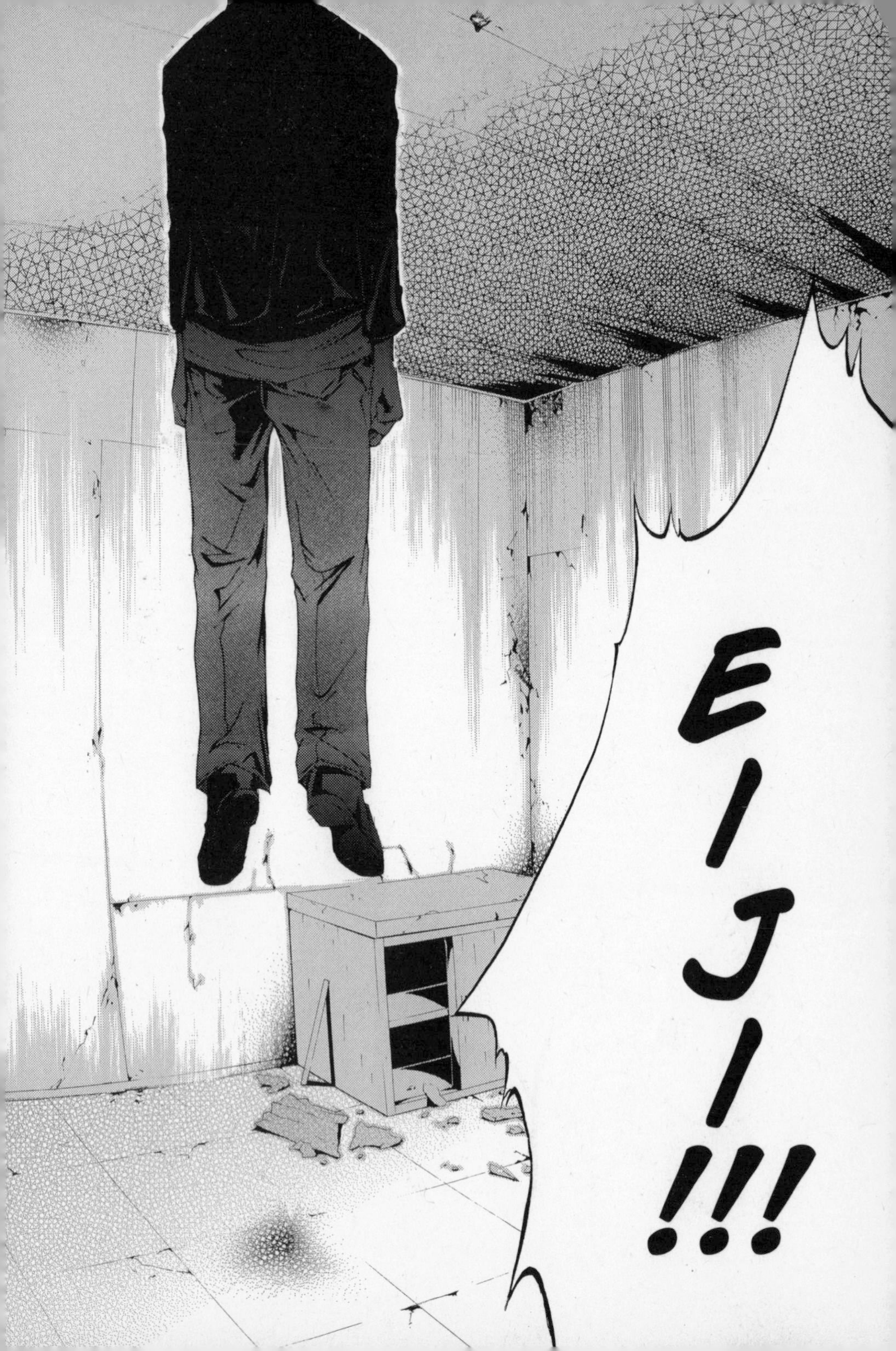
EIJI!!!

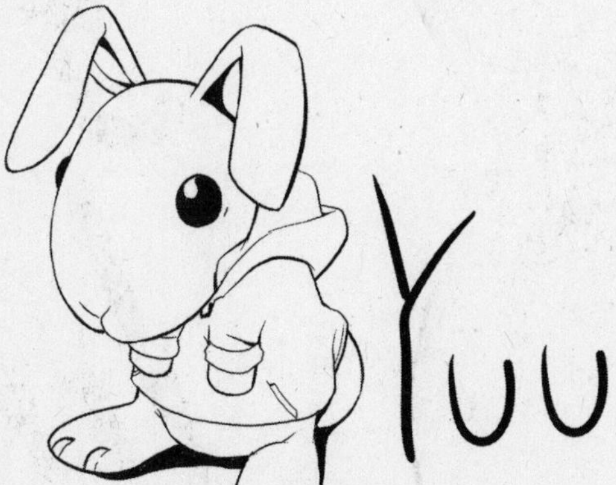
Yuu

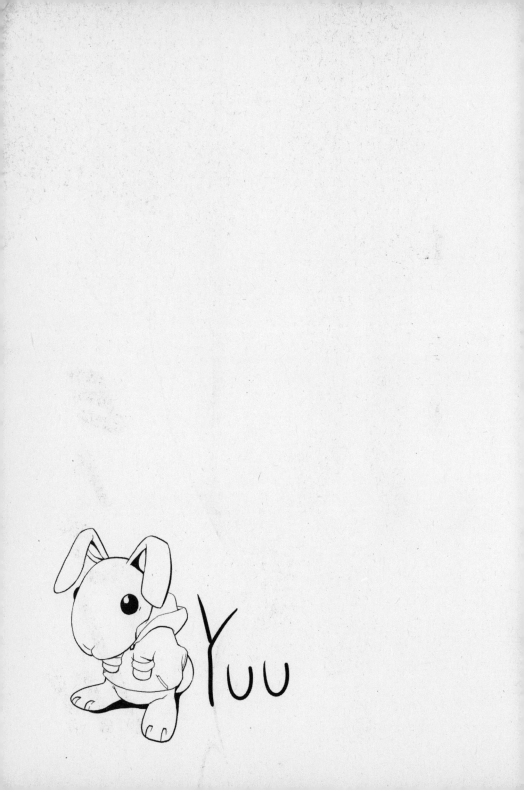

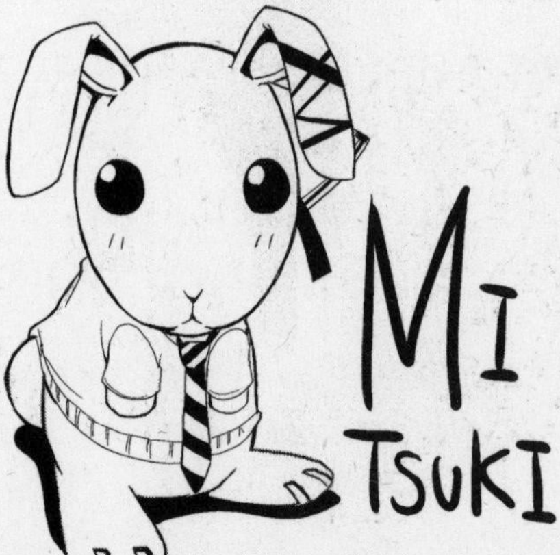
MI
TSUKI

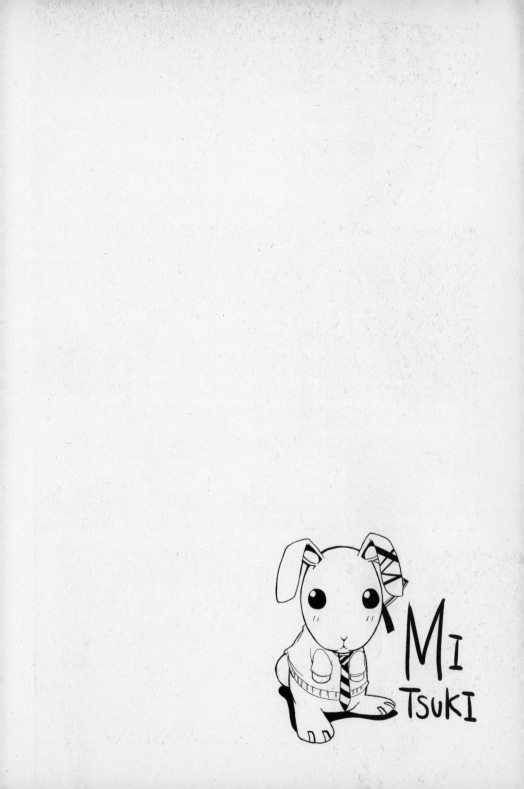

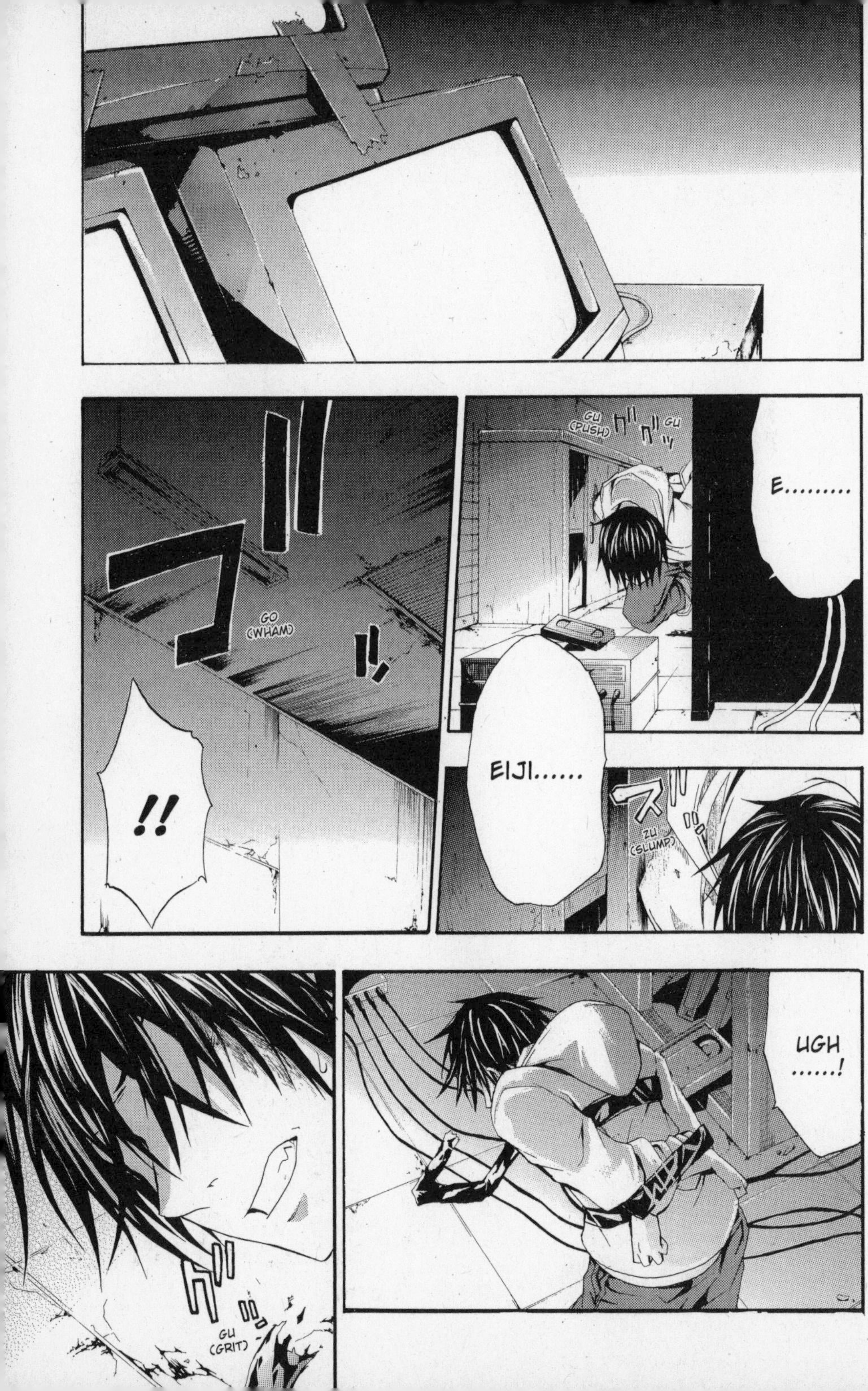
GU
(PUSH)
GU
E.........
EIJI......
ZU
(SLUMP)
GO
(WHAM)
!!
UGH
......!
GU
(GRIT)

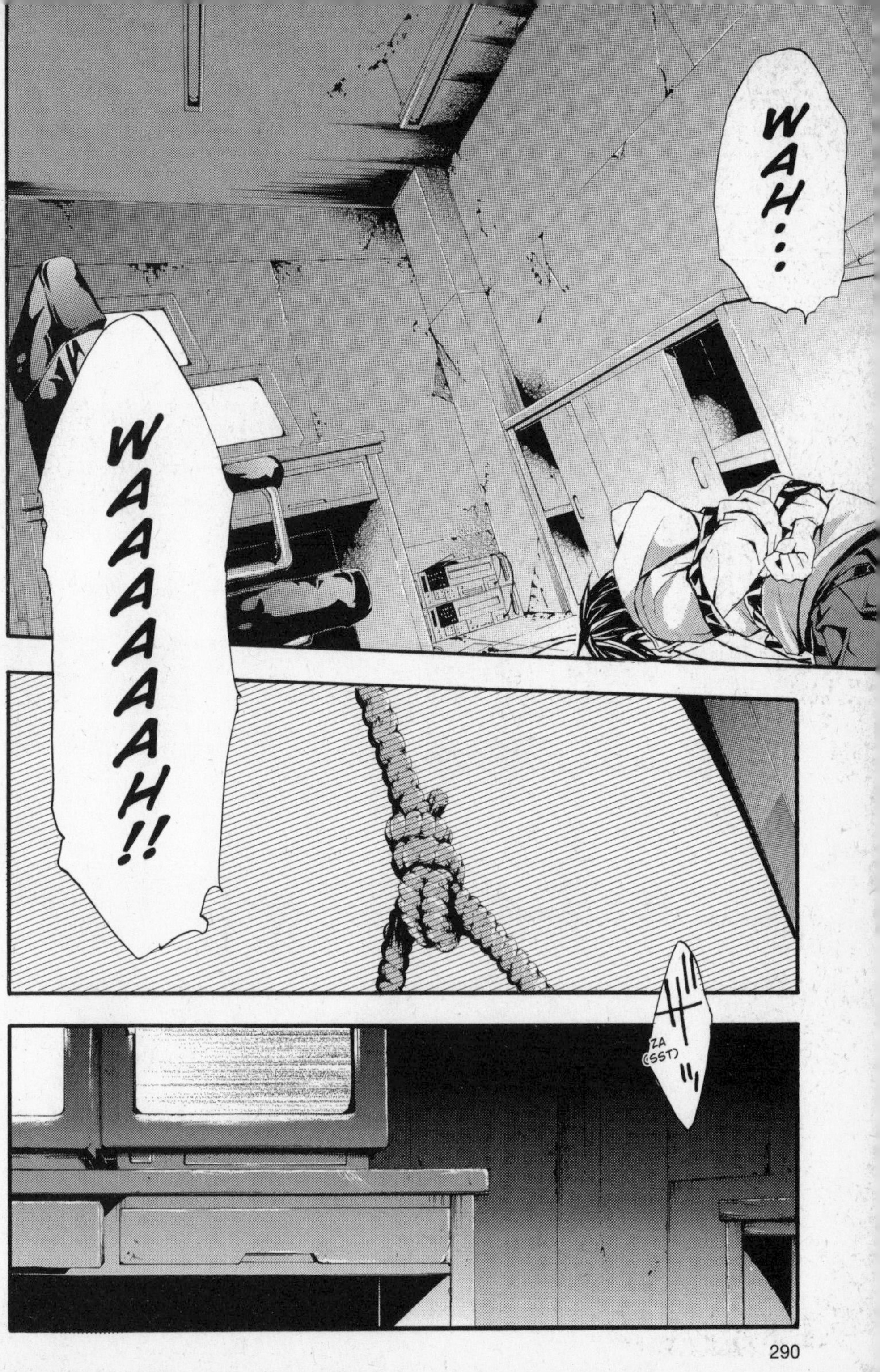
WAH...
WAAAAAAH!!
ZA (SSST)

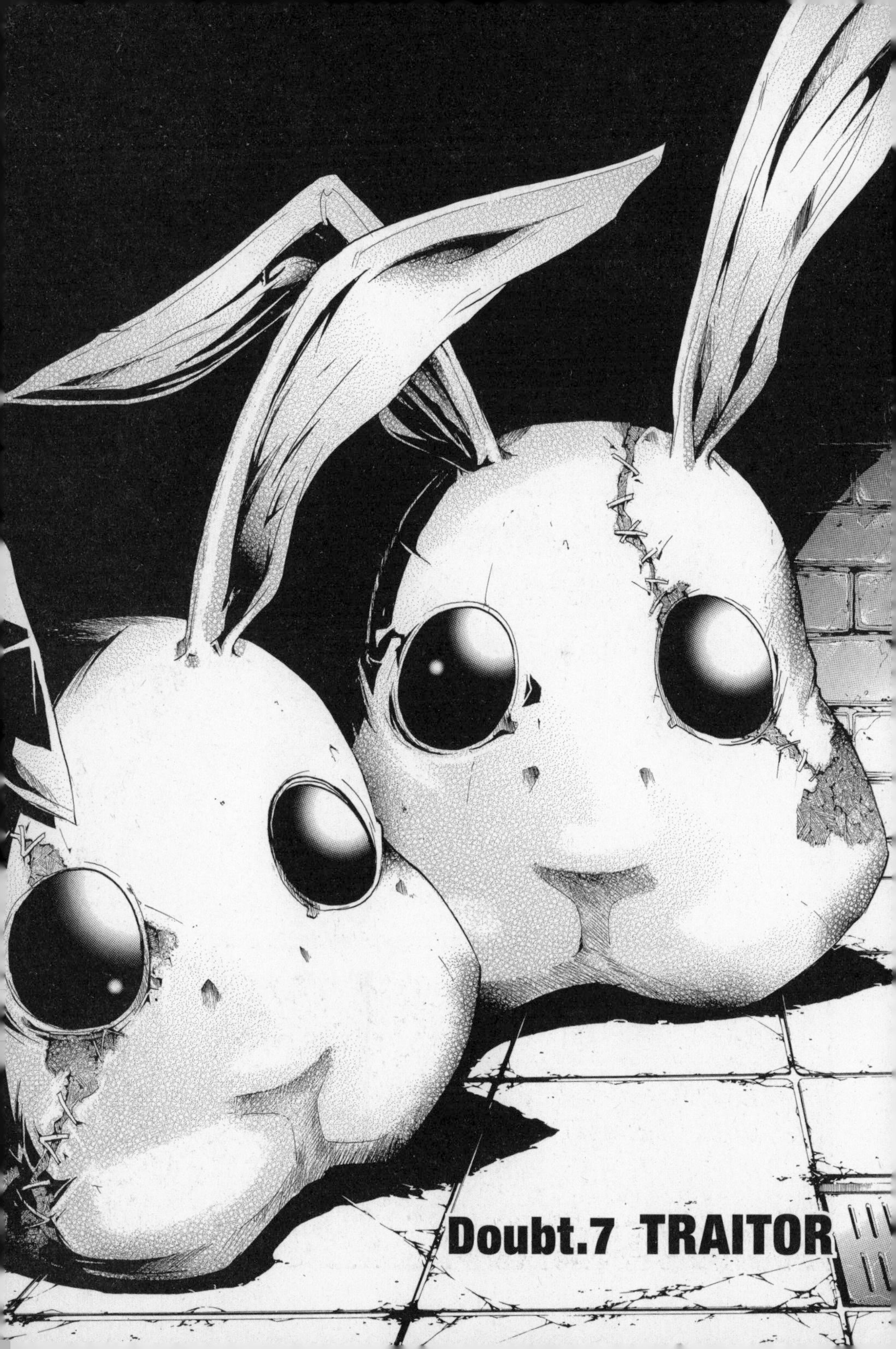
Doubt.7 TRAITOR

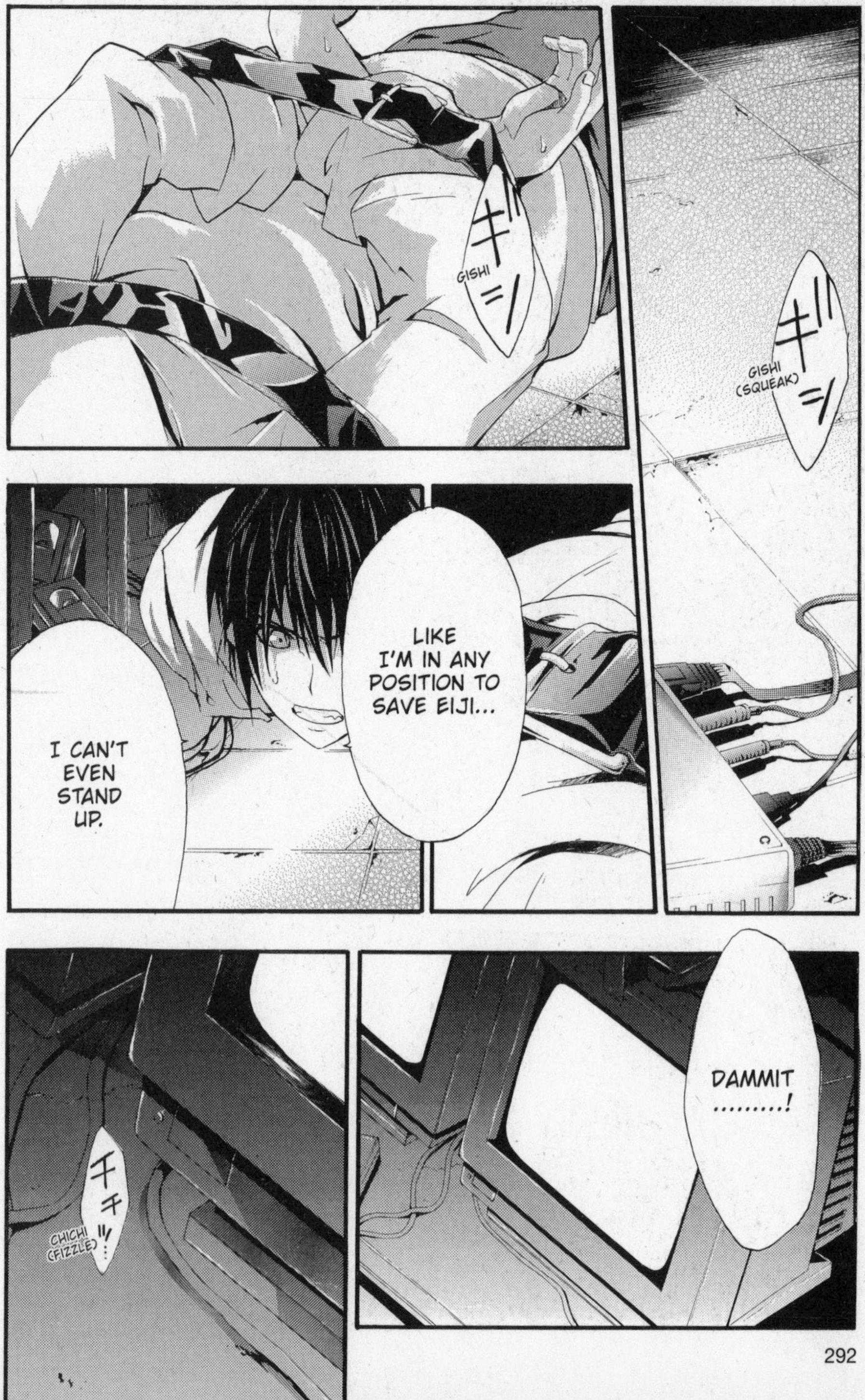
ギシ
GISHI (SQUEAK)
ギシ
GISHI
LIKE I'M IN ANY POSITION TO SAVE EIJI...
I CAN'T EVEN STAND UP.
DAMMIT ....!
チチ
CHICHI (FIZZLE)

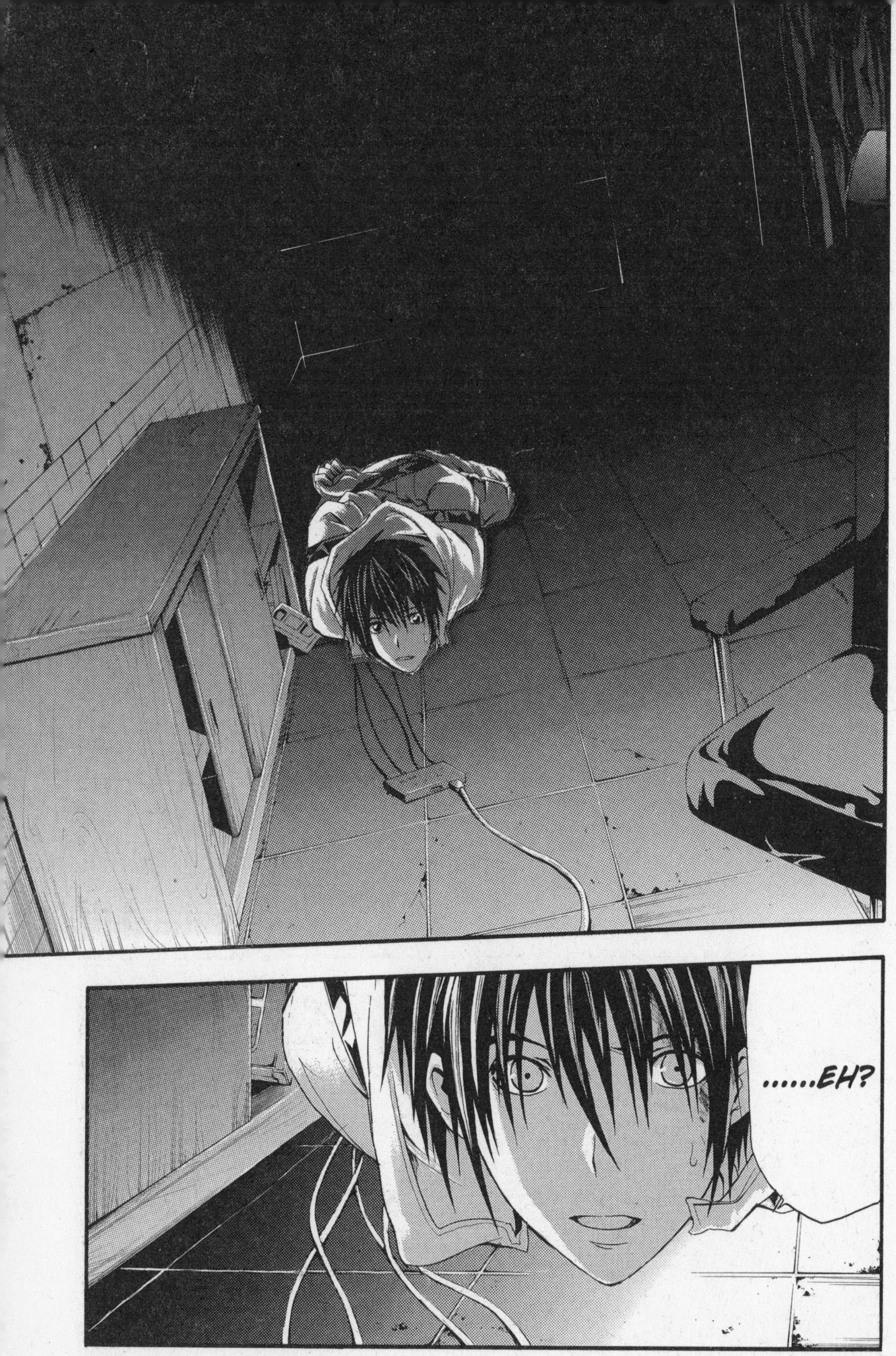
......EH?

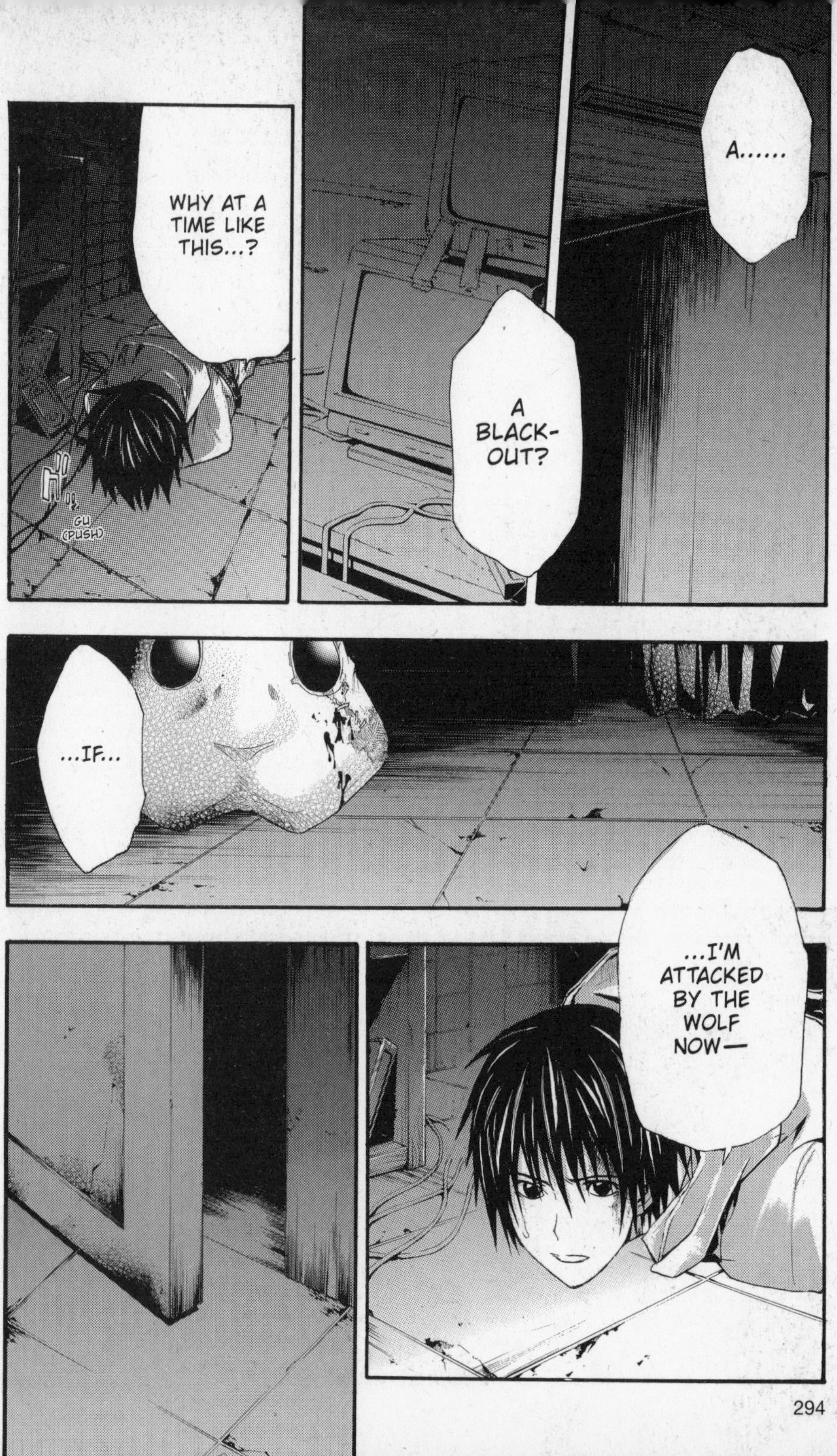
A......
A BLACK-OUT?
WHY AT A TIME LIKE THIS...?
GU (PUSH)
...IF...
...I'M ATTACKED BY THE WOLF NOW—

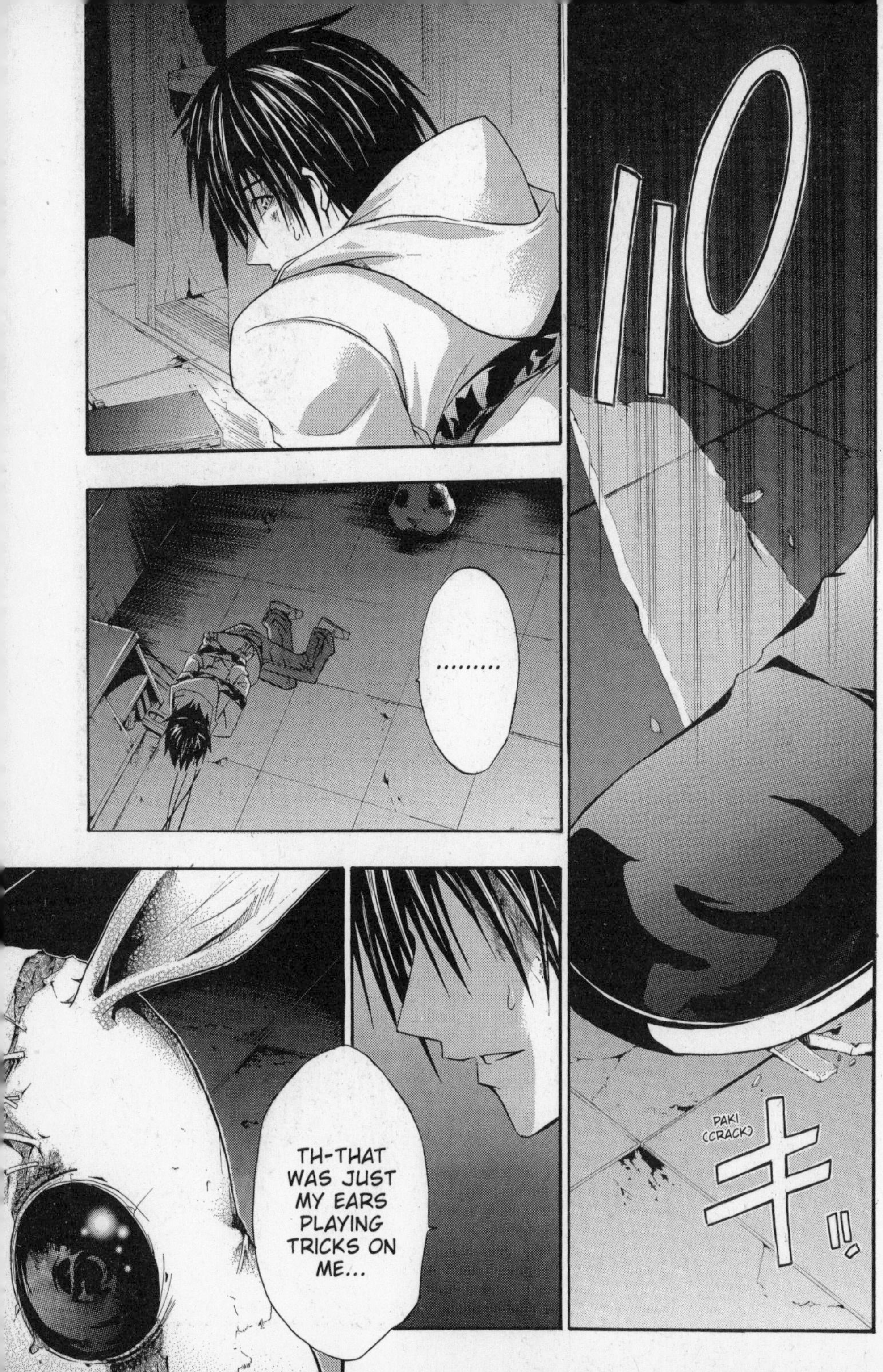
PAKI
(CRACK)
....
TH-THAT WAS JUST MY EARS PLAYING TRICKS ON ME...

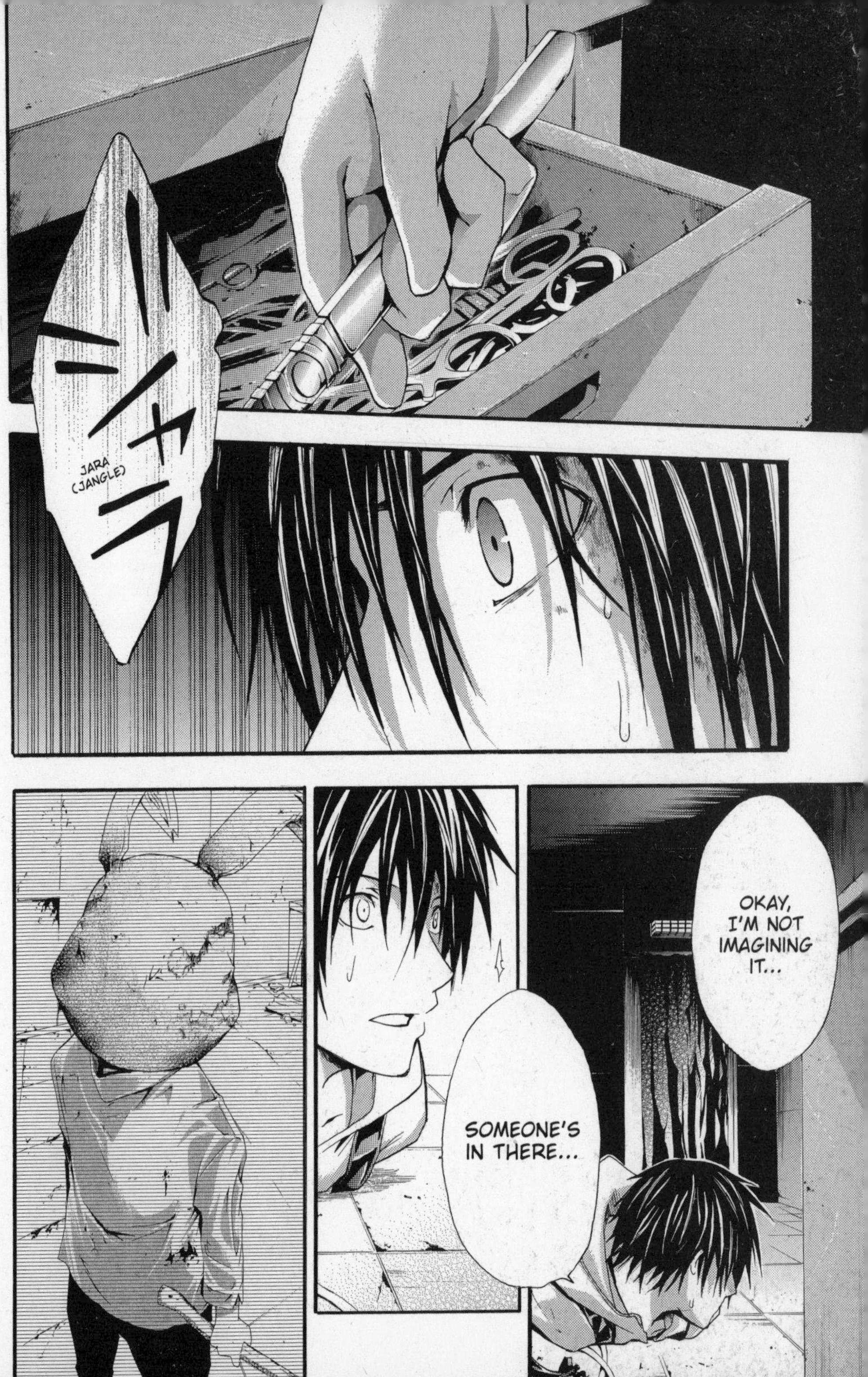
ジャラ
JARA (JANGLE)
OKAY, I'M NOT IMAGINING IT...
SOMEONE'S IN THERE...

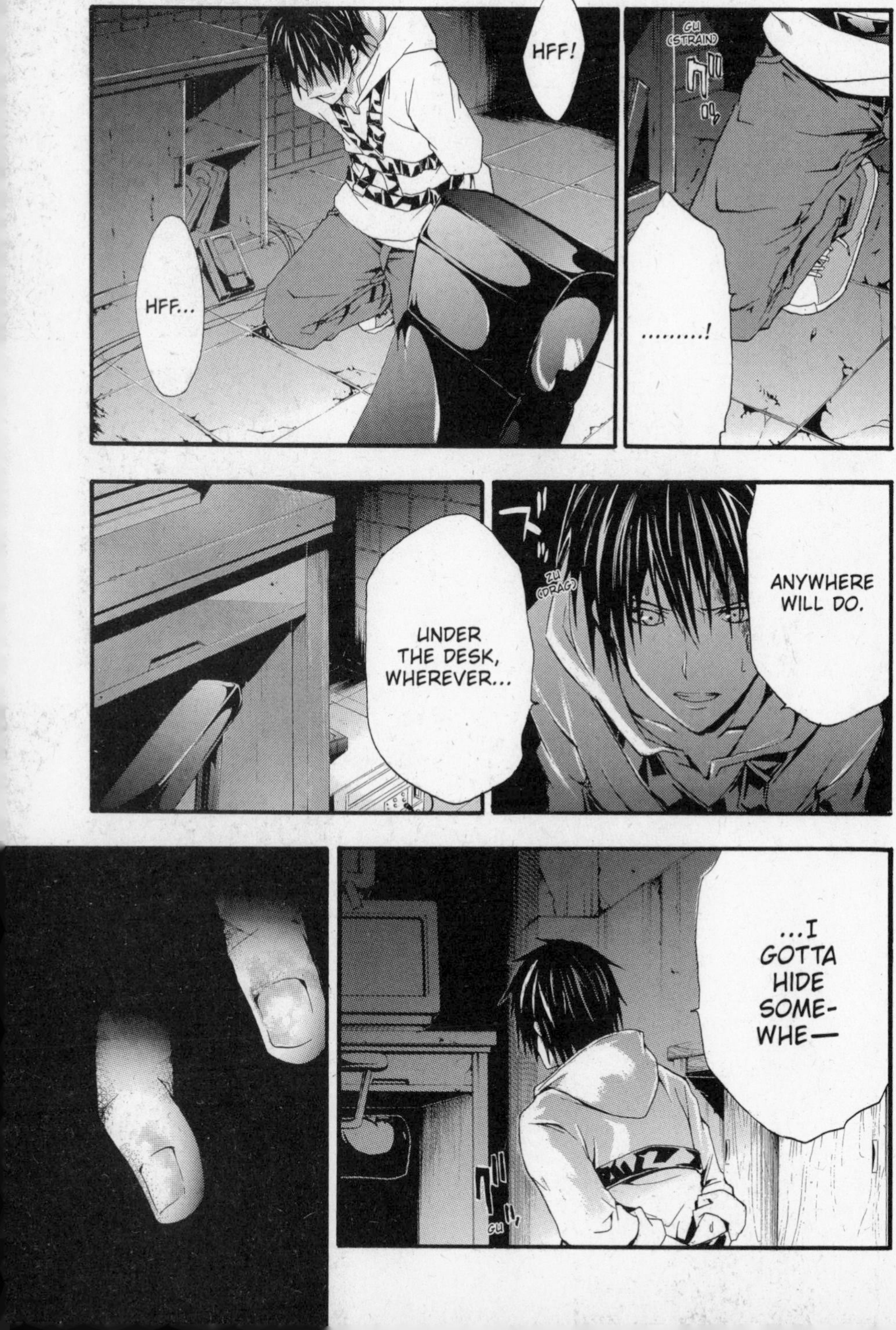
GU (STRAIN)
.........!
HFF!
HFF...
ANYWHERE WILL DO.
ZU (DRAG)
UNDER THE DESK, WHEREVER...
...I GOTTA HIDE SOME-WHE—
GU

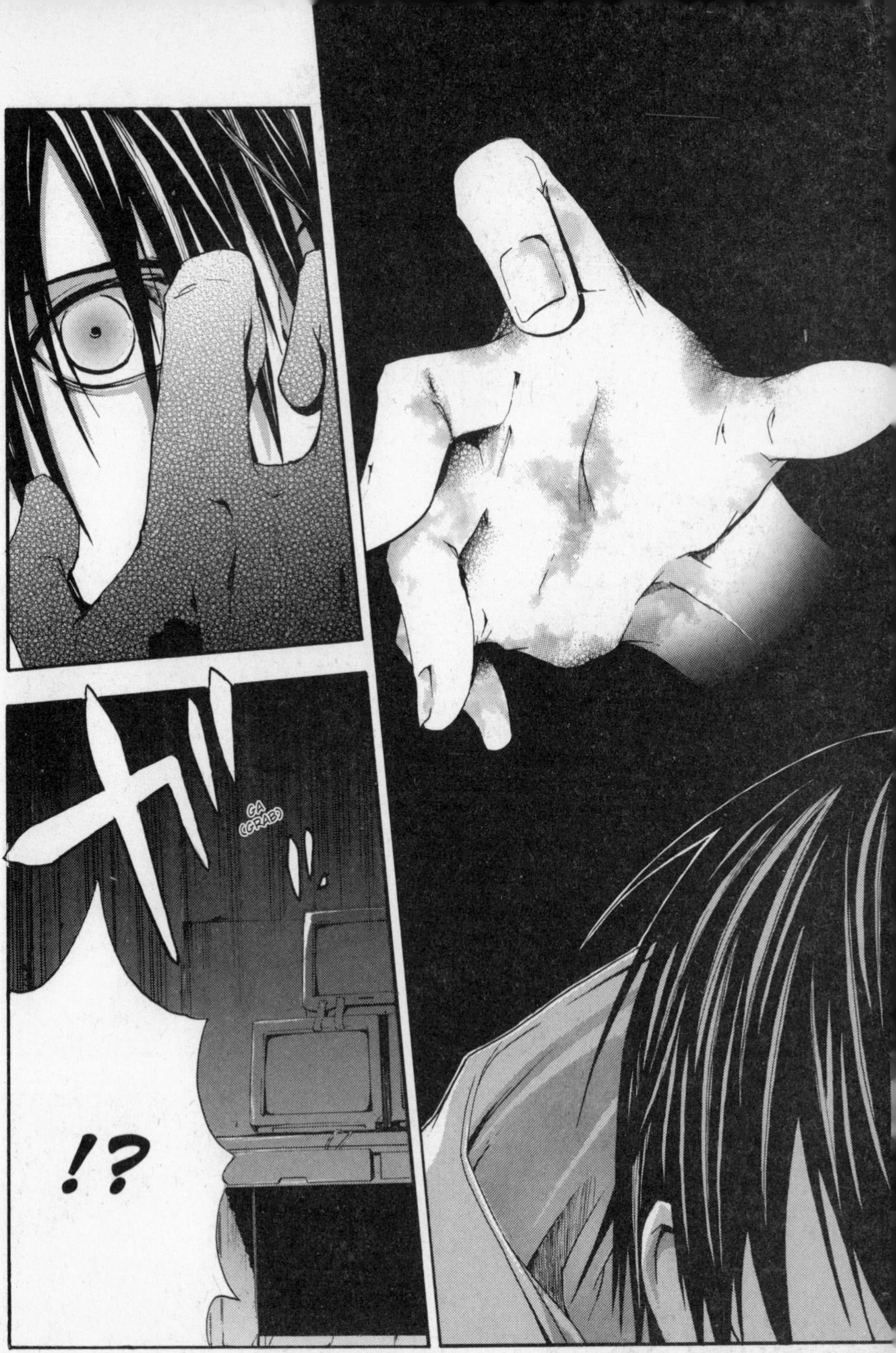
GA
(GRAB)
!?

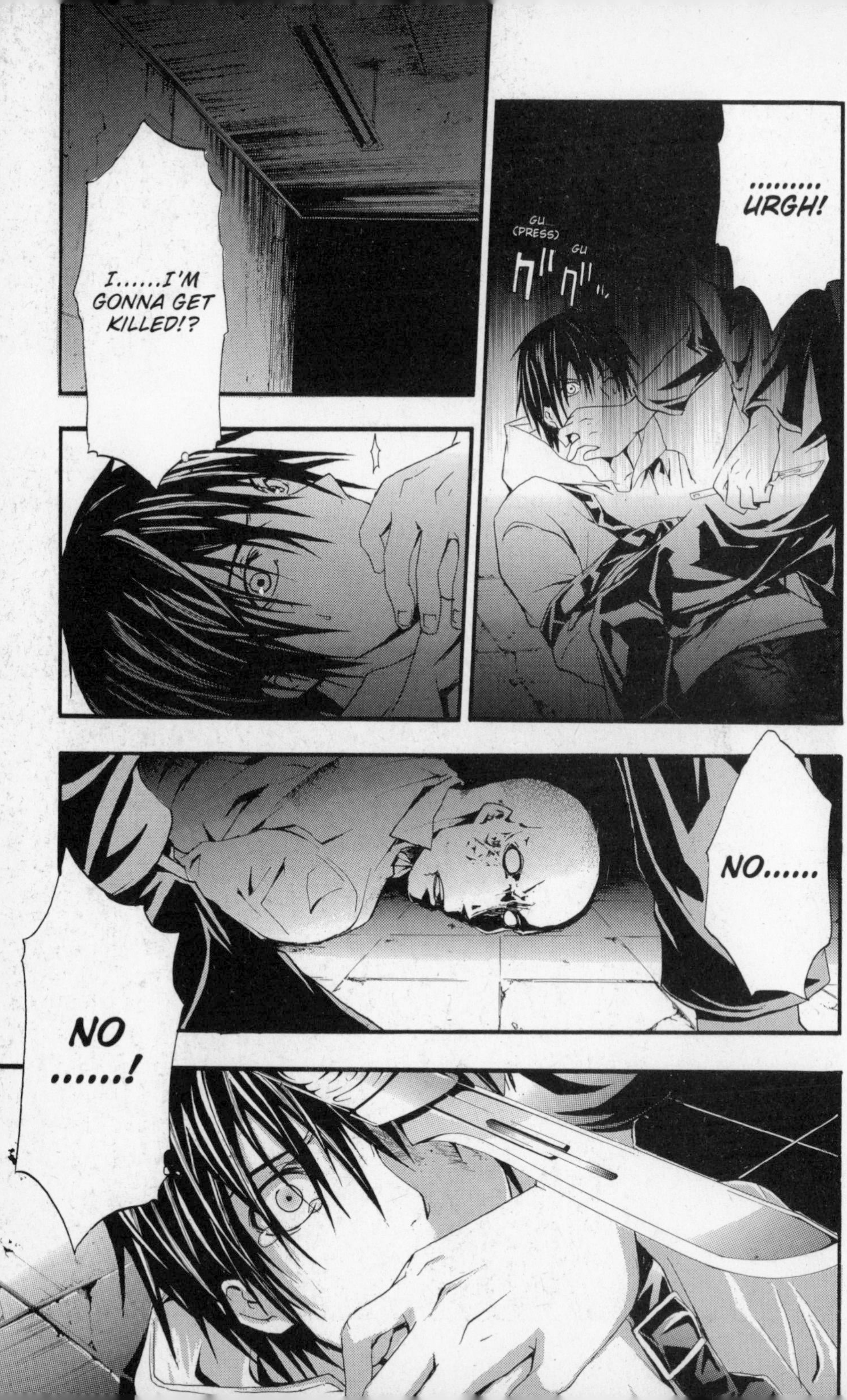

....
URGH!
GU_
(PRESS)
GU
I......I'M GONNA GET KILLED!?
NO......
NO
......!

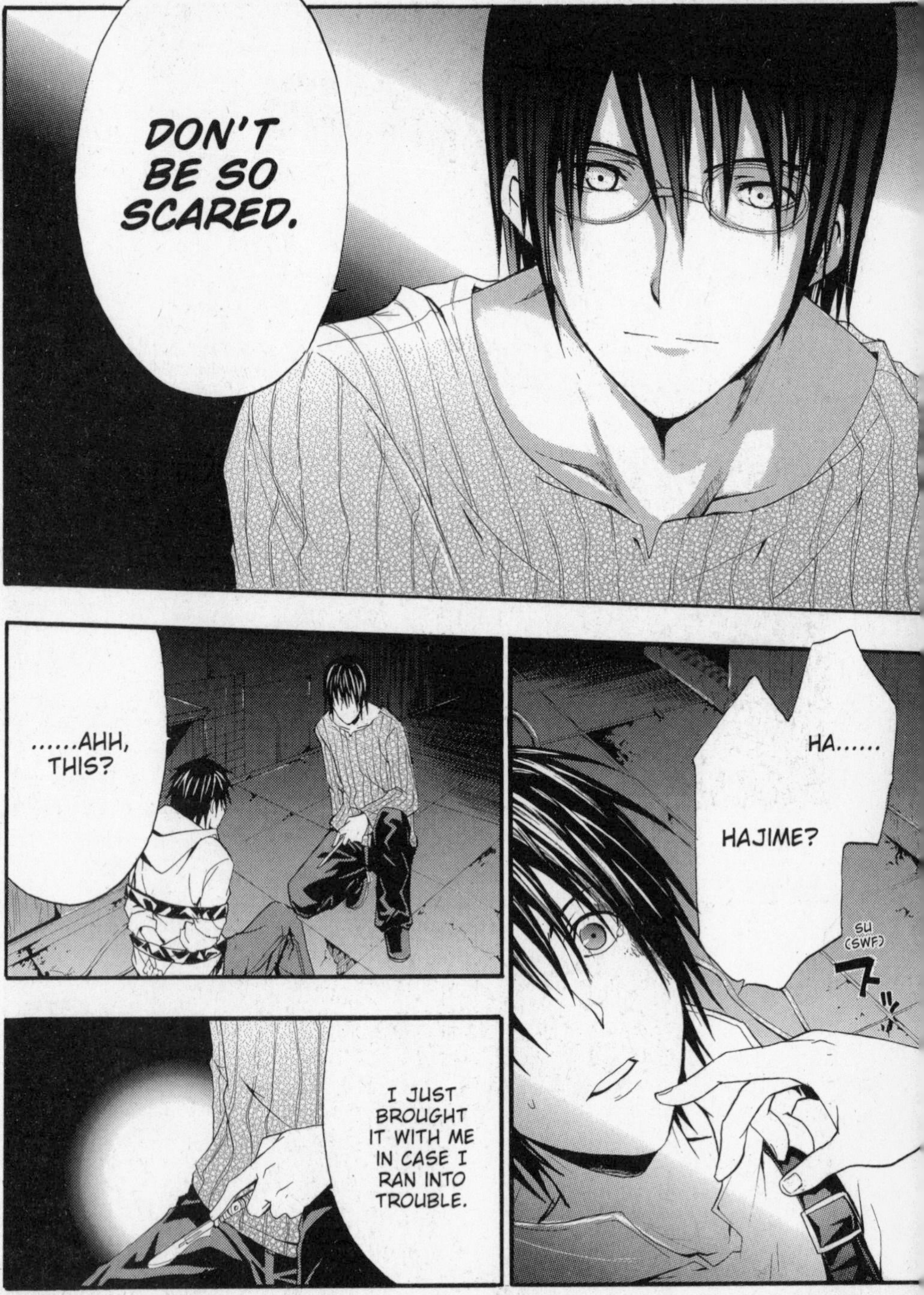
DON'T BE SO SCARED.
HA......
HAJIME?
SU (SWF)
......AHH, THIS?
I JUST BROUGHT IT WITH ME IN CASE I RAN INTO TROUBLE.

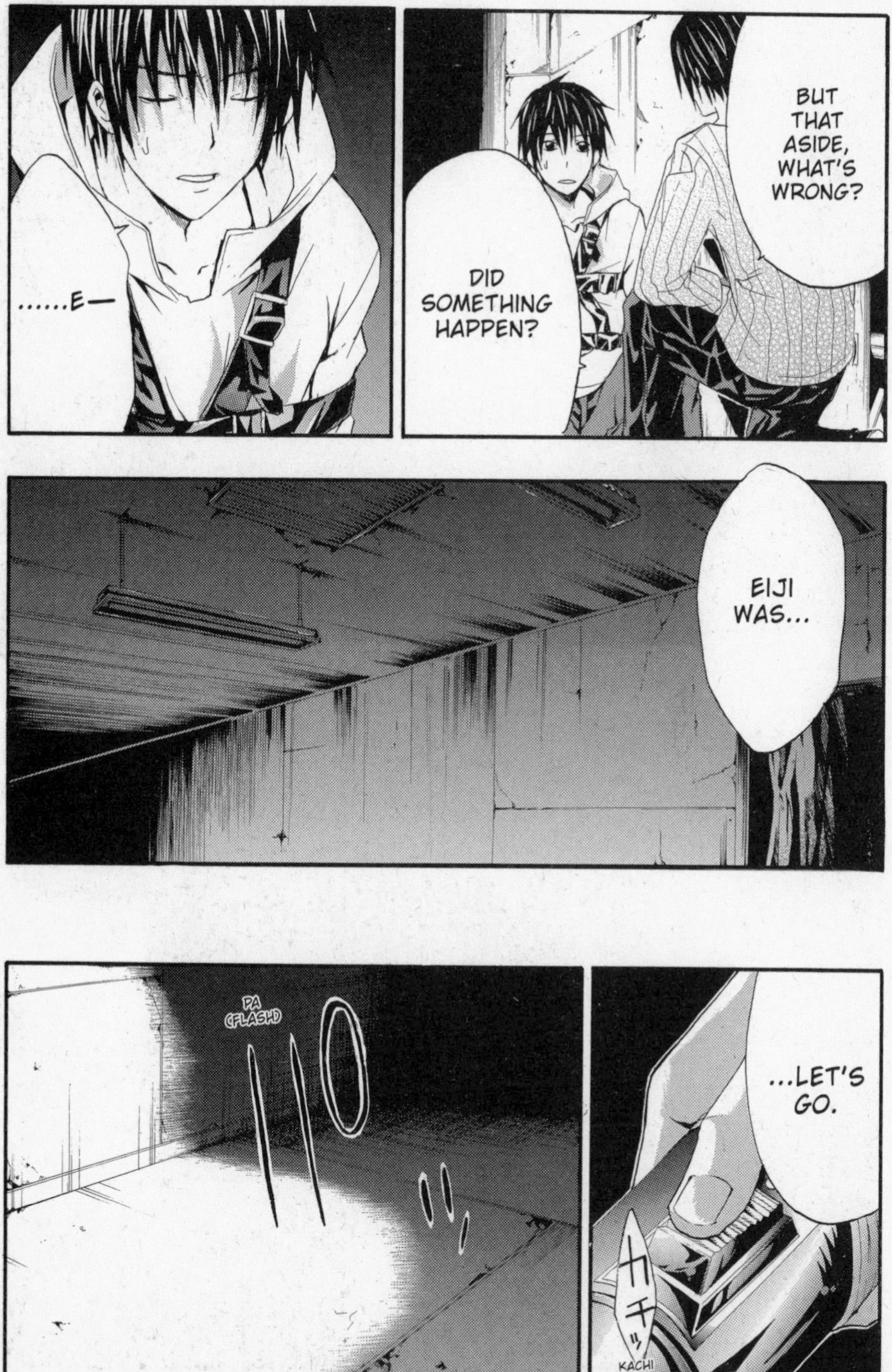
BUT THAT ASIDE, WHAT'S WRONG?
DID SOMETHING HAPPEN?
......E—
EIJI WAS...
...LET'S GO.
カチッ
KACHI (CLICK)
PA (FLASH)

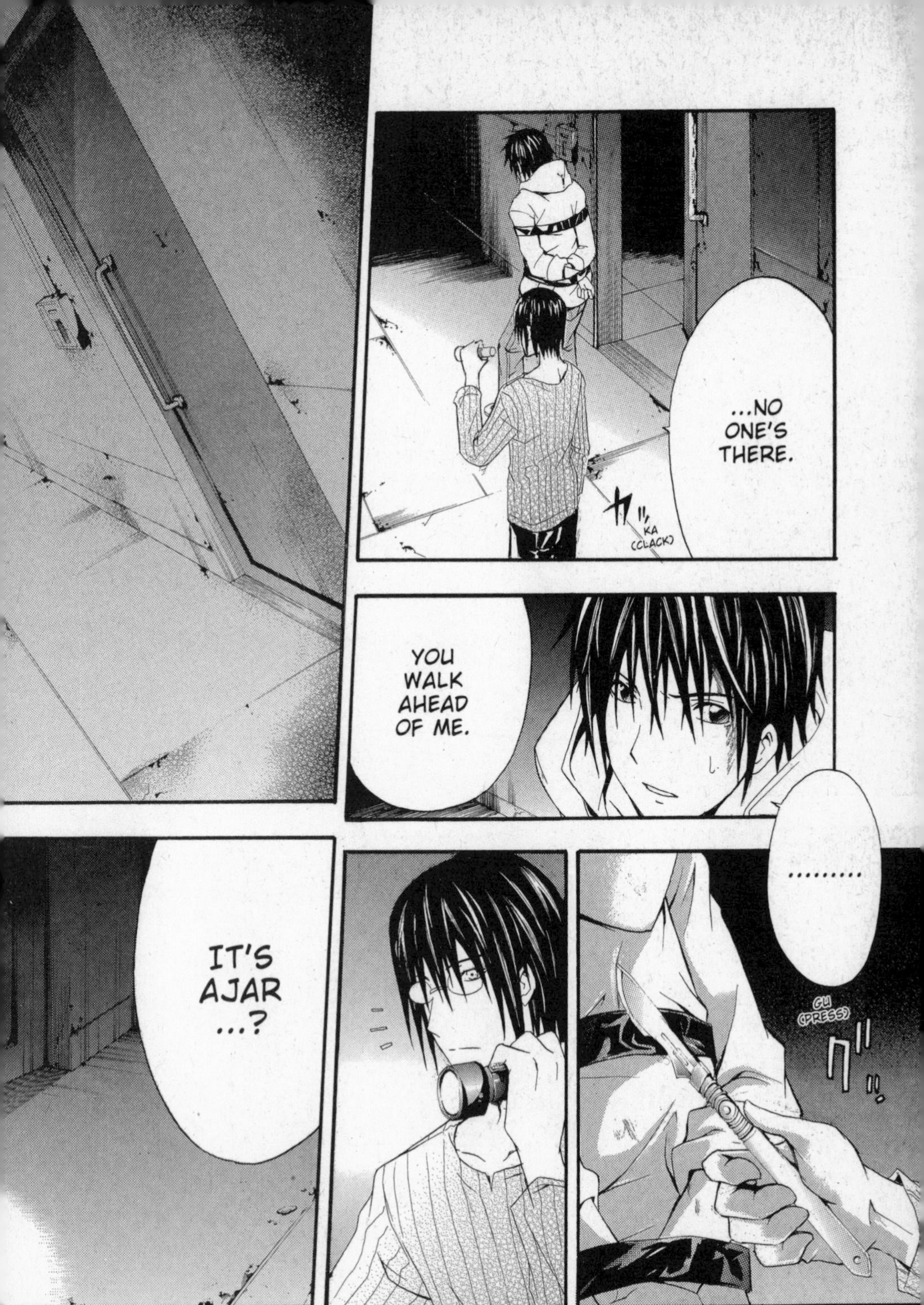
...NO ONE'S THERE.
KA (CLACK)
YOU WALK AHEAD OF ME.
....
GU (PRESS)
IT'S AJAR ...?

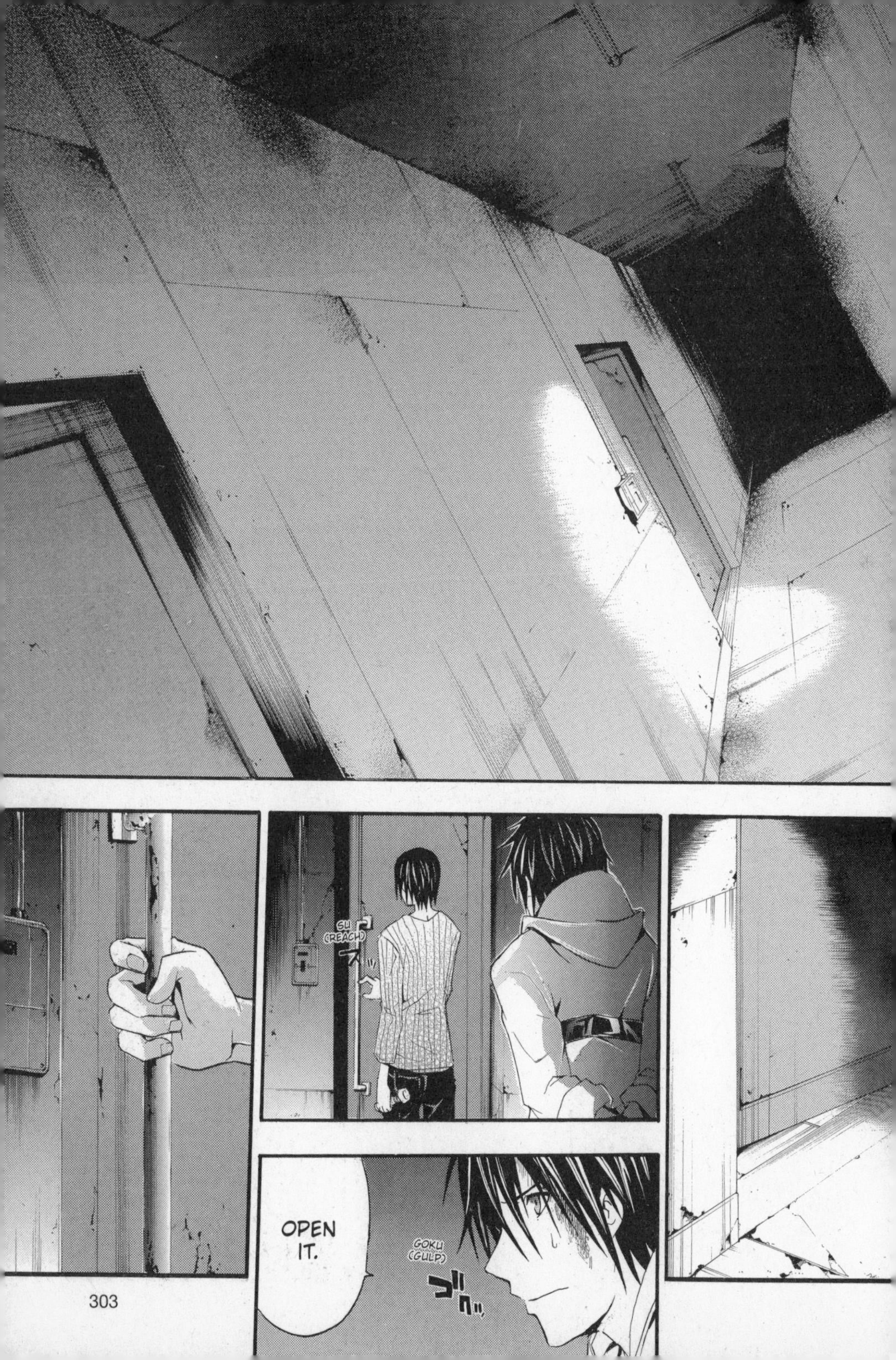
SU
(REACH)
OPEN IT.
GOKU
(GULP)

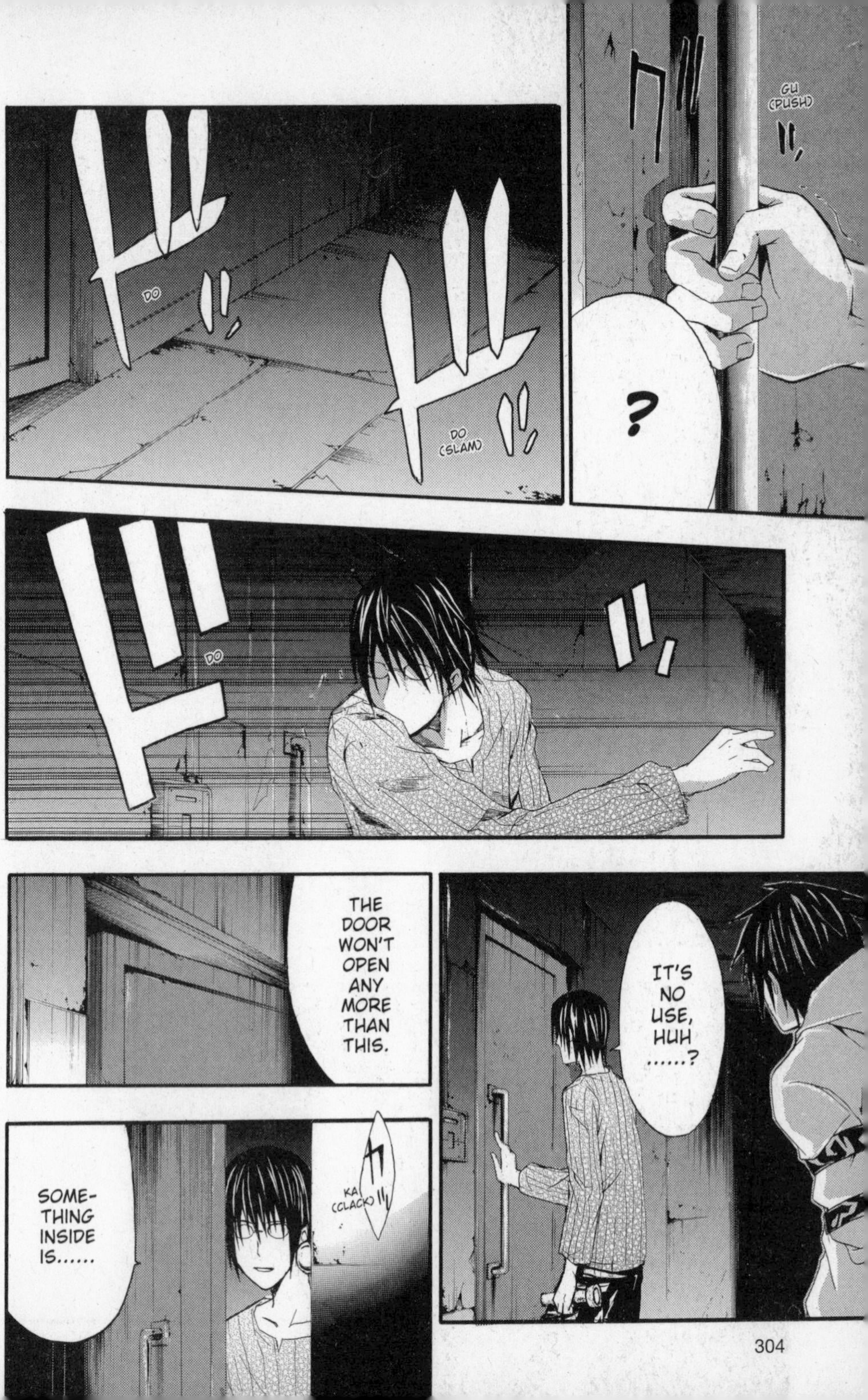
GU (PUSH)
?
DO
DO (SLAM)
DO
IT'S NO USE, HUH ......?
THE DOOR WON'T OPEN ANY MORE THAN THIS.
KA (CLACK)
SOME-THING INSIDE IS......

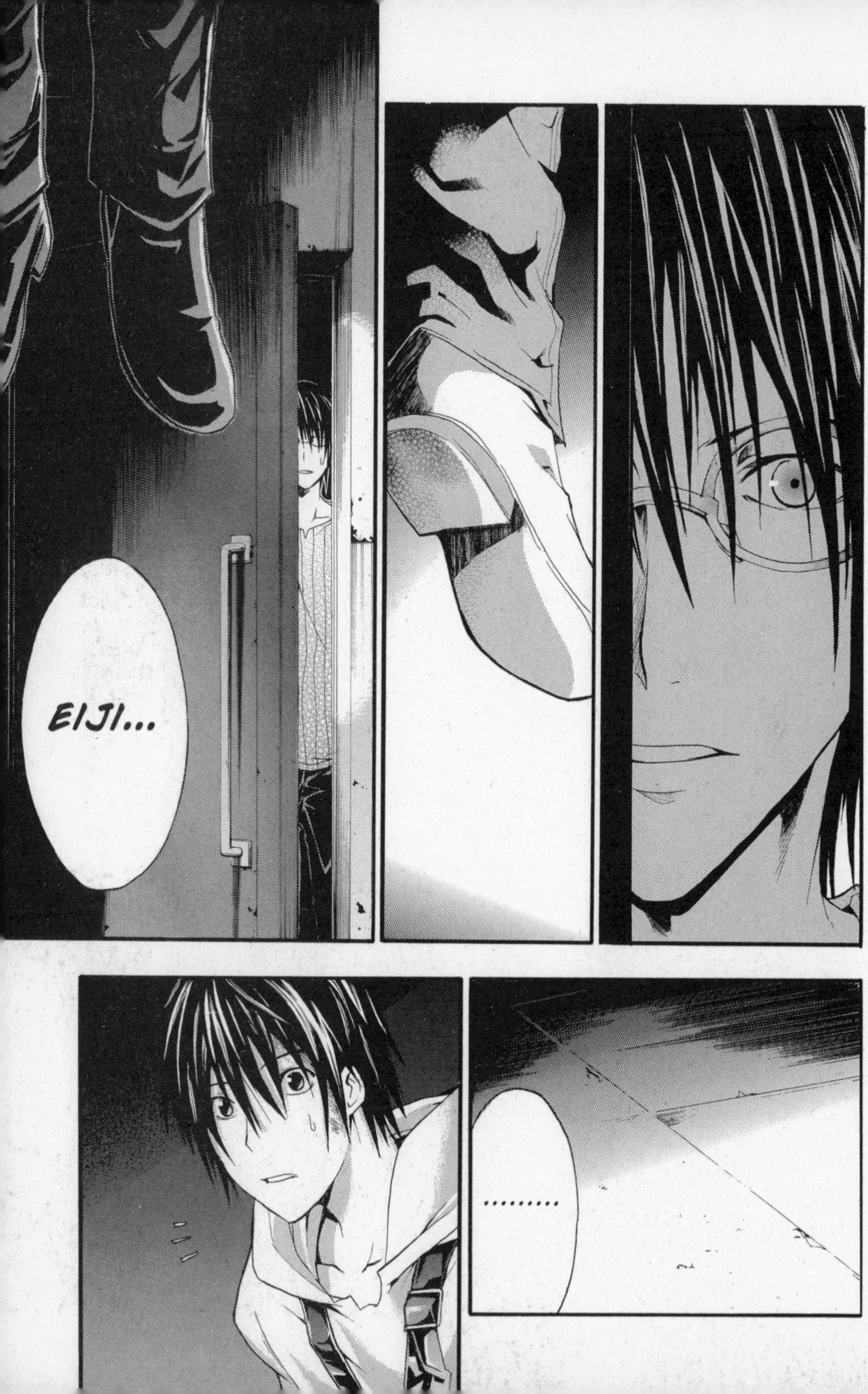
EIJI...
....

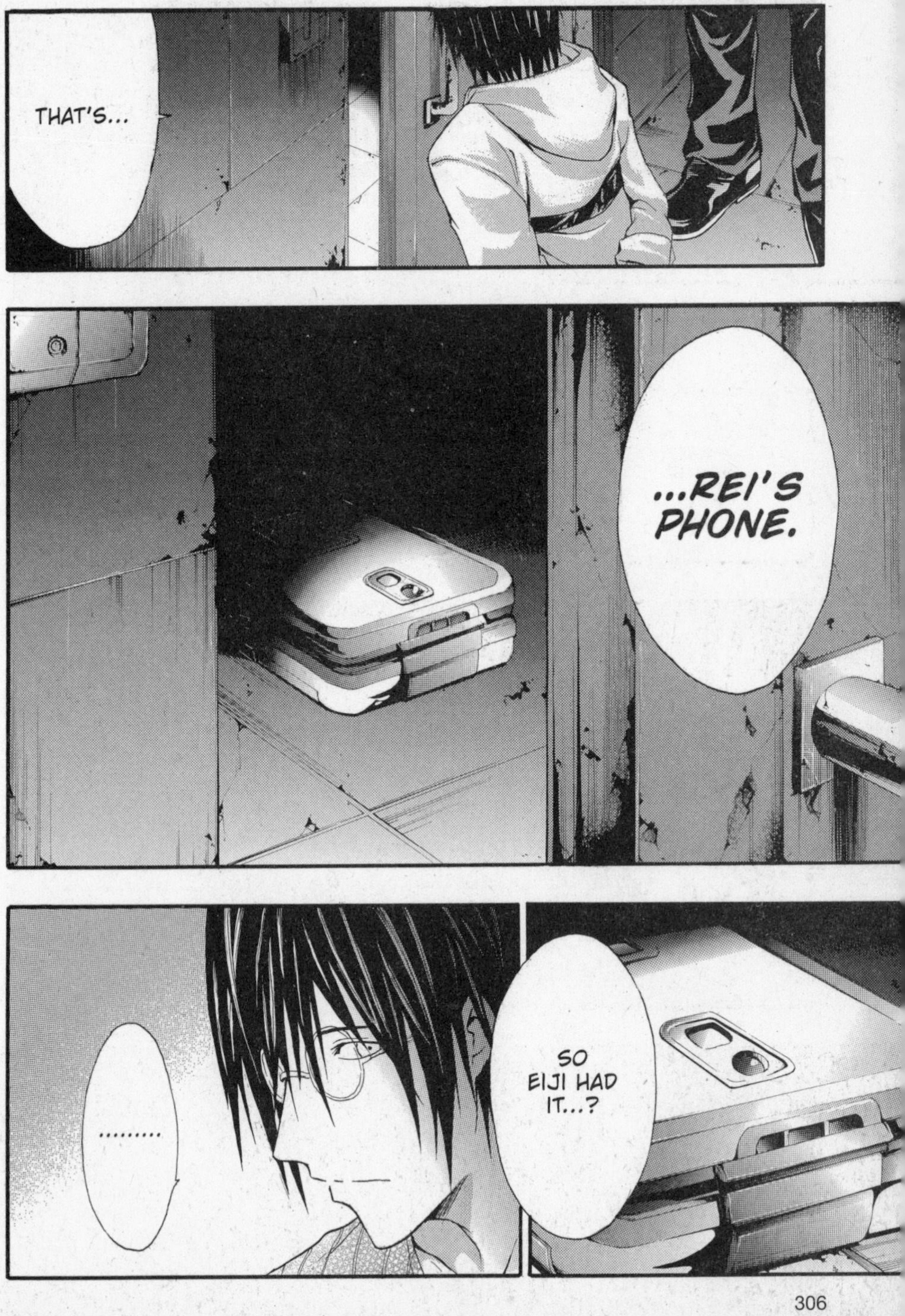
THAT'S...
...REI'S PHONE.
SO EIJI HAD IT...?
....

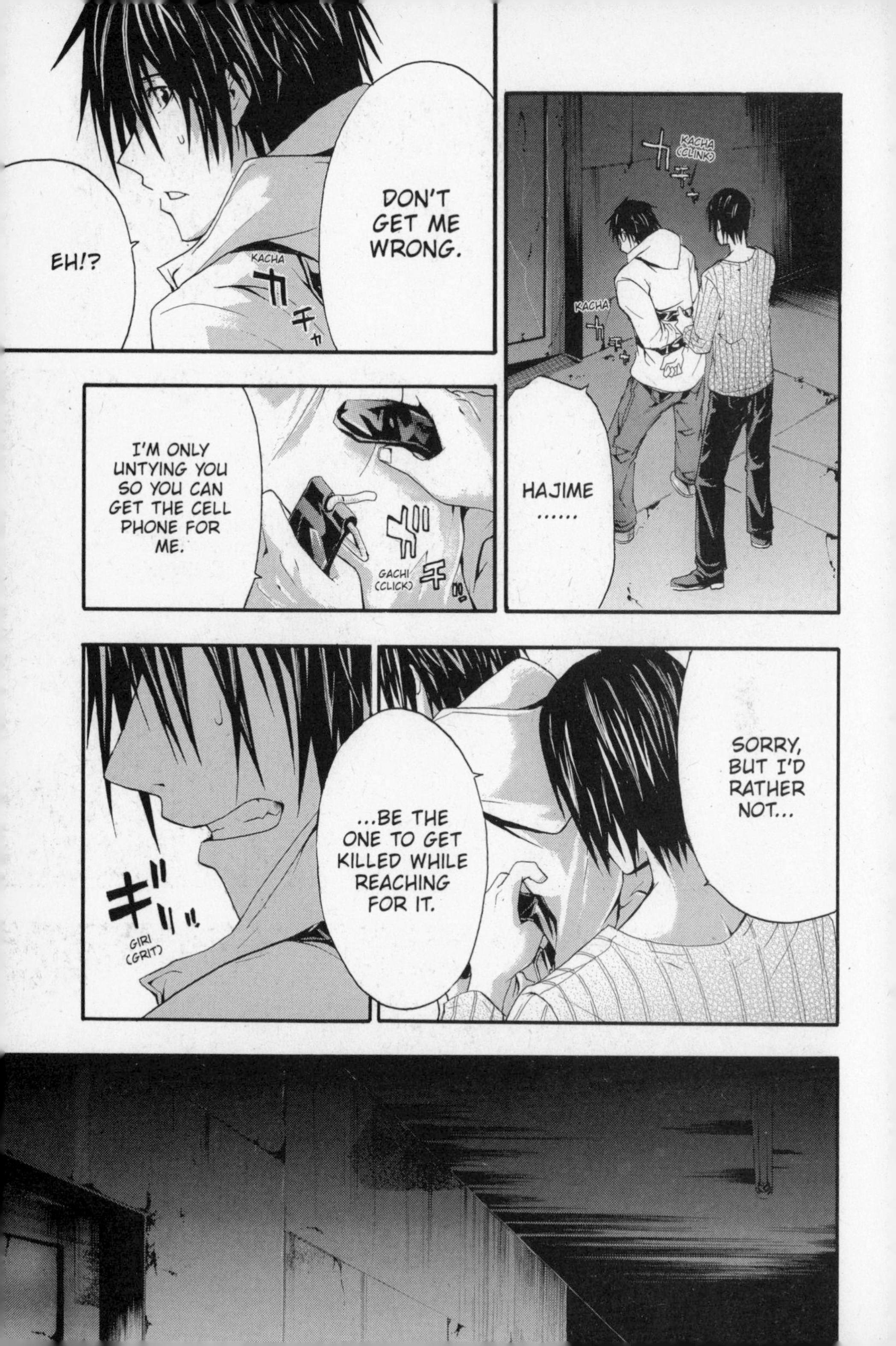
KACHA (CLINK)
KACHA
HAJIME ......
DON'T GET ME WRONG.
EH!?
KACHA
I'M ONLY UNTYING YOU SO YOU CAN GET THE CELL PHONE FOR ME.
GACHI (CLICK)
SORRY, BUT I'D RATHER NOT...
...BE THE ONE TO GET KILLED WHILE REACHING FOR IT.
GIRI (GRIT)

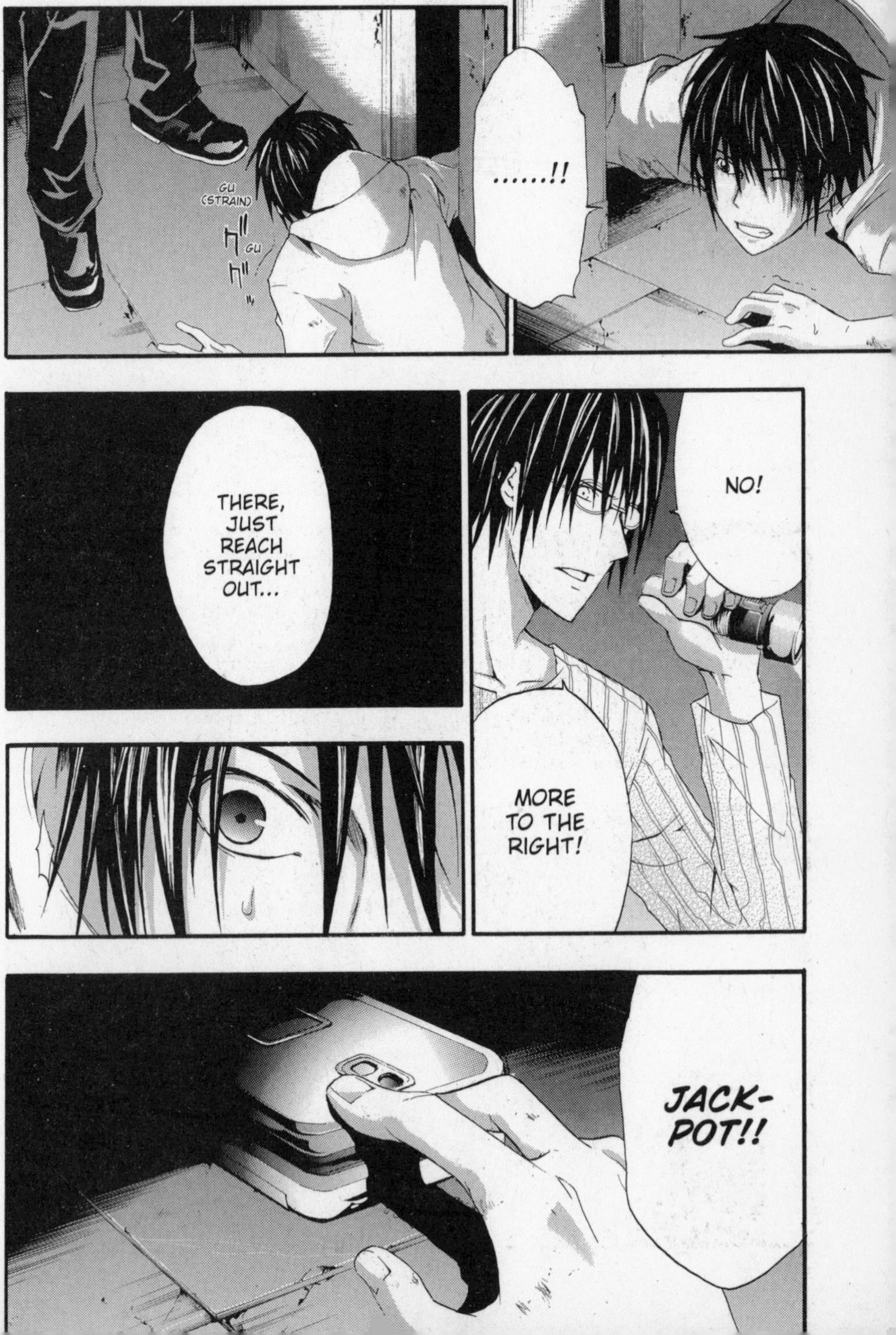
......!!
GU (STRAIN)
グ GU
グ
NO!
MORE TO THE RIGHT!
THERE, JUST REACH STRAIGHT OUT...
JACK-POT!!

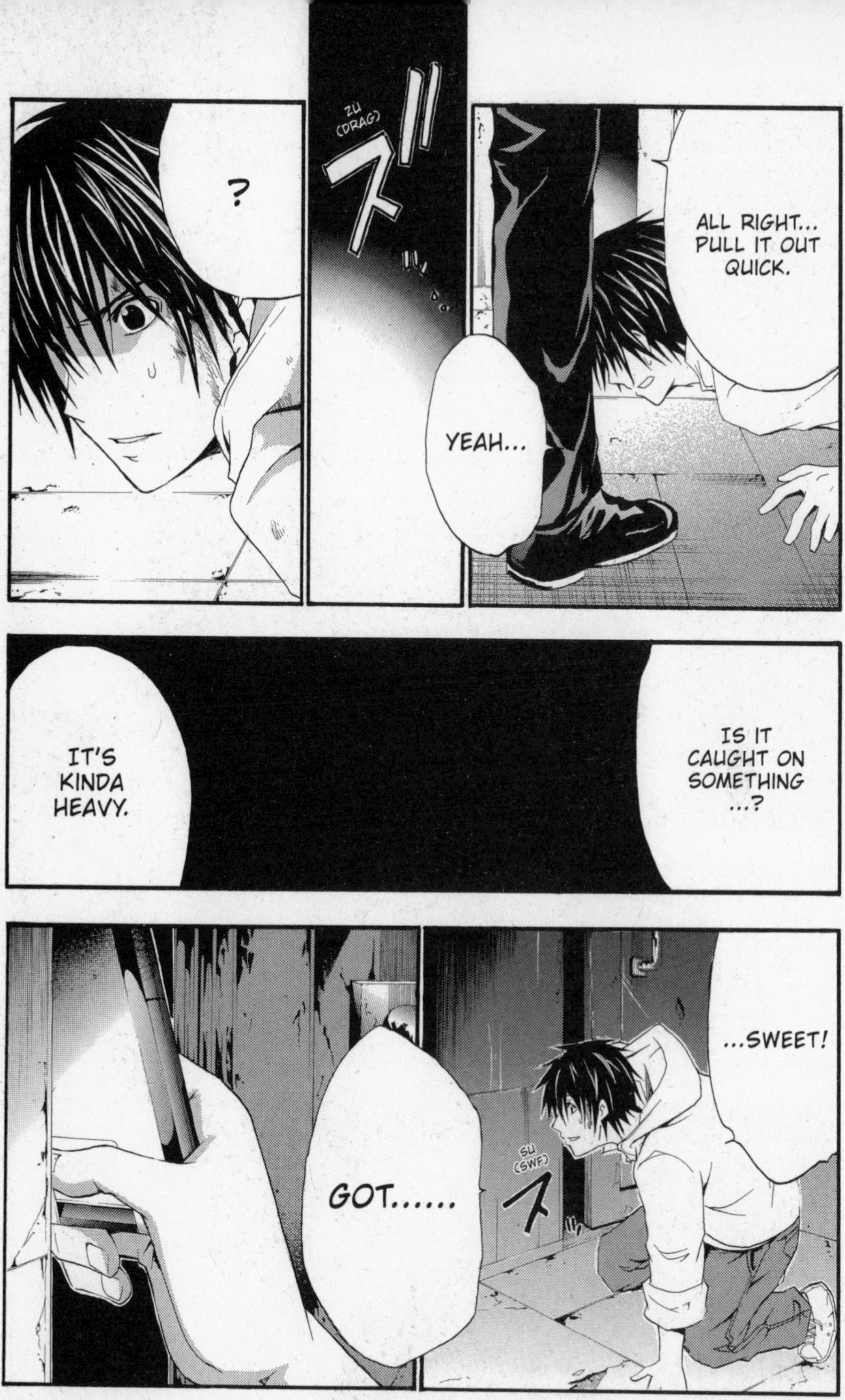
ALL RIGHT... PULL IT OUT QUICK.
YEAH...
ZU (DRAG)
?
IS IT CAUGHT ON SOMETHING ...?
IT'S KINDA HEAVY.
...SWEET!
SU (SWF)
GOT......

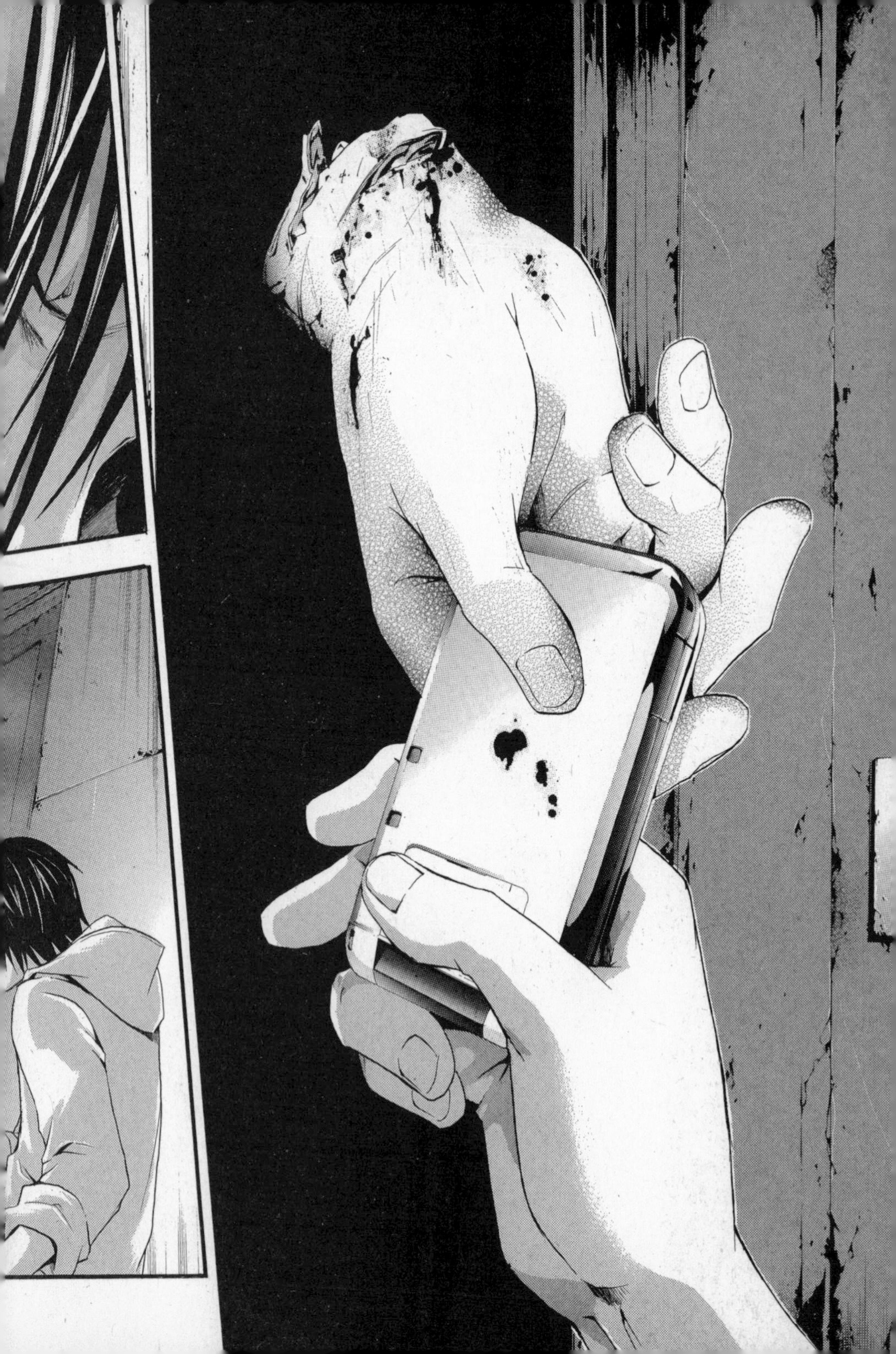

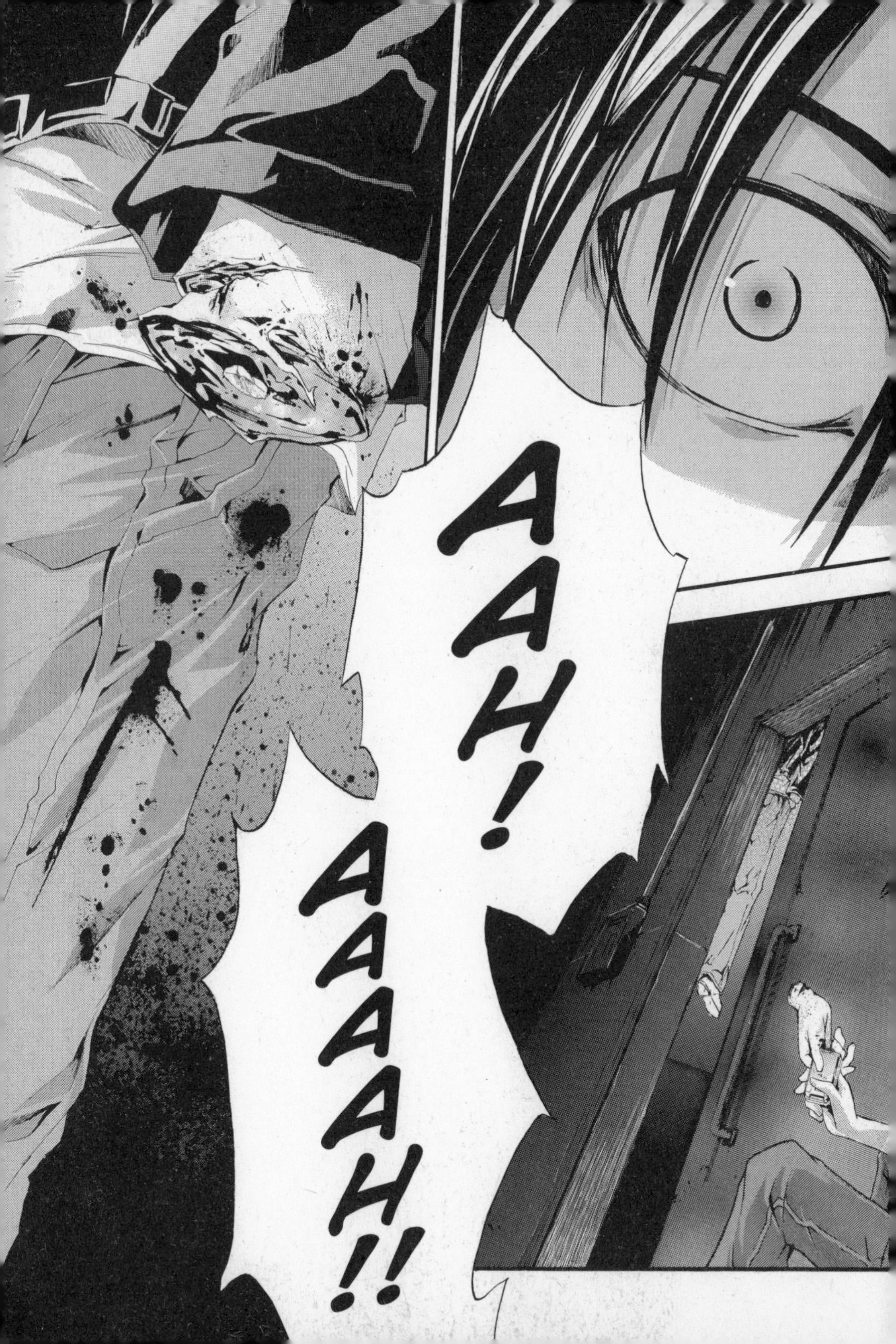
AAH! AAAAAH!!

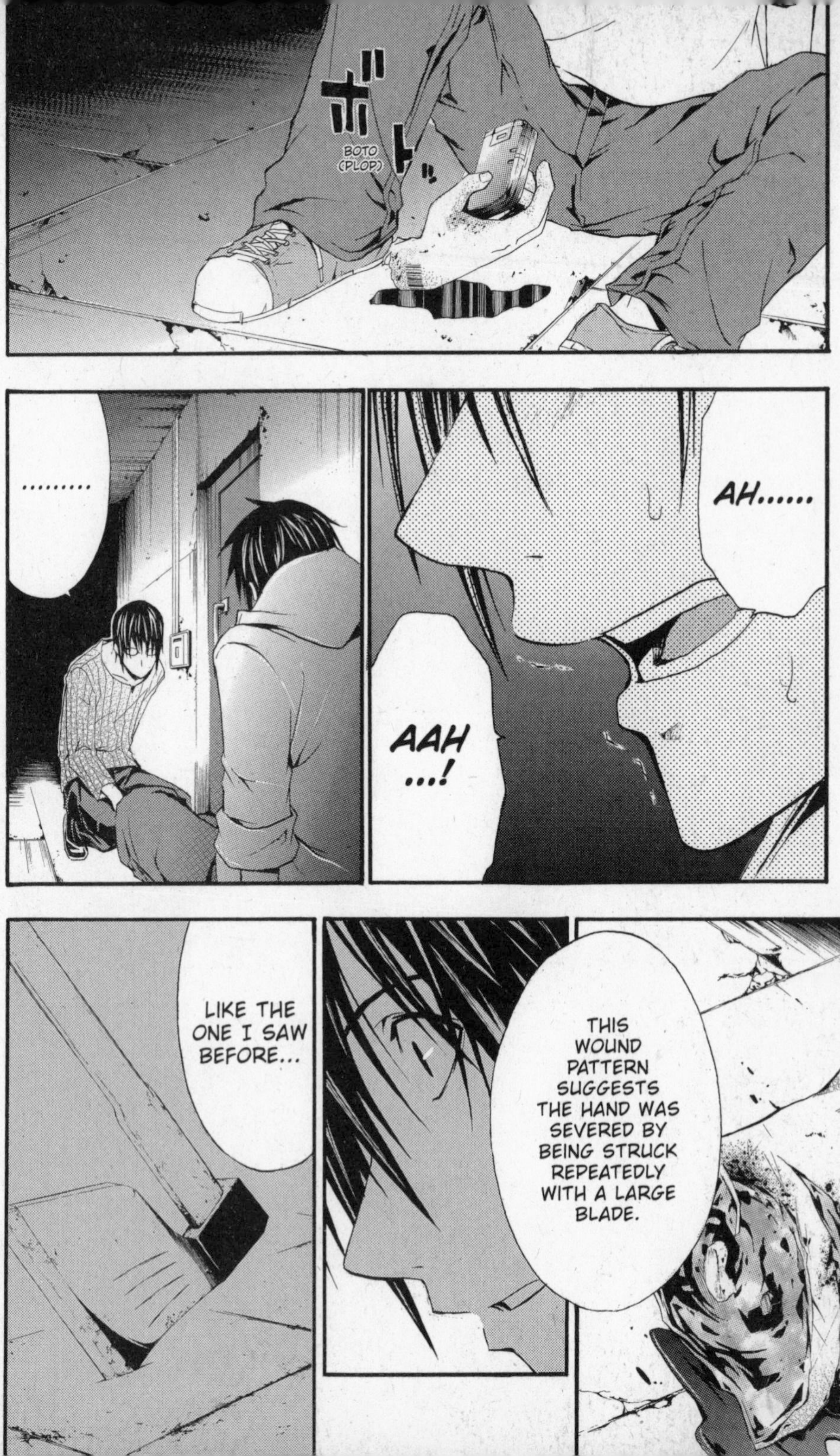
BOTO (PLOP)
AH......
AAH ...!
....
THIS WOUND PATTERN SUGGESTS THE HAND WAS SEVERED BY BEING STRUCK REPEATEDLY WITH A LARGE BLADE.
LIKE THE ONE I SAW BEFORE...

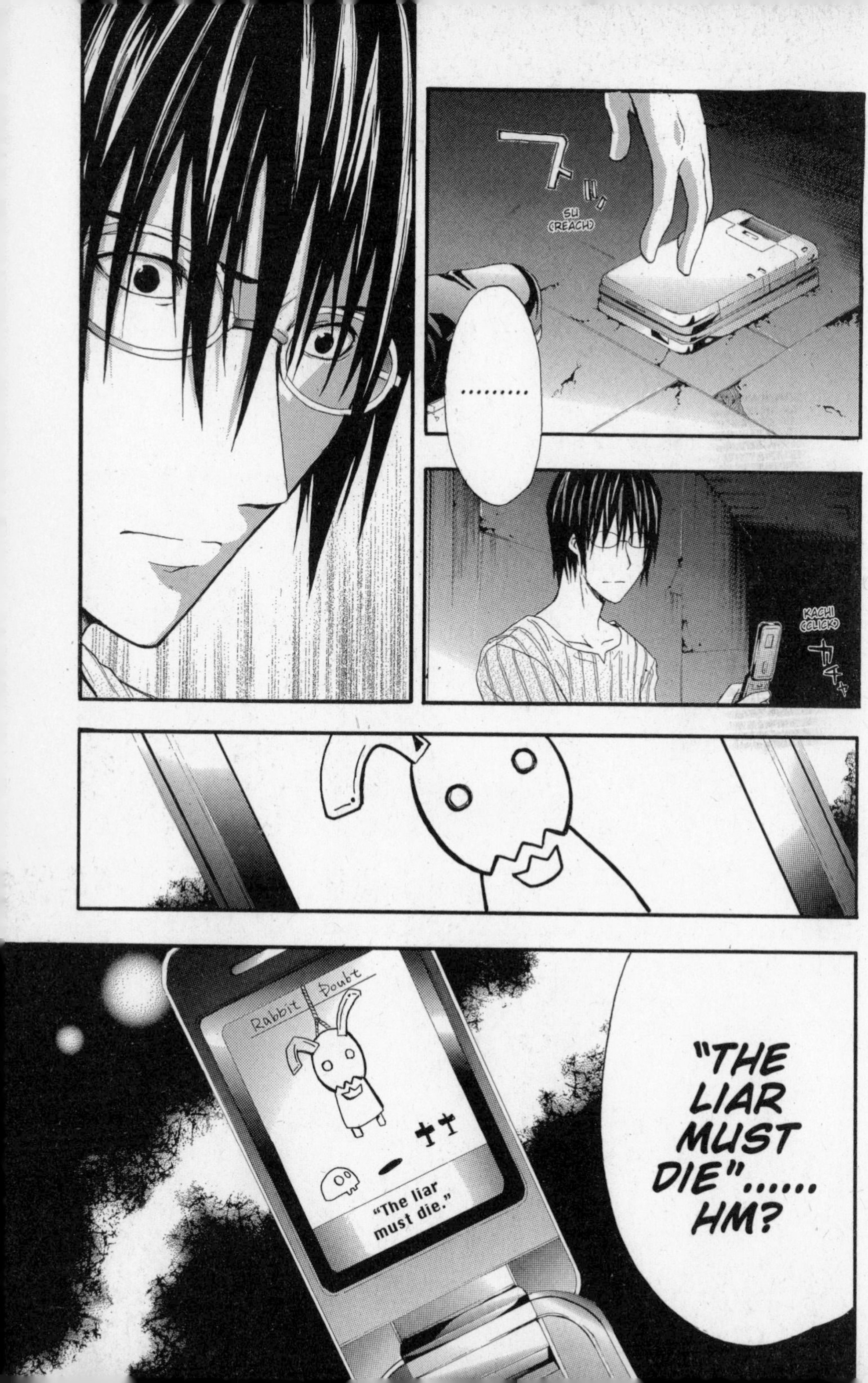
SU (REACH)
....
KACHI (CLICK)
Rabbit Doubt
"The liar must die."
"THE LIAR MUST DIE"...... HM?

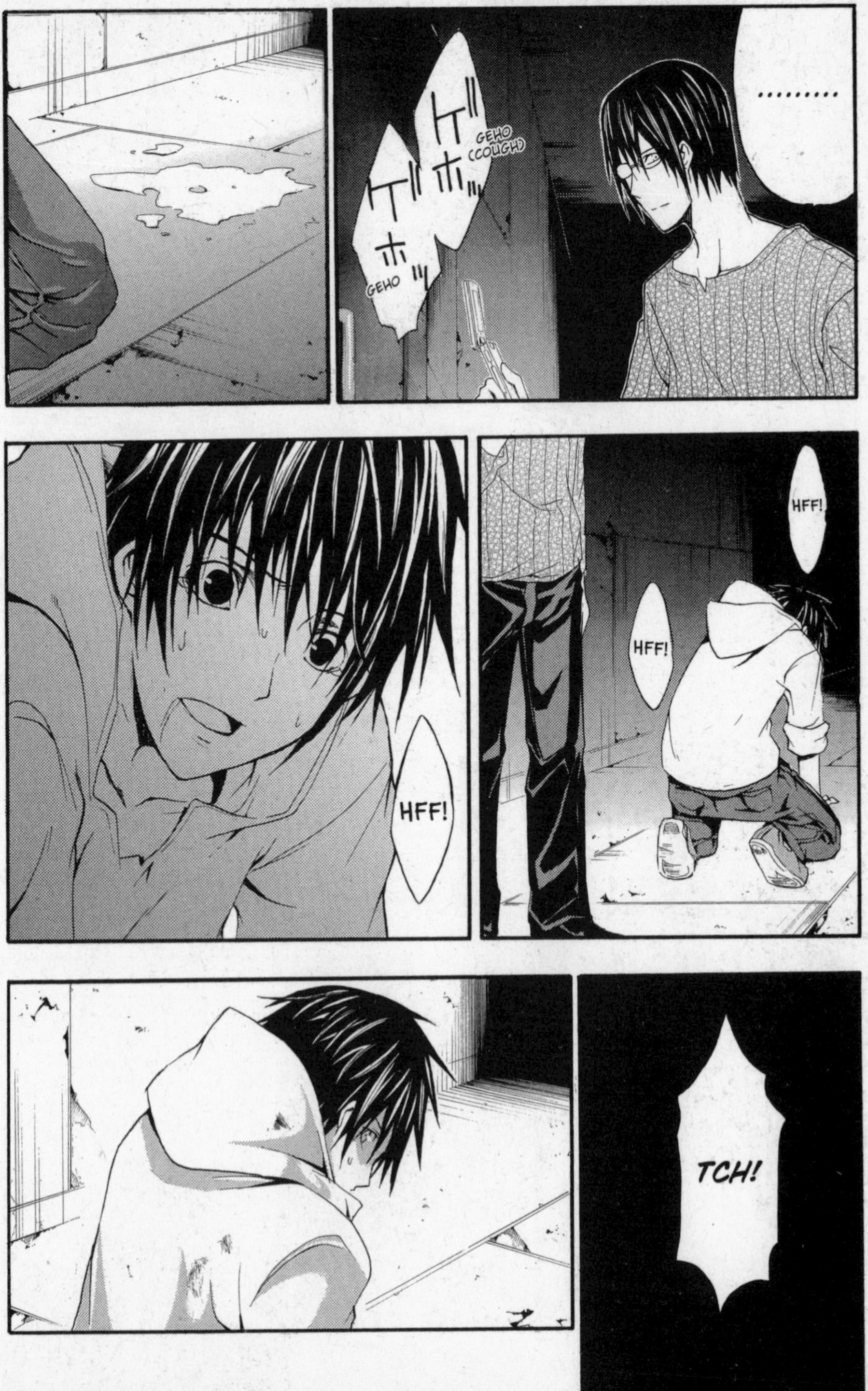
....
ゲホッ
GEHO (COUGH)
ゲホッ
GEHO
HFF!
HFF!
HFF!
TCH!

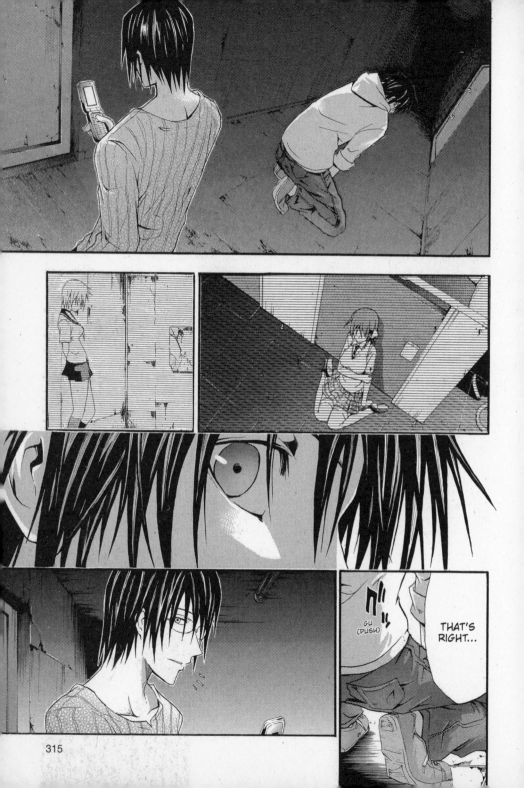

GU
(PUSH)

THAT'S
RIGHT...

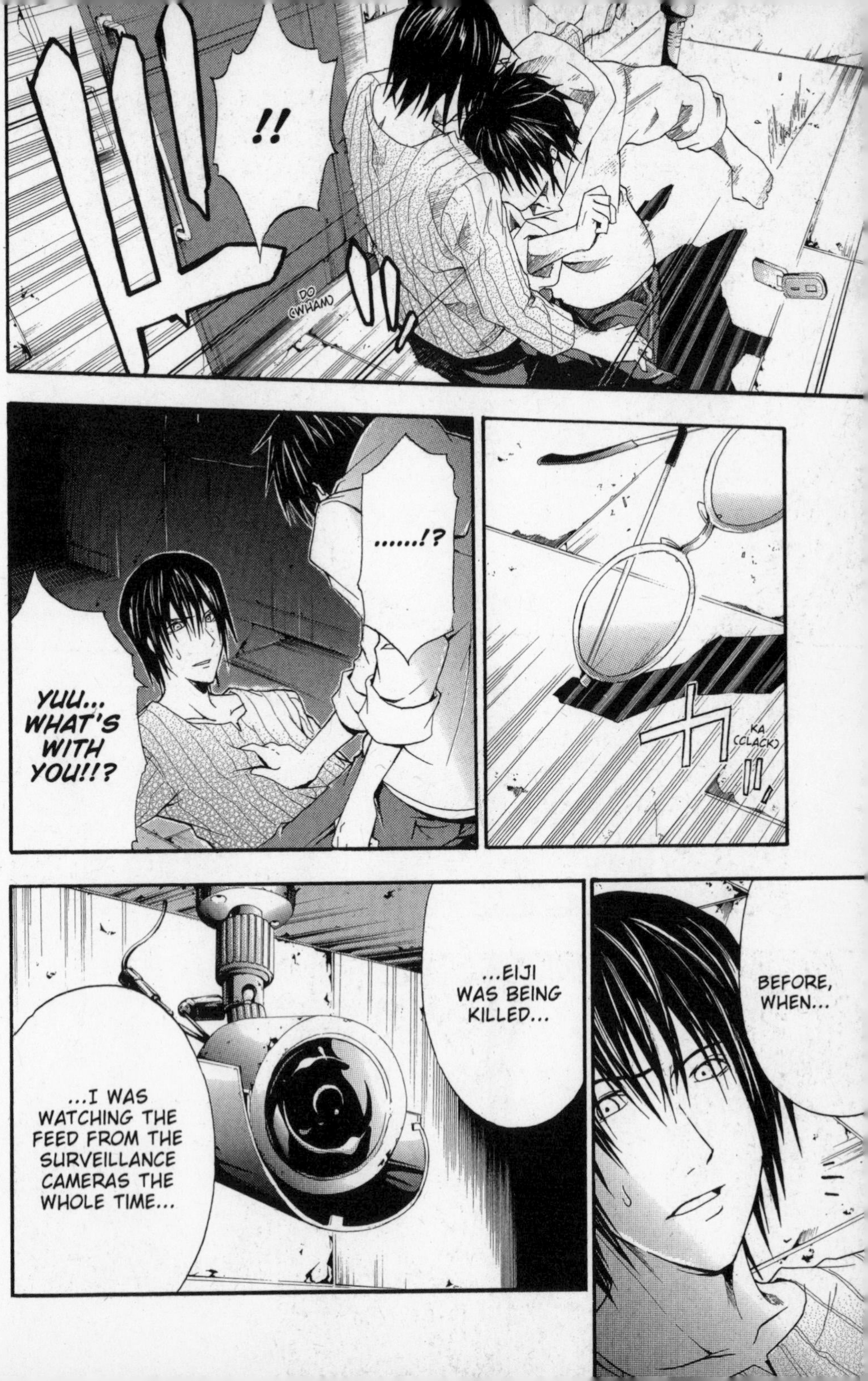
!!
DO (WHAM)
......!?
YUU... WHAT'S WITH YOU!!?
KA (CLACK)
BEFORE, WHEN...
...EIJI WAS BEING KILLED...
...I WAS WATCHING THE FEED FROM THE SURVEILLANCE CAMERAS THE WHOLE TIME...

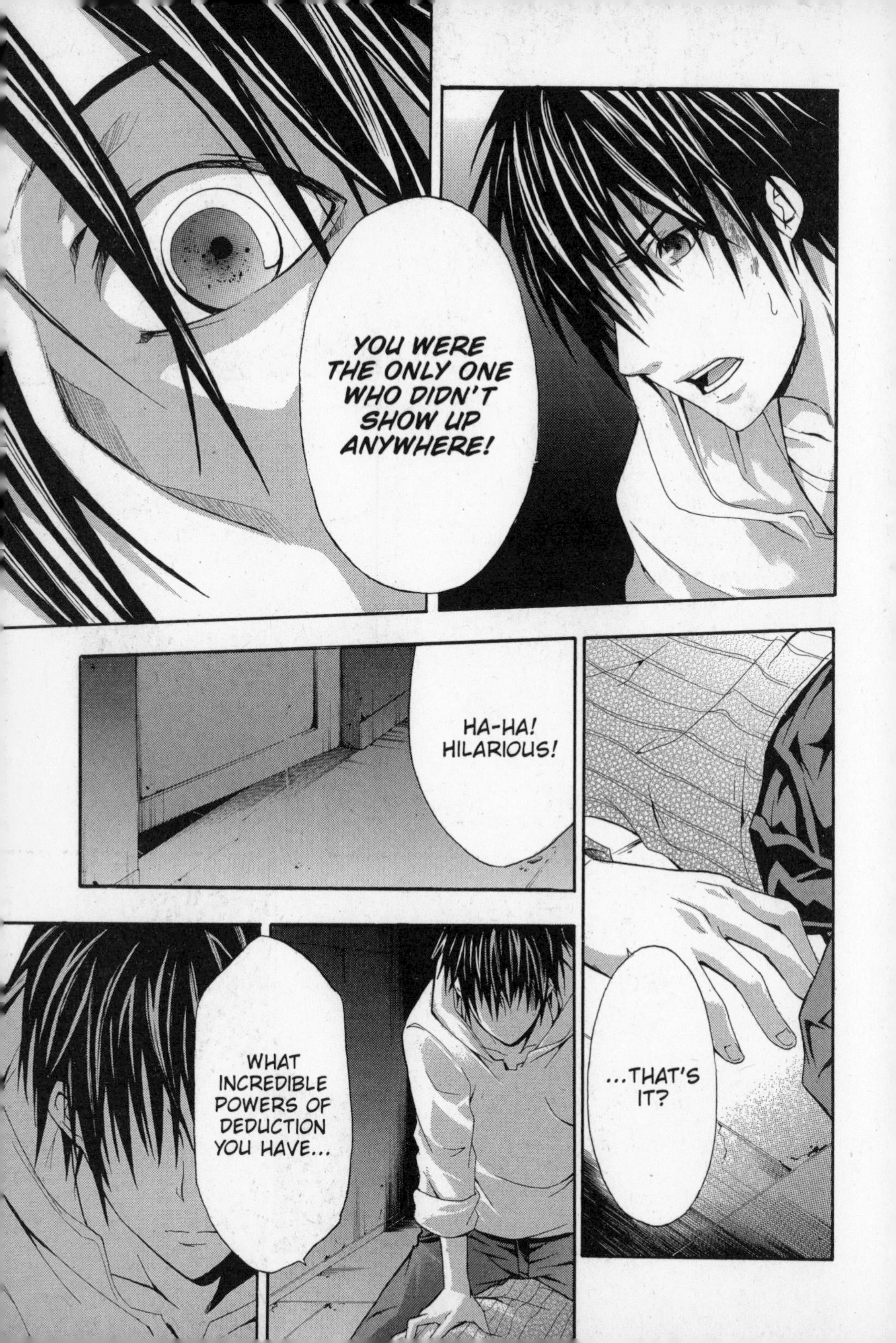
YOU WERE THE ONLY ONE WHO DIDN'T SHOW UP ANYWHERE!
...THAT'S IT?
HA-HA! HILARIOUS!
WHAT INCREDIBLE POWERS OF DEDUCTION YOU HAVE...

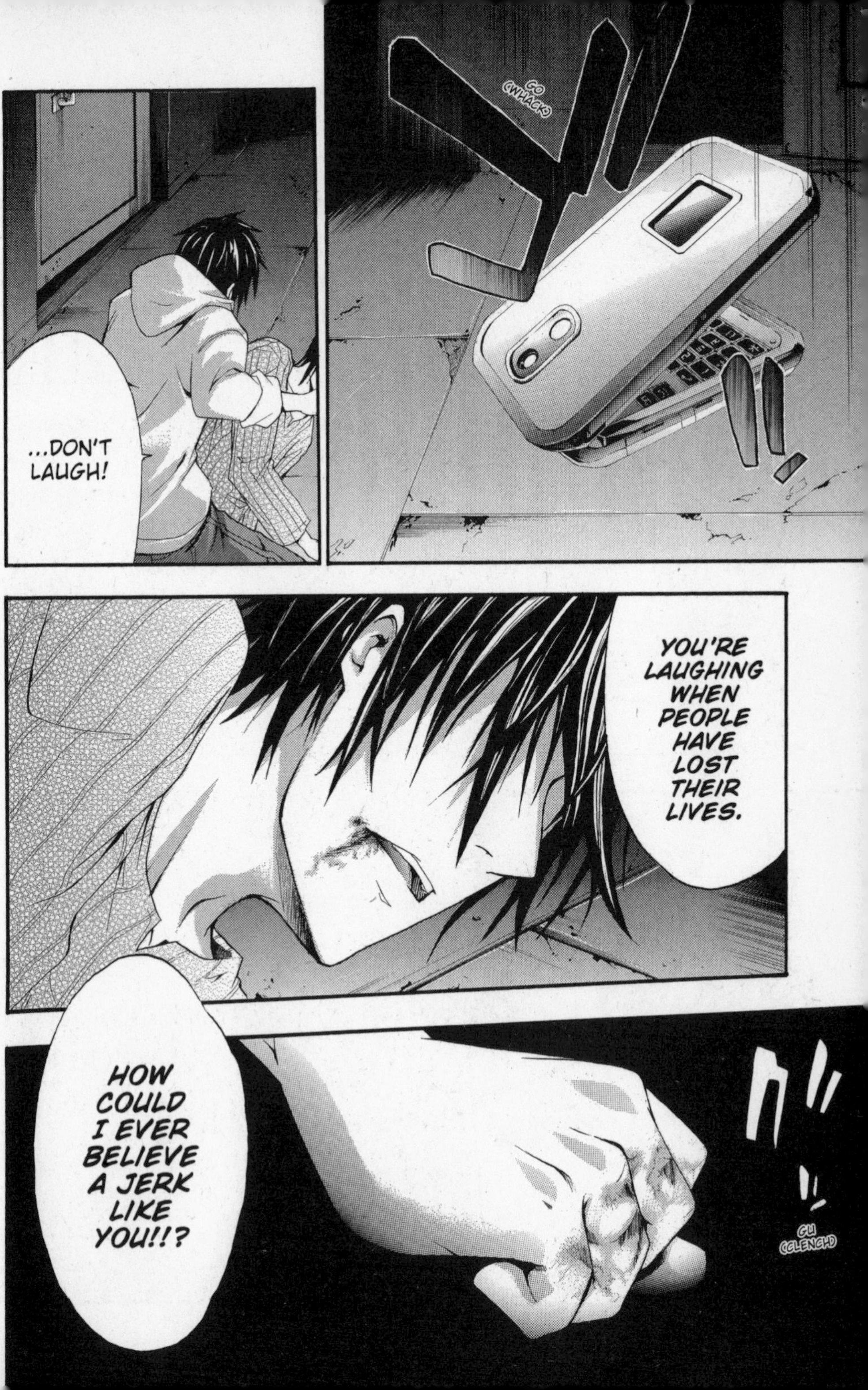
GO (WHACK)
...DON'T LAUGH!
YOU'RE LAUGHING WHEN PEOPLE HAVE LOST THEIR LIVES.
GU (CLENCH)
HOW COULD I EVER BELIEVE A JERK LIKE YOU!!?

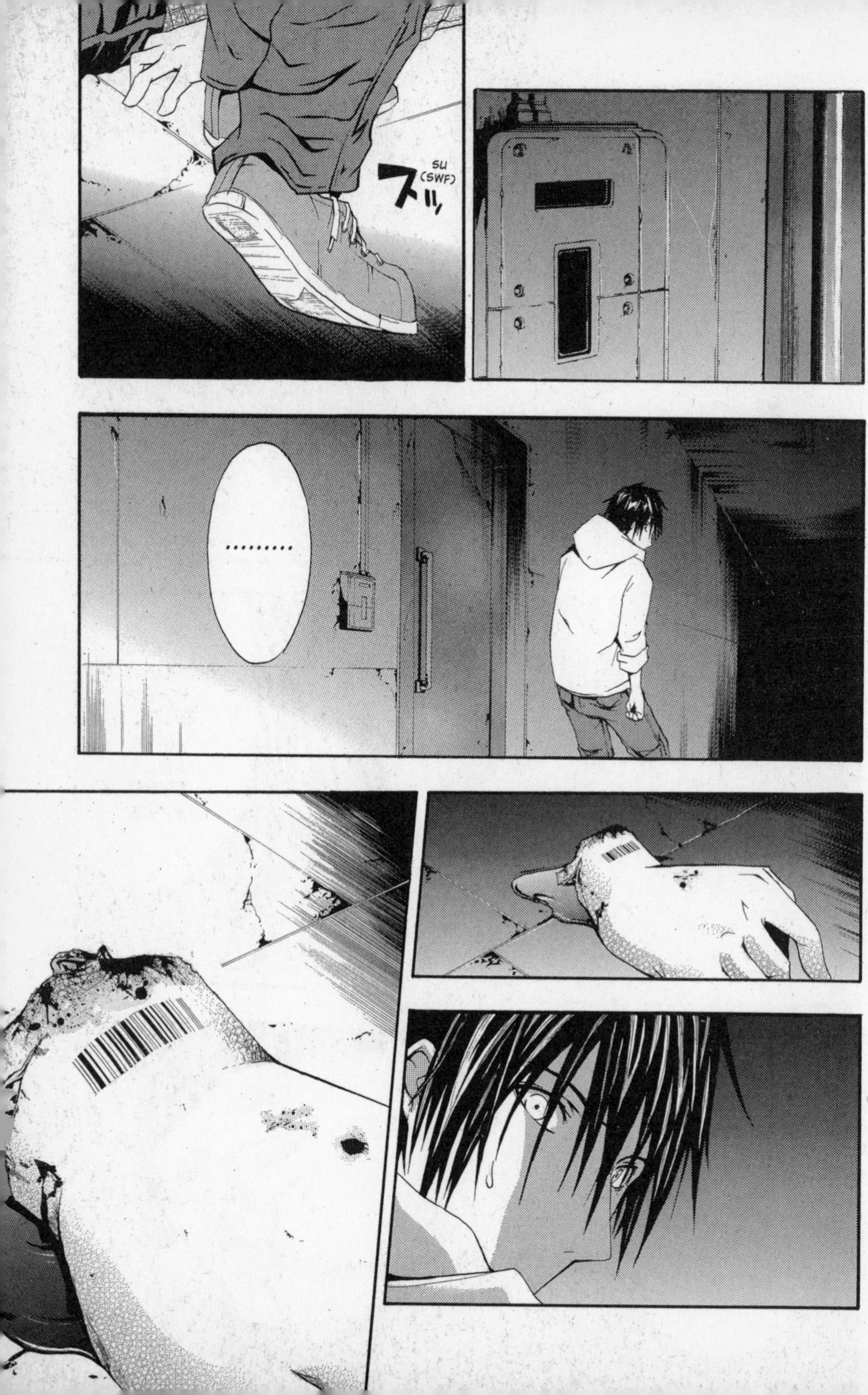
スッ
SU (SWF)
....

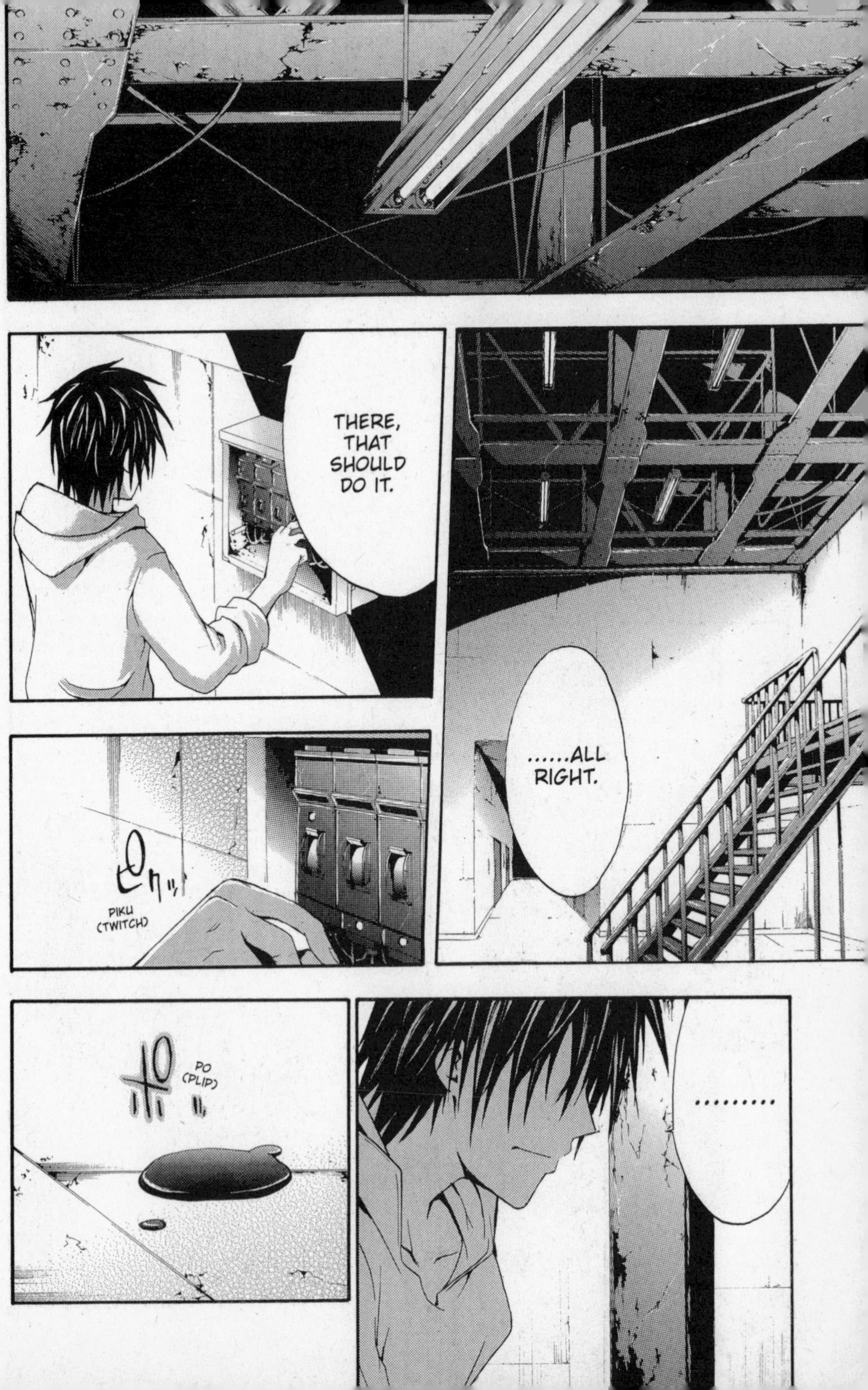
......ALL RIGHT.
THERE, THAT SHOULD DO IT.
PIKU (TWITCH)
....
PO (PLIP)

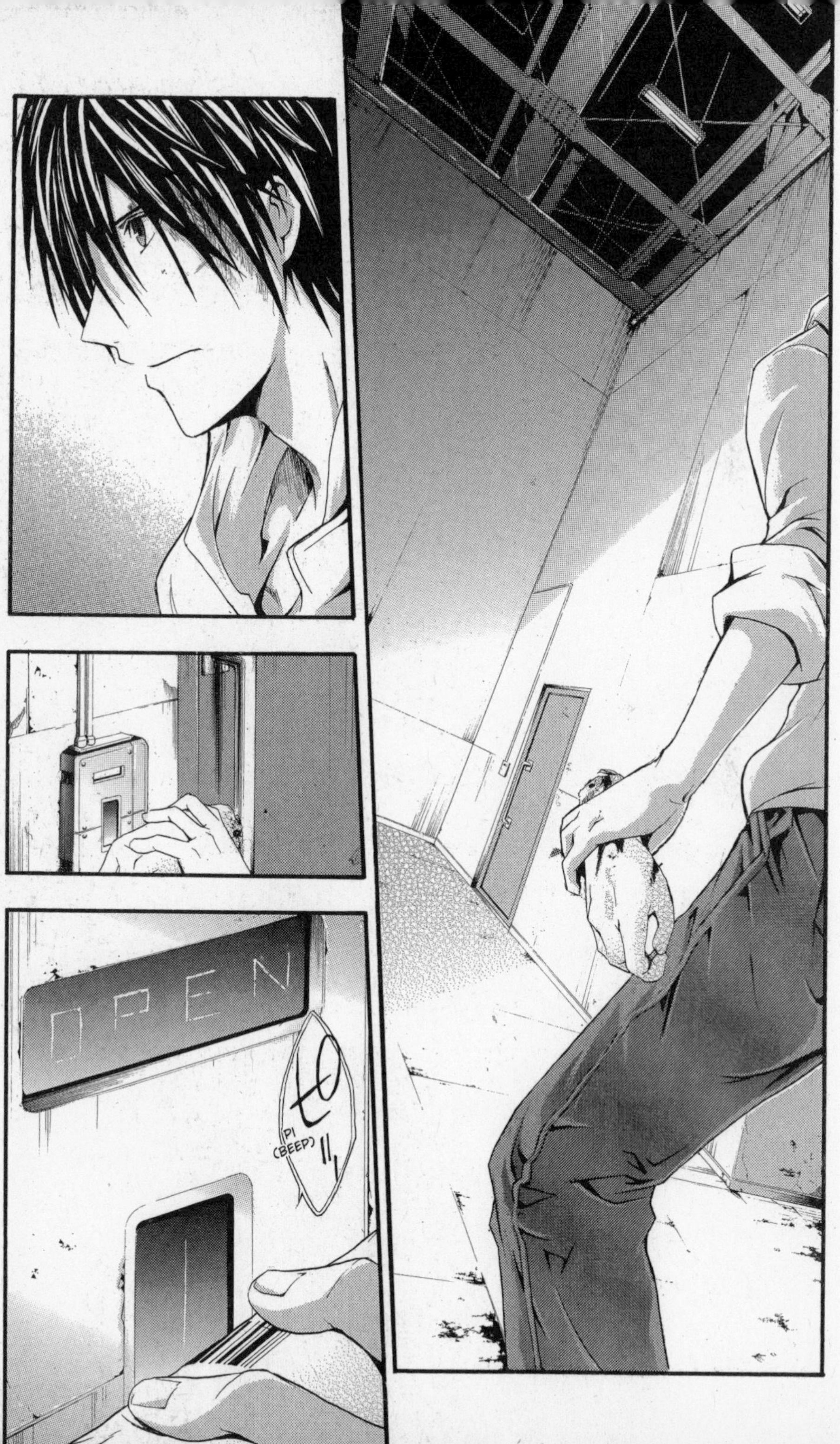
OPEN
PI
(BEEP)

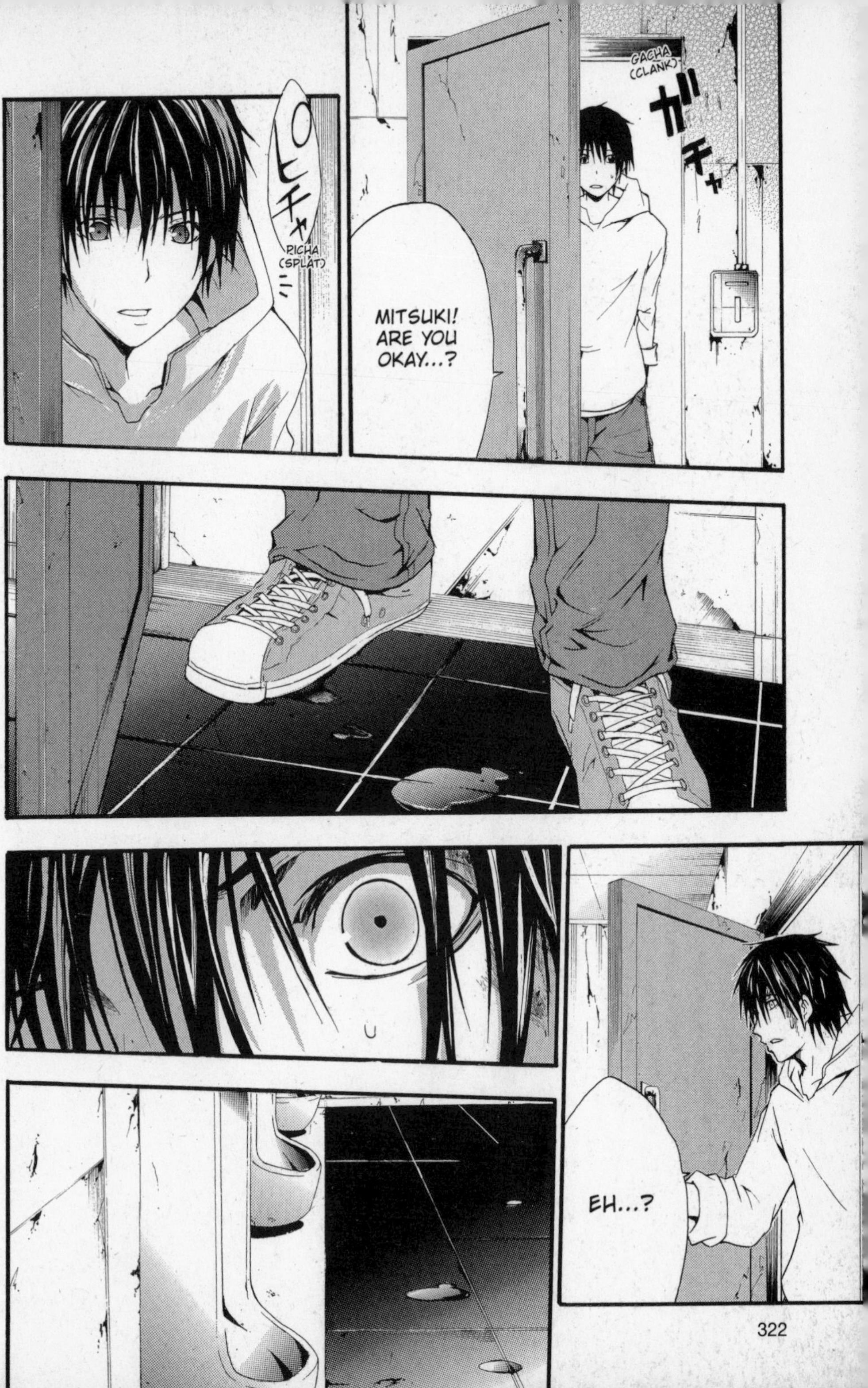
ガチャ
GACHA (CLANK)
MITSUKI! ARE YOU OKAY...?
ピチャ
RICHA (SPLAT)
EH...?

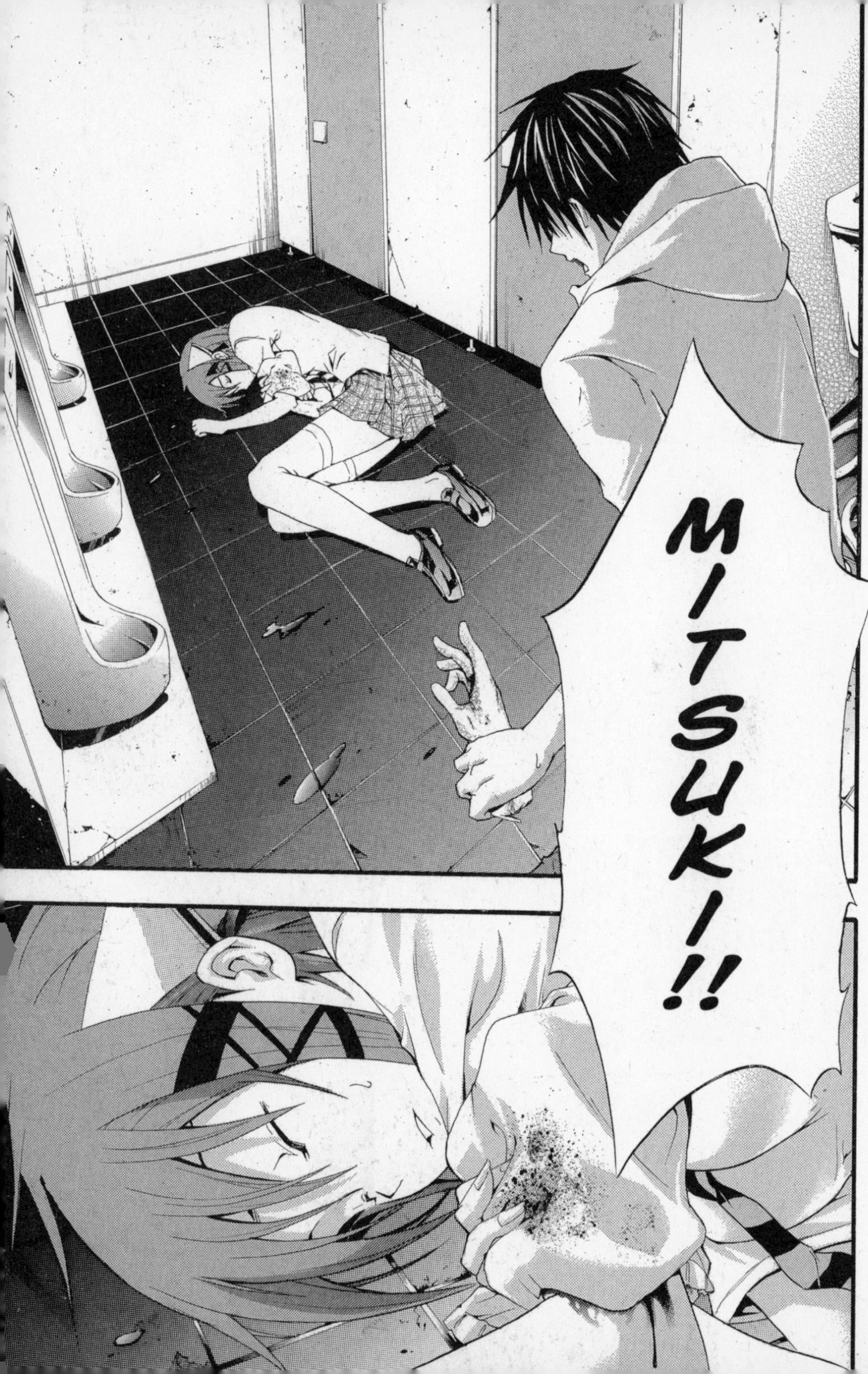
MITSUKI!!

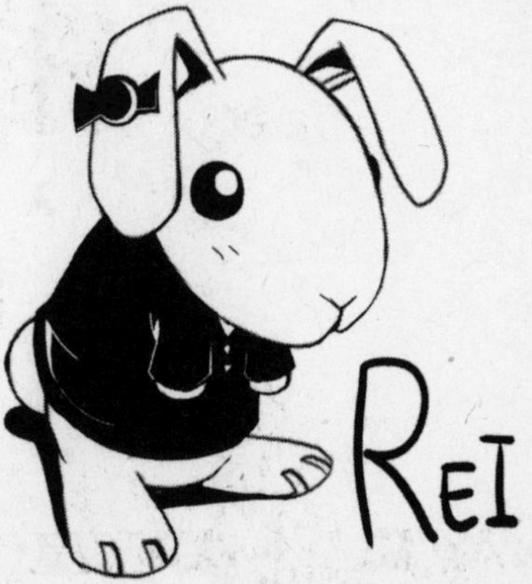
REI

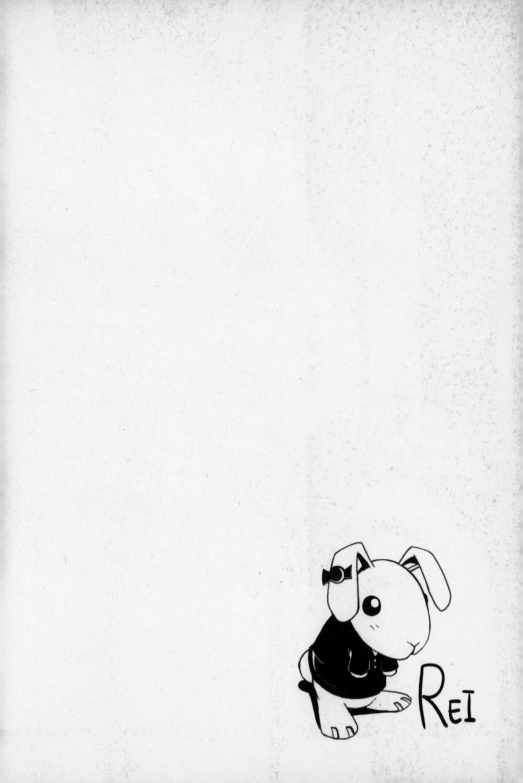

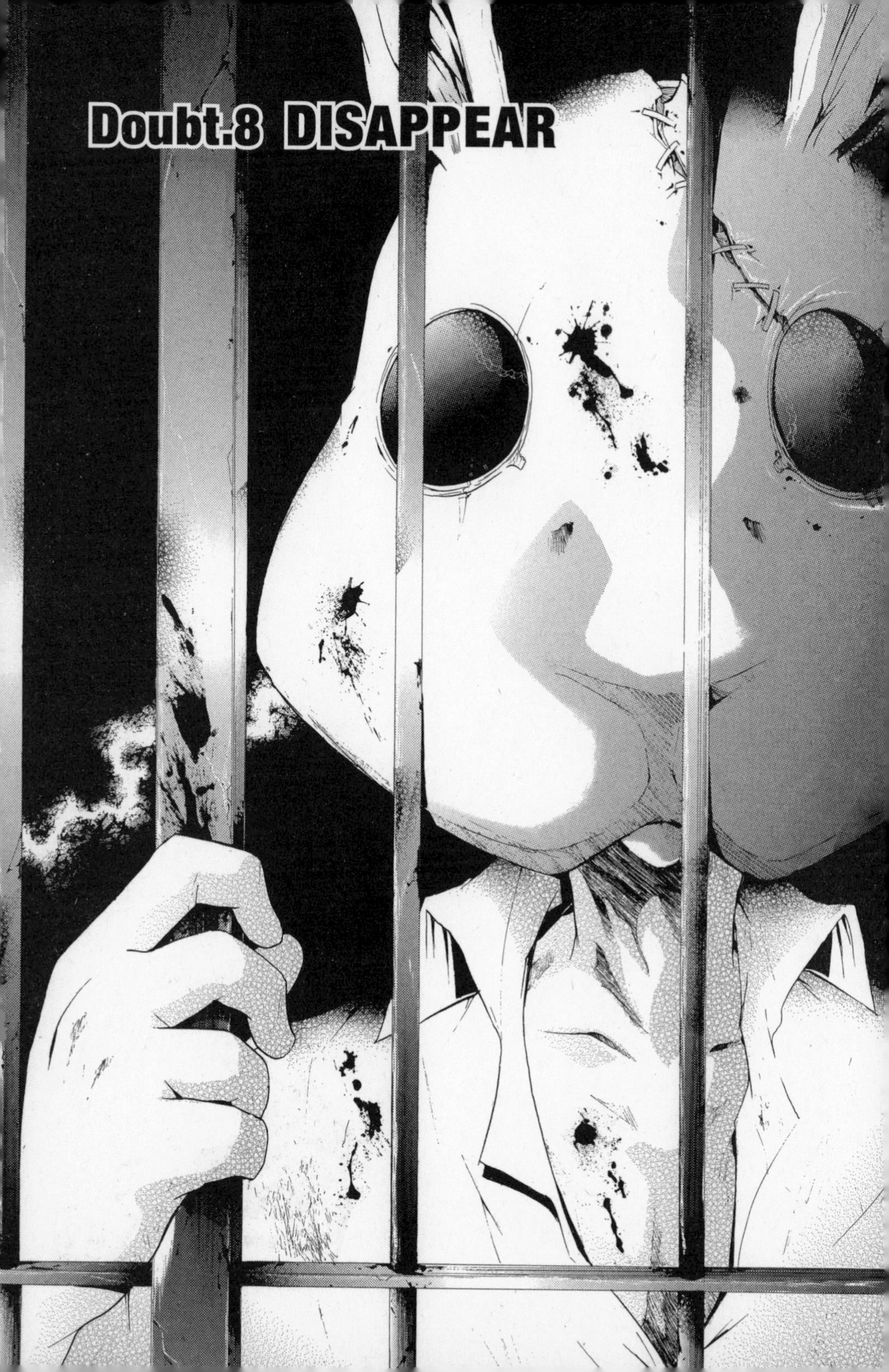
Doubt.8 DISAPPEAR

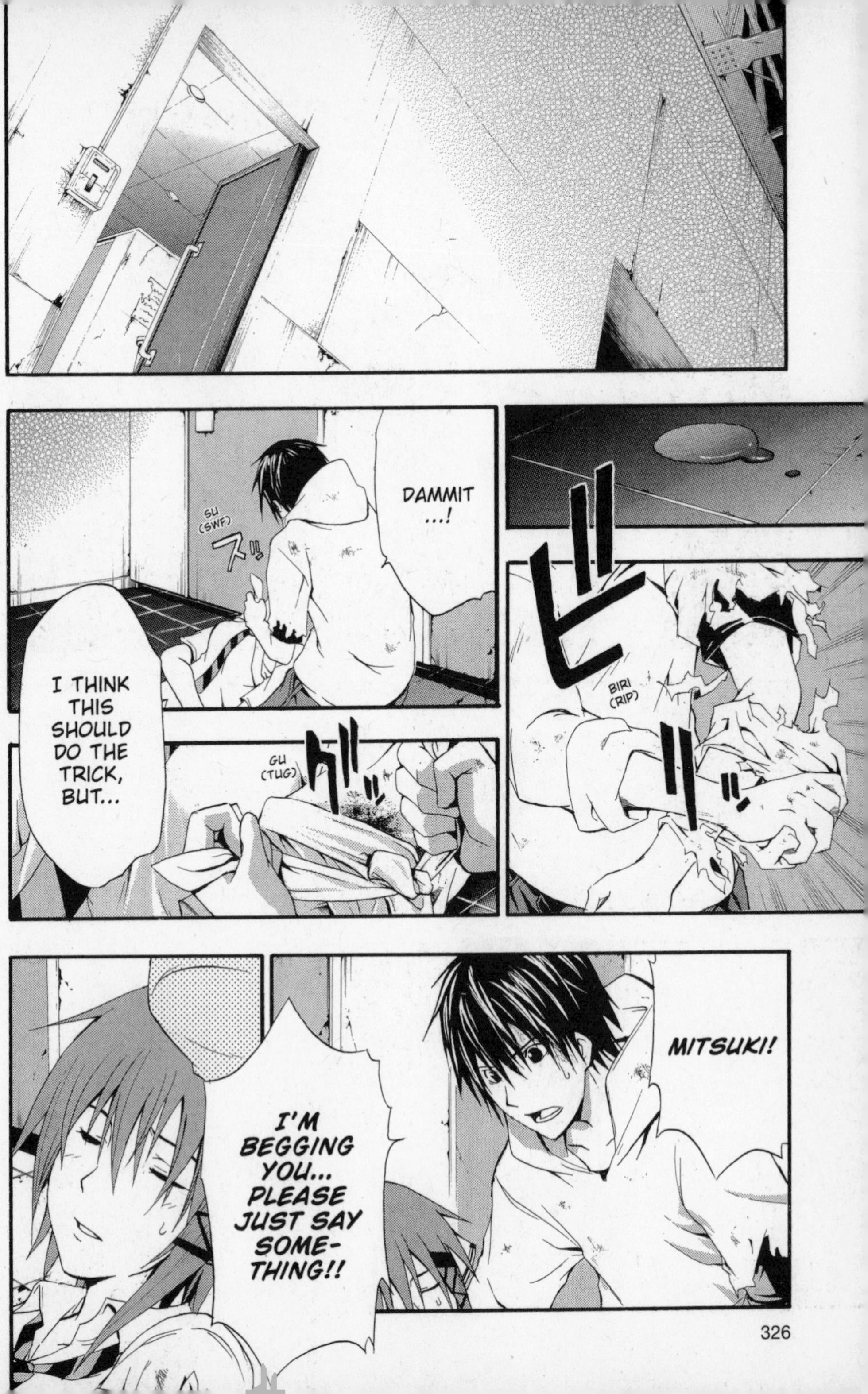
DAMMIT ...!
SU (SWF)
BIRI (RIP)
I THINK THIS SHOULD DO THE TRICK, BUT...
GU (TUG)
MITSUKI!
I'M BEGGING YOU... PLEASE JUST SAY SOME-THING!!

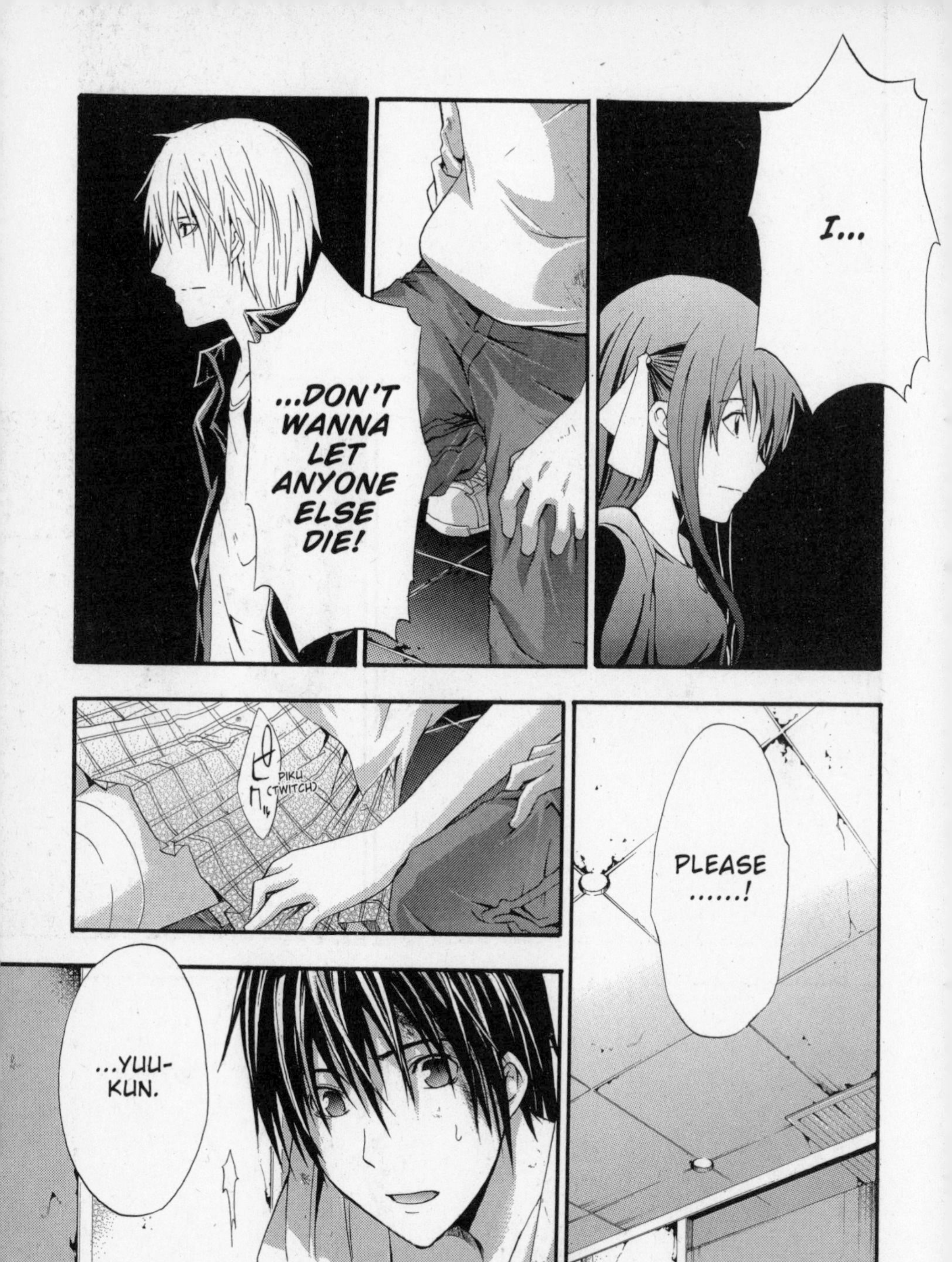
I...
...DON'T WANNA LET ANYONE ELSE DIE!
PLEASE ......!
PIKU (TWITCH)
...YUU-KUN.

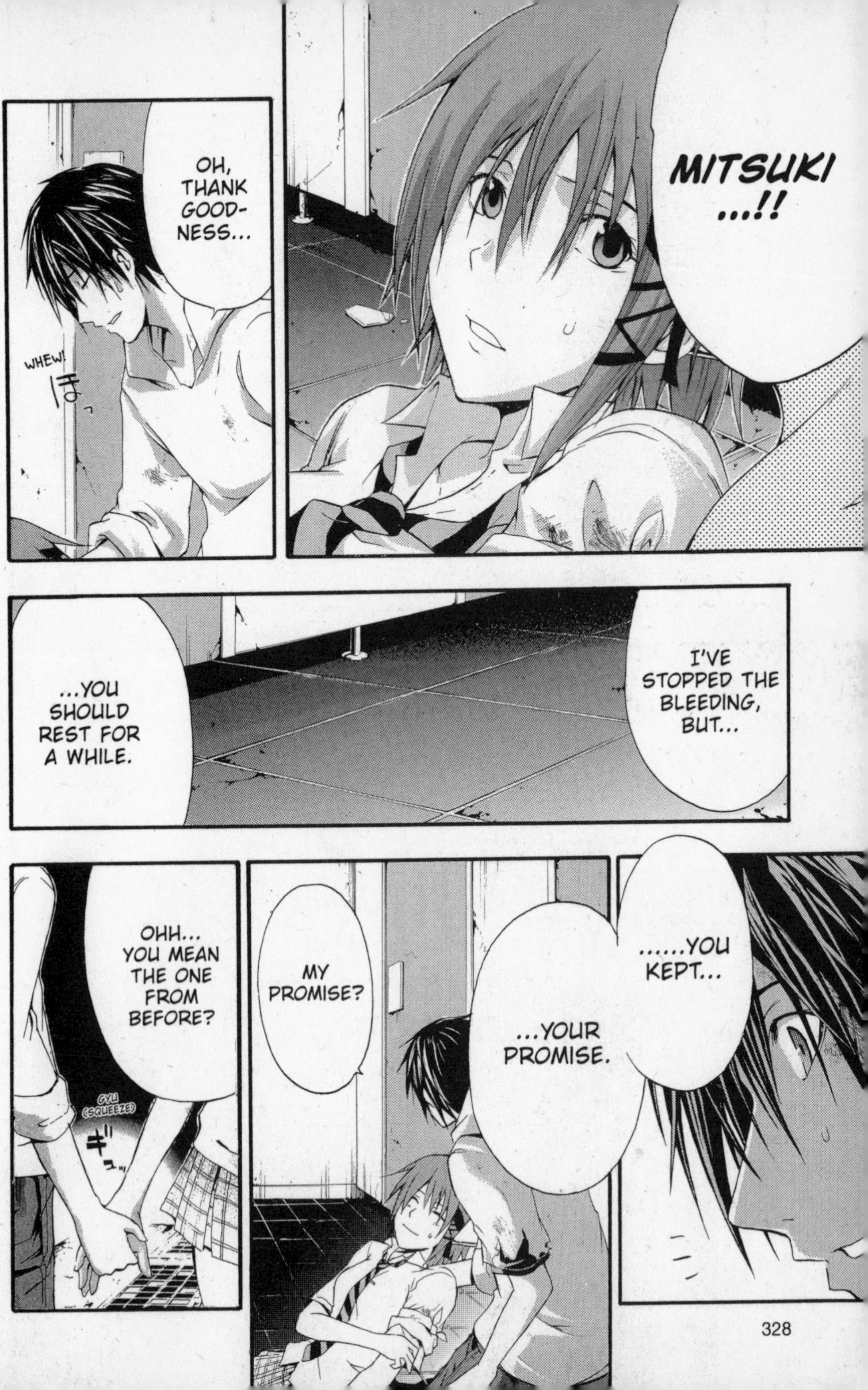
MITSUKI ...!!
OH, THANK GOODNESS...
WHEW!
ほっ
I'VE STOPPED THE BLEEDING, BUT...
...YOU SHOULD REST FOR A WHILE.
......YOU KEPT...
...YOUR PROMISE.
MY PROMISE?
OHH... YOU MEAN THE ONE FROM BEFORE?
GYU (SQUEEZE)
ギュッ

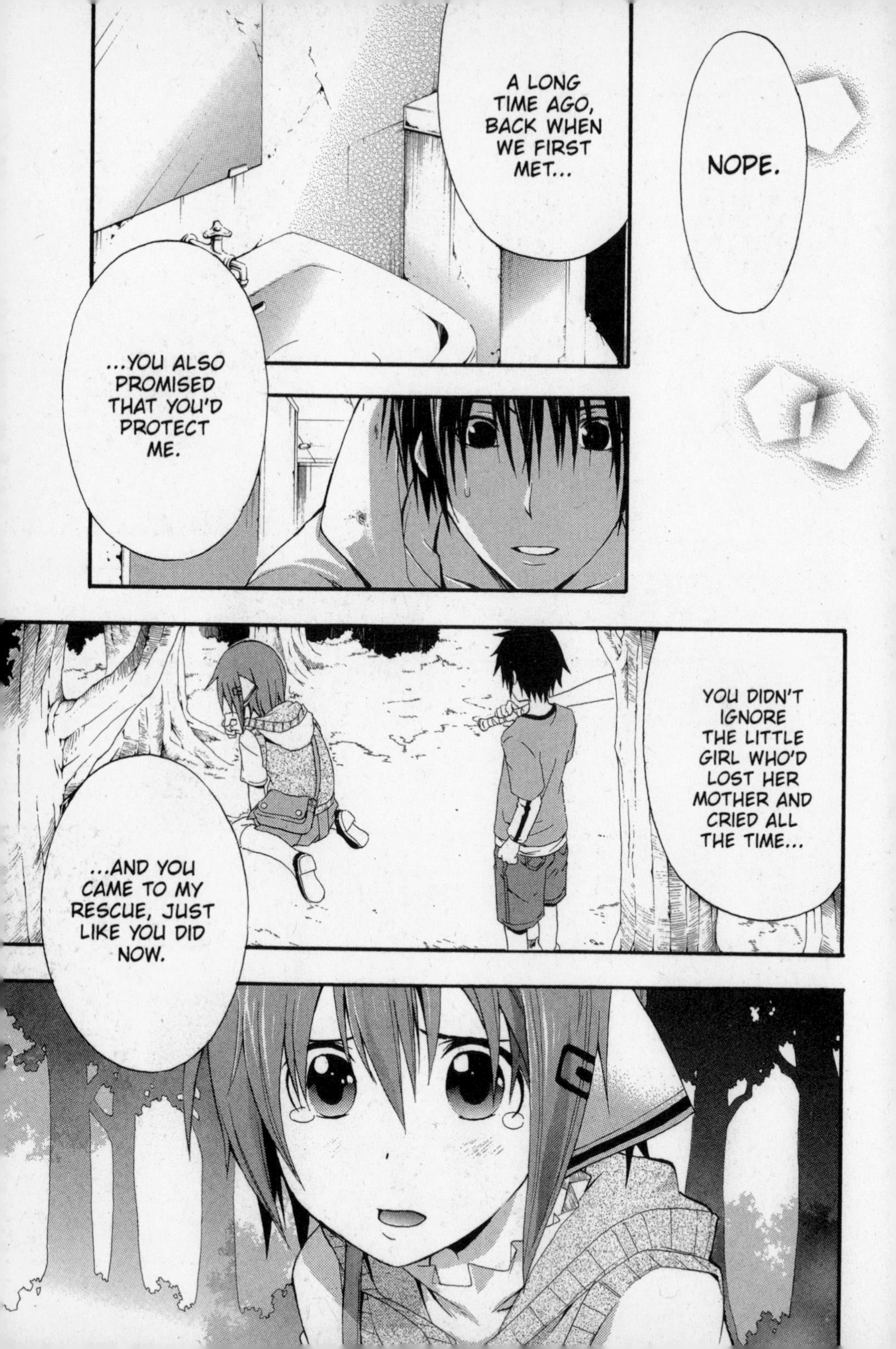
NOPE.
A LONG TIME AGO, BACK WHEN WE FIRST MET...
...YOU ALSO PROMISED THAT YOU'D PROTECT ME.
YOU DIDN'T IGNORE THE LITTLE GIRL WHO'D LOST HER MOTHER AND CRIED ALL THE TIME...
...AND YOU CAME TO MY RESCUE, JUST LIKE YOU DID NOW.

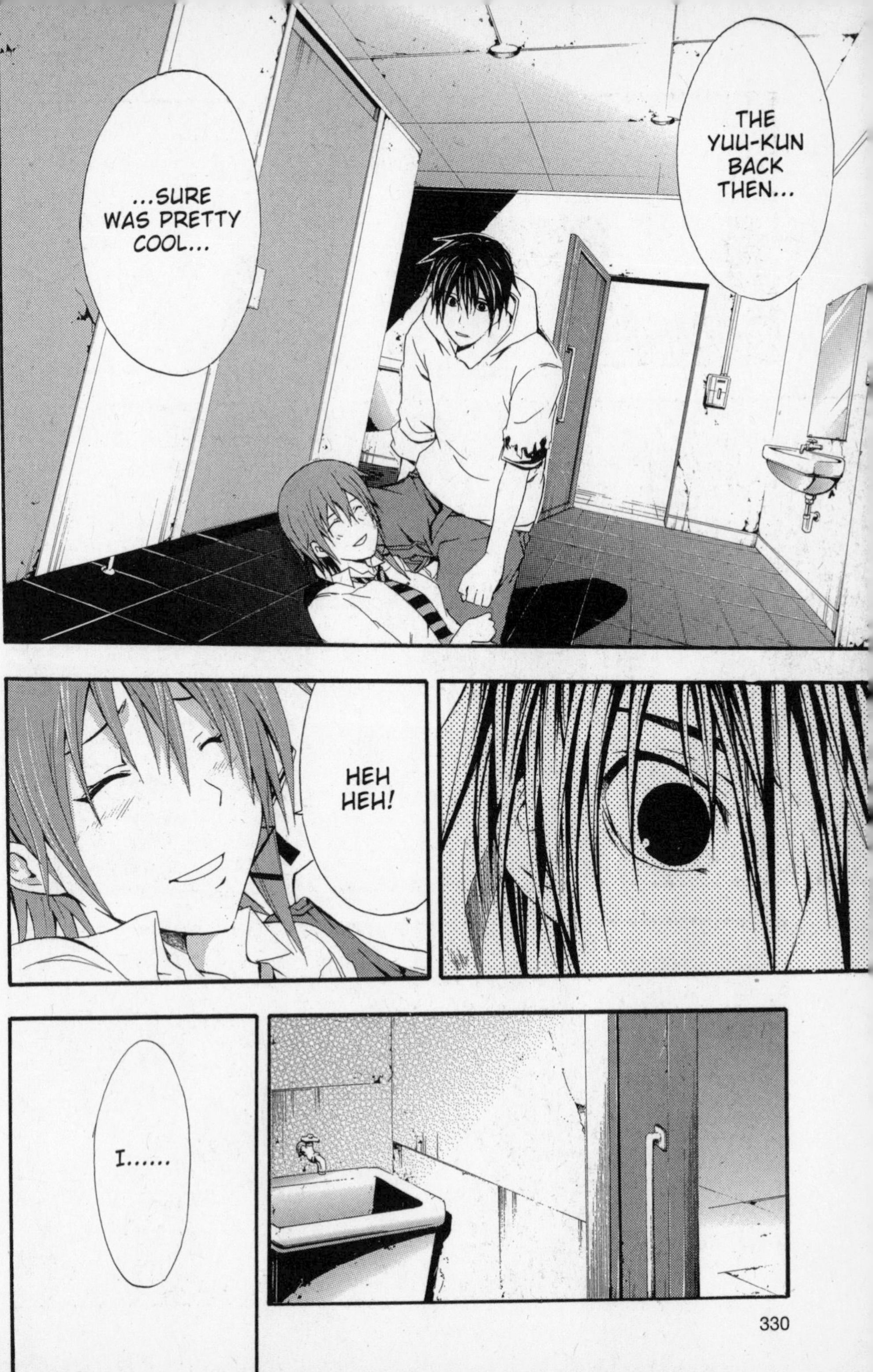
THE YUU-KUN BACK THEN...
...SURE WAS PRETTY COOL...
HEH HEH!
I......

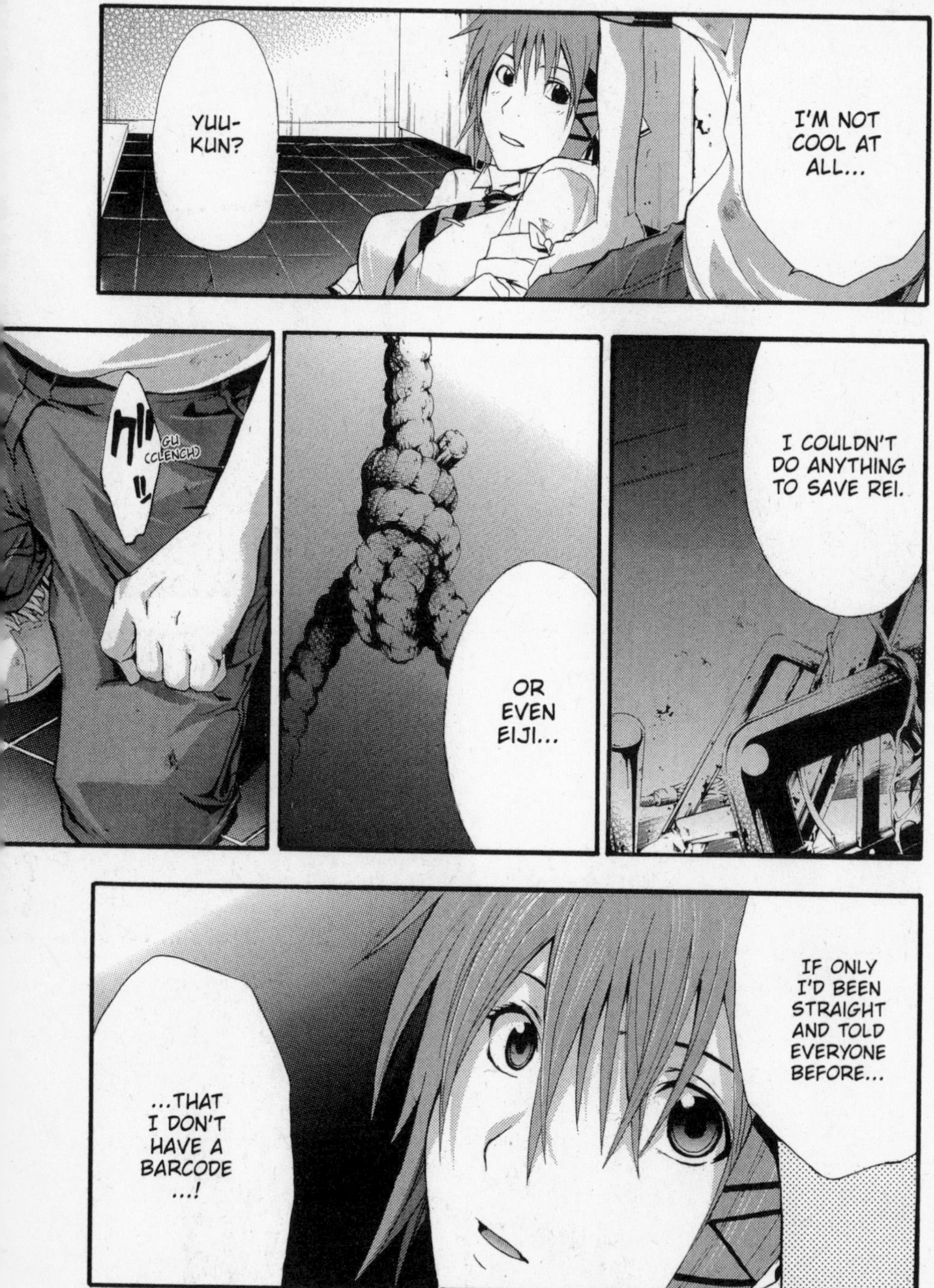
I'M NOT COOL AT ALL...
YUU-KUN?
I COULDN'T DO ANYTHING TO SAVE REI.
OR EVEN EIJI...
GU (CLENCH)
IF ONLY I'D BEEN STRAIGHT AND TOLD EVERYONE BEFORE...
...THAT I DON'T HAVE A BARCODE ...!

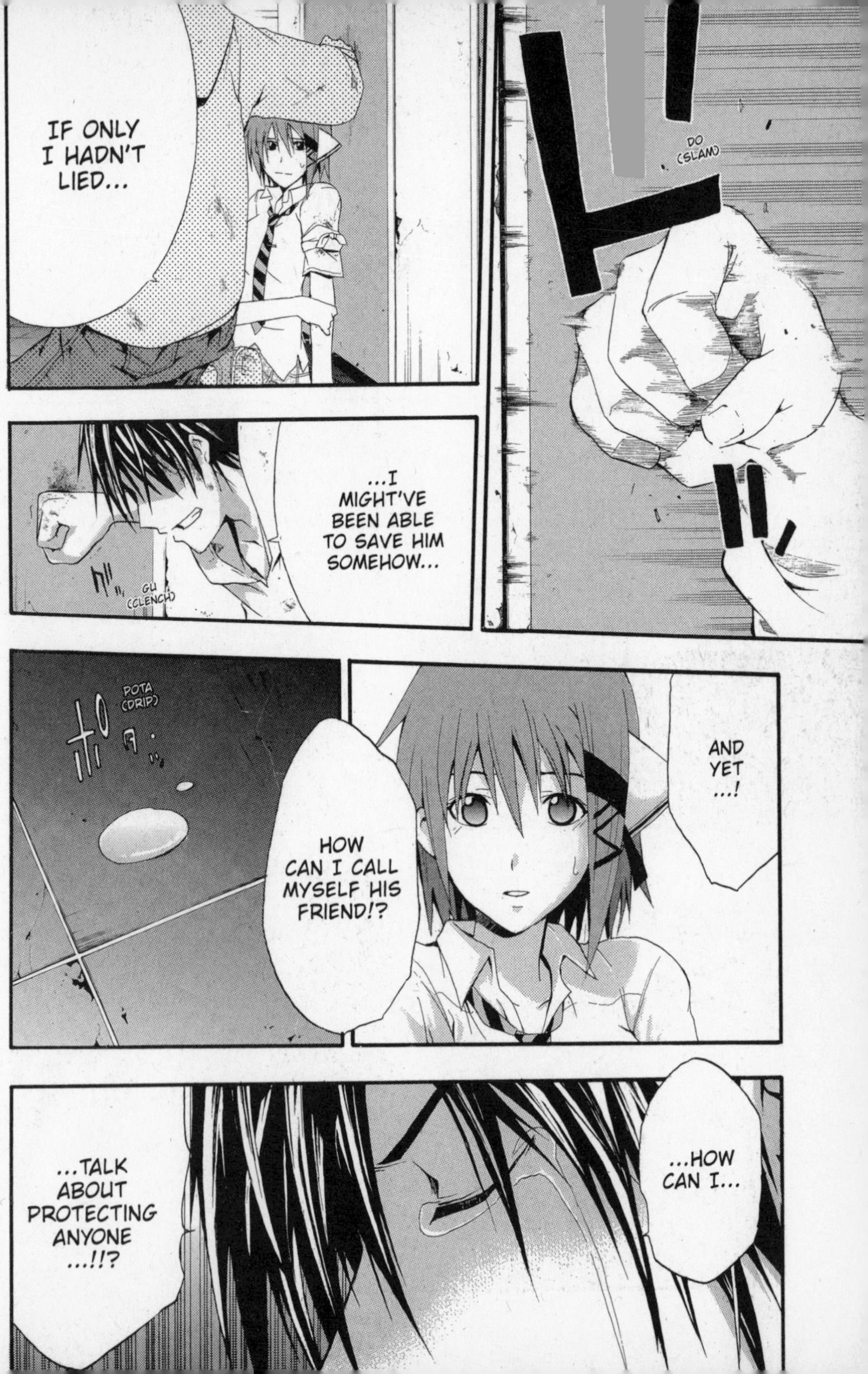
DO (SLAM)
IF ONLY I HADN'T LIED...
...I MIGHT'VE BEEN ABLE TO SAVE HIM SOMEHOW...
GU (CLENCH)
AND YET ...!
HOW CAN I CALL MYSELF HIS FRIEND!?
POTA (DRIP)
...HOW CAN I...
...TALK ABOUT PROTECTING ANYONE ...!!?

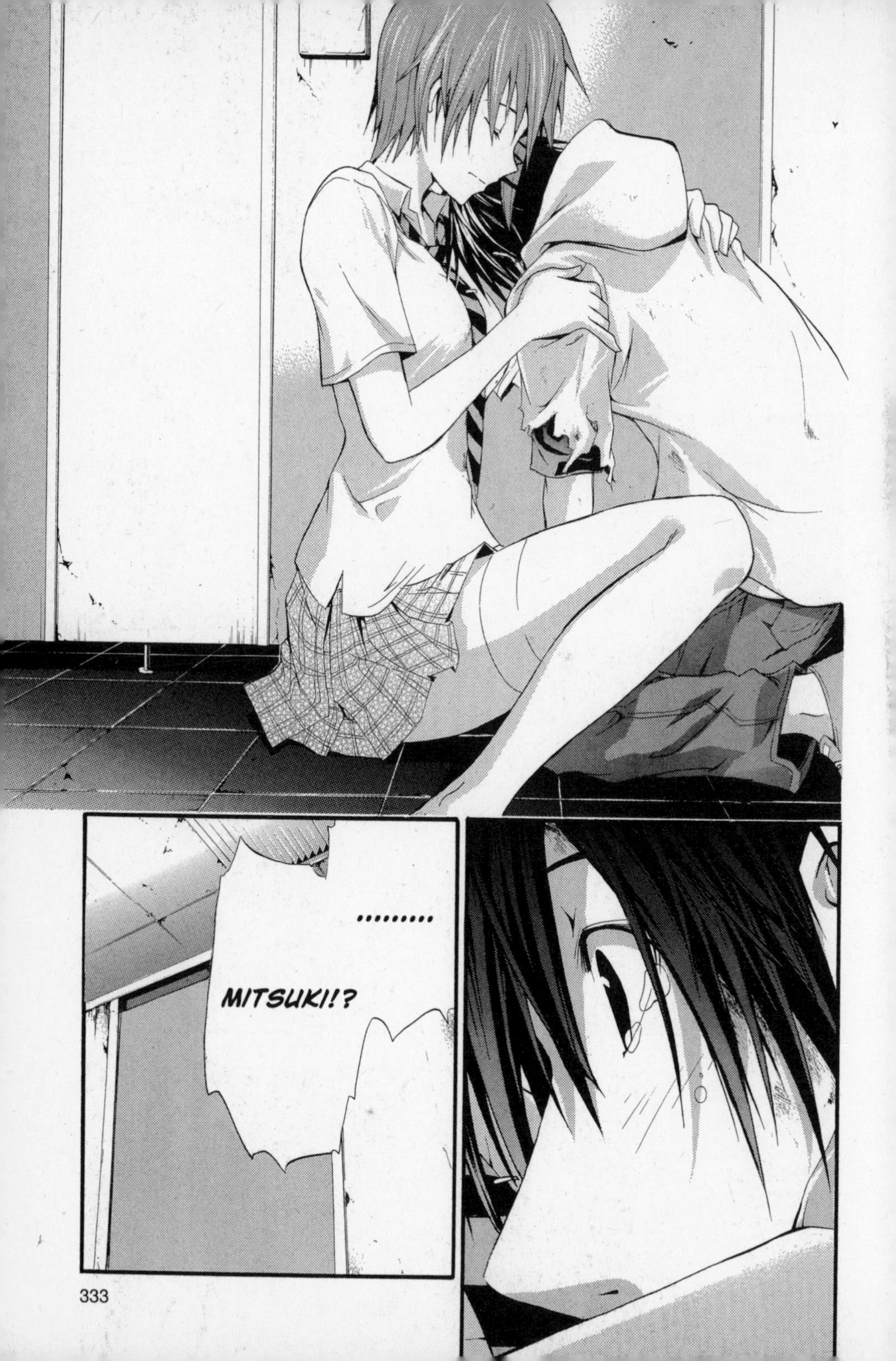
....
MITSUKI!?

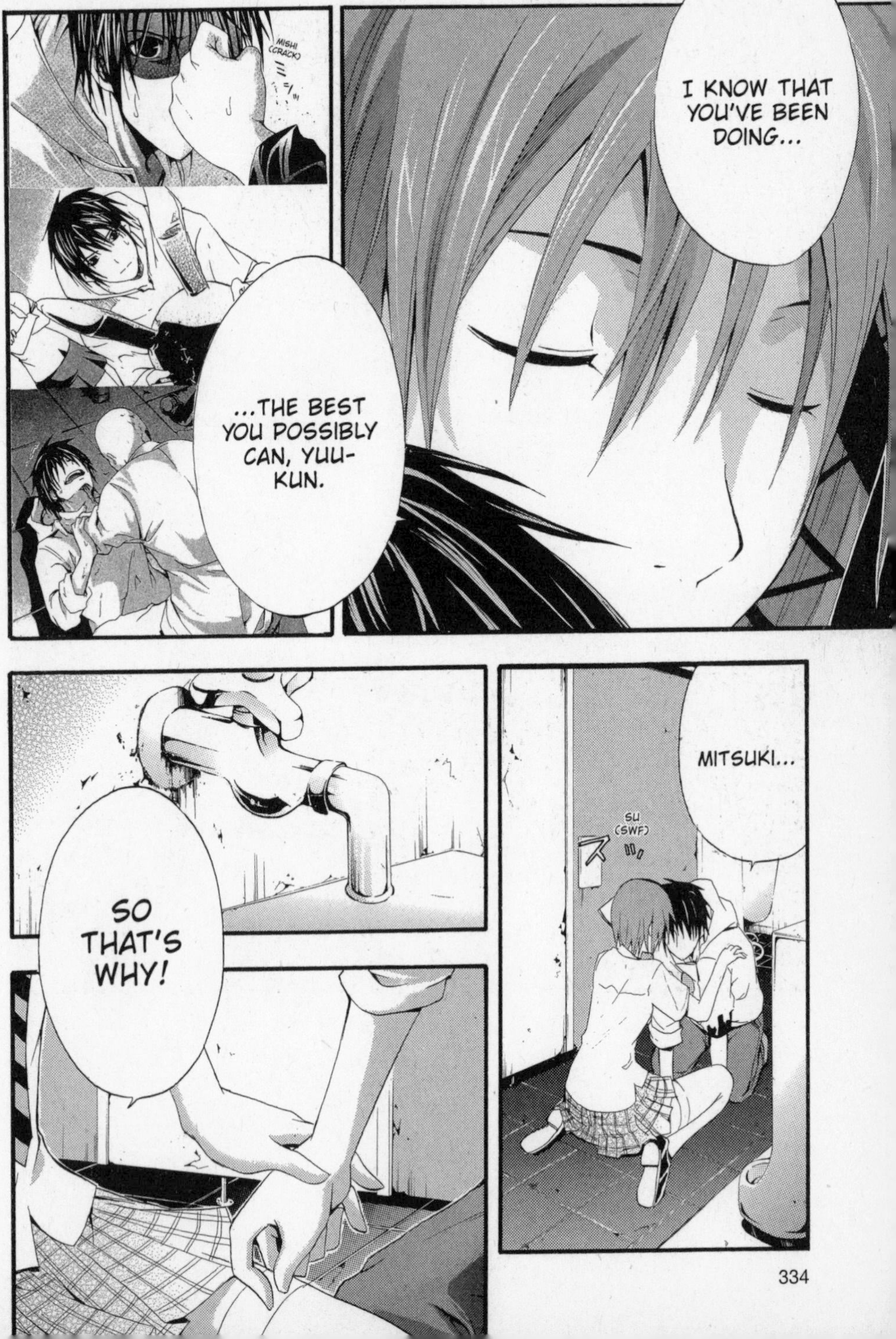
I KNOW THAT YOU'VE BEEN DOING...
MISHI (CRACK)
...THE BEST YOU POSSIBLY CAN, YUU-KUN.
MITSUKI...
SU (SWF)
SO THAT'S WHY!

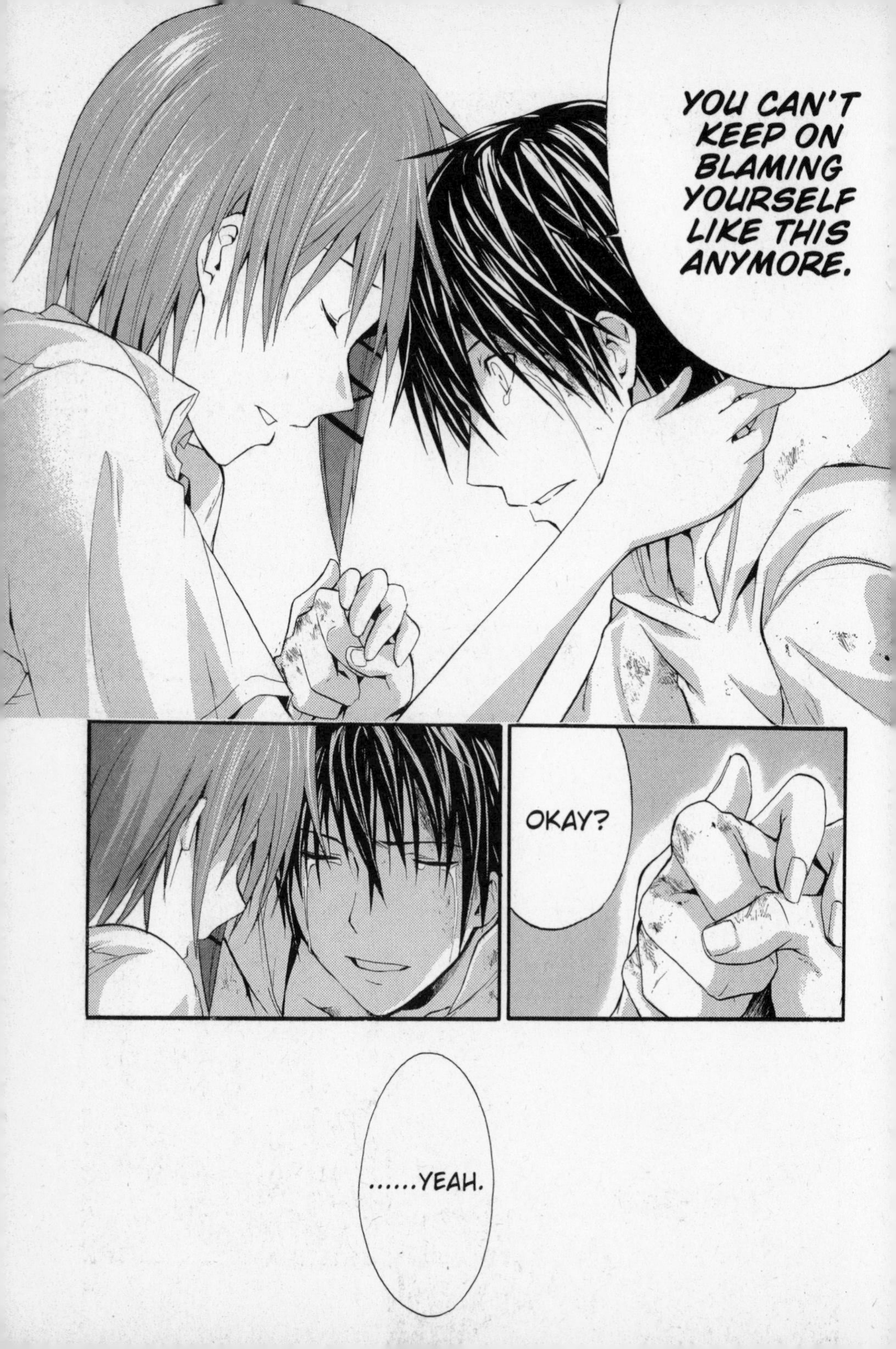
YOU CAN'T KEEP ON BLAMING YOURSELF LIKE THIS ANYMORE.
OKAY?
......YEAH.

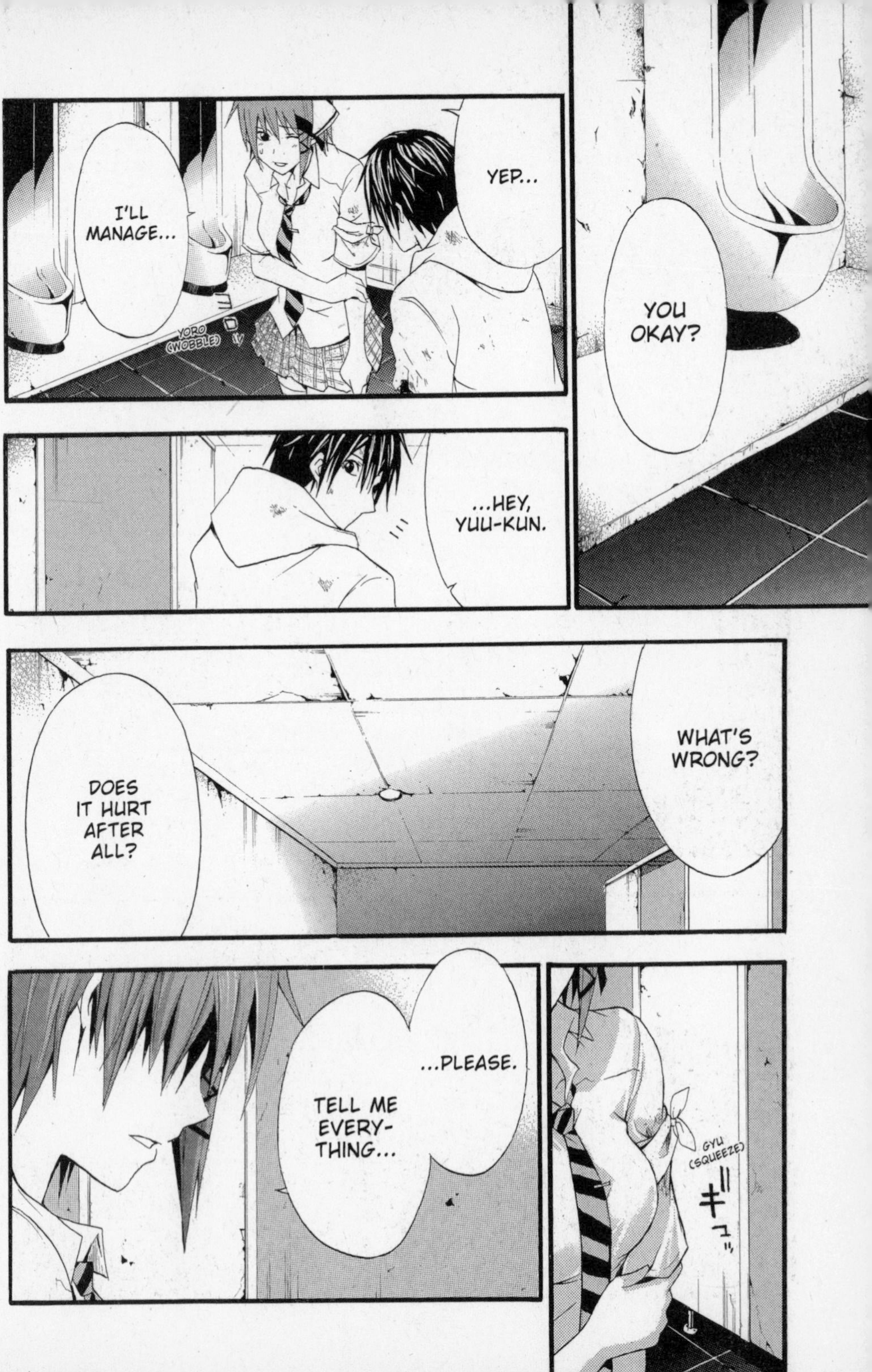
YOU OKAY?
YEP...
I'LL MANAGE...
YORO (WOBBLE)
...HEY, YUU-KUN.
WHAT'S WRONG?
DOES IT HURT AFTER ALL?
GYU (SQUEEZE)
...PLEASE.
TELL ME EVERY-THING...

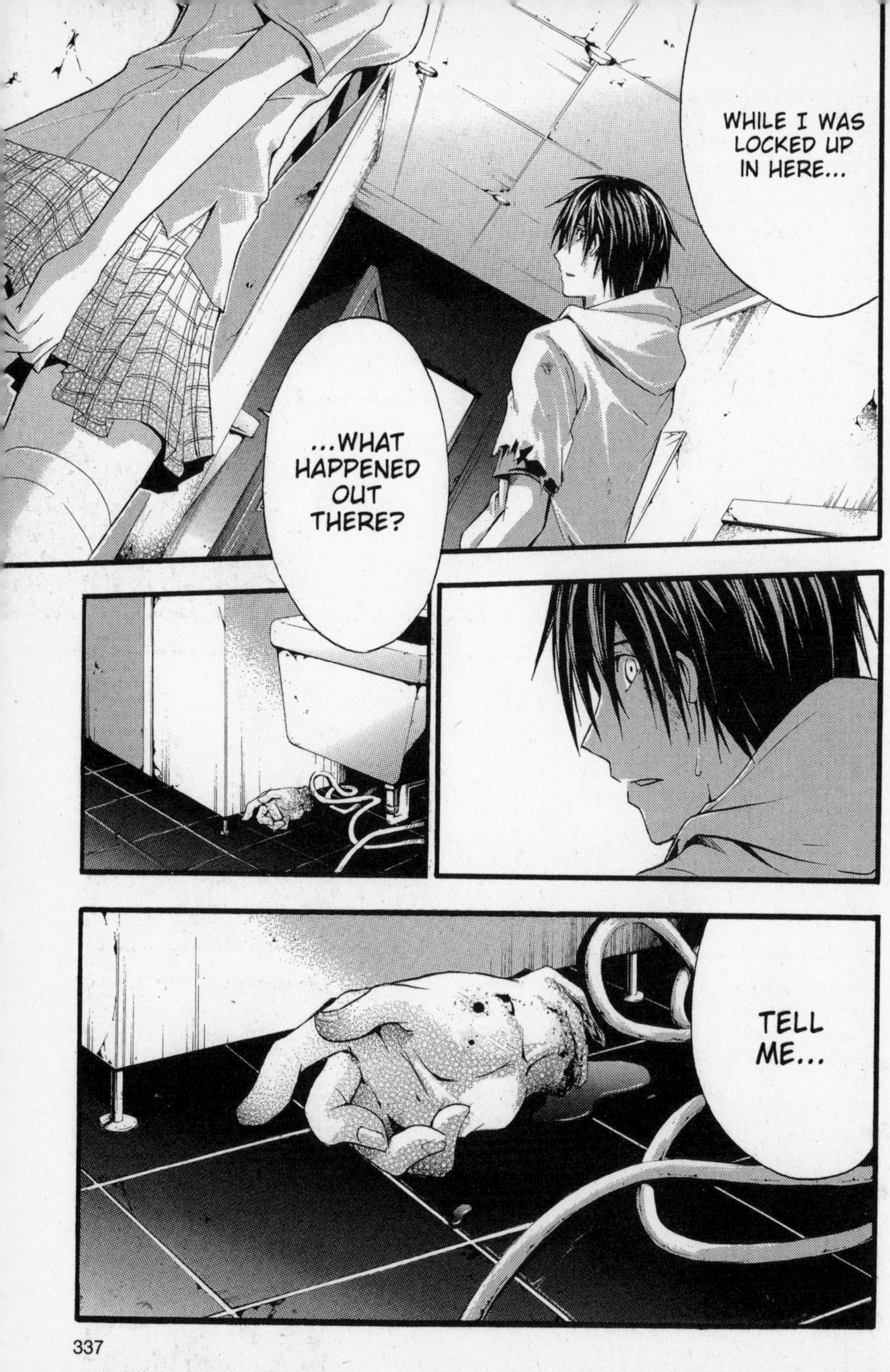
WHILE I WAS LOCKED UP IN HERE...
...WHAT HAPPENED OUT THERE?
TELL ME...

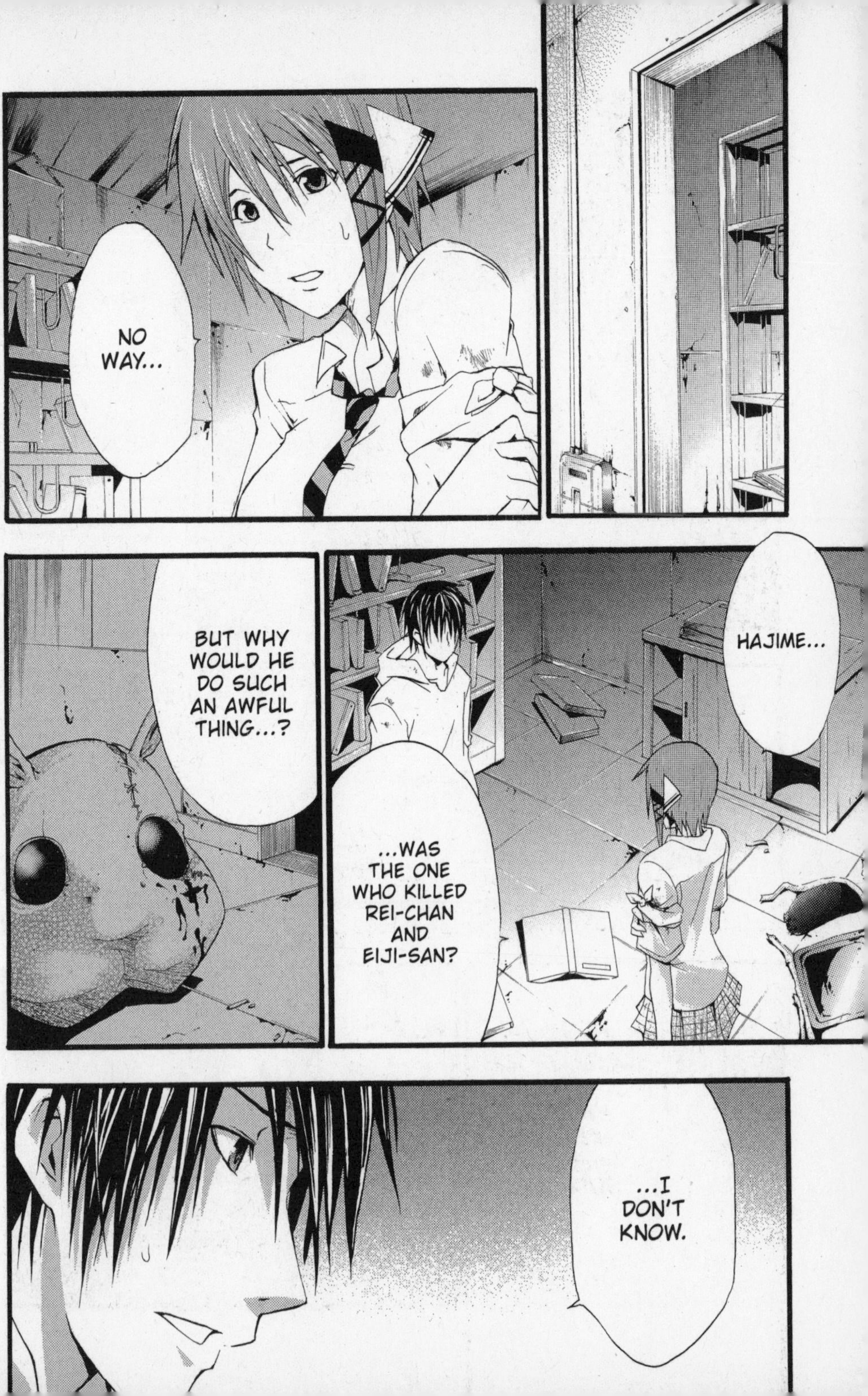
NO WAY...
HAJIME...
...WAS THE ONE WHO KILLED REI-CHAN AND EIJI-SAN?
BUT WHY WOULD HE DO SUCH AN AWFUL THING...?
...I DON'T KNOW.

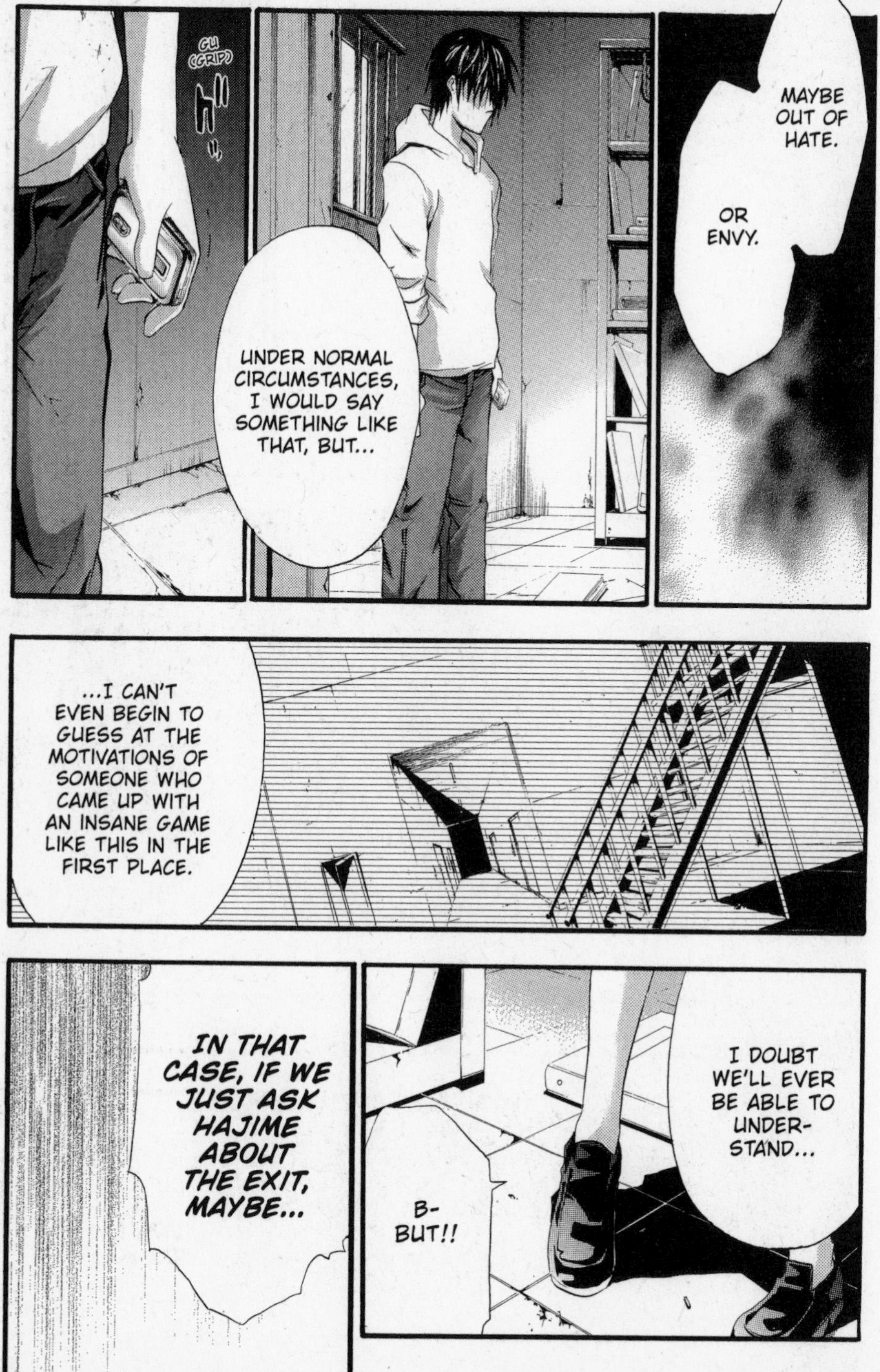
MAYBE OUT OF HATE.
OR ENVY.
UNDER NORMAL CIRCUMSTANCES, I WOULD SAY SOMETHING LIKE THAT, BUT...
GU (GRIP)
...I CAN'T EVEN BEGIN TO GUESS AT THE MOTIVATIONS OF SOMEONE WHO CAME UP WITH AN INSANE GAME LIKE THIS IN THE FIRST PLACE.
I DOUBT WE'LL EVER BE ABLE TO UNDER-STAND...
B-BUT!!
IN THAT CASE, IF WE JUST ASK HAJIME ABOUT THE EXIT, MAYBE...

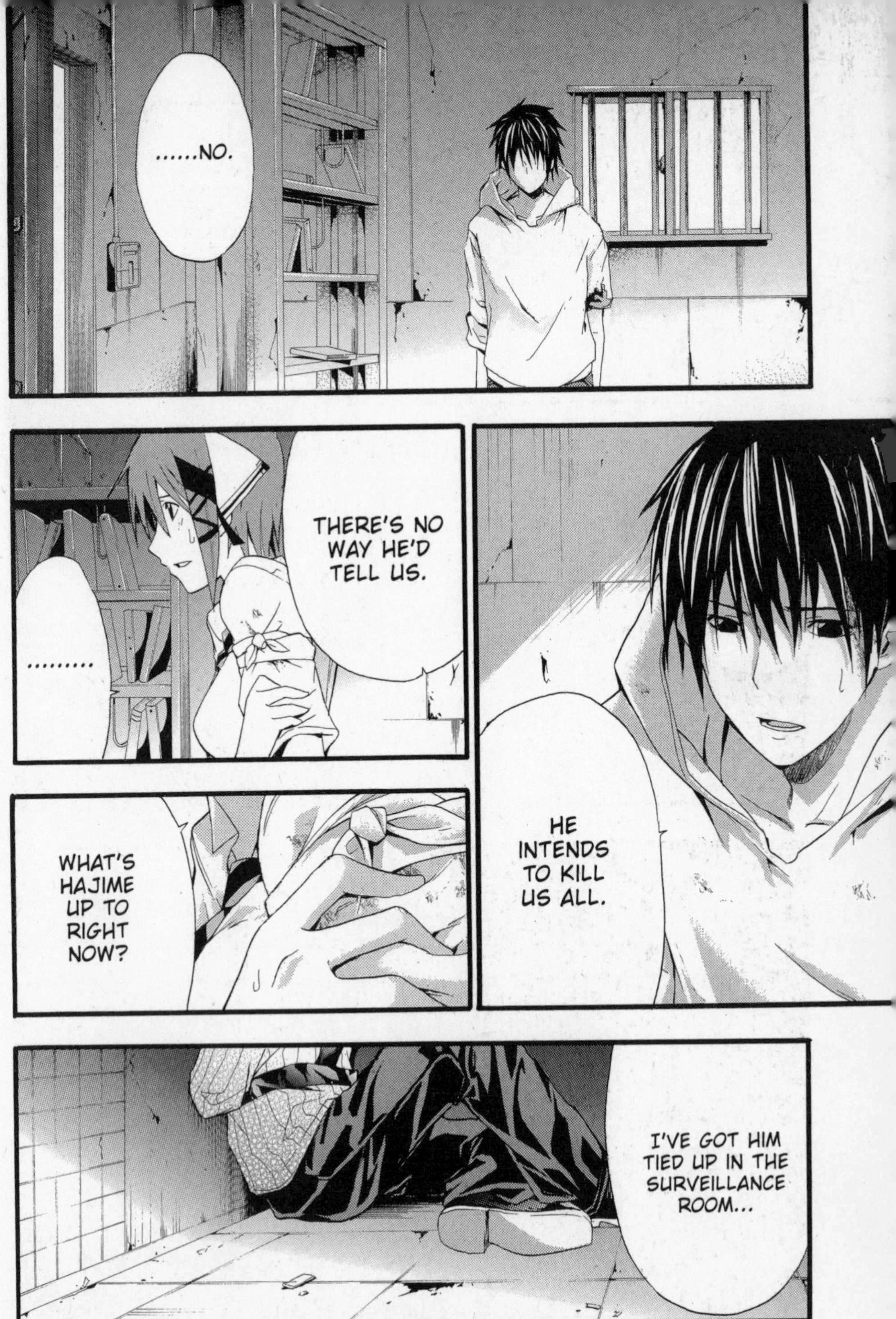
......NO.
HE INTENDS TO KILL US ALL.
THERE'S NO WAY HE'D TELL US.
....
WHAT'S HAJIME UP TO RIGHT NOW?
I'VE GOT HIM TIED UP IN THE SURVEILLANCE ROOM...

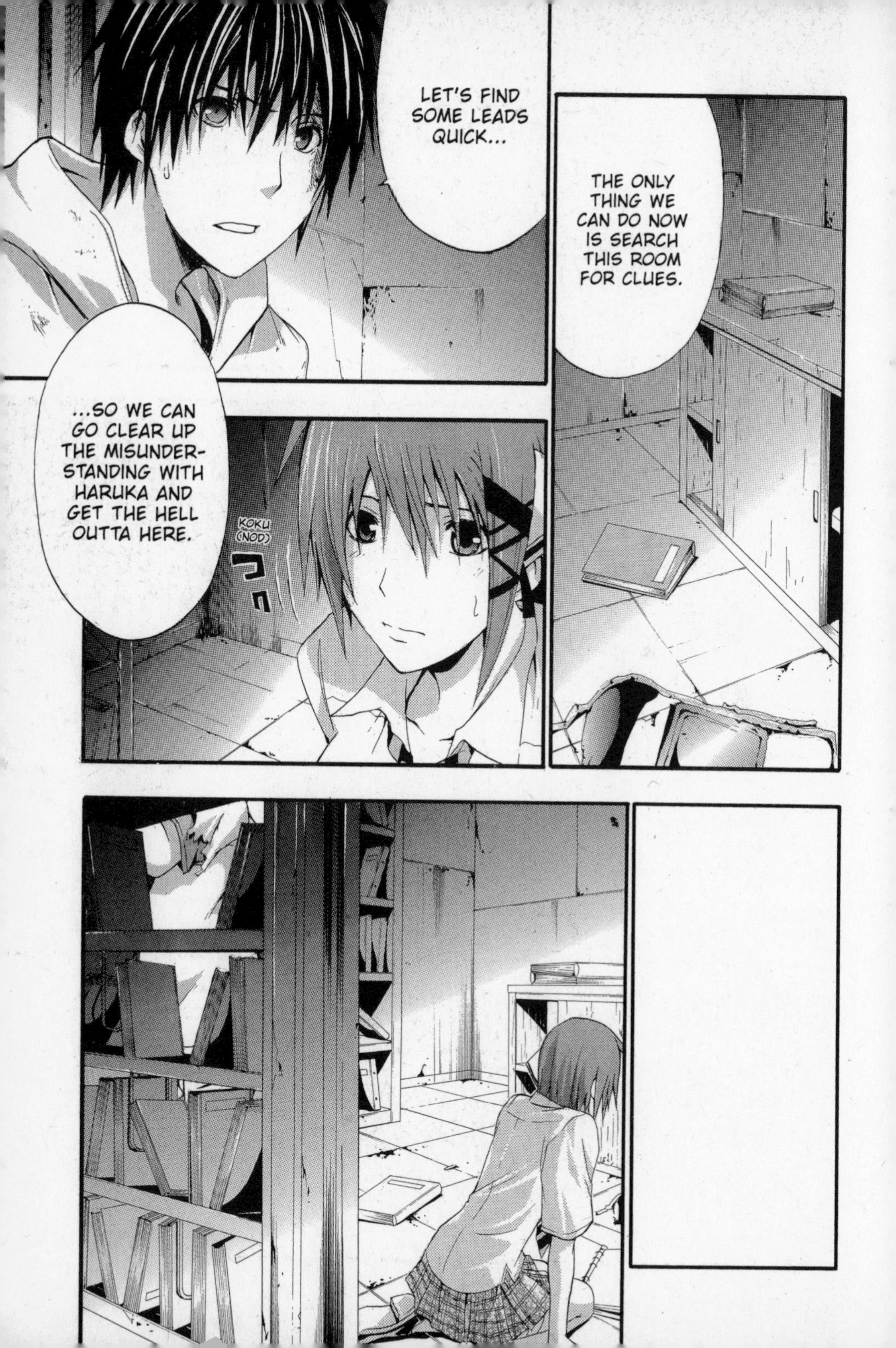
THE ONLY THING WE CAN DO NOW IS SEARCH THIS ROOM FOR CLUES.
LET'S FIND SOME LEADS QUICK...
...SO WE CAN GO CLEAR UP THE MISUNDER-STANDING WITH HARUKA AND GET THE HELL OUTTA HERE.
KOKU (NOD)

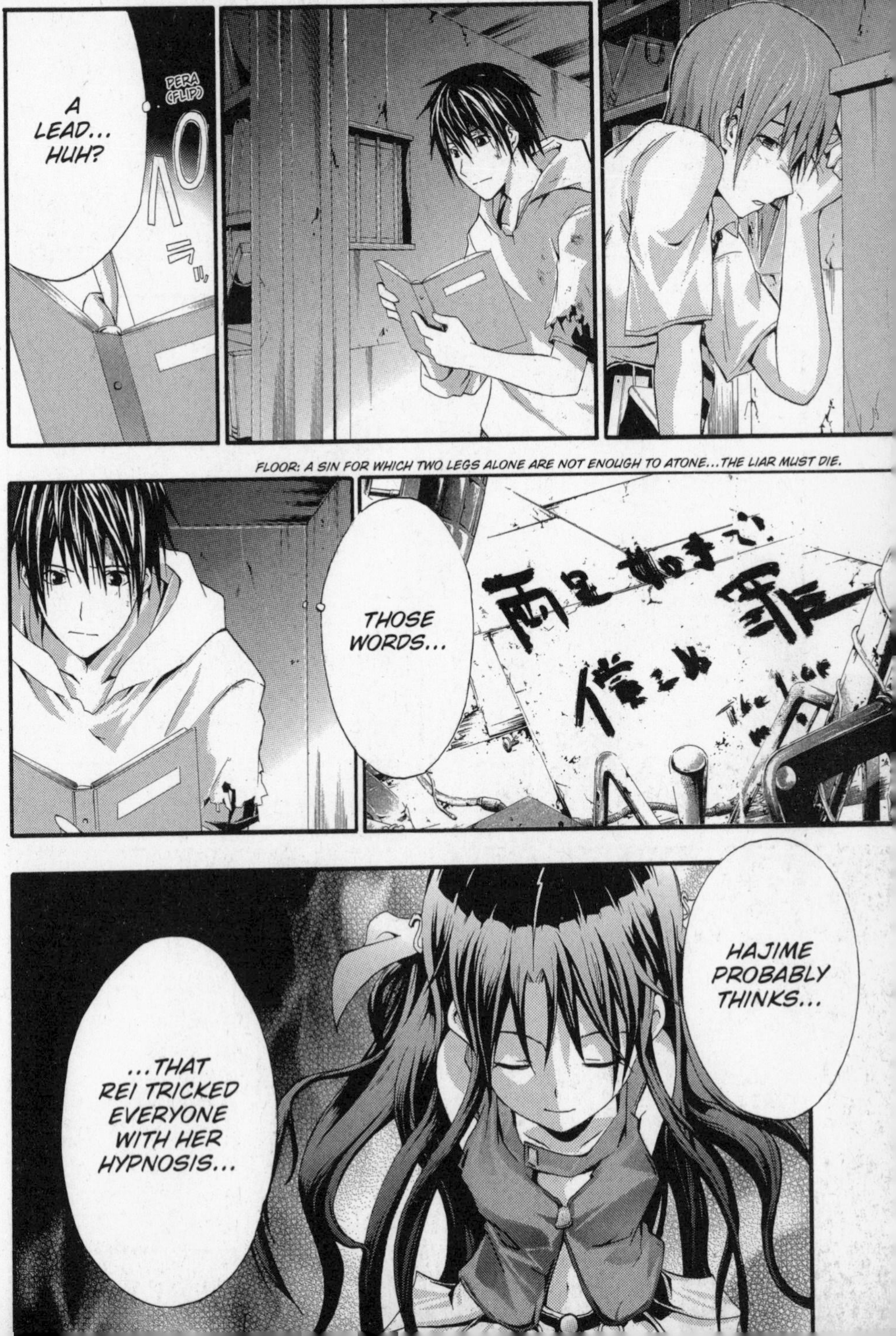
PERA (FLIP)
A LEAD... HUH?
FLOOR: A SIN FOR WHICH TWO LEGS ALONE ARE NOT ENOUGH TO ATONE...THE LIAR MUST DIE.
THOSE WORDS...
HAJIME PROBABLY THINKS...
...THAT REI TRICKED EVERYONE WITH HER HYPNOSIS...

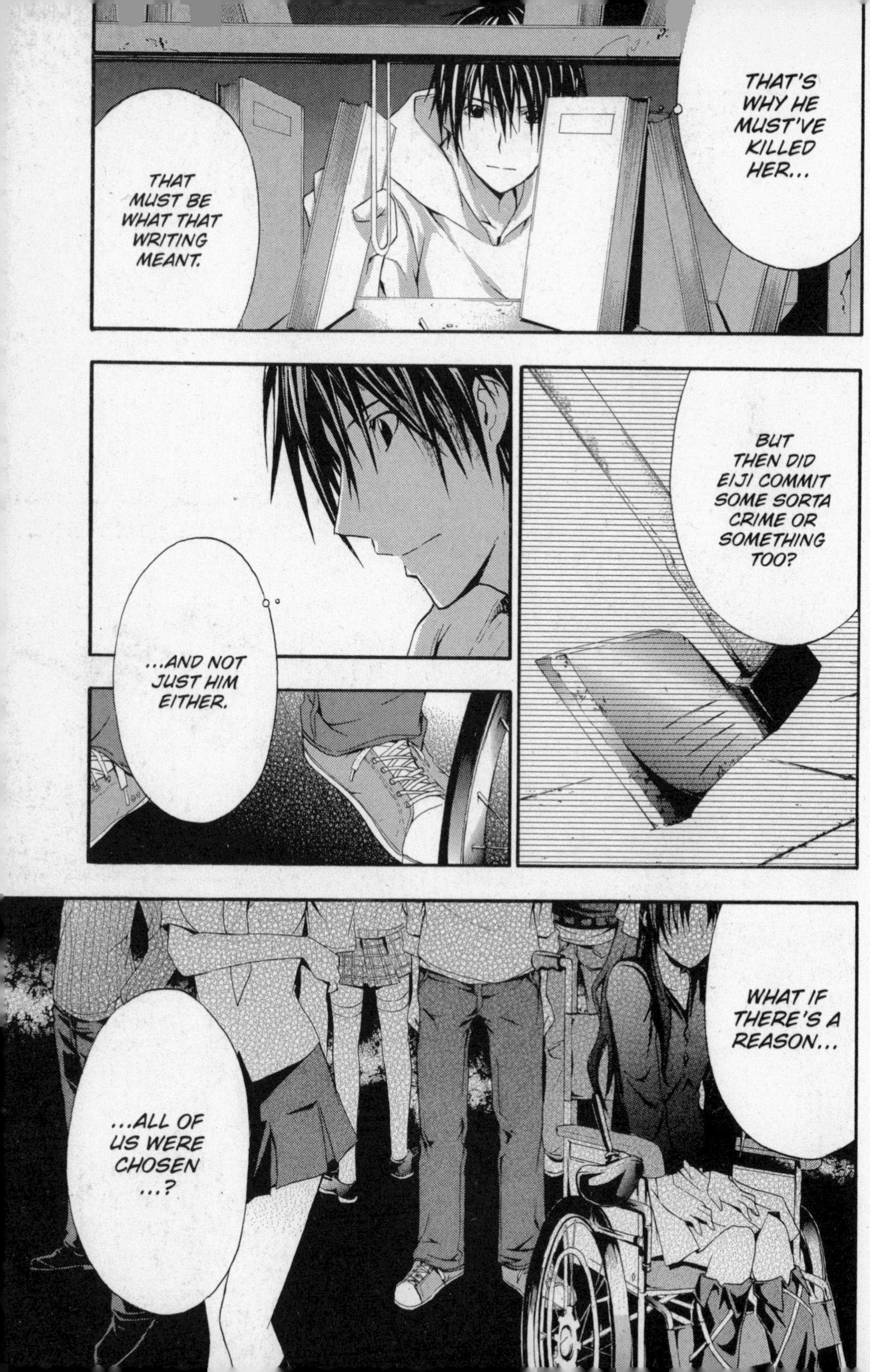
THAT'S WHY HE MUST'VE KILLED HER...
THAT MUST BE WHAT THAT WRITING MEANT.
BUT THEN DID EIJI COMMIT SOME SORTA CRIME OR SOMETHING TOO?
...AND NOT JUST HIM EITHER.
WHAT IF THERE'S A REASON...
...ALL OF US WERE CHOSEN ...?

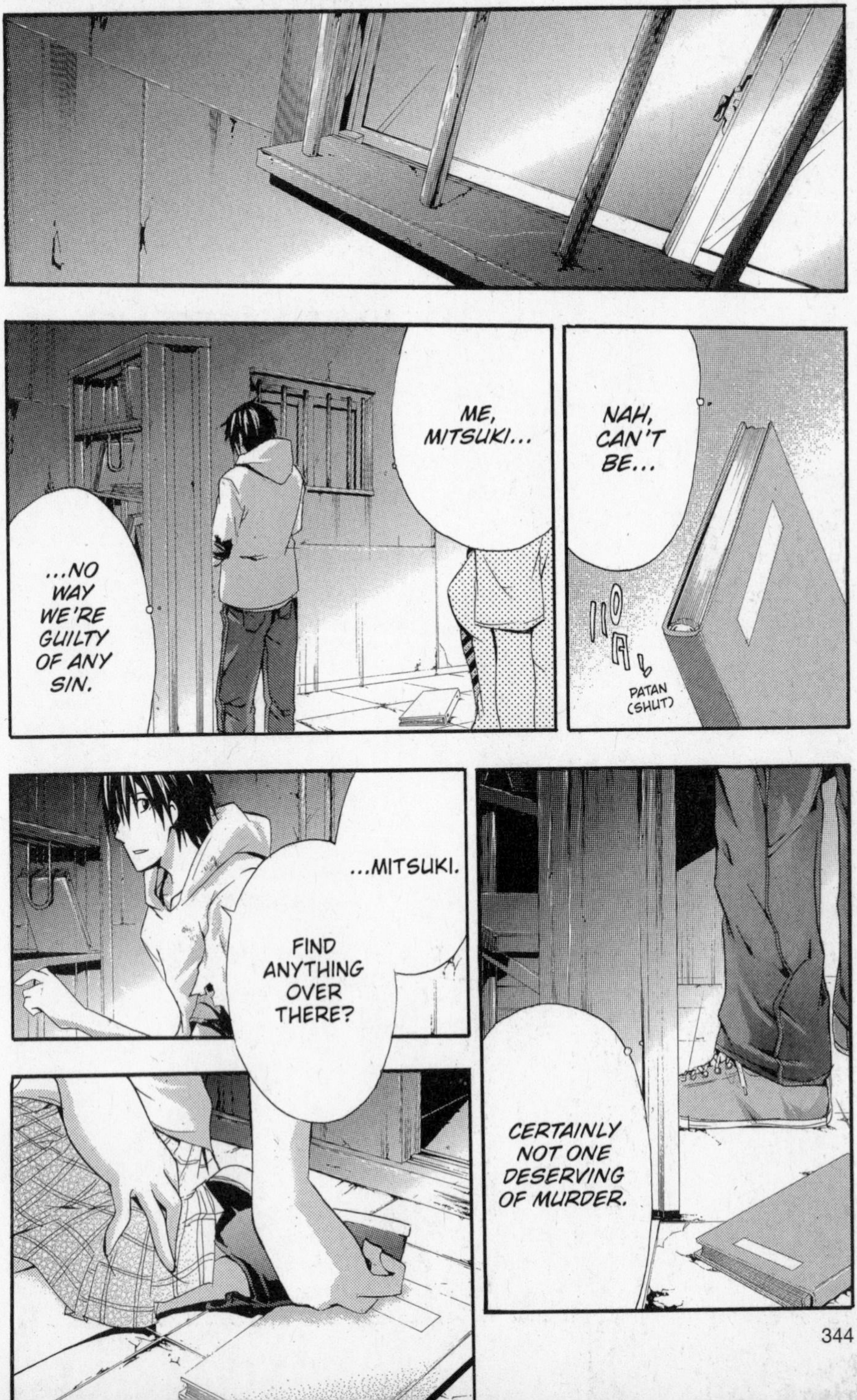
NAH, CAN'T BE...
PATAN (SHUT)
ME, MITSUKI...
...NO WAY WE'RE GUILTY OF ANY SIN.
CERTAINLY NOT ONE DESERVING OF MURDER.
...MITSUKI.
FIND ANYTHING OVER THERE?

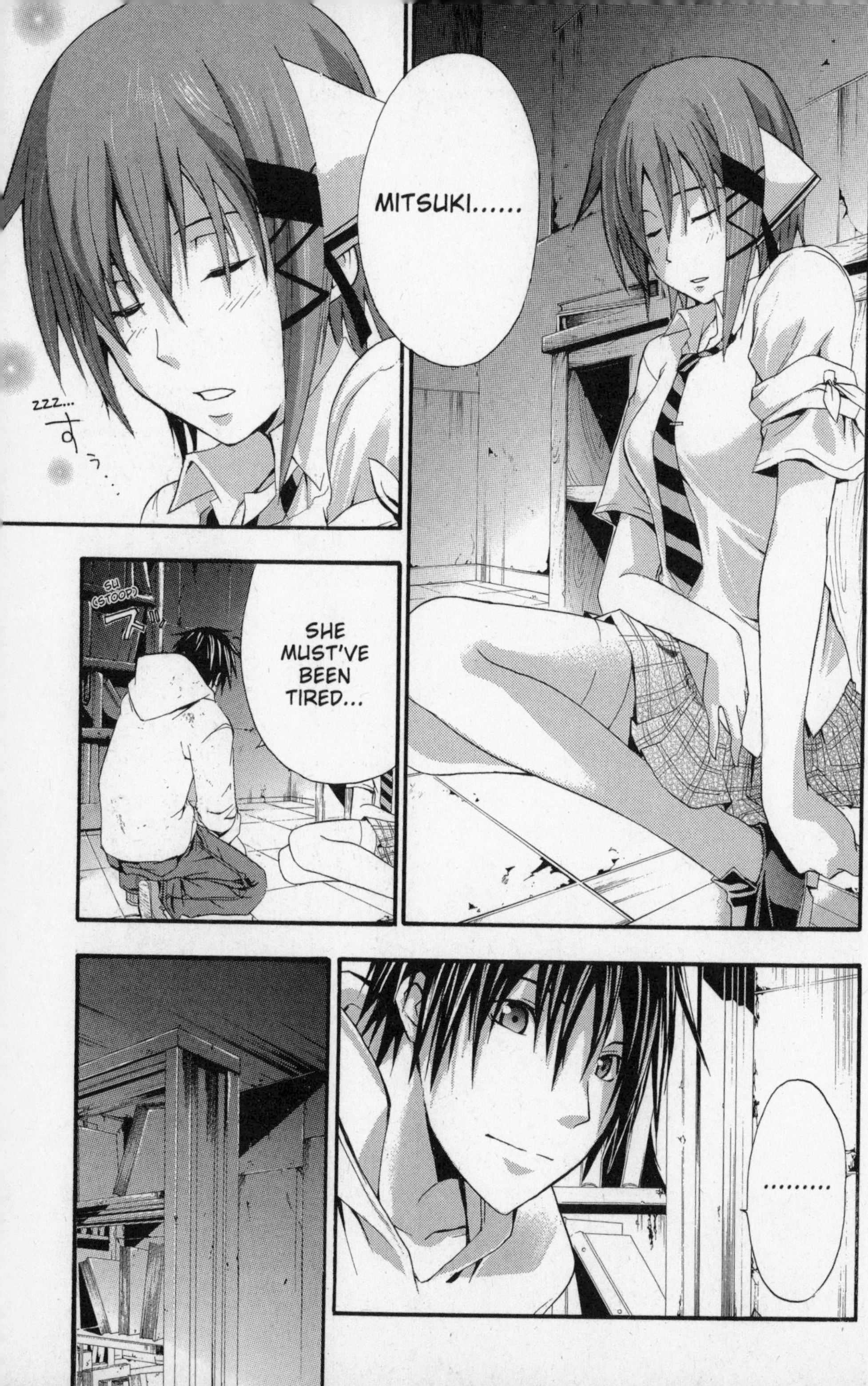
MITSUKI......
zzz...
すぅ...
SU (STOOP)
SHE MUST'VE BEEN TIRED...
....

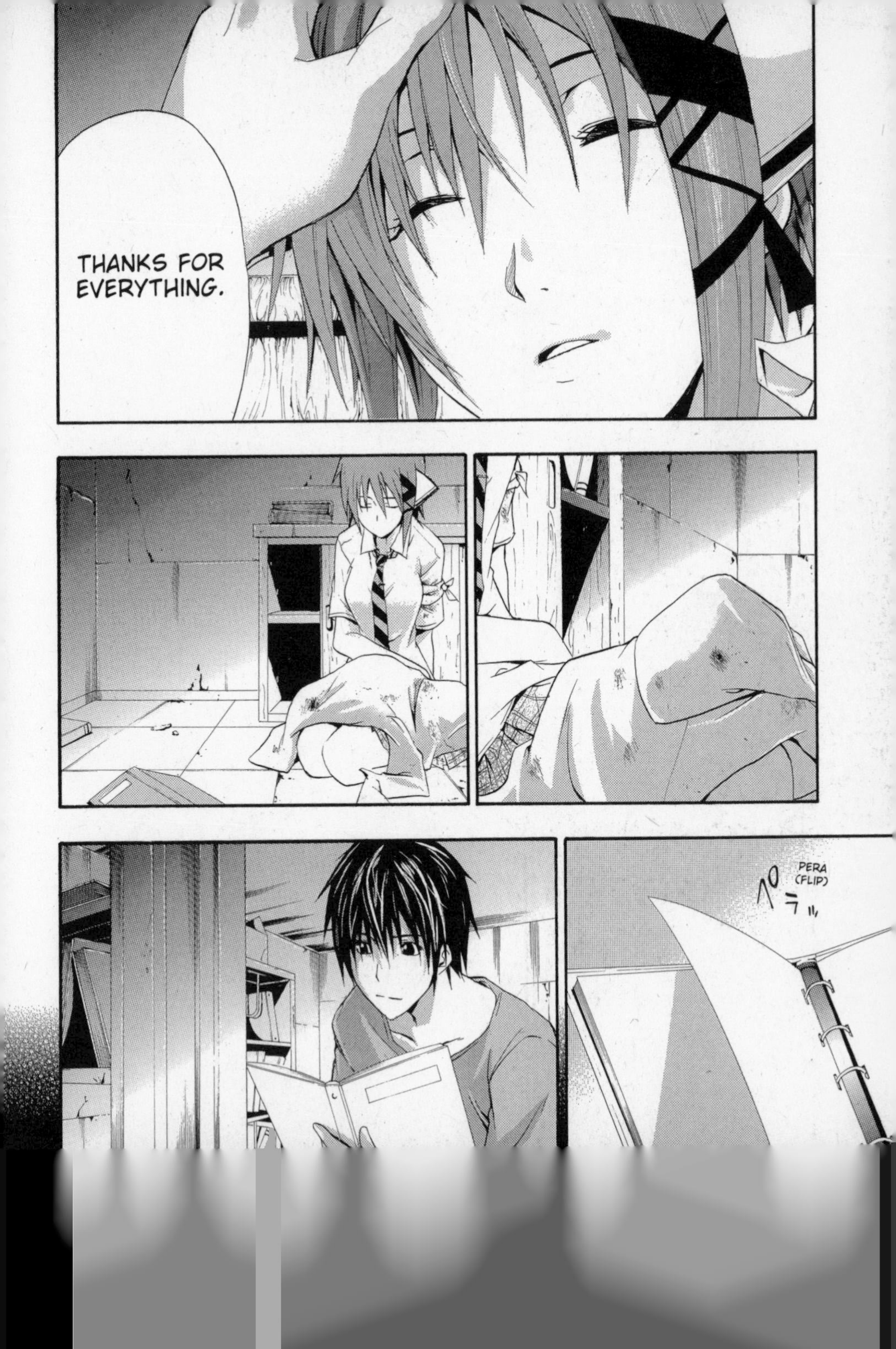
THANKS FOR EVERYTHING.
PERA (FLIP)

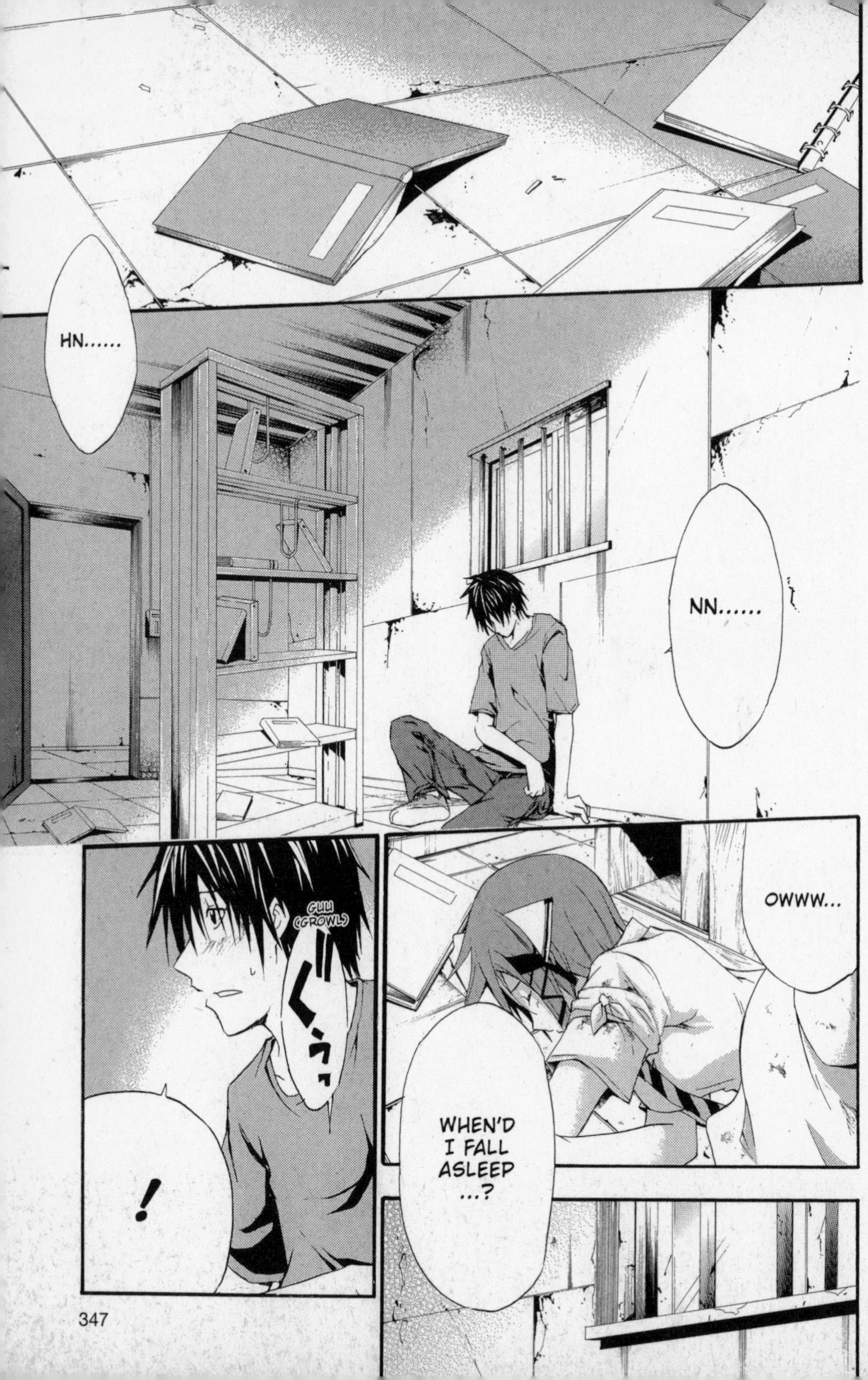
NN......
HN......
OWWW...
WHEN'D I FALL ASLEEP ...?
GUU (GROWL)
!

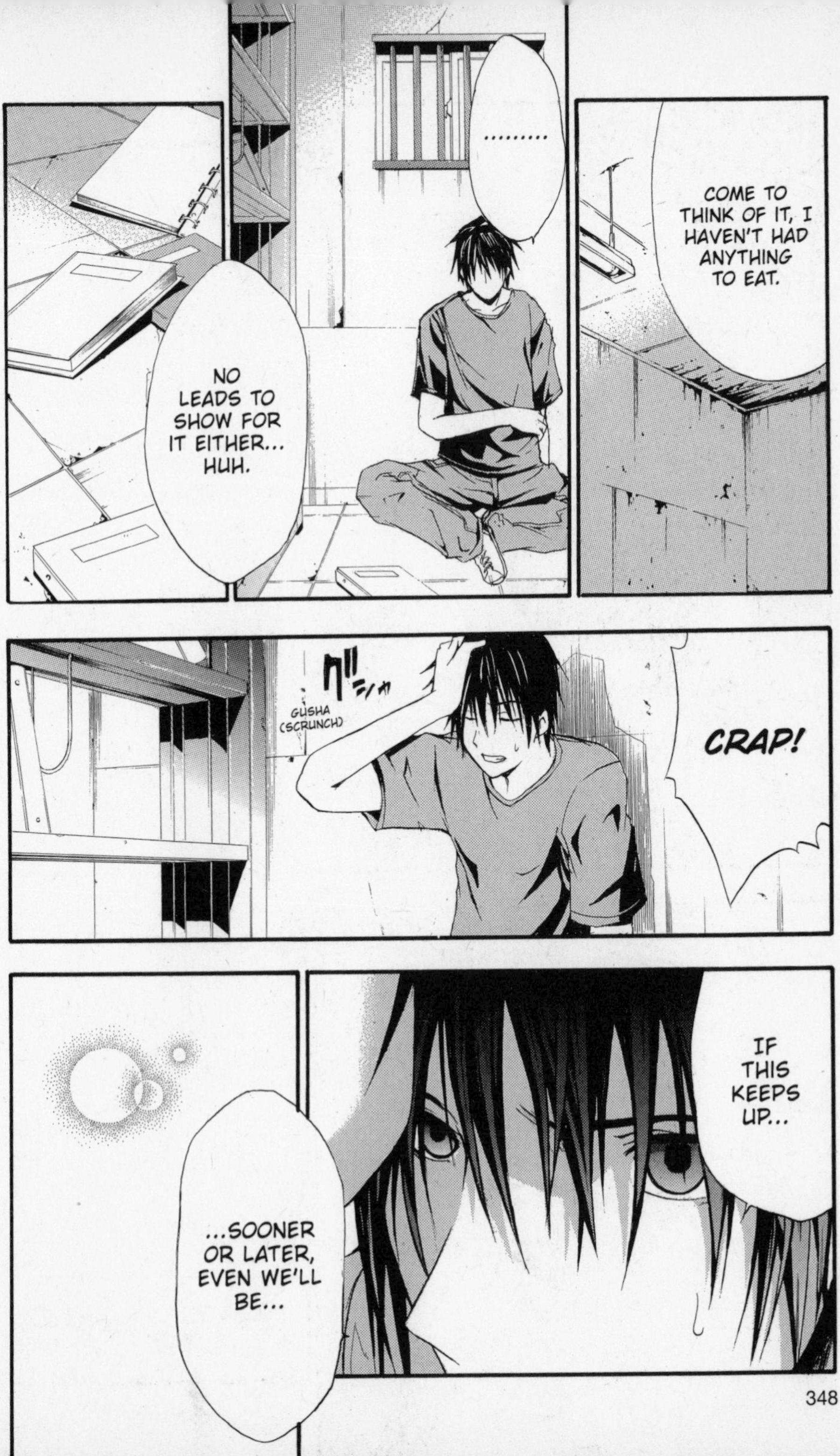

COME TO THINK OF IT, I HAVEN'T HAD ANYTHING TO EAT.
....
NO LEADS TO SHOW FOR IT EITHER... HUH.
CRAP!
グシャ
GUSHA (SCRUNCH)
IF THIS KEEPS UP...
...SOONER OR LATER, EVEN WE'LL BE...

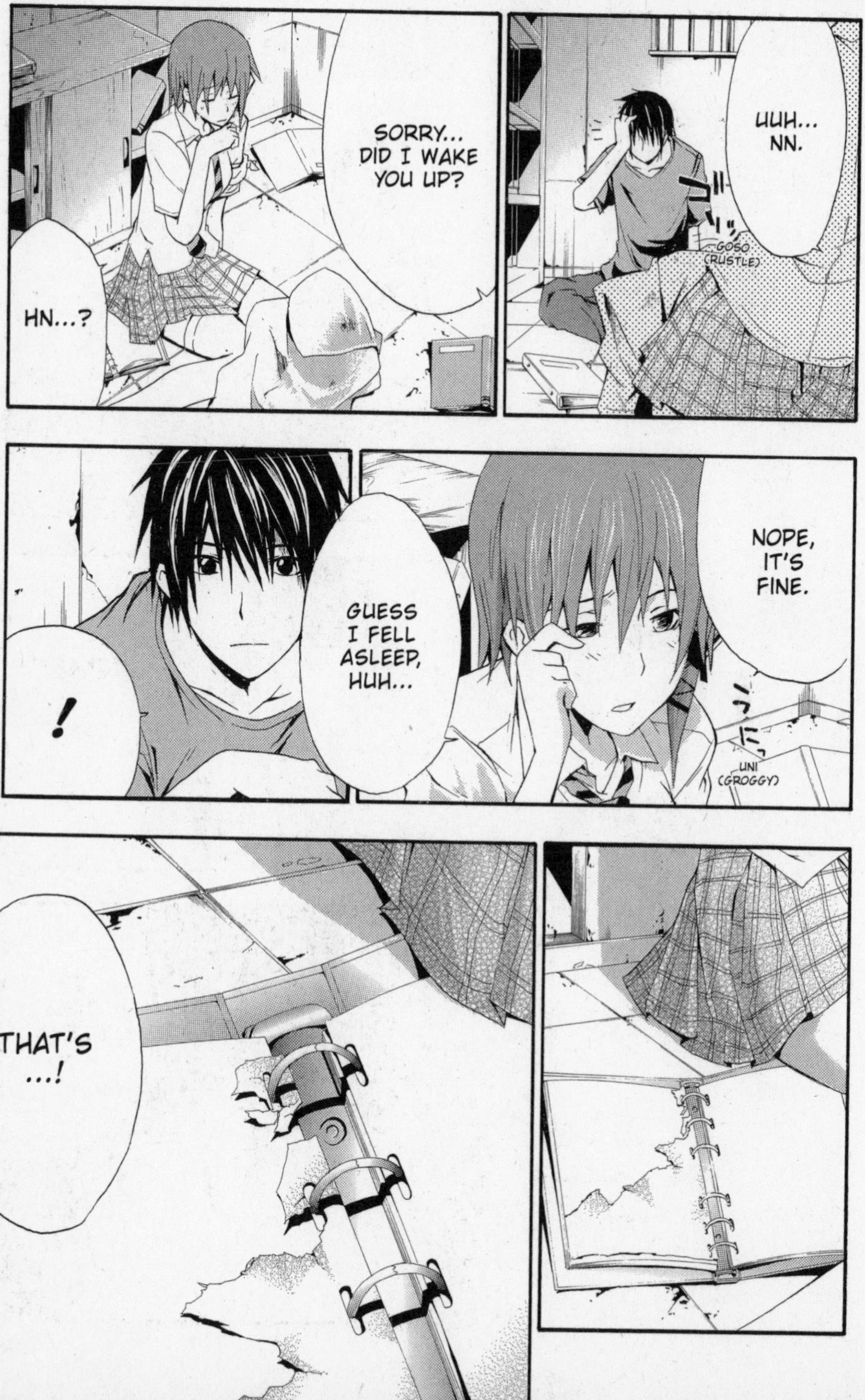
UUH... NN.
GOSO (RUSTLE)
SORRY... DID I WAKE YOU UP?
HN...?
NOPE, IT'S FINE.
UNI (GROGGY)
GUESS I FELL ASLEEP, HUH...
!
THAT'S ...!

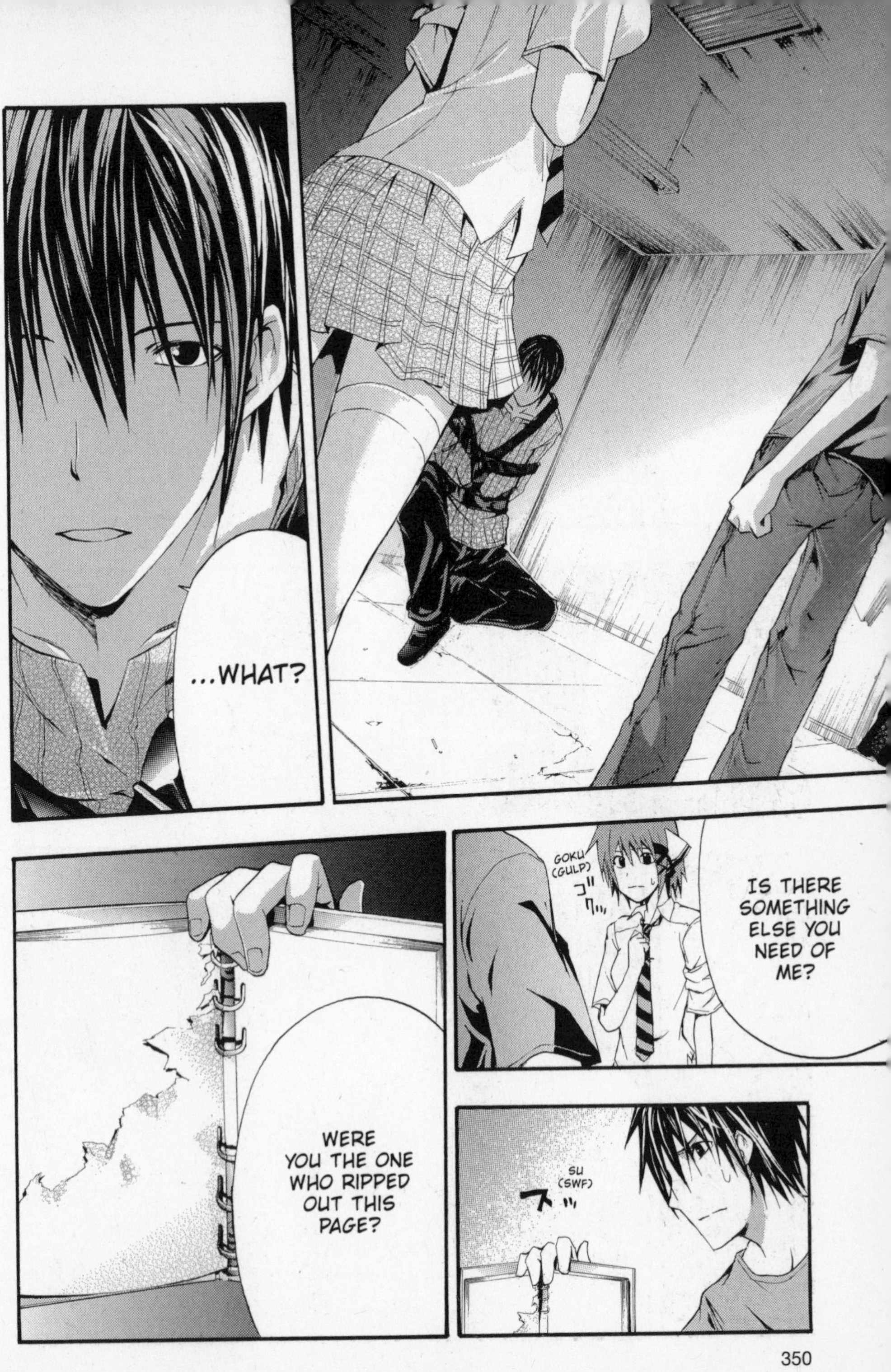
...WHAT?
GOKU (GULP)
IS THERE SOMETHING ELSE YOU NEED OF ME?
SU (SWF)
WERE YOU THE ONE WHO RIPPED OUT THIS PAGE?

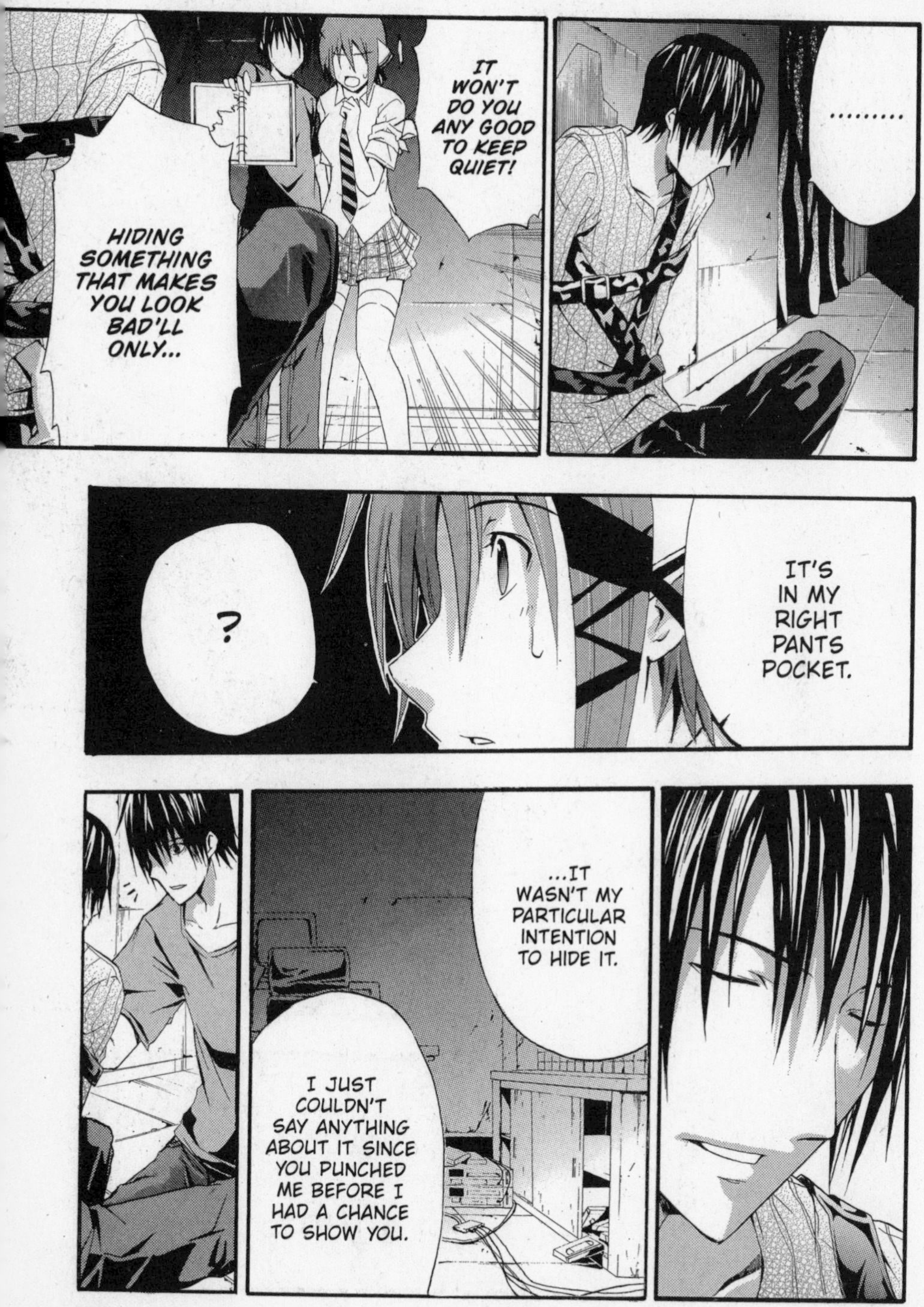
....
IT WON'T DO YOU ANY GOOD TO KEEP QUIET!
HIDING SOMETHING THAT MAKES YOU LOOK BAD'LL ONLY...
IT'S IN MY RIGHT PANTS POCKET.
?
...IT WASN'T MY PARTICULAR INTENTION TO HIDE IT.
I JUST COULDN'T SAY ANYTHING ABOUT IT SINCE YOU PUNCHED ME BEFORE I HAD A CHANCE TO SHOW YOU.

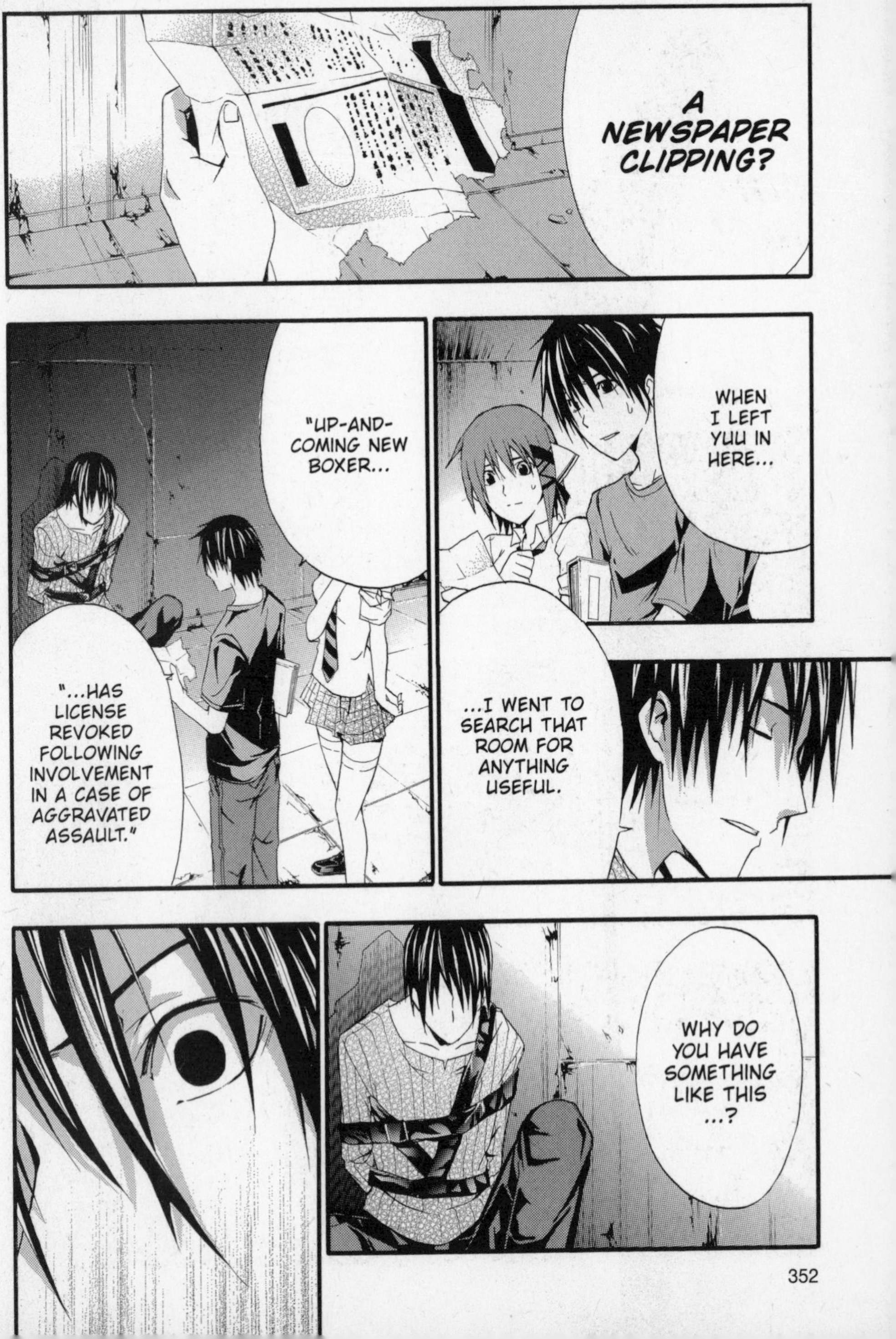
A NEWSPAPER CLIPPING?
WHEN I LEFT YUU IN HERE...
...I WENT TO SEARCH THAT ROOM FOR ANYTHING USEFUL.
"UP-AND-COMING NEW BOXER...
"...HAS LICENSE REVOKED FOLLOWING INVOLVEMENT IN A CASE OF AGGRAVATED ASSAULT."
WHY DO YOU HAVE SOMETHING LIKE THIS ...?

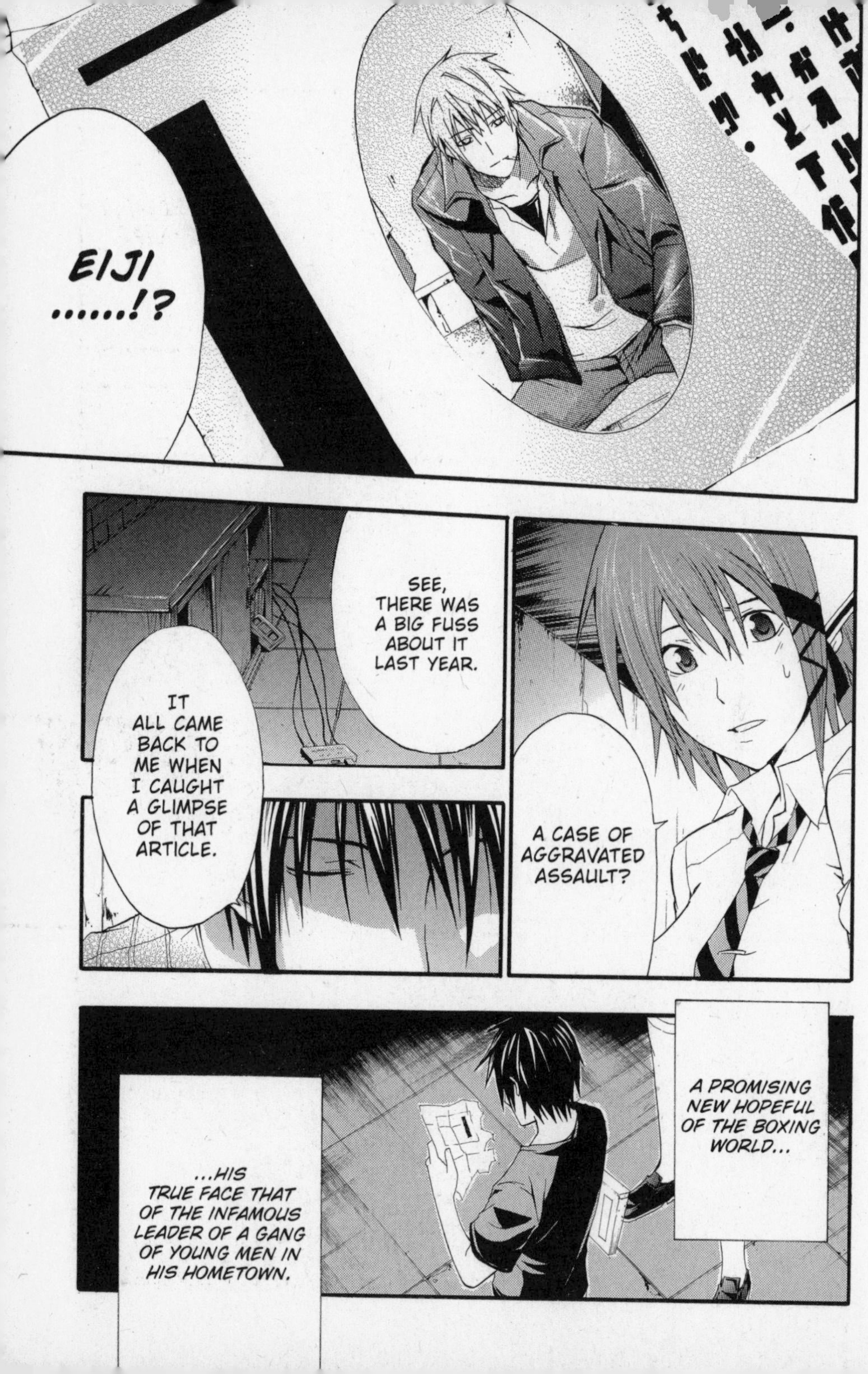
EIJI ......!?
A CASE OF AGGRAVATED ASSAULT?
SEE, THERE WAS A BIG FUSS ABOUT IT LAST YEAR.
IT ALL CAME BACK TO ME WHEN I CAUGHT A GLIMPSE OF THAT ARTICLE.
A PROMISING NEW HOPEFUL OF THE BOXING WORLD...
...HIS TRUE FACE THAT OF THE INFAMOUS LEADER OF A GANG OF YOUNG MEN IN HIS HOMETOWN.

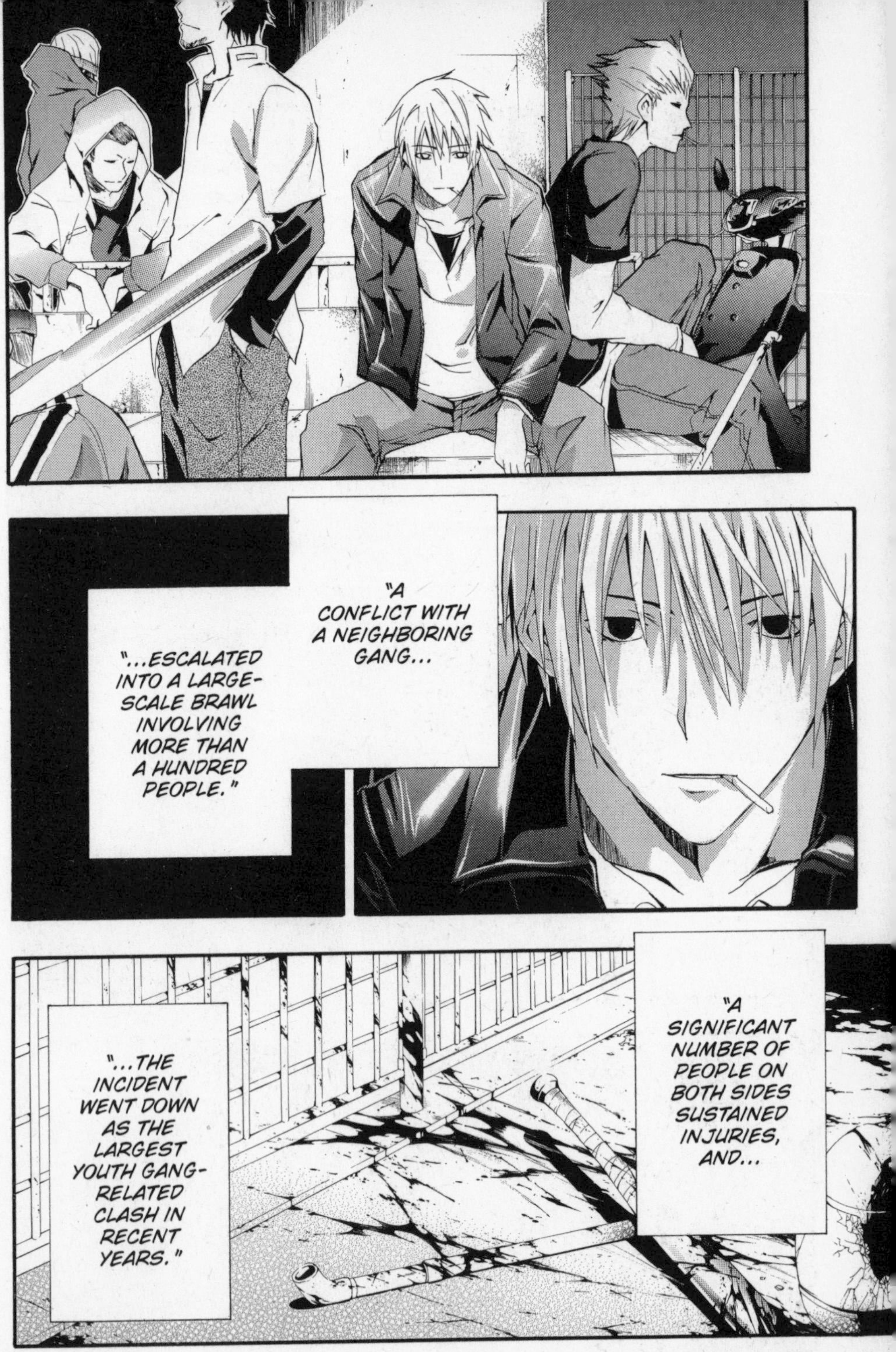
"A CONFLICT WITH A NEIGHBORING GANG...
"...ESCALATED INTO A LARGE-SCALE BRAWL INVOLVING MORE THAN A HUNDRED PEOPLE."
"A SIGNIFICANT NUMBER OF PEOPLE ON BOTH SIDES SUSTAINED INJURIES, AND...
"...THE INCIDENT WENT DOWN AS THE LARGEST YOUTH GANG-RELATED CLASH IN RECENT YEARS."

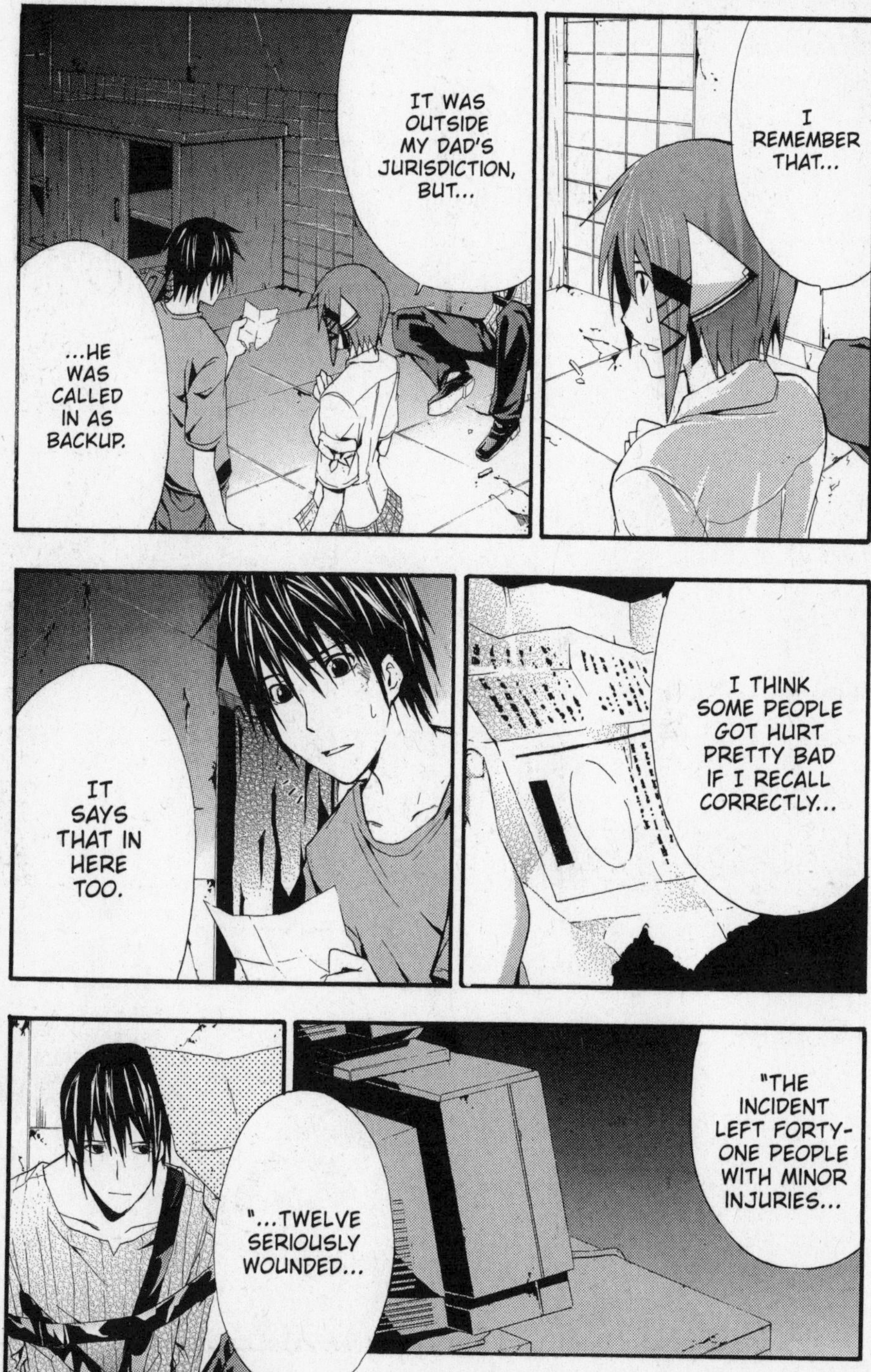
I REMEMBER THAT...
IT WAS OUTSIDE MY DAD'S JURISDICTION, BUT...
...HE WAS CALLED IN AS BACKUP.
I THINK SOME PEOPLE GOT HURT PRETTY BAD IF I RECALL CORRECTLY...
IT SAYS THAT IN HERE TOO.
"THE INCIDENT LEFT FORTY-ONE PEOPLE WITH MINOR INJURIES...
"...TWELVE SERIOUSLY WOUNDED...

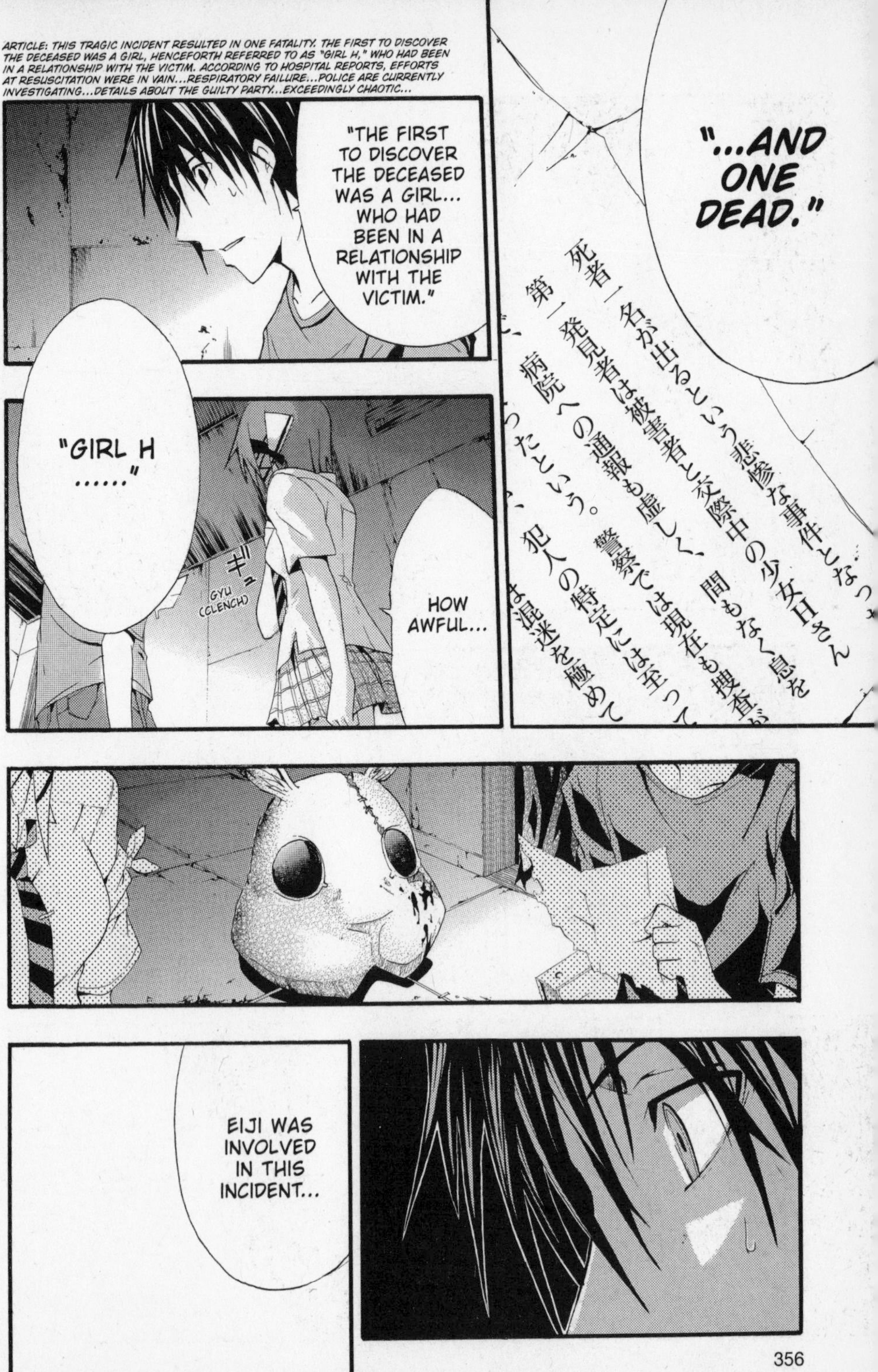
"...AND ONE DEAD."
死者一名が出るという悲惨な事件となっ
第一発見者は被害者と交際中の少女Hさん
病院への通報も虚しく、間もなく息を
ったという。警察では現在も捜査が
犯人の特定には至って
は混迷を極めて
ARTICLE: THIS TRAGIC INCIDENT RESULTED IN ONE FATALITY. THE FIRST TO DISCOVER THE DECEASED WAS A GIRL, HENCEFORTH REFERRED TO AS "GIRL H," WHO HAD BEEN IN A RELATIONSHIP WITH THE VICTIM. ACCORDING TO HOSPITAL REPORTS, EFFORTS AT RESUSCITATION WERE IN VAIN... RESPIRATORY FAILURE... POLICE ARE CURRENTLY INVESTIGATING... DETAILS ABOUT THE GUILTY PARTY... EXCEEDINGLY CHAOTIC...
"THE FIRST TO DISCOVER THE DECEASED WAS A GIRL... WHO HAD BEEN IN A RELATIONSHIP WITH THE VICTIM."
HOW AWFUL...
ギュ
GYU (CLENCH)
"GIRL H ......"
EIJI WAS INVOLVED IN THIS INCIDENT...

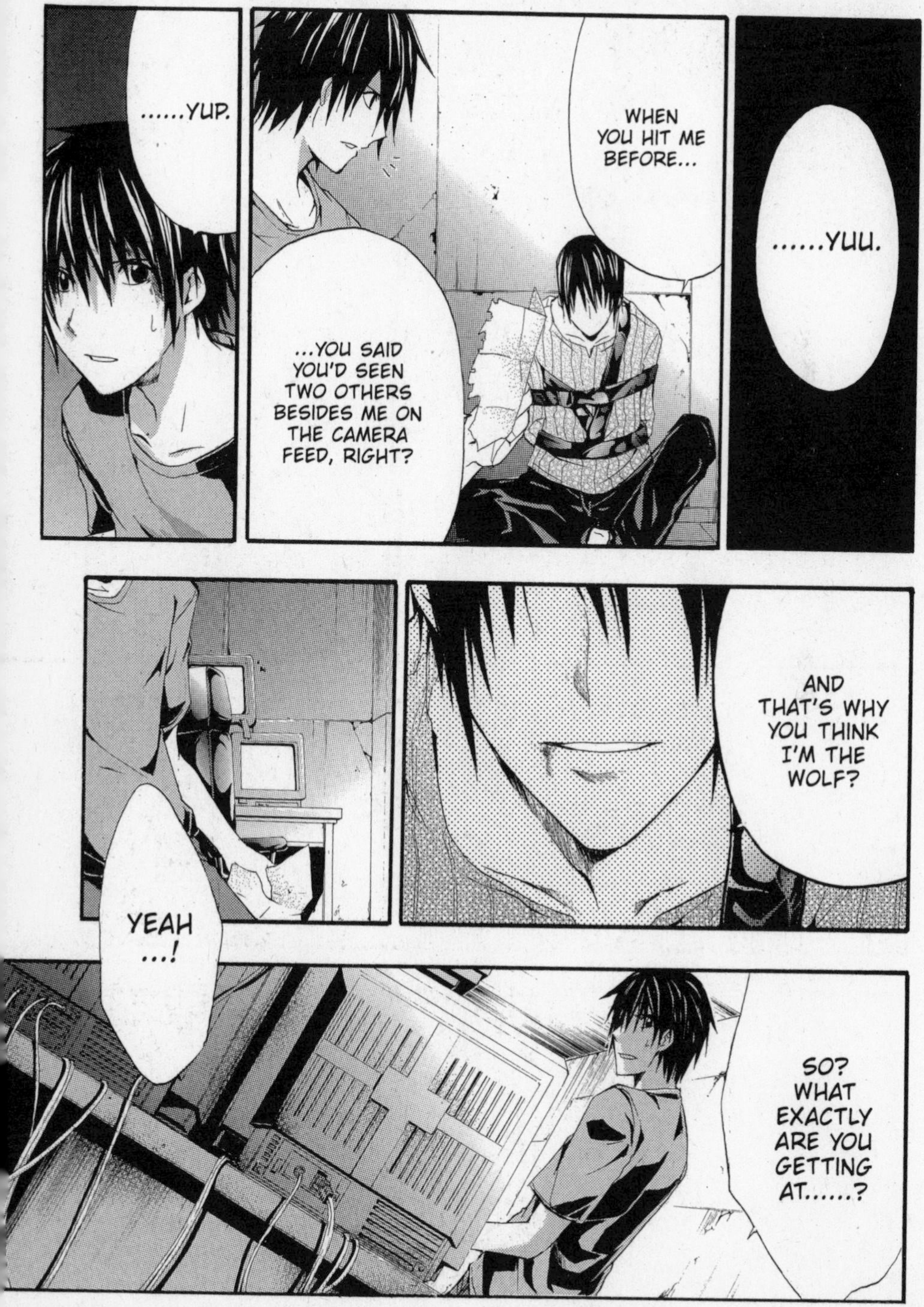
......YUU.
WHEN YOU HIT ME BEFORE...
...YOU SAID YOU'D SEEN TWO OTHERS BESIDES ME ON THE CAMERA FEED, RIGHT?
......YUP.
AND THAT'S WHY YOU THINK I'M THE WOLF?
YEAH ...!
SO? WHAT EXACTLY ARE YOU GETTING AT......?

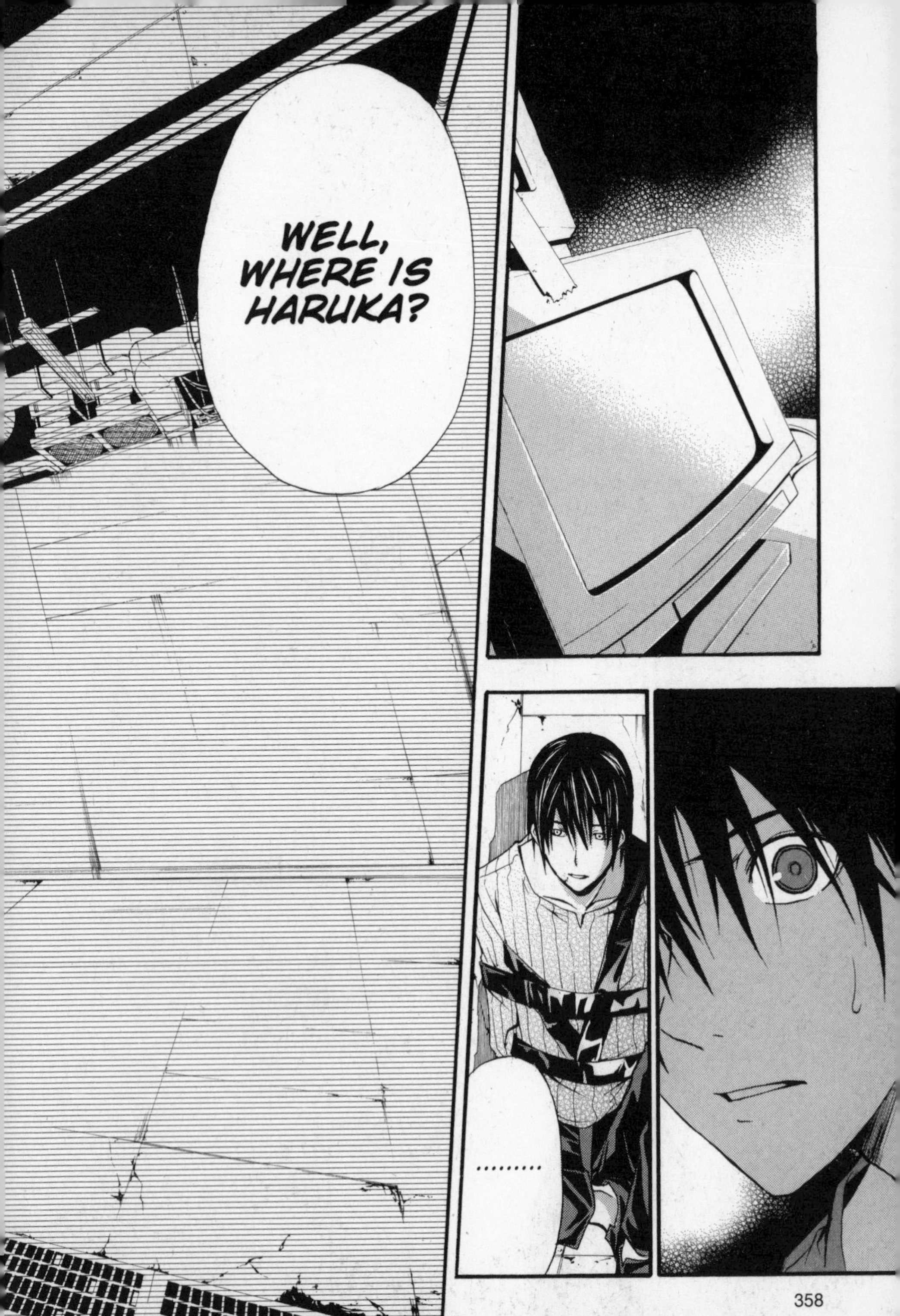
....
WELL, WHERE IS HARUKA?

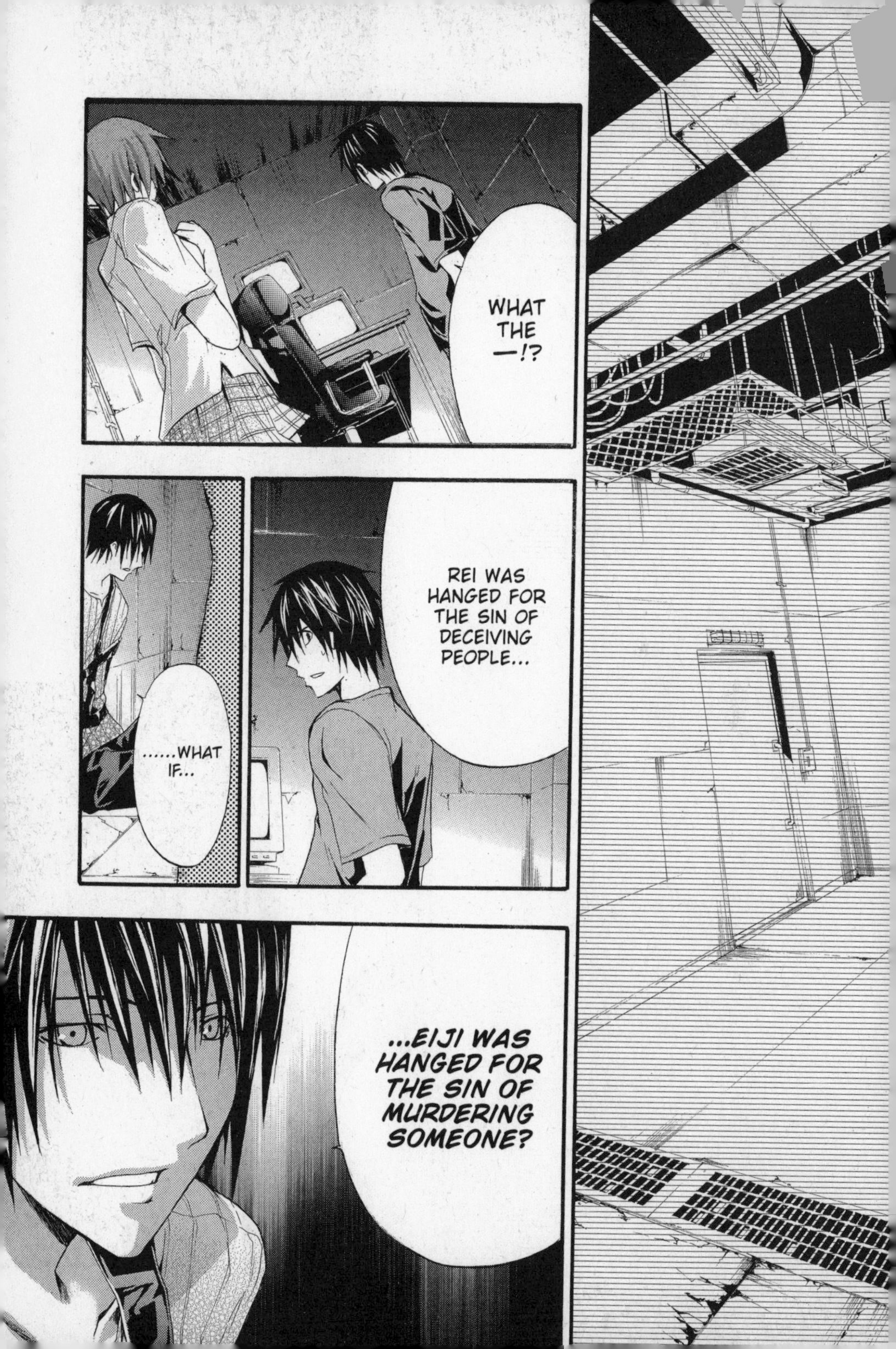
WHAT THE —!?
REI WAS HANGED FOR THE SIN OF DECEIVING PEOPLE...
......WHAT IF...
...EIJI WAS HANGED FOR THE SIN OF MURDERING SOMEONE?

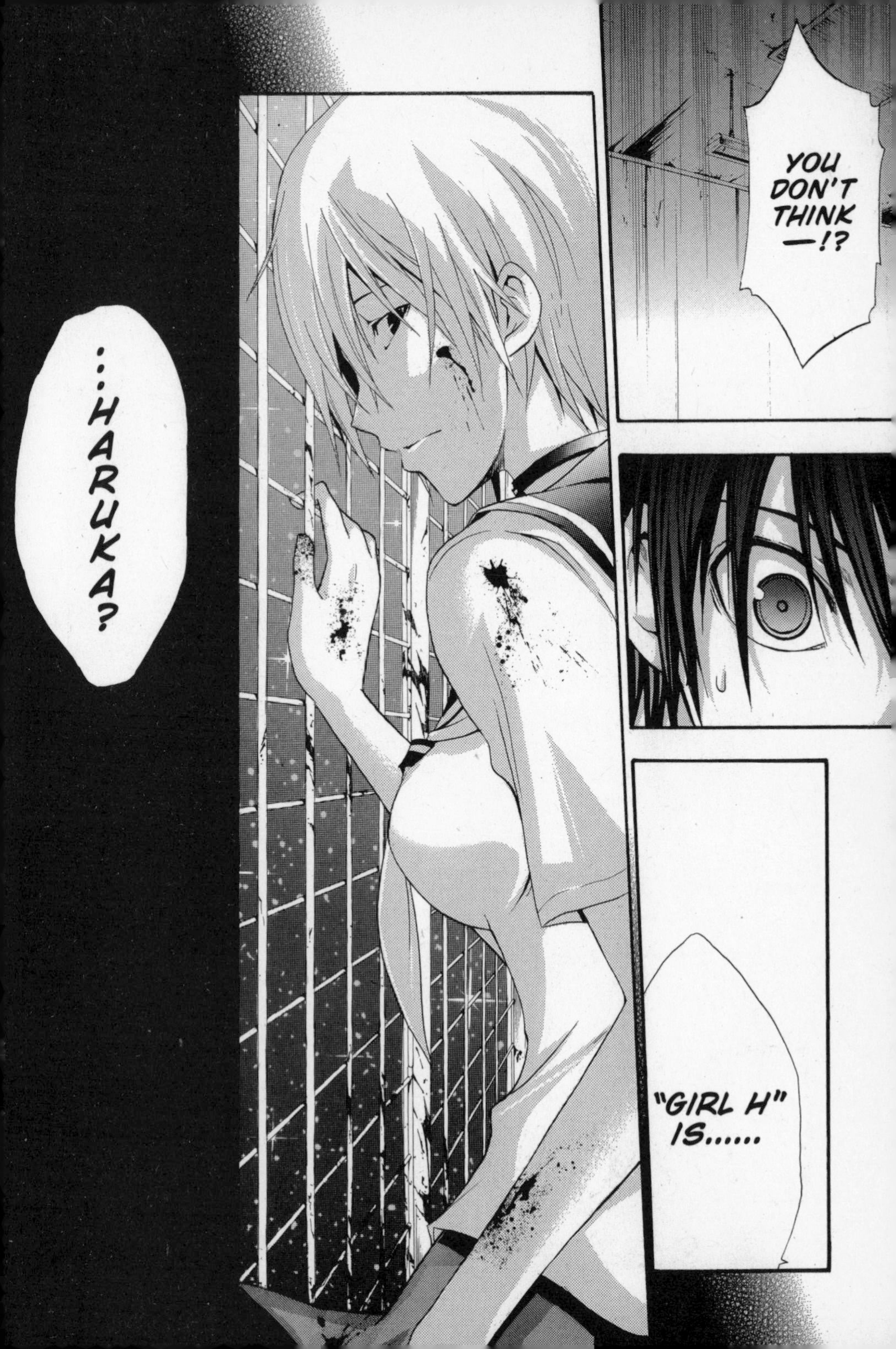
YOU DON'T THINK—!?
"GIRL H" IS......
..HARUKA?

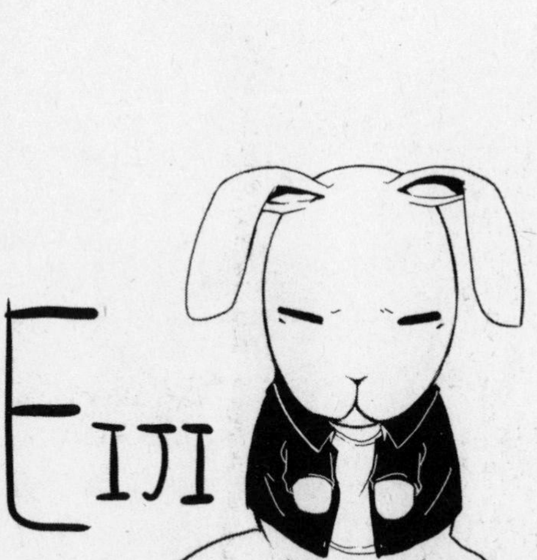
EIJI

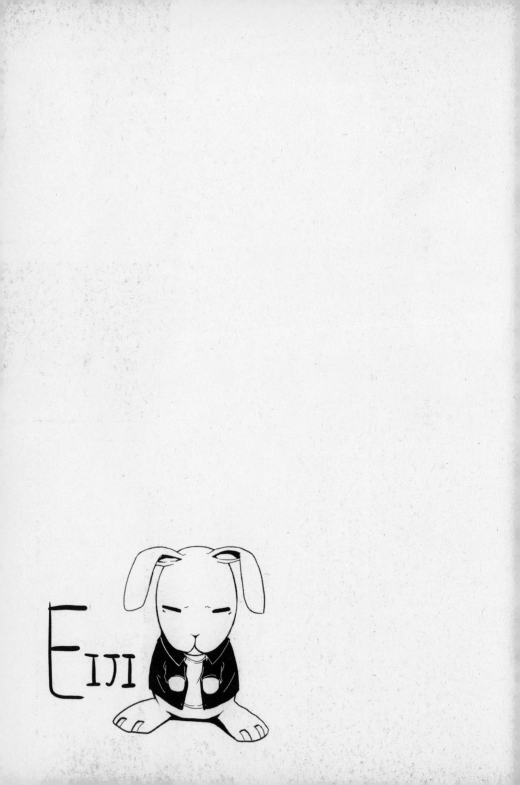

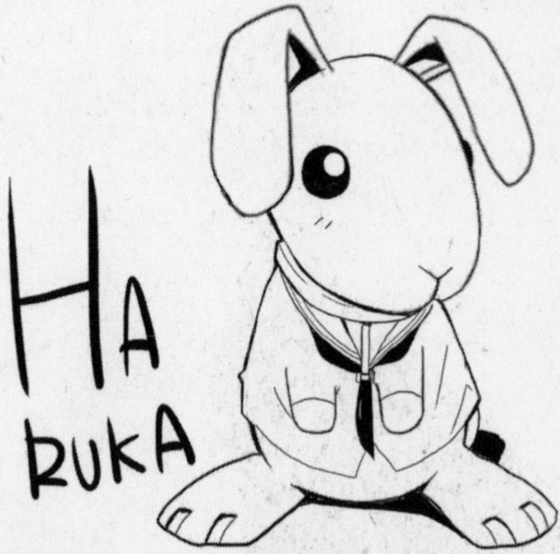
HA
RUKA

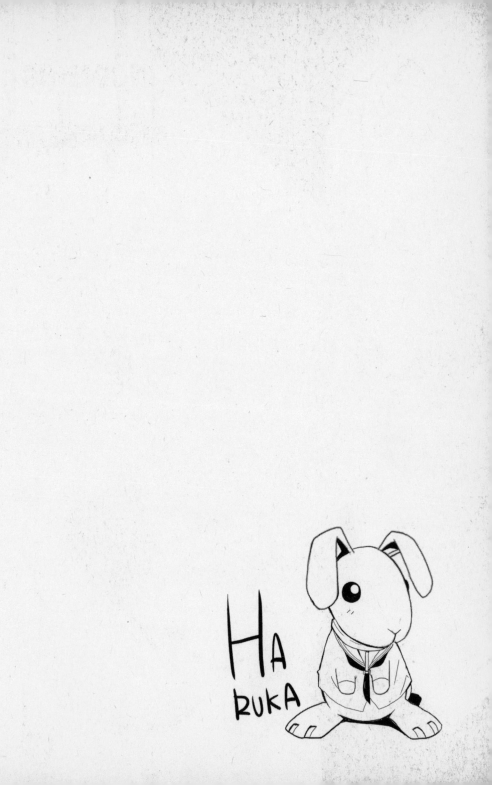

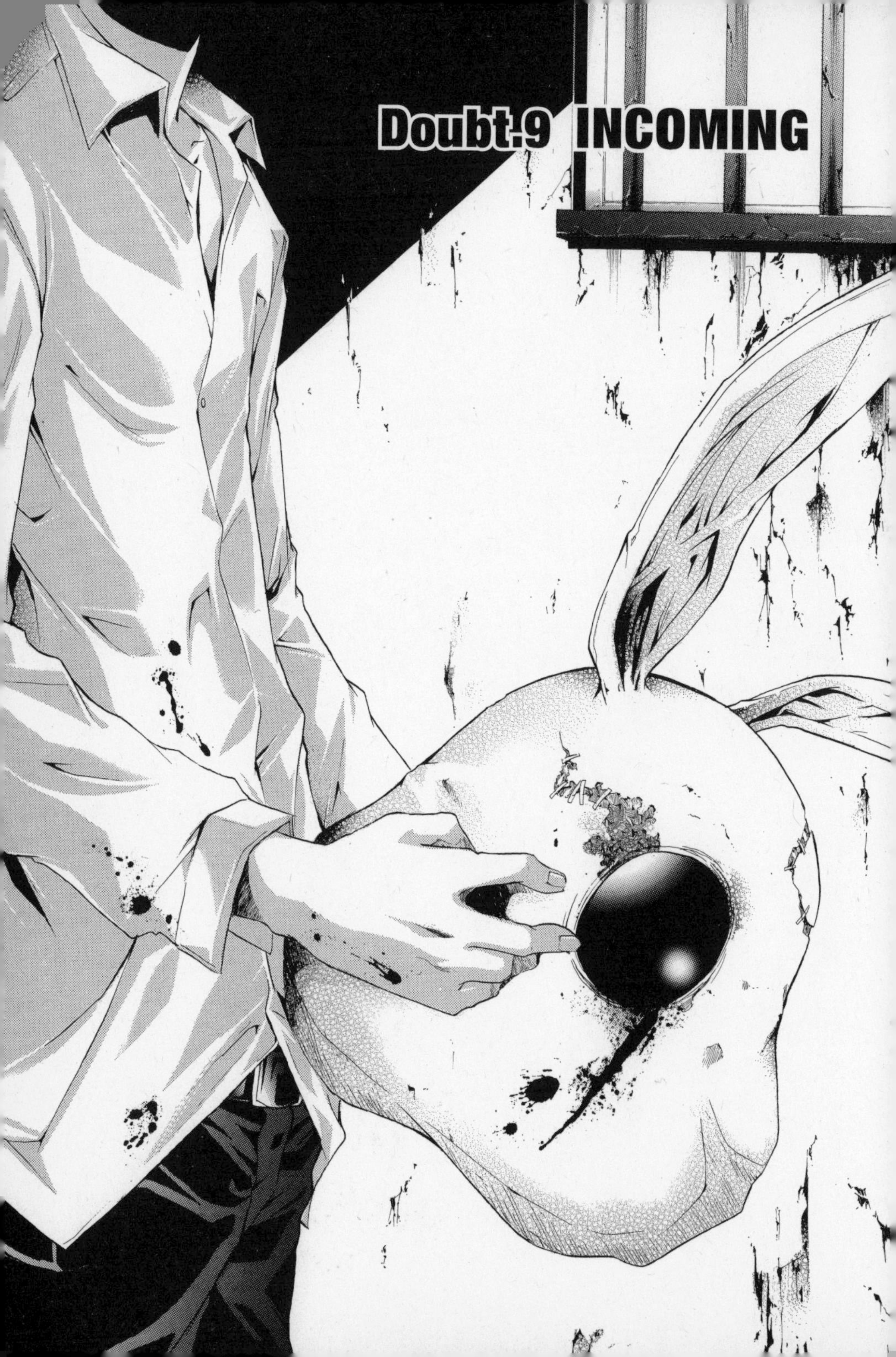
Doubt.9 INCOMING

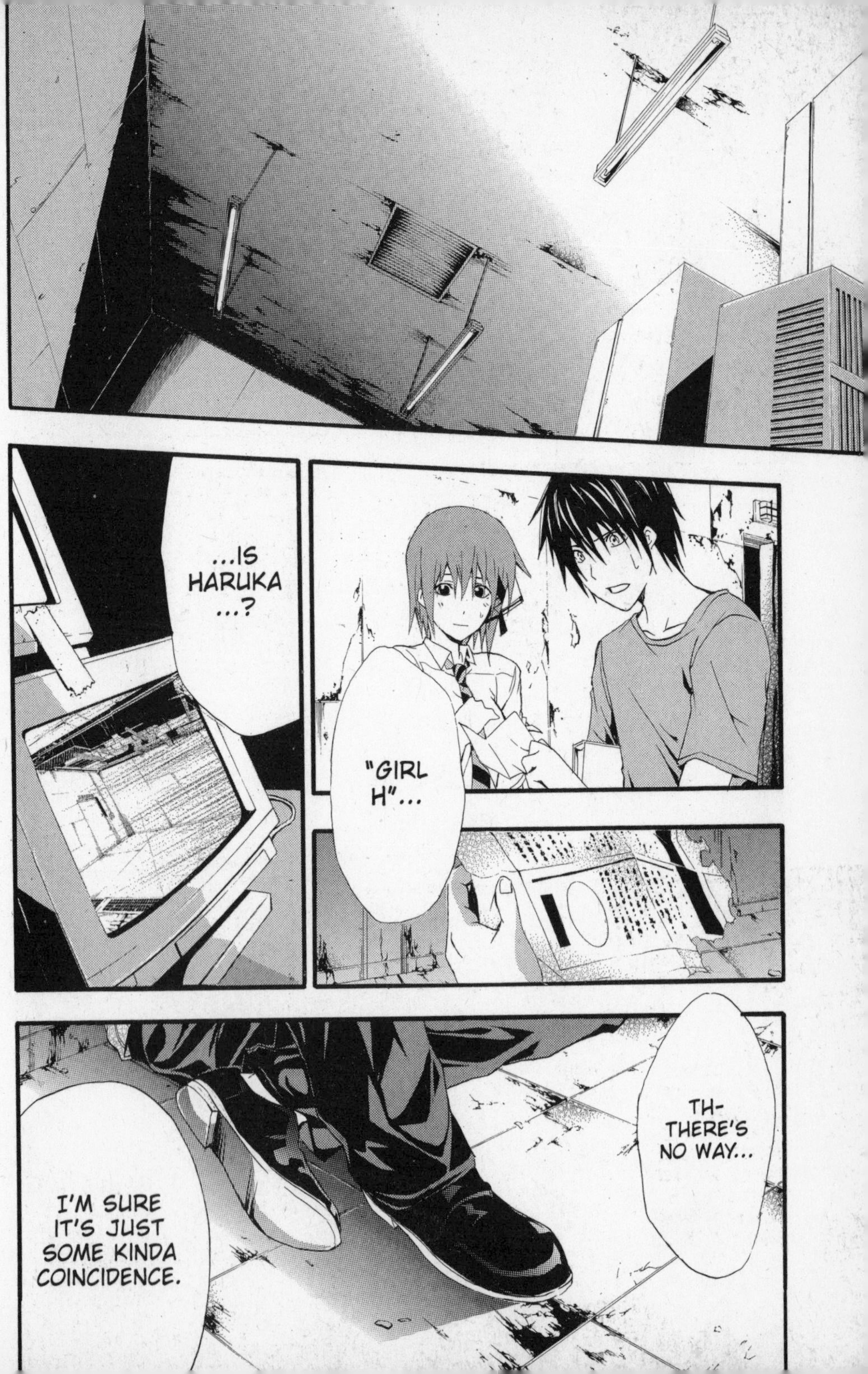
"GIRL H"...
...IS HARUKA ...?
TH- THERE'S NO WAY...
I'M SURE IT'S JUST SOME KINDA COINCIDENCE.

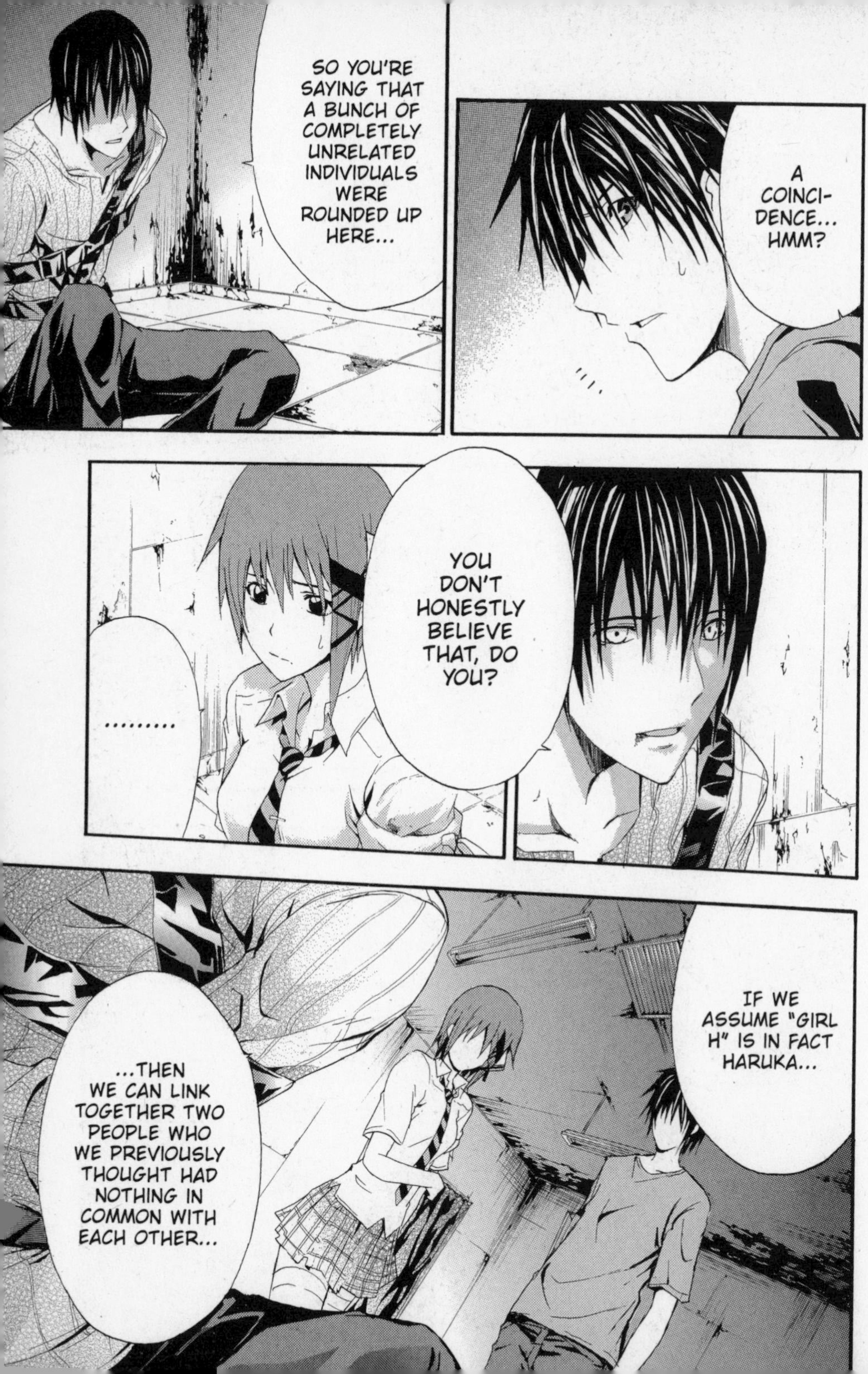
A COINCI-DENCE... HMM?
SO YOU'RE SAYING THAT A BUNCH OF COMPLETELY UNRELATED INDIVIDUALS WERE ROUNDED UP HERE...
YOU DON'T HONESTLY BELIEVE THAT, DO YOU?
....
IF WE ASSUME "GIRL H" IS IN FACT HARUKA...
...THEN WE CAN LINK TOGETHER TWO PEOPLE WHO WE PREVIOUSLY THOUGHT HAD NOTHING IN COMMON WITH EACH OTHER...

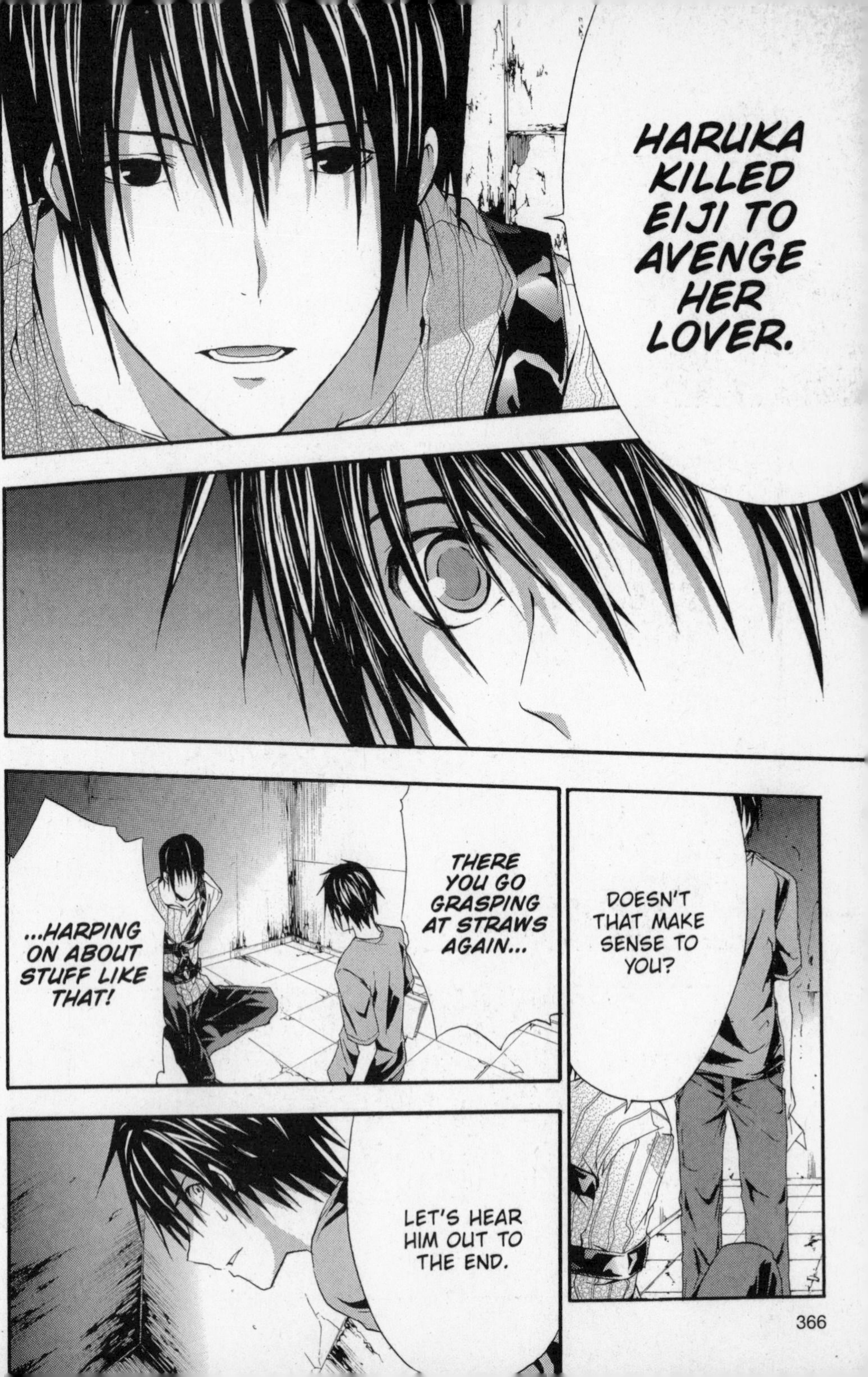
HARUKA KILLED EIJI TO AVENGE HER LOVER.
DOESN'T THAT MAKE SENSE TO YOU?
THERE YOU GO GRASPING AT STRAWS AGAIN...
...HARPING ON ABOUT STUFF LIKE THAT!
LET'S HEAR HIM OUT TO THE END.

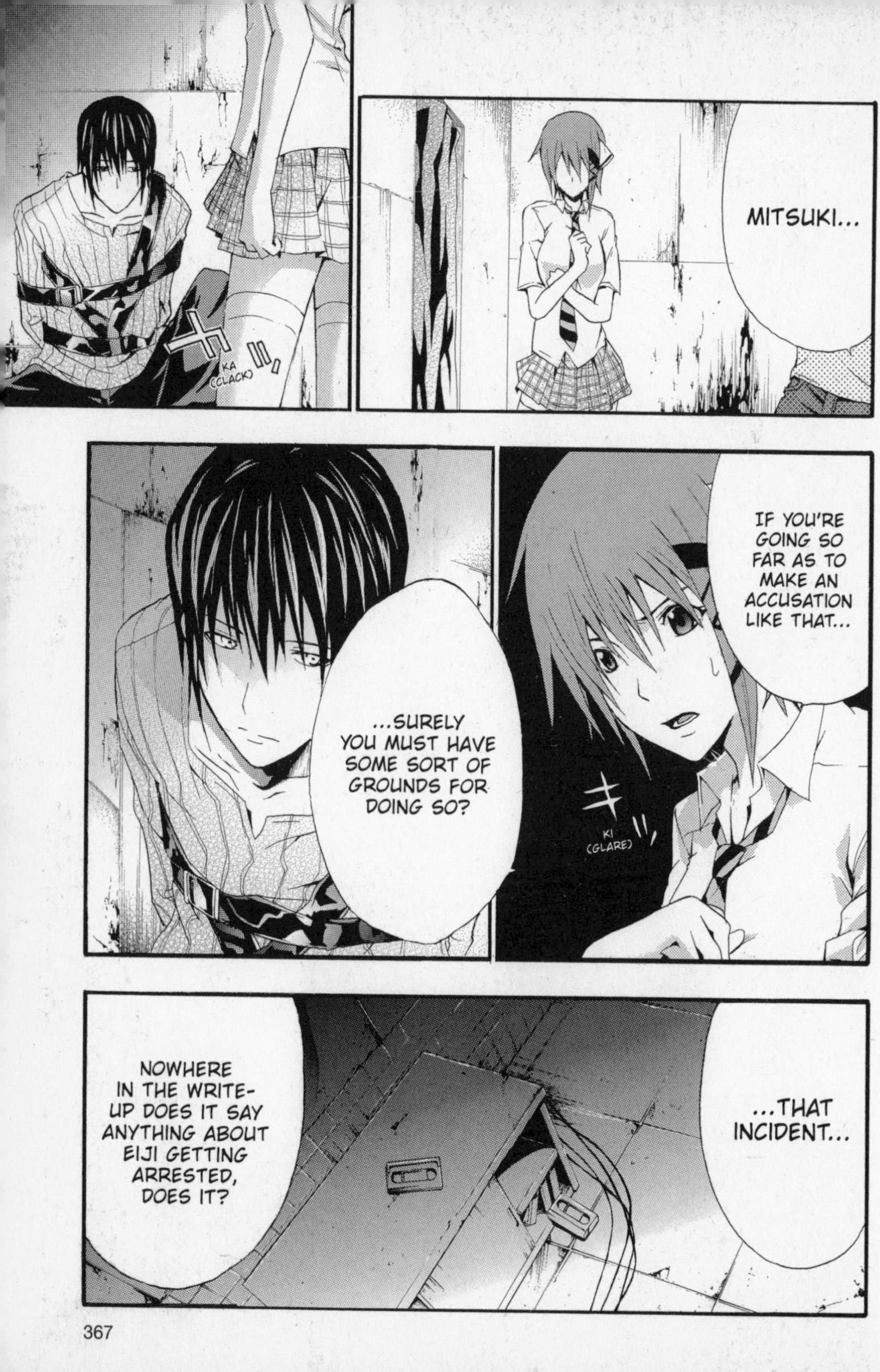
MITSUKI...
KA (CLACK)
IF YOU'RE GOING SO FAR AS TO MAKE AN ACCUSATION LIKE THAT...
KI (GLARE)
...SURELY YOU MUST HAVE SOME SORT OF GROUNDS FOR DOING SO?
...THAT INCIDENT...
NOWHERE IN THE WRITE-UP DOES IT SAY ANYTHING ABOUT EIJI GETTING ARRESTED, DOES IT?

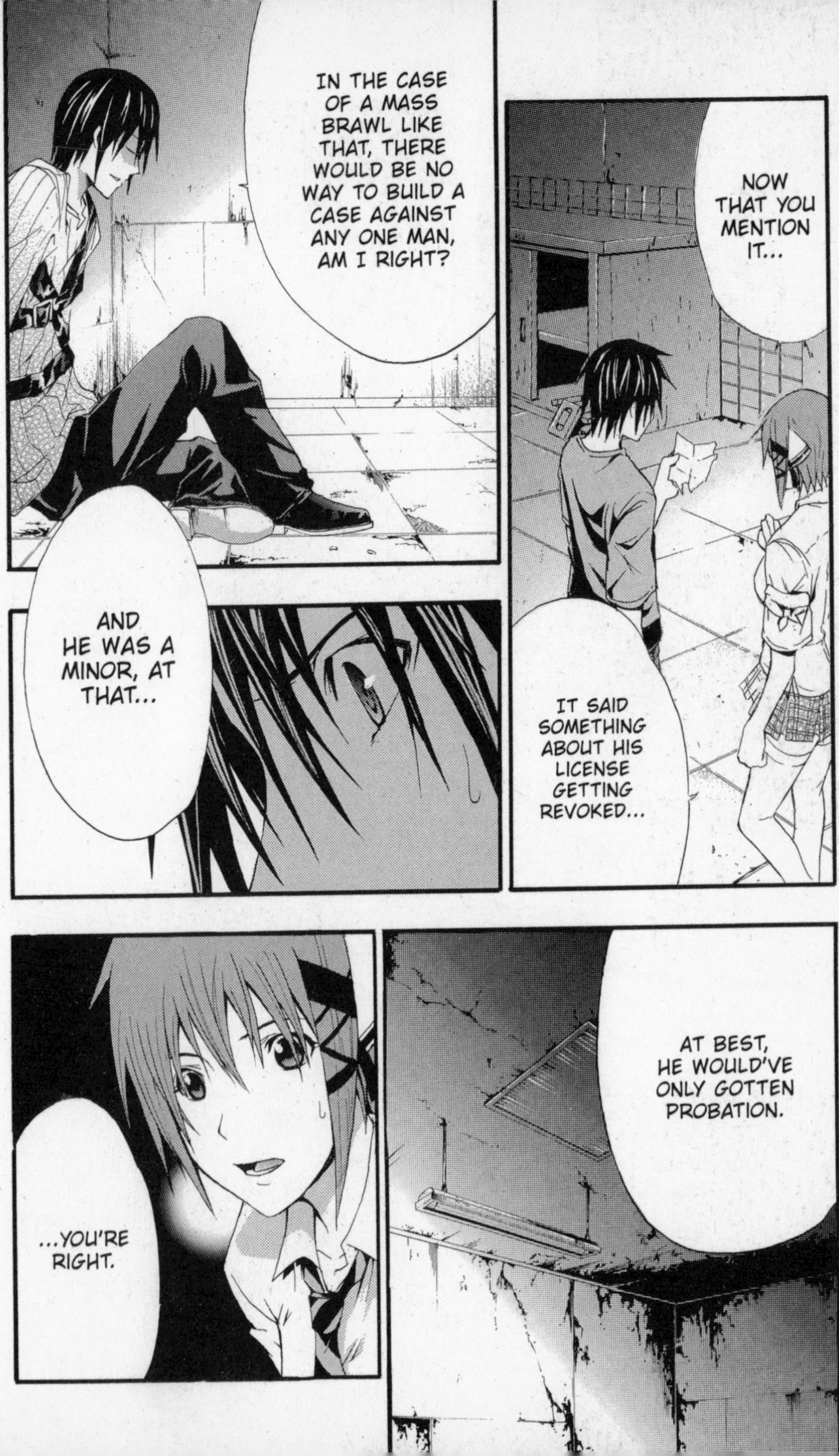
NOW THAT YOU MENTION IT...
IT SAID SOMETHING ABOUT HIS LICENSE GETTING REVOKED...
IN THE CASE OF A MASS BRAWL LIKE THAT, THERE WOULD BE NO WAY TO BUILD A CASE AGAINST ANY ONE MAN, AM I RIGHT?
AND HE WAS A MINOR, AT THAT...
AT BEST, HE WOULD'VE ONLY GOTTEN PROBATION.
...YOU'RE RIGHT.

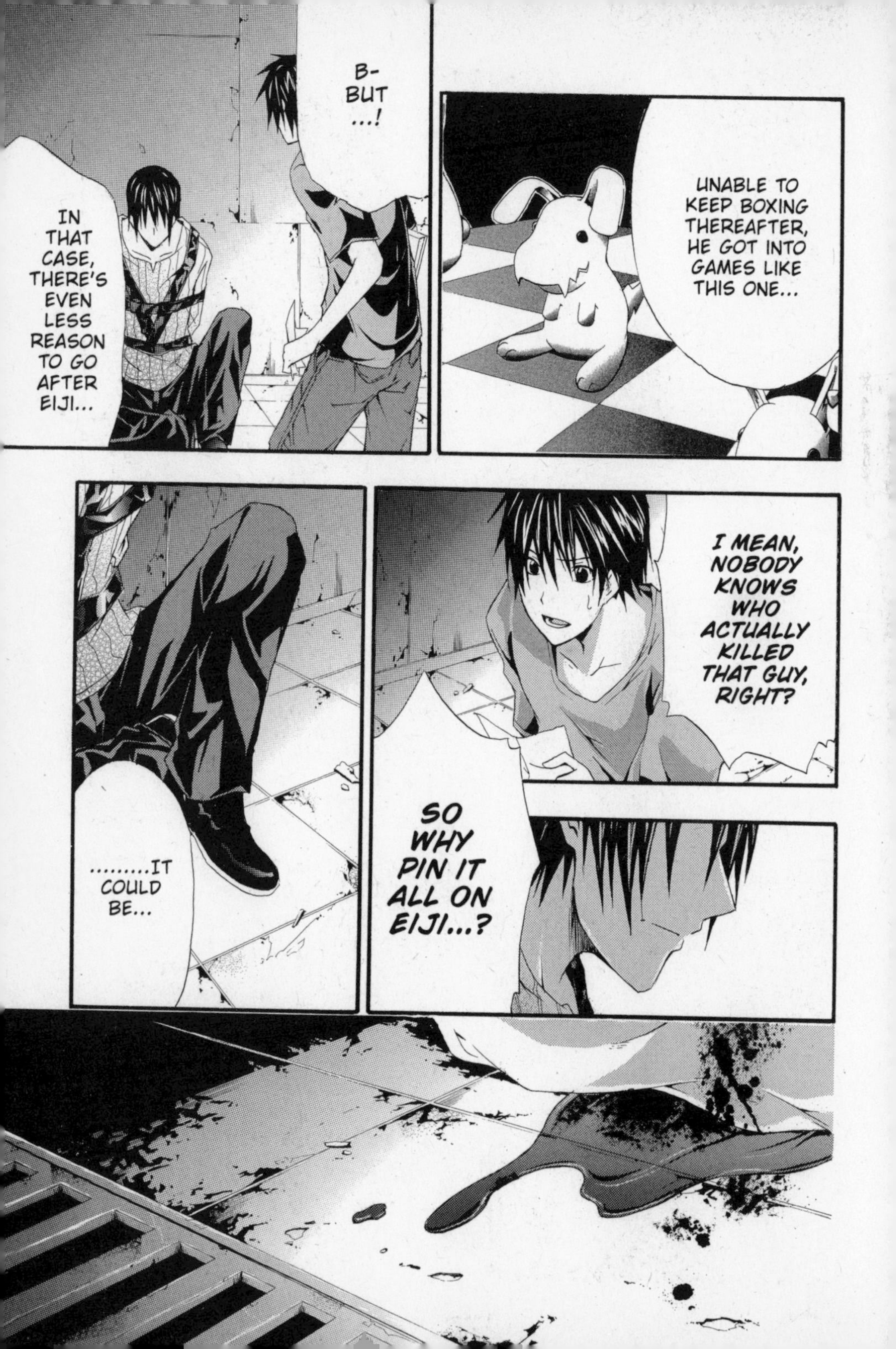
UNABLE TO KEEP BOXING THEREAFTER, HE GOT INTO GAMES LIKE THIS ONE...
B-BUT ...!
IN THAT CASE, THERE'S EVEN LESS REASON TO GO AFTER EIJI...
I MEAN, NOBODY KNOWS WHO ACTUALLY KILLED THAT GUY, RIGHT?
SO WHY PIN IT ALL ON EIJI...?
.........IT COULD BE...

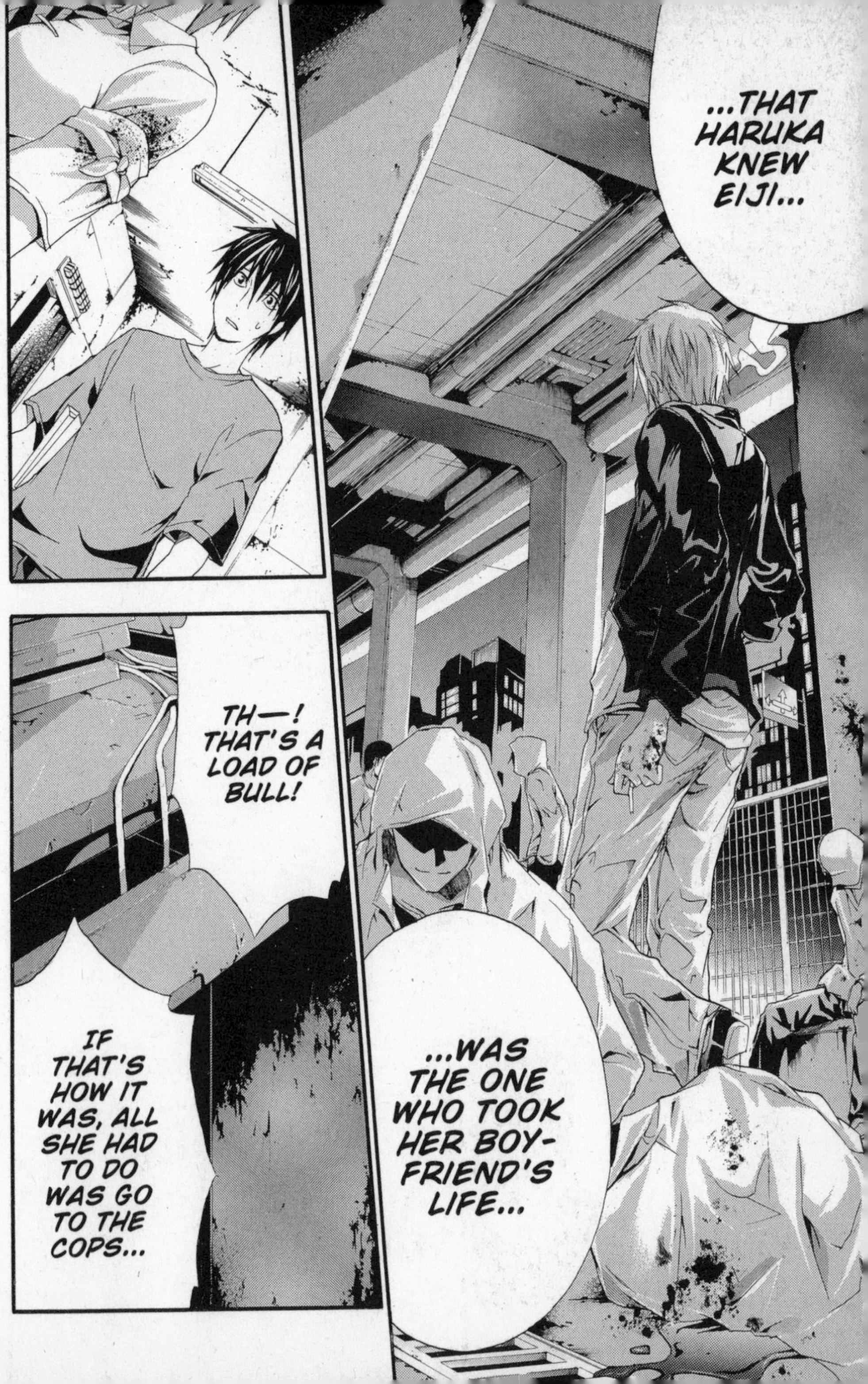
...THAT HARUKA KNEW EIJI...
...WAS THE ONE WHO TOOK HER BOY-FRIEND'S LIFE...
TH—! THAT'S A LOAD OF BULL!
IF THAT'S HOW IT WAS, ALL SHE HAD TO DO WAS GO TO THE COPS...

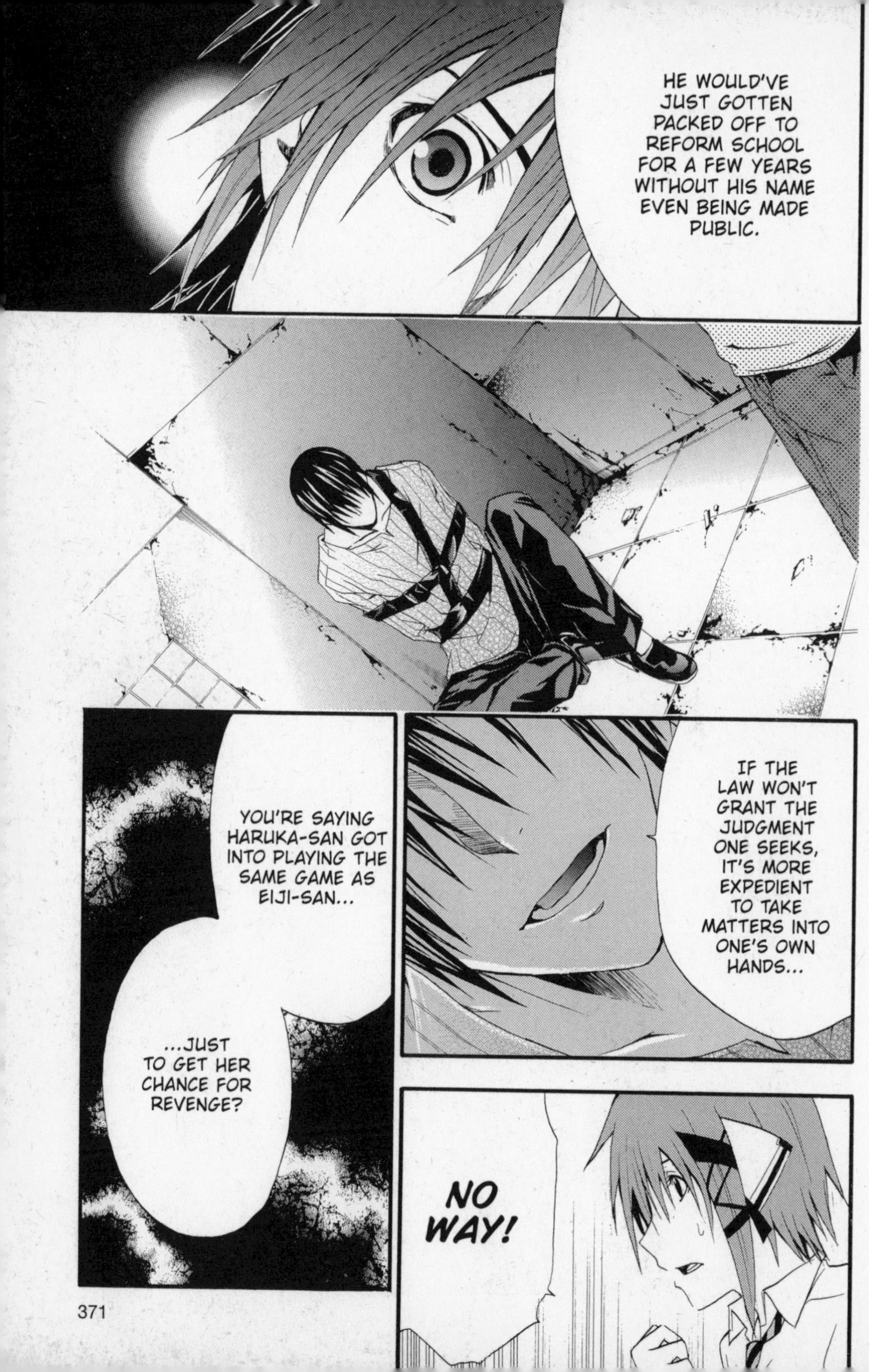
HE WOULD'VE JUST GOTTEN PACKED OFF TO REFORM SCHOOL FOR A FEW YEARS WITHOUT HIS NAME EVEN BEING MADE PUBLIC.
IF THE LAW WON'T GRANT THE JUDGMENT ONE SEEKS, IT'S MORE EXPEDIENT TO TAKE MATTERS INTO ONE'S OWN HANDS...
NO WAY!
YOU'RE SAYING HARUKA-SAN GOT INTO PLAYING THE SAME GAME AS EIJI-SAN...
...JUST TO GET HER CHANCE FOR REVENGE?

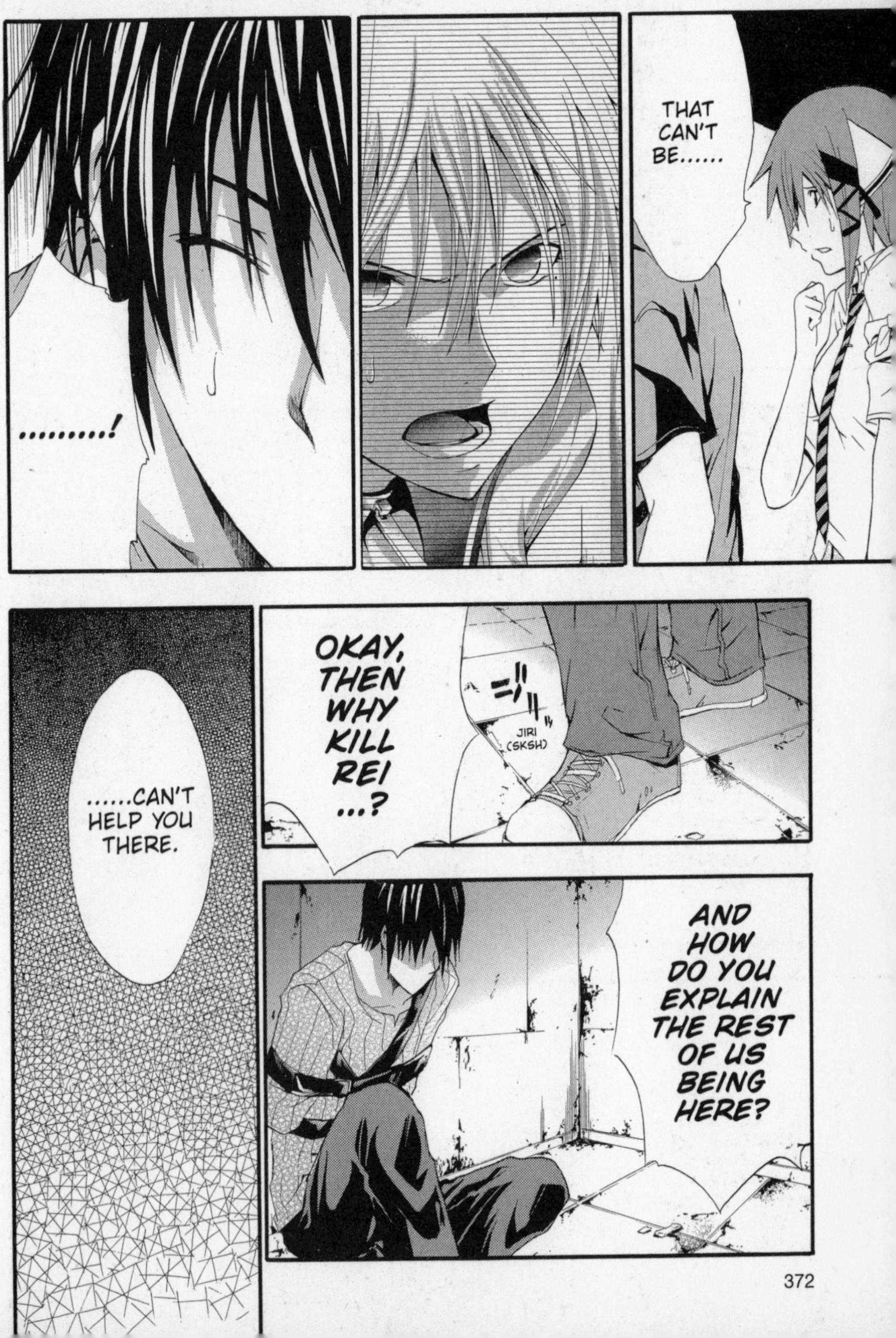

THAT CAN'T BE......
........!
OKAY, THEN WHY KILL REI ...?
JIRI (SKSH)
AND HOW DO YOU EXPLAIN THE REST OF US BEING HERE?
......CAN'T HELP YOU THERE.

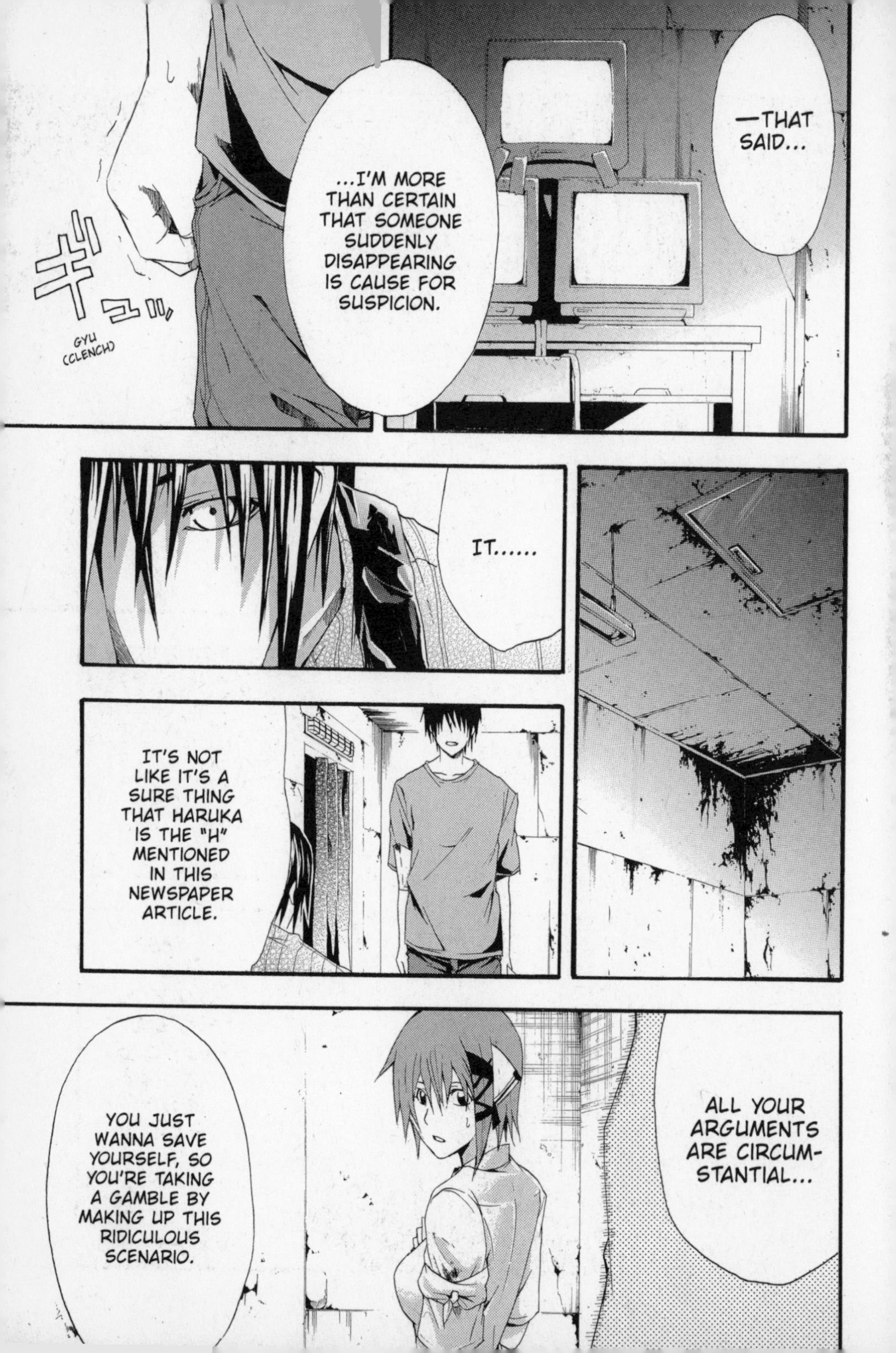
—THAT SAID...
...I'M MORE THAN CERTAIN THAT SOMEONE SUDDENLY DISAPPEARING IS CAUSE FOR SUSPICION.
ギュッ
GYU (CLENCH)
IT......
IT'S NOT LIKE IT'S A SURE THING THAT HARUKA IS THE "H" MENTIONED IN THIS NEWSPAPER ARTICLE.
ALL YOUR ARGUMENTS ARE CIRCUM-STANTIAL...
YOU JUST WANNA SAVE YOURSELF, SO YOU'RE TAKING A GAMBLE BY MAKING UP THIS RIDICULOUS SCENARIO.

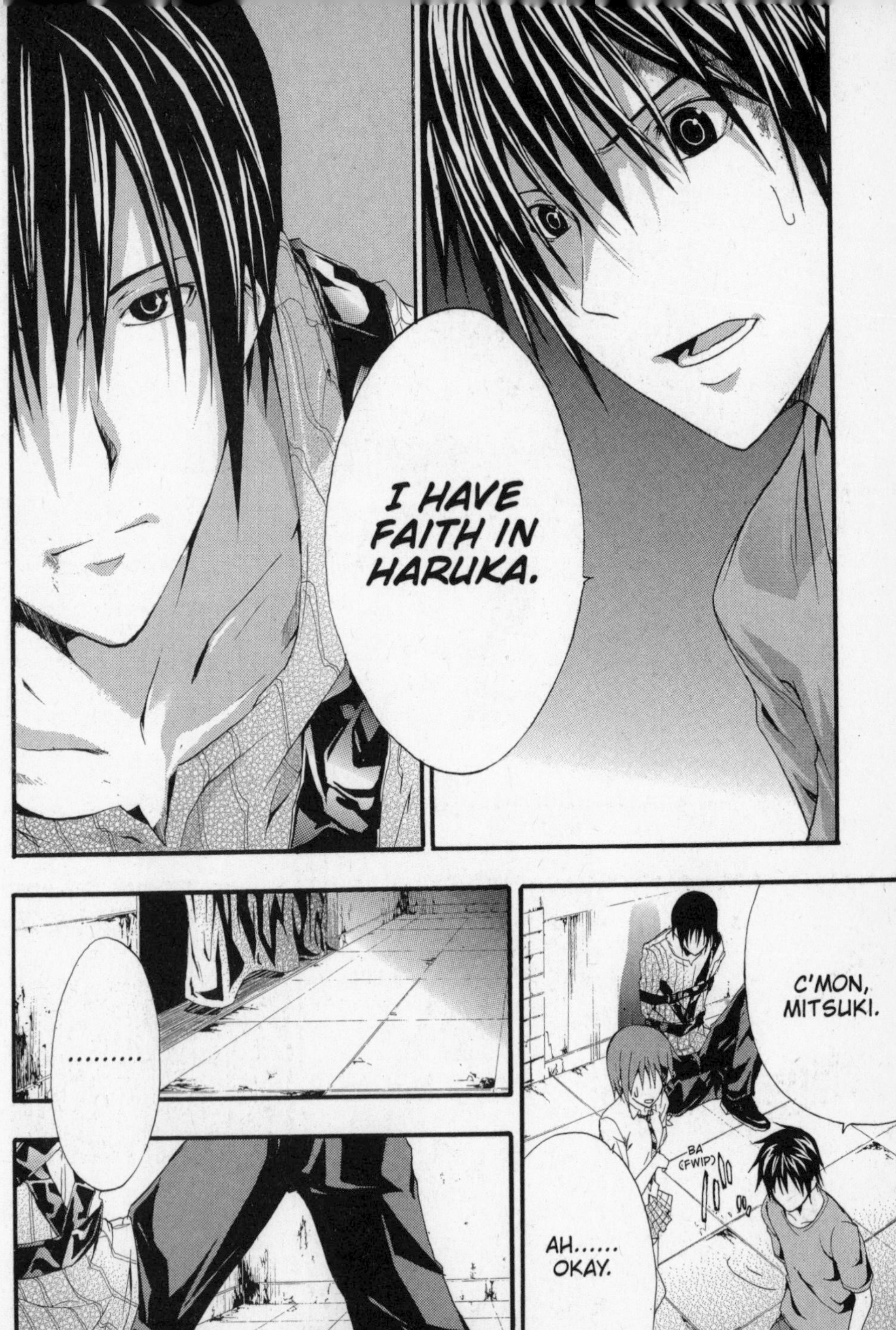
I HAVE FAITH IN HARUKA.
C'MON, MITSUKI.
BA (FWIP)
AH...... OKAY.
....

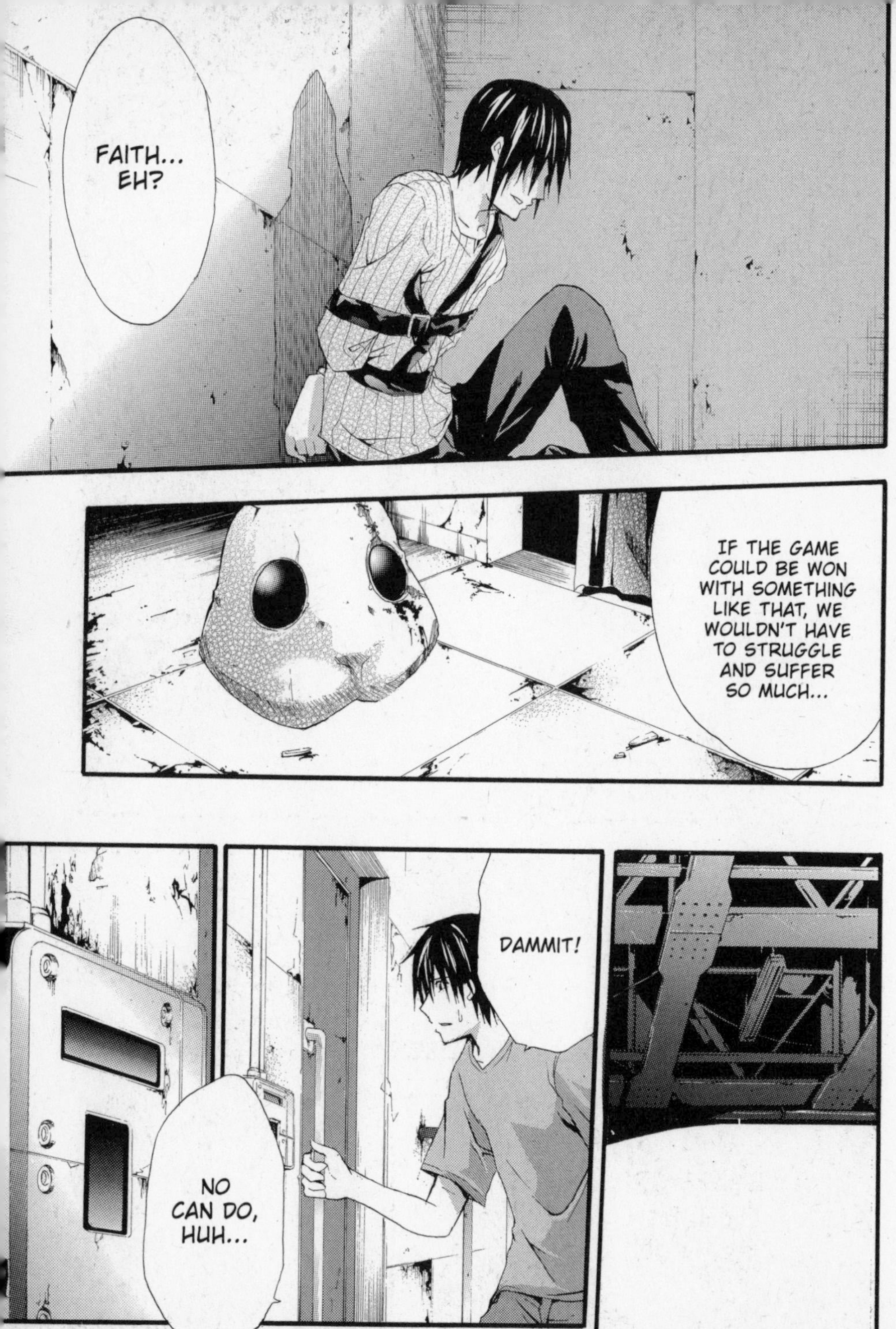
FAITH... EH?
IF THE GAME COULD BE WON WITH SOMETHING LIKE THAT, WE WOULDN'T HAVE TO STRUGGLE AND SUFFER SO MUCH...
DAMMIT!
NO CAN DO, HUH...

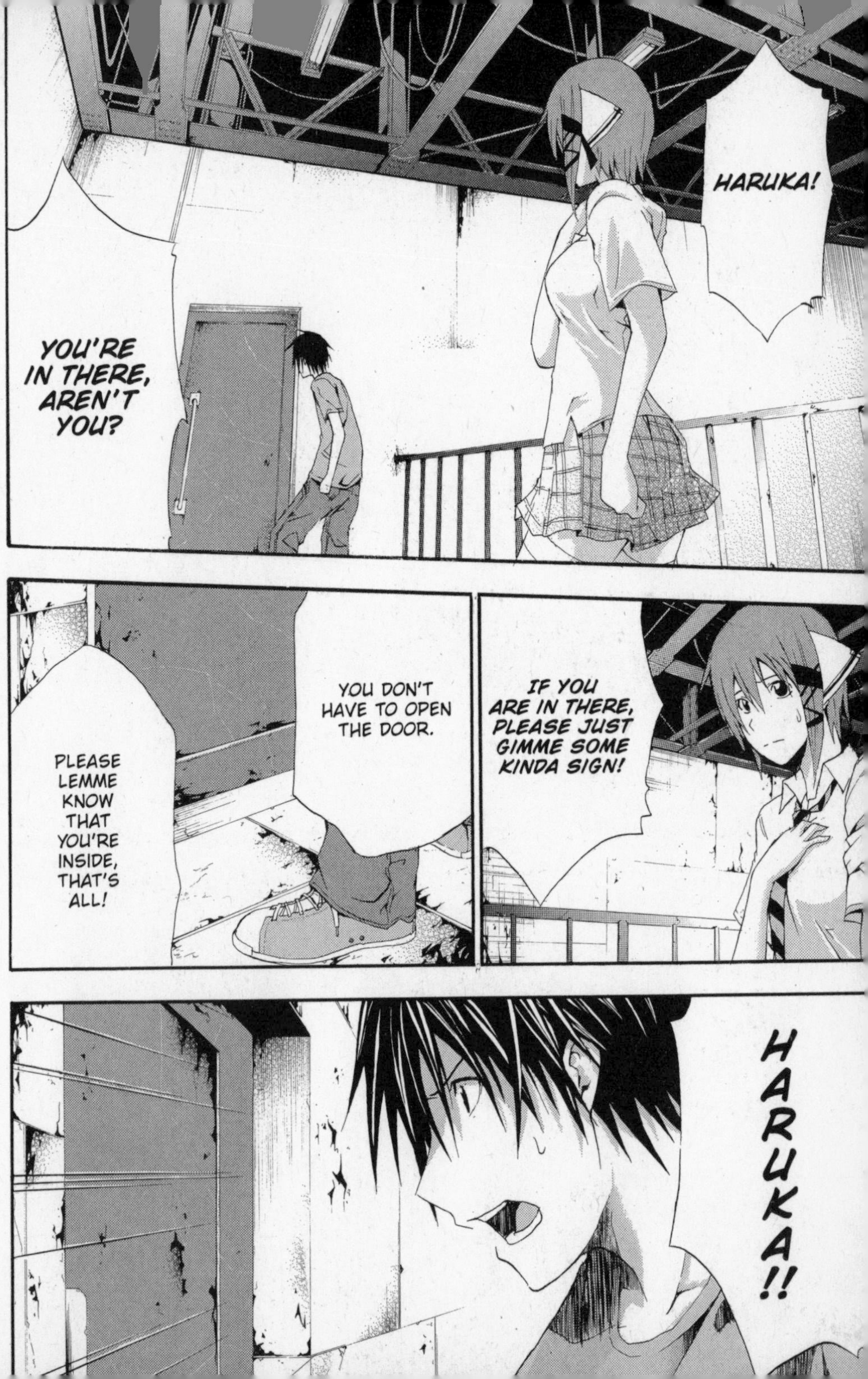
HARUKA!
YOU'RE IN THERE, AREN'T YOU?
IF YOU ARE IN THERE, PLEASE JUST GIMME SOME KINDA SIGN!
YOU DON'T HAVE TO OPEN THE DOOR.
PLEASE LEMME KNOW THAT YOU'RE INSIDE, THAT'S ALL!
HARUKA!!

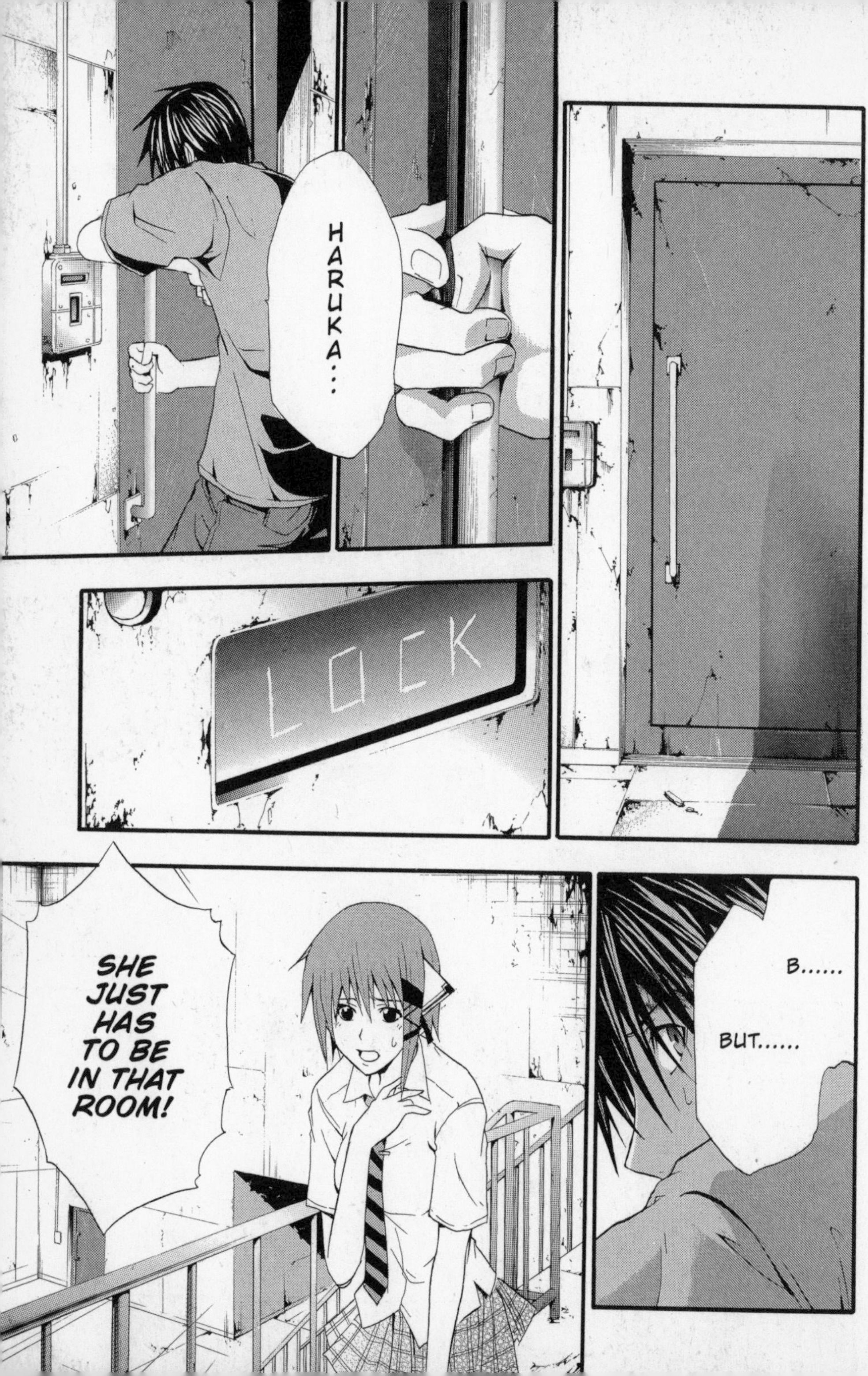
HARUKA...
LOCK
B......
BUT......
SHE JUST HAS TO BE IN THAT ROOM!

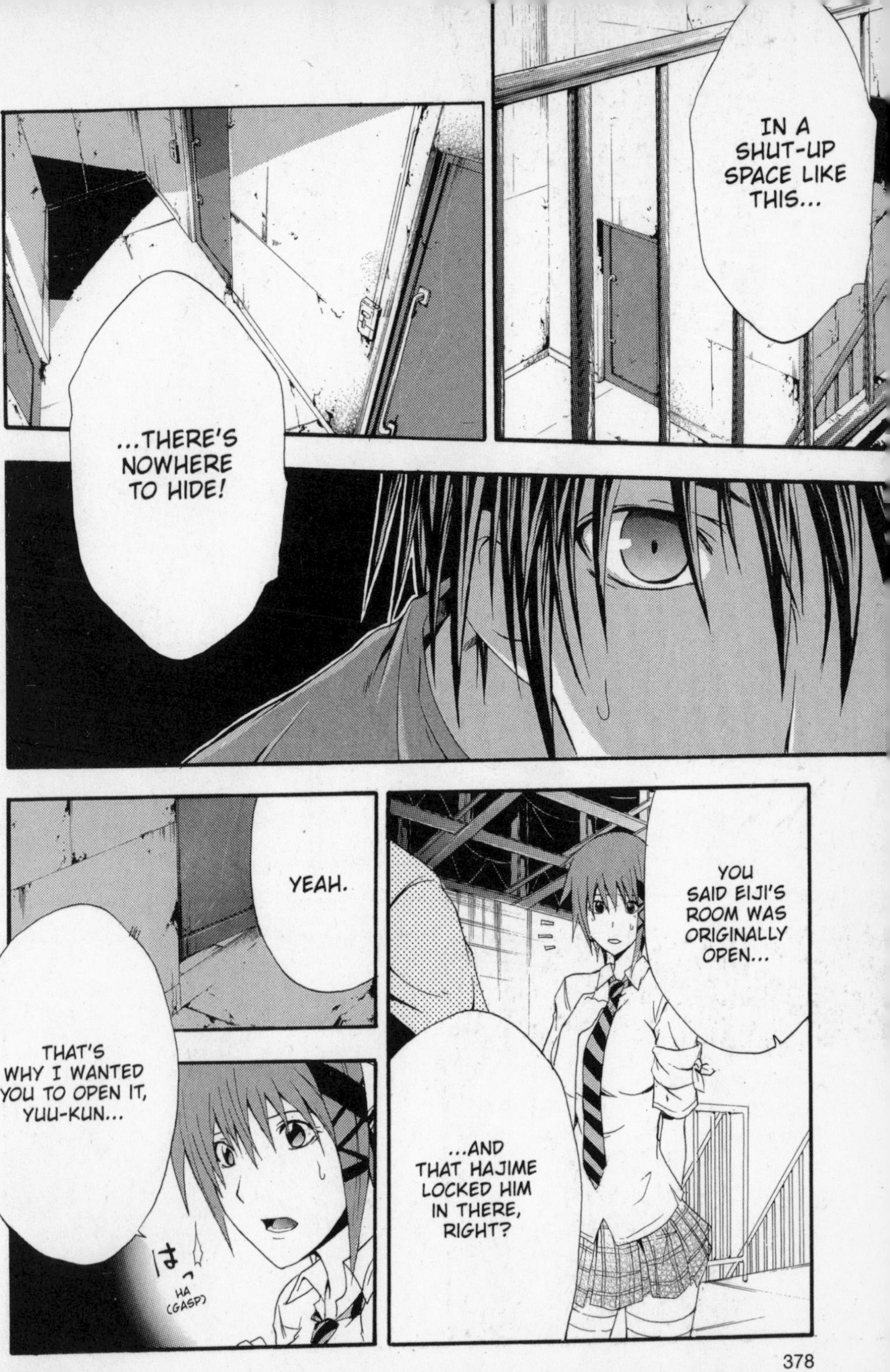
IN A SHUT-UP SPACE LIKE THIS...
...THERE'S NOWHERE TO HIDE!
YOU SAID EIJI'S ROOM WAS ORIGINALLY OPEN...
...AND THAT HAJIME LOCKED HIM IN THERE, RIGHT?
YEAH.
THAT'S WHY I WANTED YOU TO OPEN IT, YUU-KUN...
はっ
HA (GASP)

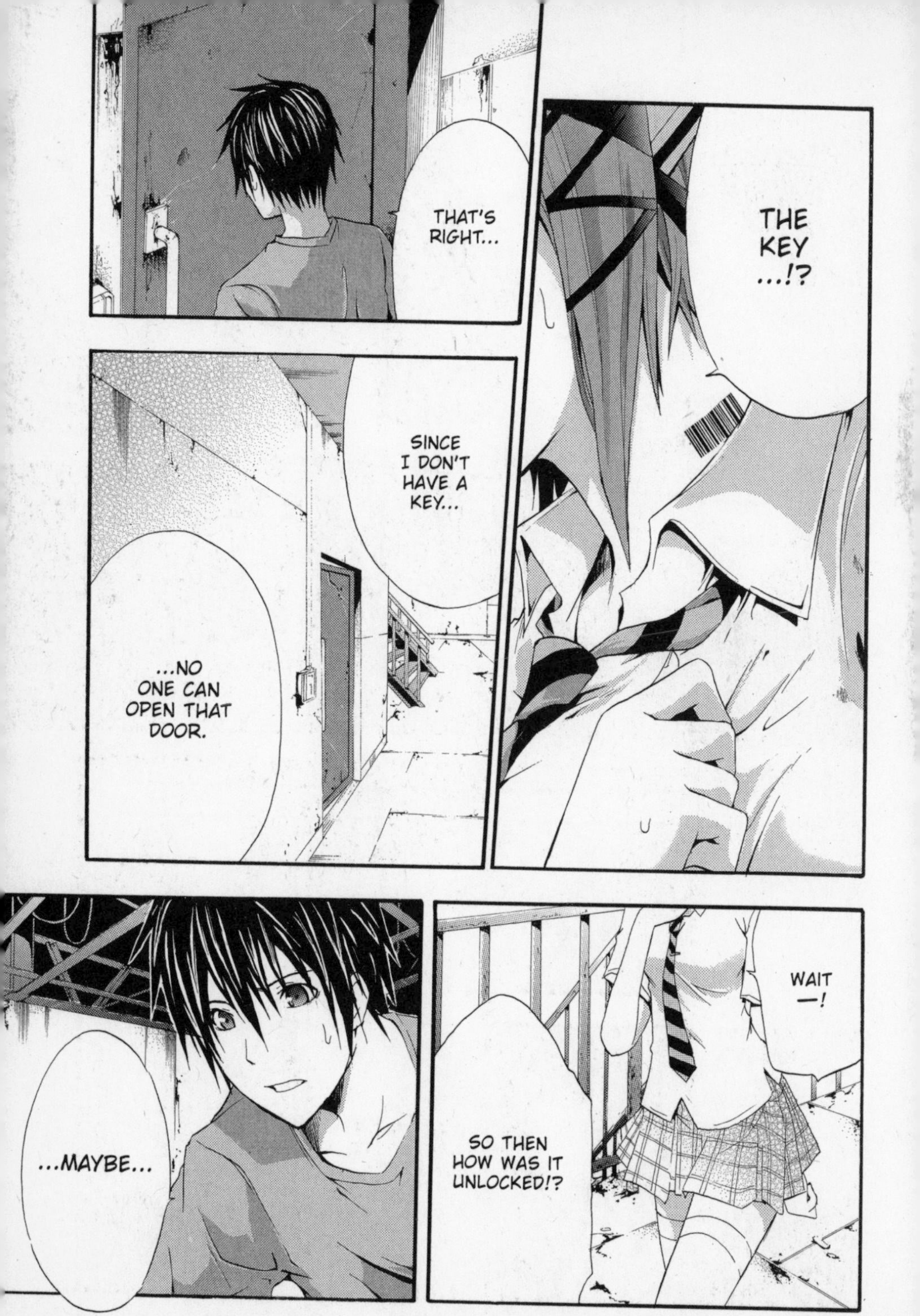
THE KEY ...!?
THAT'S RIGHT...
SINCE I DON'T HAVE A KEY...
...NO ONE CAN OPEN THAT DOOR.
WAIT —!
SO THEN HOW WAS IT UNLOCKED!?
...MAYBE...

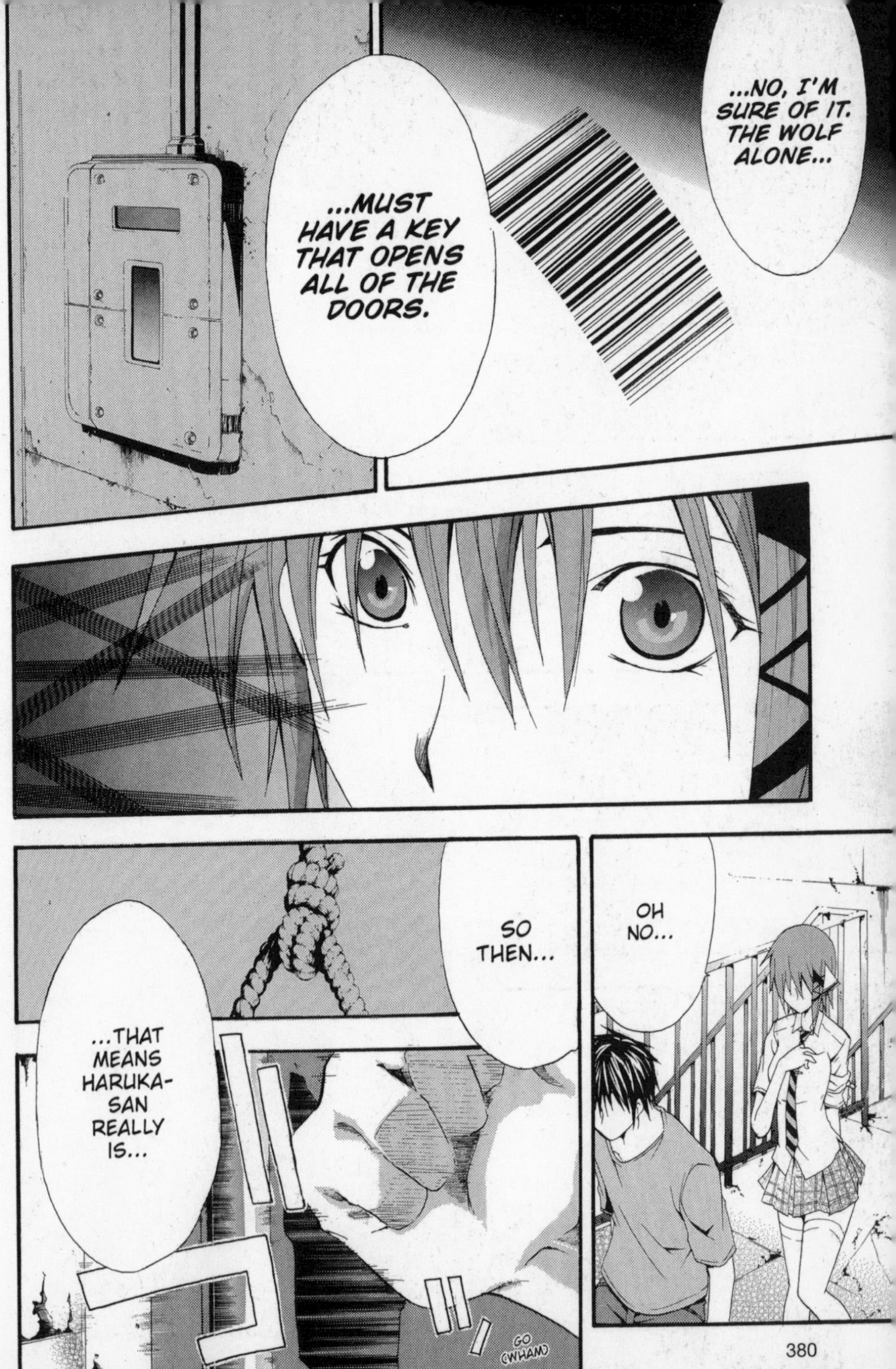
...NO, I'M SURE OF IT. THE WOLF ALONE...
...MUST HAVE A KEY THAT OPENS ALL OF THE DOORS.
OH NO...
SO THEN...
...THAT MEANS HARUKA-SAN REALLY IS...
GO (WHAM)

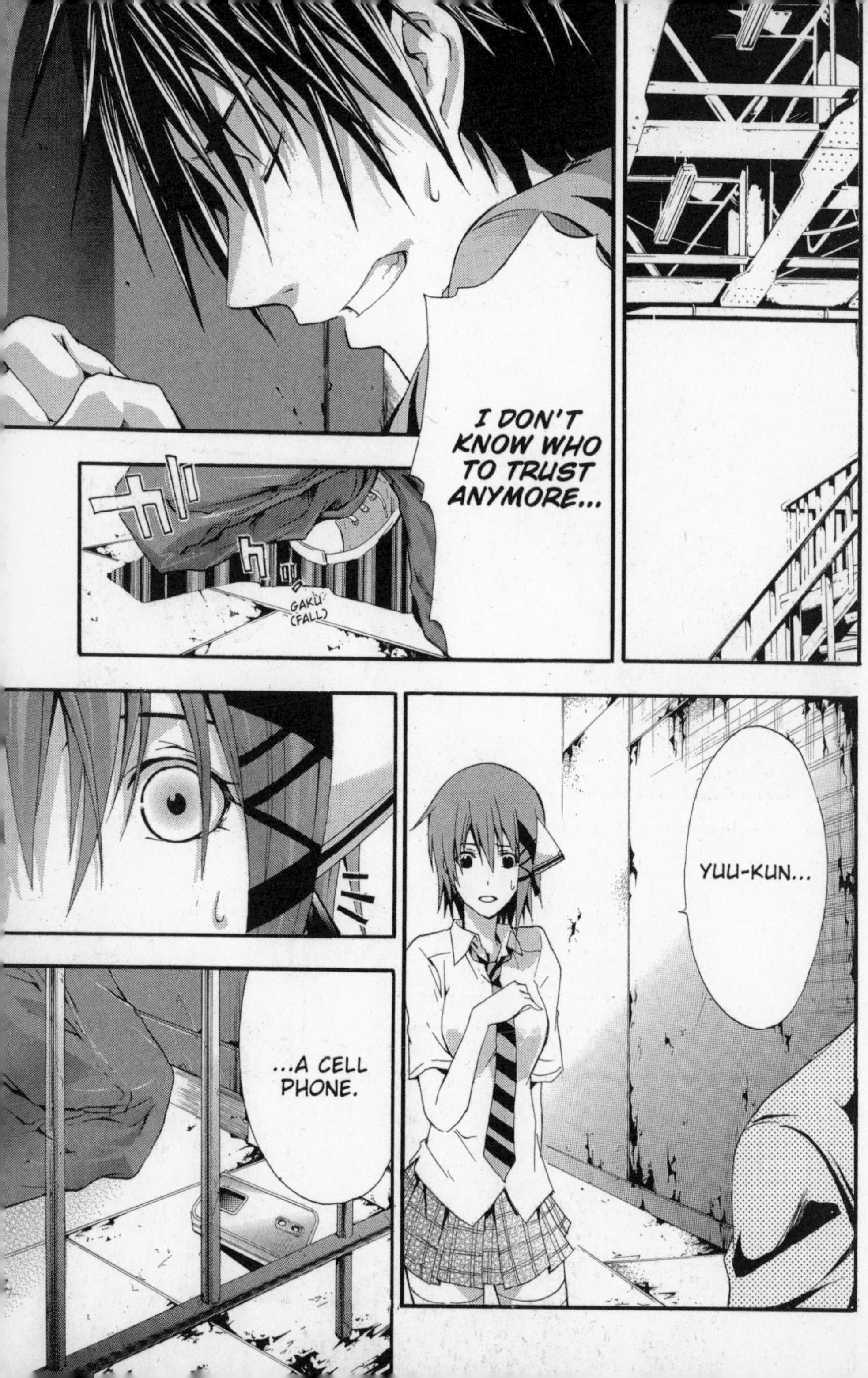
I DON'T KNOW WHO TO TRUST ANYMORE...
GAKU (FALL)
YUU-KUN...
...A CELL PHONE.

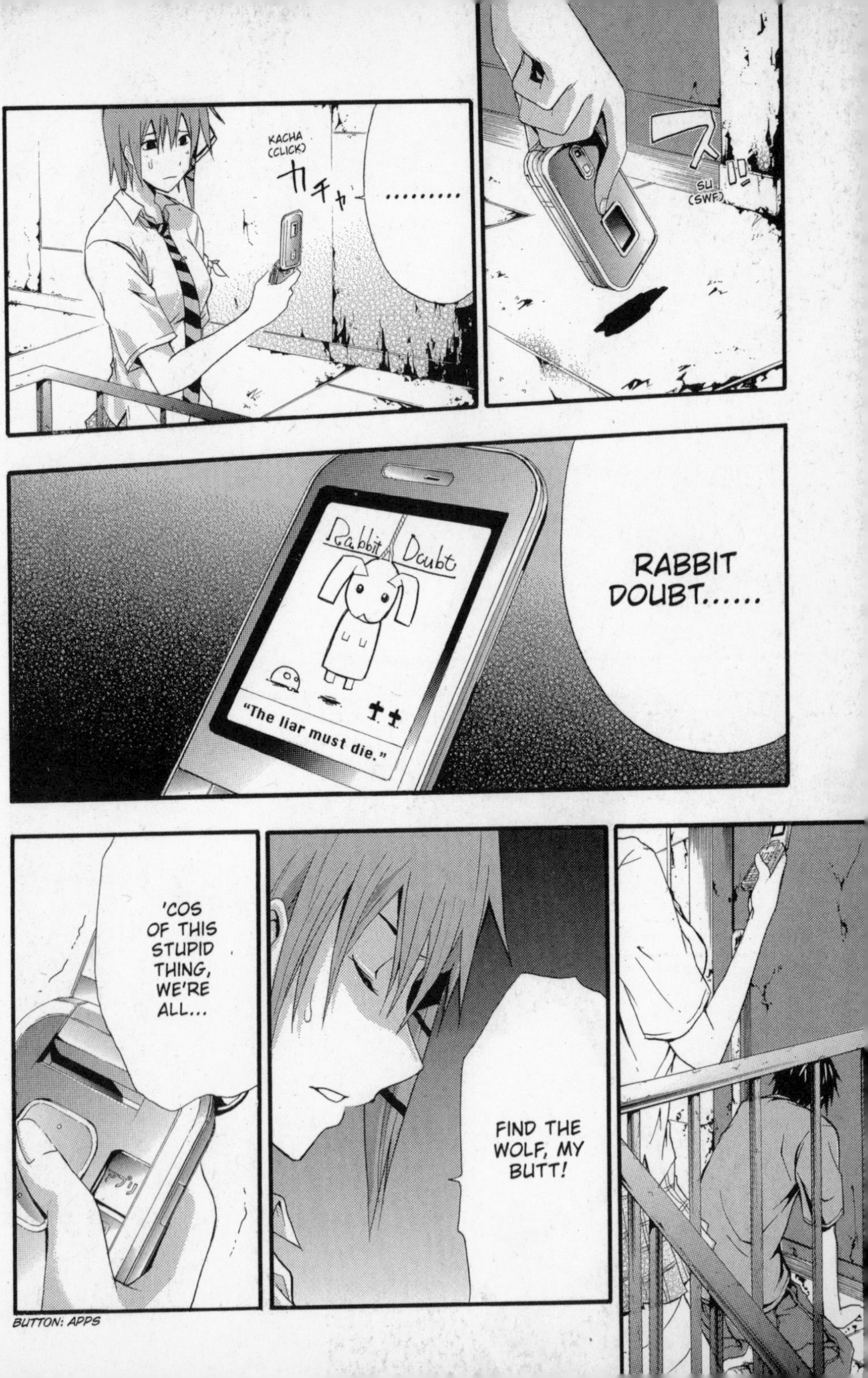

スッ
SU
(SWF)
カチャ
KACHA
(CLICK)
....
Rabbit Doubt
"The liar must die."
RABBIT DOUBT......
FIND THE WOLF, MY BUTT!
'COS OF THIS STUPID THING, WE'RE ALL...

BUTTON: APPS

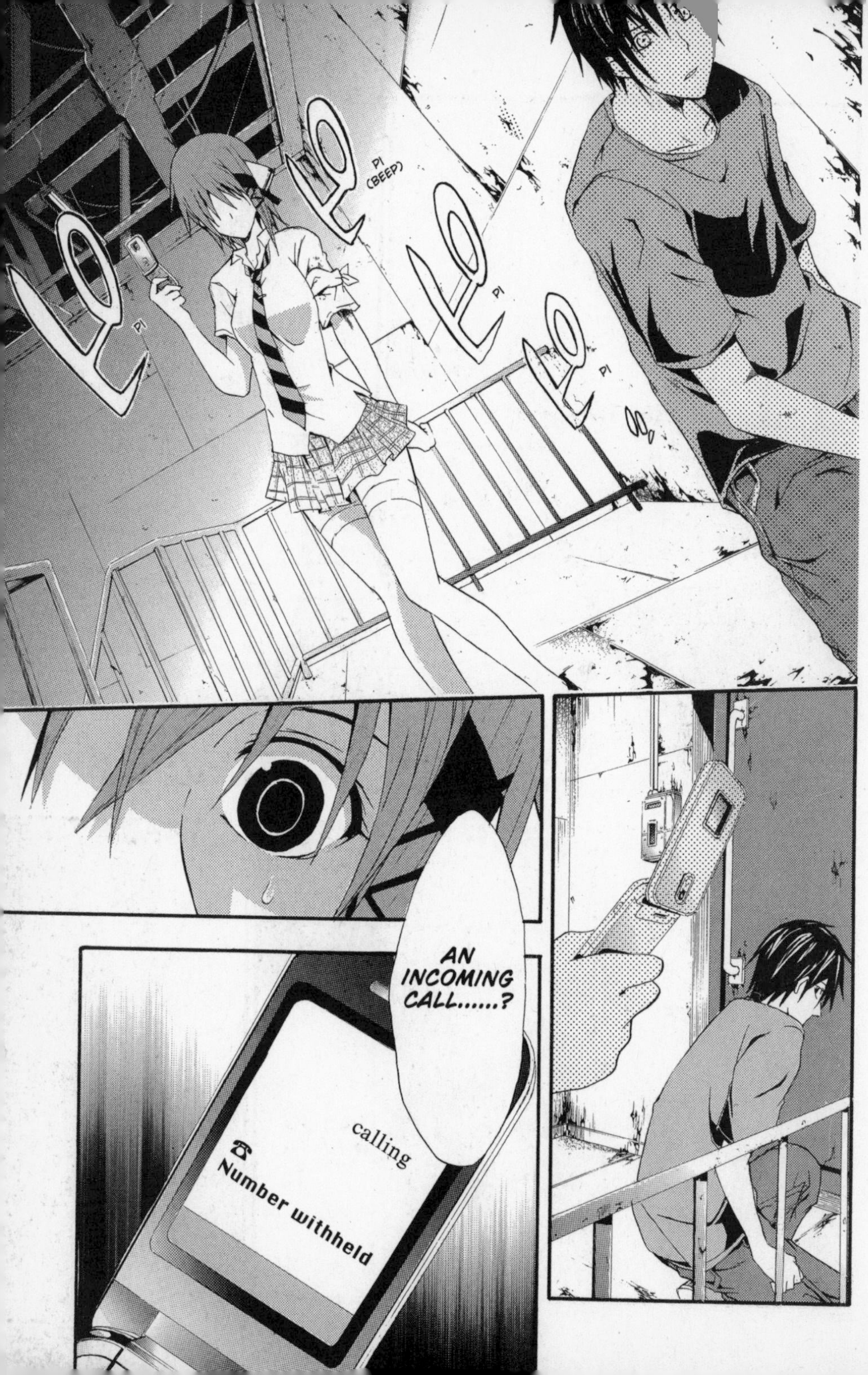
PI (BEEP)
PI
PI
PI
AN INCOMING CALL......?
calling
Number withheld

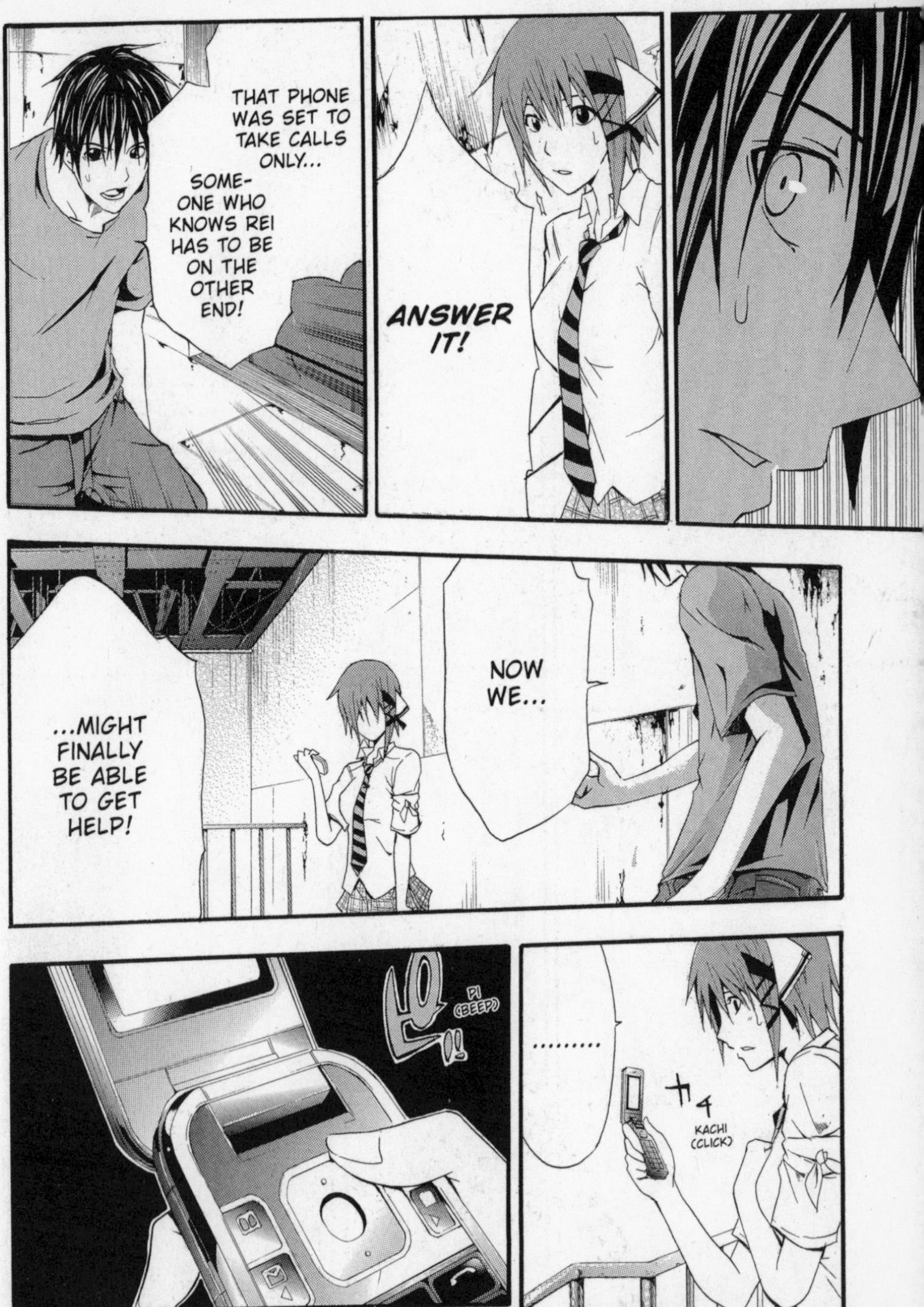
ANSWER IT!
THAT PHONE WAS SET TO TAKE CALLS ONLY...
SOME-ONE WHO KNOWS REI HAS TO BE ON THE OTHER END!
NOW WE...
...MIGHT FINALLY BE ABLE TO GET HELP!
....
KACHI (CLICK)
PI (BEEP)

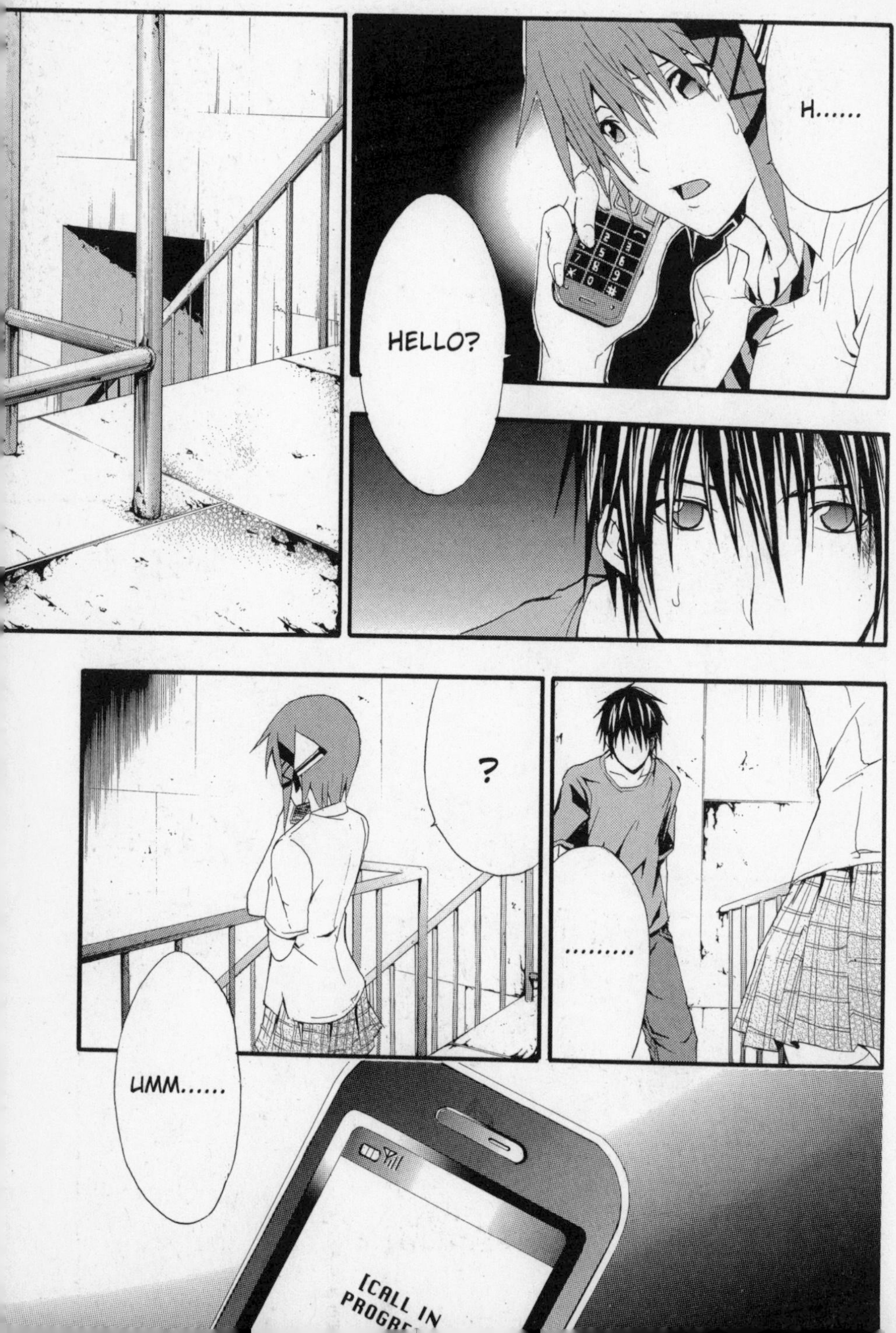
H......
HELLO?
....
?
UMM......
[CALL IN
PROGRE

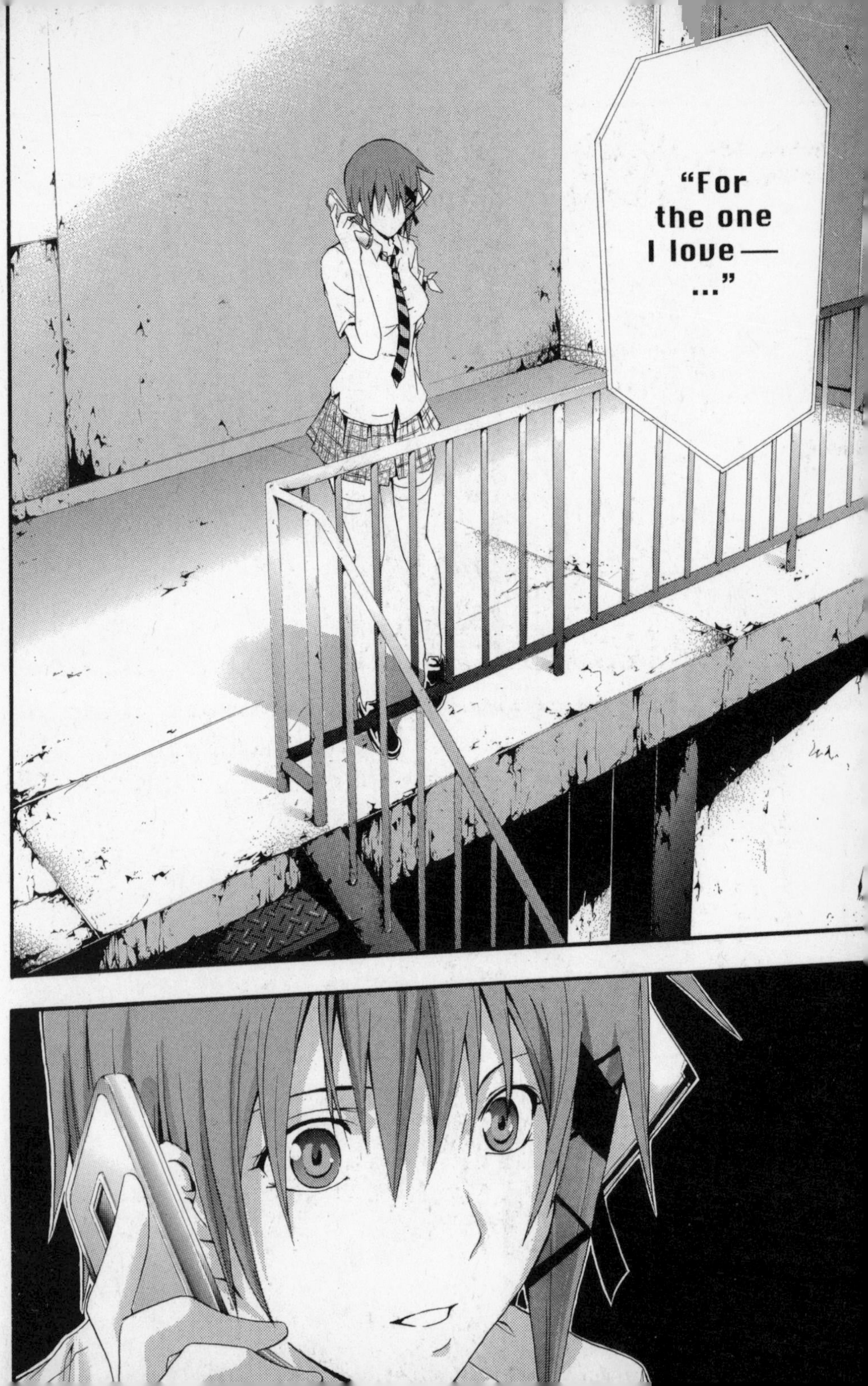
"For the one I love—
..."

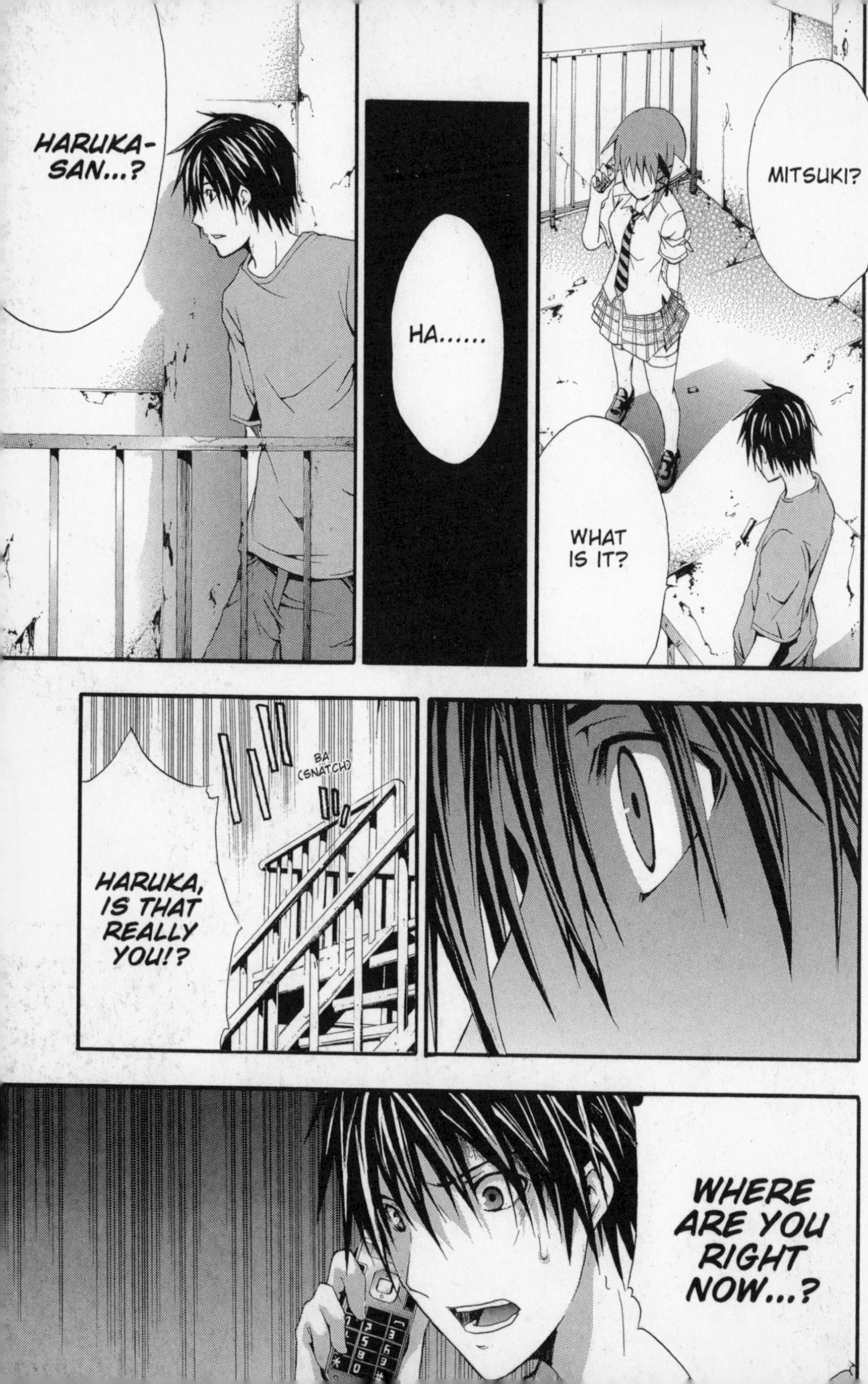
MITSUKI?
WHAT IS IT?
HA......
HARUKA-SAN...?
BA (SNATCH)
HARUKA, IS THAT REALLY YOU!?
WHERE ARE YOU RIGHT NOW...?

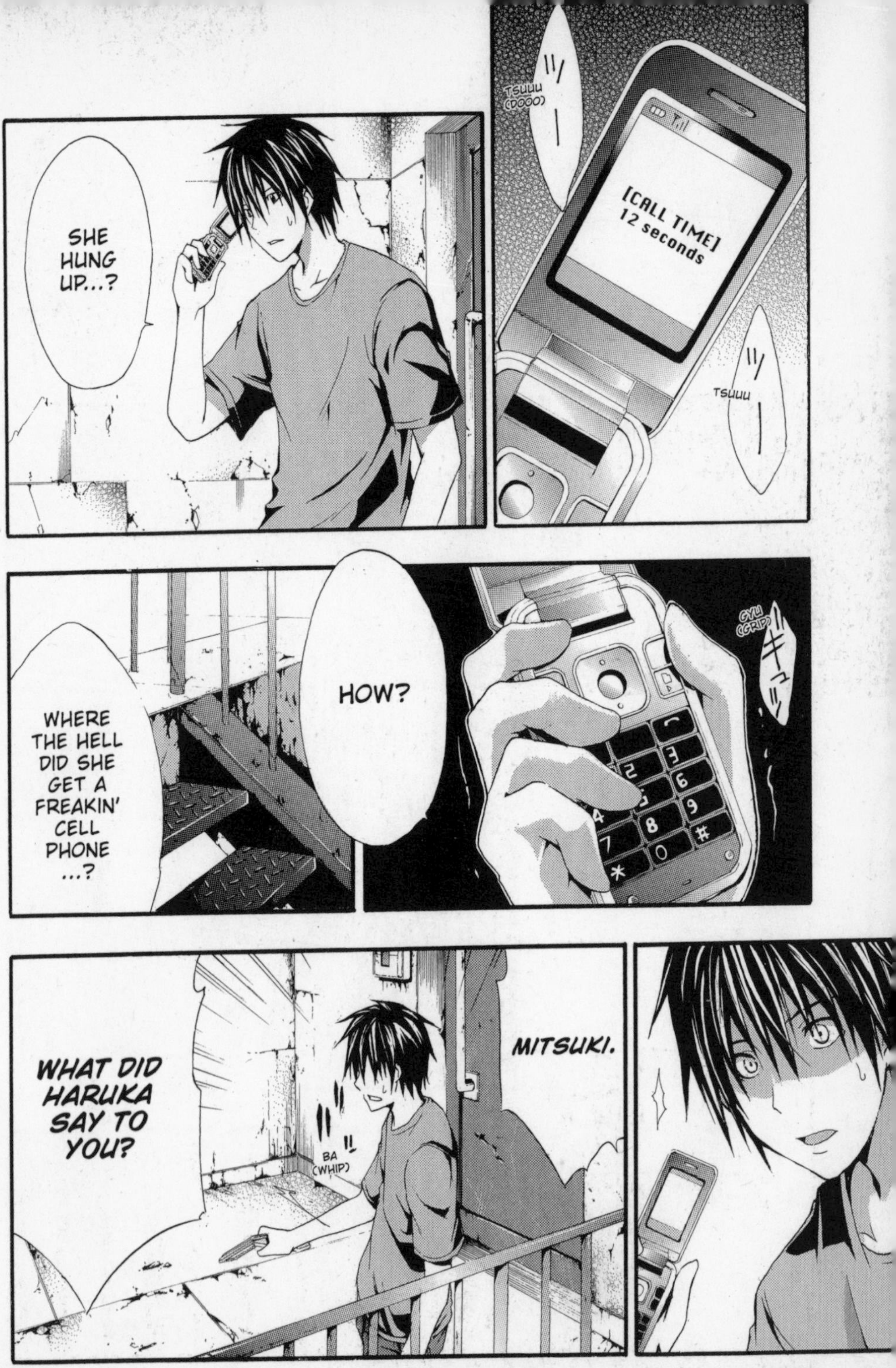

TSUUU (DOOO)
[CALL TIME] 12 seconds
TSUUU
SHE HUNG UP...?
GYU (GRIP)
HOW?
WHERE THE HELL DID SHE GET A FREAKIN' CELL PHONE ...?
MITSUKI.
WHAT DID HARUKA SAY TO YOU?
BA (WHIP)

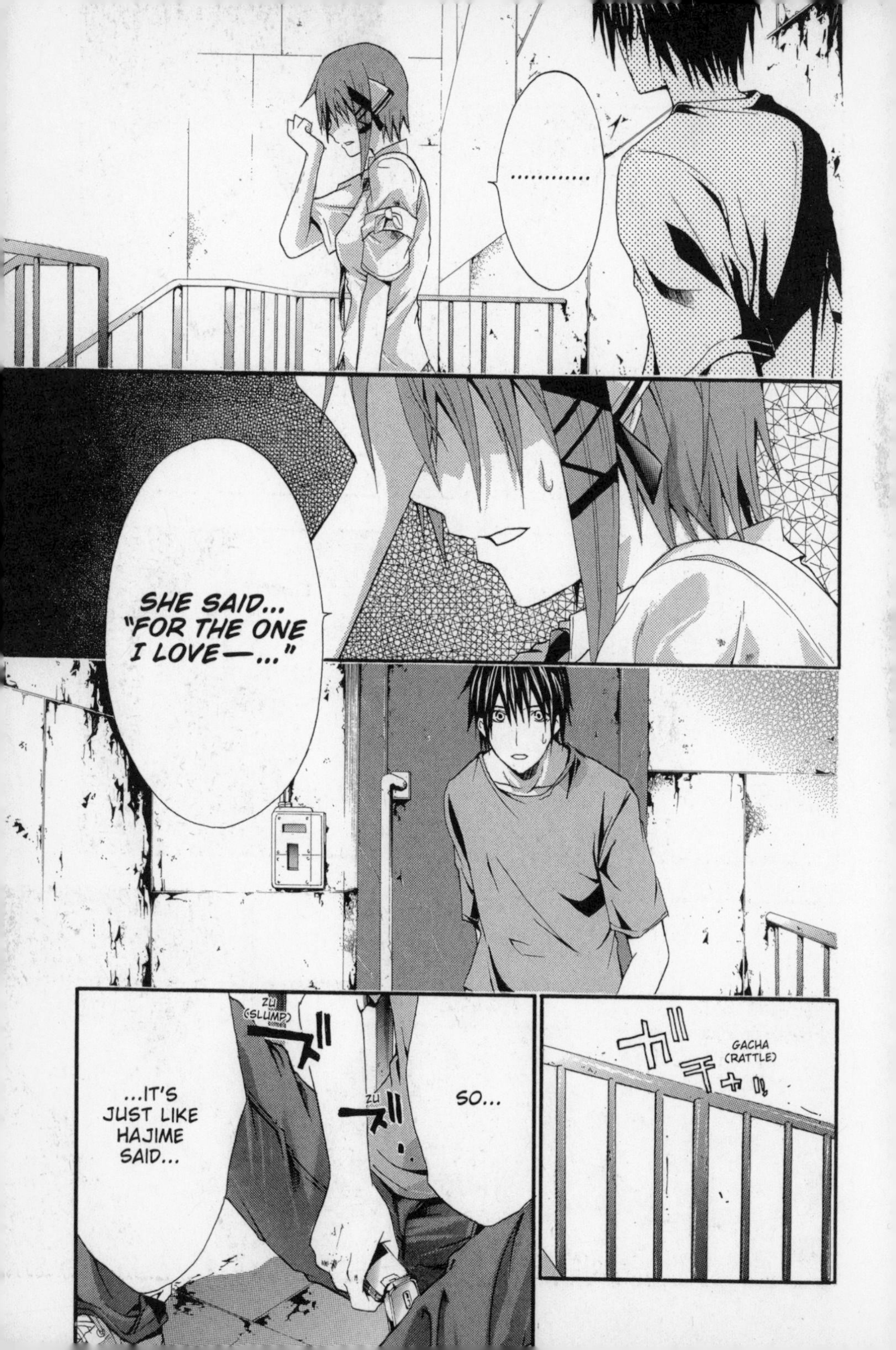
....
SHE SAID... "FOR THE ONE I LOVE—..."
ガチャ!!
GACHA (RATTLE)
ズ
ZU (SLUMP)
SO...
ズ
ZU
...IT'S JUST LIKE HAJIME SAID...

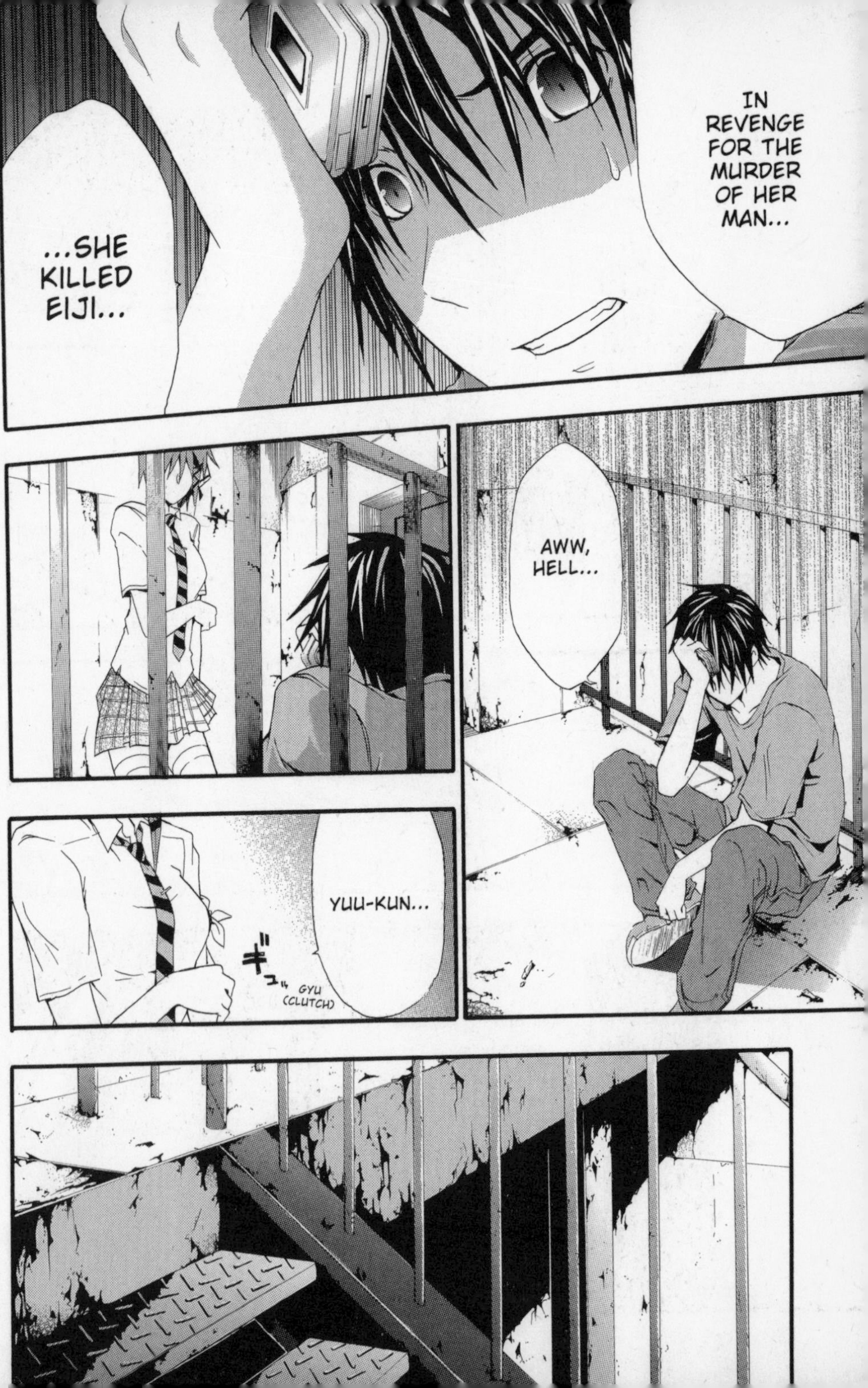
IN REVENGE FOR THE MURDER OF HER MAN...
...SHE KILLED EIJI...
AWW, HELL...
YUU-KUN...
ギュ
GYU (CLUTCH)

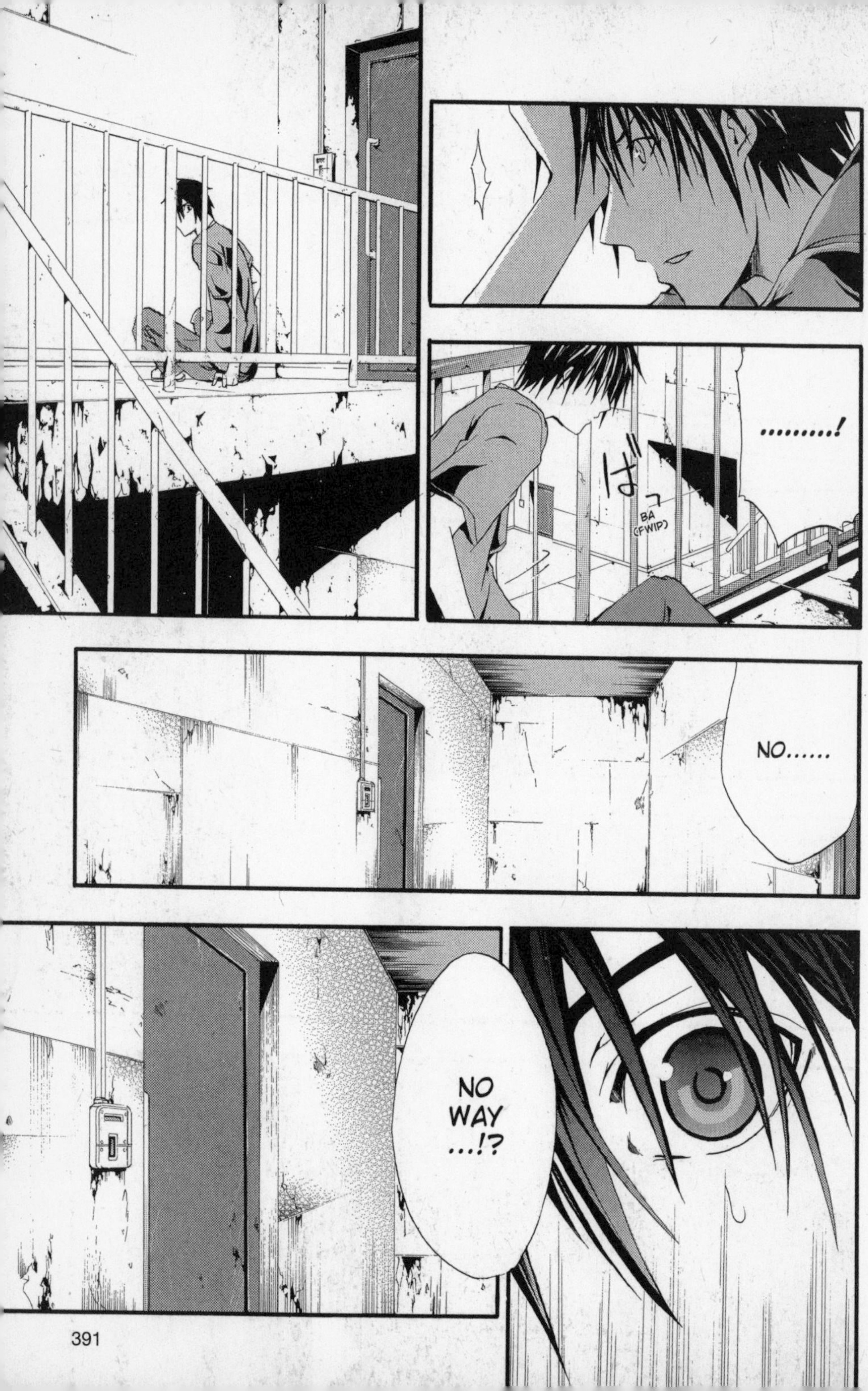
........!
ばっ
BA (FWIP)
NO......
NO WAY ...!?

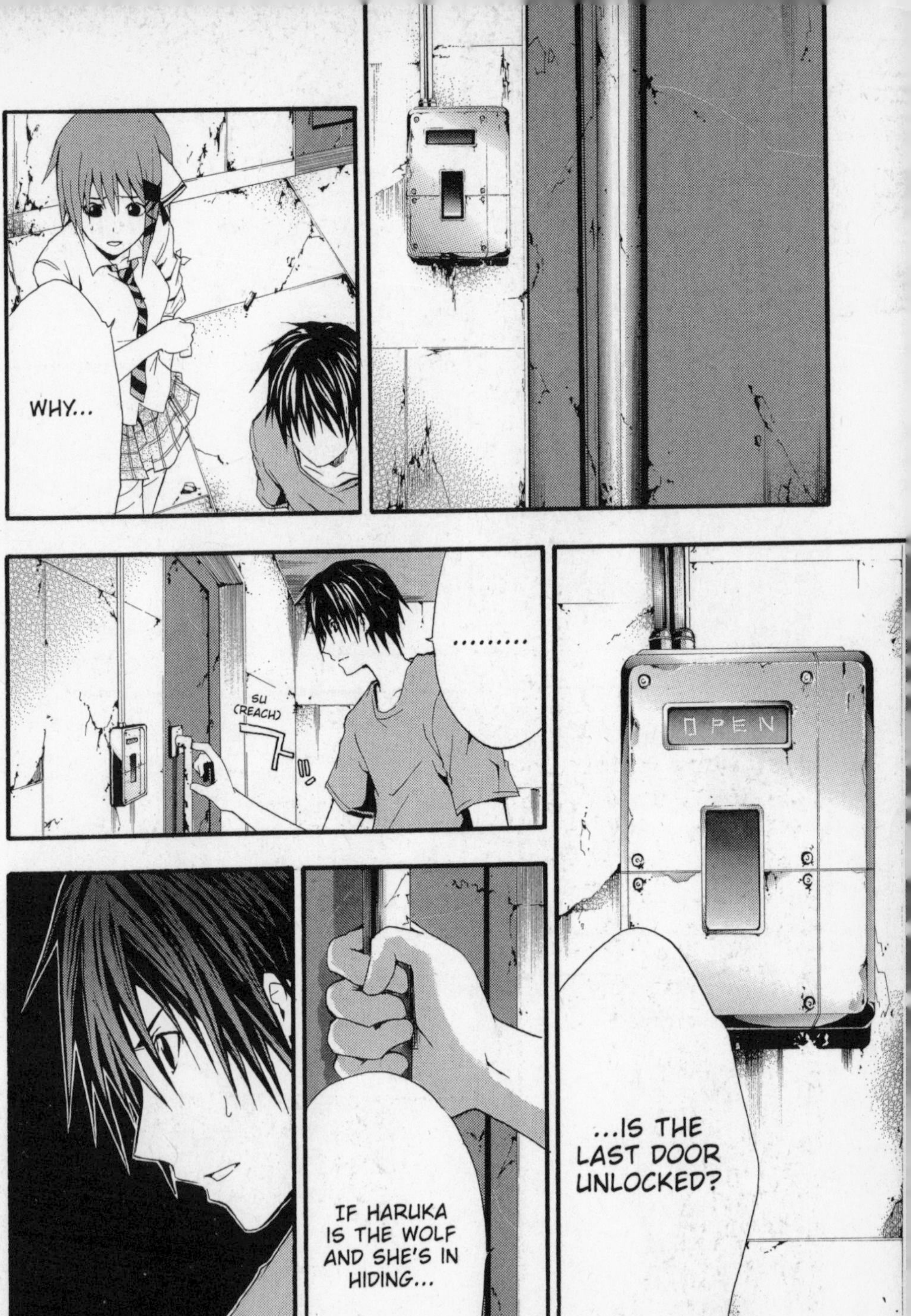
WHY...
OPEN
...IS THE LAST DOOR UNLOCKED?
....
SU (REACH)
IF HARUKA IS THE WOLF AND SHE'S IN HIDING...

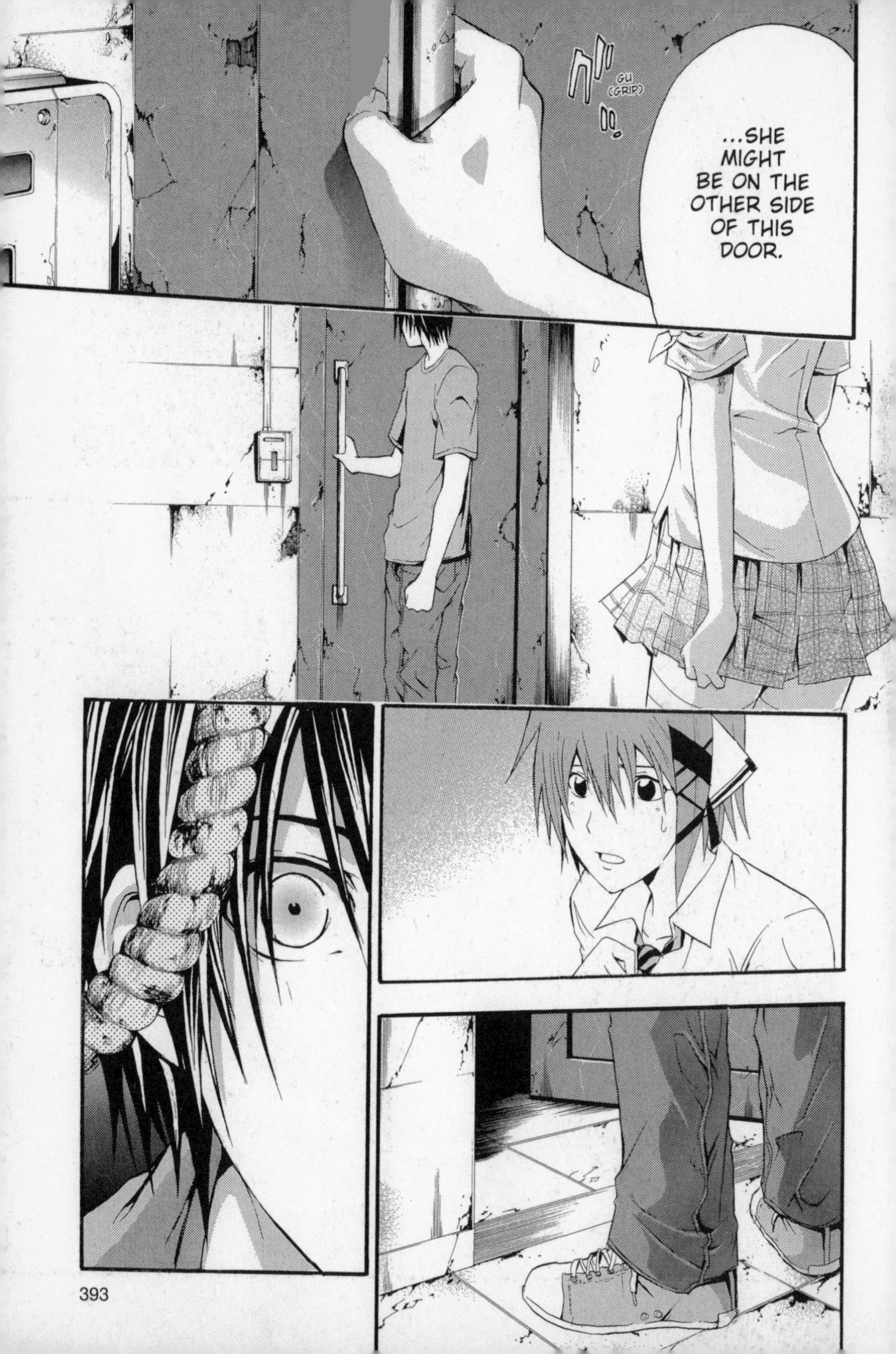
...SHE MIGHT BE ON THE OTHER SIDE OF THIS DOOR.
GU (GRIP)

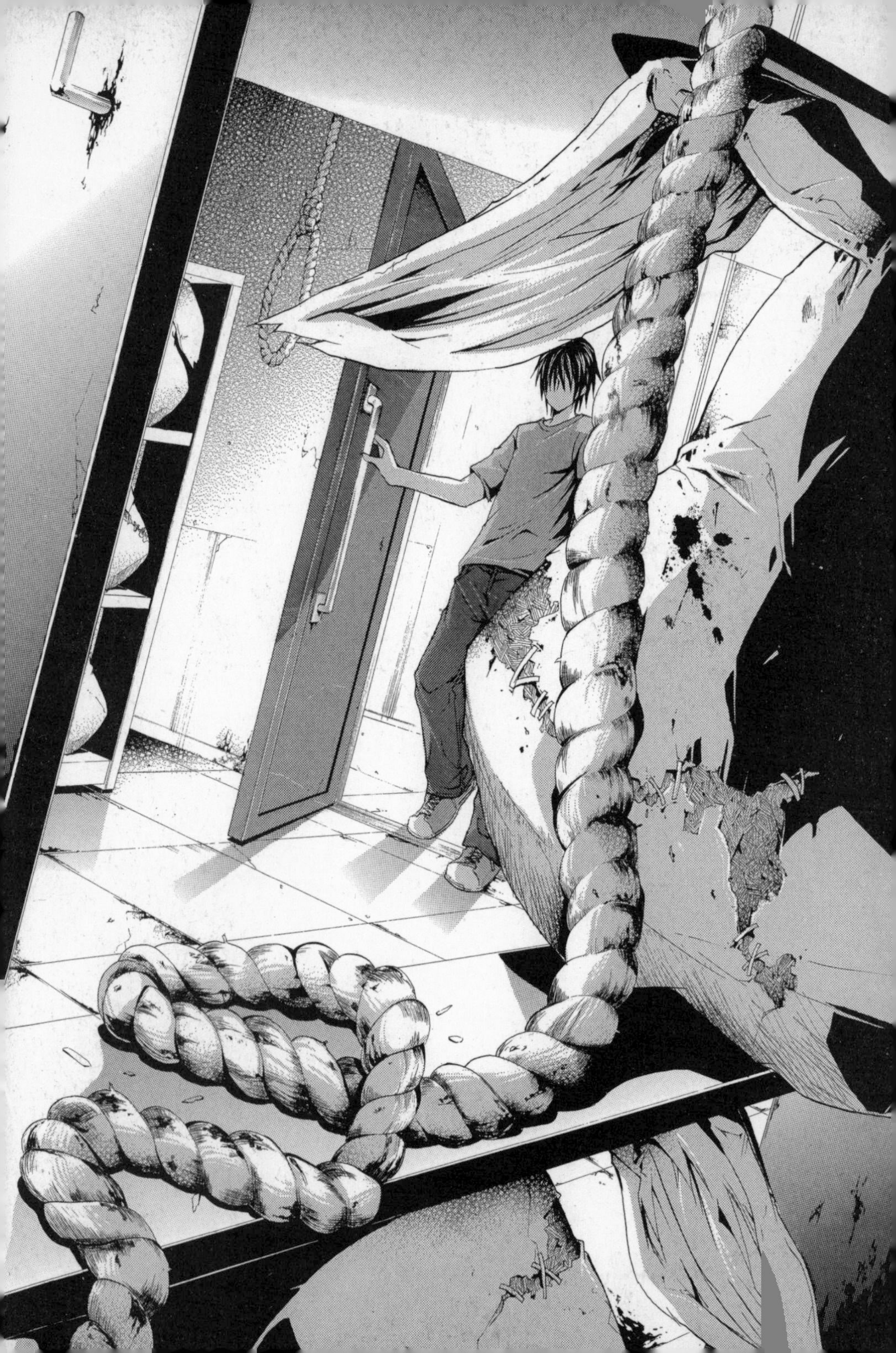

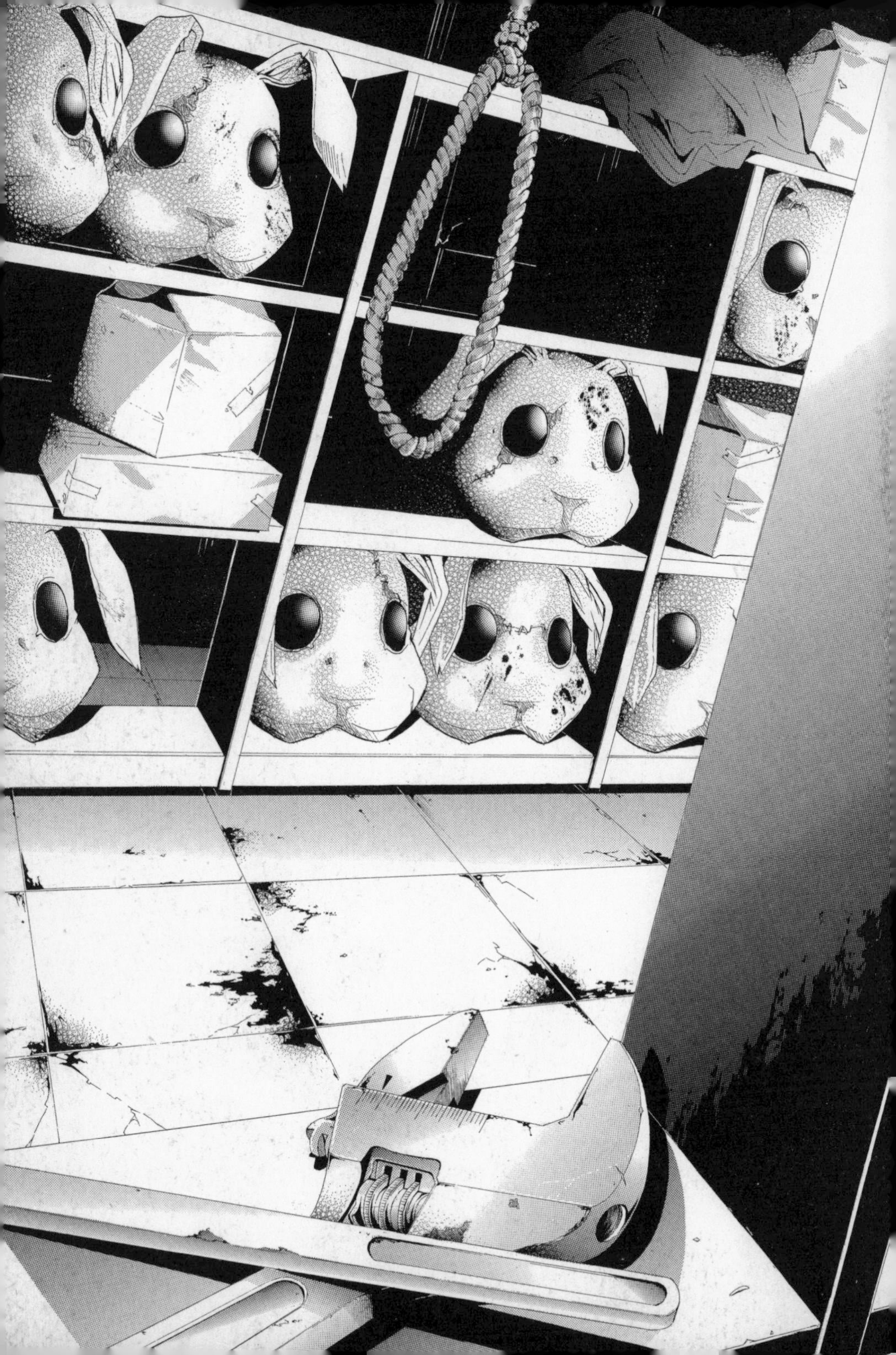

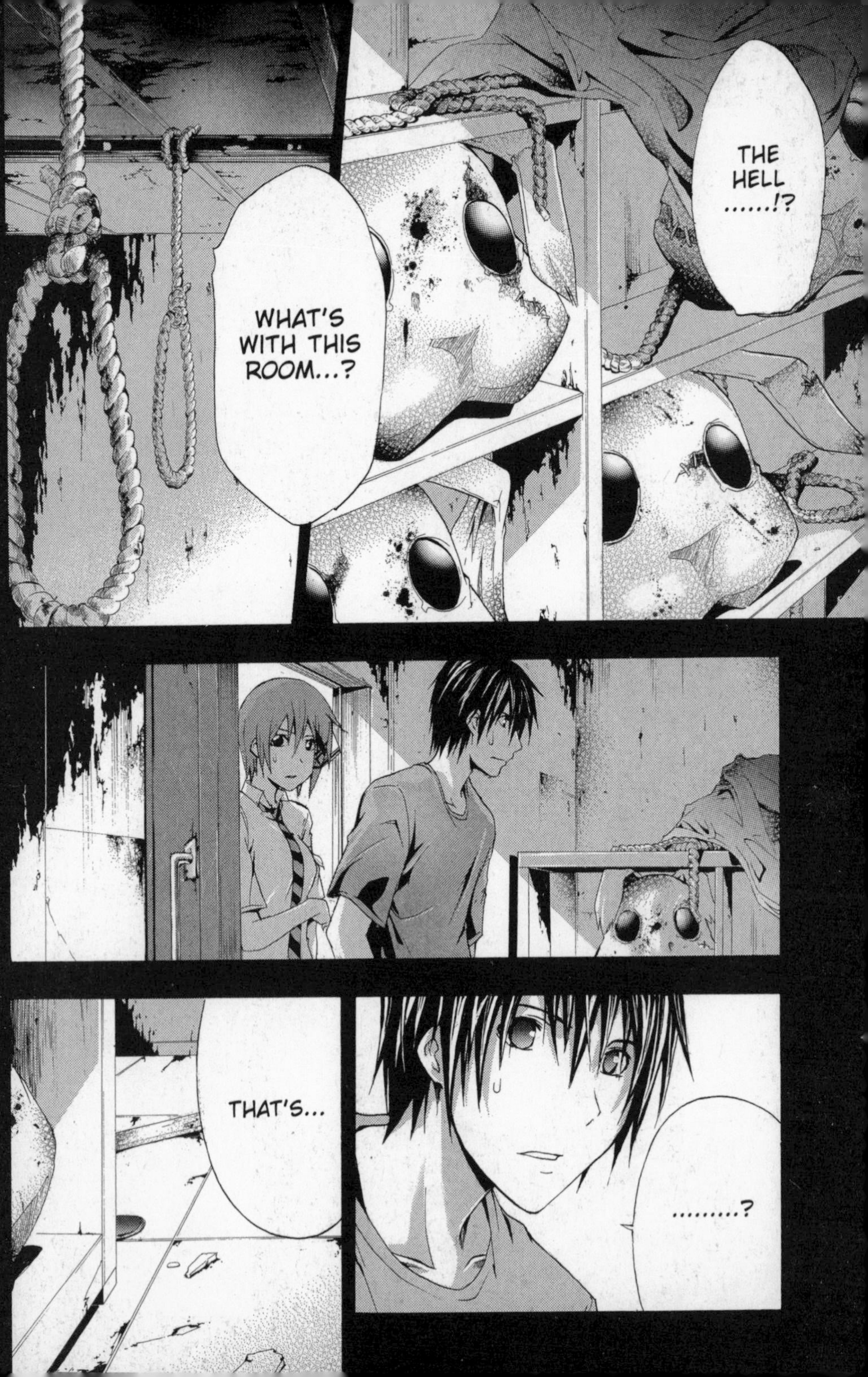
THE HELL ......!?
WHAT'S WITH THIS ROOM...?
..........?
THAT'S...

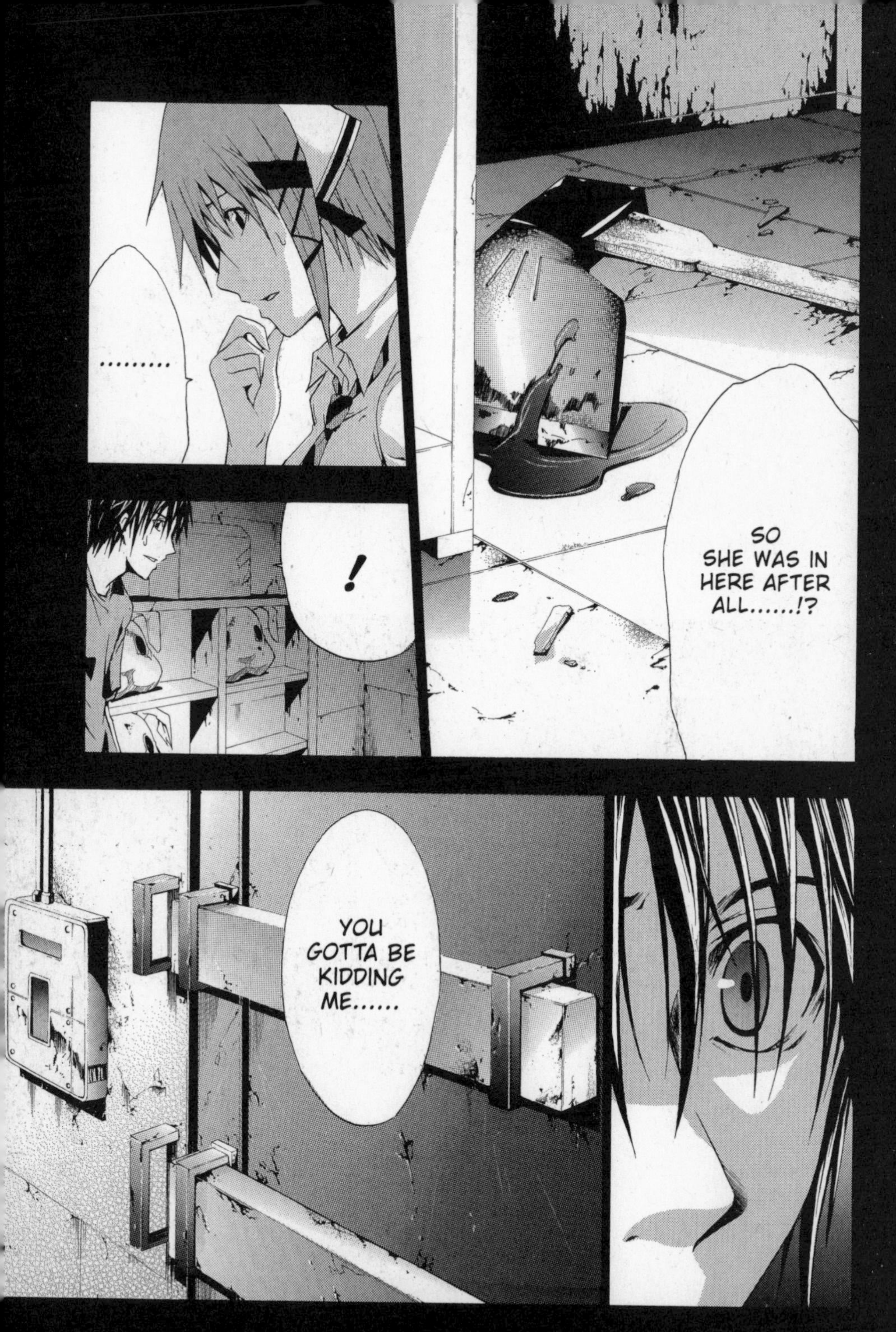
SO SHE WAS IN HERE AFTER ALL......!?
....
!
YOU GOTTA BE KIDDING ME......

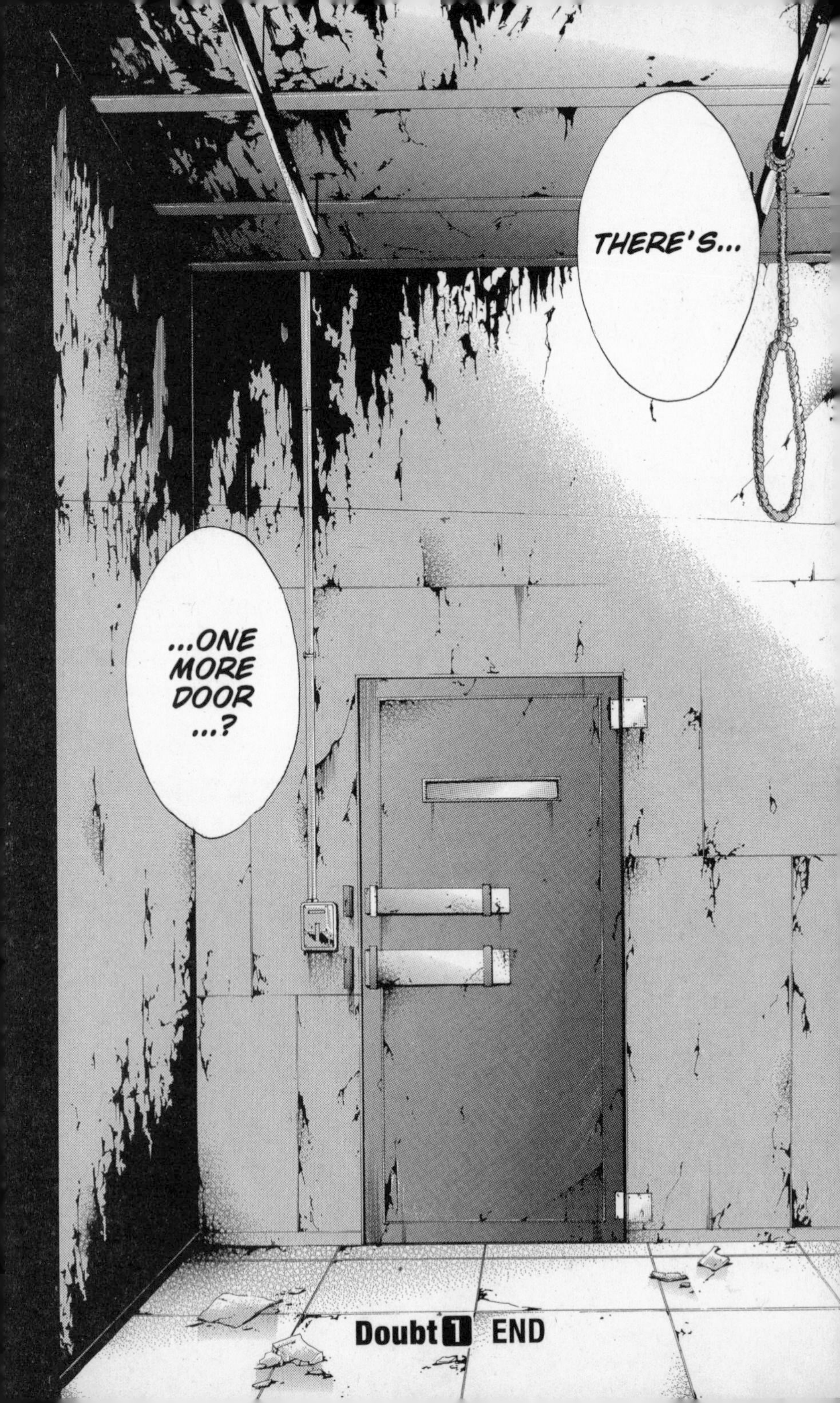
THERE'S...
...ONE MORE DOOR ...?
Doubt 1 END

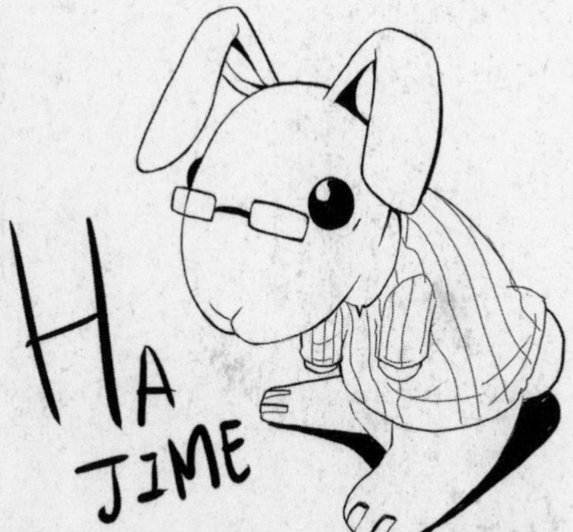
HA
JIME

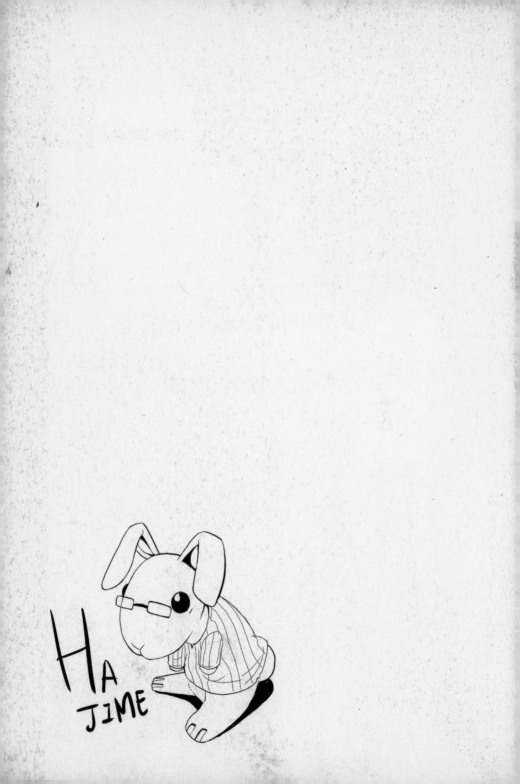

Doubt

STAFF

[MANGA]

TONOGAI

MIZOE

KATOU

MIYASHITA

KAWAZOE

SHINOMIYA

NOMURA

OIKAWA

TAKAHASHI

[THANKS]

FUJIKI

NAGASAWA

[EDITOR]

NOZAKI

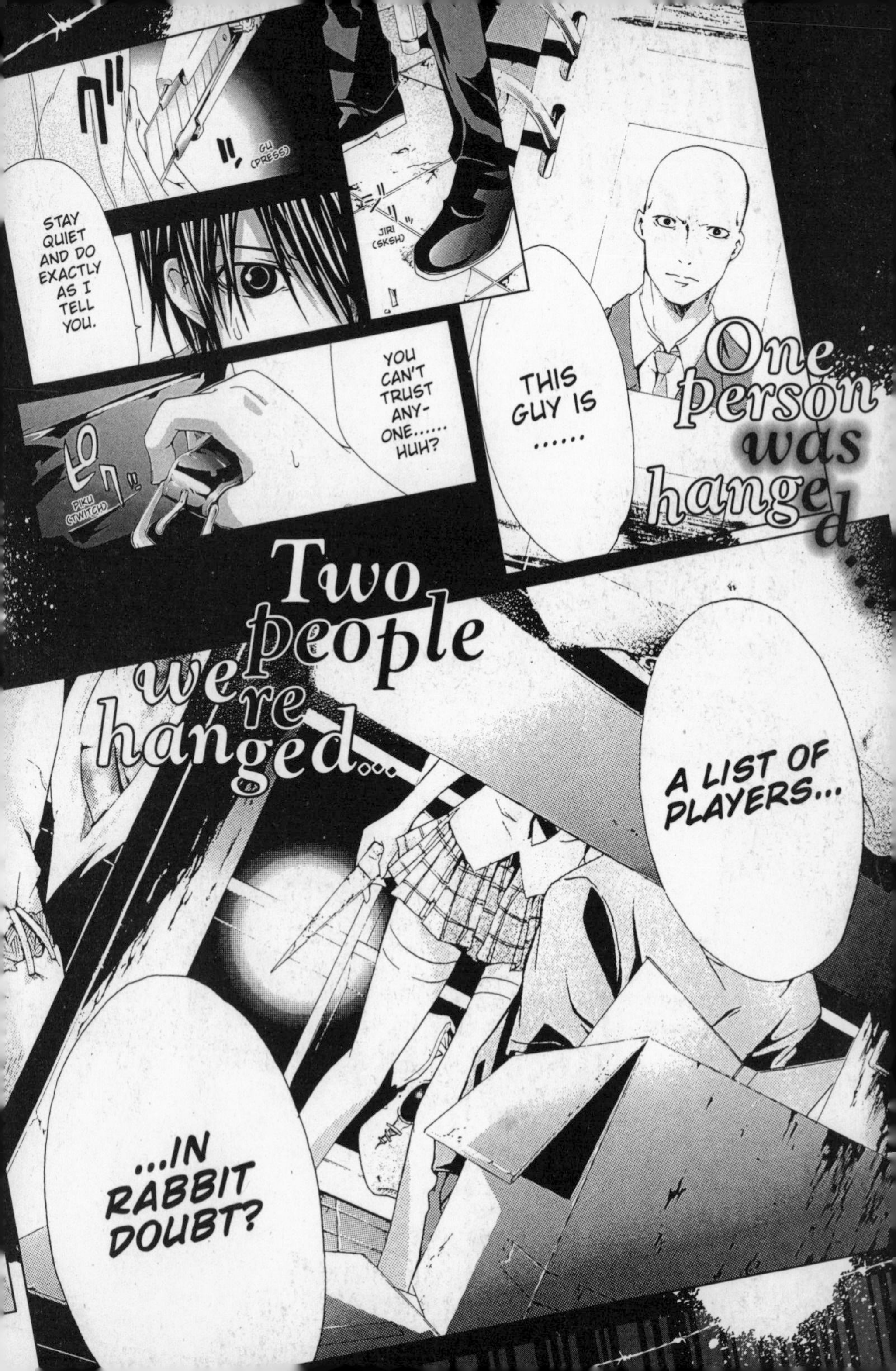

One person was hanged
THIS GUY IS ......
JIRI (SKSH)
GU (PRESS)
STAY QUIET AND DO EXACTLY AS I TELL YOU.
YOU CAN'T TRUST ANY-ONE...... HUH?
PIKU (TWITCH)
Two people were hanged...
A LIST OF PLAYERS...
...IN RABBIT DOUBT?

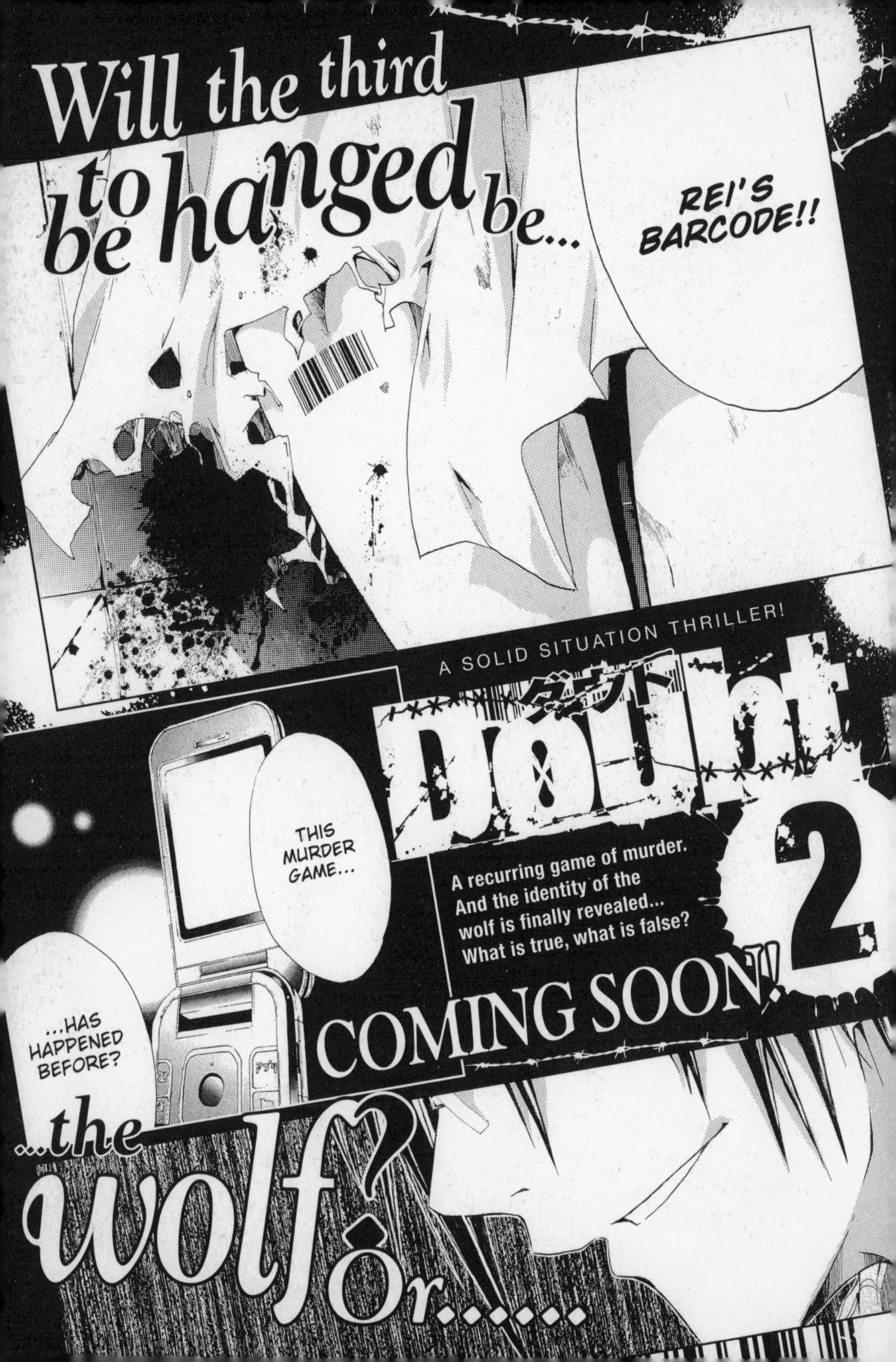
Will the third to be hanged be...
REI'S BARCODE!!
A SOLID SITUATION THRILLER!
ダウト
Doubt
2
A recurring game of murder.
And the identity of the
wolf is finally revealed...
What is true, what is false?
COMING SOON!
THIS MURDER GAME...
...HAS HAPPENED BEFORE?
...the wolf? or......

Translation Notes

Page 21
"You can smoke when you're twenty."
In Japan, you must be twenty years of age
to legally purchase tobacco products.

Page 52
"You can drink booze when you're twenty."
The legal age for purchasing and consuming
alcohol in Japan is also twenty.

Doubt

DOUBT 1

YOSHIKI TONOGAI

Translation and Lettering: Alexis Eckerman

DOUBT Vol. 1, 2 © 2008 Yoshiki Tonogai / SQUARE ENIX CO., LTD. All rights reserved. First published in Japan in 2008 by SQUARE ENIX CO., LTD. English translation rights arranged with SQUARE ENIX CO., LTD. and Hachette Book Group through Tuttle-Mori Agency, Inc.

Translation © 2013 by SQUARE ENIX CO., LTD.

Yen Press
Hachette Book Group
237 Park Avenue, New York, NY 10017

www.HachetteBookGroup.com
www.YenPress.com

Yen Press is an imprint of Hachette Book Group, Inc. The Yen Press name and logo are trademarks of Hachette Book Group, Inc.

First Yen Press Edition: April 2013

ISBN: 978-0-316-24530-2

10 9 8 7 6 5 4 3 2 1

BVG

Printed in the United States of America